erton Crandall

HERBERT HOOVER
A Biography

Books by Eugene Lyons

HERBERT HOOVER: A Biography

OUR SECRET ALLIES: The Peoples of Russia

OUR UNKNOWN EX-PRESIDENT: A Portrait of Herbert Hoover

THE RED DECADE

STALIN, CZAR OF ALL THE RUSSIAS

ASSIGNMENT IN UTOPIA

WE COVER THE WORLD (Editor)

MOSCOW CARROUSEL

SIX SOVIET PLAYS (Editor)

LIFE AND DEATH OF SACCO AND VANZETTI

Herbert Hoover

A BIOGRAPHY

Eugene Lyons

GARDEN CITY, N. Y.

Doubleday & Company, Inc.

1964

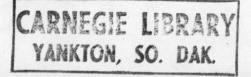

Grateful acknowledgment is made to the following for copyrighted material:

Excerpts from *Herbert Hoover, A Reminiscent Biography* by Will Irwin. Reprinted by permission of Brandt & Brandt.

Excerpts from *American Individualism.* Reprinted by permission of Herbert Hoover.

Excerpts from *American Epoch* by Arthur S. Link. Reprinted by permission of Alfred A. Knopf, Inc.

Excerpts from *The Red Decade,* published by The Bobbs-Merrill Company, Inc. Reprinted by permission of Eugene Lyons.

Excerpts from *The Memoirs of Herbert Hoover* by Herbert Hoover. Reprinted by permission of The Macmillan Company.

Excerpts from *The Hoover Policies* by Ray Lyman Wilbur and Arthur Mastic Hyde. Reprinted by permission of Charles Scribner's Sons.

Dedicated, in Friendship and Affection

to

LILA AND DEWITT WALLACE

A warm, dramatic account and appraisal of the ninety years of one of the most respected, admired — and reviled — Americans who ever lived.

HERBERT HOOVER

A Biography

By EUGENE LYONS

"From the humblest beginnings," the author writes, "he rose to transcendent heights: to the summit of his vocation, which was the mining of metals; to the pinnacle of his avocation, which was benevolence; to the highest office in the Republic."

The first President to come from west of the Mississippi was born into a poor Quaker family and early orphaned. After working his way through Stanford University, Herbert Hoover got his first job—as a common miner, at $2.50 for a ten-hour day. At the age of forty, with the outbreak of World War I, he renounced a fabulous business career as one of the world's greatest mining consultants for public service. Beginning with the epic Belgian Relief, then during the grim aftermaths of both World Wars, he organ-

(Continued on back flap)

Foreword

SIXTEEN years have passed since I wrote my original biography of our thirty-first President, published by Doubleday under the title *Our Unknown Ex-President: A Portrait of Herbert Hoover*. Nearly all of it—recast, dispersed, and for the most part rewritten—has been absorbed in this present book. The new materials added and the record of the intervening years explain and justify its issuance as a new biography.

When I first undertook the task, in 1947, Mr. Hoover gave me generously of his time. He put at my disposal private files and documents, including his then unpublished *Memoirs*. When the manuscript was completed, and again when printer's galleys were available, I asked him to read what I had written. He refused. Evidently he wished to avoid even the semblance of having influenced the content of a friendly biography.

Once, however, he did hint that he didn't like the title—specifically the description of himself as "unknown." I defended the word. He was unknown, I said, or at least insufficiently known, in the sense that the "real" Hoover had been distorted in the public mind by slanderous myths. He shrugged and the matter was not again mentioned.

But in retrospect I came to agree with him that the title, though it might have been appropriate a few years earlier, had become obsolete. Even in 1948, when the book was published, the myths were beginning to wear thin and the popular conception of Herbert Hoover was closer to reality. Certainly these sixteen years have canceled out the last excuse for considering him "unknown" in any sense.

Hoover was more than seventy-four years old when the original biography was brought out. It was a reasonable assumption, therefore, that his career was substantially completed. The assumption proved wrong. In fact the years that followed added enormously to his life's story, giving it, indeed, added dimensions of significance. I refer not alone to the important public services he performed—such as the monumental study of government operations by two successive Hoover Commissions—and the books he wrote. I refer to the profound and wholesome change in American attitudes toward the ex-President. The national conscience, deeply disturbed by Hoover's long ordeal by vilification, was eased by his vindication, and there was a universal feeling of gratitude, widely articulated in the press, that he was still alive to witness the transformation.

Disagreement with Hoover's views, of course, is still widespread. His uncompromising devotion to principle, his contempt for fuzzy-minded slogan-mongers, his defense of "old-fashioned" American and human values run counter to the dominant trends of our time. The austerity of his ethical commitments must seem "intolerant" to the moral relativists, the artisans of expediency, who for the most part run the world nowadays.

But disagreement with Hoover is no longer an occasion for ritual abuse or the impugning of his motives. It is always respectful and sometimes apologetic. Only on the more crackpot fringes of the Left do we still find the kind of Hoover-baiting familiar in the Roosevelt era, and even there it sounds archaic.

Hoover's has been an extraordinarily rich and eventful life—in a sense many lives woven into one—as engineer, humanitarian, President, author, elder statesman. It is a life that exemplified, on the highest plane, the conventional American "success story." But it contains, too, elements of immense pathos.

He is the self-made man who from the humblest beginnings rose to transcendent heights—to the summit of his vocation, which was the mining of metals; to the pinnacle of his avocation, which was benevolence; to the highest office in the Republic. Then, with startling suddenness, his destiny took tragic turns.

Rightly credited with genius in the administration of economic resources, he was fated to preside over a catastrophe of economic disintegration beyond the control of any mortal man. A Quaker whose name had become synonymous with compassion and help to the destitute, he found himself the victim of cruel accusations of callous unconcern for the sufferings of his own countrymen. From the luminous mountain peaks he was driven into the valley of shadows, there to wander for more than fifteen years in unmerited ignominy, a man mocked and defamed, pilloried and stoned, for wholly imaginary sins.

Happily the legend was dissipated in his own lifetime. The landscape of his ninety years thus has the sweep of great human drama, the counterpoint of brilliant light and melancholy shadows. He had, to quote from the final chapter in this book, "a time of crucifixion and a time of resurrection."

The drama has particular relevance, I venture to suggest, in relation to the great social changes of our time. Herbert Hoover has been the nation's most consistent, forthright, and inspiring champion of what used to be called the American way of life. But those who think of it simply as a defense of "capitalism," of the economic status quo, do not know Hoover —or the American way of life. He has thought of himself always, by a definition that was generally accepted before the Great Depression, as a liberal. In time he developed an immunity to the brickbats labeled "reactionary." Those who hurled them, being themselves materialists, failed to grasp the essentially idealistic nature of the former President's vision of the American way and his resistance to state idolatry.

The free economy is part of that vision, of course, but always with the accent on "free." Private enterprise, in Hoover's concept, is not sacrosanct, not an end in itself. He has seen it merely as the best system evolved by man for nurturing the dignity and independence of the individual. His hostility to big government and the welfare state has been tempered at all times by his humanism.

A clear head under the control of a compassionate heart has kept Hoover from succumbing to the catch-phrases and shibboleths of the hour— proof that he was never cut out to be a conventional politician. While devoting his life to helping the weak and the destitute, he never tried to flatter the masses by glorifying weakness and destitution. He sought to stir them, rather, to new strength and self-reliance.

He has not shared the besetting sin of our age, which is to regard honor and rectitude on the one hand, dishonesty and crime on the other, as relative matters, to be debated and negotiated. Without planning it, by merely acting as his mind and conscience dictated, in disregard of prevailing social pretensions and intellectual fashions, he became the spokesman and a living symbol of vital and enduring truths.

E.L.

CONTENTS

CONTENTS

I

Child of the American West

MEN rarely outgrow their childhoods. Herbert Clark Hoover was born on August 10, 1874 in what was then the largely Quaker hamlet of West Branch, in Cedar County, Iowa.

The most vital elements in shaping his character, insights, and emotions are implicit in that statement. For physically his life was rooted in the soil of the pioneer West in the last quarter of the nineteenth century, and spiritually it was rooted in the soil of God-fearing Quaker forebears. Significantly, he was destined to be the first Quaker President, and the first President born and raised west of the Mississippi.

At no point in his long and dramatic career did Hoover feel impelled to deplore or rebel against his origins, as many men must; or to resent the disciplines that a demanding religion, a primitive rural background and poverty imposed upon him. He grew sturdily and whole, without any lacerating inner conflicts. Repeatedly through the decades, at important stages in his life, he was drawn back to West Branch to refresh his instincts and associations sentimentally cherished.

Because he was poor and early orphaned, Hoover had many homes. But always they were Western homes, always Quaker homes, and never lacking in human warmth. Always he lived with relatives who not merely tolerated but wanted him. Hardships and sorrows were a large part of his lot as a child, but not loneliness or alienation. He was continually in the bosom of a large and loving family, replete with uncles and aunts and cousins, and part of a religious community in which friendship was not only a central precept but a normal, unstrained practice.

He was one of those fortunate people who "belonged" in a country and a family and a tradition, and drew strength from their wholeness.

Not until he was twenty-three, and on his way to take full command of a mature man's job in a distant land, did he set foot east of the Mississippi

1

River. In the crowded, fast-moving years that followed he was fated to plumb this planet—its breadth in ceaseless travels, its depth in ceaseless mining operations. But in his most pliant years he knew only a childhood on the Iowa prairie, a boyhood and adolescence in the rugged Northwest, a young manhood under the California sun.

In short, he was of the West, born and bred, its impress on his nature sharp and indelible. The broad horizons of the American West, its venturesomeness and self-reliance, its liberalism and tolerance, were his by natural right. Even his physique—tall, tough, equal to the most punishing exertions—bespoke the pioneer West. So did his love of the outdoors, his facility for camp life and roughing it, his lifelong passion for fishing.

The epic era of the opening of the West was tapering off at the time Hoover was born. The last free land in his native state gave out in 1875, a year after his birth. The men and the moods of that era, however, were still everywhere around him. Already the covered wagon was haloed with romance; even the stagecoach was beginning to fade out. But most of the elderly Hoovers had come there by prairie schooner only twenty years before his birth. His mother's family, the Minthorns, had come in the same fashion from Canada seven years later. A Hoover uncle drove the stage between Davenport and Iowa City.

From his own kin and others he heard fabulous accounts of Western treks bristling with Indian skirmishes. He had Indian playmates. Several times he visited relatives who served as Indian agents on reservations— once he stayed for a period of eight months—where he played and studied with Indian children and absorbed some of their skills and their lore.

The social democracy of the West into which Hoover was born was not a condescending theory. It was a living fact, inherent in a new continent in which men perforce relied on their own strength, met common dangers by pooling those strengths, and were not divided by inherited rank, prestige, or privilege. The West nurtured a new race open to new ideas, in which the individual had almost unlimited social elbow-room.

On both the paternal and maternal sides, Hoover's progenitors were members of the Society of Friends, the official name of the Quakers, as far back as they could be traced. This meant the first half of the eighteenth century in the Hoover genealogical tree and probably longer at the Minthorn end. And his Quaker heritage fitted perfectly into the regional setting. Essentially simple and democratic and tolerant of other faiths, Quakerism harmonized easily with the Western environment.

Hoover's first authenticated ancestors were Swiss: Jonas and Anna Maria Huber, who at the end of the 1600s fled from Switzerland to escape religious persecution. They settled in Ellerstadt in the German Palatinate, where their ninth child, Andreas, was born in 1723. This was Hoover's great-great-great-grandfather. At fifteen Andreas migrated to Pennsylvania, anglicized his name, then moved to Maryland, where his son John was born at Union Bridge in 1760. A decade or more later, Andrew moved his brood to Randolph County in North Carolina. There Hoover's great-grandfather, Jesse, was born in 1800.

It was Andrew's son John—which is to say the second American generation—who struck out for the Western Reserve in 1802, breaking ground near Miami, Ohio. Half a century later, in 1854, Jesse Hoover—the son of John—and his wife Rebecca made the journey by wagon to Iowa to carve out farms for a flock of tall sons in Cedar County. West Branch had been settled only a few years before and had only a few hundred inhabitants. Nearly always the Friends migrated in large groups, since their religion requires a community of the faithful for its fullest expression. A sizable part of the population of Cedar County was made up of Hoovers and the multitude of their kin by marriage.

One of Jesse's sons was Eli, who had been born at West Milton, Ohio, in 1820, and with Eli, when he came to Iowa, was his own son, Jesse Clark Hoover, born in 1846 and fated to beget a President.

Jesse set up a tiny smithy in West Branch. At the age of twenty-four he married Huldah Minthorn, from a family of six sisters and a brother who had defied Quaker pacifism by running away to join the Union Army. She had been born at Burgersville, in Ontario, Canada, in 1848—her husband's junior by two years. Her Minthorn ancestors landed in New England from England in the 1630s and were therefore among the earliest colonists. From her strain Hoover inherited some Huguenot blood.

The Friends in Cedar County, as elsewhere, wore the Quaker gray and spoke the plain speech filled with "thees" and "thous." To all of them life was earnest, without margins for frivolity or self-indulgence—although Herbert as a child observed, as he later recorded, that the women were not above some worldly pride in the silks and woolens of their ample dresses and the cut of their Quaker bonnets. To all of them "doing good" was the main justification of existence in the eyes of God.

The eldest of the Hoovers the boy knew personally was his great-grandmother Rebecca, credited with raising nineteen children besides her own brood. Born at the turn of the century, she lived until very near its close. When she died in 1896, at the age of ninety-five, Herbert was going on twenty-two. To him, as to the rest of her teeming progeny, she seemed a wonderful living link with the beginnings of the American adventure in empire-building. From all accounts she was the pioneer West matriarch of tradition in the flesh, humorous and stern, strong and energetic and wise in the ways of the open spaces; the kind of great-grandmother, one might say, whom a typical American boy would have chosen enthusiastically as an ancestress.

But Rebecca was more than that: the incarnation, no less, of the other half of Hoover's dual heritage. For she was also the traditional Quaker matriarch, pious herself and relentless in monitoring the piety and deportment of her offspring. She held herself accountable for the mundane morals and the immortal souls of three generations of them.

Of Rebecca it is reported, perhaps in exaggeration, that she opposed the screening of windows against insects as somehow a defiance of the Lord's intentions. She inveighed against worldliness even in its mildest forms, such as noisy play and boastfulness, let alone its satanic manifestations in greed or selfishness or tardy charity.

One may surmise that her grandson Jesse, named for her own husband of blessed memory, gave the old lady some unquiet moments. He was a tall, slender young man with a long beard. Though profoundly pious, he was a life-loving sort, a good mixer with an ear for gossip, for which his smithy provided a perfect listening post. "Ever happy and cheerful," the obituary editorial in the West Branch *Times* said of him when he died, even before attesting that he was "a kind husband and father, a respectful and useful citizen" who "will be sadly missed in business circles."

But Herbert's mother no doubt evened the score in Rebecca's aging eyes. Huldah had attended a Quaker finishing school and taught school briefly and was rich in book learning for her time and place. The people of her faith held education in great esteem, for women no less than for men, ranking it among the prime virtues. More important, Huldah was thrice blessed as one close to God, whom the spirit moved often and eloquently in Meeting.

Her shy spirituality made her the butt of her more worldly husband's affectionate chafing. After his death at the age of thirty-four, she became almost wholly the instrument of her spirit and was more in demand than ever in Quaker communities throughout Iowa for the beauty of her preaching. In the two years of her widowhood she took in sewing to support her three children. But her real vocation was preaching.

In any other denomination she would have become an ordained pastor; among the Quakers she had no title or parish or remuneration, except in the love of those whom she instructed. Increasingly she did receive freewill offerings to relieve her of some of the drudgery of the needle so that she might speak the word of God. Co-religionists even beyond Iowa came to know her soft, unstudied eloquence. Quite naturally, she was active in the campaigns against Demon Rum; once, her son recalled, he was "parked for the day at the polls, where the women were massed in an effort to make the men vote themselves dry."

It was while holding meetings in Springdale that Huldah took ill. She died nine days later, only two years after her husband. The editorial eulogy stressed her Christian piety, emphasizing that she had founded and been the leading spirit in a Young People's Prayer Meeting.

4

Being a little over six when he lost his father, Herbert had only the dimmest memory of him. His mother left a sharper imprint. His recollection of her was "chiefly of a sweet-faced woman who for two years kept the little family of four together." He remembered few of her words, of course, but their purport, which was love and charity, colored his mind and feelings forever. When he declared, in accepting the nomination for President in 1928, "I come of Quaker stock," it was not a casual bit of biographical information. He was offering a key to his moral essence.

In the course of his long, active life Hoover shed more and more of the externals of his fathers' faith. In his senior year in college, for the sake of the girl who was to become his wife, he learned how to dance. Later he learned to take an occasional drink in congenial company and to enjoy a good cigar, the movies, theater, and other recreations which the matriarch Rebecca and his mother rated as abominations. As a child he was chastised for fishing on Sunday; as a grownup he fished on hundreds of Sundays without a twinge of conscience. In his riper years, at the Waldorf Towers in New York, or the Bohemian Grove in California, he relished a few hours of canasta with old cronies.

But he never shed any of the spiritual precepts implanted in his heart and mind in the formative years in Iowa and Oregon. In studying his career and his ideas, one becomes more and more aware of special qualities that are indubitably of Quaker origin: his compulsive concern for the sufferings of others; his stubborn faith in the essential goodness of the individual man; a distaste for ceremony, display, and cheering crowds.

David Hinshaw, his college classmate and lifelong friend, himself a Quaker, even traces some of Hoover's faults as a President in troubled times to Quaker influences. Hoover refused to strike back at enemies or to answer charges he considered absurd; he would not carry his case—his personal case, that is, as distinct from the country's—to the American people; he ruled out showmanship and drama as demagogic and somehow immodest, this at a time when his views needed to be dramatized for a confused and frightened people. What were these, Hinshaw asks, but Quaker-like disinterest in public opinion when your conscience was clear? Why explain to men actions and motives that were understood by God? After all, the peculiar people had been conditioned through the centuries to suffer contempt and even persecution in silence.

There may be room for dispute as to the extent to which Hoover succeeded in the dedication derived from a childhood in the Meetinghouse. There can be no dispute as to motives that inspired him before, during, and after his tragic four years in the White House. Those were no sudden impulses but the flowering of seeds firmly and tenderly planted in his innermost being.

There is a pattern, we shall see, in the Hoover story and its basic design is mercy. In the long run the corrosions of political cruelty could not blur its outlines. The soft-voiced, kind-hearted woman preacher of the Friends' settlement in Iowa, though she died so young, did not live in vain.

2

Because Hoover's Quakerism explains so much about him, it is well to consider briefly the nature of that faith.

Its main elements, Hoover has written in his *Memoirs,* "were literal belief in the Bible, great tolerance, and a conviction that spiritual inspiration sprang from the 'inward light' in each individual." "The Friends," he added, "have always held strongly to education, thrift and individual enterprise. In consequence of plain living and hard work poverty has never been their lot." So far as he knew, he added, no Quaker had ever been in jail or on public relief. Probably this record has been spoiled in the age of state welfare since then. Even in the past, he remarked with his typical flicker of humor, the record was maintained in part by expelling from the Meeting erring members who could not be persuaded to mend their ways.

In the Quaker view man is born pure, though the world corrupts him, and therefore even the wicked must be cherished and succored. The Friends' code enjoins service to others not as a duty or a sacrifice but as a divine privilege; in it charity ranks above prayer and is, indeed, a sort of communion with God—with the "God" part in all mortal men.

It is a faith that has neither fixed creed nor rigid sacraments. Its imperatives are of the moral rather than the theological order. Founded in England by George Fox in 1652, the Society of Friends took its name from the scriptural injunction, "Ye are my friends if ye do the things that I command." And of the things He commanded the Friends regarded one as supreme: "This is my commandment, that ye love one another." The popular sobriquet of "Quakers" derived from George Fox's constant warning to the authorities to "quake and tremble before the Lord."

Friendship, goodness, help to the helpless, humility, a clean life filled with noble thoughts and deeds—these come closest to defining the Quaker ideal. From which it is apparent that the faith puts more store by good works in this life than eternal bliss in the next. For the true Quaker there is no sharp break between things secular and things sacred; no gap between hard-headed business, let us say, and soft-hearted religion. Worship is not a Sabbath soothing syrup for consciences snagged by weekday necessities. Honest weight and fair dealing figure in Quaker sermons and traditional maxims alongside more abstract principles.

6

Though it arose as a protest against formalized religion and the pomp of hierarchy, Quakerism in time built a formalism of its own out of its renunciations. Its dislike of ceremonials found expression in rituals of simplicity in clothes, demeanor, speech, and worship. But the order remained a church without church officials, a flock without professional shepherds. Since every human being partakes of the Godhead through his own better self, he needs no mortal intermediary for communion with the Almighty.

Worship in the unadorned Meetinghouse is silent meditation among loved neighbors, interrupted only when some Friend is inspired to speak on matters earthly or divine. The individual with the greatest moral sensitivity and the God-given eloquence to communicate it becomes a minister in effect, without acquiring titles or a privileged position vis-à-vis God. Long silences are as much a part of the worship as the eloquent preachments and discussions. Grace before meals is a minute of silence with heads bowed and eyes lowered.

In his whimsical fashion Hoover in his maturity recalled that this mode of worship was hard on children, from whom it demanded self-control and silence beyond their fidgety years. But "it was strong training in patience," he said, and conducive to habits of reticence as well.

The ethical principles of the Friends are not presented as commands surrounded by threats of hell fire but in the guise of "queries" appealing to the Christian conscience and implying their own answers. For example:

Are the necessities of the poor, and the circumstances of those who may appear likely to require aid, inspected and relieved? Are they advised and assisted in such employments as they are capable of; and is due care taken to promote the school-education of their children?

Are Friends careful to live within the bounds of their circumstances, and to avoid involving themselves in business beyond their ability to manage; or in hazardous or speculative trade? Are they just in their dealings; and punctual in complying with their contracts and engagements; and in paying their debts seasonably?

There again we can note the blending of the practical and the moral calculated to make the Quaker integral: religious in his living, and living in his religion. He is not provided with arbitrary answers but is expected to do his own spiritual bookkeeping. Quakerism at its best thus nurtures self-respect and self-reliance. It enjoins a sense of personal obligation and in turn provides scope for personal talent, for freedom of thought and conscience within the framework of the Christian ethic.

Its individualism, however—and this is helpful in appraising the one American President shaped by Quaker mores—rests not on self-interest but on usefulness to others. It is an individualism suffused by compassion,

7

and consequently at the antipodes from survival-of-the-fittest ruggedness. The Quaker ideal aims at the utmost development of the person not only as an end in itself but as contribution to the greatest good of the community of which he is a part.

Professor Rufus M. Jones was able to write that in the task of world betterment,

There is no sane and efficient program which does not include the old-fashioned Quaker faith (not sectarian) in the personal worth of the individual, a faith that a man is more precious than the gold of Ophir, a vision of the potential child of God in the submerged toiler, and, with that faith and that vision, the readiness to identify ourselves as friend with those who need us, the bestowal of personal care and sympathy, the cultivation of the spirit of consecration to the tasks and needs of the neighborhood group in which we live.

The spirit that informs such a quotation shines through much that the Iowa Quaker boy grown to manhood and eminence had to say. Who can doubt the Quaker flavor, for instance, in these words addressed by the thirty-first American President to members of the American Red Cross on April 12, 1930:

It is indeed, the spiritual in the individual and the nation which looks out with keen interest on the well-being of others, forgetful of ourselves, beyond our own preoccupation with our own selfish interests, and gives us a sense of belonging to the great company of mankind, sharing in the great plan of the universe and the definite order which pervades it.

Sentiments, these, redolent of the Meetinghouse; echoes of what he heard as a little boy from the "sweet-faced woman" who was his mother. Each community of Friends as a matter of course takes care of its own, and the many charitable enterprises of the Society—immense in relation to its small membership—are proof enough that the solicitude is not limited to fellow Quakers.

Speaking at a Quaker college in 1922, Hoover referred to the rescue work that has been carried on by the Friends from the great plague in London to the latest plague of world war:

There must be something more here than accident that our body of perhaps two hundred and fifty or three hundred thousand people of all the world, there should have been contributed to humanity during all these centuries that sense of service. . . . It is perhaps unseemly for me or for you to speak of our own, but it is well to remind ourselves for our inspiration and the inspiration of our children that there is here a tradition, there is here the motivation of some great aspiration that follows through generation after generation of our people.

I am indebted to the fine book by Walter Friar Dexter, *Herbert Hoover and American Individualism,* for some of the material in this chapter. He has pointed out, among other things, that the Quakers were the first American abolitionists. By the end of the 1700s there was no Friend in good standing owning chattel slaves; sixty years before Lincoln's Emancipation Proclamation, the Friends of Virginia directed that all those who failed to liberate their slaves be disowned by their local Meetings.

It was, in fact, their detestation of slavery which drove most of the Quakers in our South, among them the Hoovers, into the Western Reserve. The candidacy of Abraham Lincoln received virtually unanimous Quaker support. Hoover's profound admiration for Lincoln, which he evidenced in a thousand ways, was more than a personal predilection, being intimately related to his unique religious background.

II

Quaker Boyhood

FEW American Presidents had such humble beginnings and were so authentically "self-made" as Herbert Hoover. The generation that grew up after he left the White House found it disconcerting to learn that he had come up from poverty and knew the ache of hard labor. Somehow the simple facts did not jibe with their mental picture of the man.

In part this public amnesia was due to the circumstance that Hoover had succeeded in his profession early and spectacularly, so that he was a relatively wealthy man by the time the country at large became aware of him. But chiefly it was the result of the pounding propagandas of later years linking him, with intent to defame, to such symbols of presumptive iniquity as Wall Street.

Among the birthplaces of American Presidents probably only Lincoln's log cabin was more humble than the tiny gabled cottage in which Hoover was ushered into the world. The actual room in which he was delivered with the skillful help of his Aunt Ellen, volunteer midwife to much of West Branch, was about seven feet by thirteen. It was part of a simple but immaculately clean three-room, one-story house, built of upright boards and whitewashed inside and out, on the bank of the Wapsinonoc Creek, across the alley from Jesse Hoover's little blacksmith shop.

Later, when it passed into other hands, a two-story extension was built across the front of the cottage. After Hoover became President, it was fixed up as a hot-dog stand and profited on the curiosity of tourists. In 1934 Hoover's two sons bought the property; several years later their mother supervised the removal of the accretions, and had the original house restored and the grounds improved. The property was then deeded to the village and it is now preserved as a national shrine by the state of Iowa.

An engaging echo of the night of the boy's birth is available in a letter from one of his aunts. "I had spent the day with Huldah, visiting and sewing," she recalled. "Next morning early Jesse came and tapped on my window and said, 'Well, we have another General Grant at our house! Huldah would like to see thee.' So I went . . . Herbert was a sweet baby that first day, round and plump, and looked about him very cordial."

General Grant, of course, was then President. There was surely no edge of premonition in the father's boast. Millions of American fathers have announced the advent of millions of sons with that same half-earnest pleasantry.

Herbert found a three-year-old brother—Theodore, known all his life as Tad—waiting for him. A sister, May, joined them in a couple of years. Their father soon acquired a farm implement agency. As it prospered, he sold the cottage and moved into a more commodious house nearby, which is no longer extant. His was a happy little family, with flocks of relations for miles around. Of worldly goods they had little and wanted little.

Few memories of his very early years remained with Herbert. Neither in this respect nor in any other was he a precocious child. The clearest memory was literally burned into his flesh when he stepped on a red-hot chip of iron while playing in the smithy; he carried the scar for the rest of his days.

Another incident was sharp in his mind if only for the spanking it earned him. The punishment might be set down as his first sacrifice in the cause of scientific research. His father was fabricating barbed wire, which was immersed in hot tar to prevent rusting. Watching the cauldron of boiling tar outside the smithy, the boy fell to wondering whether the oily bubbles would burn and what species of tar-tinted flames they would produce. From wondering to testing was an easy step, as easy as plunging a burning fagot into the cauldron. He had his answer instantly in terrifying billows of smoke that brought the whole town, and in due time the volunteer fire brigade, running to the rescue. Ever after, Hoover has said, the sight even of a picture of a volcanic eruption revived a bit of that terror in his heart.

Because of Jesse's illness, Huldah once packed her children off to Uncle Banajah's farm. But they were soon hauled back in mysterious gloom. At home they found their grief-stricken mother and a bevy of mourning relatives around their father's bier. He had been carried off by typhoid fever. Herbert had just passed his sixth birthday.

Thereafter Huldah sewed deep into the night to nourish the bodies of her three children and read the Bible with them to nourish their souls. Herbert had read the Bible himself, in daily stints, from cover to cover before he was ten. They rarely missed worship in the Meetinghouse. Even little May was taken to the silent prayers, the institution of baby-sitters being unknown. But when summoned to give witness in some Meeting away from home, Huldah entrusted her young ones to one or another of the Minthorn or Hoover households.

Jesse left a thousand-dollar life insurance policy. Not until much later did the Hoover brothers comprehend the self-denying solicitude with which their mother safeguarded this tiny amount for their education. The sale of the farm implement business netted a small amount. This, plus the insurance money, was ultimately entrusted to Major Laurie Tatum, a lawyer living in Tipton, Iowa, legal guardian of the orphaned Hoovers, since no relative wished to assume responsibility for the "estate."

One of the memorable experiences in Herbert's childhood came to him soon after his father's death. In part to relieve Huldah of one mouth to feed, he was taken for eight months to Pawhuska, Arkansas, to live with an uncle, Major Laban Miles, United States Indian Agent to the Osage Nation.

He and his Miles cousins were the only white children on the reservation and in its school. With half-tamed young braves they explored the forests and streams, learned how to make and use bows and arrows, how to fish Indian-style, how to build a fire in the economical Indian way. Much of Hoover's love for the outdoors stems from those Osage months. His lifelong pride in the efficient building of a campfire and in open-air cookery is a measure of the zest he brought to that long-ago Indian interlude. Once, in later life, he was asked what school subject he liked best. His answer was quick: "None. They were something to race through so that I could get out of doors."

An amusing triviality of the Pawhuska sojourn stuck in his memory. A visiting missionary asked to know the subject of that day's religious lesson. The little Indians told him promptly: "Ananias set fire to his wife," which perhaps was close enough to "Ananias and Saphirra, his wife."

Before and after school hours at the West Branch Free School, Herbert, like all other boys, did the chores around the house—or on the farm when he lived with relatives—considered proper for his age, and they were not light chores. When he was old enough to know anything he knew the value of money and the virtue of frugality. In his seventh summer he earned more than five dollars picking strawberries; it was an immense sum, well worth the backaches and sunburns. With brother Tad and cousins he collected old iron for the pennies it brought.

Seven months after Herbert's eighth birthday, pneumonia struck down his mother. He recalled vividly the family council of Hoovers and Minthorns, in which a few neighbors joined. The problem, in his own words, was "not as to who should undertake the duty of raising the three or-

phans, but who should have the joy of adding them to their own broods."
Even his schoolteacher, Mollie Brown (later Mrs. Carran) put in a bid
for Herbert. As an unmarried lady, however, she was not considered
equal to the responsibility.

In the end Grandmother Minthorn took in May; the Aunt Ellen who
had helped bring him into the world and her husband, Allan Hoover,
acquired Herbert; and Theodore went to live with another uncle.

The Allan Hoovers lived on a farm outside of West Branch. For nearly
two years Herbert's life was therefore adjusted to the routine of a typical
farm of the period. Nearly half a century later, speaking in Iowa in the
course of a campaign swing through the country, he alluded to the extent to which those pioneer farms were self-contained:

We ground our own wheat and corn at the mill, we slaughtered our hogs
for meat; we wove at least part of our own clothing; we repaired our own machinery; we got our own fuel from the woods; we erected our own buildings;
we made our own soap; we preserved our own fruit and grew our own vege-
tables.

Only a small part of the family living, he pointed out, came by trade
with the outside. About 80 percent of what farms produced, they con-
sumed, with about 20 percent sold in the market to purchase the small
margin of necessities and to pay interest on the mortgage. The farm families were thus very little affected by economic conditions in the country
at large. Recessions and depressions barely touched them. However, illness and death took a more tragic toll—witness the death of his own parents in the prime of life. Herbert himself successfully negotiated mumps,
measles, croup, diphtheria, and chicken pox.

There was no dearth of tough work for a vigorous, intelligent boy on the
farm of old. Its economic system, he was to write with a touch of whimsy,
"avoided class conflicts, labor boards, and arbitration. It absolutely denied
collective bargaining to little boys. The prevailing rate for picking potato bugs was one cent a hundred, and if you wanted firecrackers on the
Fourth of July you took it or left it." Young Hoover took it.

At Uncle Allan's he found a great friend in cousin Walter. Together
they walked to and from school—a mile and a half each way—or, in winter
weather, rode mounted double on a farm horse. They shared friends, activities, confidences. The autograph of a girl classmate, which survived
into her maturity, carried this inscription: "To Addie, Let your days be
filled with peas, Slip along on slick as greese. Herb Hoover." What was
lacking in spelling was made up in sentiment.

The chubbiness of his childhood was giving way to the tall, muscular
leanness of boyhood. The babyish diminutive of Herbie was giving way to
the more manly appellation of Bert. Except for the accent of special af-

fection, as if he were a favored child, he was as completely the son of the house as any of his cousins there. In 1907 Hoover was to express his abiding love for his Uncle Allan by naming his second son for him.

2

Outwardly the first ten years of Hoover's life would appear restrained and even cheerless. Twice he was orphaned and passed from relative to relative. But we make a mistake to look on the life of a child with grown-up eyes.

When he was running the vast Belgian Relief enterprise, Hoover constantly traveled from his base in London across the Channel en route to Holland, Belgium, Germany, Switzerland, sometimes Paris, then back to London. Under wartime conditions these trips, from 1914 to 1917, entailed many hours of waiting for delayed boats and trains. To utilize the time he decided to write "a sort of record of my varied life for my two sons."

It was not intended for publication, of course. But ultimately, more than thirty-five years later and virtually unedited, it became the first part of the first volume of his *Memoirs*. This casual record, written at odd times over several years and entirely from memory, is both detailed and accurate. More remarkable, in view of his subsequent public image, is the fact that the narrative is often playful in tone and pervaded throughout by human warmth. It opens with these words:

I prefer to think of Iowa as I saw it through the eyes of a ten-year-old boy. Those were eyes filled with adventure and great undertakings, with participation in good and comforting things. They saw days of stern but kindly discipline.

The Quaker way of life was not too conducive to the high spirits of a healthy and growing boy. Existence seemed a jungle of "don'ts," but there were ways of getting around some of them. His early love of reading had to be indulged half in secret, for even *Robinson Crusoe* and the tales of James Fenimore Cooper were too secular for the taste of his elders. His family was "unwilling in those days to have youth corrupted with stronger reading than the Bible, the encyclopedia, or those great novels where the hero overcomes the demon rum."

Comforts were scarce (but not really missed, since they were not known) and money scarcer. Hard toil—weeding, currying the horses, milking, gathering fuel, even dishwashing—were a matter of course for all youngsters. Yet the view from this boy's vantage point was cheerful and exciting. It appeared, indeed, a happy time of endless wonders. And the wonders were not a mirage of middle age. Hoover had been back to check his memories and found them quite true and exceedingly good. The sites of his childhood were not much changed and each of them stirred echoes of all-suffusing joys and high moments of discovery.

There was, for instance, Cook's Hill, "where, on winters' nights, to satisfy our human craving for speed, we slid down at terrific speeds, with our tummies tight to homemade sleds." There was the shallow swimming hole under the willows down by the railroad bridge from which one returned caked with "clean and healthy mud." It was "hard to keep from pounding the mud with your hands and feet when you shoved off for the thirty feet of a cross-channel swim."

A galling episode was connected with trapping. Under the boys' code of the period captive rabbits had to be brought home alive. Brother Tad knew just how this should be accomplished, having studied the instructions in his surreptitious reading of *Youth's Companion*.

One cold morning, having caught a rabbit, Tad was set to put his superior knowledge into practice. He prepared to puncture holes back of the rabbit's knee joints, through which a string would then be passed and tied for complete security. All that Herbie had to do was to stand still in the snow and hold the animal, while Tad made ready to ply his not oversharp knife.

But alas, the resistance of the wiggly bit of fur was too much for the younger boy's frozen thumbs and squeamishness. "I was not only blamed for its escape all the way home and for weeks afterward," he would record, "but continuously for years. I never see rabbit tracks across the snowy fields that I do not have the painful recollection of it."

There were pigeons in the woods and prairie chickens in the hedges for young hunters equipped with bows and arrows. "The Ritz has never yet provided game of such wondrous flavor as this bird plucked and half-cooked over the small boys' campfire." And above all there was the fishing:

We were still in that rude but highly effective epoch of the willow poles with a butcher-string line and hooks ten for a dime. And the dime was hard to come by. Our compelling lure was a segment of an angleworm and our incantation was to spit on the bait. We lived in a time when a fish used to bite instead of strike and we knew it bit when the cork bobbed. And moreover we ate the fish.

In all respects his remembrances of Iowa food were "of the most distinguished order." In the decades that followed he partook of what the most famous restaurants in the great capitals of the world had to offer but was "still sure that Aunt Millie was the better cook." In visiting this aunt in his mature years, he "challenged the dear old lady, then far along in years, to cook another dinner of the kind she had provided on Sabbath days when we were both more youthful. She produced that dinner, and I am able to say now that if all the cooks of Iowa were up to Aunt Millie's standard, then the gourmets of the world should leave Paris for Iowa."

The Burlington railroad provided fascinating treasure trove. Its tracks were ballasted with glacial gravel and the youngsters, by diligent search, found "gems of agate and fossil coral that could, with infinite backaches, be polished on the grindstone. Their fine points came out wonderfully when wet, and you had to lick them with your tongue before each exhibit."

Because we know the answers at the back of the book, the temptation is to detect the great geologist of the future in the little lad sorting stones at the track. Then one recalls that his playmates were no less engrossed in the game but did not grow up to be miners. The temptation is even stronger when we learn of the story told in the 1920s by the eighty-eight-year-old Dr. William Walker.

Dr. Walker was the West Branch dentist and collected stones as a hobby. "Many an hour," he reported, "Herbert spent in my office poring over specimens while other children played. And gradually there was born in the boy the determination to win an education. For so often I would have to say, 'I don't know' in answer to his questions. That never satisfied him."

When Secretary of Commerce Hoover visited West Branch he did not fail to call on the dentist and—proving the absentmindedness of some Cabinet members—forgot two fifty-dollar bills on the old man's mantlepiece. But one suspects that the good dentist assigned a role to his geological collection not uninfluenced by later knowledge.

Actually the earliest recorded ambition of Herbert was to drive a locomotive. Dr. Walker was right, however, in surmising that the boy hankered for learning, especially the kind one picked up outside of school rooms. He took after his mother in his hunger for knowledge and his idealistic urges, even as he took after his father in his humor and mechanical bents.

There was a well-remembered vacation which Herbert spent with an Uncle Pennington Minthorn in Sioux County, Iowa. The uncle was breaking in a prairie farm that summer. For the boy it was thrilling to live in a sod house and ride the lead horse of a team plowing up virgin soil. Any such farm "was a Montessori school in stark reality," as he put the matter long afterwards.

His earliest awareness of the stir of national events was a torchlight parade in the Garfield campaign. There were only two or three Democrats in West Branch—one of them conveniently a drunk and therefore a living reproof to the Democratic Party. It must have been ritual rather than vote-getting that accounted for the parade. In Hoover's mind it would loom larger and brighter than any of the thousand parades he was fated to suffer as a man.

No, it was decidedly not an unhappy childhood. Maybe it should have been, but it wasn't, any more than Huckleberry Finn's or Tom Sawyer's. Bereavements and sorrows, big and small, were blotted out by the "glories of snowy winter, the joining of the neighbors to harvest, the gathering of apples, the pilgrimage to the river woods for the annual fuel and nuts," and a thousand other momentous events.

One thing is sure. There was in Hoover, then and thereafter, no trace of self-pity when he contemplated his childhood in Iowa—and in Oregon after that. He never felt that destiny had shortchanged him. He came out of his first ten years with a strong body, a lively mind, and a spirit richer than he could himself suspect.

On taking inventory of his enduring memories and his earliest influences, he was able to state without reservation: "It is the entry to life which I could wish for every American boy and girl."

3

In late 1884, when Herbert was more than ten, no doubt after another family council, he was told gently, "Thee is going to Oregon." That meant the hurt of separation from his whole West Branch world, but it also meant a thrilling journey by train across the Rocky Mountains to the fabulous Northwest, there to join the most respected of his uncles—Dr. Henry John Minthorn, country doctor, missionary, teacher, Civil War veteran. The tears that filled the boy's eyes connoted not only the pain of parting but the joy of anticipation.

Dr. Minthorn had practically demanded that his sister's boy be surrendered to him. His only son had just died and it seemed to him right that one of Huldah's orphans be sent to fill that place in his home and heart. And he had another argument on his side, one that carried immense weight. He had just been put in charge of a new school, the Friends Pacific Academy, forerunner of today's Pacific University, so that Herbert could continue his schooling without touching the tiny estate left by his parents.

And so his demand prevailed. Loaded down with blessings, sound spiritual counsel, a roll of bedding, and a huge hamper of provisions— meats and breads cooked and baked by Aunt Millie—Herbert made the seven-day journey by migrant train to Oregon. A family named Hammil, making the same journey, agreed to take him in charge. On the way the boy wrote long letters to his beloved schoolteacher, Miss Brown, describing his fellow passengers and complaining that the Rockies were not as rocky as he'd expected—just dirt.

In Portland he was collected by a taciturn uncle in the familiar Quaker garb and conveyed to the new Friends' settlement called Newberg on the Willamette River, about twenty-two miles southwest of Portland. Aunt Laura and her three daughters were boiling pear butter for the winter when their kin arrived from "the East" and graciously invited him to eat all the pears he wished. Never having tasted the fruit before, he proceeded to gorge himself, with the result that he could not look at a pear again without wincing.

There was plenty of work to spare for a strong lad in a family of girls. He became valet to the doctor's team of ponies and frankly disliked the task; he milked the cow, split the firewood, helped his uncle clear tracts of fir forest. And, of course, he was put to school at once. What with study, the Meetinghouse, and letter-writing to Iowa, he was busy enough. One of his first summers in Newberg he took a job weeding onions in the bottomlands north of the town at fifty cents a day; the thirty dollars he brought back and conserved made him feel rich and almost independent.

He found ample compensations for the hard labors. There were the great wheat fields he loved to watch; the rivers swarming with fish; the forests. He wondered whether he could ever absorb this new, more rugged land to his heart's content. In time he did, for a boy's hours are many times longer than a man's hours. Somehow he found the leisure to play baseball with new friends, to build dams, hunt for grouse and, of course, fish for trout.

Above all, there was Uncle Henry John himself, a university man whom he found endlessly romantic. For this uncle had driven teams for the "Underground Railway" in Iowa as a boy, had run away from home to enlist in the Union Army, and had taken part in the Battle of Shiloh. In his nephew's eyes he was a character right out of a forbidden book. Besides doctoring, Henry John superintended the new school, where he taught history and literature, took a leading part in the affairs of the Friends, and of course cared for his homestead.

Sometimes the boy accompanied him on visits to patients, which usually meant jogging along rough and often hub-deep mud roads for hours. They would take turns driving the team. And though the doctor was sparing in words, his strong sense of duty demanded that these intervals be used to instruct his nephew.

Herbert thus learned a lot about physiology in health and in sickness. He learned even more about Indian history—Dr. Minthorn had set up Indian schools in his time and, in fact, first came to Oregon as a U. S. Indian Agent. Many of those jogging hours were also devoted to American history, with special reference to its central event, which was of course the Battle of Shiloh.

Not all Quakers are pacifists and certainly Dr. Minthorn was not one. "Turn your other cheek once," he instructed the boy, "but if he smites you then punch him." He had another favorite maxim of his own making which registered on Herbert's mind: "The meanest thing a man can do is to do nothing."

The boy had a will of his own which at times, as in all normal families, clashed with his uncle's. There was even a period when Herbert stalked out in anger and boarded with other relatives. It could not have been serious, for when the Minthorns moved to Salem, the capital, he went along. He was then fifteen and the transfer marked the end of his basic schooling.

Salem was already a thriving city of eight thousand. The doctor had gone into the land-settlement business with Charles Moore, Ben Cook, and other Quaker friends. The entrepreneurs had bought several square miles of fat land and were parceling it out as orchard plots to new settlers. They drew up truthful but enticing descriptions which were spread throughout the country, and their salesmen met new arrivals at Portland to explain the fruit-raising opportunities near Salem.

To Herbert fell the post of office boy for the Oregon Land Company, as the venture styled itself. His salary was fifteen dollars a month and in time it was raised to twenty. Except for a short break, during which he drove the first horsecar in Salem, he remained office boy until he left for college at the age of seventeen.

The title made him in effect a general utility man. From the man who kept the books he learned the rudiments of bookkeeping. Briefly, indeed, he considered that as a career, but the specimen of the trade closest at hand was a dour and unhappy Scotsman and that served to dissuade him. With the help of the secretary, Miss Laura Hewitt, he learned how to type passably well—a skill that would prove helpful in the years immediately ahead. He took a hand also in drafting advertisements and blueprinting roadways and plottings.

One night a creditors' meeting was taking place at the company office. It grew stormy and was getting nowhere. Suddenly the lights went out and the gathering perforce dispersed. Dr. Minthorn was locking up when he caught sight of his nephew, a guilty grin on his face.

"Did thee turn out the lights?" he asked in sudden comprehension.

"Yes," the boy admitted. "They were only running up the gas bill. There was no use in that kind of talk."

Together with the office boy of another firm, Herbert once took a flier in business. A sewing machine agent had his shop on their street. Since he accepted old machines as part of the purchase price of new ones, and wrecked them as thoroughly as he could, he had a dump of smashed metal in his backyard. The boys paid him twenty dollars for the junk, after which they labored for weeks sorting parts and rebuilding machines. But even at a dollar apiece they could find no buyers for the resurrected goods. They lost their twenty dollars but, as Hoover later put it, they "learned a powerful lot about the insides of sewing machines."

Ben Cook, one of his employers, was more than willing to discuss his former office boy when Hoover had become a great figure in the great world. It was Cook, along with Laura Hewitt and other Salemites who knew him "when," who launched a Hoover-for-President committee in Oregon thirty years later. Young Bert, he told inquirers, impressed them especially with his extraordinary memory. They came to refer to him as a walking encyclopedia, for he knew the status of all deals, the contents of all letters, and the whereabouts of all documents.

"He was on the jump when there was anything to do," Cook testified, "but the moment he was through, out would come his geometry or algebra or history, and he'd sit, shoulders hunched over the little table in the corner, preparing for college."

Others, too, remembered him primarily in that studious posture. He was at the age when reading can become an absorbing passion for some boys. A Miss Jane Gray—he never forgot her name or his debt to her—made the reading of good books among Salem boys her mission. She introduced him to Dickens and Scott and other classics, and before long there were few books in Salem libraries which he had not read.

His main contact with national affairs was through an elderly and argumentative Democrat named Hobson and his cronies. They came from time to time to the office of an evening to argue with the Quaker Republicans. "The debate," Hoover has attested, "invariably ended with complete disgust of each one at the obstinacy and low intelligence of the others."

Herbert had made up his mind to go to college. More than that, to a college of his own choice. Catalogues from all kinds of institutions were delivered to his address. He knew that Dr. Minthorn could wangle a scholarship in some small Quaker college, but his mind was increasingly fixed on science and engineering, departments in which Quaker schools were not interested.

When a business school was opened in Salem, young Hoover promptly enrolled for evening classes. Luckily one of the teachers was deeply interested in mathematics and was delighted to discover that the youngster had a natural aptitude for it. Thus Hoover was guided through elementary algebra and geometry at odd hours and at no cost except time.

In conversations with his associates Hoover sometimes recalled how the dream of engineering was brought to the surface of his thought:

An engineer from the East—a Mr. Robert Brown—drifted into the office on some mission and made the acquaintance of the office boy. In the course of our talks he discussed the advantages of college training for a profession. He spoke much of engineering.

For a year I mulled over it, talking to all who would listen. I haunted the little foundry and sawmill and the repair shops of the town. I collected catalogues and information on engineering universities. I was determined to become an engineer. My leanings had been initially on the mechanical side. But I had visited a mining prospect in the Cascades with a mining engineer who persuaded me that his branch of the profession offered more choice. His study of the geology of the mines and his conclusions therefrom that the mine was no good excited my imagination.

Then the dream found a focus for action. Reports began to appear in the local press about a new university being founded at Palo Alto, near the southern shore of San Francisco Bay, by the wealthy Senator Leland Stanford, as a memorial to his only son who had just died at the age of sixteen. It was to be a progressive institution, with the stress on technical and scientific disciplines and "usefulness" as its guiding ideal. A young scientist and educator who had already made a name for himself, Dr. David Starr Jordan, had been secured as president and was gathering a faculty of broad-minded teachers not yet set in rigid academic patterns.

Hoover, having received advance literature on the Palo Alto project, put away all other catalogues, for he knew where he was going. At the same time his heart was filled with despair: he had not attended high school and the requirements for entry seemed far beyond his capacity. He studied harder than ever, on the chance that he might crash through.

His lack of preparation was only half his problem. The other half was the opposition of Grandmother Minthorn, who had come to live in Oregon, of Henry John and others to a secular institution and one, moreover, without background. This once, however, they realized that Huldah's son, though pliant in other matters, could be obstinate on essentials.

Happily the announcement of the entrance examinations to be held in Portland indicated that they would be conducted by a well-known mathematics professor, Joseph Swain—and providentially Dr. Swain happened to be a prominent Quaker. A university with which he was connected could not be iniquitous, so the family opposition crumbled.

The completion of the new university was scheduled for the very month in which Herbert would turn seventeen, August 1891. That spring he went to Portland and diffidently, more than a bit scared, presented himself to Dr. Swain. He did not pretend that he was fully prepared for higher education but took all the exams. Though he failed in many subjects, he impressed the Quaker educator with his proficiency in mathematics, at least as far as he had gone, and with his eagerness and general intelligence. In his fumbling efforts Dr. Swain discerned solid abilities and a firm character.

He talked to the boy at length. In fact, he accepted an invitation to visit the Minthorns and other admirers in Salem. It seemed clear that Herbert could not afford several years of preparatory school. It was now or never. Dr. Swain proposed that he come to Palo Alto a few months ahead of time, get some coaching, and take a few examinations again. Thus it was decided.

It was a worried, immature, gangling boy who set out for California that June. He was tall for his age, lean and strong, toughened by pioneer life; his round, serious face under a mop of light brown hair was tanned and handsome and his jaws were set in high resolution.

He carried with him all his earthly goods: two suits of clothes, a bicycle, and $160 of savings—to which the family added fifty dollars more. He knew also that he could draw on his one-third of the money left by his parents and tended by Mr. Tatum. Another Salem boy, the son of the local banker, was his traveling companion; the banker insisted on paying Hoover's fare in consideration of some tutoring in mathematics for his son.

In the morgue of a Portland newspaper there was a yellowing clipping which told—accurately, we can but hope—about Hoover's departure:

Finally, when the time came to leave Oregon friends for the big university, Grandmother Minthorn went down to the depot at Salem with her boy.

"I think thy mother would like to see thee now," she said, when Bert stopped to kiss her soft withered cheek. "Thee has always been a good boy, Bertie. I shall always pray that thee does a conscientious work."

"Thee will have cause to be proud of me someday," Bert promised with a smile whimsical enough to cloak his emotions.

In his narrative for his sons, Hoover wrote of the adolescent years in the Northwest:

Oregon lives in my mind for its gleaming wheat fields, its abundant fruit, its luxurious forest vegetation, and the fish in the mountain streams. To step into its forests with their tangle of berry bushes, their ferns, their masses of wildflowers stirs up odors peculiar to Oregon.

III

Student at Stanford

PALO ALTO in 1891 was not even a railroad stop. The two Salem boys alighted at Menlo Park and found a hack to take them to the rambling country house on the outskirts of the university grounds where early arrivals, faculty and students, were put up. They naturally hastened to inspect "Stanford farm," as the campus-to-be was irreverently nicknamed for some time; the mission-style quadrangle of buildings and the accessory structures had been deployed on what used to be a hayfield.

They found buildings unfinished, dormitories draped in scaffolding, workmen rushing the job in anticipation of hordes of students. The sawing and hammering and swishing of paint brushes said, "Hurry, hurry!" The freshness of the institution, as if it were being made ready especially for them, thrilled the more sensitive students. It was all at the greatest possible remove from the sense of hoary age which is the trademark of a Harvard or a Yale.

In accordance with Dr. Swain's arrangements, Herbert moved into the Adelante Villa, where a Miss Fletcher gave him board and lessons in the subjects he had yet to take. This time he passed the entrance examinations, just barely and with a few "conditions"; one of them, English, only because he never got around to it, was to plague him at the end of his Stanford sojourn.

Discovering that he was short one subject for the minimum entry requirements, he analyzed the electives and decided to stake all on elementary physiology. Fortified by the reading of two textbooks on the subject in two nights, he took the test and passed—a demonstration of his exceptional memory and a providential dividend on those long rides with his country doctor uncle.

The truth is that Dr. Jordan and his associates were not overly hard on applicants for matriculation in that first season. They were less concerned with academic records than with the applicant's appetite and potential for learning. The misfits could be weeded out later, as indeed they were, wholesale.

About two weeks before the school doors opened, Hoover moved into Encina Hall, Room 38, and tradition has it that he was the first person to sleep under its roof. With the help of Dr. Swain, and by virtue of his experience as an office boy, he got a job at once at five dollars a week in the university office, where he helped to register the swarm of boys and girls from all over the country, but mostly from the West.

Hoover was the youngest student in that first Stanford class. For a boy reared in tiny towns and on farms, with little scope for his vigorous but largely unawakened intelligence, the life at the college was endlessly colorful and stimulating. Stanford had drawn to itself a unique and highly varied aggregation of both students and teachers.

The faculty was made up for the most part of men and women eager to break the traces of academic orthodoxy; they were keen on the slogans of "usefulness" which then had a ring of bold modernity. The student body counted young people from every layer of American society. Many of them, like Hoover, had only a sketchy kind of education picked up between chores, on the run; probably they would have been sent home for finishing courses by the established institutions. Others were well-to-do young intellectuals attracted by the progressive aura around the new venture. There were many, too, who came because Senator Stanford had made provisions for good students in bad circumstances; more than one of them had reached California by "riding the rods."

Here were wider human horizons than Hoover had as yet glimpsed; exciting mental contacts; startling political and religious views, each of them personalized in some classmate. From all reports he said little and listened a lot. There was about him a wordless eagerness. When he did offer an opinion it was succinct and impressively to the point, so that his presence among them registered—not dramatically, as in the case of the extroverts, but slowly, like an unfoldment.

The official opening ceremonies took place on October 1, 1891, with the Stanford family, state dignitaries, and leading Californians in attendance. An aroma of paint and fresh lumber hovered over the oratory. Something about the brand-newness of the place, the Santa Cruz foothills in the background, the noise and enthusiasm, so different from the conventionally hushed university atmosphere, gave the occasion a "gold rush" feeling; and some of the big, raw-boned students in the audience fitted perfectly into that fancy.

"All that we can do for you," said Senator Stanford, "is to place the opportunity within your reach. Remember that life is, above all, practical;

that you are here to fit yourself for a useful career; also, that learning should not only make you wise in the arts and sciences, but should fully develop your moral and religious natures."

And the youthful president, David Starr Jordan, said:

Our university has no history to fall back upon; no memories of great teachers haunt its corridors; in none of its rooms appear the traces to show where a great man has lived or worked. No tender associations cling ivy-like to its fresh new walls. It is hallowed by no traditions. It is hampered by none. Its finger posts all point forward.

Hoover was mightily impressed. Stanford was to become the physical and intellectual focus of his life, and in turn he was to bring enormous prestige and an array of practical activities to the school. He was fortunate: among the men he met there, classmates and teachers, he found a large number who were peculiarly congenial to his own type of mind and ideals. They were to figure among his dearest friends and most trusted co-workers in engineering, in social work on a grandiose scale, in vast public services. Within the precincts of Stanford he was to meet the woman whose devoted love and fine intellect were his greatest possessions forever after. Never were a young man and a young university more perfectly suited to one another.

The need to make a living would rarely be far from his mind—not as a worry but simply as a problem to be solved. In partnership with two other students he organized a newspaper route. Then he started a laundry service. Every Monday morning he collected bundles of soiled clothes, each Saturday afternoon he delivered the clean parcels. After a while he was able to hire helpers and leave himself free for other work, and in time leased these businesses to others, drawing a small but steady income from them. In his junior year he sold the laundry agency for thirty dollars. Also, at the suggestion of a new friend, they started a co-operative residence for students in Palo Alto, but this he soon abandoned because it took him away from campus interests.

Despite these multifarious activities, he made the freshman baseball team as shortstop. Alas, he stopped one a bit too short, spraining a finger so badly that he had to drop out. That was the end of his athletic career; except, as we shall see, as organizer and coordinator of all athletic and other student enterprises.

Dr. John Branner, the head of the department of geology and mining, was delayed until early in 1892. With his arrival, Hoover's real vocation began. Luckily for him there were only eleven students in the first geology class, so that he had the kind of personal tutelage which penetrated deeply. Of Dr. Branner he would write, in the fullness of time, "I came under the spell of a great scientist and a great teacher, whose friendship lasted over his lifetime."

He was a remarkable educator and human being, this professor, besides being among the foremost geologists in the United States. From the first he recognized in the gangling, immature-looking Quaker boy an aptitude for his specialty that had in it elements of genius. In need of a part-time secretary, and learning that Hoover could type, he engaged him forthwith, at thirty dollars a month.

When summer vacation came along, moreover, he obtained for his favorite student a job with the Geological Survey of Arkansas. Its assignment was to map the geologic outcroppings on the north side of the Ozarks. Mostly Hoover went about on foot and alone. The hill people, being afraid of all "government agents" who might interfere with their moonshining, wondered aloud whether this one was a spy. His attempts to explain the purpose of the survey only strengthened their suspicions, so he "finally gave up trying."

Always, however, there was a friendly family to give him a night's lodging. Hoover returned from the Ozarks "lean as a greyhound, as hard as nails, and as brown as a berry"—and about two hundred dollars ahead for the sophomore year.

As was perhaps to be expected, several students griped about Hoover's "pull" with Dr. Branner. Overhearing this talk, the geologist explained patiently that it wasn't pull that served Hoover but a sterling character. After indicating the way most men fumbled a job at hand, he said:

But I can tell Hoover to do a thing and never think of it again. If I told him to start to Kamchatka tomorrow and bring me back a walrus tooth, I'd never hear of it again until he came back with the tooth. And then I'd ask him how he had done it.

2

At Stanford, as at older universities, there was a snob element. As if to compensate for the lack of campus traditions and for the presence of a lot of backwoods boys and girls, the fraternity and sorority groups put an extra polish on their exclusiveness and refinement. The quiet boy who delivered papers, collected laundry, and worked in a professor's office could hardly rate with that element. Besides, Hoover naturally fell in with the original thinkers, the radicals, the doers among his classmates. In what was partly a social and partly a political alignment, he gradually assumed a share of leadership on the "progressive" and "populist" side.

The Greek-letter minority had taken most of the control of student activities into its hands. It was in the sophomore year that a young crusader appropriately named Zion raised the banner of revolt. He was more generally known as "Sosh" from the initial syllable of the sobriquet "socialist" thrown at him, and "Sosh" he remained even when he was a conservative businessman in San Francisco decades later. The great war between the Frats and the Barbs—short for "barbarians"—was under way. It raged for two years and smoldered for many years thereafter. Hoover, without seeking it, became the chief strategist and one of the leaders of the Barbs.

The most barbarous of the Barbs were the students so poor that they lived in the "camp," a row of workers' shacks left over from the period of the construction of the buildings. Though Hoover could afford to live in Encina Hall and had some "swells" among his friends, the "camp" dwellers looked upon him as morally if not physically their own.

To Hoover, therefore, "generalissimo" Zion assigned the job of "delivering the camp vote." This he duly accomplished in a series of bull sessions in the shacks. Personable male Barbs were assigned to work among the girls, apparently with first-rate results. The outstanding freshman of that year joined lustily in the fight on the Barb side of the barricades. His name was Ray Lyman Wilbur, then known on the campus as Rex Wilbur; many years later as Prex Wilbur when he became president of Stanford; and still later as Secretary of Interior Wilbur in the Hoover Cabinet.

The campaign was so hot that the faculty was a bit alarmed. Dr. Jordan wondered in so many words whether he was nurturing "a little Tammany Hall" in the university. When the votes were counted, the Barbs had won virtually all the offices, though by narrow margins, and Hoover, for all his anxiety to remain in the background, was given a lion's share of the credit.

During his second summer vacation, in 1893, and again thanks to Dr. Branner's recommendation, Hoover was hired by the United States Geological Survey, as cub assistant to Dr. Waldemar Lindgren. It was the luckiest of his many breaks. Dr. Lindgren was a top-shelf geologist. Three months by his side, ranging "in the glorious High Sierra, the deserts of Nevada, and among the mining camps where vitality and character ran strong" were the equivalent of a dozen years in school laboratories. As always when he worked with superior men, Hoover found in Dr. Lindgren a permanent friend and technical associate.

Most of the work was done on horseback on this assignment, and Hoover never thereafter had much use for horses. They offended his engineering sense. He would write for his sons:

In these long mountain rides over trails and through the bush I arrived finally at the conclusion that a horse was one of the original mistakes of creation. I felt he was too high off the ground for convenience and safety on mountain trails. He would have been better if he had been given a dozen legs so that he had the smooth and sure pace of a centipede. Furthermore, he should have had scales as protection against flies and a larger water-tank like a camel. All these gadgets were known to creation prior to the geologic period when the horse was evolved. Why were they not used?

But more than the horse disturbed him. Constantly during that summer he thought of the problems of the university. The many campus activities were run haphazardly; some of them had been monopolized for the profit of special groups; most of them suffered from chronic deficits. By the time he returned for his junior year a detailed plan for reform had taken shape in his mind. He presented it to Rex Wilbur, Herbert Hicks, Lester Hinsdale, and other Barb leaders.

The end product of their discussions was a campus constitution, written by Hoover. With only slight changes it is still the basic student charter of the university. It provided for a better articulated student organization, with responsibility and full accountability for all activities, whether intellectual, artistic, or athletic. Its key official would be a paid treasurer, whose job it would be to make activities pay off and to present regular, audited statements of receipts and expenditures. By thus organizing the finances—and this was characteristic of Hoover's special blend of idealism and practicality—it would be possible to help deserving students in distress.

When the caucus was ready to announce the plan, it insisted that Hoover run for treasurer under the new constitution. He refused. Since it was a paid office, he pleaded, the opposition might charge that he had initiated the project to make himself a job. Only the argument that the Barb ticket could not hope to win without him finally swayed Hoover—but on condition that, constitution or no constitution, he would not accept a salary. And that's how it was—he served as treasurer without a cent in remuneration, though the enormous work the office entailed cut into his other earnings.

The Barbs this time won overwhelmingly and the Hoover charter became campus law. To the supervision of the laundry route, his work for Dr. Branner, his heavy schedule to make up conditions, he now added responsibility for the "gates" at all university activities, from theatrical shows to football games. His was the principal headache when the till was empty; when sickness or some other trouble afflicted a worthy student; when funds were needed for uniforms or to finance a team sent to play off-campus.

The fact that he prospered under the staggering load must be credited first to his unusual physical stamina; secondly, to his natural gift for organizing time, for doing one thing intensively then turning to the next with equal concentration; thirdly, to his ability to spot able men and entrust them with adequate authority; and finally, to that amazing mental grasp which enabled him to soak up effortlessly the knowledge for which others had to slave and sweat.

He flunked only one course—German—but he did not get as high marks in other subjects as he might have with more effort. He was content with lesser grades because that left him margins of time for the extracurricular education that he regarded as no less important, such as attending lectures in biology, evolution, religion, a dozen other subjects, and for a lot of unassigned reading.

The Stanford athletic field was not yet fenced in. Hoover stationed assistants at strategic points to collect entrance fees—usually a quarter—from all comers. At a baseball game one day Hoover observed that a dignified, bearded old gentleman had been allowed to enter free. The collectors had simply lacked the nerve to demand a quarter from that eminent guest.

Hoover did not relish the job either; but the team's finances were weak, and duty was duty. When the blushing Hoover made his stammering demand, former President Benjamin Harrison proved that he was no gate-crasher. In recalling the episode, ex-President Hoover declared, "Justice must occasionally be done even to ex-Presidents and I here record that he took two more tickets." An embarrassing moment of the same order occurred on a subsequent occasion, with Andrew Carnegie in the culprit's seat and Hoover again doing the dirty work of extracting the entrance fee.

A combination lecture and concert forum was being operated by an enterprising student as his private business and private risk. On leaving college he willed the business to Hoover, to whom its amalgam of culture, enlightenment, and money-making appealed strongly. And thus he found himself also in the role of impresario. He did not do too badly in that role, though he came a few croppers. One of his more unprofitable "attractions" was a young Nebraska congressman who, being virtually unknown, failed to draw a crowd. A few years later his name would have jammed the largest auditorium in California, for it was William Jennings Bryan.

And once Hoover bit off more than he could chew. With an associate he sponsored a concert in San Jose for the celebrated and high-priced Polish pianist, Ignace Paderewski. Admission prices were of necessity stepped up, to cover the artist's minimum fee of two thousand dollars. But evidently Paderewski's celebrity had not yet impinged on that corner of California. The famous musician found himself facing infamous voids in the concert hall, and the impresarios found themselves four hundred dollars short. Hoover offered his personal note, based on nothing but good faith, of course. But the famous guest graciously canceled the obligation and everything ended happily, except that it left Hoover penniless for a while.

Some twenty-five years later, at a great public reception for Hoover in the city of Lodz, the same Paderewski, as Prime Minister of Poland, thanked the American for having saved tens of thousands of Polish lives. Understandably, he did not recall the San Jose incident. In his response to the President's eulogy, Hoover refreshed his memory of that occasion. Thunderous applause testified to the general conviction that the four hundred-dollar debt had been repaid in full.

3

When the last summer vacation arrived, between the junior and senior years, there was some uncertainty whether a geologic survey post would be open for him. With several classmates equally in need of making a few honest dollars, Hoover therefore went into the sign-painting business, of all things. They obtained commissions from San Francisco businesses to paint and erect in the Yosemite Valley "eyesores" advertising their wares.

The boys had no more than reached the valley when a telegram overtook them. It notified Hoover to report immediately to the survey party. The entrepreneurs had put their available cash into the purchase of materials. Upon turning their pockets and wallets inside out they confirmed the sad truth that all together they did not have enough money on them to pay his stage fare to the railroad. Herbert Hoover set out on foot. He walked eighty miles in three days, arriving in time.

That summer's expedition through the High Sierras, again under Dr. Lindgren's command, saw the cub geologist blossom into a real assistant. It was exacting but invigorating toil, on horseback most of the day, under the open skies most of nights. The spirited conversation of his mature companions fascinated the college student. Since many of them worked in Washington agencies, he learned a great deal not only about geology and mining but about the operations and eccentricities of government.

When the maps of the survey were published by the Government Printing Office, lo and behold! Hoover's name appeared beside Dr. Lindgren's in the credit lines. That was the first public recognition to come to Hoover in his chosen field of endeavor—an unsolicited compliment by a man at the top of the profession to a beginner on the lowest rung. Among the multitude of honors that were to descend on him through the years, Hoover would rank this one in a class by itself.

As the youngest member of the expedition he was made the disbursing officer, which made him responsible to Uncle Sam for every penny spent. That burdensome distinction netted him an amusing story for his fat repertoire of personal experiences, though it was not in the least amusing at the time.

On awaking one morning the party discovered that one of the pack mules was dead. It devolved on Hoover and two witnesses to report the loss and all attendant circumstances. As disbursing officer he was personally responsible for the full value, which was sixty dollars. An autopsy revealed that the mule, which had been tethered to a tree, had scratched his head with his hind foot, which got tangled in a halter rope; in trying to jerk out of the dilemma he evidently had broken his neck.

The report that in time reached the appropriate officials in Washington set forth these lugubrious facts. Some weeks later Hoover was officially advised that mules do not scratch their heads with their hind feet and that sixty dollars had been deducted from his salary! Dr. Lindgren insisted on absorbing the loss, vowing that he would collect it from some "damned bureaucrats" when he got back to the capital. The geologist, however, did not know the stuff of which bureaucrats are made. Some years later Hoover engaged him for consultation work in Australia. Dr. Lindgren's first words when they met in Melbourne were:

"Do you know that that damned bureaucrat never would pay me the sixty bucks! And do you know that I have since seen a hundred mules scratch their heads with their hind feet!"

Later Hoover found and bought a statuette of a mule contemplatively caressing his head with a hind foot, but Washington never restored the deducted money. Showing that there are mules of various breeds.

How did the twenty-year-old Hoover look to his classmates? Fortunately we have an expert answer from a specialist in observing his fellow men, the celebrated journalist and author Will Irwin. Will came to Stanford in 1894, when Hoover was in his final year. In the fullness of time Will wrote:

Entering as a freshman, my first impression of Hoover, our most eminent senior, resembled that of some great impersonal force. Jack Reynolds and Jule Frankenheimer, the uncheckable halfback; Phat Browning, the mighty football captain; Charlie Field and Edward Maslin Hulme, the university poets; Bledsoe and Magee, the statesmanlike intercollegiate debaters—them one cheered or joked from the bleachers.

But Hoover, while he walked humanly among us, was a kind of legend too; a supernally able personage. We both lived in Encina dormitory, so I must have seen him constantly at meals. I was playing football, so I must have beheld him conferring with Walter Camp, who coached us that year. Yet I have no concrete memory of him until that day when, playing center on the freshman team, I broke my ankle. . . .

Among those who came to visit him was Hoover. Will Irwin continues:

I have carried for more than thirty years the picture of him as he stood framed by the yellow door of my dormitory room. He was tall—just under

31

six feet—broad-shouldered, lean of figure. He wore one of those double-breasted blue suits which have since become almost a uniform with him. He had a slight stoop which, you felt, came rather from excess muscular development of the shoulders than from the midnight oil.

As he contemplated the damaged member, he carried his head a trifle to one side—another trick of attitude which marks him to this day. He had mouse-colored hair, as stubbornly straight as an Indian's, and hazel eyes so contemplative that they seemed dreamy. His round but powerful face had not a straight line in it. That oddity, I have noticed since, often characterizes the physiognomies of extremely able men—O. Henry and Lord Northcliffe, for example. He stood with one foot thrust forward, jingling the keys in his trousers pocket; a little nervous trick which he has never overcome.

Others present expressed sympathy for the wounded football player. But Hoover went into action, unobtrusively. He consulted the nurse about needs and the cost of an operation. He wrote a telegram to a San Francisco physician and sent one of the boys to file it. He was, in short, in quiet and efficient control. Irwin recalled:

He did not say a word of sympathy for me—in pain and forever out of football—but I felt it nevertheless. Then at the door he turned for an instant and jerked out: "I'm sorry." Just that; but it was as though another man had burst into maudlin tears. The crown of that personality was shyness.

Then and there, I suppose, I put myself under his leadership. That kind of thing was always happening at Stanford. Even men who opposed him in the "great frat-barb war," coming afterward into association with him, began to lean on his sane and unruffled judgment. The whimsies of life have permitted some of us to follow him since in affairs and struggles whose actors were kings, principalities and powers, dynasties and armies, violences of which the nineteenth century never dreamed, incredible human sacrifices, Godlike benevolences. But the game was the same. . . .

Will Irwin's appraisal, except that it was conveyed with the color and clarity of a professional writer, was par for the course among those who remembered and described Hoover in the college years. Without exception they underlined his great ability, his restraint, his diffidence, and his compassion.

4

Stanford being a co-educational university, we may safely suppose that girls were the principal scholastic interest of the boy students, or at any rate second only to football. Dozens of those boys have reminisced about the future President who walked in their midst. But one finds no reference to any "heart interests" credited to Hoover. Except one, and that one became his mate for life.

Since young Herbert was normal and prominent and strikingly good-looking, we must rely on his shyness and his earnestness to explain that hiatus. It seems clear that he had neither the time nor the talent for light flirtations. He did not learn to dance until his senior year, and that only so that he could squire the one and only "heart interest" to the proms.

This was before the Hollywood era and the word "glamorous" was not yet in common circulation. But it would have fitted Lou Henry, the daughter of a small-town banker in Monterey, California. Her looks and her horsemanship aroused about equal admiration when she enrolled as a freshman. Lou was tall, slim, beautiful rather than pretty, with a mass of brown hair over a high forehead. She was the outdoors type, strong and supple. As a matter of course she was installed in one of the swankier sorority houses.

And amazingly for a girl in those days, she had elected to major in geology. She had heard Dr. Branner lecture and her intelligence, which was of a high order, had been aroused by the fascination of this planet's structure. For Hoover, when he got to know her, the amazement was raised to a dimension of the miraculous when he learned that she had been born, of all places, in Waterloo, Iowa, only seventy-eight miles from West Branch and but four months after his own birth. It all seemed pre-ordained.

Lou's father, Charles Delano Henry, was born in Ohio and served in the Union Army in the Civil War. He learned the rudiments of banking in Waterloo, and in 1884 moved to Whittier, California, where with others he started a bank. In 1890 he moved to Monterey, founding the Bank of Monterey of which he remained president for many years. Lou was his only child.

From the day she entered Stanford, she subsequently informed Hoover, she had heard of him. He seemed the key man in every extracurricular enterprise, and his prowess as a geologist had become legendary. She imagined him, she said, as a mature, probably bearded, giant.

One afternoon, in his laboratory, Dr. Branner was showing the tall freshman girl an interesting pre-carboniferous specimen. Lou Henry paid no attention to the suntanned, straight-haired, rather immature-looking boy who stood nearby. She was too accustomed to that stare of fascinated admiration on his face to think anything of it.

Then Dr. Branner addressed him by name. "What is your opinion, Hoover?" He never got an answer. Hoover was tongue-tied and turning color. Whatever his opinion of the pre-carboniferous specimen, which he had himself brought from the Lindgren expedition, there was no doubt about his opinion of the contemporary specimen of womanhood in the laboratory.

33

Thereafter he was zealous, far beyond the call of duty, in helping her with geology, one of his obligations as an employee of the department. The blessed duty, as he would write for their sons, "was stimulated by her whimsical mind, her blue eyes and a broad grinnish smile that came from an Irish ancestor."

One story, solemnly recorded in a book, is that Lou Henry's sorority sisters objected to the social visits of a student whom, for all his reputation, some of them still remembered as their laundry collector. Lou is supposed to have packed her things and moved out in a huff. Whether the story is true deponent sayeth not. Suffice that the pre-carboniferous acquaintance flourished into an enduring and almost flawless human partnership.

For a moment, as the final university hours approached, it looked as if the old "condition" in English might prevent Hoover's graduation with his class. The tragedy was averted by Dr. Branner and other professors formally attesting that the boy's English was not merely adequate but superior.

Herbert Clark Hoover received his sheepskin, inscribed "Bachelor of Arts in Geology," in May 1895. Indubitably he was the outstanding student in the first graduating class of the new university. He was within three months of his twenty-first birthday. He has written:

I listened to Dr. Jordan's fine Commencement address with my mind mostly on the sinking realization that a new era was opening for me with only forty dollars in cash and the need of finding an immediate job. The depression of 1893 had reached the Pacific Coast in 1895. I had lived all my life in hard times. But I had never heard of depressions. No one told me there was one on foot. So I did not need to worry about that. Nor did I have to worry about what the government was going to do about it. No one was crying over "helpless youth" for that matter.

He avoided tearful farewells from campus friends—"I just assumed that I would see them again." The boys and girls attracted by the new university must have had, he said, "some special streak of enterprise." In any case, its first five or six classes produced an extraordinarily high ratio of graduates who in due time won leadership and fame in their various fields. For himself, they produced enduring friendships and loyal associates in important private and public undertakings in all the years to come.

How he felt about leaving Lou Henry he did not record—clearly his shyness did not permit this—but perhaps it needed no recording. The separation must have been a painful trial for both of them, since they were betrothed in their hearts. In the next three years, while Lou Henry completed her college education, Hoover, starting at the very bottom of his profession, would rise rapidly to posts normally beyond his years. He would be able to see her only a few times, but they carried on a large correspondence.

He had worked his way through college with forty dollars to spare as basic capital for starting a man's life work.

I V

Australian Gold

THE most famous alumnus of Leland Stanford University, Class of 1895, was making the Commencement address to the graduating Class of 1935. The country was deep in the mire of depression. He had no illusions about the kind of economic world those boys and girls, clutching their sheepskins, were setting out to conquer. But it was not in Herbert Hoover's nature to counsel defeatism or flaccid reliance on government "youth projects." He believed profoundly that American opportunity, though comatose, was not dead. His mind reached back across the chasm of four decades.

Some years ago [he said], I marched up, as you do, to receive the diploma of this university. For me, as for some of you here present, the occasion was somewhat distracted by the sinking realization of a shortage of cash working capital and the necessity of finding an immediate job.

Put into economic terms, I was earnestly wishing some person with a profit motive would allow me to try to earn him a profit. At the risk of seeming counterrevolutionary or a defender of evil, I am going to suggest that this test for a job has some advantages. It does not require qualifications as to ancestry, religion, good looks, or ability to get votes.

I did not immediately succeed in impressing any of the profit-and-loss takers with the potentialities of my diploma. The white-collar possibilities having been eliminated, my first serious entrance into the economic world was by manual labor. But somehow, both in the stage of manual labor and in professional work, I missed the discovery that I was a wage slave.

He did discover the wretchedness of unemployment as the last of the forty dollars he possessed on graduating melted away, and later, between manual jobs. He learned to know, in his own words, "the bottom levels of despair . . . the ceaseless tramping and the ceaseless refusals" at employment offices.

He headed, naturally, for the Sierras, where he had ranged with government surveying gangs, in the mining areas of Nevada City and Grass Valley. His engineering degree netted him only pitying smiles; hard-boiled "practical" mine bosses did not quite trust the "effete," diploma-bearing animal. It was best, he found, to dress rough, postpone shaving, try to mangle your grammar, and say nothing about your education—for the time being.

Both his money and his credit at a shabby hotel were about exhausted before he got his first job. It was at the Reward Mine, but the name evidently did not apply to him. His reward as an underground "mucker," pushing a car into which he had shoveled wet dirt and rock at the lower levels on the ten-hour night shift, was two dollars a day in a seven-day week. In a couple of months, however, he was promoted to helper on a drill and attained the social status of a miner.

Laid off by Reward, he had an interval of "ceaseless tramping" that ended with a job at full miner's wages at the Mayflower Mine. His shift boss had some kindly advice: "Get in there and dig. You need a nose for gold. It can't be learned by sticking your nose in a book. You'll develop it by working where the gold is." The fact that this superior took to calling him "the Professor" didn't improve his standing with fellow miners, but in time they came to like and to accept him.

Most of the miners in that district were Cornishmen, speaking their ancestral dialect, which was colorful enough, whether in sacred disputation on religion or in profane times of cussing. After a while they took the grammatical college man to their grimy bosoms. Some thirty-three years later those of his fellow workers who survived organized a Hoover committee and carried every Cornish vote in the valley for the Republican ticket. Always, as miner or mine manager, Hoover left a trail of friends and admirers.

His brother Theodore had been forced to leave school in order that their sister May might continue her education, after Grandmother Minthorn died. They were living in Berkeley, California, where Theodore was employed as a linotyper. Having saved a hundred dollars, and learned invaluable lessons about mining and miners, Herbert joined them. For the first time since her death, Huldah's three children kept house together. Harriet Miles, one of the cousins who had sat with Herbert in the Indian school in Pawhuska, came to live with them.

Just as soon as Hoover began to earn money, he insisted that Theodore resume his education at Stanford. After a successful engineering career the elder brother returned to their common alma mater as Dean of the Engineering School.

Over in San Francisco the reigning mining expert was an American of French birth named Louis Janin. Though he was too big-hearted and easygoing to be the richest mining man in the West, he was acknowledged as the ablest. Wherever men picked the bones of this crusty old planet for mineral wealth, there Janin's reputation extended. Hoover took his courage in tow and called on this gentleman.

Janin was a stout, garrulous, and amiable fellow. Fledgling engineers by the dozen came to him for work, any work; it meant a lot to have the Janin imprimatur on your career. He let them down gently. He took the boyish Hoover, for instance, to lunch in his club and ordered wine and spent more on the repast than his guest possessed in all the world. Not only was there no opening in his firm, he explained, but there was a long waiting line of experienced and well-recommended men. Just to emphasize how hopeless the situation was, he remarked that the only job vacant in his organization was that of copyist. Which was Janin's blunder or, as it turned out, his good fortune.

"That's fine," the young man said in substance, "I can typewrite and I have a pretty good handwriting. When do I report for work?"

The jovial Janin roared with laughter. He was cornered. As Hoover had calculated at once, a copyist close to the throne was more strategically located than an engineer on a waiting list. He got the job. Within a few weeks Janin assigned him to a chore of research in northern Colorado. He was so well impressed with the report that copying went by the board.

This was the last time Hoover ever applied for a job—thereafter the jobs applied for Hoover.

As Janin's respect for the young man's abilities mounted, the assignments became more important. One of these called for a survey on a mine in the Sierras. When Janin remarked on the completeness of the resulting report, Hoover said quietly, "I worked underground in that mine, pushing a car."

Another assignment took him to Steeple Rock, New Mexico, as assistant to the mine manager. He had sampled some tough camps by that time, but this was the toughest yet, a frontier "set" of the sort Hollywood Westerns would one day immortalize in celluloid; a place, as Hoover put it, that "practiced a good deal of original sin, especially after paydays." It was one of the jobs that helped temper the steel under his shy exterior. He went about his duties among assorted desperadoes with a six-shooter on his hip and a rifle in his saddle guard. There was no jail in the camp, but a deep abandoned shaft did as a substitute. The manager just lowered malefactors into the pit and threw the rope after them, pending the arrival of the sheriff.

A mine is not merely a hole in the ground. It is a complex problem in machinery, supplies, transport, power, water, and a thousand other elements. It is a problem in choosing and weeding men, improvising quick answers to sudden technical questions. Hoover was being paid more by

Janin with every passing month, but the knowledge and insights he gathered could not be measured in dollars and cents. His gift for detail and organization and estimating men, and that sixth sense about metals and fuels which is inborn, came to the surface almost from the start.

After about a year in the field, Janin decided he needed Hoover in the home office. The firm had been engaged as expert counsel in a great mining litigation in Green Valley. The briefs had been prepared by Judge Curtis Lindley, tops in his profession. But Hoover had one advantage over the judge—he had worked in Grass Valley pits and surveyed every acre of the sites involved. So he tore the briefs apart, steered the great lawyer in the right directions, and helped win the case. And the old human pattern was repeated: Judge Lindley became his devoted lifelong friend.

By that time Janin knew that he had a "gold mine" in the young Quaker. It must be set down as evidence of his Gallic gallantry, therefore, that he released the boy when a great opportunity showed up.

A gold rush was then under way in central Western Australia. "The City" in London was the money center of the world. Through its counting houses millions of pounds sterling were being funneled into the new developments at the antipodes. And The City had a healthy respect for American gold-mining methods and American engineers. In October 1897, Louis Janin received a cabled inquiry from the venerable firm of Bewick, Moreing and Company, the most highly esteemed concern of mining consultants in England.

They had been retained by clients as agents on ten Australian gold mines, as well as an array of prospecting sites. Huge investments were at stake. They needed a young man, as the job would be extremely strenuous—but not too young, as it required thorough experience; say a man of thirty-five.

Janin reported afterward that Hoover stared in speechless awe when he was offered the post. Six hundred dollars a month sounded like sudden wealth, but what mattered more than money were the horizons for expansion, the headlong plunge into the very center of the profession. Though Janin did not conceal his candidate's relative lack of experience, he sent the kind of answer that clinched the appointment. In indicating that his protégé was not yet thirty-five, he was well within the truth—by twelve years, in fact.

And so the Iowa lad said farewell to Lou Henry, now a junior; they were not exactly engaged but there was between them what in that time was called "an understanding." He took leave of his family and friends. On the advice of Janin, he bought himself his first dress suit. At the insistence of his friend Lester Hinsdale, he also bought a sporty Scotch tweed suit. A year later Hinsdale received from Australia a package containing the suit, with a note that said, "Since you like it, take it. I haven't worn it yet."

Herbert Hoover was off on an adventure that would make him as familiar with Australia and China and India, with South Africa and the interior of Russia, as he was with West Branch or Newberg. On his way eastward he paused at West Branch, where assorted Minthorns and Hoovers marveled at his rapid rise to man's work, for they remembered him as a very average little boy.

Then he crossed the Mississippi for the first time, headed for New York, for London, for Australia, for the world.

2

The seven thousand-ton White Star liner that conveyed Hoover across the Atlantic "proved unable to overcome the waves to my satisfaction." In due time he presented himself at the imposing offices of Bewick, Moreing. If Charles Algernon Moreing, who was head of the firm, and other dignitaries were astonished by his youth, they were too well bred to comment on the crime. Besides, they went immediately into a detailed examination of the Australian problems with him and realized that there was nothing juvenile about his mind and temper.

A weekend at Mr. Moreing's elegant estate for the final consultations turned up one minor terror for which even the New Mexican experience had not prepared him. His name was Buttons and he sniffed audibly at the scantiness of the American's wardrobe; worse, he insisted on helping a grown man dress! Only the dress suit (as Janin may have foreseen) mitigated the butler's contempt.

It was a long journey—by way of France, Italy, Egypt, India: "History became a reality and America a contrast," Hoover would sum it up. Having arrived in Albany, the port in Western Australia, he had to spend two tedious weeks in quarantine, smallpox having been discovered on board the ship. Then, three hundred-odd miles inland by a just-constructed single-gauge railroad, and he was at Coolgardie, one of the gold-mining areas assigned to him.

Americans, knowing the feel of California in '49 from their literature, can more readily visualize Coolgardie, Kalgoorlie, Leonora, and the other mushrooming towns in the Australian desert; though even the "forty-niners" had far more comforts and amenities. It was a flat and desolate land of vast distances covered with low, bristly sagebrush, where the mercury rarely dropped below one hundred even at night; a land in which water was almost as valuable and more rare than the gold for which thousands of men were hunting feverishly. Only the "Persian carpet of many-colored immortelles," as Hoover described it, spread once a year after the brief rainy season, broke the monotony of the parched and cracked landscape.

It was a sultry, dusty, insect-ridden world of clapboard and corrugated iron shelters, unlicked men, vile liquor, and soaring hopes that too often petered out in sordid defeat. No one has recorded what the mine managers and engineers and miners, many of them grizzled veterans, thought of the boy sent to lead them. What is known is that very soon he became "the Chief" to his men. A later generation would take for granted that this title derived from his term as President of the United States; actually it began when he was twenty-three, and "the Chief" he remained to those associated with him in all the years that followed.

Hoover inspected the mines, discounted those that seemed to him uneconomic, and focused his energies tenaciously on the few that showed real promise. Coolgardie, for instance, he canceled out early; Kalgoorlie proved profitable. He brought in specialists from all parts of the world, but mainly from California. He laid out plants, ordered American equipment, and introduced processes that were new to Australia, or just new. Rapidly he carved islands of order out of a turbulent sea of chaos; for the first time certain financiers began to see a profit on their investments.

The inspection of new prospects meant days-long journeys, astride Afghan camels in the first period, because of the water shortage; later, when the government put in a four hundred-mile pipeline which brought fresh water from the coast, horses were used. For the rest of his life the very sight of a camel made Hoover a little seasick. In installments of thirty or forty miles a day, he traveled with the nauseous caravans from one of his mines to another; or on the trail of rumors that sometimes made millionaires in London and New York and more often fizzled out in disappointments.

The life was every bit as strenuous as the Londoners had promised. Of nights, when the rest of Kalgoorlie or Leonora was loud with payday guzzling and brawling, Hoover was in his sweltering corrugated offices, working and planning. He seemed detached, above the fevers of the place and time, a cool mind clicking away in the swirling excitements.

Now he had plenty to report to the blue-eyed girl still at Stanford. Some of the things he described she could understand perfectly, being a geologist herself—the new filter process he had introduced, for instance. He had adapted it from one used in sugar refining and in time the whole mining industry employed the process. And there were bits of humor to transmit too. The burro who ate wax matches, starting an internal blaze that had to be put out with water through a funnel. The vegetable garden he tried to coax into being in defiance of parched soil and salty water,

netting two pathetic cabbages at a cost of only $250 a head. The eccentric
characters who gravitated to a boom region.

Once the British aristocrat who was Governor-General of Australia
visited the district and was conducted by the reception committee to a
mine under Hoover's management. In his usual garb when at work, a
pair of overalls, the American conducted his guest personally down the
shaft. When they came up on the surface the Governor graciously thanked
the nice young man—and gave him a five-shilling tip.

On one of his early camel treks, 150 miles into the interior, Hoover
camped overnight near a prospect which the owners, a group of Welsh-
men, called "Sons of Gwalia." They took him through their primitive mill
and "showings." Others had seen the place—it was one of dozens of hope-
fuls—and moved on. But Hoover, with that sixth sense to guide him,
stopped short. He knew at once that this was "it" and negotiated an
option.

It required a special kind of courage for a man of twenty-four to urge
upon his home office, on his own judgment, an investment of half a million dollars; $250,000 for a two-thirds interest in the property and $250,000
more for working capital. London followed his hunch, voted him ten
thousand dollars a year to manage the mine, and gave him a small interest in the enterprise. In the next fifty years the Gwalia mines produced fifty-five million dollars in gold and ten million dollars in dividends.

Hoover was too busy to be lonely. He found tag ends of time, moreover,
to indulge his great hunger for reading; not only the English and French
classics, economics and technological tomes, but the classics of antiquity
became part of his mental equipment. And despite the normal quota of
failures, he had the deep satisfaction of achievement. Recalcitrant mines
began to hum and pay off. Areas that did not even have a name a year
earlier were turning swiftly into populous and prosperous communities.
The Gwalia workings, to which he now gave his major time, were yielding the yellow metal beyond his own high expectations. He was able to
send money home to his family and toward the support of needy friends.

In retrospect he was to write of this period: "To feel great works growing under one's feet and to have constantly more men getting good jobs
is to be master of contentment."

His name was beginning to appear in mining journals and even on the
financial pages of London papers. Melbourne and Sidney publications
respectfully solicited his views on this and that. In Australia miners talked
of him as "Boy Hoover" with an intonation that meant "boy wonder."
There were some who dubbed him "Hail Columbia" Hoover—H.C.
being conveniently his initials—because of the zeal with which he pushed
American machinery, men, and methods.

Beginning in Australia and in his fifteen subsequent years of engineering, Hoover played an important role in "Americanizing" the mining industry of the world. More than any other one man, he enhanced the prestige of his country in this specialized field. It was a prestige translated through the years into thousands of jobs for American engineers and in American plants supplying the equipment for their work.

Once, at the Gwalia site, a lanky young man of Scotch extraction, John A. Agnew, came looking for employment. He was a graduate of the University of New Zealand with only a few months of experience in mining. Hoover put him to work underground and kept an eye on him. In a few weeks he made Agnew shift boss and later mine superintendent. Until 1914, Agnew continued to work under Hoover and thereafter rose to leadership in the British mining profession. Before his death, in 1939, he commanded the largest group of mines of any engineer in the world.

The Agnew story was not exceptional. For all the time Hoover "panned" for dependable men as eagerly as a lone prospector pans for gold. When he found them they usually remained "Hoover men" in all his future operations, not only in industry but often in public service.

All the same, after nearly two years in the Australian deserts, homesickness was beginning to gnaw at Hoover's nerves. A girl in Monterey (Lou Henry had now graduated with honors and was back home) certainly had much to do with his condition. He was planning to go home for a visit when a cable reached him which settled the immediate future neatly and dramatically. It came from Peking, China, and was signed by his boss, Charles Algernon Moreing. There was work to be done in China.

Two messages went forward simultaneously over Hoover's signature, one to Peking and the other to Monterey, California. The first was an emphatic Yes to Moreing. The second was an affectionate request for a Yes, and it arrived with record speed.

V

Adventure in China

Hoover journeyed to the second stage of his great adventure, China, by way of England and California. When he reached London in January 1899, he was no longer self-conscious about his youth, no longer intimidated by the magnificence of offices or the snobbery of butlers. He had proved himself and justified Janin's trust. No one cared now whether the man who activated the limping Australian properties and developed the fabulous Sons of Gwalia was twenty-five or eighty-five.

From Mr. Moreing, now back home, he got a fill-in on his new assignment.

China was in the throes of the short-lived "reform and progress" movement under the so-called Young Emperor, Kwang Hsu. The Celestial Empire seemed ready for Westernizing influences to unlock its sealed-up natural resources. The principal European nations shoved and bribed and intrigued for privileged positions in the process.

The Chinese-owned Chinese Engineering and Mining Company was floating a large bond issue in England, France, Belgium, and Germany, and it was in this connection that Mr. Moreing had gone to Peking. The company owned coal mines and cement plants and was raising the capital in part to construct a coal-loading port at Chingwangtao on the Gulf of Chihli.

The nominal Chinese manager of this company was a former stable groom risen to political power and wealth by devious routes, one Chang Yen-mao. The Young Emperor had also put him at the head of a newly established Ministry of Mines. Chang was looking for a foreign specialist as his right-hand man in the government and in the company. The European nations, snarled in a great knot of partnerships and rivalries, each

44

maneuvering for a juicier bite of roasted China, coveted that post under Minister Chang.

Moreing had sensibly counseled Chang to choose an American and thus bypass the whole pack of diplomatic intriguers. Chang agreed, and Moreing produced the man. The job involved a dual responsibility: manager of the coal and cement corporation and director of all Celestial Mines, known and especially unknown, under the Young Emperor's conniving minister. It carried a combined salary of twenty thousand dollars and all expenses.

The coal and cement end was clear enough. It meant building rail lines and an ice-free port, organizing production and transport—practical work for a superbly practical man. The Chinese Government end was exalted but nebulous, intangible and shadowed by palace intrigues. It was to remain nebulous to the finish. Even before Hoover reached China several months later, the Young Emperor had been dethroned and imprisoned by the Empress Dowager, his mother. Leading "reform" officials among the courtiers were being executed or forced to flee for their lives and the Westernizing plans, mining included, were left in mid-air. The wily Chang was among the few who survived the tempest. But much of this was still in the future.

Lou Henry became Mrs. Herbert Hoover in her parental home in the picturesque mission town of Monterey on February 10, 1899. The Henrys were Episcopalians but the girl had already announced her intention to join the Society of Friends. There being no Quaker Meeting in Monterey, a civil ceremony was decided upon. A Catholic priest who was a friend of the family, Father Ramon Mestres, officiated in his capacity of civil magistrate.

The following day the newlyweds sailed from San Francisco, loaded down with all the books on Chinese life, history, and customs they could corral. A month's voyage across the Pacific was their honeymoon, a rented dwelling in the foreign compound in Peking was Lou's bridal house. While her husband threw himself into the complex affairs of his new jobs, she turned the house into a home. For this she had a unique talent which eased their lives in a dozen foreign settings for twenty years to come. She mobilized the usual battalion of Chinese servants and began the systematic study of the Chinese language, with excellent results.

Anyone who has lived in a foreign colony in the East knows the elaborate structure of social life and protocol that prevails there. Both his business and official positions entitled Hoover and his bride to top-shelf social status. But the multilingual colony found them disappointing and even alarming in their choice of friends, native and foreign, on the basis of personal predilections and with small regard to social lines. Then and ever after, the Hoovers had no patience for the rigamarole of "society."

It was a comparatively simple matter to import a few of his associates from Australia and get the work going for the Chinese Engineering and Mining. The harbor of Chingwangtao was cleared and port construction speeded despite freezing weather. Rails were laid. The twenty-five thousand Chinese in the coal mines and cement plants were kept busy, at wages higher than they had ever known before.

But the Ministry of Mines was another matter, for here politics and intrigue, not engineering, set the pace. Logic dictated intensive research on coal, iron, steel, zinc, and copper. These were the resources readiest at hand and the things the Chinese people most needed. Minister Chang, however, operated on a devious political logic of his own. He was hoping to dazzle the Empress, fortify his official status, and incidentally get his hands on treasure at government expense by locating gold. Pressed for permission to dig coal and iron where they existed, Hoover was shunted repeatedly to prospecting for gold where it might or might not exist.

It was primarily on the search for the yellow metal that Hoover and several of his assistants traveled thousands of miles, endured hardships, and on occasion fought off bandits. The most distressing of those hardships was the magnificent style in which, as plenipotentiaries of a self-important Minister with public funds to burn, they were obliged to move. Gold or no gold, the search had to build "face" for Chang.

The first of these expeditions was typical, both in its scale and its futility. It was into Jehol, to a site about 150 miles from the railroad. Hoover had his first taste of Chinese pomp and inefficiency, of magnificence tempered by bedbugs. He needed only a few specialists, a cook and interpreter, a few good ponies and pack mules. But only the most ponderously showy setup would do for an exalted Minister's Director of Mines in the Celestial Empire traveling on affairs of state.

On the railway leg of the trip Hoover was invited to share a private car occupied by one of the most prominent and truly patriotic leaders of China. Tong Shao-yi, a graduate of Columbia University, was the director of the Northern Railways of China and the largest Chinese stockholder in the coal and cement company which Hoover was managing. In the years to come Tong would twice serve as Prime Minister of China. The friendship of the two men, who thus met casually in travel, was to last for decades, as long as the Chinese statesman and financier lived.

At the railway destination Hoover and his companion, geologist George Wilson, found their expedition awaiting them in noisy and panoplied grandeur. Twenty officers commanded a hundred cavalrymen. There were flocks of graded officials, servants, grooms, coolies, some two hundred animals, and mountains of luggage. The cavalcade, when finally it began to roll, was slow-moving and uncomfortable but vastly impressive, with banners flying, advance heralds, and rear guards.

For all of Hoover's impatient pushing, the monstrous magnificence rarely made more than twenty-five miles a day. Nights were spent in bug-infested inns. Meals were lengthy and overloaded rituals. The cook, unhappily, had once worked in the French Legation and carried away the conviction that important foreigners must be served five courses, against their will if need be and even if some courses were of necessity the same ingredients in different disguises. In the end Hoover adjusted himself with a sigh to the Chinese tempo and caught up on his reading. Finally the cavalcade reached the gold-mining interior of Jehol.

The advance heralds had done their work all too well. Thousands from miles around awaited the "foreign mandarin" who, so the story went, had magic "green eyes" that saw through earth and solid rock to the gold below. He was trailed by fascinated men, women, and especially children who spied on his every magical move.

The reports on gold in Jehol were true enough. The site was being worked now, as it had been for centuries, by the crudest methods. But Hoover and Wilson established quickly that the best veins had been exhausted long ago. The current workings were thin and would not justify exploitation with modern machinery. Their most memorable find was a foreman who had once worked in California and greeted them solemnly with all the English he had retained: "Hello, boss!"

The interpreter assigned to Hoover had some trouble translating his Chinese emotions. Things that were bad he described as "damn" and things that were disastrous (which were a lot more frequent) as "really damn." No doubt he had a name, but to Hoover and the mining staff he was known only as Really Damn.

Local expectations of magic gold discoveries by the green-eyed one reached a pitch where a blunt announcement of failure might have precipitated riots. Really Damn therefore explained to the populace with elaborate apologies that the foreign mandarin's findings could not be disclosed except to a most exalted personage in Peking. The exalted personage, His Excellency Minister Chang, was disappointed but not discouraged in the great search, so that other such journeys followed.

The mining industries in China were in fantastic confusion. Westerners were grabbing concessions with the connivance of grafting officials. Freebooters of a dozen nationalities were scheming deals and compounding overlapping contracts. Great dignitaries were selling properties that did not belong to them. There were no laws, or too many laws, and no trace of a national policy to guide officialdom.

The best thing that Minister Chang could do, if he were really concerned for the obligations of his office, was to impose some order on this confusion. Such was the burden of Hoover's advice. "In the freshness of youth," he was to recount later, "it seemed to me that the beginning must be a systematic mining law requiring development and production with equal rights to all nationalities but under full control of the government."

In line with this purpose Hoover made a study of Chinese mining legislation, of existing or projected concessions, and then drafted a decree regularizing the rules of the game. Its fundamental aim was to safeguard the Chinese people's ownership of their natural resources and to guarantee proper royalties for the government and decent conditions for Chinese labor.

It was one of the first attempts to protect China against the encroachments of foreign exploiters and native greed. A few high-minded men, such as Tong, fought for it. Chang and his brood of foreign hangers-on sabotaged the project. Possibly they knew better than the idealistic young Californian that no logical order could prevail in the face of the cyclone of violence just then being brewed in the Peking palace and beyond.

Hoover did bludgeon Chang into authorizing a survey of coal deposits west of Peking. The field outlined by the American engineers contained more anthracite coal than all the known deposits in the world combined. It was to become a prime objective of Japanese imperialism, then of Russian imperialism, in the half-century ahead.

The gold hunt went forward in flea-bitten splendor. Always the journeys were gummed up by grandeur. They followed the rainbow paths of rumor to Shantung, Shansi, and Shensi, Manchuria, and the Gobi Desert. Mrs. Hoover went with her husband on some of them. Coolies trotted alongside with gaudy but empty sedan chairs to prove that it was not poverty but eccentricity which induced the foreign pair to ride horseback like commoners. At provincial capitals there would be elaborate receptions and exchanges of gifts with local overlords; among them they found a few men of great wisdom, culture, and charm.

No high-powered Americans could crash through the millennial layers of ceremony and seemliness. If they found no gold, they found food for thought and matter for a lifetime of reminiscence. There were also episodes of danger to add spice to the futilities.

Perhaps the most memorable of the expeditions was the one that took Hoover as far as Urga (Ulan Bator), the Mongolian capital in the Gobi Desert. The thirty-nine days were largely wasted as mining research but highly rewarding as cultural experience. Little had changed since the land was described by Marco Polo in the Middle Ages. Hoover made a state call on the Dalai Lama or Living Buddha. He found the deity pedaling a bicycle in great glee around the inner court of the lamasery and was entertained with gramaphone records; these Western marvels to relieve the tedium of godhood were the gifts of the local Russian consul.

The wanderings under banners and military escort took Hoover to the Kalgan Gate in the Great Wall of China. Forced by weather to remain there for several days, he was rewarded by spending Christmas Eve and the following day at the large, long-established Catholic American mission in the area. He was greatly impressed with the school, the medical clinic, and the selfless devotion of the missionaries, doctors, and teachers. Four secondhand footballs had reached the mission among Christmas gifts from the United States. Hoover volunteered to teach the game to the children, though the ground was covered with snow. Some three hundred boys and girls showed up, and soon were lustily kicking the four balls around simultaneously in a version of the game improvised for the occasion.

The travels took him also to points on the Yellow River. His advice was wanted on how to tame that beast, which periodically drowned millions in its floodings. Though it was outside his special competence, he offered concrete suggestions that, in the light of time, proved highly sensible.

All his journeys netted reports in which he pleaded for the abandonment of the search for gold and pointed to by-product discoveries of promising deposits of less glamorous metals. He came to know more about the underground treasures of China than any other man of his time. Meanwhile the coal and cement work went forward on a constantly enlarged and more profitable scale.

2

All his efforts were soon to be washed out in tidal waves of hatred and violence. Rumblings of anti-Western rebellion echoed through China. Sporadic attacks on foreigners were flowing into a torrential explosion. A society that called itself I Ho Tuan—the Mailed Fist, which the Europeans called "The Boxers"—was rolling up massive force. It was an amalgam of political fury, racial hatred, and religious fanaticism, pledged to drive all foreign devils into the sea and to destroy all Chinese who had trafficked with foreign deviltry. Whether the Empress Dowager backed the movement was not clear, but clearly it was a reaction against her son's earlier reform and modernization efforts.

Returning from a wearing trip, Lou Hoover developed sinus trouble. Because the physician they trusted most was living in Tientsin, Hoover decided to transfer his operational headquarters to that city—a move that had unexpected consequences. By May 1900 more and more stories of missionaries murdered, their women tortured, and Chinese "collaborationists" (to borrow a word from the future) hacked to death began to filter through. Hoover decided to call in all his men from the field; the decision undoubtedly saved many lives.

By the end of May the foreign settlements in Peking and other cities were beleaguered. About eleven hundred sailors and marines of half a dozen nationalities arrived in Tientsin from the warships anchored at Taku. Unfortunately they brought only one cannon and a few machine guns. Some optimism was sustained, however, because a local Imperial army of twenty-five thousand under foreign officers and with foreign equipment was deployed in the Tientsin area. It was generally regarded as dependable.

"There exploded in the faces of two twenty-six-year-old peaceful Americans," we read in Hoover's *Memoirs*, "an event that was to modify their lives, and also give them something to talk about for 'the rest of their born days.'" The Boxer Rebellion engulfed Tientsin.

The foreign compound of Tientsin was an elongated area of several parallel streets, in all about a mile long and a quarter of a mile deep, with the river on one side and the thickly populated and highly scented Chinese city on the other three sides. On June 13, 1900, the storm broke. The "dependable" army turned its guns on the foreign officers, killing a few while the rest fled to the compound. It was war, with the chances of survival for those trapped in the compound seemingly remote.

As the foremost civilian, Herbert Hoover at twenty-six thus found himself, in fact though not in title, the commander-in-chief in an unequal struggle. The ranking naval officer, a Russian colonel named Wogack, assumed military command. To Hoover fell the technical responsibilities and, no less important, the organization and husbanding of food supplies and water. This, indeed, was his first experience as food controller.

The foreign colony numbered around three hundred, some eighty of them Americans. More than a thousand Chinese, most of them Christians, also sought refuge in the settlement. In addition, Minister Chang Yen-mao and Tong Shao-yi, with their families and retinues of subordinate officials —in all about six hundred souls—crowded into the compound and became Hoover's personal responsibility.

Having discovered a providential supply of sacked rice, sugar, and other staples in warehouses, Hoover soon had more than a thousand terrified Chinese and all the able-bodied Westerners at work building barricades with these sacks. Overnight the settlement was shielded on its three land sides, with its troops stationed at dangerously wide intervals.

That the ill-armed naval contingents and civilian volunteers held off the swarms of attackers for more than a month seems in retrospect almost incredible. What they had in their favor was compactness of strategic position, discipline, and intelligence. Had the Boxers and Chinese soldiers had a plan, any plan—had they attacked from all three sides at once, for instance—the defense probably would have crumbled.

Every man, woman, and child had specific duties to perform on a twenty-four-hour schedule. The waterworks, unfortunately, were outside the barricades. Squads of daring men, Hoover often among them, stole out night after night, worked the pumps and the boilers, and returned before dawn with supplies of safe water. A herd of cattle was salvaged and, under Mrs. Hoover's direction, provided milk and some meat.

It was estimated that sixty thousand shells were fired into the compound during a month that seemed years long. Casualties were heavy. Only two doctors and one trained nurse were on hand to care for the wounded. Hospitals were improvised and Mrs. Hoover made their smooth functioning her chief duty. "There were no pacifists in the settlement," Hoover had cause to explain years later. Enemy artillery ignited fires faster than the harried defenders could put them out.

There was a terrible night when hysteria got the upper hand. Some stray bullets started the dangerous rumor that refugee Chinese within the compound were sniping. Messengers rushed into Hoover's home with the news that an undisciplined British bully, a Captain Bailey, had aroused a mob and rounded up the six hundred Chinese under Hoover's care. Drumhead trials were under way, with mass lynchings to come.

When Hoover, on a bicycle, hurried to the scene he found that Chang, Tong, and other outstanding persons had already been "found guilty." Bailey only laughed at his protests and threats. Hoover rushed to Colonel Wogack's headquarters and in a few minutes returned with enough force to disperse the mob and rescue all the Chinese.

And there was a day when a shell burst through Tong's roof, killing his wife and a baby daughter. Hoover, who lived across the street, rushed into the burning house and carried two of Tong's little daughters to safety through a hail of bullets.

About eighteen years later, when Hoover was American Food Administrator in Washington, the Chinese Ambassador, Wellington Koo, invited him and Mrs. Hoover to dinner. At one point Mrs. Koo said smilingly, "Mr. Hoover, we have met before. I am Tong Shao-yi's daughter whom you carried across the street during the siege of Tientsin."

About forty-six years later Hoover was in Shanghai in the course of a globe-girdling mission for President Truman. A Mrs. Chew, married to a former Chinese Ambassador, asked for an appointment. Her errand, it developed, was to thank him for saving her life. She had been among the children he had protected against the lynch mob.

Toward the end of the month of siege the joyous news came that fifteen hundred American Marines and Welsh Fusiliers were on their way from

Taku. The following day they arrived, with Marine buglers at their head. Of all the music he had ever heard, Hoover likes to tell, there was none so beautiful as "There'll Be a Hot Time in the Old Town Tonight" as rendered by the approaching buglers.

Women and children were evacuated by the river route. Mrs. Hoover and several others insisted on remaining at their posts. She had become expert in bicycling close to walls to dodge bullets, as she went between her home and the clinics. Once a bullet did puncture her bicycle tire. Late one evening she was at home, playing solitaire to rest her nerves. Suddenly a shell burst through a window, exploded, and shattered the front door. Mrs. Hoover shrugged and kept on playing.

The reinforcements were too small to assure safety. Fighting continued and there were many dark moments. But they had brought artillery and machine guns. With the American Marines there also had come a few American correspondents. One of them was the renowned Frederick Palmer. Another was the aging California poet, Joaquin Miller, representing the Hearst press. Miller became something of a problem. Having gotten his fill of Tientsin color stories, the old gentleman made arrangements to start out for Peking by rickshaw. The chances of his getting through alive were not one in a hundred but he would not listen to reason. In the end Mrs. Hoover bribed the rickshaw boy to desert him, stranding the bard in relative security.

About the middle of July the danger was ended. The Boxer uprising had been crushed. The siege of Tientsin was far more costly in blood and more desperate for the besieged than the one in Peking, but it received less than its due share of fame. The Boer War in South Africa was under way at the time; the beleaguerments of Kimberley, Mafeking, and Ladysmith are celebrated episodes, yet all three together suffered fewer casualties than Tientsin.

3

With the end of danger also came the end of solidarity among the foreign military contingents and the governments behind them. The Empress Dowager and her court fled from Peking to the interior and China seemed about to be dismembered. A wild grab for Chinese wealth began, and the properties under Hoover did not escape.

The Russian Army seized the coal mines and carted off carloads of machinery to Manchuria. The harbor works at Chingwangtao were grabbed by the British Navy. Germans took the coal yards at Tientsin and Taku. The American Army helped itself to the company's fleet of a dozen transport vessels, while Japanese forces took over the offices in

Tientsin. The local Chinese peasants, too, dug into what remained, in particular carrying off the railroad tracks.

To salvage the bondholding interests, the company was reorganized as a British corporation. This was done on Minister Chang's own initiative, as the best hope of regaining possession of the looted assets. The deed of property was in Moreing's name. Certain rights were reserved, of course, for the Chinese owners, but control shifted from China to a European group—a fact which very nearly cost Chang his head. Hoover signed for Moreing, subject to later London approval, then departed for England.

The Hoovers journeyed to London by way of the Red Sea. The reorganization was approved and several millions in additional capital were raised. Hoover was reappointed general manager at an increased salary with a minor stock interest. At the same time a young Belgian diplomat already in China, Chevalier Edmond De Wouters, was detached from his legation to deal with the five foreign powers and the Chinese government in the effort to reassemble the company properties.

Hoover and his wife decided to go back to China by way of the United States, thus circling the globe. Early in 1901, after leaving Lou Hoover in Japan for the rest she badly needed, he headed for Shanghai. Transportation having been utterly disrupted, Hoover and several American and British officers chartered a twelve hundred-ton steamer in Shanghai to take them to Chingwangtao. The harbor was still choked with floating ice. The ship rammed its way as far as possible, after which the passengers, lugging their suitcases, stumbled seven miles inland in the dark, in sub-zero temperature, to the railway station. Before daylight they were able to stop a troop train which took them to Tientsin.

The Ministry of Mines having expired in the melee, Hoover now had only one job on his hands, but it was a fantastically complicated one. He surveyed the depredations and demanded return of properties and reparations for damages from the five foreign governments involved. The engineer had to turn diplomat, in association with Chevalier De Wouters. Delicate negotiations and not so delicate threats were needed to extract the various grabs from the various grabbers, while adjusting the conflicting foreign and Chinese claims.

In the end the properties, or their equivalent in money, were restored and in time the enterprise began to function again. The American Army made a compromise cash settlement for the boats it had commandeered. As for the purloined machinery in Manchuria, the Czar's government finally agreed to its return—after which it had to be ransomed piece by piece from his army officers. Even the rails came back, through Hoover's simple expedient of advertising a reward and immunity to villagers who would bring them back.

Productivity expanded swiftly. The original Chinese stock, in the new

European issues, rose 500 percent in the stock markets of the world. On his authority from the foreign owners, De Wouters negotiated a settlement with Chang and his assortment of Chinese claimants, assuring them certain face-saving titles and functions and a bloc of stock. Hoover had no direct authority in the negotiations, but he approved the arrangements as just to all concerned, subject to approval by the corporation's principals in Europe. A memorandum embodying the terms was signed.

In the autumn of 1901 Hoover was informed that a Belgian syndicate had quietly bought up enough stock to assume control of the company. Soon thereafter the Belgian representative, Emile Francqui, arrived to take over. One of his first acts—over the indignant protests of Hoover—was to repudiate the De Wouters-Chang memorandum, alleging fraud on the Chinese side.

This act was to have absurd but annoying repercussions for Hoover decades later, when he found himself neck-deep in American politics. Though he had scant respect or affection for the wily Chang, ex-Minister of Mines, he felt that the Chinese had both moral and legal justice on their side. He supported them against the Belgians and, failing to win his point, refused to remain as general manager despite Francqui's urging. There was a lot of plain speaking between the American and the Belgian. They parted in a mood far from cordial, never suspecting that they were destined to work together intimately on a larger stage in a world war thirteen years later.

Chang, now discredited with his government, saved his head only by promising to obtain justice in the courts of England. The litigation he instituted, revolving around the validity of the memorandum, dragged on for almost six years. Hoover was not personally involved. But he did testify, and his evidence, wholly pro-Chinese, was the most influential element in ultimately giving the Chinese a substantial victory. He had simply told the truth as he saw it, and won the gratitude of Chinese leaders.

From 1920 forward, however, political enemies in America, having obtained a grotesque version of the story, tried to use it as a smear brush on Hoover's character. Amazingly, they turned the facts inside out and accused him of having "exploited" the Chinese. The senseless libel showed up again when he ran for President; it became, indeed, a staple of abuse in anti-Hoover articles and books. Quite unable to decipher the intricacies of the business, opponents sought to distort his help to the Chinese into its very opposite.

But that, of course, is running far ahead of our story. Hoover was winding up his affairs and preparing to return to California when he received a cabled offer of a junior partnership from Bewick, Moreing and Company. He accepted. His four and a half years in the field had made him indispensable to the London organization. Already his name loomed large in the mining world.

With Mrs. Hoover, he went on to California for a brief vacation; then they proceeded to London. He was just over twenty-seven but professionally a veteran, knowledgeable and tempered by years surcharged with experience and human drama. He had some money laid aside and profitable interests in Australian and Chinese mines. He had superb health, a matured mind, a record of leadership under the most difficult circumstances.

Hoover had learned only about a hundred Chinese words, but these he used in *sotto voce* conversations with his wife, who spoke the language with some facility. As a hobby, Mrs. Hoover had taken up the collection of antique Chinese white and blue porcelain of the Ming period. Magnificent displays of these antiques were to form part of the decor in Hoover homes in all the turgid years to come.

From his two and a half years in China, Hoover emerged with a genuine respect for the Chinese people. He was to write long afterward:

The impression I held of them, is one of abiding admiration. Here 90 percent of a huge mass live so close to the starvation line that someone falls below it in nearly every village every year. Yet they live with patience and tolerance. They have the deepest fidelities to family ties and the fullest affection for their children. They work harder and more hours than any race in the world. True, they are superstitious beyond belief, but they have a vivid sense of humor. They are courageous, as witness the armies they have created. They are highly acquisitive, and one need have little fear that this great mass will ever be communists for long.

One can only hope that his judgment on the last statement will ultimately be affirmed by events.

VI

The Great Engineer

Y EARS after he had resigned from the profession, political propaganda succeeded to some extent in putting an accent of irony into the phrase. But Herbert Hoover was in sober and literal fact the Great Engineer.

In all the history of mining industries there have not been a dozen men in a class with him for scope and comprehensiveness of accomplishments. This has been the considered opinion of the mine engineering fraternity, a clannish and hard-boiled group without inhibitions in appraising their own practitioners.

They attested their judgment continually through the years by loading him with all the honors, titles, offices, and medals he was willing to carry. To them Herbert Hoover was an incandescent name long before the world at large became familiar with it. In his early thirties he was widely regarded in his profession as the world's outstanding mining engineer and administrator; by the time he was forty this regard was unanimous.

There were greater experts in this or that specialized branch of the field—geologists, metallurgists, power engineers, chemists, construction engineers. These were often the specialists he employed, deployed, and directed simultaneously on thirty or forty great enterprises in many parts of the world. But there were few men, if any, who could compare with Hoover for his extraordinary blend of technical knowledge, organizing ability, and business acumen.

As our twentieth century went into stride, it was insatiably hungry for metals and fuels. Never had so much of the stuff of a technological civilization been turned up in so many places; and nearly everywhere the sure mind of Hoover directed some of the exploring, appraising, digging, smelting, and transportation of this stuff. In the course of his engineering

56

career an aggregate of at least a million workers were employed in projects where he played a decisive role. At the time he quit, at the outbreak of World War I in 1914, more than 150,000 were drawing their pay from mining works with which he was connected.

In the thirteen years after he left China he girdled the globe eight or ten times. These years divide into two periods. During the first, for about seven years, he operated as a junior partner of Bewick, Moreing and Company; in the following six years, from July 1908 until mid-1914, he functioned as a free-lance engineer and consultant.

With the London firm he served primarily as the practical engineering executive in the field. It was a field that stretched from Colorado, California, and Canada to Europe, the Middle East, Australia, South Africa, and India. In his period of free-lance operations he had dozens of top men in the profession under his command, not exactly as partners but as associates participating in the profits; he fitted the man to the job as required. The geography of his career expanded to take in Russia and Egypt, Latin America and Abyssinia, Scotland and Korea, the United States and Alaska —place names which indicate the breadth of the activity without defining it in full.

Whatever his official offices, his real offices were ships and trains that sped him from one enterprise to another. At every port he found stacks of urgent mail; at every telegraph office, urgent cables. His principal filing system was that phenomenal brain of his, that "card-index memory." It became a commonplace in his life to hasten from thirty degrees below zero in Siberia or Korea to 100 degrees in the shade in the Malay Straits or the Levant.

Despite the extent and global dispersal of his labors, he managed to keep abreast of books and ideas and political tides. He used the leisure of travel to read and to study; to write technical papers and to publish a mining textbook; to translate, with Mrs. Hoover, a medieval classic of metallurgy that had stymied the classicists; to lecture in mining schools and assume growing responsibility for the affairs of Stanford University.

Political currents had direct impact on so many of Hoover's interests that he was necessarily concerned with the intricacies of world events. But that aside, his boundless curiosity led him to observe, compare, make inner judgments. He had started with the heritage of American and Western and Quaker precepts and preferences. Now he was testing these in the crucibles of worldwide realities. He was hammering out his philosophy of life, his social and economic views, on the anvil of direct experience. Few Americans destined for public leadership have been so close to the multitudinous world, its dizzying patterns and contrasts, its varieties of peoples, customs, and ideas.

A telescoped recital of his engineering career, such as this must be, conveys an impression of hurry, crowding, excitement. A lesser man would have been an ulcerous wreck under the strain. But Hoover had the ability to carry towering loads with a genuine nonchalance. He remained unhurried and unexcited. He knew how to dismiss the trivial and secondary, to focus on essentials. He had a talent for keeping jobs apart in his emotions, so that the griefs of one—and he had his normal share of disappointments—did not intrude to color and dampen another.

In only one of those thirteen years did he fail to spend some time in his native land. Mrs. Hoover was by his side in most of his earlier wanderings. Then, increasingly, the education of their two sons kept her more and more at home—which usually meant London or California. One of these boys, it was reported, traveled around the world twice in his first year. Be that as it may, it is a fact that Herbert, Jr., born in London in 1903, set out for Australia in his fifth week; and that his brother Allan, born in 1907, likewise in London, went promptly on a journey to Burma, likewise at the advanced age of five weeks.

We find Hoover asserting in his notes that "traveling with babies is easier than with most grownups." Whether his wife concurred in that opinion is open to some doubt. But she toted her boys in baskets to the most outlandish segments of the world map under the most trying circumstances; she toted them on horseback and camelback, on passenger liners and freighters and tugs. She shielded them successfully against Arctic cold and tropic heat, against mosquitoes and sandstorms and polluted water.

For Lou Henry knew that her husband, paradoxical as it may sound, was at heart a homebody who abhorred hotels and was deeply attached to familiar things, to his own house and furniture and flocks of pets. No matter where the tom-tom of professional duty summoned them, California, and specifically Palo Alto, provided a geographical and sentimental anchorage. It was the fixed point of their compass of hopes and plans. There they acquired their permanent family seat—first a six-room cottage and much later a more elaborate house on the campus of Stanford University.

In London, where the Hoovers spent more time than in any other spot except California, they occupied first a suburban cottage, then a city apartment; but finally they rented a spacious and rambling old place near Kensington Gardens, known for generations as the Red House. It had a large garden and was shaded by a spreading oak tree. Vernon Kellogg, who knew its hospitality well, described it as a "bit of transplanted America, and, in particular, a bit of transplanted California." Hundreds of Americans learned to value its homey flavor. They came to know the dog Rags, and the Persian and Siamese cats which were so often on Hoover's lap, the pigeons in the garden, and the boys' menagerie in the upper rooms.

Men and women with famous names and gilded titles came there, but only because the Hoovers judged them interesting and genuine. For the Hoovers steered clear of Society with a capital S. An evening's guests might count an eminent statesman or financier, but it was likely to include also a prospector fresh from the Klondike, a writer or painter, a railroad man from India, a Quaker acquaintance from back home. But always there were people, always there was lively talk and the friction of clashing views.

Small wonder that the Hoovers retained a nostalgic feeling for the Red House. In a letter written to his wife many years later, after revisiting the place, he told her how he persuaded the butler, with the help of a ten-shilling note, to let him enter the place:

> To the left was the oak-paneled library with its fine fireplace and its leaded glass bookcases—the same as ever. I imagined again, sitting on the opposite side of the desk from you, with the manuscripts and reference books of Agricola piled between us, as we worked over the translation of *De Re Metallica*. Again I saw "Pete" at the little table in the corner, making marks and announcing that he was writing a book too; and "Bub" clambering into his mother's lap and demanding to know what the book said.
> The dining room was the same walnut-paneled room and evoked all kinds of memories of the multitude of happy gatherings which had filled it. The living room had been redecorated from its old neutral tints to modern white French and was a "repellent stranger."

The background of a happy, harmonious family life must be taken for granted as one follows the "public" Hoover, engrossed in great affairs of business or service to his fellow men. It would help sustain his courage and nourish his self-confidence in times of ordeal as outsized as his triumphs.

2

An account of Hoover's engineering, in the context of his long and diversified life story, has to be deplorably abbreviated; a mere sampling to suggest its dimensions and its special Hooveresque flavor must do.

Bewick, Moreing and Company managed other people's properties or served as technical advisers on a fee basis plus a small share of the profits. No two contracts were exactly alike. The company might be called in to save an ailing enterprise, if possible, or to improve a healthy one. It appraised new mining prospects and, if the findings were encouraging, followed through with their development. It worked with investment groups in mining as the technical experts on new or old operations.

Hoover, like the other junior partners, received an agreed percentage of all earnings. The firm's deed of partnership specifically forbade any member to engage in stock market speculation. They made a lot of money, but never by manipulating pieces of paper or "mining" too-eager investors. On the contrary, their special function was to restrain speculation by uncovering the hard facts under glittering claims or appearances.

Their most valuable stock-in-trade was rigid honesty and dependability. It was on competence, on stepped-up production, on reduced costs —often on the liquidation of uneconomic or played-out mines—that the income of the organization depended. Though the youngest and newest member, Hoover was therefore well within its policy in warning the industry and the public on many occasions against the speculative booms associated with mine financing.

The technical journals of those years contain interviews and articles in which he assailed high-powered promoters and warned the gullibles who let themselves be snared by promises baited with exaggerated figures. He set himself boldly against the gaudy promotional aspects of the business in a more concrete fashion also: he dared to deprecate bonanzas. The vitality of mining, he argued, rested on hard work and rational production, not on the sensational accident. He was convinced early that gold mining was the toughest and least remunerative branch of the business. For him the backbone of mining was the exploitation of large bodies of low-grade ores. He preferred a stable and continuous business to the spectacular flash in the pan. And as he went deeper and deeper into the industry he did not hesitate to make these views known.

His most dramatic victories were not in gold but in zinc and lead and coal; in transforming abandoned low-grade workings into steady profit-makers; in finding access to deposits long considered inaccessible. In his opinions and methods he was therefore at the opposite pole from what American journalese implies by the word "promoter," pronounced with a grimace. His professional judgments helped raise millions to finance old and new projects, but only after he had investigated them personally and only on the basis of a full and frank picture of the potentials involved. Always his profits or losses were related to output and costs of production, never to the ups and downs of investment fever charts. His name as a consultant or on a board of directors in the mining world became a guarantee against promotional shenanigans.

At the turn of the century the mining booms wrecked more fortunes than they made. There had been plenty of self-delusion and plain fraud. The get-rich-quick artists feared firms like Bewick, Moreing. It was often after the bubble burst, when alarmed stockholders sought to salvage some of their millions, that honest technicians were called in. Not once but dozens of times Hoover took over mismanaged, overexpanded, seemingly hopeless mines; in a year or two or three he made them solvent and profitable. "We were engineering doctors to sick concerns," as he phrased it himself.

So many people had been brutally burned in the boom fevers by the time Hoover joined the firm that there was a veritable epidemic of contrite honesty. More and more owners seemed eager to jettison the inflated illusions and establish their mines on a solid businesslike foundation. This reaction against the boom and false optimism brought more and more business to the organization.

When he joined the firm, it held contracts to some twenty mines in different parts of the world, as well as two large exploration syndicates searching for new mines. The business included coal mines in China, Wales, and the Transvaal, a tin mine in Cornwall, gold mines in Western Australia, New Zealand, South Africa, and West Africa, copper mines in Queensland and Canada, a lead-silver mine in Nevada, a turquoise mine in the Sinai Peninsula of Egypt. Bewick, Moreing worked out of branch offices in New York, Kalgoorlie, Melbourne, and Johannesburg.

Hoover's first journey as field man was to Australia, via Suez and Ceylon. In the three years since he had pioneered there, the gold properties as a whole had deteriorated sadly. The continent down under was nursing a hangover after the intoxicating boom. British and Colonial methods had displaced American in many areas. Ruthlessly he closed down some mines and set out to restore the vitality of the others. He brought over fifteen university-trained American engineers, introduced new machinery and methods, centralized the buying of supplies, and in general tightened and streamlined the operation. The improvements in total production and flow of profits were soon manifest.

On board ship, en route to Australia, Hoover met a prominent English investment banker who was to become not only a source of business but, more important, a close and faithful friend. Francis Govette was going to Kalgoorlie to inspect two important mines which had been made the objects of scandalous promotions. Indeed, the chief culprit had committed suicide after being convicted of criminal fraud. Govette had been brought in with full authority to clean up the mess.

Not a mining man, Govette, after a few days in Kalgoorlie, found himself utterly bewildered and turned to Hoover. He asked Bewick, Moreing to take over the technical and financial reorganization of his mines. Hoover did so well with this assignment that Govette in the years that followed turned over a lot of additional business to the London firm. Moreover, this proof that "sick" properties could be restored to lusty health—watched by the entire industry—brought others into the fold. Hoover went on to New Zealand and other areas before returning to England in the fall of 1902.

3

Toward the end of the year the firm suffered a terrific body blow and Hoover happened to be the one to take its full impact. He had been in London only two months at the time and his whole British experience came to less than three months. Mr. Bewick, who was no longer active in the business, was off hunting moose in Canada. Mr. Moreing was off hunting tigers in Manchuria. Hoover faced more frightening animals virtually alone.

On reaching the office one morning, he found a bulky letter on his desk marked "private and confidential." It was a twenty-page handwritten confession—by A. S. Rowe, long the chief accountant of the firm and a junior partner. Rowe was a middle-aged, conventional fellow of excellent repute: the last man who would have been suspected of the nerve and the imagination for large-scale embezzlement.

But there it was, the fantastic confession, ending with a hint of suicide. The very evils the firm was fighting had ensnared its own trusted accountant.

For a long time, Rowe revealed, he had been speculating in American railroad stocks, and had resorted to criminal fraud to cover mounting losses. Now he was a million dollars in the hole—a million dollars he had in part stolen from the firm's cash but mostly raised by issuing forged certificates of stock, forged checks, and using other thieving devices. It was a defalcation on a breathtaking scale, with clients of the firm as the principal victims. The specific frauds and forgeries were neatly listed— Rowe was a conscientious bookkeeper.

Failing to reach the senior partners by cable, Hoover acted on his own. He summoned a few of London's leading financiers and mine specialists among his acquaintances, including Francis Govette. They sat open-mouthed as he read them the confession. The only thing quite clear was that Bewick, Moreing was under no legal obligations whatsoever; they could not be held accountable for the forgeries.

One of the older men turned to Hoover. "Young man," he said, "you are new in the firm and new in English business. We would all like to help you. We would first like to know if you have any ideas as to what you would like to do."

Hoover answered promptly, "I would *like* to pay every dime over the counter, whether we are liable or not."

The tension was relieved when the questioner declared that under the circumstances "tuppence" would be a better expression than "dime." The young partner did not need any more advice than that. On his own authority, at the risk of Moreing's later disapproval, he issued a statement to the press. It set forth the facts of the disaster, indicated that the firm was legally in the clear—then pledged that every tuppence would be made good notwithstanding.

This demonstration of integrity beyond the call of legal duty—a million dollars beyond it—made more of a sensation in London than the defalcations themselves. Hoover's unpleasant task was to call each of the defrauded individuals and companies in turn to appraise them of the size of their losses, promising to make good on them. It was a week before the tiger-hunting Moreing got the shocking news. He instantly approved Hoover's conduct and assumed 75 percent of the obligations; the rest was assumed by Hoover and another junior member.

In one swoop the greater part of the young American's savings from five grueling years in Australia, China, and elsewhere were thus wiped out. Some of his surplus in the next few years, too, went to pay off the Rowe crimes. Deliberately he had chosen to assume what was for him a heavy financial burden: the voluntary restitution of another man's thefts.

Hoover's personal standing as well as the reputation of the old firm were immensely enhanced by this episode. It became one of the great legends of business probity. Their clientele grew enormously, so that in the long run the million came back with interest in the form of new business. Surely it is one of the brightest pages in any man's business record. But there are no limits to political legerdemain. Even this episode would in the future be "processed" into another smear on his character in anti-Hoover propaganda.

Rowe did not commit suicide, but fled to Canada, leaving his wife and children destitute. He was caught and convicted. Mrs. Hoover—and this is a fact London did not know until long afterward—helped to care for Rowe's innocent family until he finished his ten-year term.

Not all of Hoover's missions, of course, panned out. There was, for instance, the Lodder River System, a gold-bearing site in Victoria, Australia. By the magic of frenzied finance, six million dollars of investors' money had been sunk into the development—two in actual equipment and construction, four in speculations—and lost. Its chief promoter took his own life when his house of stock certificates tumbled around his head. The desperate investors hired Bewick, Moreing to study the picture.

The junior partner reported that there was only a marginal chance of making those mines yield; the geological conditions made retrieval of the gold almost impossible. A subterranean river under lava deposits had to be overcome. Hoover brought over Dr. Lindgren, his former boss on those college-vacation surveys, to study the problem. In full awareness of the heavy odds against them, the investors decided to throw two million dollars more into a final salvaging effort. Hoover thereupon undertook the greatest pumping operation in mining history, but finally the Lodder System had to be abandoned.

For contrast we have the famous Broken Hill operation, also in Australia. In that silver-lead district there were great mountains of "tailings," the residue after silver and lead had been extracted. They were regarded as waste, millions of tons of it, because no one had succeeded in processing the zinc and other by-products out of this slag. Hoover acquired some five million tons of the tailings for the group that had hired his firm, as well as an array of low-grade mines which others had dismissed as worthless.

In the following years Broken Hill saw many false starts and failures. But Hoover was convinced that the key to unlock the treasure-house could be found. He initiated pertinent research not only on the scene but in the London laboratories. In the end he found economic methods of salvaging the zinc from the tailings and for making the despised low-grade ores pay dividends. He worked out the so-called "flotation" process, which thereafter became standard technique for the industry. Broken Hill evolved into one of the world's richest sources of silver, lead, and especially zinc. Its output from Hoover's time to the early 1940s was estimated at four hundred million dollars.

His explorations took Hoover to Mt. Sinai for the Government of Egypt. The turquoise was there in abundance, but there were no buyers to justify its large-scale mining. This semi-precious stone, highly prized in the days of the Pharaohs, had lost its appeal in the intervening millennia. Incidentally, however, the Cornish miners who worked on this site stumbled on a great store of artifacts which excited archaeologists.

Hoover engineers made a survey of the resources of the ancient land of Abyssinia on the invitation of its Emperor, the Conquering Lion of Judah. The results were completely discouraging. Hoover was to remark decades later that if Mussolini had studied the resultant reports he might have been dissuaded from his bloody Ethiopian aggression.

4

By all odds the most formidable, heart-breaking, and in the long run most fabulously productive of Herbert Hoover's labors were in the nearly inaccessible reaches of Burma, not far from the frontiers of China and India. With Mandalay as base of operations, he started his investigations late in 1904 while still with Bewick, Moreing, but they continued deep into his free-lancing period—reversing the roles at that point by engaging his old firm as technical managers.

It took him more than five years, as one of his biographers put it, "to transform some deserted works in the heart of a jungle into the foremost producer of its kind in all the world." Hoover made a number of extended sojourns on the site, with his family installed in a leased house in Mandalay, and it was to be the last of the mining properties in which he would retain a financial interest. Indeed, the Burma mines became the foundation of his personal fortune, which, however, was never as great as common report claimed.

Like many others in the business, Hoover had heard about the abandoned silver mines in the impoverished Shan State. It had been the fabled source of Ming silver. Worked as early as the year 1400, it seemed to have petered out by 1850 and was now being scratched on the surface in a most primitive and profitless fashion.

On his homeward journey from a survey of tin mines in Penang, Hoover made the acquaintance of a railroad contractor named A. C. Martin, who was building a strategic railway from Mandalay to Lashio near the Chinese frontier. Martin spoke excitedly of the centuries-old lead and copper mines in Shan, which he had recently leased from the Indian government. He was anxious to interest Bewick, Moreing in them.

With some American and English associates, Hoover's firm took an option on a controlling interest and sent a young engineer on a scouting trip. His report sounded too enthusiastic to be true—at least half a million tons of slag and labyrinths of ancient workings still far from exhausted. Skeptical, Hoover sent a more experienced American engineer, C. D. Clark, to doublecheck. Clark's report, in April 1905, was even more ecstatic.

Hoover thereupon went himself. The site, he found, seemed to have been deliberately placed by a perverse nature behind almost impassable mountain barriers and impenetrable jungles. But what he saw convinced him that the building of roads, the laying of rails across two mountains, the throwing of bridges across dizzy gorges, the excavation of vast new tunnels through the old workings, were justified.

The native prince of Sawbwa of the Shan State was an Oxford-educated young man living in genteel poverty. He realized that the activation of the virtually abandoned mines might solve his own and the principality's economic problems—as, indeed, it did eventually—and was therefore zealous in his cooperation.

Hoover and Clark experienced hardships and dangers as they crawled, sometimes on hands and knees, through diggings a hundred to five hundred years old. The incident that they would never forget came the day they realized, on penetrating a considerable distance into a narrow tunnel, with only a lighted candle as weapon, that a Bengal tiger had preceded them—the animal's footprints were quite fresh. They beat a hasty retreat. Said Hoover subsequently, "The tiger, fortunately, was not of an inquisitive turn of mind and did not come out to greet us."

A few years later, having built a deep two-mile tunnel through the crumbling labyrinth, Hoover christened it the Tiger Tunnel. The Shan prince mobilized thirty thousand of his people, at good wages, to do the work blueprinted by Hoover and his staff. For the first time, Hoover broke his rule of not investing much of his own money in a new venture. He put most of his savings, and more as he earned it, into the Burma mines. By 1908 they yielded their first substantial hoards of metal, though full production was not reached until 1916. From one of the wretchedest of the principalities, the Shan State became the most prosperous.

Tunnels had to be driven deep and far to get at virgin deposits. A huge smelter was erected on the grounds, as well as mills, hydroelectric plants, houses, towns, schools, and hospitals. In thirty years the mines gave the world 1,500,000 tons of lead, with silver, zinc, and other products in proportion. They gave employment to some hundred thousand Chinese, Shans, and Indians and are still accounted the world's leading silver source. Hoover sold his interests in the Burma mines in 1918.

In the summer of 1904 Hoover went to South Africa to inspect and negotiate with a coal company and some gold mines under Bewick, Moreing management. Beneath the coal mines, it was ascertained, there were extensions of the Rand gold-bearing veins. As a result of these negotiations, the coal mines were in due time converted into very successful gold mines.

It happened that at this time the Rand mines in South Africa had begun to bring in Chinese coolie labor, seasonally as required. The American engineer had no more to do with this than you or I. But for a long time the falsehood that he "exploited coolie labor," based in part on the South African situation, held an honored place in the panoplied legend of his wickedness.

One of the ironies of the situation is that the Chinese laborers fought and schemed and even killed for the privilege of being exploited. They earned enough in the Transvaal in a few months to sustain their families for a long time in China. The greater irony is that Hoover was outspoken in opposition to this and to any other "cheap labor." As a mine administrator, not as a humanitarian, he contended that the cheapest labor is the most expensive, in that it is the least productive. Speaking before the Chamber of Commerce in the Transvaal, he cited his lower costs per ton in Australia with labor that was paid decent wages and provided with

66

decent living conditions. Excerpts from the speech are on record in the London *Chronicle* of the time.

Four years later he was to enlarge on this judgment in lectures at Columbia and Stanford Universities, as well as in his book *Principles of Mining*. He could point to the Broken Hill development which, in times of widespread strikes and quarrels in Victoria, Australia, never lost a day for such reasons. The remarkable fact is that there were virtually no strikes or lockouts in any Hoover-run mines in places where others were wrestling with these problems. "Our operations were a demonstration of an industrial fundamental—greater technical service, more labor-saving devices, lower costs, and larger production at higher wages," in his own words.

He believed that honest labor unions fitted well into this formula. In reading words like the following from his book on mining, bear in mind that he was talking to management, not to the public; and that this was 1908, when such views sounded radical and heretical to most businessmen:

As corporations have grown, so likewise have labor unions. In general, they are normal and proper antidotes for unlimited capitalistic organization. . . . Given a union with leaders who can control the members, and who are disposed to approach differences in a businesslike spirit, there are few sounder positions for the employer, for agreements honestly carried out dismiss the constant harassments of possible strikes. Such unions exist in dozens of trades in this country, and they are entitled to greater recognition. The time when the employer could ride roughshod over his labor is disappearing with the doctrine of *laissez-faire* on which it is founded. The sooner the fact is recognized, the better for the employer.

In that passage on labor-management relations he went on to dispute the orthodox economic assumption of the period that workers were a "commodity" and wages governed by laws of demand and supply. "In these days of international flow of labor, commodities and capital," he wrote, "the real controlling factor in wages is efficiency." More efficient production, he contended, could be the common ground for cooperation between labor and capital: "No administrator begrudges a division with his men of the increased profit from increased efficiency."

5

Hoover's contract with the managerial firm was running out in mid-1908. He decided not to renew it, despite flattering inducements to stay on offered by Mr. Moreing. The business of the firm had tripled in the seven years and Hoover was given major credit for the growth. His share of the fees made him among the best-paid mining engineers of all time.

The hope of being able to spend more time in the United States and with his family was basic to that decision. However, he was so much in demand in so many places that the free-lancing years proved to be, if anything, more crowded and hectic than those that preceded. He did not create a formal company—his offices in New York, San Francisco, London, and subsequently in St. Petersburg and Paris carried only the simple inscription, *Herbert C. Hoover.*

John Agnew developed into a kind of Chief of Staff, with men like Gilman Brown, Dean Mitchell, Louis Chevrillon, Amor Kuehn, T. J. Jones, and Hoover's brother Theodore running major offices and handling major technical jobs. "Ours was a happy shop," Hoover could write. "There was the sheer joy of creating productive enterprises, of giving jobs to men and women, of fighting the whims of nature and of correcting the perversities and incompetence of men."

The continuing demands of the Burma project kept may of his top men busy. In 1910, at the behest of a group of Japanese bankers, he went to Korea to appraise copper and gold mines. His frank assessment ended the bankers' dream. That same year he made his first professional visit to Russia, with dramatic results in terms of mining successes.

The most notable of the Russian enterprises was on the Kyshtim estate, in the Urals, near Yekaterinisburg. The estate took in an area as large as a small European country. It had provided an extravagant living to a distant branch of the Romanoff family for many generations but had been continually mismanaged and depleted. Some hundred thousand workers and peasants dependent on its mines, forests, and accessory activities were sunk in poverty and ignorance.

The current owner, Baron Mellor Zakomelsky, had invited a Russian-born Briton, Leslie Urquhart, to refinance and activate his properties. The baron, according to Hoover's testimony, was genuinely concerned about improving the lot of the population. Though Urquhart plowed under huge sums of investor money, the estate went from bad to worse. In 1909, therefore, he called in Hoover, in the capacity of "doctor of sick mines," to save the patient—and Hoover did.

He judged the latent possibilities of Kyshtim favorably and was assured a free hand in their development. He brought in experienced engineers from Butte, Montana, where geological conditions were analogous. He built modern furnaces, provided economic transport facilities, and erected factories to process some of the Kyshtim iron and steel into salable finished products. Almost at once the estate began to show profits, this despite—or because of—the fact that American management paid the highest wages in all Russia and raised living standards for a hundred thousand souls. The fame of this achievement spread through the sprawling country, and representatives of the Czar's family called in Hoover to survey all the Romanoff mining properties, the so-called "Cabinet" mines.

A curious sidelight: A book written by an American correspondent in 1891—*Siberia and the Exile System* by George Kennan, an uncle of the George Kennan who was to be the U. S. Ambassador to Soviet Russia—gave Hoover valuable clues to possible mineral deposits in the Cabinet group. The book had created a sensation as an exposure of terror and convict labor in Russia, so that the first Kennan became celebrated as a great friend of that country; in later decades, alas, correspondents who exposed worse terror and greater convict labor were too often assailed as "anti-Russian reactionaries."

In any case, Hoover read Kennan carefully, and from his eyewitness accounts obtained leads to Czarist mines that might be worth examining. The most promising, he found, were in the Altai Mountains in the southern reaches of Siberia. Again he conquered problems of inaccessibility to begin development of what turned out to be one of the most extensive and richest bodies of ore ever discovered on this planet. Ten million dollars were raised to finance what became known as the Irtysh Mine.

By the time the Russian Revolution canceled out all of Hoover's labors, the Kyshtim works in the Urals were earning a profit of two million dollars a year for Baron Zakomelsky and the investors, and it was only in its initial stage. When the Bolsheviks took over, the management had to flee for their lives, and within a few months the whole enterprise was paralyzed and on the rocks. However heart-warming the theories of public ownership may be on paper, in practice they merely restored the old misery, hunger, and desolation. The fate of the Irtysh Mine under the new management was no less disastrous.

What was lacking, as Hoover later explained, was the "tuned intelligence" that spells the difference between profitable and losing operations. By 1923, when Hoover's famine relief men were in the Kyshtim region on their errands of mercy—under the American Relief Administration—they found that little remained of the great enterprises. Local people, recognizing one of the old American engineers among the relief workers, begged him to transmit a message signed by a large group of workers. In time Hoover received it: a touching and pathetic message, imploring him to come and give them work again, promising that they would be "good and obedient."

These Russian developments showed that wealth could be produced with free labor where slave labor—Czarist or Communist—failed. In the 1920s conscienceless stories based on falsehoods were to be spread far and wide, especially from the so-called Left, alleging that Hoover's opposition to the Soviet regime was motivated by his hopes of retrieving those properties. Actually he had disposed of all Russian interests years before the Revolution. Even if he were the sort of man to adjust his principles to prospects of profit, therefore, he stood to gain exactly nothing by an overthrow of the Soviet regime.

This summary account does not begin to do justice to his record as the Great Engineer; one might as well try to pack the contents of a department store into an overnight bag. Only another engineer, one associate explained, can comprehend fully the quality of Hoover as a creative miner: the fertility of his technical devices, the daring of his concepts. The greater the obstacles, it seemed, the keener his determination. He used camels to haul timbers 175 miles through mountain country. He based vast smelting and manufacturing ventures on wood fuel, "extracting the last by-product of charcoal as part of an interlocking conservation scheme." He recovered ores in our own West with entirely new procedures in underwater dredging. In his field he was distinctly the innovator, the revolutionary.

The immensity of his professional commitments, as has already been indicated, did not restrict Hoover's mental horizons. In the course of his travels he absorbed a whole library of classic and modern writings, along with the key technical and engineering books of all centuries and all countries. He was fascinated by the ancient cultures, human and technical, which still showed above ground, like the open ends of antique "workings," in the life of millions of human beings.

One of the old books that intrigued him was the celebrated *De Re Metallica*, published in 1556 by a German scientist of that century who used the pen name Agricola. Though scholars had often tried to translate it into French, English, and German in the intervening centuries, they had given up the task as hopeless. To begin with, the book was written in a vulgate Latin which scholars found insuperable. Second, it was a technological work, abounding in nomenclature and formulas which the Latinists could not decipher. Since there were no ancient Latin words to describe many medieval engineering processes, Agricola apparently had invented them or transliterated them from German and French expressions into a Latin of his own coinage.

On and off for years Hoover, and even more so Mrs. Hoover, who was the Latinist of the family, had played with the book, translating passages for the fun of it. The mining ideas of 1556 presented quite a challenge to a couple of young Stanford alumni. For instance, Agricola took into account the mischief-making role of "gnomes" and how to propitiate them.

By 1907 they decided to tackle the translation in earnest. They carted their notes and manuscripts with them all around the world. It became their principal "game" for spare time and during long journeys. They found excuses for visiting the actual mine sites in the Alps and elsewhere which Agricola mentioned, and made researches in Saxony where he had written the volume. Sentence by sentence, paragraph by paragraph, they read the 350-year riddle. It was in many ways a job of scientific detective work. They carried out Agricola's formulas in laboratories to check their own intuitive translations. By dovetailing known facts they deduced obscure meanings. And in five years they were ready with the first accurate rendition of the classic in English.

Some years before, Hoover had helped to put his friend Edgar Rickard into business in London as a publisher of technical journals dedicated to greater appreciation of American methods, men, and machines. The business had prospered. Rickard now sponsored the publication of Agricola in a large and elegant format, bound in white vellum like the original medieval edition, and reproducing the original woodcuts and initial letters. Issued in a limited edition, it quickly became and remains to this day a valued collector's item. The translation, of course, was signed jointly by Lou Hoover and her husband.

6

Repeatedly during these years Hoover contemplated retirement, which to him meant the funneling of his energies into some kind of public service on a full-time schedule. Financial reverses and the appearance of exciting engineering challenges interfered. But the dream was never far from his consciousness. It edged close to reality in 1908, about the time he severed relations with the London firm.

He accepted an invitation at that time to deliver a series of lectures to the engineering students of his alma mater and took under serious advisement its invitation to join the faculty. But the Burma and a few other huge enterprises were "cooking" and could not be left on the fire without endangering other people's investments. Hoover repeated the lectures at Columbia University and they became the substance of his *Principles of Mining*, published in 1909. The book remained a standard college text for decades and is still widely consulted.

Increasingly Hoover concerned himself with the affairs of Stanford. As early as 1909, in a talk to students, he proposed that they erect a building to house all their organizations, what he called the Stanford Union. The idea was immediately adopted and he made an initial gift of ten thousand dollars toward the project. Ultimately the Hoovers contributed one hundred thousand dollars to help make the Stanford Union building a reality. In 1912 he joined the university's Board of Trustees and played a role in the appointment of his old geology professor, Dr. Branner, as President. Because of advanced age, Branner soon retired and was succeeded by Hoover's classmate and devoted friend, Dr. Ray Lyman Wilbur.

Because it seems to reflect the quintessence of Hooverism, one episode deserves to be put on the record. (It was told publicly for the first time in 1948, in the original version of this biography, and since then has been confirmed in Hoover's *Memoirs*.) Though its principal characters were Jews—as they were in the first Noel story of all—it is in a sense a Christmas story. The Hoovers were in California for the holidays and the episode began on the day after Christmas of 1913. That was when Hoover stepped into the Bank of California to cash a check and was buttonholed by the bank president, Frank Anderson, who told him a sad tale:

Two great California families, Sloss and Lilienthal, were on the brink of bankruptcy. They had overextended their business operations and found themselves unable to meet a mountain of notes, mostly personally endorsed, falling due in the days ahead. The families were meeting at that very moment to wrestle with their troubles, involving ten first-rate companies and related enterprises, sixty million dollars in various securities, and some four hundred banks. The bankruptcy would deliver a terrible blow to the whole state and might, indeed, touch off fears in larger areas.

What the Lilienthals and Slosses needed, Anderson thought, was a cool outside mind—a Hoover mind—to help them. Would he consent to talk to them? He did, immediately. They took him fully into confidence. He appraised their troubles as another case of mismanagement and tangled finances, for the two families were people of sterling honesty. Thankfully they accepted his advice to fight it out and placed themselves under his monitorship.

For nearly ninety days and nights, Saturdays and Sundays included, while his multifarious personal affairs waited, Hoover worked with these people, their lawyers, their bankers. The details are too ample and too complex. At times he staved off creditors by the sheer force of his reputation for probity. He reorganized some companies, merged others, and carefully husbanded every resource to prop up a leaning tower of finance.

He got wind, for instance, of the fact that Sloss, Sr. at his death had left two million dollars for his wife, now ninety years old. Her sons, even in their extremity, did not wish to alarm the matriarch whom they all adored. Hoover took it upon himself, however, to visit her. The grand old lady understood at once. She told him with a smile that fifty or a hundred thousand dollars would be more than enough to keep her for such years as remained to her—the rest was at his disposal. Hoover insisted on leaving her a quarter of a million and covered the rest with securities in her sons' businesses. The $1,750,000 was crucial in paying overdue interest and saving the Sloss-Lilienthal empire.

What would his fee be for salvaging the great fortune? The grateful families were not only ready but eager to pay anything he would ask.

Over their violent protests, he got the full amount he asked for: nothing. He had not injected himself for profit, he explained patiently, and therefore could accept no payment. Another contingent of Hoover cultists was born in those tense three months, and California did not even suspect that it had been rescued at the brink of possible panic.

In 1914, though he could not himself know it, Hoover was at the end of his professional life—on the threshold of a second and greater career as humanitarian and public servant. He was by then a man seasoned by unique experiences; with a great surgeon's sureness of touch in handling practical affairs; with a mind not only vast in expanse but rich in depth, like the most generously endowed of his many gold and silver mines.

Practically unknown to the public at large, he was the most famous of all in his own field. To hundreds of men and women who had worked with him or under him he was "the Chief." They were not merely Hoover people but Hoover zealots. The best of this human crop was to follow him into his new career, on a full or part-time basis, as devotedly as they had followed him from Australia to China, from China to Russia and back again.

Though he had lived so much abroad, he was profoundly American. In a sense he was a self-chosen apostle of American technology to the technical heathens of the globe. The sobriquet "Hail Columbia" had stuck, and with good reason. But he was American in a far more significant way. Having sampled every living and moribund civilization extant, he had developed an ever-deepening and ultimately a passionate patriotism for his homeland. America seemed to him, with all its faults, not simply an extension of European civilization but a new civilization, unique and integral, and rooted in concepts of human freedom.

As an Iowa Quaker he had been, one might say, born a Republican. And it was the Republicanism of Iowa Quakers—at bottom populist, liberal, grass-roots in quality—that meant anything to him. He enrolled as a Republican the first time he was old enough to do so, in Berkeley, though he was off on his life's work before he could vote. In 1912 he supported Theodore Roosevelt's Bull Moose movement against the regular Republicans.

In the spring of 1914 he accepted an extracurricular assignment from his adopted state in connection with the Panama-Pacific International Exposition scheduled to take place in San Francisco, to celebrate the opening of the Panama Canal. European nations showed themselves reluctant to take part; perhaps it seemed to them pretty far away. Hoover was asked, directly and through his associates in various capitals, to do something about it. He agreed to try.

Had it not been for this assignment, he most likely would not have been in London when the fatal shot was fired at Sarajevo on June 28,

1914. The whole pattern of his life might then have been altered. Among other things, that shot shattered the delicate diplomatic negotiations on which he was engaged for the exposition. Already he had succeeded in getting Germany, France, and England to reverse previous decisions not to participate, and he was working on other governments.

His wife and sons joined him in London immediately after school closed for the summer vacation. It would enable them to enjoy another of those too-rare intervals of normal family life. Little did they dream that normal life, for them and for most of mankind, would seem a bright memory and a forlorn hope in the months and years ahead.

The Hoover whose fortieth birthday was celebrated with his little family and a few intimate friends on August 10 at the spacious Red House was a self-made man in the finest American tradition, with many of the authentic Horatio Alger trimmings. The West Branch blacksmith's orphaned son stood at the pinnacle of his chosen profession, well-to-do, respected, rich in friends. Yet it was a somber celebration. For Germany had declared war on France exactly a week earlier. The modern scourge of total war had begun to engulf the blundering human race for the first but, alas, not the last time.

VII

Hoover Chooses Public Service

T H E outbreak of war in 1914 stranded nearly two hundred thousand Americans, among them some thirty thousand vacationing school teachers, amid the dislocations and hysterias of Europe. Tens of thousands of them were piling into London, bewildered, frightened, and often penniless. Banks had ceased to honor American checks and other paper. On the Continent, too, our consulates, legations, and embassies were besieged by hordes of these trapped men, women, and children. Frontiers were being closed without warning. Ships were scarce and growing scarcer. It was a tangle of confusions touched by panic.

On Monday afternoon, August 3, a bank holiday in England, the United States Consul General in London, Robert P. Skinner, telephoned Herbert Hoover. He was in a mess, he announced. Hundreds of anxious and indignant tourists were milling within and around his consulate, demanding help. What could Mr. Hoover suggest? Hoover's office was only a block from the consulate and he hurried to the scene.

"I did not realize it at the moment," he would write in the future, "but on this Monday my engineering career was over. I was on the slippery road of public life."

He met the immediate crisis in the consulate by scraping up a few hundred pounds in cash and improvising an exchange-and-loan office. The clamorous Americans were lined up before five desks manned by Hoover friends. Those who had dollars or could make out checks received some English currency in exchange; the rest received ten-shilling loans against I.O.U.'s. That would tide them over until a sensible repatriation plan could be worked out. Hoover was touched especially by the plight of the teachers "who had pinched, saved and planned for this one trip to Europe all their lives." In them he saw the beloved teachers of his own boyhood.

A worse crisis had that same day overwhelmed the American Embassy. It was beleaguered not by hundreds but by thousands. They insisted loudly and indignantly that Uncle Sam, in the person of Ambassador Walter Hines Page, "do something" forthwith. They were citizens and taxpayers, weren't they? Uncle Sam was momentarily as flustered as his nephew Skinner. And learning that this fellow Hoover had taken over in the consulate, he hastened to dump the whole muddled emergency in his lap.

A self-constituted committee of the less excited Americans, headed by Oscar Straus, called a mass meeting at the Savoy Hotel that evening to consider the situation. At the Ambassador's request, Hoover attended it. The gathering ended with Hoover holding the bag of responsibility. The challenge of an emergency was perhaps what he needed at the moment —purposeful action was always his best medicine. "The wreck of the past week," he would explain subsequently, "had left me stunned and un- strung. It was hard to become accustomed to world wars. But the troubles of the American tourists served to reduce the feeling of helplessness."

Hoover's own house was in serious disarray. The war had upset his mining empire, at some points disastrously. But the bigger problem un- loaded on him by Uncle Sam took priority. Within twenty-four hours a new American committee, mostly composed of his own business associates and friends, was functioning in a stratum of calm above the storms of confusion. Willing men and women among the hordes of refugees were mobilized and soon Hoover had "a volunteer staff of five hundred of the most capable people in the world." At his initiative, similar committees were formed in other European centers. Mrs. Hoover rallied women in the American colony for a women's division to care for unaccompanied women and children.

In a few days the improvised refugee rescue mission was operating with reasonable speed if not altogether smoothly, in rooms provided rent-free by the Savoy Hotel. It had the combined attributes of a bank, shipping company, diplomatic agency, and tourist bureau, with charity and social service functions thrown in for good measure.

Large numbers of Americans were evacuated from difficult zones, cared for at points of concentration, and in time shipped home. It was done so quietly, so expeditiously, with so little ballyhoo, that only a few realized they were witnessing a miracle of organization and efficiency. Somehow Hoover found the staff, the cash, the food, the clothes, and above all the passenger ships, so that by the time Congress appropriated a million dol- lars for the job of repatriation, much of it had already been done.

After the first tide of tourists and teachers there came a great flow of destitute Americans—mostly naturalized citizens fleeing wartorn countries where they had been living and working. The officials sent from Washing-

76

ton to oversee the operation handed it over to the Hoover committee, with a sigh of relief.

This was the first time Americans outside the mining and financial communities became truly aware of the man Hoover. And American correspondents had their first taste of a public figure who seemed strangely determined to keep himself out of the public light.

In six weeks the Hoover "show" handled about 120,000 Americans in varying degrees of distress. Over and above the crucial banking services for those with money, the committee raised and distributed substantial sums on a charity basis. Its personnel worked day and night; though they could not guess it, this was for many of them a dress rehearsal for rescue tasks on an unprecedented scale to begin in the near future and to last nearly nine years.

Along with the organizational efficiency there was great faith. With a few friends whom he drew into the gamble, Hoover induced one bank in London to cash any kind of American paper, on his personal pledge to make good any losses. Obviously there was neither the time nor the machinery for checking credit ratings. Before the exodus was completed, over $1,500,000 had been cashed. That was the extent of the gamble. But faith was vindicated: less than three hundred dollars was lost in the big transaction.

In the avalanche of work and worry there were nuggets of diversion. Hoover recalled, for instance, the old lady who would not board a ship without his written guarantee that there would be no U-boat attacks. Under the circumstances even Great-grandma Rebecca would have tolerated the little deception as Hoover obliged with a document. Then there was the woman, being repatriated at public expense, who declared a hunger strike for better accommodations than steerage. She was maneuvered into a seat in a committee lunchroom, where the odors of edibles broke her resistance in a few hours.

Hoover liked to recount also the complex woes of a rich man's daughter from Lansing, Michigan, who had lost her ten trunks, including a trousseau, before she reached London from the mainland. Papa came through with money to replace the trousseau. Having bought the best that London had to offer, the girl consigned the packages, for safety's sake, in care of the committee at the Savoy. That was her mistake, for the committee had an Old Clothes Department to which all gifts of clothes were delivered as a matter of routine. The women in charge were astonished but pleased by the windfall of finery, and some of their humble clients found themselves more elegantly dressed than ever before in their lives. The blunder was not discovered until Miss Lansing came for her packages a week later. Papa threatened to sue but thought better of it.

Then there was the American Wild West show which descended on the Savoy in full Indian and cowboy regalia but totally broke. It had traveled a long way, from Poland in fact. The troupers had lost or sold their animals and orthodox clothes as they proceeded, saving only the costumes on their backs. London had something to stare at while they waited to be transported to the United States.

So little suspicion did Hoover have of what history was preparing for him that he made reservations to sail with his family for America. With his stranded countrymen under smooth control, he was organizing his private affairs with a view to a long sojourn in California. The gods who preside over such ironies looked on and smiled in knowing amusement.

2

Let us turn back for a moment to 1907. Hoover came up from his desert diggings to greet Dr. David Starr Jordan, in Melbourne on vacation. After he had caught up with the Stanford news and gossip, he was willing enough to answer his old "prexy's" questions about his work and plans.

"I have run through my profession," Dr. Jordan remembered him saying. "It holds nothing more, except money, of which I have enough already. . . . When I return to London, I think I shall resign, and after a while go back to America to see if there is not some form of executive position in which I can serve my country."

He did resign, as we have seen, but he did not retire. Five years later a prominent journalist, Will Irwin, waiting for his ship in a European port, ran into Hoover on his way back from Russia. They picked up the threads of their old campus friendship and talked, as boyhood acquaintances will, of their hopes for the future.

As Irwin recalled their conversations, Hoover thought he was getting closer to the financial independence mark when he could give up business without being unfair to his dependents. "What then?" Irwin wanted to know. Hoover did not have a precise answer. The nearest he came to formulating that persistent inner nudging was to declare that he was "interested in some job of public service—at home, of course."

Other friends of that period recalled similar allusions to public service. But perhaps money-making is a little like drink to an alcoholic: he resolves to quit when he has had "enough" but never recognizes the "enough" point. It is probably a fact that for Hoover wealth was never an end in itself but the means to an end: the self-sufficiency that would allow him to serve his fellow men. It was not, in his case, a dream of self-abnegation but of self-fulfillment. He talked of doing something for humanity and his country in the way other young men talk of achieving yachts and country estates. He simply had a gnawing hunger of the spirit and promised himself to indulge it as soon as he could afford it.

In accepting a trusteeship at his alma mater, in consenting to represent the Panama-Pacific International Exposition abroad, he was edging closer to that reserve vocation. Yet, had it not been for the war, he might have been held in the groove of international mining by the inertia of business triumphs and the magnetism of ever larger engineering problems. The great cataclysm of 1914 forced the decision.

He was preparing for the journey across the Atlantic with his family when an engineer whom he knew only slightly, Millard Shaler, came to see him on September 25. Shaler had just arrived from Brussels, the captive capital of a conquered nation, and was full of the horror of its expanding tragedy.

Belgium imported at least 75 percent of its breadstuffs and 50 percent of other foods. The German invaders were requisitioning local supplies, so that stocks were dangerously low and sinking fast. The 7,500,000 inhabitants were helpless prisoners, ringed by German bayonets on land and by Allied blockade on the coast. The same was true of the 2,500,000 people in northern France overrun by the Germans. A terrifying catastrophe was clearly in the making unless help from the outside came quickly.

Shaler and other Americans stationed there had formed a Committee for the City of Brussels, with Daniel Heineman as chairman and a brilliant young diplomat serving as Secretary of the American Legation, Hugh Gibson, among the members. For the Committee, Shaler had bought twenty-five hundred tons of food but was finding the British officials obdurate about allowing its delivery to Rotterdam for transshipment to Brussels. Hoover steered the engineer to Ambassador Page, who had the plight of the Belgians close to heart. With the Ambassador's backing, Hoover induced the British to grant a permit for the twenty-five hundred tons, accompanied by a Foreign Office warning that this was the end of such nonsense: let the Germans feed their captives!

Other emissaries from Belgium kept arriving in London in the following days and weeks. All of them sought out Hoover. All of them told gruesome stories of creeping starvation, with epidemics around the corner. Belgian industry had all but collapsed. Currency was losing value fast and, in any case, there was less and less to buy. A large-scale relief effort by neutrals, meaning Americans, was indispensable.

On October 18 Hoover was summoned to the U. S. Embassy. There he found the Belgian Minister, Hugh Gibson, Chevalier Emile Francqui, and a Baron Lambert. They talked relief and they spelled it Hoover.

Now there is a curious counterpoint in the music of Hoover's life. Repeatedly the episodes and personalities of one phase show up dramatically in another, like recurrent themes. It was a Belgian group, back in 1901, which had precipitated his withdrawal from China; now it was the travail of Belgium that would hold him in Europe. The financier with whom he had parted in anger in China thirteen years before, whom Hoover's testimony helped defeat in the celebrated Chang litigation in London courts, had in the meantime emerged as the head of the leading Belgian financial house. And now this same Francqui was again in London, pleading for swift aid to his cornered and famished nation.

At one point Francqui rose impulsively and approached his old adversary.

"Mr. Hoover," he said in substance, "I owe you an apology. You proved right in the Chinese matter. We in Belgium and northern France are faced with life and death for millions of our people. You alone have the setting for the job. If you will undertake it, I will either serve under you or retire from any connection with it."

He argued that any true relief effort must be headed by an American and that Hoover, with his worldwide experience and close-up knowledge of transportation, was that American. The Ambassador, Gibson, and everyone else backed up this logic. They all understood and acknowledged the extent of the sacrifice they were urging upon him.

War conditions had endangered Hoover's far-flung business interests and required his personal attention more compellingly than ever. Valuable cargoes on the high seas had to be shunted to new destinations; smelting plants were caught in belligerent areas; large numbers of men and women who looked to his London office for orders were suddenly cut off by closed frontiers. At least a dozen major and twice as many lesser undertakings were at stake. Consulting fees netting him over one hundred thousand dollars annually were involved.

Moreover, he was in an ideal position to make himself one of the world's richest men if he chose. Hoover happened to have the inside track in the race for base metals, especially zinc and lead, at the start of a war in which these products would be worth their weight in gold. A large slice of the world's available sources of war minerals was directly or indirectly under his control, and there were few people alive with such intimate knowledge of untapped areas of supply.

The group met again for discussion. Hoover asked the Belgians and Americans for a day or two to ponder his personal position. For a relatively young man with a profound sense of obligation to his family, it was not an easy decision that he faced. Though a man of wealth, he was far from the goal he had set for himself as the measure of independence.

Besides, more comprehensively than the others, Hoover saw the towering difficulties of the proposed enterprise in compassion. As he summed it up in retrospect, "It was not 'relief' in any known sense. It was the feeding of a nation." And it presented problems "for which there was no former human experience to turn to for guidance." It would mean finding food for ten million people, transporting it across oceans infested with submarines and hair-triggered mines, and delivering it across the physical and red-tape obstructions of belligerent navies and armies. It would mean finding the money to buy the supplies, building an apparatus for their equitable distribution, and seeing to it that none of them fell into the hands of occupying forces.

For some future playwright with the insight to dramatize the Hoover story there is a superb scene ready-made—the scene in which a forty-year-old American must choose between incalculable wealth and the arduous, usually thankless career of public service. There was never any real doubt that this Quaker would accept the challenge of monumental human misery. From the beginning, even before he explicitly accepted the job, he took the lead in planning the effort. Clearly he was already committed in his heart. His immediate problem was whether to retain his business empire or to renounce private ambitions altogether.

Will Irwin, in London as war correspondent for the *Saturday Evening Post* and a number of newspapers, was living with the Hoovers at the Red House. During the crucial night when his host wrestled with the problem, he would record, he heard Hoover discussing the problem with his wife, then pacing his room for hours. But in the morning, when Hoover came down to breakfast, he seemed unusually serene.

"Well," he said to his friend, sensing perhaps that Will had followed the inner struggle, "let fortune go to hell."

He said it as casually as if he were canceling a weekend vacation, rather than giving up the near-certainty of immense wealth. Recalling the moment, Irwin wrote afterward: "I felt then, I know now, that I had witnessed a significant moment in history." It was a decision that would affect the lives of literally hundreds of millions of human beings—since Belgium was only the first act in the long-term drama of benevolence. From that moment the story of Hoover became part of the substance of world history. Never had a great business career been so sharply renounced for a greater career of service.

To his associates he announced simply, "The business is in your hands." He apologized for leaving them on their own at a trying juncture and promised to be available for advice should crises arise. But they understood, as he wished them to understand, that he was through with mining and active money-making. He transferred to them all the lush fee contracts and resigned from a score or more directorates, retaining only a nominal and inactive place on the board of the Burma Land Mines.

So little suspicion did Hoover have of what history was preparing for him that he had made, and canceled, several reservations to sail with his family for America. After the great decision, the family sailed without him. Announcement of their safe arrival took the form of a jocular cable from the older son reporting his conquest over seasickness and the consumption of seven cream puffs in one Atlantic day. The English censor was never quite convinced that it was not a code and mumbled pointedly about the penalties for espionage.

One evening in the last week of October, Hoover met Ambassador Page, Chevalier Francqui, and others to inform them that he was accepting their proposal, but on two conditions: first, that he be allowed to serve without pay; and second, that he was to have full command and authority, as the job could not be done by "a knitting bee."

Those present saw him glance at his watch, then leave the room briskly. In a few minutes he returned. Later Page asked him why he had absented himself so abruptly. Hoover explained that he wanted to catch the New York market before it closed for the day; he had placed an order for ten million bushels of Chicago wheat earmarked for Belgium, at his own risk.

The following morning he met with the Americans whom he had summoned to his office: Millard Hunsiker, John White, Edgar Rickard, Millard Shaler, John Lucey—all engineers—Hugh Gibson, Ben S. Allen of the Associated Press, and a banker. In a few minutes the relief enterprise was born and christened: Commission for Relief in Belgium (C.R.B. for short). It was not a corporation but a partnership, and that meant unlimited financial responsibility. The banker withdrew.

Like nearly everyone else at that time, these men assumed that the war would be over in the spring, so that it was just a matter of "tiding over eight months until the new harvest." Writing in the early 1920s, Hoover said:

> The knowledge that we would have to go on for four years, to find a billion dollars, to transport five million tons of concentrated food, to administer rationing, price controls, agricultural production, to contend with combatant governments and with world shortages of food and ships, was mercifully hidden from us.

It was John White who remarked at the initial session, "We are about to handle millions of dollars. Some day some swine will rise up and say we either made a profit out of this business or that we stole the money." (Not one but many such swine did in fact arise.) At once Rickard was dispatched to confer with Sir John Spender, head of the leading British firm of auditors. Sir John not only undertook to audit accounts, do all the bookkeeping with his own staff, and countersign all checks, but to do so gratis, except for the modest salaries of the men he would have to place in C.R.B. offices all over the world.

From that day forward Hoover never accepted for his private use a dollar in payment for any of his manifold public services. He paid his own travel and out-of-pocket expenses. His salaries as Secretary of Commerce, and then as President, went into a special fund for disbursement in full for charitable causes, to raise wages of aides who needed it, or to pay for expert personnel not provided by official budgets. Money that came to him for writing or speaking went likewise to private charity and public causes.

Associates on his new course, from 1914 on, if in a position to do so, followed the Chief's example in refusing remuneration and in paying their own expenses. More than that, they contributed money to enable others, who had no means of their own, to work with Hoover on projects of benevolence. No Quakers themselves, merely out of affection for the Chief or through conviction, they lived by his Quaker dictum that public service is a God-given privilege, not a business. In addition, of course, they recognized the force of his familiar adage that people in public life must have "glass pockets."

VIII

The Belgian Relief

A BIBLIOGRAPHY of books, pamphlets, and articles about the Belgian Relief runs to several closely printed pages. Its major facts and incidents might be crammed into a large volume, its human content can never be compassed by words. Here we can only hope to suggest the magnitude of the undertaking, the uniqueness of the problems it posed, the single-minded devotion and immense competence of the man who carried it through successfully.

It was not only a new kind of task for Hoover, remote from his past experience, but a new phenomenon in the experience of the human race. In solving its piled-up problems and resolving its never-ending crises there were no precedents to draw upon. But the precedents it set would help others in the future, in war and in peace in two score countries, to organize and administer analogous projects. Unknowingly, Hoover and his staff were pioneering total relief for the coming world of total disasters.

Though the job was 90 percent American, Hoover wisely put other neutrals well in the foreground. His honorary chairmen included the key Spanish and Dutch diplomats; the Scandinavians shied away for fear of embroilment in the war. In Belgium itself Francqui headed up a National Committee comprising the most eminent citizens; it tended to become the focal point of Belgian unity, faith, and morale in the years ahead. Provincial and city committees were then formed to do the local work of distribution. Until the Armistice four years later, some fifty thousand Belgians were engaged in the enterprise, all volunteers or at most drawing only regular rations as wages. Another personality out of Hoover's China period, Chevalier Edmond De Wouters, acted as liaison officer between the C.R.B. and the National Committee.

At the same time Belgian Relief Committees for fund-raising were built up all over the world, from Britain and Sweden to Japan and Latin America. The largest network was in the United States: a national headquarters in New York and subsidiaries in forty states and hundreds of cities. Charity drives, even if highly successful, could provide only a small part of the money required—it was a job for governments. Hoover knew this. But the little was welcome and the very process of soliciting funds stirred up the public sentiment needed to sustain official cooperation.

The logic of the operation, given the suspicions of both sets of belligerents, placed all responsibility for local distribution upon the Hoover organization. Before long the Americans were administering a perfectly coordinated rationing system, assuring that the richest and the poorest got no more than their prescribed share of calories. They ran flour mills, bakeries, dairies, a dozen other industries, and commanded the entire agriculture of the nation. In the "operational" zones of France, where Germans helped cultivate the land, it was Hoover's delicate and heart-wrenching task to negotiate the apportionment of the crops between the armies and the population.

One day, in the organizational stage, a young man named Perrin C. Galpin arrived at Hoover's office to offer his services. He was a Rhodes scholar at Oxford and he thought that nearly all his fellow Rhodes-men would volunteer, too, if asked. He was right. In a few days fifteen "of the finest and most courageous American youngsters ever born"—Hoover's accolade—left Oxford for Brussels. Galpin and a number of others remained "Hoover men" for the rest of their days.

The C.R.B. was able to pick up twenty thousand tons of wheat and other foods at once in Holland and rushed them by canal transport to the hardest-pressed Belgian cities. Some sixty thousand additional tons from overseas were delivered in the next six weeks. A start was thus made. The plan set eighteen hundred calories a day as the survival minimum, with supplements to children, expectant mothers, and the sick.

All the Belgian cash reserves abroad were assigned to the Hoover group. They were lamentably small, about six and a half million dollars, and soon exhausted. To keep the ten million people alive, the Committee needed at least twelve million dollars a month, plus another ten million dollars to cover supplies "in the pipe lines" on their way to the stricken areas. The figures kept rising, of course, due to the rise of food prices in world markets and ever-steeper costs of ship charters, so that in the last years the monthly budget stood at twenty-five million dollars.

"In order to assure the trans-ocean stream of food for the next few weeks," Hoover later revealed, "I had incurred a debt of $12,000,000 over and above our assets. I had financed these purchases by personally accepted trade bills payable on arrival of the ships at Rotterdam."

The indispensable immediate need, from the first day, was to obtain the help of combatant governments, including large financial subsidies. To grasp the nature of this problem, we must bear in mind that on both sides of the war military minds were in control. As the struggle resolved into a stalemate of bloody attrition and wild hatreds, the human element was all but forgotten. It was Hoover's task to make the voice of crying children heard above the roar of battle, and he had only neutral sentiment and influence to use as megaphones.

To an English critic of some phase of the work, Hoover once said that the job was "like trying to feed a hungry kitten by means of a forty-foot bamboo pole, said kitten being confined in a barred cage with two hungry lions."

One of these lions was the helmeted Germany, the other was the Allies. Bitter opposition to feeding the Belgians and constant interference with the work came not only from the Germans. British and French leaders, too, had to be sold on the idea or bludgeoned into cooperation with the big stick of public opinion in the neutral nations. The most intense hostility to feeding the occupied sector of France, for instance, came from French leaders. In England, to the very end, a powerful group led by Winston Churchill, First Lord of the Admiralty, and Lord Kitchener, then the War Minister, was loud and sometimes effective in blocking the C.R.B.

Even after British subsidies had been firmly negotiated, this group continued to snipe at the C.R.B. Once the naval authorities, presumably with their First Lord's blessing, filed with the Foreign Office charges against Hoover personally as a spy working for the Germans! "Our staunch friend, Sir Edward Grey," Hoover would record, "had these charges referred to a King's Bench Court for a private investigation. After tedious hearings we were exonerated and eulogized."

The strategy of blockade became increasingly important in Allied thinking. Fear that some of the food funneled into Belgium might leak to the Germans outweighed sympathy for the victims. "Let the Huns provision the territories they have overrun," many top Allied leaders thundered. "If they cannot or will not do it, the blood of the victims will be on *their* heads, not ours. Let the world see the bottomless brutality of these beasts, even if innocent lives are lost."

The Germans at their end demanded the lifting of the blockade. "Stop your naval war on civilians," they howled, "and there will be no relief problems. Why should we let you feed the Belgians and the French while you are starving German women and children? Allow the feeding of all or none! Besides, this is a total war, not a parlor game. We can't have a lot of neutrals in our operational zones spying on us and lying about us." It was a point of view that became more insistent as the extreme jingo mood and Junker control deepened.

Moral and humane appeals were so much thistledown in the fierce winds of hatred. Hoover had to rely on more solid arguments, the kind that were veiled threats. Persistently, until the day America entered the war, he forced the belligerents to realize that neutral—and primarily American—opinion would be horrified by the mass starvation of helpless noncombatants. The surest way to drive America into the Allied camp, he convinced the Germans, was to starve the Belgians. The surest way to alienate America, he convinced the Allies, was to block the relief of Belgium.

President Wilson, the entire American diplomatic corps, and most U.S. newspapers sided with Hoover. But there was a vocal minority at home, headed by Senator Henry Cabot Lodge, attacking his efforts as pernicious "entanglement" in foreign wars. Hoover could address the fighting nations with the authority of three leading neutrals. American Ambassador James W. Gerard in Berlin, the corresponding American diplomats in London and Paris, and their Spanish and Dutch colleagues fought continuous battles to keep the "forty-foot bamboo pole" from being knocked out of Hoover's hands.

At critical junctures, however, it was Hoover himself who rushed from one capital to another and at times to the secret German headquarters at Charleville on the fighting front to save his work from annihilation. In a little over two years he crossed between England and the Continent, across the mine-infested English Channel and North Sea, forty times. Few ordinary Belgians and Frenchmen knew by how thin a margin they were rescued again and again from the lingering death of starvation. "He is the best diplomat of us all," the Spanish Minister told relief workers in Brussels.

The British had a plausible alibi for withholding cooperation. They demanded solid German guarantees against diversion of relief supplies. Hoover's first visit, after Brussels, was therefore to Berlin. The opposition in Germany seemed insuperable. Neutral diplomatic pressures had failed to budge the military clique. It was a cold opposition, mechanical, impersonal, seemingly impervious to common sense, let alone common humanity. Hoover talked to key political and military leaders, one by one and in groups; he talked for hours, for days. Because they had hopes of keeping the United States neutral, they listened—and finally capitulated almost on his terms.

Berlin agreed to facilitate the supplying of conquered areas, under written guarantees that not a morsel of home-grown or imported food reached German mouths. They allowed a considerable freedom of movement for relief workers and undertook to halt the requisitioning of Belgian food and cattle then under way. The Reichsbank agreed to support food loans of from fifty to one hundred million dollars for the C.R.B., secured by Belgian bonds.

Returning from Berlin with these assurances—and, incidentally, with the conviction that the war would be long drawn—Hoover then tackled the British Government. Again it was a titanic struggle. The Cabinet appeared opposed to the whole American scheme. They attached high hopes to the blockade; they had more urgent uses for food and ships; and they resented the interjection of humanitarian questions into a "realistic" struggle for existence. Hoover wore them down by the sheer logic of his position, reinforced by the threat of American indignation. Ambassador Page was a tower of strength for him in these prolonged duels.

2

Lloyd George was not yet head of the Government, but he held a key post and swung enormous weight in the Cabinet. He began a decisive conference with the American engineer in a frankly hostile spirit. Other leaders present let the shaggy little Welshman conduct the debate while they listened. Immunity for relief ships from Allied seizures, unhampered passage through blockade lines, large British financial support for the Belgian Relief—these were the issues at stake.

At the end of a long afternoon, Lloyd George announced, "I am convinced." He asked the American to prepare a statement embodying his arguments for presentation to the full Cabinet. When they met again, Lloyd George shook Hoover's hand warmly. "You've put up a great fight —and you've won," he said. Over the protests of Churchill and Kitchener, the British Government had acceded to all of Hoover's terms—and voted one million pounds a month to "the Hoover Fund."

The toughest opposition of all was put up by Paris. When finally France did come around—aware that it could not appear less humane than the Germans and the British—its contributions were made indirectly, through an ostensibly private channel. Three million dollars a month reached the C.R.B. punctually from a "private" source, though it was an open secret that it came from the French Treasury.

Unhappily, few arrangements with governments at war settle anything clearly or for long. The proof of the pudding was literally in the eating— whether the Belgians and the occupied French would have enough to eat to sustain life. There were conflicts of authority between central governments and local military and naval commanders to be adjusted. There were individual officials who refused to cooperate. Where the delay of a consignment meant hunger for hundreds of thousands, red tape must be slashed and special privileges exacted by sheer nerve—and Hoover always had enough of this in reserve.

The British, fearful that the enemy might seize supplies without warning, insisted that no more than four weeks' imports be accumulated at Rotterdam, the port of entry, and in Belgium at any time. This made it necessary that the flow of supplies be constant, uninterrupted, and accurately estimated—a formidable assignment under war conditions. And it was just one of a long array of tough assignments.

Bursts of opposition in the United States, reflecting isolationist passions, were also a continuing problem. Twice they forced Hoover to rush home to mend fences. In a personal interview, Senator Lodge threatened him with imprisonment under the moldy Logan Act prohibiting private citizens to deal with foreign governments. Fortunately the President and virtually the whole press rallied behind Belgian Relief and the threats came to nothing. It was on the first of these visits home that Hoover first met Woodrow Wilson; their admiration was instant and mutual. He also met ex-President Theodore Roosevelt, who thereafter threw his formidable weight behind the relief effort.

"In time," Hoover was able to write, "we won the confidence of both belligerent sides and became a sort of neutral state of our own. We in effect issued our own passports and visas." For a period, indeed, the Commission even printed what amounted to its own currency: scrip that was universally accepted in Belgium because it could pay for food rations.

By dint of diplomatic pressures, the C.R.B. obtained from the Germans immunity for its ships on seas swarming with submarines and paved with mines. At its peak the Commission operated a fleet of sixty cargo ships totaling nearly three hundred thousand tons, under its own charter and flying its own flag—the initials C.R.B. in red on a white field—as well as four hundred barges plying between Rotterdam and Belgian ports. Every Hoover ship had the words *Commission for Relief in Belgium* painted on its hull in huge white letters for visibility. Despite this, even before the start of unlimited U-boat warfare, nineteen of these ships were lost, at least three sunk by submarines. German apologies and indemnities could not restore the lives lost nor the badly needed ships.

Hoover was the one man who moved freely across all frontiers and all military lines. He was head of a new Great Power, employing political and moral authority exceeding that of many real nations. Its country and its capital were on no map, but they coincided with what remained of decency and Christian sympathy in the fevered world. "A piratical state organized for benevolence," a British diplomat called it.

The actual feeding process was not, as many people assumed, all charity. Most Belgians could afford to pay for their rations, provided it was made available. Hoover's most brilliant fiscal improvisation was perhaps in making the profits on sales to the solvent cover the cost of caring for the indigent. This necessitated procedures of great complexity.

The whole operation was divided into two branches, "Provisioning" and "Benevolence," each run as if it were a separate function. The number of people dependent on straight charity naturally increased as the war dragged on. Toward the end, half the population in occupied Belgium and northern France was on the Benevolence side of the ledger.

Some three million children were fed by the C.R.B. directly, over and above the rationing mechanism. The techniques worked out in this connection were adopted all through Europe after the war. Then, after the Second and greater World War, they were applied in more than forty countries, with a number of graduates of the Hoover staff in Belgium prominent in administering them. Hoover would write in due course:

From the rebuilding of the vitality of the children came the great relieving joy in the work of the Belgian Relief. The troops of healthy, cheerful, chattering youngsters lining up for their portions, eating at long tables, cleaning their own dishes afterwards, were a gladdening lift from the drab life of an imprisoned people. And they did become healthy. When the war ended it was found that children's mortality and morbidity were lower than ever before in Belgian and French history.

The Commission was even able to finance some building and loan associations to keep them from going under. It paid the salaries of minor judiciary, police, and certain other officials; social stability was essential to limit German intervention in daily life.

A typical sidelight on the Benevolence work: Belgium's largest cottage industry had been, for a century, the making of hand lace. It was providing a livelihood to some fifty thousand families when war broke out. With the world market cut off, there was danger that the skills passed down through the generations would be forgotten. C.R.B. therefore arranged to buy the lace in return for rations. At the war's end the Commission had four million dollars' worth in its warehouses. To everyone's astonishment, the lace found a ready market and the families—an accurate account having been kept—received unexpected dividends.

Nations at war competed for the food resources of the neutral world; nations not yet at war were building reserves as insurance against the future. It was in that kind of world market that the C.R.B. found rice in Rangoon, corn in Argentina, beans in Manchuria, wheat and meats and fats in the United States—150,000 tons of food every month. Even keener and tighter was the competition for shipping tonnage, but in this, too,

Hoover succeeded, though repeatedly vessels on which he counted were snatched from him by the Allies for military uses.

An anecdote has come down from those years that tells much about the man in command. Hoover was pressing a British Admiralty official for a permit to export certain supplies. Of what use would the permit be, the official objected, when there isn't a single ship available? "We've got the ship," Hoover said quietly, "and it's already loaded."

Gloom deepened in January 1917, when the Germans announced their unlimited submarine warfare. In the following sixty-five days, until the United States entered the war, the promised immunity began to fade out. Eight C.R.B. ships were sunk by submarines, four more by mines. Deliveries plummeted from 150,000 tons a month to an average of under 25,000. Not until the Allies began to provide military escort was the situation partially remedied.

As American involvement became inevitable, Hoover transferred the formal direction of C.R.B. to the Spanish and the Dutch, although he continued in real command in the wings—at the same time that he served as wartime Food Administrator in Washington. It is a commentary on the efficiency of the whole mechanism that it functioned without serious breakdowns until the Armistice.

The roster of the C.R.B. leadership included many names that were to figure importantly in national affairs in the future. Their aggregate abilities were strikingly high. Yet the fact that their work was so incredibly effective amid the passions and disorientations of war can be explained primarily by the personality of Hoover. This was the unanimous verdict of those closest to the effort, whether Americans or Europeans. Not one in the group ever defected or ever wavered in his loyalty to the Chief. Dr. Vernon Kellogg, who was in this devoted company, wrote:

> Those of us who have lived through the difficult, the almost impossible days of Belgian Relief . . . have come to an almost superstitious belief in his capacity to do anything possible to human power. . . . People sometimes ask me why Hoover has such strong hold on his helpers. The men of the C.R.B. know.

Hugh Gibson, in *A Journal from Our Legation in Belgium*, wrote that the Relief

> is without doubt the greatest humanitarian enterprise in history, conducted under conditions of almost incredible difficulty. . . . In its inception and execution, the work of the Commission is distinctly American. Its inception was in the mind of Herbert Hoover; in its execution he had the whole-hearted assistance of a little band of quiet American gentlemen who labored in Belgium from the autumn of 1914 until we entered in the war in April of 1917. . . . It was the splendid human side of the Commission that made it succeed in spite of all obstacles.

3

Men and women with only a normal endowment of physical, mental, and spiritual stamina cannot survey the story of the Belgian Relief without marveling how one man could have carried that load. The historians of the Commission can organize their materials, analyzing each of the categories of problems separately. Hoover had to resolve them simultaneously, day by day, often hour by hour. "Whether internal distribution, care of the destitute, or shipping were relatively the worst problems I could never decide," he was to say in retrospect. "No one day went by without a fight to keep part of the mechanism from breaking down."

It was a mechanism that had its wheels and pistons and fuel dispersed over half a dozen countries, most of them ringed with steel. His every crossing of the North Sea was related to a pressing crisis, and involved the risk of being blown to smithereens by mines or too-eager U-boats. Yet, as we have already noted, it was in part on these sea journeys that he wrote a charming story of his life for his boys; its placid, sometimes droll style hardly suggests the conditions under which it was composed.

On his hurried American visit in January 1917, Hoover accepted an invitation to address the New York Chamber of Commerce. This, he wrote afterward, was his "first public address of any pretension—and certainly the public received it with patience." Which is an indication of the extent to which Hoover escaped public appearances.

"He is a simple, modest, energetic man who began his career in California and will end it in Heaven; and he doesn't want anybody's thanks," Ambassador Page reported to President Wilson at the start of the Belgian Relief. Hoover, incidentally, developed a towering esteem for the Ambassador, which was fully reciprocated. This is the more noteworthy because they did not see eye to eye on the issue of American entry into the war, Page being for it and Hoover against.

The first announcement of Belgian Relief had been made, on Hoover's insistence, in Millard Shaler's name. But after that Hoover could not keep his name from skyrocketing without seeming to evade his responsibilities for all that transpired. Those most directly connected with the press and public relations aspects of the job, men like Will Irwin and Ben Allen, have attested (in pride mixed with annoyance) that the Chief hampered their work by rejecting endless openings for capitalizing on his personal exploits. The American press, keen as always on the scent of personalities, clamored for "human-interest stuff" about the head of the greatest relief effort in history up to that time. The little they got was without the help, and frequently in defiance of, Hoover himself. "Play up Belgian Relief," he kept instructing his press staff, "not Hoover."

He could not sidetrack the fame that was his destiny. It was a time of warriors and politicians of war, but slowly the name that symbolized humanitarian impulse and the code of mutual help impinged on world consciousness until it overshadowed most of the rest. Diplomatic pouches reaching Washington and private reports to the President bulged with praise for Hoover that had in it overtones of awe.

As was to be expected, various belligerent governments bid for his services, dangling titles and honors before his eyes. He was so horrified by these hints that they were not repeated. And private groups (as Mr. Page informed Wilson in one communication) besieged him with fat offers if he would resign and go to work for them. Obviously they did not understand Hoover; like the politicians of a later day they mistook him for one of their own.

Not a word about the relief organization could appear in the German-censored Belgian press. Nevertheless, Hoover's name was known and venerated. During his periodic visits in Brussels, sometimes accompanied by his wife, he strove to remain out of sight. His shyness in the face of acclamation came close to a phobia. Besides, pro-American demonstrations in a conquered area would have alarmed the conquerors and endangered the work.

Yet word of his presence in their midst did spread now and then, and tens of thousands of simple people found their own way to express gratitude. During one visit, for instance, they came to the Legation door day after day—singly or in twos, to avoid the appearance of a demonstration—and left their "cards"; these ranged from elegantly embossed pasteboards to scraps of butcher paper with a name scrawled on it. Each day, as another huge pile of these tokens was deposited on Hoover's desk, he fingered them pensively, sighed, and returned to his chores.

Once, after Hoover had completed a conference with a Junker officer in Brussels, the German said, "Well now, Herr Hoover, as man to man, what do you get out of all this? You are not doing it for nothing, surely." The American felt it was futile to explain. For that matter, a few Americans back home had as much difficulty understanding or believing disinterested service as the German.

He did have to explain, in detail, when a question of the same order was put by the Minister of Foreign Affairs of Spain, where Hoover had stopped on his return from his second visit to America. It was clear to him then that the United States would soon cease to be a neutral. Formal administration of the C.R.B. had to be transferred to other hands.

"What is your salary, Mr. Hoover?" the Foreign Minister in Madrid asked archly. "What do your assistants get? What salaries will our nationals receive?"

The expression on the Spanish politician's face showed that he did not quite believe his guest's assurances that neither he nor his top associates were being paid. Their Spanish successors before long proved quite generous in assigning themselves salaries and other emoluments.

Continually the Commission assumed heavy financial obligations without knowing precisely when and how they would be made good. One of Hoover's remarkable accomplishments was his success in forcing the reluctant Allies to provide large subsidies, either in outright grants or in loans to Belgium. Before the job was wound up, the British Government had contributed $109,000,000; France, $205,000,000; the United States, mostly in the period of its belligerency, $386,000,000. World charity added $52,000,000 to the grand total.

The final auditing by Sir John Spender's organization covered nearly a billion dollars. (The internal food supplies administered by the Commission came to roughly another billion, but did not fall into this audit.) Because so many hundreds of Americans and thousands of Belgians gave their time and unlimited energies without pay, *the overhead costs came to less than half of one percent* (0.43%). This was a record well-nigh miraculous. Many efficient charities are pleased if they can hold their overhead under 20 percent; the administrative expenses of UNRRA after World War II, a comparable undertaking, came to about 20 percent.

For Hoover, as he phrased it himself, it was "a gigantic trust executed in the name of the American people, the luster of which should be protected from defilement by any person in the future." In the perspective of time, despite the zeal of political enemies, the luster remained undimmed and undefiled. It was an undertaking which, while it fed the body of Belgium, also fed the soul of America. For it was the practical expression of our country's revulsion against man's inhumanity to man.

So extraordinary was the "tuned intelligence" behind the gigantic labors that when it was all over there was a balance of thirty-three million dollars. Most of it was distributed to needy Belgian educational institutions. The rest went into establishing a program for a Belgian-American educational exchange of professors and students that is still going strong.

4

There is a touch of pathos in the desperate attempts the Hoovers made to maintain a near-normal family life. Their plans on this score were repeatedly wrecked by the demands of work on hand. In the three years after the start of the war, Hoover was with his sons an aggregate of less than six months.

Having placed her boys in school in Palo Alto in October 1914, Mrs. Hoover rejoined her husband in London. But the following May she had to rush back to California to take care of the children—then back to London. Toward the end of 1915, reluctantly, they brought them to England and placed them in a small private school.

Mrs. Hoover was herself deep in the Belgian Relief, as well as in activities for the needy in Britain. She established a knitting factory to give jobs to women left without means because of the war, the finished products going to the troops and to the destitute. Her principal activity, however, was the hospital she established at Paignton, supported, managed, and staffed by Americans for the duration of the war.

With American participation in the war coming closer, the Hoovers late in 1916 thought it best to transfer their sons once more to California. The boys had acquired an Oxford accent and this, their parents frankly revealed, was one compelling reason for getting them back to America. Mrs. Hoover and the boys bade farewell to the Red House, with its quaint garden and its multitude of happy associations, in genuine sorrow. They realized it was probably forever.

5

Sir John Spender's audit barely indicated the dimensions of the achievement. The major crises and the major victories, the million human incidents and heartaches, do not show up in the final accounting. There were dread moments when the entire Relief seemed doomed to collapse, and other moments when Hoover threatened to call the whole thing off unless London or Berlin yielded to his demands. The episodes of stark tragedy and pathos and humor have filled books, and in all of them the figure of an Iowa Quaker orphan grown to manhood looms heroically, unforgettably.

A British journalist who worked for some time under Hoover in these years, F. A. Wray, subsequently tried to convey his judgment of the man. I quote only a few sentences:

An utter absence of "side," coupled with a very kindly and a completely unassuming manner, were the characteristics which struck one at the outset. Throughout the entire time he was running the biggest individual job in the world he put on no more airs than the simplest citizen. One could size up in a moment his terrific determination, his extraordinary grasp of detail, his tremendous efficiency.

Very few men have drawn forth so great a degree of loyalty in his associates. My own connection with the Belgian Relief was typical of Hoover methods. I received a telegram reading: "Want you for Rotterdam tomorrow." It was taken for granted I would go. Every preparation had been made, down to the last detail. I left London at 3 A.M. next morning.

During the life of the C.R.B. and after it was dissolved Hoover evaded all honors so far as he could without giving offense. At a meeting with King Albert in the sliver of Belgian soil that remained unconquered, he explained patiently why he wanted no decorations and the King understood. But then and on other occasions, Hoover sometimes added with a twinkle that his hard-working assistants collected "buttons" and ribbons. As a result, his associates in Belgian and later relief work—men like Rickard, Tuck, Pate, Galpin, Strauss—had stacks of those "buttons." "They're really for the Chief—I'm just the custodian," Admiral Strauss told me.

The problem of how to express a nation's eternal appreciation must have bothered King Albert of the Belgians. He respected Hoover's feelings in the matter. But one day, when Hoover was visiting him after the Armistice, the King informed him that his Government and Parliament had created a new Order to be bestowed upon only one person and to expire with that person. Then he solemnly bestowed upon his guest the title of Friend of the Belgian People, carrying with it honorary citizenship. Hoover accepted, and was handed a Belgian passport marked "Perpetual."

Since the French Government was directly concerned in the relief work, the auditors in 1919 submitted the tremendous accounting to Paris for its final scrutiny. The French sent it back untouched. "We have tasks more pressing and more fruitful," they said, "than questioning the integrity of Mr. Hoover."

Nineteen years after the completion of the Belgian Relief, Hoover yielded to many urgings of the Belgian crown and press that he revisit their country. He was received as a national hero. But what touched him most deeply was a meeting of the old National Committee which had coordinated the work inside the country. The Committee had been composed of Americans and over ninety leading Belgians. It had met once a month during the four years of captivity. Let Hoover himself report on that gathering:

After our final meeting dissolving the Relief in August, 1919, the *Comité* had never met again, even for social purposes. In the meantime Emile Francqui, the Chairman, had passed away. But with the exact old protocol at its former hour and place, the Vice Chairman Emile Janssen and the Secretary van Bree had summoned this special meeting of the *Comité*. Of the Americans, Hallam Tuck, Perrin Galpin, Millard Shaler and myself were present. We all occupied our old seats.

The Chairman, with a formality that for the moment covered his emotion, declared that the agenda for the day had but three items—to call the roll, to honor the dead, to renew friendships built in time of trial. I have seldom been more affected than by that roll-call and the frequent reply, *"Mort."* More than one-third of the chairs were empty. Many of the chairs were occupied by men obviously feeble with age, all of them under great emotion at so vivid a reminder of those who had passed on. It was then I realized that while I was in my forties during the war our Belgian colleagues had been composed of the old and tried men who were then mostly twenty years my senior.

Every article in the room and every word revived memories of men who had risen to great acts and great days. Some way a great spirit flowing with human devotion flooded the room. We all had difficulty in completing our sentences.

I X

Food for Victory

WHEN Colonel Edward M. House, Woodrow Wilson's man Friday, came to Europe in 1915 and again in 1916 to explore the chances of a mediated peace, he consulted at length with Herbert Hoover. For Hoover was the one American in a position to see Armageddon whole, from the vantage points of self-righteous leaders in Berlin, London, and Paris alike; through the eyes of generals who walked with death and little children who walked with hunger.

Sadly he told the shrewd little emissary and his friend in the White House why their "peace without bitterness" was a fantasy far removed from the blood-drenched earth of Europe. He told them that in this war, as in few before its advent, people hated their enemies more than they loved themselves. What they wanted was not peace but victory, not victory but vengeance. Even those leaders in the warring countries who were sickened by the prolonged slaughter dared not make an open move—they would have been crucified by their own people. Europe was pinioned by hate.

Hoover blamed this in large part on the fact that hunger had been turned into a weapon—a weapon which made the young, the aged, and the women its first and sometimes its only targets. Soldiers, munition workers, and others doing needed war work would always be fed; only the "useless" masses could be starved by blockades. He therefore urged President Wilson to begin the crusade for a compromise peace with practical measures to reduce the prevailing temperatures of hatred. And that, he argued, could best be done by ruling out starvation of civilians as a war strategy.

He wanted the President to use his immense influence to cut enough holes in the surface and U-boat blockades to let through subsistence food for noncombatants, under absolute neutral controls. It was a less showy program than peace-now advocates in America at the time were agitating for, but closer to the realities. Hoover would never be popular with the kind of idealists who require big daily helpings of soul-stirring but futile rhetoric. The pragmatic ingredients in his makeup would never allow nebulous emotions, however noble, to drown reason.

But he was at one with certain liberal and socialist groups in the United States, at least in the first two and a half years of the conflict, in opposing American military participation. His reasons, of course, were of different character; he often explained them to Ambassador Page, Colonel House, and through them to the President. The fact, when the chips were down, that Hoover became at once a key figure on Wilson's war team is proof enough that the President had not misunderstood those reasons.

Hoover was much too close to the war to invest it with any romantic glamor. Having dealt continually with both sides on the rock-bottom questions of humanity, he could not agree that either side had a monopoly on justice or on wickedness. Beyond most Americans he was aware of the thousand-year historical conditioning, the deep-rooted power politics, behind the struggle. He doubted "our ability to change those forces and, in consequence, to make a lasting peace." Wilson's heartbreak at Versailles would demonstrate how right he was. Hoover was convinced, moreover, that the moral, economic, and military might of the United States "would enable us to dominate the peacemaking more effectively" if it were not among the nations physically exhausted and emotionally implicated in the bloodletting.

The German declaration of unlimited submarine warfare early in 1917 helped to temper Hoover's opposition to American entry in the war. His conversion may have been hastened by the sinking of Belgian Relief ships in disregard of Berlin's pledges. The ten million lives in his care were for Hoover a very personal responsibility.

Also, the collapse of the Romanoff dynasty, giving the peoples of Russia a chance for freedom, seemed to him to take some of the smell of cant out of the war-for-democracy slogans. This despite the fact that Hoover was not as optimistic as President Wilson about the prospects in Russia. Will Irwin remembered him saying, after the downfall of Czarism:

This revolution will be difficult to stabilize. There have been centuries of oppression. There is no large middle class. There is almost total illiteracy in the people. There is no general experience in government. Russia cannot maintain a wholly liberal republic yet. Revolutions always go further than their creators expect. And in its swing, this one is more likely to go to the left than to the right.

Congress declared war on April 6, 1917. On May 3, 1917, at the President's request, Hoover returned to the United States. His reputation had flourished enormously. Despite himself, the Great Engineer had emerged as the Great Humanitarian. Why he was returning was apparent enough, and the press headlined him as the "Food Czar" and "Food Dictator."

In the months before his return, he had made for Mr. Wilson quiet surveys of food, shipping, and other elements of the war and had conferred with Allied leaders and experts on their problems. From the first, "food mobilization" had been recognized as America's number one obligation if and when it joined the war. The formation of a special agency to deal with every phase of food provisioning was the President's suggestion, but the availability of Hoover doubtless hastened the decision. In conference with Wilson, on May 5, Hoover accepted the invitation to organize and head up this agency. He made the same stipulations he had made in assuming the Belgian burden; first, that he was to receive no pay, and second, that he was to have full authority.

The second of these cut across the President's predilection for group leadership through boards and commissions. Wilson, moreover, may have been disturbed by the "Food Czar" headlines. But Hoover had a semantic inspiration which made it somewhat easier for the President to accede to his demand. Let the agency, he proposed, be called an Administration and its head an Administrator. (In the future, under the New Deal, Hoover was to smile wryly as he watched the mushrooming of his inspiration until Washington was cluttered with assorted "administrations.") On May 9, the American Food Administration was launched.

Hoover knew the seriousness of food shortages in Europe. He was aware that in Allied thinking bread ranked with bullets in any inventory of war priorities. The continuous and sufficient flow of food was second in importance only to military action in defeating the Central Powers. Our problem, as Hoover saw it, was "to squeeze out enough exports from the United States, the West Indies and Canada to make up the large deficits of our Allies and certain neutrals, and to do so with a minimum disturbance to our economy."

This was the task that he undertook. So brilliantly did he perform it that neither soldiers nor civilians on our side had to go on short rations for a single day in the final nineteen months—the American months—of the war. Thus he rates with the prime architects of the victory. That was what General Pershing meant when he wrote a personal message to Hoover, "whose contribution to the success of the Allied cause can hardly be overestimated."

The prevailing system of food management in belligerent European countries was on a strictly regimented basis. One man controlled crops, rations, prices, everything, and enforced his orders by police methods. Few of these "dictators" lasted more than six months. Even before he returned to the United States, Hoover had made up his mind that the system of coercion, undesirable per se, was particularly unsuited for Americans. They could be led, he believed, but not driven.

His American Food Administration offered the largest and the most successful practical test of the principle of voluntary cooperation in modern times. At the armistice, it had some eight thousand full-time and 750,000 part-time volunteers throughout the nation. The paid employees —fifteen hundred in Washington and sixty-five hundred in local offices— were almost entirely clerical.

Supplementing President Wilson's detailed statement on the food challenge on May 19, Hoover issued a press release which said in part:

The whole foundation of democracy lies in the individual initiative of its people and their willingness to serve the interests of the nation with complete self-effacement in the time of emergency. I hold that democracy can yield to discipline and that we can solve this food problem for our own people and for our allies by voluntary action.

The techniques of his Administration, too, were almost exclusively of the voluntary varieties. This Hoover regarded as the best defense against "Prussianizing the country." Some twenty million individuals—housewives, restaurant managers, food processors, wholesalers, retailers, shippers—signed pledges making them "members" of the Food Administration, as attested by a certificate and lapel buttons. Committees of volunteers without any police power enforced conservation in public eating places. Representatives of the provisioning trade groups, summoned to Washington, enthusiastically accepted Hoover's proposals for a voluntary War Committee in each group to make and enforce the necessary rules. There was no rationing. The Administration made constant requests and recommendations but issued few "orders."

In applying the principle of voluntarism, Hoover looked on the great saving of money as the least of its benefits. He believed then—as he did a dozen years later in setting up nationwide relief organizations during the Depression—that a paid bureaucracy, tending to expand and perpetuate itself, is a blight on any such undertaking.

Another aspect of the Food Administration policy, similarly related to his concept of a democratic society, was his belief in the utmost decentralization, in local and state responsibility, as against the alternative of politicalized federal control through arbitrary central "directives." Every state had its own food controller, who in turn worked through city and county units of volunteers familiar with local resources, conditions, and psychology.

This, of course, did not obviate the need for intense thinking and planning at the center. Hoover put his view in one sentence in testifying before a Senate committee on the Food Administration Bill: "My idea," he said, "is that we must centralize ideas but decentralize execution."

While in sympathy with the President's reluctance to entrust excessive authority to an individual, Hoover argued that the cure of inefficiency was worse than the disease of single direction. As one commission after another bogged down, he kept pressing Wilson to expand the practice of holding one man responsible for major undertakings. In several instances he produced the man to fit the job. Before many months there were single administrators with adequate authority to command fuel, railways, shipping; there was a War Trade Board and—under Bernard M. Baruch—a streamlined War Industries Board.

On Hoover's recommendation, these single directors, along with the Secretaries of the Departments involved in the war effort, were constituted as a War Council. It met regularly to discuss and synchronize policy and adjust operational conflict. Hoover was thus at the heart of the war effort, privy to all its problems, and among the closest advisers to the Commander-in-Chief.

Wartime agencies in Washington were notoriously overloaded with retired military men and civilians in the gaudiest military regalia they could wangle. There was about them the noise, the excitement, and the confusion of a continuous parade. The Food Administration was an exception. In both looks and mood it was all civilian and businesslike—"the only war agency which wore no bells and costume jewelry," as Hoover later put it.

A more impressive fact, perhaps not unrelated, is that it emerged as the only major war agency that was not investigated by Congress after the shooting was over, though it had handled transactions totaling seven billion dollars.

2

The very landscape of America shrieked the reminder, "Food Will Win the War!" and the American people responded magnificently. Every housewife felt herself a soldier in a war on waste in the kitchen and in the dining room. Meatless and wheatless days, new dietary habits to release the grain and fats needed for the armies and export, the "clean-plate" ideal, and a hundred other devices depended for success on the willing cooperation of the average American. A new verb entered the American language: "to Hooverize," meaning to conserve. The saving of food became a sort of game for young and old. Parents, Hoover would record, imposed eating disciplines on their children—"and blamed it on me."

The bill establishing Hoover's agency gave it important regulatory powers, through licensing of food manufacturers, jobbers, and wholesalers, as well as retailers doing more than one hundred thousand dollars of business a year. It provided no controls on farmers, stock growers, and other primary producers, or on the immense army of retailers below the one hundred thousand dollar line, or on the ultimate consumer.

The power to withdraw licenses for violation of wartime rules and other punitive provisions was used sparingly. The spirit in which Hoover dealt with business interests was indicated in the statement outlining the aims of the agency:

The Food Administration is called into being to stabilize and not to disturb conditions and to defend honest enterprise against illegitimate competition. It has been devised to correct the abnormalities and abuses that have crept into trade by reason of the world disturbance and to restore business as far as may be to a reasonable basis.

The businessmen of this country, I am convinced . . . realize their own patriotic obligation and the solemnity of the situation, and will fairly and generously co-operate in meeting the national emergency. I do not believe that drastic force need be applied. . . . But if there be those who expect to exploit this hour of sacrifice, if there are men and organizations scheming to increase the trials of this country, we shall not hesitate to apply to the full the drastic, coercive powers that Congress has conferred upon us in this instrument.

The later fable that Hoover was a know-nothing supporter of *laissez-faire* capitalism, come hell or high water, looks pretty silly when matched with such statements. But he did devote much thought and effort to safeguarding the normal economic processes. The whole complex of raising, processing, and distributing food remained less controlled and closer to normal in the United States than in any other warring country.

As Food Administrator he did not rely blindly on the laws of demand and supply. He imposed a web of regulatory restraints which enabled those laws to operate without going haywire. Unrestricted price competition in a world at war, he said, would not curtail consumption by armies —costs did not matter in that domain—but would strike at the living standards of the lowest-income groups. He did not hesitate to use abnormal methods for the abnormal times, always with the admonition that government interference was one of an array of war evils and must be dispensed with at the earliest moment.

"This agency represented the first assumption by the American government of great economic power," Hoover would attest. He was determined to limit what he considered the dangers inherent in this novel fact by keeping it maximally voluntary in character and by "quick dissolution after the war."

The control of wheat, the most vital single food item, he achieved through the United States Grain Corporation, which was the sole channel for military and export provisioning. It was capitalized at its peak at five hundred million dollars and served as a stabilizing force for producer and consumer alike. On its liquidation at the end of the war it returned to the Treasury every dollar it had drawn, plus a reasonable interest. The same was true of the Sugar Stabilization Board; its record stood up in sharp contrast with the vast losses wrapped in scandals suffered by some other wartime economic agencies. The Food Administration as a whole returned to the government, on its windup, a profit of some fifty million dollars.

After poor harvests in 1916 and 1917, an exceptionally harsh winter punched holes in 1918 estimates. By the end of 1917 surpluses were close to the exhaustion point. Meanwhile Hoover's observers on the scene and Allied statesmen clamored for quantities far above those planned. In January, British Food Controller Lord Rhondda, cabled:

Unless you are able to send the Allies at least 75,000,000 bushels of wheat over and above what you have exported up to January first, and in addition to the total exportable surplus from Canada, I cannot take the responsibility of assuring our people that there will be enough food to win the war.

America came through. Reporting to the President at the end of the initial year of operations, Hoover could show exports not only of wheat but of all other essential foodstuffs between 35 and 50 percent above the preceding year; this despite the always larger demands of our own military establishment.

Whether the United States should dispatch a great expeditionary force to Europe, as was being urged by General Pershing but not yet by the Allies, was a problem not only of strategy but also of provisioning. The critical element was shipping. In April, the month we entered the war, over 850,000 tons of merchant ships were sunk; five hundred thousand tons were sent to the bottom in each of the four following months. Hoover did not oppose the sending of troops. He did insistently warn both the President and Pershing that it would be dangerous to undertake the transport and supply of a huge army across the Atlantic until at least two new policies were adopted.

First, he said, Britain and France must abandon their long hauls for food and supplies from the Southern Hemisphere, China, and other distant areas, and depend solely on North America; by thus shortening the routes, a substantial amount of merchant tonnage would be released for other uses. Second, he pleaded (as did many others) for a massive naval convoy system to contain losses from submarine raids.

Under the hammer blows of German victories, both these measures were adopted in March 1918. The accuracy of Pershing's conviction that American manpower must be thrown onto the scales, as well as the cogency of Hoover's views, had become all too obvious. Shipping losses were sharply reduced by the convoy system and more tonnage was made available through Europe's exclusive reliance on food from the United States, Canada, and the West Indies. Within seven months two million Americans were transported to France and turned the tide of battle in our favor.

Nearly a quarter of a century later, in the midst of the Second World War, Hoover's relation to the expeditionary forces would be mercilessly twisted out of shape. At the behest of the Roosevelt administration, Senator Theodore F. Green of Rhode Island made a speech charging that Hoover had opposed sending American forces to France. Actually, as we have seen, he opposed it only until adequate shipping could be assured. Hoover demanded and received apologies for the attack from Secretary of War Stimson and others involved in the strange falsification, though not from the Senator.

The only serious attack on Hoover during the life of the Food Administration came from Senator James A. Reed of Missouri. The real target was President Wilson but some of the most intemperate language was addressed to Hoover. In remarks to reporters, Reed suggested that Hoover had made personal profits on the Belgian Relief.

It was then that John White remembered his prophecy, on the day in 1914 when the Relief was launched, that one day "some swine" might arise and make just such charges. He cited the minutes of the meeting where he had made that forecast, leaving no margin for doubt as to the identity of the "swine." The Senator retorted with what he perhaps considered the supreme insult: that White was an Englishman! Again White went to the records and proved that his family had deeper roots in America than Reed's. The press and radio made the most of the bickering and the Senator, one hopes, wished he had not impugned Hoover's honesty.

In July 1918 Hoover went to London and Paris, accompanied by his young secretary, Lewis Strauss, and Dr. Alonzo Taylor, to confer with government heads and food controllers of the Allied nations. The result was the formation of an Allied Food Council, under Hoover's chairmanship, to improve coordination of provisioning.

In a book of reminiscences, forty-odd years later, Lewis Strauss—by then an Admiral—refers to a banquet honoring Hoover, at which Lloyd George said: "It seems to me, Mr. Hoover, that you represent not only the United States but also Merciful Providence. We are no longer aliens, foreigners to one another; we now disagree with the same violence and familiarity as if we were members of the same Cabinet."

Even while he sat in the inner councils of the war effort, Hoover wept inwardly for the increasingly hungry children and women in Germany and Austria. In the mood of the time, his concern for the starving in enemy countries seemed bizarre if not unpatriotic. Washington and other Allied capitals were shocked when he proposed again, now that the United States was at war, that the blockade be relaxed enough to permit the feeding of enemy children and weaker women.

Their shock did not deter him. He drew up a concrete plan for providing such relief through neutral organizations, under airtight guarantees, basically along the lines of the Belgian precedent. He argued that this would in no way alter the military equation. Because he knew that mere appeals to decency and charity would be a waste of breath in a time of inflamed hatreds, his arguments were practical rather than sentimental. But under these public arguments was his private compassion for Man Crucified, which for him did not stop at any geographical or racial lines.

His proposals, of course, were rejected as visionary. Wilson was sympathetic, but London and Paris would have none of this humanitarian softness. In the perspective of time, who can be so sure that the Hoover idealism was not the most *practical* of the alternatives? Hatred, like love, can become romantic beyond reason and logic. He would write of the First World War in the midst of the Second:

I did not myself believe in the blockade. I do not believe in starving women and children. I do not believe it was the effective weapon of which the Allies were so confident. And above all, I did not believe that stunted bodies and deformed minds in the next generation were the foundation upon which to rebuild civilization.

In the peace terms submitted to the Germans toward the finish there was a clause committing the victors to helping feed the vanquished. It was Hoover who drafted it and then fought fiercely for its inclusion in the Peace Treaty. Though his draft was watered down, it did acknowledge the principle.

Hoover's desire to feed enemy children even while the war was at its height deserves to be underlined. It called for moral courage of a high order. Some Americans actually professed to see in that solicitude for innocent victims of the holocaust only another "Hitler lover." From the perches of their propaganda and official respectability they hurled insults not only at Hoover but at anyone who dared mention ordinary human obligations. Cynics all, wandering without compass in their ideological jungles, they could no longer recognize human beings under political labels—not even just-born babes.

Had the Hoover approach prevailed to a greater extent in World War I, the chances of a Hitler emerging would probably have been reduced. There would have been fewer of those "stunted bodies and deformed minds" in the postwar generation.

3

But let us return to the Food Administration.

Inevitably there was some profiteering on food which a rigid police system might have curbed, although the black-market evils associated with rationing and police controls in other countries raise some questions even on that score. Hoover showed scant sympathy for the leeches. In July 1918 he proposed to the President that the nation's tax power be used to siphon off excess profits into the public coffers—the first "excess profits tax" proposal in American history. At Wilson's request he put the idea into a letter addressed to Senator Furnifold McL. Simmons of North Carolina.

Though his special assignment was food mobilization, Hoover played a large part in the whole civilian strategy for victory. His worldwide experience gave his voice a resonance in the War Council that often made it decisive in formulating policies. No less often, of course, he fought for lost causes in the Council room and the private chambers of the President.

We have cited the frustration of his view on feeding enemy children. Another notable failure relates to Russia after the Bolsheviks seized power.

In the light of Hoover eyewitness knowledge of Russia and the Far East, the President asked for his opinions on the proposed Japanese invasion of Siberia. Hoover counseled against this with all his energy. Whether the Japanese succeeded or failed, he insisted, the invasion would only serve to rally the people behind the extremist regime; besides, if the Japanese succeeded in occupying any portion of eastern Siberia, they would try to hold it forever as a reward. But Wilson, reluctantly, submitted to Allied pressures and the invasion went forward, with a token American force taking part primarily in order to restrain Japanese territorial appetites.

While stimulating the production of food and directing its deployment, Hoover did not lose sight of the certainty that all Europe, winners and losers and neutrals alike, would face shortage and in huge areas outright famine when the fighting ended. He created gigantic surpluses; either they would be needed to see the Allies and America through another year of war or, as he ardently hoped, to start the tasks of rehabilitation after victory.

As early as mid-September 1918, when the Battle of St. Mihiel seemed to point to German defeat, Hoover began to revise food policies on a postwar basis. It amounted to a sharp switch of vantage points from war management to relief and economic rehabilitation. He had unlimited backing from the President, who called the salvaging enterprise "second only to the mission of our Army."

On November 11, the day of the armistice, Wilson authorized the conversion of the Food Administration into a new relief agency—dealing with problems Hoover had already surveyed. The rapid dismantling of the domestic operation was Hoover's immediate concern. He put Edgar Rickard in charge of the Washington office; within sixty days its staff of three thousand was reduced to four hundred, with matching reductions on the state and local levels.

For operational purposes the Belgian Relief was too useful to be canceled out at once. At the request of both Belgium and France it was kept intact until July 1, 1919. Throughout his term as American Food Administrator, Hoover had carried factual though not formal responsibility for the C.R.B. The neutrals in charge constantly looked to him for guidance and action in crises. There was the time, for example, when Hoover discovered that the American military leaders, with the support of their British and French counterparts, were about to seize three hundred thousand tons of C.R.B. shipping for military uses. At once he protested to Wilson, Lloyd George, and Clemenceau: the shipping was not molested.

Many of the American names that figured in the Belgian story showed up again in the Washington story. Now Washington men appeared in the great postwar operation. Hoover was developing a corps of specialists in the new science and art of provisioning entire nations. Having begun by caring for ten million, they continued by dealing with the food needs of two hundred million, and ended with administering the relief of four hundred million on an entire continent.

In mentioning Dr. Ray Lyman Wilbur, Julius Barnes, Robert Taft, Dr. Alonzo Taylor, Ben Allen, John White, Edward M. Flesh, Christian Herter, Judge Curtis Lindley, H. Alexander Smith, Joseph P. Cotton, Dr. Vernon Kellogg, Dr. Raymond Pearl, Edgar Rickard, and Gertrude Lane, we are only sampling names in a long and honorable list of Americans who shared Hoover's laurels. The sincerity of the Chief, the confidence he inspired, evidently attracted men and women of exceptional quality. The great majority of them went on to become Cabinet members, Senators, college presidents, authors, editors, and business leaders.

Lewis Strauss merits special mention, if only because he joined at the very bottom—as office boy. "At twenty-one," Admiral Strauss has written,

"I had the extraordinary good fortune to become private secretary to Herbert Hoover." It was the start of a lifelong friendship, he said, that became "almost filial."

Actually, the secretarial post was a later development, by some weeks. Since the age of sixteen, Lewis had been a "drummer," selling shoes in the Carolinas, Georgia, and West Virginia. He had done well and saved what, for a boy, was a considerable amount of money. Rejected for military service because of defective eyesight, he went to Washington determined to see Hoover and volunteer for the food effort.

Told that the Chief was too busy, the young man stubbornly sat in the outer office for hours and finally intercepted Hoover as he was leaving for some urgent appointment. In one long and fervid sentence he told Hoover that he wanted to help—without salary, of course. Let the mature Strauss take up the story: "He looked at me with a puzzled smile and asked, 'When do you want to start?' 'Right now,' I replied. 'Take off your coat,' he said, and left. These ten words were the only exchange I had with him for a matter of weeks."

Strauss began as office boy and not long thereafter Hoover made him his private secretary. While with Hoover in Paris he met Mortimore Schiff, of the famous banking firm of Kuhn, Loeb & Company. Schiff, impressed by the young man's ability and personality, offered him a job as soon as Hoover could release him.

When Strauss left for America, he carried a closed envelope from Hoover addressed to his new employer, not to be opened until he returned home—"sealed orders," the Chief declared. "It contained a two-page letter in his own hand which was an endorsement beyond my deserts," according to Strauss. In the decades that followed, Strauss became a leading financier, an Admiral for his services in the Second World War, Chairman of the Atomic Energy Commission after the war. Whatever his employments or his titles, he remained always a "Hoover man," subject to call for any assignment.

At Food Administration headquarters, Hoover's secretary kept hours almost as long as those of the Chief. They usually started work at 7:30 in the morning and knocked off at 7:30 in the evening. Often Hoover remained after young Strauss left, working deep into the night. One morning the secretary was horrified to discover that the desk drawer in which he kept confidential documents had been forced, and some of the papers removed. He was about to call for the Secret Service when Hoover came in. "I picked the lock of your desk last night," he explained. "Needed some of those papers."

The biggest dividend Hoover received from his war work was the company of his reunited family. In 1917, after the close of the school term in Palo Alto, Mrs. Hoover and the children—now fourteen and eleven—

moved to Washington. The boys were enrolled in the Friends' School. After a few months in a house on Sixteenth Street, Mrs. Hoover succeeded in renting the old Adams residence on Massachusetts Avenue.

This became the warm center of Hoover's life. There were times, because of the hotel and housing shortage, when as many as forty friends and Food Administration personnel found shelter in the Hoover home. In addition, since Hoover did considerable entertaining for the Government, the house provided hospitality to such wartime visitors as Arthur Balfour, Marshal Joffre, Jan Paderewski, Thomas Masaryk, Lord Reading, and Fridtjof Nansen.

Blessed escape from the heavy official burdens came on Sundays, whenever Hoover could manage it. The Rickards and a few other families close to the Hoovers held regular Sunday picnics. The world's leading metallurgical engineer joined with the bevy of children building dams across streams and canals, and at roaring campfires. In the winter, ice skating led the program of fun. Forever after, Hoover and his wife would look back on those Sundays as among the happiest times of their family life.

X

Crusade against Chaos

WHAT would happen to the populations of Europe after the years of bloodletting, destruction, and suppurating hatreds? The question was never far from Hoover's mind in the climactic year of the war. Better than most, he understood that the coming victory would create more problems than it solved, and that for some three hundred million human beings the paramount problem would be that of sheer physical survival.

Hoover saw, with obsessive clarity, the looming chaos which, if it were not checked resolutely and in time, could suck all mankind into its vortex. It would be a fateful race, he never tired of warning, between relief and total collapse, anarchy, Bolshevism. "To make the world safe for democracy," the slogan for which thousands of Americans were giving their lives, could be turned into cruel irony if hunger and disease opened the floodgates to tyranny.

And he saw, no less clearly, that only his own country could hope to head off the disaster. Only the United States had the necessary resources and at least a modicum of emotional perspective. The European nations were too deeply embroiled in territorial and power contests, secret treaties, and blood feuds of revenge.

Neither the Peace Conference nor inter-Allied agencies, he was convinced, could be trusted with a veto over American benevolence. In a cable to his London representative on Armistice Day he made clear that the U.S. "will not agree to any program that even looks like Inter-Allied control of our economic resources after peace." This applied not only to relief and rehabilitation but to larger—and, as Hoover viewed it, sinister —Allied plans for a species of world economic dictatorship. The idea was to pool all resources of the victorious nations, then use that command of food, shipping, finance, etc. to impose rigid controls on the whole globe for years beyond the conclusion of peace.

It was as ambitious a power play as had ever been attempted—and Hoover would have none of it. He believed, on the contrary, that the global economy must be restored to a normal peacetime basis as soon as possible; that nations must be helped, not hampered, in working out viable systems of life.

His success in defeating the Allied design for worldwide economic supremacy, though rarely noted by historians, deserves a high place in any inventory of American influences in this period. Hoover convinced President Wilson on this issue and then had a free hand in canceling out the whole scheme. Patently, an economic pool without America would be an empty cistern. In a message to the American contingent in London he said: "At the Peace Conference the economic power of the United States must be entirely unrestricted, as this force in our hands may be a powerful assistance in enabling us to secure acceptance of our view."

The critical element in "our view," for Hoover, was the unimpeded right to feed the starving continent and restore its economic health. The flow of life-sustaining supplies, he knew, would be dammed by Allied politics, blockades, and above all by the contempt for human life bred by the holocaust. He would use American wealth, prestige, and idealism to the limit: "We consider ourselves trustees for our surplus production of all kinds for the most necessitous and the most deserving. We feel that we must ourselves execute this trusteeship."

The enemy countries were being ravaged by hunger and disease. Except for Belgium, the occupied and soon to be liberated nations were in no better case. And after four years of blockade the neutral countries, too, were in a tragic plight. Half of the European population was in a condition of actual or near-famine; the rest suffered shortages in varying degrees. Industry, transport, currencies, and even governments were in assorted stages of collapse.

Food reserves on the Continent were at the vanishing point as the Armistice approached, with the next harvests ten months away. An exceptionally harsh winter blanketed Europe. Already starvation was reaping its own harvests of death and disease. In the eighteen enemy and liberated countries, ten to twelve million children—always Hoover's measure of conditions—were in a state of advanced undernourishment.

Months before the end of hostilities, in anticipation of victory, Hoover had surveys made of the world's exportable foodstuffs and of Europe's likely postwar needs. His relief ships, filled with food staples, were steaming toward Europe before the fighting ceased. Some of them were unloading their cargoes in Copenhagen, Rotterdam, Antwerp, Amsterdam, and Mediterranean ports within forty-eight hours after the Armistice was proclaimed—and returning for more. By mid-December, one month later, one hundred cargoes were on the high seas or in European ports.

"At one time," Lewis Strauss has recorded, "we had in excess of a billion pounds of fat and a hundred thousand bushels of wheat stored in those ports, all of it on Mr. Hoover's personal obligation for an amount exceeding five hundred million dollars. He had made a decision to feed the starving in Europe or to go gloriously broke."

Angry outcries from Allied quarters, charging high-handed violation of the blockade, came quickly. Hoover took them in stride. "Starvation does not await the outcome of power politics" was his guiding formula. Frustrated in his efforts to feed at least the neediest children in enemy countries while the war was on, he was determined to repair the failure as soon as possible after the war ended. His instructions to representatives on the scene were that, wherever possible, food must be made available first to children.

President Wilson, as has been noted, authorized an extension of the Food Administration functions to embrace Europe, the European phase being designated as the American Relief Administration. The War Department agreed to turn over to Hoover its large stocks of surplus food, medicine, and clothing in Europe. No less vital, it accepted his proposal that the repatriation troop ships, when the evacuation began, would carry food cargoes on the Europe-bound half of their round trips.

Hoover was about to undertake one of the greatest responsibilities ever placed on one pair of shoulders. Having accepted the responsibility for Belgium and German-occupied France, this American found himself on a road from which there could be no turning for a man of his background and native instincts. The greatest relief job in history, dwarfing the Belgian operation which it now absorbed, was under way.

Having started the flow of food, having selected veterans of the Belgian Relief and the Food Administration for key posts across the seas, Hoover sailed for Europe on the *Olympic* on November 17, six days after the Armistice. With him were Robert Taft as legal adviser, Dr. Alonzo Taylor as adviser on nutrition, Julius Barnes, the executive head of the Grain Corporation, and of course his "jewel of a secretary," young Strauss. Because understanding and support at home were important to the new crusade, he issued a parting statement to the press.

In view of later controversy, his emphasis on Germany is noteworthy. "What is desired most now is for Germany to get on some sort of stable basis," he argued. "Unless anarchy can be put down and stability of government can be obtained in the enemy states, there will be nobody to make peace with and nobody to pay the bill."

The Hoover who went to Europe was no longer the tyro who, in Belgium, had to learn and improvise. By now he knew more about food, its processing, its administration, its shipment, than any man alive. And he had the immense advantage of a battalion of experienced and deeply loyal associates and field men.

In London he met, in his own phrase, "a rude awakening." He found the atmosphere miasmic with intrigue, suspicion, rivalry, and assorted greeds. In the hour of triumph, a spirit of vindictiveness ruled men's minds and hearts. The Allies distrusted each other while sharing a common distrust of "foolish American idealism."

Wilson might be a Second Messiah to Europe's common people, but to the victorious statesmen his zeal for justice, beginning with the Fourteen Points, was an embarrassment. Hoover's own single-minded concern for the wretched masses seemed to them rather quixotic. The greatest famine since the Thirty Years' War, he soon discovered, didn't seem to disturb his British, French, and Italian confreres.

He discovered, too, that they had not given up their grand design for pooled economic might. Hoover's insistence upon American economic autonomy seemed to them as captious as General Pershing's insistence, the year before, upon an independent American military command.

Evidently they had decided to lead Hoover to the mountaintop for a glimpse of personal glory. Lord Eustace Percy came to see him privately. In the name of Britain and France he offered Hoover the chairmanship of a World Economic Council if he would withdraw his opposition. That would in effect make him the global economic czar for years to come: "the Foch of the world!" as the emissary phrased the temptation.

On a subsequent occasion Hoover, with a straight face, made a counterproposal: that the economic management be divided among the Big Four in the same proportion as their respective contributions to the "pool." That ended the discussion, since the American contribution would have been overwhelmingly larger than the other three combined.

Hoover left London on December 12 and two days later opened the fifty-room headquarters of the American Relief Administration in Paris, at 51 Avenue Montaigne. With the authority and help of General Pershing and Admiral William S. Benson, the U. S. Chief of Naval Operations, he drew about twenty-five hundred officers and men from the Armed Forces for his operation. Thousands of the men in uniform who were specialists in civilian life—engineers, physicians, executives, railway and communications experts, scientists, scholars in uniform—were eager to volunteer for the exciting peace project. Hoover had the pick of the crop. Many of these recruits, as in the past, remained dedicated "Hoover men" for the rest of their lives.

These men and others were quickly deployed through the length and breadth of Europe, and redeployed thereafter as critical situations developed. While inter-Allied agencies and at times the exalted Peace

Conference itself were still debating relief and economic policies, Hoover went about his chores. By actually opening operations as an all-American enterprise, he was to attest later, "I had done away with the pool and Allied control of American resources in one act."

In January the Supreme War Council finally set up a Supreme Council of Supply and Demand and, making the best of an accomplished fact, named Hoover as its Director-General. By February the new body was still mumbling along ineffectually and Hoover asked for its dissolution. On the spot he drafted a resolution in less than fifty words, duly accepted, substituting a Supreme Economic Council, with himself as chairman, its functions sufficiently broad to permit him to operate without excessive interference.

Hoover thus wore many hats. He was the U. S. Food Administrator, head of the American Relief Administration, Chairman of the U.S. grain and sugar agencies, of the Belgian Relief Commission, and now of the high-sounding Supreme Economic Council. It was hard to know under which of these assorted authorities he and his staff did what they did. But it mattered not, for they did what had to be done in disregard of formalities.

In practice, the hatless Hoover sufficed. Though it embraced a congeries of titles and functions, mostly conveniently vague, the Hoover apparatus was close-knit by loyalty to its Chief and welded by a unifying mind. In Europe, as in Washington, the men on the job had almost limitless autonomy within the bounds of a set of "centralized ideas." "It did not occur to hungry nations," he would recall, "to ask whether my activities had been visaed by other Allied governments. . . . Never did we make a request that was not instantly law." He had the full and enthusiastic cooperation of the U. S. Armed Forces.

Credentials bearing Hoover's signature were honored on frontiers and in government offices where mere passports, the American included, only aroused suspicion. Somehow the many official designations of the enterprise got translated, from Finland to Greece, from the Atlantic to the Urals, into "the Hoover organization."

The continuing blockade was the most galling of many obstructions. The struggle to remove it or to mitigate its effects took up much of Hoover's time and energy. With Admiral Benson's salty blessings, the blockade was simply ignored in the ports of liberated and neutral countries. The Admiral had made it clear that if ships flying the American flag were molested, the U. S. Navy would know what to do. They were not molested. Neutral governments were apprised that their orders for food in America would be filled, blockade or no blockade.

The enemy countries, however, presented a different problem. The Allies clung to the theory that starvation was their indispensable weapon in forcing the defeated nations to swallow unconditionally the peppery dishes being prepared for them in Paris. It was a theory disguised as strategy but, at bottom, related to a craving to inflict maximum punishment.

In the United States, too, Hoover's solicitude for the people of defeated countries drew a barrage of attack, on and off the floors of Congress. At times he felt it necessary to defend his views. We Americans, he said in one broadside, have been brought up "not to kick a man in the stomach after we have licked him. . . . We have not been fighting women and children and we are not beginning now. . . . No matter how deeply we may feel at the present moment, our vision must stretch over the next hundred years and we must write now into history such acts as will stand credibly in the minds of our grandchildren." But Congress, in voting one hundred million dollars for European relief, specified that not a penny of it must reach former enemies.

The Allies remained impervious to either the logic of humanity or of political wisdom. They could not be moved by reports of worsening conditions, not even by the fact that Communists already controlled three German cities (Hamburg, Munich, and Stettin) and were gaining the upper hand in Hungary.

Month after month Hoover and other Americans pleaded for a relaxation, if not full removal, of the blockade. They bombarded the Big Four with memoranda and warnings. To point up the fatuity of French opposition, they exposed the illicit sale of large quantities of textiles to Germany, for gold, by French traders. At one meeting of the Peace Conference Hoover exclaimed:

The uses to which blockade of foodstuffs is being put are absolutely immoral. I do not feel that we can with any sense of national honor or dignity longer continue to endure this situation. . . . I wish to solemnly warn the Conference as to impending results in total collapse of the social system in Europe.

The American delegation, under the direct impact of Hoover's persistence, finally decided to back him. On March 7, 1919, Hoover again faced Lloyd George, as he had faced him nearly five years earlier on the Belgian tragedy. The Commander of the British Occupation Army in Germany, General Plumer, was present. Evidently this soldier's reports had moved the British leader. The General repeated them now—none of it news to Hoover. The rank and file of his army, Plumer said in substance, were sickened by the horrors; they could no longer stand the sight of bloated children rummaging in the garbage like famished dogs.

At this confrontation Hoover accused the British of sabotaging the relief of millions while mouthing hypocrisies. In the end, Lloyd George again professed himself convinced. The following day he came through brilliantly in supporting Hoover before the War Council. He heaped hot coals on Clemenceau, despite the fact—more likely because of the fact—that the British were almost equally to blame. Hoover won. The blockade, so far as food and medicines were concerned, was lifted at once, the rest to come later that month.

"You may start your shipments," one of the French delegates said smilingly, in acknowledgment of defeat.

"They started weeks ago," Hoover replied grimly.

In which he was merely telling a remarkable truth. The moral courage of the man showed up repeatedly in the way he started relief shipments for the stricken areas on his own authority long before the diplomatic opposition had been removed—often long before the physical roadblocks of wrecked transport had been removed.

It was a victory that left Hoover with a heavy heart notwithstanding. The four months of senseless delay had cost thousands of lives and left hundreds of thousands of children impaired in body and mind. It was Hoover's contention, in years to come, that this maimed generation gave Hitler much of his support among the German youth and helped bring him to power. This was not the wisdom of hindsight, for he had warned against just such consequences when he was fighting against the blockade.

Nearly a generation later, when vilification of Hoover was still the hallmark of accredited New Dealers, one of them chose the ex-President's fifty-sixth birthday, August 10, 1940, publicly to pervert the blockade story. In a broadcast that day Elmer Davis accused the "heartless" Hoover of having "continued the food blockade for many months after the war." After this topsy-turvy error was called to his attention, Mr. Davis did not consider it necessary to make a correction.

2

Hoover was not a member of the Peace Mission in Paris, though he shared rooms with the American delegates at the Crillon and remained in daily, sometimes hourly, consultation with them and with President Wilson. In many ways he was their most valuable liaison with the European actuality, screened from their view in conference halls by competing ambitions and warborn delusions. The Hoover organization, with human tentacles in twenty-odd countries of the shell-shocked continent, was the main and often the sole reliable source of current economic and political information.

The Big Four and their droves of assorted experts lived in a wilderness of committees and commissions dedicated to fooling each other and especially successful in fooling themselves. But the several thousand "Hoover men" lived amid the rubble and depravities of war's aftermath. They dealt in concrete detail, not in diplomatic formulas, with famine and typhus, transport and telegraph lines, coal and iron, with the immediate human consequences of hatreds in eruption and hopes in collapse.

Hoover at the Peace Conference was concerned, as he phrased it, "with the gaunt realities which prowled outside." These, unhappily, were not rated as primary problems by most of the embattled peacemakers. Later, looking back, they had reason to know—and a few had the grace to admit—that their sorry peace would have been buried in an avalanche of death, with Bolshevism feasting on the putrefaction, had Hoover failed to deal swiftly and ably with those "gaunt realities."

An English delegate, the economist John Maynard Keynes, wrote in retrospect:

Mr. Hoover was the only man who emerged from the ordeal of Paris with an enhanced reputation. This complex personality . . . his eyes steadily fixed on the true and essential facts of the European situation, imported into the Councils of Paris, when he took part in them, precisely that atmosphere of reality, knowledge, magnanimity, and disinterestedness which, if they had been found in other quarters also, would have given us the Good Peace.

The ungrateful governments of Europe owe much more to the statesmanship and insight of Mr. Hoover and his band of American workers than they ever appreciated or ever will acknowledge. The American Relief Commission [Administration], and they only, saw the European position during those months in its true perspective and felt toward it as men should. It was their effort, their energy and the American resources placed by the President at their disposal, often acting in the teeth of European obstruction, which not only saved an immense amount of human suffering, but averted a widespread breakdown of the European system.

Once, when General Pershing was asked what precisely was Hoover's position, he replied, "Mr. Hoover is the food regulator of the world." If that was too broad in some respects, it was too narrow in many more respects. Relief, after all, is not just a matter of finding and handing out victuals. It involved demolition of towering political barriers and imposing patterns of order in areas of anarchy.

In every country and community the local leadership had to be found, organized into working committees, then trained and supervised to guarantee fair, economical, effective distribution of supplies. Relief involved shipping, money and credit, harbors and railroads, fuel and power, and virtually all other economic factors. Hoarded supplies had to be requisitioned, agriculture restored, new rationing plans devised.

What began as relief expanded unavoidably into large-scale rehabilitation. Hoover was by no means the "economic dictator" he was labeled in the world press, but he was the economic activator in nearly all the defeated and liberated nations. Out of abysmal chaos he helped conjure the minimum of order which made a return to approximate normality possible.

Before the work was completed, his comrades in benevolence were operating telegraph lines, canals, ports, railroads, coal mines, hospitals, nurseries—this over and above the vast primary tasks of gathering food, financing it, hauling it from overseas, then deploying it like divisions of a great liberating army to combat hunger, pestilence, and moral disintegration where those ruthless enemies were in occupation. Repeatedly cargoes being rushed to one destination had to be suddenly switched to some sector where danger was more urgent. A hundred times anarchy was headed off in the nick of time by the arrival of bread and medicines.

Will Irwin, who reported the spectacle as a foreign correspondent, would write: "I think of Hoover as a chess master, playing twenty games at once, and most of them blindfolded." The Chief worked from twelve to eighteen hours a day seven days a week.

War is a discipline—its end spells confusion. Civil conflicts were under way in Russia; territorial, ethnic, and dynastic conflicts were under way in the Baltic and Balkan countries and in the bleeding fragments of the Austro-Hungarian empire. Eastern Europe from Finland to the Levant was an economic shambles and in political convulsions. Germany presented a bloody froth of violence on a great sea of lethargic miseries.

Civil wars more terrible than ordinary wars were being fought in the debris of a civilization in dissolution and the American conscience could not always remain neutral. The marvel of it was not that Americans made political mistakes but that they made so few. When they could, they threw their weight on the side of democratic or at least less bloody forces.

The great common hatred that had held the Allies together exploded into a lot of little hatreds that drove them apart. Hoover was one of the few, along with Colonel House, Secretary of State Robert Lansing, and Bernard Baruch, who had urged Wilson not to go to Europe. They believed that his voice would carry farther coming from the White House than face to face with the hagglers and bargain-hunters of European power politics.

Within days after his arrival in Paris on December 15, the President asked Hoover for a briefing on the general situation. He got a frank answer that disturbed and probably exasperated him. As Hoover recalled the long interview afterward, he painted for the Commander-in-Chief a grim picture of "greed, robbery, power, sadistic hate, and revenge" in individuals; "fevered nationalism, imperialism, militarism, reaction, determination to decimate and dominate" in nations. He said he found

119

no tolerance, integrity, or generosity among the winners—not merely toward the losers but toward one another.

Wilson demurred, insisting that his friend was too harsh. But about two months later, alluding to that earlier conversation, a wiser Wilson said sadly to Hoover: "I have often agreed with you."

On a landscape of riotous passions and deep despairs, trampled by War and Death, now rode the other two Horsemen of the Apocalypse, Famine and Pestilence. Hoover's expert investigators found an annual death rate as high as 30 percent in some Baltic and Balkan cities; children with the swollen bellies of the last agonies of hunger in Germany, Hungary, Poland; cannibalism in Armenia and other places; women tearing the flesh off rotting horses with their bare hands; skeletonlike children and grownups scavenging in offal heaps everywhere; human flesh on sale in open markets.

As we have already indicated, Hoover felt that he could not wait for the statesmen to formulate decisions. While they argued, he acted. His field men were told in effect: "Feed the starving by any means, only quickly." When necessary these men blustered and bluffed through opposition to move cargoes, commandeer railway cars and locomotives, turn mansions into canteens and hospitals. Hoover men on their own in isolated places exercised power that was as often assumed as assigned. They talked owners into reopening factories and farmers into resuming planting beyond their own needs.

The thrilling story has come down of a lone doughboy accompanying a trainload of food destined for Vienna from an Adriatic port. Somewhere in the Balkans the train was stopped by military guards and ordered to unload its cargo. The American soldier had no notion of the local politics of the situation, so he jumped on the locomotive and ordered the engineer to put on full steam. He covered the flabbergasted guards with an automatic and the train pulled out. He "wasn't working for no kings or generals," he said in reporting the incident; he took orders only from the Chief. It was typical of a thousand such incidents in a thousand tight spots.

There were touches of humor to relieve the tension on the Avenue Montaigne. Once, for instance, a telegram arrived from Vienna: "Have arranged sell Galicia ten locomotives for eggs. How many eggs to a locomotive?" What the American did with the reply was never learned, for it read: "Does not matter. We have no confidence in the age of either."

An American officer on the staff once came to see Hoover in Paris. He was troubled and wanted to make a clean breast of something, and this is the story he told:

Civil war was raging in Dalmatia. The officer and two doughboys were caught in a crossfire on a mountain road above Cattaro. On investigating they discovered that the entrenched armies, perhaps a thousand guerillas in all, were willing to call the battle off, but neither of the commanding generals dared to lose face by crying "Uncle." Neither would surrender to the other.

That was simple, the officer pointed out—they could both surrender to America with their honor intact. In drawing up the formal capitulation paper, however, he became alarmed about involving the United States of America in a foreign fracas, so he wrote in "United States Food Administrator" instead. In a ceremony staged in the best movie tradition, he collected swords from the two generals, after which he put members of their armies to work reloading the trucks.

But he got to worrying whether he hadn't put the Chief on a diplomatic spot by using his name, and here he was in Paris explaining it all. Hoover, with a straight face, demanded to know what happened to the swords. The officer still had them. In that case, he ruled, if his guest would give him one and keep the other as mementos of the Dalmatian peace, the episode would be considered liquidated. Later Hoover wrote him that he was "of the stuff that had made America a great country."

Multiply this little drama by a thousand and we begin to feel the texture of the continentwide crusade against hunger and chaos.

XI

Salvaging a Continent

MEN like Robert Taft, Dr. Alonzo Taylor, Dr. Vernon Kellogg, and Lewis Strauss from the Food Administration assisted Hoover in Paris. They were joined by dozens of graduates of the Belgian crusade, among them some of the former Rhodes scholars. Hugh Gibson, by that time First Secretary of our London Embassy, was assigned to Hoover as diplomatic go-between with other governments.

These men were rushed without prior notice to danger spots when necessary. Gibson, for instance, at Hoover's request was designated Minister to Warsaw when conditions in Poland deteriorated. Additional men were detached from the Army, Navy, and Marines as the operation needed them. Many of these men made themselves so indispensable that they were engaged by various governments to remain as advisers after the relief organization was dissolved. Like their chief, those of his top assistants who could afford it worked without salaries.

A white-and-gold house on Rue Lubeck in the Trocaderao district, run at their own expense as a cooperative boardinghouse, became home for the duration for Hoover himself (when he was not at the Crillon) and some thirty of his associates. The big edifice boasted only four baths and there were many other housekeeping problems. Hoover had mobilized an Army private of his acquaintance as general handyman in the house. Not until later did he discover that this man in turn had mobilized sixteen other doughboys by simply claiming that "Hoover wanted them." Since he had chosen well—chauffeurs, a tailor, assistant cooks, mechanics—the Chief accepted the accomplished fact with equanimity.

On Avenue Montaigne the fifty rooms were full of men, mostly in uniform, the clatter of typewriters, adding machines, telegraph instruments, the voices of direction and instruction, and sometimes beefing. The walls were covered with ocean maps upon which little flags showed where hundreds of ships were and where they were going, as well as charts of some twenty-five countries showing their food stocks on hand and what they would need in the next month. There were no photographs of starving children, no evidence that all this machinery had to do with human travail.

The work in the flesh-and-blood countries mirrored on the charts was the opposite of mechanical. It was vibrant with drama and challenge. The very news that Hoover was back on the job in Europe, having spread from the Atlantic to the edges of Russia, "acted like magic in restoring hopes to these despairing millions," Vernon Kellogg attested from direct observation. He added: "It is owing more to Hoover and his work than to any other single influence that utter anarchy and complete Bolshevik domination of eastern Europe was averted."

There was an American aspect of this gigantic enterprise that closely concerned Hoover. By the summer of 1918 there had been good grounds for hoping that the German armies would soon be routed. But those responsible for uninterrupted and even stepped-up flow of food across the Atlantic could not gamble on a hope. They dared not relax the building of safe stockpiles.

On Armistice Day, the United States was therefore caught with huge quantities of provisions and immense new farm productive capacity. Agriculture had expanded to the tune of fifteen million tons of exports as against a prewar five million tons. Unless Europe, weeping and begging for food, could receive it quickly, collapse of farm prices at home and an economic debacle seemed in the cards.

In fighting for the right to rescue Europe, including the vanquished peoples, from famine, Hoover was also fighting to safeguard the farm and food industries in the United States. It was a case of economic imperatives at home and humanitarian imperatives abroad coinciding—with Allied suspicions, continuing blockades, and appetites for vengeance sitting stubbornly athwart the roads to both sets of goals.

Hoover was successful in clearing the roads, but not without sweat and tears. The very Congressmen and editors who belabored him for trying to "feed the Huns" were giving him hell for the dangerous food surpluses. On the latter score his critics did not know the half of it. Not until the peace had been signed did the public learn, for instance, about the Battle of the Pork which he had fought almost singlehandedly in behalf of farmers, packers, and a dozen related groups in the United States.

Surplus breadstuffs could be bought and stored by the Grain Corporation, but pork products were perishable. All the Allies had placed huge orders, and America had extended itself to meet these demands. With the war's end those orders were abruptly canceled. Hoover argued and pressed and threatened until practically every pound of that pork was taken up—by England, France, the Belgian Relief, and the American Armed Forces. We tell it here in one sentence, but it sums up dozens of conferences, months of labor, endless negotiations.

Hoover held the line on pork prices. Those whose economic lives he saved never realized how near they were to misfortune. American and Allied troops during those months had cause to grouse about their monotonous diet of ham and bacon. They could not guess that they were eating for the safety of farms and jobs in America.

There can be little of chronological order in telling the story; too many things were being done simultaneously in too many places. The succession states in central Europe had purloined one another's rolling stock and cut the Austro-Hungarian railway system into five national segments. Hoover's men succeeded in crashing through inflamed nationalisms to restore transport. To move their cargoes they reopened canals, put choked harbors into condition, found and reconditioned rolling stock, and supervised some thirty thousand miles of railway lines.

When it became apparent that near-collapse of the Silesian and Polish coal industries was blocking reconstruction in half the continent, Hoover was obliged to take over in that domain. Colonel Anson C. Goodyear, selected for the post by General Pershing, and his American staff doubled coal output in a few months. In August 1919, a bloody local war erupted in the Silesian coal area between Poles and Germans. Almost alone, the colonel "raced from one side to the other and finally stopped it." The coal was being mined again.

Once trains were moving, under American control, it became possible to arrange exchange of coal, oil, other vital commodities between countries on a barter basis. One of the monthly reports from Vienna suggests the nature of this strange trade:

Lubricating oils being exhausted, Colonel Jones was sent to the Polish oil fields where he loaded ninety-two cars with petroleum products. While he was doing this, the Ukrainian and Polish troops were fighting for possession of the fields. He succeeded in getting his cars out to Prague and Vienna.

Under escort of one U.S. corporal, two hundred carloads of tannin were shipped from Serbia to Poland in exchange for two hundred carloads of oil products. A trainload of manufactured goods was sent from Vienna to Galicia in exchange for forty-two cars of eggs and other edibles. "Altogether in Gregory's territory (headquarters in Vienna)," Hoover would report, "we exchanged over 150,000 tons of food and other commodities besides coal under American escorts. In addition we negotiated the purchase of 42,000 tons of grain in the Banat and shipped it to Austria and Hungary."

These are only samples of the process, throughout the continent. Because no American cash was involved, the barter transactions did not show up in the final accounting or statistics, but they played their role in stemming the tides of hunger and breakdown.

The telegraph and telephone lines between the enemy and Allied portions of the continent had, of course, been utterly disrupted. Yet rapid communications were essential for the relief operation. At Hoover's suggestion, the U. S. Navy solved this problem in the early months. Admiral Benson stationed an American destroyer or cruiser in all the vital ports. The wireless of these vessels, along with wireless equipment in the main relief offices on the continent, provided a workable network.

The improvised radio system, however, expired in February, when the Navy began pulling out its ships. It fell to Hoover, consequently, to open a continentwide telegraphic network, which in that period was a far greater feat than it sounds. Although intended for the relief work, the network was soon being used by press correspondents (with a neat profit for relief purposes) and even by some governments.

Because old and new governments were fearful of espionage, codes were forbidden. This did not bother resourceful Americans with a rich native slang at their command. In their dispatches one eminent statesman always figured as Mutt, another as Jeff, a third as the Chump. The jargon of baseball and "craps" did yeoman service for private communications.

The most famous of these dispatches derived from the turgid political situation in Hungary after the fall of Bela Kun's hundred-day Communist regime. Under Rumanian patronage, Archduke Joseph had assumed power in Budapest. The regional relief director, Captain Tom Gregory, had instructions to inform him that the Allies wanted no Habsburg for that job. On August 23, 1919, over his own wires, Hoover received the following telegram:

"Archie on the carpet at 7 p.m. Went through the hoop at 8 p.m."

When Hoover reported the accomplishment of the mission to Clemenceau, the old Tiger, who had lived in America and appreciated its humor, appropriated the telegram as a souvenir.

2

The shocking reports of the depredations of the typhus louse in the war zones of a shattered Russia could no longer be ignored when the epidemic, like a conquering army, began to move into Lithuania, Poland, the Ukraine, Rumania, and Serbia. Nearly a million cases of the dread disease were totaled in those areas, with tens of thousands of deaths. Each day the pestilence marched farther westward. All of Europe was menaced.

The most authentic and alarming information on the typhus scourge naturally came to Hoover, who alone among the peacemakers in Paris had representatives everywhere. He pressed the Supreme Council to take action, but to no effect. Then he asked the American Red Cross to accept the challenge, only to be informed with regrets that the task was far too big even for the Red Cross. So, with a sigh, he shouldered that battle too.

With Colonel H. L. Gilchrist of the Hoover organization in charge, and additional personnel drawn from the U. S. Armed Forces, Americans formed a battle line that stretched from north to south across the continent. The American Army contributed vast amounts of medical and hospital supplies and equipment. In time a few of the Allied and neutral armies also came through. The German Reichswehr turned over millions of dollars' worth of delousing machinery.

No one was allowed to pass the battle line from east to west without a certificate of delousing. Having strayed to the wrong side of the *cordon sanitaire,* even Hugh Gibson had to obtain a delousing certificate the hard way despite his diplomatic eminence. Steadily, month after month, the line was pushed eastward and finally total victory could be announced.

In the scheme of this biography there is, unfortunately, no space for detailed recitals of how the crusade was fought and largely won in each of the individual countries. Every one of those battlefields provided enough drama, sorrow, satisfactions, and even humor to fill volumes—and, in fact, a few such volumes have been written.

Consider the Baltic wedge where three newly hatched republics—Lithuania, Latvia, and Estonia—had their violent being. Their aggregate population was under five million, but their aggregate sufferings and bloodlettings were almost incalculable. Regimes rose and fell in cyclones of terror, with Bolshevik buzzards always hovering over the debris. Latvia writhed in agony nearly six months under a Soviet frenzy of loot and slaughter. In Riga the streets were still littered with corpses when American food arrived to the rescue.

Hoover learned of one minor but heartwarming incident in the relief of Riga which merits telling. A Yankee sergeant asked if there was still an American consulate in town and was directed to an obscure address. Tacked on the door was a small American flag and under it a typewritten notice in Lettish and English warning the world in general not to molest the premises, and signed "Acting Consul of the United States of America."

The sergeant knocked. After a while a girl peeked out. She was quite obviously frightened and starved. At the sight of the American uniform she burst into tears of joy. It turned out that the girl was an American of Lettish origin, the stenographer in the consulate. When everyone else retreated before the Germans she chose to hold the fort, and promptly reopened her "consulate" when the war ended.

Much shrill nonsense has been written by Communist propagandists about Hoover and the short-lived Red regime of murder under Bela Kun in Hungary. It was the fixed policy of the Relief not to deliver supplies to governments anywhere which could not be trusted to distribute it equitably, without political bias. That by definition ruled out Communists, who openly treated food and famine as "weapons of class war."

Yet Hoover insisted that twenty-five trainloads of supplies en route to Budapest at the moment Kun seized power be delivered to its destination, since the preceding Hungarian government had paid for them. He made the one condition that Americans control the distribution. The Supreme Council at first opposed this Hoover decision but in the end agreed, with the proviso that no more shipments be made as long as the Communists were in power.

Just as soon as the Kun mob was ousted, at the initiative of the trade unions, provisioning was resumed. Hungary's ordeal, however, was only beginning. The attempt to install a democratic government was frustrated by invading Rumanian forces, which looted even children's homes and hospitals. Then, when a Habsburg was installed, it was a Hoover man —we have already cited his cryptic message—who unseated him. A new, more representative government followed.

Now, as in the Belgian work, Hoover was especially vigilant for the well-being of children. Subordinates, knowing his softest spot, could get anything they wanted from him by showing that it involved relief for the little ones. In part his lifelong concern for the young rested on cold logic —without a healthy, normal new generation there could be no hope for the future. But that was merely the façade for a solicitude of the heart. The fact is that the very thought of children in pain or in hunger struck the deepest core of his being.

Beyond the general rationed relief he therefore set up special services which in time embraced eight million boys and girls in Poland, Finland, Czechoslovakia, Armenia, and other countries. He organized them on an almost entirely private charitable basis, raising the funds through philanthropic, religious, and private sources. In Germany he arranged for the child relief to be conducted by the Friends (Quaker) Service Committee; in Armenia, by the Near East Relief. For years after the main and official assignment was completed, the feeding of needy children continued, under Hoover's watchful eye.

3

Finland, independent after its long subjection to Russia, was in a desperate economic plight. A deputation of its leading citizens called on Hoover soon after he arrived in Paris. He saw to it that enough emergency supplies were switched at once from other destinations to Finland to take the sharp edge off hunger until he could organize the large-scale rescue work. This he did so well that a new word was added to the Finnish language—*hooveri*, meaning deeds of benevolence.

Political stability was essential to Finland's recovery and that required, in the first place, recognition of its nationhood by the Big Four. Hoover dedicated himself to this objective. Having convinced Wilson that the action could not wait for the Peace Treaty, Hoover with the President's backing then won over Clemenceau. Finnish independence was acknowledged. Major Ferry Heath, in charge of relief operations in Helsinki, received the news in a confidential message from an American colleague in Paris before the formal announcement. "The recognition of Finland," it said in part, "has been brought about entirely by Mr. Hoover by his urgent and repeated representations to various governments."

A substantial part of the Hoover organization's energies and resources were funneled into Poland, perhaps the most tragically stricken country in Europe. The relief mission, headed in its initial stage by Dr. Kellogg, later was run by Colonel William R. Grove, assisted by other Army men and one brilliant civilian, Maurice Pate.

This newly constituted nation of twenty-eight million souls had been brutally mangled by four separate invasions, the last being a full-scale Soviet bid for conquest. The Polish people were reduced to indescribable destitution. Typhus and assorted other killers swept the land unchecked, while bloody political struggles did the rest.

In the end "the Colonels," an army group with Joseph Pilsudski at its head, assumed power. In an effort to contain factional violence at least until the famine and pestilence could be checked, Hoover proposed that Ignace Paderewski, the great pianist beloved by all Poles, be named Prime Minister, under Pilsudski as "Chief of State." This was done. With relative internal tranquillity restored, the tasks of feeding the hungry, stemming disease, and reactivating the nation's economy could be tackled in earnest.

Paderewski felt that a visit by President Wilson, as token of American friendship, would help his country's morale. The President, unable to comply, asked Hoover to go in his stead. For both Poland and Hoover it was to prove a memorable experience.

In a special train, accompanied by an impressive group of American "brass," Hoover reached Warsaw on August 12, 1919. The reception, in its official aspects and in the great outpouring of popular emotion, no doubt achieved the political purpose Paderewski had hoped for. Hoover, diffident and unhappy as the object of adulation, went through the paces from a sense of duty. Hugh Gibson, as the American Minister to Poland, did what he could to shield the Chief against excessive public demonstrations. Yet one of these was to remain among Hoover's most cherished memories. In his mind, always after, it outweighed the mountain of medals and scrolls that would come to him through the years. The inspiration for it was Paderewski's.

One day, at an old race track in the capital, Hoover took a salute of affection from some fifty thousand children, many of them brought from schools and soup kitchens in other cities by the trainload. Hour after hour they passed before the reviewing stand in untidy formation, most of them carrying tiny American flags made of paper. Boys and girls from five to twelve years of age, a lot of them in tattered, nondescript clothes, they looked well fed and happy: a cheering, laughing, high-spirited army.

In the reports on conditions in Poland brought to him at the war's end, Hoover had been touched to the quick by a casual observation that there was no sign of children playing on the streets of Warsaw, Cracow, and other cities. Here—as Paderewski, always the artist, meant to convey—was the noisy, living proof that eight months of American care had taught these children to play and laugh again!

Thousands of the youngsters, having come directly from their American hot lunch, brought their tin cups along and waved them aloft like banners. Never before or since has there been a stranger, more moving parade, or one more happily in consonance with the nature of the man being greeted. The head of the French Military Mission, General Henrys, was so overcome with emotion that he left the stand to hide his tears. He paused to remark to Hoover in a choked voice, "There has never been a review of honor in all history that I would prefer for myself to that which you received today." Hoover was himself too close to tears to reply.

At one point in the march of the tiny tots an astonished rabbit leaped out of the grass and started down the track. That was too much of a test for the decorum of the little paraders. Thousands broke ranks and dashed wildly after the rabbit, laughing and shouting. Having caught the animal, they brought it triumphantly to Hoover as their token of love. Vernon Kellogg tells the rest:

"But they were astonished to see, as they gave him their gift, that this great strong man did just what you or I or any other sort of human being could not have helped doing under the circumstances. They saw him cry."

4

Sprawling Russia, riven by violence, presented a special problem. After the overthrow of Czardom, Hoover urged that the fledgling democracy receive food and medical supplies. No one listened. Had the Allies mustered the wisdom to provide timely and generous support to the moderate forces under Kerensky, the handful of fanatics led by Lenin and Trotsky might never have succeeded in seizing power—hunger, surely, was their strongest ally.

Hoover had also counseled Wilson against sending American troops to Russia in the small-scale and futile intervention of 1918–19. The President, however, yielding to Allied pressures, dispatched small token forces to Archangel and to Siberia. In Paris, Hoover was almost alone in the upper stratum of advisers to plead for relaxation of the Russian blockade to allow food and medicaments for children to enter. Moreover, he fought against the proposal by Churchill, in the name of the British Cabinet, for a united Allied invasion of Russia. The American opposition helped defeat that plan.

In the confusion of our time it is almost forgotten that the Lenin-Trotsky group did not overthrow the old regime or "make the revolution." On the contrary, the Bolsheviks hijacked the revolution from its makers, the people of Russia, washing out in blood the first attempt to establish a democratic way of life there. But in 1919 such simple truths were too fresh to be overlooked. Hoover's sympathy for popular Russian aspirations was even deeper than his detestation of the Bolshevik doctrines and methods. On March 28, 1919, he wrote a letter to Wilson outlining his views on the Russian problem. At one point it said:

It simply cannot be denied that this swinging of the social pendulum from the tyranny of the extreme right to the tyranny of the extreme left is based on a foundation of real social grievance. The tyranny of the reactionaries in Eastern and Central Europe for generations before the war, the sufferings of their common people, is but a commonplace to every social student. . . . The poor were starved and driven in the presence of extravagance and waste.

But the Communist cure seemed to him worse than the disease. Having indicted the Red terror in scorching language, Hoover declared that some way must be found, notwithstanding, to bring help to millions of starving Russians. If the Soviet Government should prove willing to remain within fixed frontiers, renouncing plans to carry its minority domination into neighboring countries, he said, the outside world—and America in the first place—should agree to provide adequate and completely non-political relief.

Specifically, he proposed to President Wilson the formation of a commission headed by a prominent neutral acceptable to the Kremlin and operating on about the same basis as the Belgian Relief. Wilson approved, and Fridtjof Nansen, the celebrated Norwegian polar explorer, was selected by Hoover to head up the project. Then the Big Four, in an exchange of letters with Nansen, accepted the Hoover plan.

Clemenceau was frankly reluctant and contemptuous. Indeed, French sabotage delayed Nansen's formal message to Lenin, dated April 17, by more than two weeks, during which the French press assailed the idea and limited it in a way that made Moscow's rejection a certainty. When Chicherin, the Bolshevik Foreign Minister, finally received and answered the Nansen proposal—an answer again delayed by accidents that were not accidental—it was in the negative, as expected. Hoover was profoundly disappointed and, rightly or wrongly, blamed the French more than the Russians for the failure of his intercession. Subsequently he wrote:

I believed that the reply left a crack open, and that the many words were for internal [Russian] consumption. I wanted to pursue the question further, but the French in the meantime emitted vociferous denunciations of the whole business and so the effort died at no cost but words.

Knowing what we know today about the Bolshevik mentality, Hoover was probably naïve in believing Lenin might have agreed to compromises of any sort. The Kremlin then had high hopes (as it was to have them a second time after World War II) that all Europe would go Communist. What were a few million Russian corpses more or less against the interests of world revolution? But the Russian people, if and when they emerge from the yoke of their Red masters, will learn for the first time that the same Hoover who fed them in later years had tried desperately to bring them relief as early as 1919.

5

The general public knew little of the role played by Hoover in the Paris negotiations, but insiders at the Peace Conference were unanimous in appraising it as large and enlightened. He saw in dismay that a peace of vengeance was being hammered out, in cynical defiance of the Wilsonian principles. Like other liberals on the scene, Hoover was especially distressed by the economic absurdities that were being compounded.

The President of the United States, increasingly weary, despairing, and in failing health, struggled to keep his head above the quagmires of intrigue. More and more, perhaps unwisely, he went along with decisions he deprecated, in the belief that the all-important objective, his League of Nations, warranted some sacrifice of lesser things.

European statesmen, while treating the American President with demonstrative deference in public, in private did not conceal their contempt for his "foolish idealism." In the memoirs many of them eventually wrote, their references to Wilson were faintly patronizing, even when they praised him, and in a few instances the overtones of mockery were audible.

Unhappily for mankind, in Paris in 1919—as in Yalta a quarter of a century later—an ailing American President helped fritter away the fruits of victory.

Hoover was among those alarmed by the course of negotiations. He was outspoken, though he had reason to know that the President, more and more sensitive to criticism, would not be grateful for his candor. On April 11, 1919, he addressed a long memorandum to Wilson which amounted to a reminder of Wilsonian principles. Two of its paragraphs are especially revealing of his mind and his feelings as the end of the Peace Conference approached, and they throw some light, incidentally, on Hoover's controversial views in a war yet to come:

It grows upon me daily, that the United States is the one great moral reserve in the world today and that we cannot maintain the independence of action through which this reserve is to be maintained if we allow ourselves to be dragged into detailed European entanglements over a period of years.

In my view, if the Allies cannot be brought to adopt peace on the basis of the Fourteen Points, we should retire from Europe, lock, stock and barrel, and we should lend to the whole world our economic and moral strength, or the world will swim in a sea of misery and disaster worse than the Dark Ages. If they cannot be brought to accept peace on this basis, our national honor is at stake and we should have to make peace independently and retire.

Hoover did not set himself up as a prophet. He was simply an open-eyed, highly trained American who had been more deeply immersed in European reality than any other American in Paris. Certainly the disaster and misery and medieval darkness he foresaw came soon enough, in immense and bitter measure.

One of the "entanglements" against which he was on the alert was the "mandate" system, under which the colonial holdings of defeated nations were being divided among the Allies. Wilson was inclined to credit the theory that this was a plausible experiment in "trusteeship." But Hoover saw the mandate as a "euphemism" for the old-style imperialism and "one of the most monumental attainments of old diplomacy." He could discern no genuine difference between rule by mandate and plain colonialism.

He was therefore thoroughly worried when, in mid-May, Lloyd George and Clemenceau proposed that America accept a mandate over both the Russian and Turkish portions of Armenia, as well as Constantinople and the Dardanelles. Wilson, Hoover learned, was tempted by the scheme and, in fact, had approved in principle a suggestion by Colonel House that Hoover himself be appointed Governor of the mandated areas.

"I was greatly distressed at this whole idea," Hoover would report, "and argued at length with the President that we should not undertake it. I thought, aside from its other disqualifications, it was wrong because it would involve America in the whole power politics of Europe."

He succeeded in persuading Wilson to delay a decision until an American mission examined the project on the spot. The mission, headed by General James G. Harbord, included several experts from Hoover's own staff and designated by him. Some months later it brought back a gloomy and adverse report and the whole plan expired by default.

At four in the morning of May 7, Hoover was awakened in his Crillon apartment to accept a confidential printed copy of the completed draft of the Peace Treaty just delivered to him. He read it in bed until dawn, in mounting sorrow. He felt that the document did not so much mark the end of a war as the prelude to another war.

Agitated and depressed, he dressed and went for a walk in the deserted streets of Paris to think about what he had just learned. Suddenly he found himself face to face with another agitated and sorrowful figure, General Jan Christiaan Smuts of South Africa. Then a third man joined them: John Maynard Keynes. All three recognized at once what had driven the others to the streets! They compared notes, agreed that the document was "terrible," and undertook to do what they could to have the more senseless clauses modified.

That morning Hoover called together the "thinking men," as he put it, in his organization for breakfast. For some hours they discussed the most grievous elements in the treaty. Later that day the three men who had met in the dawn got together again, along with Vance McCormick, to devise tactics for obtaining vital changes.

One of the strangest, saddest dramas in modern history was then played out, without the public being aware of it. This group and others drawn into it by their conscience had some degree of success with the chief architects of the treaty: Lloyd George, Clemenceau, and Orlando. But Wilson opposed all revisions! Having approved the treaty provisions, often in sorrow and against his own better judgment, he now felt honor-bound to defend them. The circumstance that he had already suffered a mild stroke, concealed from the world, could have blurred his judgment. In any case, it was Keynes who then coined the aphorism that "Lloyd George, having bamboozled Wilson, could not unbamboozle him."

On June 3 Hoover and others met with Wilson in an attempt to make him recognize weaknesses that could still be repaired. The forthright and emphatic presentation by Hoover irritated the President and he made sharp replies. Two days later, at the request of Secretary of State Lansing, Hoover put his criticisms of the treaty into a memorandum which the Secretary turned over to the President.

In a few days, Hoover had his last important discussion with Wilson. He departed crestfallen, knowing that he was in the Presidential dog-house, to which Colonel House and others had preceded him. Except for a formal farewell on the station platform when Wilson left Paris, the two men were not to meet again while Wilson was in the Presidency. It was part of Wilson's fast-gathering tragedy that, precisely when he needed them most, he had in effect dismissed House, Hoover, and the others who had disagreed with him.

On Saturday, June 28, the Peace Treaty was signed in the Hall of Mirrors at Versailles. At the glittering ceremony, the delegates of the Central Powers, who signed without reading, were not the only ones with heavy hearts and somber premonitions.

Hoover's principal tasks in Europe were ended. Under the law, American relief and rehabilitation had to be wound up. There were many pressures on Hoover to extend the work for another year and he could readily have found the means. But he believed that "continuance beyond peace and harvest would undermine the very initiative and the economic structure of the states concerned." His knowledge that good harvests were in prospect helped firm up this judgment.

Three months after the fifty rooms on Avenue Montaigne were closed, a plaintive note reached Hoover from a humble sergeant who had been checking railway cars in central Europe and sending in reports to the vacated headquarters. The "forgotten man" wanted to know when he would be relieved.

Hoover remained in Paris until September. Again he had been sepa-rated from his family for over ten months. A few weeks before the end, Mrs. Hoover and their younger son, Allan, came to Paris to be with him and to accompany him home. The boy teamed up with another twelve-year-old, General Pershing's son Warren. Under the firm guidance of an Army sergeant, the youngsters saw more of the sights of the capital and its environs in several weeks than their fathers had seen in years.

Amazingly, considering the scope of his activities, Hoover found time to promote a side project he had dreamed up in late 1914 while crossing the North Sea. He was reading a book by Andrew D. White, president of Cornell University, in which the scholar complained about the disap-pearance of contemporary documents and other materials on the French Revolution. There and then Hoover decided that this must not happen to the records of the war then under way and its aftermath. The idea of a systematic collection and preservation of current documents was born.

Soon thereafter he initiated what came to be known as "Operation Pack Rat." Agents and friends and public officials were asked to salvage printed and other data, large and small, that might be helpful to future historians. He continued to gather and hoard such historical materials while he was Food Administrator. After the Armistice he put the unique undertaking on an organized basis.

He brought a seasoned historian, Professor E. D. Adams, to Europe and provided him with an operating fund of fifty thousand dollars to direct the collecting. More than a dozen historians were detached from the Army by General Pershing to help him. Every one of the scattered relief missions had the preservation of local documents among its tangential assignments.

The data flowed into central repositories in ever greater volume. The collapse of old governments made their archives available—successors were not reluctant to put some of these into American hands. New leaders, when routed by oppositions, similarly confided their records to Hoover's keeping. Before long, ships returning to the United States after delivering supplies carried large cargoes of these historical materials.

Hoover's interest in this enterprise would never flag. In the midst of other and always staggeringly heavy burdens, even while in the White House, he continued to raise the money and find the trained men to build his library of contemporary source materials. On the grounds of Stanford University there stands today a beautiful towerlike edifice—the Hoover Institution of War, Revolution, and Peace—as a living monument to his imagination and enterprise. The building, dedicated on June 20, 1941, houses the largest such collection in the world and draws to it scholars and researchers from all nations.

All in all, in the twelve months following the Armistice, the Hoover organization brought from overseas and distributed twenty-seven million tons of food, seed, clothing, medical and other supplies, valued at five and a half billion dollars.

The figures, of course, tell only a small part of the story. They do not include food imported by the Allies from countries other than the United States, nor the imports by neutrals under Hoover coordination. They do not include the hundreds of thousands of tons of provisions and equipment the organization made available, as already indicated, on a barter basis. Above all, they do not reflect the human content of the undertaking.

The Hoover men provided the initial push that started the machinery of normal life rolling in over twenty countries. They became the mouthpieces of stricken populations reaching out for a modicum of freedom.

Without ever putting it into such words—for they were practical workers, not sentimental phrasemakers—they served as the conscience of mankind. The humblest among them shared the sense of having taken part in great and fine deeds.

The American post-Armistice contribution, though recorded on the books as a businesslike operation based on credits and contracts, came in truth to three billion dollars of charity. "From an American point of view," Hoover would state, "the British, French and Italians were, for the twelve months beginning with the Armistice, as much on relief as Poland or any other country. They had to be loaned the money to buy their imports, and there was no probability they would repay the loans." And, indeed, they never were repaid. Of the European beneficiaries of the "second American crusade," only one—Finland—ultimately paid for what it had received. The others, through necessity or by political sleight-of-hand, managed to repudiate their obligations.

It was essential that Hoover make a final personal inspection of relief centers in the major countries. Try as he did, he could not avoid public meetings, demonstrations, press eulogies, sermons on his work. The prestige which American idealism had lost in Paris it regained through the length and breadth of Europe, wherever "Hoover relief" had penetrated.

In September 1919, when the date of his impending departure was announced in the European press, there was an extraordinary outpouring of gratitude—a deluge of letters, telegrams, resolutions, from every country on the continent. Hoover was understating the facts when he wrote:

They came from Presidents and Prime Ministers of Britain, France, Italy, Belgium and all the other countries we had served. They came from my colleagues in every country. They came from His Holiness the Pope, the heads of the Greek, Armenian, and Lutheran Churches. An especially affectionate message was from my old friend, Cardinal Mercier. But the most touching of all were the volumes which arrived over the years containing literally millions of signatures of children, with their own illustrations.

Hoover's last call before leaving France was upon its Prime Minister. Clemenceau was in a gloomy frame of mind. "There will be another world war in your time," he told the younger man, "and you will be needed back in Europe." To lighten the gloom, Hoover asked in parting, "Do you remember Captain Gregory's report on the decline and fall of the Habsburgs?" Clemenceau chortled. He pulled a drawer and brought out the original telegram. "I keep it close by," he said, "for that was one of the few flashes of humor that came into our attempts to make over the world."

Europe did not forget. Countries, cities, villages, and millions of in-

dividuals, respecting Hoover's known aversion to decorations and citations, found other ways to convey their gratitude. Dozens of cities struck
special Hoover medals in his honor. Warsaw erected a statue to him in
one of its parks. Nineteen years later, visiting that city again, he was told
that the head of the statue probably had been blown off. "In any event,"
he reported, "I found I was headless at that time—and no doubt continue
so under the communist regime."

He might have checked on this, but didn't, when he found himself
in the Polish capital once more in 1946, while on a round-the-world
trip for President Truman. He was conferring with a group of Polish
Communist officials one day. Suddenly a woman turned to him and said
in substance: "I am one of the children you fed after the First War. If it
were not for you, Mr. Hoover, I would not be alive now—and I guess the
same is true of others in this room." True it was: one after another, the
officials smilingly acknowledged that they had been sustained by Hoover
charity as children. At a public meeting in Belgrade, during the same
1946 trip, the Communist Foreign Minister of Yugoslavia in his speech
made the identical admission for himself.

In all of the twenty-odd countries after the war, names of ancient
streets and squares and parks were discarded in favor of the name of
Hoover. The aggregate signatures of collective letters and scrolls to which
he alluded, often bearing the names of entire communities, came to
nearly four million.

XII

Back Home from Europe

THE forty-five-year-old Hoover who sailed for home on the *Aquitania* in late September 1919 was a tired man. "A weary Titan," Keynes called him. He had simultaneously commanded campaigns on a score of fronts in a continental war on disaster in many shapes. Not one of his stalwart lieutenants could keep pace with him, for few human beings are endowed with such reserves of stamina and inner discipline.

But the weariness was more psychic than physical. He was surfeited with human wretchedness and political duplicity.

It was a deeply saddened Hoover who left Europe. The general is sustained by the passion and pageantry of war, by the goad of a tangible foe. But Hoover had dealt with plodding, depressing, amorphous materials of famine, typhus lice, human wreckage, and economic rubble—in a war without true end, in which amelioration rather than the glory of victory was the best one could hope for. Moreover, he had seen at intimate range the emergence of frightening ant-heap ideologies, blotting out a century of liberal progress. He was one Republican who had no delusions about "normalcy" for his own land or the world.

In the nature of public life, he had been subjected to some attacks. His most humane impulses, particularly his concern for the health of the enemy's children, had been misconstrued and assailed. And he lacked the thick skin of a natural politician.

With every aching muscle and nerve he yearned for an interval of leisure and forgetfulness, for the simple amenities of a close family life. His diffidence kept him, in his writings, from overt expression of sentiment on the personal level. Yet a great love and admiration for his wife shines through in an occasional phrase. He hoped, he would recall, "to

138

renew association with a great lady and two satisfactory boys." He needed them as much as they needed him.

Besides, now that he paused to survey the landscape of his life, he realized that his wealth had been seriously depleted. He had had no time to give to the several companies in which his savings were invested. Expenses, paid out of his own pocket, had been an increasing drain as his prominence and obligations expanded. After a good long vacation, he promised himself and his friends, he would begin to repair the family fortunes.

The idyll crumbled rapidly, since it was based on the naïve supposition that he could retreat into a sheltering obscurity.

On the *Aquitania* he was apprised that the American Institute of Mining and Metallurgical Engineers had arranged a banquet in his honor in New York and that, of course, he would make "a few remarks." The prospect cast a shadow over the journey. From the sheaves of invitations, demands, and offers awaiting him it was clear that his countrymen were massed to block his retreat.

Hundreds of letters and telegrams a day reached him, each a trap baited with heart appeal to snare his time and energy. Hoover had underrated his own fame and his hold on the country's imagination. Worse, his very reticence, the edge of mystery, added dimensions of popular interest in him. A New York *Times* opinion poll on the ten most important living Americans showed him high on the list. He found it all disturbing and vaguely depressing.

After the New York reception Hoover went on to California. But cables, telegrams, letters, and phone calls pursued him even to the hills and streams when he went camping and fishing with his family.

For a man like Hoover it was one thing to say that he would now devote himself "to a reasonable existence," quite another to brush off calls to duty. He was conscious of his own tensed powers at the zenith of his maturity. His experience and intuitions, ripened into a philosophy of life, weighed on his spirits like a public trust. In declining various services being urged upon him, he felt almost as if he were deserting in a time of danger.

Paul Warburg, the eminent financier, had just organized the International Bank of Acceptance. He invited Hoover to join, on any terms he wished. It was an opportunity to enter the world of finance at the top and he was tempted. But he turned down the offer, and other such temptations. If he went back to private business, he explained, it would be in his familiar engineering world. Months before, he had informed President Wilson of his hope of returning to his own profession.

Hoover actually went so far as to open an engineering office in San

Francisco. First, however, he would have a long draught of that "reasonable existence." With their old cottage on the Stanford campus as base, he took the "great lady" and their boys, now twelve and fifteen, on motoring trips into the hills, the car loaded with the paraphernalia of camp life and fishing.

As ramparts against the avalanche of invitations and requests, for a few weeks at least, he drafted and made public a whimsical set of resolutions. For a month, he said, he would accept no telephone calls and read no letters longer than one page. He would make none of the sixty-four speeches he had been asked to make, and the public should be "gratified to find a citizen who wants to keep still." He offered "this intimate disclosure of private affairs," he concluded, "so that it may be clear that I contemplate no mischief against the Commonwealth."

But imbedded in the statement was one proviso which was an unwitting revelation of his ambivalent state of mind as he faced the future, namely: "All this is subject to the reservation that nothing turns up to irritate my conscience or peace of mind." The double pull on his emotions—toward private life and toward public service—is thus quite evident under the beguiling tone. The fact is that his conscience and peace of mind were indeed deeply disturbed. He could not slough off his sense of personal responsibility for the fate of his country.

He had returned to an America that was in a confused, restive, and in some areas embittered state of mind. The descent from the heights of wartime dedication had begun. A sobering cynicism was the hangover from patriotic intoxications. Counsels of violence, intolerance, and social extremism were gaining ground. Having seen the results of similar moods in Europe, he was worried for his native land. The zeal for making the world safe for democracy was petering out in impatience to withdraw from the world altogether.

Almost despite himself, Hoover was soon thoroughly implicated in public business. Though he had been disheartened by the Peace Treaty, he urged that the United States ratify it notwithstanding. With all its faults, he felt, it was better than no treaty as a counterweight to chaos and a prop for the new representative governments in Europe. By the same logic, he joined with ex-President Taft, Charles Evans Hughes, Elihu Root, and other prominent Republicans in pleading for ratification—with a number of reservations—of the League of Nations Covenant.

Thus the pressures from without, and even more so the pressures from within, proved too strong for him. "Reluctantly I gave way to conscience" was his own summation. Despite his flirtation with a return to engineering, he was soon drawn into full-time political and humanitarian chores. With his tendency to statistics, he compiled an inventory of what he did in the seventeen months between his departure from Europe and becoming Secretary of Commerce. He made forty-six speeches, presided over fifteen public meetings, issued thirty-one press statements, wrote twenty-eight magazine articles, testified nine times at Congressional hearings, and made four extensive reports on various subjects.

The symbol of the urge to privacy, for the Hoovers as for millions of American families, was a "dream house"—in Palo Alto, of course. Half a dozen years earlier, Mrs. Hoover had leased land on a nearby Stanford campus hill with an exciting view of the mountains and the bay. She had worked with architects on preliminary drawings of a spacious western-style dwelling, with flat roofs and ample provisions for outdoor living. Often, through the years, she and her husband had discussed the house-to-be, savoring it in anticipation.

Now, at last, Mrs. Hoover began actual construction. Two years later the house was finished and, miraculously, it matched their dream. But by that time Hoover was Secretary of Commerce in the Harding Cabinet. It would be twelve years, and the children would be grown up, before the family could finally occupy the house on a more or less continuous basis.

There was a lot of unfinished business that he could not evade. He must give a detailed accounting to the Supreme Economic Council, the U. S. Congress, and the American people of the billions of dollars and a multiplicity of organizations under his stewardship. His was the only major wartime agency that was not investigated by Congress; the records were too clear and invulnerable.

His, too, was the main responsibility for setting up endowments with the thirty-three million dollar residue in the coffers of the Belgian Relief. When the task was in order, he put Perrin Galpin, the former Rhodes scholar, in executive command. Above all, there were the seven or eight million children in central and eastern Europe still dependent on American charity. He proceeded to raise the money and kept his hand on the machinery of this enterprise for years. Until then the American Relief Administration had been an official agency for administering the one hundred million dollars appropriated by Congress. Hoover reorganized it on a private basis and its initials, ARA, became a beacon of hope wherever disaster struck.

A number of groups were active in helping the European peoples: the Red Cross, the Friends, the Jewish Joint Distribution Committee, and the Knights of Columbus, among others. Hoover persuaded them of the advantages of common fund-raising. Accordingly they all joined in forming the European Relief Council under his chairmanship, with Franklin T. Lane as treasurer and Christian A. Herter as secretary.

The initial drive raised the necessary thirty million dollars. Its main technique was a series of "Invisible Guest" dinners throughout the country, at one hundred to one thousand dollars a plate. The "Invisible Guest" was a needy child. The meal served, on tinware, was a typical relief luncheon. The largest of these dinners, in New York, netted three million dollars, including a one million dollar contribution by John D. Rockefeller, Jr.

Special emergencies arose frequently and were duly met. For instance, some two hundred thousand destitute intellectuals in Europe—writers, artists, doctors, lawyers, professors—were provided with food and clothing. To facilitate relief gifts by individual Americans to relatives and friends in Europe, Hoover developed the "Food Draft" idea. At his request, some five thousand banks sold, without charge, drafts in units of ten dollars payable in relief packages on the other side of the Atlantic. A total of eight million dollars was thus transferred, with a profit of six hundred thousand dollars which the ARA applied to the children's relief program.

In 1920 Hoover was elected President of the American Institute of Mining and Metallurgy, and also of the American Engineering Council, representing all organizations in this field. Characteristically, he used these offices at once for a practical objective.

Under the aegis of the Council, he initiated a study in depth of waste in industry. It confirmed what he had suspected: that about 25 percent of the costs of production could be saved without affecting wages or increasing the work load. The report, titled *Waste in Industry*, published in 1921, became a milestone on the American road to greater efficiency and productivity. Hoover was by that time in a position, as Secretary of Commerce, to help translate the findings into voluntary action by the country's industrial community.

2

Before leaving California, Hoover was handed a protocol job which harked back to his Belgian adventure. At the invitation of Congress, the King and Queen of the Belgians in October 1919, paid a visit to the United States. Apprised of President Wilson's serious illness, the royal pair fell in with a State Department suggestion that they spend in California the week originally apportioned to the White House.

Accordingly Hoover was asked whether he could put them up at his "estate." Their party, he was informed, counted only forty persons. Since there was only one spare bedroom in the cottage constituting the whole of the Hoover "estate," that presented problems. In the end he found two actual "estates" in Santa Barbara which, by dint of crowding, could care for twenty each.

The generous hosts and other local folk collected plenty of "buttons" for posterity, and the royal couple had a wonderful and unconventional time. Santa Barbara at the time still boasted an old-style sheriff complete with boots, a ten-gallon hat, and a brace of six-shooters. The sheriff and his deputies assumed the task of guarding King Albert's quarters. Monarch and sheriff became good friends at once. Being shy on protocol, the sheriff addressed his charge as "Oh, King," until someone set him straight and he switched to "Your Majesty." His Majesty, however, would have none of that and requested him to switch back to "Oh, King."

San Francisco staged a great parade for the royal pair. But the mayor, James Rolph, Jr., coming up for re-election the very next day, was scared to death that the Order of the Crown, Second Class, awarded him by King Albert, might cost him the votes of anti-royalists. Hoover stepped into the great emergency by proposing that Rolph accept the award not for himself but for the city. The election, if it had really been in jeopardy, was saved. Many years later, when Rolph (by then governor) died, Hoover was among the pallbearers. On the governor's breast, he noted, lay the Belgian Order of the Crown, Second Class.

Hoover had served the Democratic administration loyally, in a nonpartisan spirit, during the war. In the Congressional campaign of 1918 he wrote a letter urging, in view of the war, the election of men who would support the President without regard to party. Doubts were thus fostered about his own party affiliations.

Actually he was an enrolled Republican from his twenty-first birthday. He joined the National Republican Club and supported Theodore Roosevelt in 1912. Nevertheless, the liberal New York *World* and a number of prominent individuals urged his nomination as Democratic candidate for President. He was obliged to attest firmly that he was a Republican.

Over his protests, amateur groups across the country formed Hoover-for-President Clubs. Several times he publicly, but without success, asked them to desist. In scattered districts, where he could not stop it, his name was placed in primaries, both Democratic and Republican. In Michigan, he drew the largest vote of any candidate—in the Democratic primary. A man who had served with Hoover in the Wilson administration, Franklin D. Roosevelt, wrote to Josephus Daniels that "Herbert Hoover is certainly a wonder, and I wish we could make him President of the United States. There could not be a better one."

Only in California, then a Republican stronghold, was Hoover entered in the primary contest with his consent. He was motivated by conscience rather than any mistaken hope of winning. Senator Hiram Johnson was seeking the Republican nomination for President on a violently anti-League program. Pro-League Republicans urged that a heavy Hoover vote in California, though short of victory, would demonstrate that the party was deeply divided on this issue, and not unanimously against American entry. Hoover drew 210,000 primary votes against Johnson's 370,000. This was substantially better than his supporters had hoped.

At the Republican convention, Hoover was put in nomination; but the nomination, of course, went to Senator Warren G. Harding. During the campaign Hoover delivered, in his own words, two "poorish speeches," which Will Hays, the National Chairman, thought "too objective." Evidently partisan passions were not in Hoover's nature.

After the election, Harding offered Hoover a choice between the Interior and Commerce Departments. Because he considered reconstruction and national development the most important immediate tasks, Hoover indicated his preference for Secretary of Commerce, though the Department of Interior was considered more important. Behind the scenes, the designation of Hoover for any Cabinet position was being fought by the more conservative party leaders. However, since they wanted Andrew Mellon as Secretary of the Treasury, Harding had a weapon ready. He told them in effect: "Mellon and Hoover or no Mellon."

While the politicians were haggling over his appointment, Hoover was confronted with another temptation, perhaps the strongest in his life, to return to private business and immense wealth. In January 1921, Daniel Guggenheim went to see him. The Guggenheim brothers owned the greatest mining and metallurgical company in the world, one of the most fabulous empires of wealth in America's history.

The brothers, Daniel explained, were getting old, and their sons were not interested in taking over. They needed someone to carry on—and had decided that Hoover was the man. Their offer was without precedent in the annals of business: a full partnership and a guaranteed *minimum* income of $500,000 a year, this in a period of relatively mild income taxes.

Hoover asked for a week to think it over. As on that critical occasion in London in 1914, he and Mrs. Hoover weighed the alternatives—the selfsame alternatives, great fortune or public service. Not even their closest friends, let alone the public, realized the nature of the sacrifice he was making when he announced his readiness to serve as Secretary of Commerce. In his forty-seventh year, Hoover gave up a slice of the Guggenheim empire and half a million dollars a year for life for the uncertainties and headaches of a political office paying fifteen thousand dollars a year.

The plans for economic reconstruction Hoover was already drafting were so far-reaching that they would unavoidably impinge on the spheres of agriculture, labor, finance, even foreign affairs. He wanted the President-elect and prospective Cabinet members to know this in advance, to preclude subsequent misunderstandings. Harding and his appointees went along with these conditions and Hoover accepted the post of Secretary of Commerce.

3

To fill out the picture of Hoover's career as humanitarian, we must deal here with the relief of famine in Russia, 1921–23, though it does some violence to chronology.

For some three hundred Americans who took part in the operation inside Red Russia it was to remain the crucial experience of their lives; because of the exceptional number of writers among them, several books and scores of articles have been published on the subject. Here is the story in the most summary fashion.

In 1921 a great drought in the Ukraine and the Volga valley, the breadbaskets of Russia, caused terrible famine. The economic barbarism of the regime had stripped the peasants of their normal food and seed reserves. Civil war had wrecked transport and dislocated distribution. Everything thus conspired to multiply the horrors of the catastrophe.

That July the celebrated Russian novelist, Maxim Gorki, appealed to the American people for aid. Hoover responded at once. The ARA was eager to help, he said, but must make a number of reasonable conditions, such as the release of Americans held in Soviet prisons, full freedom of travel for relief workers, complete control of distribution by the ARA, equal treatment for all Russians regardless of "class origins" and political views in apportioning help. At the same time he pledged that the undertaking would be rigidly non-political at the American end.

On August 20 an agreement was signed in Riga by Maxim Litvinov for the Soviets and Walter Lyman Brown for the Hoover organization. The first American meals were being served in Kazan, in the heart of the famine zone, one month later.

Hoover had dispatched Colonel William A. Haskell, the man who headed up relief in Armenia immediately after the war, to examine the Russian famine situation. "Death was only a few months away for millions of people," Haskell reported, and the worst epidemic of infectious diseases in modern history was gaining ground.

Following the Riga agreement, Hoover sent two other veterans of his rescue missions, Dr. Vernon Kellogg and former Governor James P. Goodrich of Indiana, into the dying areas. Their findings were soul-rending. The death tolls were rapidly mounting. In the hospitals, clinics, children's homes, tens of thousands were in indescribable agony, totally without food and medicines. The earth had been picked clean of the last tailings of the 1920 harvest, the trees were being stripped clean of their bark. All dogs and cats had already been eaten and everywhere there were reports, and some evidence, of cannibalism. Diseased human corpses had to be guarded against hungry mobs.

The ARA made the distressing information public. Its appeals had to overcome the general American abhorrence of the Lenin-Trotsky regime of terror. With the support of Charles Evans Hughes and others in the new Administration, Hoover convinced President Harding that humane considerations must have the right of way over political objections.

Although the Russian tragedy coincided with hard times at home, the American people responded generously. There was little hope, in view of deep anti-Soviet sentiment, that the government would contribute. But Hoover did induce Congress to divert to famine relief the eighteen million dollars in profits still in the Grain Corporation account. From the War Department and the Red Cross he obtained millions of dollars' worth of medical supplies and equipment. Various American religious and ethnic charitable organizations pitched in with funds and personnel. With the Kremlin's consent, grudgingly given, about eleven million dollars from the Russian gold reserves abroad was added. The rest, in a total of nearly ninety million dollars expended in a little over two years, came from private contributions.

James Rosenberg, lawyer and philanthropist, many years later described to me a scene which constitutes a sufficient answer to subsequent Communist slurs on Hoover's motives in undertaking the gigantic relief enterprise: In August 1921, at the request of Secretary of Commerce Hoover, representatives of many social work agencies met in Washington to plan cooperation on the Russian appeal. Rosenberg was there for the Joint Distribution Committee. At one point in the proceedings a woman raised doubts about the wisdom of the whole business.

"Mr. Secretary," she said, "aren't we going to help Bolshevism by feeding these people?"

Hoover's renowned calm broke down. He sprang to his feet and banged the table angrily. "Twenty million people are starving," he exclaimed. "Whatever their politics, they shall be fed!"

The problem for him was not whether the Russians should be aided but how to do it most swiftly and effectively. Command in the field was assumed by Colonel Haskell, with hundreds of American volunteers to help him. Thousands of Russians, too, volunteered to work under the ARA banner, with only their rations as compensation. Many of these Russians were to be rounded up, imprisoned, or exiled on trumped-up political charges after the relief job was completed.

At the peak of the famine the Hoover organization was feeding eighteen million people. Great numbers of peasants had fled the parched provinces in the forlorn hope of finding food in the cities. They were drawn back by Hoover's insistence that the starving be fed only in their own villages and towns. His purpose was to assure the planting of a new crop with ARA seed when the drought was over.

On July 10, 1922, when the relief work was in full operation, Maxim Gorki wrote to an American woman in Berlin, evidently in response to some inquiry. The name of the woman and the circumstances of the exchange are not available, but the original of the three-page letter is in the possession of an American journalist, Isaac Don Levine.

The novelist told the woman that "the famine is greater and more ominous than all that is being said and written about it." He urged that there be no relaxation by people of good will. Of the American mission he wrote:

I think that the work of the Hoover organization is, by its scope, an unprecedented phenomenon in history. Never before has any one country come to the relief of another with such generosity and such munificence of resources and means. Hoover's agents are really people of courage. I do not exaggerate if I will call them heroes. America has a right to be proud of her children who are so splendidly and fearlessly toiling on the vast fields of death, in an environment of epidemics, barbarization and cannibalism.

But while Russia's great novelist and close friend of Lenin was extolling the American spirit, the Soviet dictatorship was deliberately making life difficult for its foreign benefactors. Almost from the start Colonel Haskell had cause to complain of "lack of cooperation" by the authorities, broken promises and interference by Secret Police agents swarming around the ARA. Again and again Hoover was forced to threaten to end relief—a threat that always brought Moscow to its senses for a while. ARA men rode relief trains to prevent plunder en route.

The climax came in the spring of 1922, when the Soviet Government began to seize whole trainloads of provisions. The depredations stopped only after Hoover showed, both by words and deeds, that he really meant to call off the whole undertaking.

With the harvest of 1922, the worst of the famine was over, but the care of about three million children and a million adults continued into the winter of 1923. Once more Hoover had to rally the American people to give their dollars. In a speech at this time he reproved those who allowed their anti-Soviet feelings, which he fully shared, to cancel out their humane instincts. "I would rather have implanted the love of the American flag in the hearts of millions," he said, "than to have added to the American Navy all the battleships that the Atlantic could float."

The full-blown Communist charges that the Hoover relief had been a cover for political activity are of much later vintage. But even while the ARA work was under way, American Communists, fellow travelers, and their retinue of befuddled innocents staged a dress rehearsal of that outrage to come. They undertook some fund-raising for famine relief in competition with the ARA and, because Hoover would not endorse their organization, proceeded to smear him heavily.

The main Leftist relief committee was headed by one Walter W. Liggett, with an impressive list of respectable supporters as façade—one of the earliest "front" organizations. The moneys collected were funneled into the Friends of Soviet Russia, an undisguised pro-Communist outfit. Many years later a Congressional committee established that these groups had operated with Kremlin approval, and that mighty little of the funds collected, over a million dollars, ever reached the starving Russians. Most of the evidence was provided by defectors from Communism, among them Dr. David Dubrowski, the very man who was sent over by Moscow to organize the Communist fund-raising.

From 1928 to 1934 I resided in Soviet Russia as United Press correspondent. By that time Hoover had become a standard target of Communist vilification the world over. But I can testify that his name was still remembered and venerated among the Russians, including some Russians who were obliged to attack him publicly. I met dozens of people who said they owed their lives to the Hoover relief, hundreds who were anxious for Americans to know that the "real Russia" was neither forgetful nor ungrateful.

During World War II, Americans were frequently told by Soviet officers and soldiers with whom they came in contact that, as children, they had been saved from death by the ARA.

When the relief was wound up, the Soviet press began to pay off in the coin that has made Communist sportsmanship notorious. Hoover, the papers said graciously, had provided food only in order to undermine the Soviet regime—in the hope of getting back "his mines in the Urals." Hoover, of course, never owned any such mines, having served as consultant on a fee basis. But mere truth did not deter American comrades and others from repeating the lie.

Officially, however, the Soviet Government did present Hoover with an illuminated scroll expressing extravagant appreciation. Dated July 10, 1923, signed by Leo Kamenev as acting President and by other top commissars, it said in part:

In the name of the millions of people who have been saved, as well as in the name of the whole working class of Soviet Russia and of the Confederated Republics, and before the whole world, to this organization and to its leader, Mr. Herbert Hoover . . . and to all the workers of the organization, to express the most deeply felt sentiments of gratitude, and to state that all the people inhabiting the Union of Socialist Soviet Republics never will forget the aid rendered to them by the American people, through the agency of the American Relief Administration, holding it to be a pledge of the future friendship of the two nations.

Maxim Gorki was even more ardent in his thanks, in a letter to Hoover:

In all the history of human suffering [I know of] no accomplishment which in terms of magnitude and generosity can be compared to the relief that you have actually accomplished. . . . Your help will be inscribed in history as a unique, gigantic accomplishment worthy of the greatest glory and will long remain in the memory of millions of Russians . . . whom you saved from death.

Kamenev and most of the other commissars under Lenin who signed the scroll were eventually murdered by Stalin. Their expressions of gratitude and their pledge of friendship have been blotted out in the official Soviet histories. Even Nikita Khrushchev, though he had denounced Stalin as a mass killer and a madman, found occasion—while in the United States as an honored guest of the American Government!—to disparage the relief episode.

The transformation of Hoover from an officially recognized savior of Russian lives into an official villain provides an extraordinary case history of Kremlin duplicity. The *Great Soviet Encyclopaedia,* in 1926, still recorded the life-saving episode but lied about its dimensions. Only ten million had been fed, it wrote, at a cost of one and a half million dollars; actually some eighteen million had been fed, at a cost of nearly ninety million dollars.

By 1950, in a new edition of the *Encyclopaedia,* there was no mention of lives saved but only an accusation that the ARA had helped "saboteurs to blow up Soviet industry." Two years later Senator William Benton of Connecticut, translating from the most recent edition, could write that "the article converts Herbert Hoover into the murderer of millions of Russians, instead of the savior of millions from starvation, as reported a generation earlier."

But that wasn't the end of it. In 1958 the Kremlin completed the job of historical mayhem. Hoover had been invited by Belgium to the World's Fair in Brussels, where he made a speech defending liberty and humanism. The Moscow press thereupon devoted four columns to smearing Hoover and his "notorious" ARA, which "shamelessly covered its aid to all and sundry enemies of Soviet rule with its alleged concern for the hungry."

When shown this piece of fiction, Hoover said: "I can at least take satisfaction that liquidation by propaganda is not as fatal as that by machine gun in a muffled cellar."

XIII

An Old-style Liberal

O N March 4, 1921, the Senate confirmed Hoover's nomination as Secretary of Commerce. He was plunging into another of his many lives. This offers a convenient point in time to examine his basic social philosophy. At bottom he was a man of action, a pragmatist, who rejected the tyranny of congealed ideas. Our economic system, he always emphasized, "is not a frozen organism" but a living, changing way of life. Yet he was to adhere to a consistent philosophy, in essence, through all the years.

He had lived and worked in areas of our planet where variants of old and new social systems were on view. Each of these he had studied, not in an academic vacuum but in relation to the others and to his American background. In Europe he had found himself at the center of what he called "a gigantic laboratory of fierce ideas and changes." Invariably he related these to his native heritage. During his entire European experience he "had been trying to formulate some orderly definition of our own American system." Feeling that he had come close to such a definition, he was impelled to share it with his countrymen.

This was the design of his many addresses and magazine articles, and of his many practical proposals. His views had "jelled." With the same gift that had made him so successful in mining, he was separating the gold from the dross, the lofty verbal trimmings from the basic American realities. Hoover was knowingly engaged in setting forth his assessment of American civilization, its strengths and its weaknesses, its potentials for constructive advance and its vulnerabilities to destructive forces agitating the world.

As he saw it, the American system was good and viable, despite its many lacks. To tamper with its basic mechanisms would be to kill the goose that laid the golden eggs of American greatness. But he did not consider it immune to the "infections from European ideologies." "We had a large sprinkling of intellectuals who, stimulated by the fumes from the cauldrons of Europe," he would write later, "were promulgating the idea that there was merit in a mixture of these new systems."

The survival of the American way of life, Hoover said in many of his speeches, called not only for the negation of patent medicines but for positive and resolute corrections of "marginal faults." These included "the twelve-hour day in a few industries; an unequal voice in bargaining for wages in some employment; arrogant domination by some employers and some labor leaders; some fortunes excessive far beyond the needs of stimulation to initiative; survival of religious intolerance."

Insistently he pointed out that our children's health and welfare were neglected in large backward areas; that labor's rights to legitimate union organization were being unfairly obstructed. He called for higher inheritance taxes to unfreeze "inactive capital" and deflate the power of big fortunes. He proposed rigid controls over banking and stock promotions—a particularly unpopular notion destined to be denounced as almost "un-American."

At the end of 1919 President Wilson called together an impressive conference of industrialists, labor men, and public representatives, to seek remedies for the growing labor troubles. William B. Wilson, Secretary of Labor, was chairman but Herbert Hoover, as vice-chairman, presided over and guided the deliberations during three months of almost continuous sessions. The final report, of which Hoover was rightly regarded as the chief architect, was hailed by progressives and assailed by standpatters.

For the first time, an independent body of experts urged collective bargaining by agents of labor's choosing. The report supported the right to strike and proposed plans for amicable adjustment of disputes. It asked for the end of child labor, advocated reduction of hours of labor. Another "first," it recommended development of plans for national old-age insurance.

When Hoover accepted an invitation to address the Boston Chamber of Commerce, he chose to defend this controversial report. As he expected, the applause when he finished "would not have waked a nervous baby." Few then would have called him a conservative, no one in his senses would have called him a reactionary. In 1920, as one historian recently pointed out, Hoover was "the darling of the progressives who still clustered about the figure of the fallen Wilson." Though he avoided the progressive label, Hoover probably did not consider it entirely unjust.

His concern for children, well known by that time, found voice in his speeches before the Associated Charities of San Francisco and, a year later, the Child Hygiene Association. More general compulsory education, systematic health inspection in schools, hot lunches in schools in certain areas, and of course the elimination of child labor were among the suggestions in his program. Ultimately he succeeded in creating the American Child Health Association, with adequate private funds and staff, and remained its guiding spirit for a great many years.

Such concrete proposals indicate the direction of Hoover's thinking and interests. In this context we must recall again, also, his investigation, through the engineering society, of waste in industry. Improved conditions for the masses, as he saw it, must come from greater and more efficient production; in his own words, "We must push machines and not men and provide every safeguard of health and proper leisure."

Words were not Hoover's most effective tools. As a literary stylist he will certainly not be bracketed with Jefferson, Lincoln, or Wilson—to mention Presidents who, as Hoover, did their own writing. Yet he proved himself effective when, in his middle forties, he was ready to present the ripened fruit of his years of pondering. He was not elegant or scintillating; too often he relied on phrases worn thin from much usage. But he achieved his aim, which was not sensation but lucidity.

In 1921 he distilled much of his thinking on the country, present and future, in a long essay published in book form in 1922 under the title of *American Individualism*. It might with equal pertinence have been called American Liberalism, for that is what it came down to. In his writings, as a matter of fact, he sometimes used the terms interchangeably.

Already Bolshevik and other collectivist dogmas were eroding the concept of liberalism. In time they were to make "liberal" almost a synonym for its antipodes—state regulation, totalitarianism, the melting of the person into some abstraction of collective, society, or class. Men and women robed in self-righteousness would before long purloin the vocabulary of liberalism and progress for their most illiberal and retrogressive beliefs, in the most remarkable semantic conquest of all time. That social mongrel, the "totalitarian liberal," would take command at the Left and would push genuine liberals into the Right, where many of them felt that they did not belong.

But in the 1920s that semantic expropriation was still in an early stage. The vulgarization of liberalism which was to be its death sentence had not yet gone so far that an instinctive liberal like Hoover needed to apologize or to dissociate himself from the imposters. The kind of "progressive" who whooped it up for concentration camps, slave labor, and one-party regimes was yet to emerge in his full panoply of unreason.

The more reactionary Republicans and the manipulators of "invisible government" who feared Hoover and fought him—who tried to keep him out of Harding's Cabinet—were quite justified. They sensed the implications of his assertion that "No civilization could be built or endure solely upon the groundwork of unrestrained and unintelligent self-interest."

2

A personal philosophy is significant largely in the measure that it is impersonal and universal. Hoover's "orderly definition," first presented at this time and fortified in later years, is meaningful because it is close to the core of traditional American insights. It did not once occur to him to claim originality. He sought merely to give conscious shape to the nation's historical memories, preferences, and urges. He was not so much expounding his own creed as affirming what he considered the quintessential American creed.

In the title of his book, *American Individualism,* the first word had for him equal weight with the second. "Our individualism," he said, "is in our very nature. It is based on conviction born of experience." The individualism he championed was not a party program or an academic concept, but the pragmatic principle of American life as a whole. It was not, that is to say, a dogmatic belief to be held inviolate—in the way that orthodox socialists, for example, hold to "economic determinism" and Leninists to "dialectic materialism."

American individualism, as Hoover described and defended it, was not a law handed down from some sociological Mt. Sinai. It was simply a system that had worked—worked so well in its American version that the American people were incomparably better off, healthier, better educated, and freer than any other people in recorded history. Because it was a living fact, not a fixed dogma, its economic, political, and ethical contents were intimately interwoven, and each inseparable from the others. To revolutionize one of these elements—the economic system, let us say—without revolutionizing the others in about the same measure was therefore impossible. It is well to understand this thesis in appraising Hoover as President and after his retirement from the White House.

He claimed for this individualism no miraculous powers which, applied anywhere, would evoke an American style of life. He saw it rather as a peculiarly American flowering. Nor did he claim for it the arrogance of perfection. On the contrary, the will to cure shortcomings and injustices without destroying the whole system was a vital part of the genius of individualism.

It was a system, moreover, that had its own "dialectic," as Marxists would put it. It contained seeming opposites in a balanced whole. In it the supremacy of the individual was combined with a passionate concern for the well-being of the community. "We have learned," Hoover wrote,

153

"that social injustice is the destruction of justice itself." American individualism saw the successful society as the by-product of free and wholesome individuals. It regarded as degenerate the society, however great its material achievements, in which personal values are discounted or wholly proscribed. "Progress of the nation is the sum of progress of its individuals," he wrote. And at another time: "The primary duty of organized society is to enlarge the lives and increase the standards of all the people." Which is to say that organized society is not an end in itself. It has no prerogatives to which individual men and women must knuckle under—except, of course, the rights needed to protect the individual.

In the spectrum of social ideas this view—which is old-fashioned American liberalism unalloyed—is at the remotest remove from totalitarianism in any of its guises. It accepts the human being, not state or race or class, as the unit of social bookkeeping. Virtue, it assumes, resides in the person and not in any impersonal entity like society. Its final tests of the good, the true, the beautiful are in the effects on individual men, women, and children.

Hoover did not allow himself to be trapped by any of the free-enterprise absolutes. For every attack on socialism, there was in his writing and thinking a corresponding attack on selfishness. His experience as a self-made leader was tempered by his Quaker certainty that man is his brother's keeper.

"Private property is not a fetish in America," he wrote in the book, citing the cancellation of the liquor trade without a cent of compensation as one proof that property rights are not dominant. Then he added: "Our development of individualism shows an increasing tendency to regard right of property not as an object in itself, but in the light of a useful instrument in stimulating the initiative of the individual." Where control of property and control of government fall into the same hands, individualism must react to prevent this monopoly of power.

Hoover would have none of the wasteful equality that averages human endowments; it was for him at the opposite pole from the equality which provides unlimited room for each person to develop to the utmost the best that is in him. He argued, therefore, for diversity as against uniformity, for individual creativeness as against adherence to prescribed patterns:

Amid the scene of growing complexity of our economic life, we must preserve the independence of the individual from the restraints of government, yet by the strong arm of government equally protect his individual freedom, assure his fair chance, his equality of opportunity from the encroachments of special privileges and greed for domination by any group or class.

The concept of *laissez-faire* capitalism, he believed, had been canceled out in the United States decades earlier, when we passed the Sherman

Anti-Trust and the Interstate Commerce Commission laws. Free economy by his definition implied opposition to monopoly, whether in the mild forms of business oligarchies or its virulent extremes of government regimentation. For Hoover, capitalism carried to its utmost logic in one direction would be anarchy; in the other direction, fascism. He noted "two schools of thought: one that all human ills can be cured by government, and the other that all regulation is a sin." And he rejected both schools.

Hoover's individualism had nothing in common with dog-eat-dog, survival-of-the-fittest behavior and rationale. It is not an ideological cover for exploitation of the weak by the strong, but implies at every point a moral obligation toward the weak. Its true concepts are not in Adam Smith or Darwin, but in the Hebrew prophets from Moses to Jesus who prescribed love of one's neighbor as the first law for man. "Our individualism insists upon the divine in each human being," Hoover wrote.

In the very first pages of *American Individualism* he declared:

Individualism cannot be maintained as the foundation of a society if it looks only to legalistic justice based upon contracts, property, and political equality. Such legalistic safeguards are themselves not enough. In our individualism we have long since abandoned the *laissez-faire* of the Eighteenth Century—the notion that it is "every man for himself and the devil take the hindmost."

We abandoned that when we adopted the ideal of equality of opportunity— the fair chance of Abraham Lincoln. We have confirmed its abandonment in terms of legislation, of social and economic justice—in part because we have learned that it is the hindmost that throws the bricks at our social edifice, in part because we have learned that the foremost are not always the best nor the hindmost the worst—and in part because we have learned that social injustice is the destruction of justice itself.

We have learned that the impulse to production can only be maintained if there is a fair division of the product. We have also learned that fair division can only be obtained by certain restrictions on the strong and the dominant. We have indeed gone even further in the Twentieth Century with the embracement of the necessity of a greater and broader sense of service and responsibility to others as a part of individualism.

He insisted that "the most potent force in society is its ideals." America "has become not merely a physical union of States, but rather is a spiritual union in common ideals of our people. . . . Out of such variety comes growth, but only as we preserve and maintain our spiritual solidarity."

He was at all times aware of the risks:

No doubt individualism run riot, with no tempering principle, would provide a long category of inequalities, of tyrannies, dominations and injustices. America, however, has tempered the whole conception of individualism by the injection of a definite principle, and from this principle it follows that attempts at domination, whether in government or in the processes of industry and commerce are under an insistent curb.

The principle to which he referred was "an equality of opportunity" backed by "that sense of service that lies in our people." Nations which have learned from America, he believed, have gained in temporal and spiritual vigor. The symbol of that experience has been the pioneer, sensitive to "the challenge of opportunity, to the challenge of nature, to the challenge of life, to the call of the frontier." And these challenges, as he saw it, could never be exhausted: "There are continents of human welfare of which we have penetrated only the coastal plain. The great continent of science is as yet explored only on its borders."

The individualism of the Old World, to Hoover, was far removed from the American brand, because it had been superimposed on the remnants of feudalism, on class stratifications. America was, for him, not an extension of European culture but a fateful break with that culture. For himself, he testified:

My faith in the essential truth, strength, and vitality of the developing creed by which we have lived in this country of ours has been confirmed and deepened by the searching experiences of seven years of service in the backwash and misery of war. . . . And from it all I emerge an individualist—an unashamed individualist. But let me say also that I am an American individualist.

3

"In every society," Hoover wrote at this time, "there will always be at the bottom a noxious sediment and at the top an obnoxious froth." He did not agree with those who in anger or impatience demanded that the entire society be jettisoned because of those unpleasant excrescences. For this he was denounced as a radical at one extreme and a reactionary at the other. In truth he was an earnest reformer—though not the kind who is willing to kill the patient for the sake of a beautiful operation. In the sense that Hoover wished to safeguard the central values of the American society, he was ever the conservative; sometimes especially so when he seemed most radical to reactionary critics and most reactionary to radical critics.

His lifelong emphasis on child welfare—his automatic acceptance of the child as the test of a community's health—had in it the primordial logic of the farmer's concern with the new crop. It was in the pattern of his life that one of his first public addresses after returning from Europe was on this theme:

If we could systematically grapple with the whole child problem in the United States, if we could insist on the proper conditions of birth, upon proper safeguarding of their general health, on proper education, we could then say with confidence that . . . in twenty years . . . public health, efficiency, sanity, morals, and stability of the whole population would be advanced beyond anything that any nation has yet aspired to.

His subsequent pleas for a Constitutional Amendment to outlaw child labor were consistent with this earlier sentiment.

From the first, as we have indicated, Hoover supported a sensible, socially responsible labor unionism. Writing in the *Saturday Evening Post* (December 27, 1919), he said:

The organization of workers to better the conditions of labor is undoubtedly a safeguard of equality of opportunity and in accord with basic principles. The essence of combination of workers is collective bargaining and the recognition of the right to combine cannot be separated from the right to bargain collectively.

Every combination, he added by way of caution, "can be used for domination of the community," whether it be labor or farmers or capitalists. In July 1920 he wrote:

No one doubts that the modern consolidation of the employers over large units of employees gives every justification and right for the organization of the employees similarly into units for the exertion of equality in bargaining powers.

He was, of course, too optimistic in supposing that "no one doubts" this view. There were plenty of doubters and they bore no great love for Hoover in this connection. It is worth recalling in this context that in 1922, as a Cabinet member, Hoover firmly protested federal injunctions against railwaymen on strike; and that as President he signed the bill which outlawed "yellow-dog" contracts in the face of loud protests by industrialists.

His thoughts on taxation as an instrument of individualism he embodied in a 1921 memorandum to the President which said in part:

If we are to lessen the stifling of initiative we should make lower schedules applicable to individual incomes from wages, salaries, professions, and business transactions, than to those from dividends and interest and rents. That the government takes up to 50 percent of the profits from professional earnings or business transactions, while the individual takes all the risks, is intensely discouraging to initiative. It is fundamentally wrong to charge at the same rate these two types of income, "earnings" and "property income," because a person who possesses "property income" has already the capital protection of his dependents while a part of "earned" income must be put aside for such a purpose.

157

I am not attempting to make a full inventory of Hoover's views, but only to suggest their temper and direction. Hoover demanded government regulation to curb runaway speculation and in particular rigid supervision of "blue-sky" promotions. Small wonder that the stand-pat schools of business and political leaders began to look at him through narrowed eyes, as a possible mischief-maker. Certainly Hoover, far from being the "mossback" of the future propaganda version, was in the front ranks of American liberalism. Where his path diverged more and more from those of the "official" liberals who in time obtained a monopoly of the designation was in his abhorrence of excessive government, distrust of bureaucratic agencies, insistence on decentralizing political authority. Yet he acknowledged the widening role of government in the economy.

To curb monopolistic and autocratic trends in business "and yet maintain the initiative and creative faculties of our people"—this was the problem for Hoover. Neither of the purposes, he declared, was served by an approach to socialism, however it might be camouflaged. Nationalization of business or commerce is itself the ultimate monopoly, and the most dangerous because it puts economic and political power in the same set of hands. The difference between trusts running the government and government running the trusts is more seeming than real. Perhaps he put his awareness of the risks of state regimentation into one meaningful sentence when he said in 1929 that "every time the government is forced to act, we lose something in self-reliance, character and initiative."

Hoover despised the "strong men," the ruthless ones so fashionable between the two world wars—whether economic oligarchs or political oligarchs. Strength without compassion ever seemed to him a species of savagery. To the new-styled "liberals" who took small account of the individual and his freedoms, men like Hoover no doubt seemed leftovers from a bygone epoch. To the monstrous Darwinists of "social engineering" which treats people as the raw stuff for experiments, men like Hoover were scarcely comprehensible. They dismissed them sneeringly as "old-fashioned," Rotarian, reactionary, and worse.

Neither the piecemeal presentation of Hoover's definition of the American system in speeches nor its organized presentation in print created much stir. None of it was strange to American ears. It seemed to most Americans, in the early 1920s, simply a summation of widely held and quite respectable liberal ideas—sufficiently "left of center" in their day to annoy extremes, but not enough to shock anyone. They had been so much a part of the mental climate in America that few had felt it necessary to articulate them in such plain and succinct fashion.

XIV

Consulting Engineer to the Nation

THOUGH they held their quota of griefs and disappointments, his nearly eight years as Secretary of Commerce were among the happiest and most creative in Herbert Hoover's life.

The long separations from his wife represented great trials. Now she could be with him. She bought a comfortable old brick house at 2300 S Street. With the talent for homemaking which her husband inordinately admired, she brought order and beauty into the acre of neglected garden, making it the chief attraction of the home, and she had an ample rear porch built for out-of-doors dining and entertaining.

More important, it was a home overflowing with affection and friendship, constantly filled with associates and friends so dear that they were part of the family. In Washington, moreover, the solace of a Quaker Meetinghouse that they had missed in their constant travels was again open to them. Soon after settling down in Washington, Mrs. Hoover accepted the national presidency of the Girl Scouts, an organization to which she devoted a great deal of her time for the next two decades.

Herbert, Jr., at eighteen, entered Stanford University in 1921. During vacations he managed to find jobs at manual labor, usually in or near mining operations. His brother Allan enrolled in Stanford in 1925. Both boys had attended public high schools, which their parents preferred to private schools. They were healthy, stalwart lads, with the normal assortment of pets, when living at home, and hobbies wherever they lived.

As always, vital work was Hoover's main and often his only "recreation." His secretarial staff became inured to working two or more nights a week at his home. He labored prodigiously and had the satisfaction of seeing concrete achievements, spread through the length and breadth of the country he loved.

One of Hoover's predecessors as Secretary of Commerce, Oscar Straus,

assured him that a couple of hours a day would be all that the post entailed. Few men had ever given it more. The accepted idea about its
scope was the jest that the Commerce Secretary was expected only "to
put the fish to bed at night and turn out the lights around the coast."

This was not Hoover's idea of any job. The Enabling Act establishing
the Department had not skimped on territory: "To foster, promote and
develop the foreign and domestic commerce, the mining, manufacturing,
shipping and fishing industries, and the transportation facilities of the
United States."

The new Secretary meant to explore the whole of that immense province and, as we noted, obtained Harding's support for his ambitious intentions before assuming the post. At his suggestion, in 1925, the Bureau
of Mines and the Patent Office were transferred from the Interior Department to Commerce, where they seemed to him to belong. For every major
industry he formed a specialized commodity division, each manned by
experts drawn from the staffs of its trade association and trade journals.
Later, Housing, Aeronautics, and Radio divisions were added. Hoover
made his Secretaryship a full-time office, and full time in the Hoover
dictionary was a literal phrase.

Within a year or two after he took over, Commerce ranked with State
as the most influential executive departments. Somnolent bureaus were
awakened to dynamic activity; routine functions suddenly blossomed into
service stations and repair shops for the nation's entire economy. Even
"putting the fish to bed" ceased to be a joke, now that the nursemaid
began replenishing rivers, fighting pollution, protecting Alaskan salmon,
and serving as patron of all amateur fishermen as president of the Izaak
Walton League.

The manpower assigned to the Department was hardly sufficient for
its new enterprises, and Congress was slow in authorizing additions. Hoover hired two secretaries and three assistants at his own expense, at a cost
far exceeding his salary. These personal employees included young Christian Herter, who one day would serve as Secretary of State under President Eisenhower, and others who would play notable roles in a national
life—a commentary on Hoover's instinct for able men.

The spirit in which he tackled his new opportunities was well described
by his friend Mark Sullivan, the journalist-historian:

One may say that Hoover has regarded our entire business structure as a
single factory, conceiving himself, as it were, consulting engineer for the whole
enterprise. Having this conception, Hoover set about applying to the whole
business structure of the United States principles similar to those which Henry
Ford applied to the manufacture of automobiles.

Shallow comment on this massive effort judged it merely in relation to
Hoover's genius for efficiency. Hostile comment related it merely to prof-

its. Both failed to comprehend that for Hoover efficiency was a tool, not a goal. The goal was set by his social conscience, his concept of the good life for America.

His eight-year offensive against waste rested on a revolutionary idea: the enrichment of existence for the whole population through maximum use of modern productive potentials. In the voluminous record of that offensive there is scarcely a trace of the profit urge per se. Its whole purport is to provide more of the necessaries and luxuries of life for more people. The riches siphoned off by material and human waste, it insisted, spelled the difference between comfort and penury for tens of millions. In 1919, before he was in the government, he outlined the underlying idea in a magazine article thus:

The standard of living is the quotient of the amount of commodities and services that are available among the total population. Therefore the standard cannot be maintained or improved unless there is a maintenance and increase in the production of commodities and services up to the maximum need of the entire number. There is no equality of opportunity to the consumer with deficient production.

The ancient dream of an economy of abundance, asserted not as a rhetorical hope but as a practical plan, was Hoover's theme in accepting the presidency of the American Engineering Council in November 1920. That was when he mobilized seventeen top engineers and set them to find the "leaks" of wastage. They worked without remuneration. In a foreword to their report four months later Hoover wrote:

We have probably the highest ingenuity and efficiency in the operation of our industries of any nation. Yet our industrial machine is far from perfect. The wastage of unemployment during depressions; from speculation and overproduction in booms; from labor turnover; from labor conflicts; from intermittent failure of transportation of supplies of fuel and power; from lack of standardization; from loss in our processes and materials—all combine to represent a huge deduction from the goods and services that we might all enjoy if we made a better job of it.

To correct this situation was the program he sought to work out beginning on March 4, 1921. The warning at this early stage against "speculation and overproduction in booms" was made in a time of relative depression. He would reiterate it constantly in the boom years that followed.

In launching a Committee for the Study of Business Cycles, in September 1921, he declared:

Booms are times of speculation, overexpansion, wasteful expenditures in industry and commerce, with consequent destruction of capital. . . . It is the wastes, miscalculations and maladjustments, grown rampant during the booms, that make unavoidable the painful process of liquidation. The obvious way to lessen the losses and miseries of depressions is first to check the destructive extremes of booms.

No more than his listeners could he suspect that when the prophecy came true, its miseries would be blamed on the prophet.

Hoover's was a program aiming at the abolition of poverty through the fertility of modern science and technology. And he applied it not by compulsion of law but on the principle of voluntary cooperation which had served him well in the past. His primary method was to convene representatives of some segment of the economy, large or small, direct their attention to their own problems, then guide them in the search for solutions. More than three thousand such conferences were held in the eight years. Few of them failed to agree on some measures of standardization or simplification of processes that would cut waste and benefit all elements, from workers to owners.

At the end of his two terms, in accepting the Republican presidential nomination, he would say:

My conception of America is a land where men and women may walk in ordered freedom in the independent conduct of their occupations; where they may enjoy the advantages of wealth, not concentrated in the hands of a few but spread through the lives of all; where they build and safeguard their homes, and give to their children the fullest advantages and opportunities of American life; where every man shall be respected in the faith that his conscience and his heart direct him to follow; where a contented and happy people, secure in their liberties, free from poverty and fear, shall have the leisure and impulse to seek a fuller life.

There, except for those who chose willfully to misconstrue him, was the ideal symbolized picturesquely in the much-maligned formula of "two chickens in every pot and a car in every garage." Hoover, it happens, did not himself use those words. They were written by someone for a political advertisement during his presidential campaign. But he would not repudiate them, despite the mockery to which they were later subjected.

2

Unfortunately the most important facts do not always make the most interesting reading. At the risk of wearying the reader, we proceed to list some of the myriad objectives set, and in substantial measure achieved, by Hoover's crusade for conservation and expansion of national wealth as Secretary of Commerce:

Elimination of waste through improved equipment and methods in railroad transportation; better and fuller use of water resources for cheap transportation, flood control, reclamation, and power; enlarged electrification to save fuel and labor; reduction of seasonal fluctuations in employment in construction and other industries; reduction of waste in manufacture and distribution through more rational standardization of sizes, qualities, and processes; more uniform business documents and book-keeping methods; government aid in development of pure and applied science looking to labor-saving devices and practices; cooperative marketing and better terminal facilities to avoid waste in agricultural distribution; greater commercial arbitration to cut down the wastes of litigation; reduction of losses through preventable labor-management conflicts; a scientific approach to reducing industrial, traffic, and other accidents; preservation of competitive freedom and protection of the public interest in new fields like aviation and radio.

This inventory is far from complete. Each of the items was sufficient to occupy one man for a lifetime. Hoover undertook them all simultaneously and made some progress in all. He thought of them as facets of the same problem of achieving abundance. And despite the intervening tragedies of depression and war he remained convinced that it is a proper goal for the human race. In the physical sense, he remained convinced, grinding poverty is no longer inevitable. It is a leftover from a primitive past, perpetuated by inertia, greed, and human stupidity. With the advent of new sources of energy, with the marvels of the new chemistry, with modern facilities for exchanging the world's total products, the civilization based on abundance which was impossible in the past has been brought within the compass of possibility.

To trace Hoover's activities in each of the categories he tackled would require many volumes. The Department of Commerce, without benefit of new laws or powers, stimulated self-regulation for efficiency in literally scores of economic pursuits. Through thirty or forty "commodity divisions" it provided the data and guidance on which exports and imports flourished as never before.

It linked all the elements in the process—actual and would-be home-owners, craft unions, builders, architects, financiers, in a coordinated drive called "Better Homes in America." Meanwhile the Secretary undertook to solve a housing problem close to home, in Washington itself. He lined up the banking and building support for the construction of comfortable small apartments for federal employees, on a self-liquidating basis at lower than prevailing rentals. The scheme was wrecked, however, by real estate interests.

An amusing by-product of his Department's action in the unfolding radio industry involved the famous woman evangelist, Aimee Semple McPherson. The eloquent lady built a radio station in connection with her

Los Angeles tabernacle, but could see no reason why she should not use any wavelength and power volume she pleased. When the Department of Commerce intervened, she denounced it—and its Secretary in particular—for thwarting God's freedom of speech.

In the end Hoover sent a young radioman to manage the McPherson station to keep it from meandering from channel to channel. The radio troubles were cured, but the young man, alas, embroiled himself in an alleged love tangle with the evangelist that made sensational headlines for months.

In these years, as always, child welfare occupied a lot of Hoover's attention. He coordinated existing health and educational agencies for children and took the lead in most of the fund-raising efforts in those connections. The designation of May Day as "Child Health Day" grew out of his suggestion.

The Department explored water resources and started processes that ultimately gave the nation great hydroelectric stations, deepened waterways, and improved flood control. Hoover, in 1922, was the first high official to envision in detail and formally propose what in due time became the St. Lawrence Seaway. By 1924, he was chairman of a United States St. Lawrence Commission to negotiate with a corresponding Canadian commission. Negotiations were slow but his initiative eventually led to the great waterway now in operation.

Hoover personally administered a twenty-million-dollar fund for research in pure and applied science. He simplified and systematized standards and sizes in hundreds of fields as various as paving blocks and the care of child health. There were, indeed, few corners of the national economic landscape where he did not penetrate, and at all times by stimulating voluntary action in a spirit of mutual understanding.

The planning and stimulation of a whole nation's economy has been tried before and since—in our own time in fascist and Communist states —but only on the principle of unlimited coercion. Always they have failed because without freedom there can be no sufficient incentives. Always their substance was eaten away by the blights of bureaucratic profligacy and the dead weight of regimentation.

Hoover tried it, insofar as one man with limited authority in a limited time could do so, on the principle of free consent. He did not fail. The hundreds of gains he made have not all been dissipated. The techniques he pioneered remained as a permanent addition to the functioning of our economy. Principles of self-regulation and cooperation he was first to promote have been so widely accepted that few realize how new they are.

He met many and serious setbacks, of course. For instance, he failed to obtain the better control of banks and financing for which he pleaded. President Coolidge, content with the prosperity of the moment, repeatedly yielded to financial interests in blocking his Secretary of Commerce. The President "rejected or sidestepped all our anxious urgings and warnings to take action" on "the rising boom and orgy of speculation," Hoover would recall in after years. As for the professional speculators and economists drugged with optimism, they called Hoover a "spoilsport" and "crepehanger." They resented such a typical Hoover warning as this:

No sensible businessman wants either a boom or a slump. Our working folk should dread a trade boom above all things, because it means an aftermath of unemployment and misery. Our farmers should resent a boom, because they inevitably get the worst of the deflation which is bound to follow.

In 1925 Hoover's spirited objections were successful in blocking an expansion of credit by the Federal Reserve Board, under pressure from domestic and foreign sources. He stood up to the combined authority of Benjamin Strong of the Federal Reserve, Montagu Norman of the Bank of England, Charles Rist of the Bank of France, Hjalmar Schacht of the Reichsbank, and Bertil Ohlin of Sweden. In a letter to one of the Reserve governors, referring to policies then under consideration, he declared that the proposals meant "inflation with inevitable collapse which will bring the greatest calamities upon our farmers, our workers, and legitimate businessmen."

With paper fortunes being pyramided into super-fortunes on thin margins and Wall Street bucket-shops multiplying, the voice of common sense was drowned out. Two years later the "easy money" policies were put over despite Hoover. As he had clearly foreseen, the immense new credit inflation fed the speculative madness. Probably Montagu Norman, Schacht, and the others, sustaining speculative booms in their own country with vast American loans, would have succeeded in 1927 in any case. But their victory was made easier by the diversion of Hoover's total energies at the time to a gigantic life-saving task: the removal of 1,500,000 people from the path of great Mississippi floods.

Neither did Hoover get very far in his campaign against foreign and home-made cartels for price-fixing and apportioning markets. To him these devices were fascist in essence and a menace to the individualist economy he was defending. He did in some degree liberate the country from complete dependence on sources of rubber under cartel controls by encouraging rubber plantations in other areas, especially Latin America. And he did lay down policies which preserved the radio airwaves for the people—"this is just as important as to keep the channels of navigation open to ships," he said—and ruled out their monopolization.

One of the defeats he felt most keenly was in the realm of bureaucracy. He had initiated various studies of the operations of the government, exposing the kind of duplication of effort and outmoded methods which would not be tolerated in any rationally run private enterprise. Again and again he demanded action to cut waste in federal administration. But there were too many vested political interests in the status quo; he could get no action.

3

Depressions after periods of boom are no new phenomenon. Another arrived early in 1921, in the first year of the Harding administration. Never in the past had the federal government assumed any responsibility in such emergencies. A depression was something that "ran its course," like measles.

But Hoover, against the dominant opinion in his party and in the Cabinet, decided to "do something." By September unemployment had assumed serious proportions and the winter ahead promised to be hard and bitter. With Harding's approval, he therefore called a conference of some three hundred leaders of industry, agriculture, labor, banking, and finance. The time for passive waiting had passed, he told them in an opening address—in modern society the pain and suffering are too great to let nature take its cruel course:

There is no economic failure so terrible in its impact as that of a country possessing a surplus of every necessity of life in which numbers, willing and anxious to work, are deprived of these necessities. It simply cannot be if our economic and moral system is to survive.

Hoover believed that the groups represented at the meeting could meet the challenge within the framework of our free economy. "It is not consonant with the spirit of institutions of the American people that a demand should be made upon the public treasury for the solution of every difficulty." Instead he called for "the mobilization of cooperative action of our manufacturers and employers, of our public bodies and local authorities, and if solution could be found in these directions, we would have accomplished more than the care of our unemployed."

The self-help he asked for was forthcoming. The conference established branches in every state where unemployment was grave and the state branches created subcommittees in cities or counties. A special committee on unemployment, under Hoover's personal direction, was set up in his Department to coordinate and guide the effort. Federal, state, and municipal governments worked together to provide or speed up public construction. In many areas, at Hoover's urging, available jobs were shared to avoid layoffs.

At its peak this depression saw five million unemployed. Then the many measures undertaken under Hoover's direction, plus "the natural recuperative power of the country," eased the situation. By the spring of 1922 the depression was over. The nation had lived through the winter without real suffering.

Long before he entered the government, Hoover had spoken out vigorously against the ten- and twelve-hour day and the seven-day week which prevailed in the steel and some other industries. The subject was one of his main concerns when he became Secretary. Immediately he undertook an investigation which gave him ammunition in the form of clear and incontrovertible information. Then, on May 18, 1922, he got Harding to call Charles Schwab, Elbert Gary, and other top steel men to the White House.

The President let Hoover run the show. Its leaders squirmed as he spread the record of their industry. It was clear to him from their attitude that they would not move unless dynamited by public opinion. He had small faith in the committee under Gary, which they agreed to set up to "look into the problem." Hoover therefore deliberately broke the story to the press. The President, he told the American people, was attempting to persuade industry to adopt a reasonable working day. He had the engineering societies issue a report in support of the President—with an introduction signed by Harding which Hoover had written.

The Gary committee, obviously stalling for time, delayed its report until June 1923. Hoover expressed publicly his own and the Administration's impatience and disappointment, thus feeding fuel to the fires of popular resentment. The steel industry capitulated. When Hoover reached Tacoma to join Harding on July 3, he was just in time to write a few powerful paragraphs into the President's Independence Day address, announcing the voluntary abolition by industry of the twelve-hour day and the eighty-four-hour week.

The language was so different from the rest of the speech that Harding stumbled over the passage in reading. While the great assemblage wildly applauded the announcement, the President whispered to his neighbor on the platform, "Damn it, Hoover, why don't you write the same English as I do?"

We can only mention a few of the myriad episodes of Hoover's fight for justice to labor. Dismayed by a federal injunction against striking railway workers, he sought Secretary Hughes's support in the matter. Knowing that Attorney General Harry M. Daugherty was the chief culprit, they decided to tackle the issue at the very next Cabinet meeting, in Daugherty's presence. Hoover broached the subject, Hughes backed him up with a learned legal opinion—and Daugherty, on Harding's order, undertook to have the injunction vacated.

Among the strikes in which Hoover acted as mediator for the President was that of the railway shopmen. His chief difficulty was not with labor but with the railroad interests. Their committee of two hundred tried to repudiate terms agreed to in principle by its negotiator, Daniel Willard of the B & O, but Hoover was in no mood to permit this, and confronted the railroads' committee. He said later:

I certainly had a freezing reception. Paradoxically, my temperature rose somewhat and I delivered a modest preachment upon public relations which, to most of them, only branded me as a wild radical. Among other things I stated that such attitudes would sooner or later bring great disaster upon industry itself.

One durable result of these strike negotiations was the Railway Labor Mediation Board, an idea developed by Hoover and put into law by Congress.

4

Herbert Hoover had lived and worked for many years in tough mining towns, among hard-drinking, hard-playing men, without being one of them. In those lusty gambling and toping crowds the straitlaced young Quaker must have seemed incongruous. If he was not resented, and even inordinately admired, it was because he was the best miner of them all.

The same edge of incongruity attached to him when he found himself among the "Ohio gang" who had the run of the White House under Harding. After a sad experiment or two the President had sense enough no longer to invite Hoover (and for that matter Charles Evans Hughes, Andrew Mellon, Will Hays, Vice President Calvin Coolidge, and certain others) to his poker parties.

But the President and his Secretary of Commerce became close friends. The man from Ohio, being without illusions about his own limitations, liked to consult Hoover on all sorts of problems. He took pride in the well-stocked Hoover mind and Hoover's rigid moral principles. It was known to insiders that the President repeatedly went to bat for his Secretary against Senator Boies Penrose and other Republican bosses who feared Hoover's progressive innovations.

Harding, according to Hoover, was a dual personality: a man of noble instincts with a weakness for ignoble company. He "sincerely wanted to be a good President" but could not cut himself off from high-binding cronies. There was a juncture when Hoover was so distressed by some of Harding's associates and the whole poker aura that he discussed seriously with his wife the temptation to resign. The importance of the work he had in hand—and the President's cooperation in that work—swung the balance in favor of sticking it out.

In the spring of 1923 an official of the Veterans' Bureau, in the course of a Senate investigation of its activities, committed suicide. Then, shortly before President Harding went on his trip to Alaska—the trip which was to end in his sudden death on the return stage—one of his friends in the Department of Justice, Jesse Smith, took his own life. Though Harding enjoyed an amazing popular affection, ugly rumors were already in circulation.

On his summons, the Hoovers joined the President at Tacoma on July 3. As soon as they boarded the ship, they noted that the President was morose and distraught, his genuine gaiety of the past now a transparent mask for inner distress. He played bridge from breakfast to past midnight, as if it were a drug. Hoover and other guests organized a schedule of relays to keep Harding supplied with partners and yet escape the treadmill for a while. "I grew a distaste for bridge and never played it again," Hoover said.

A few days out, on the way to Alaska, after a gloomy luncheon, the President asked the Secretary of Commerce to come to his cabin. He had obviously mulled over what he intended to say, for he at once asked a startling but carefully formulated question:

"Hoover, if you knew of a great scandal in our Administration, would you for the good of the country and the party expose it publicly or would you bury it?"

Hoover replied without hesitation, and the answer no doubt was what the shrewd Harding expected. "Blow it out at once," he said. "The blowing will prove the integrity of the Administration."

Then he asked for particulars, and Harding seemed willing. He had heard some rumors of irregularities, he said, centering around cases in the Department of Justice involving Jesse Smith. He had sent for Smith one evening and informed him, as a matter of friendship, that he would be arrested the following morning. That night Smith burned a lot of papers at home and killed himself. Harding, however, gave Hoover no intimation of the nature of the irregularities. When asked whether Attorney General Daugherty was mixed up in the affair, the President "abruptly dried up" and the interview terminated.

Did Harding give anyone else on board that much of a glimpse of what was preying on his mind? Hoover could not know. Not until the Teapot Dome and other scandals broke many months later did he realize the nature of the weight on Harding's mind.

When the President took ill in Seattle on July 27, his personal physician diagnosed poisoning from bad seafood. A younger naval doctor attached to the party suspected a heart ailment and Hoover, on his own responsibility, wired ahead to his friend Dr. Ray Lyman Wilbur, himself a physician, to have heart specialists meet the presidential train in San Francisco. The President's party stopped at the Palace Hotel, where the specialists at once confirmed that it was heart trouble. Harding died on the evening of August 2, expiring while his wife was reading him a magazine article.

Had he been planning to "blow it out" on his return to Washington? Did the knowledge of the piracies committed by his "gang" hasten his death? No one will ever know the answers. "People do not die from a broken heart," Hoover was to write in the perspective of the years, "but people with bad hearts may reach the end much sooner from great worries."

In the housecleaning under President Coolidge after the scandals a man of sterling integrity, Harlan F. Stone, became Attorney General. Stone asked Hoover to recommend an able and reliable man to head up the Federal Bureau of Investigation. The Secretary recommended a namesake who was no relative, J. Edgar Hoover.

Inevitably, in the course of Herbert Hoover's subsequent career, snide charges were made that he had known about the scandals in the making. They were untrue, of course, and easily refuted. Hughes, Mellon, Hoover, and a few others in the Administration lived in a different world from the one inhabited by Harding's cronies.

After the President's death, citizens in Marion, Ohio, his home town, raised funds for a magnificent mausoleum. When it was built, the cautious Calvin Coolidge, fearing that it might be a political liability, resisted pressure that he take part in dedication ceremonies. The dedication was postponed and Hoover, as President, did participate. Loyalty to the President who had been his friend took precedence over political considerations.

"Those with Harding on his last trip," he said in Marion, "came to know that here was a man whose soul was being seared by a great disillusionment. We saw him weakened not only from physical exhaustion but from great mental anxiety." The crimes of his playmates, he believed, "never touched Warren Harding," who was "a man of delicate sense of honor" and "passionate patriotism."

A stage director could scarcely have figured out a sharper contrast to Harding than his New England successor. Lusty, open-handed hospitality, a bit on the rowdy side, gave way in the White House to quiet and parsimonious hominess. Coolidge's favorite recreation—the myth of taciturnity notwithstanding—was conversation. He often invited Hoover alone of an evening for a few hours of "gab," and drew on his store of Yankee stories as they discussed public affairs and people.

Coolidge also had a store of wisdom, which he passed on in copybook style. "If you see ten troubles coming down the road," according to one of his home-brewed proverbs, "you can be sure nine will run into the ditch before they reach you and you have to battle with only one of them." He was a lucky President—the man who followed him discovered that when ten troubles came down the road they somehow multiplied to a hundred by the time they arrived. After Hoover was elected in 1928, Coolidge offered him some fatherly advice of the kind that helps explain his reputation for silence:

You have to stand every day three or four hours of visitors. Nine-tenths of them want something. If you keep dead still they will run down in three or four minutes. If you even cough or smile, they will start up all over again.

Coolidge proved far less interested and less cooperative than Harding in the ambitious reforms of his Secretary of Commerce. The charge that would one day be made against Hoover—the charge of "doing nothing"— did apply to Coolidge. Letting things ride amounted to a passion with him. The less we meddle with them, he believed, the more chance nature has to work its ancient healments.

Hoover's zeal to reform things therefore disturbed the President. He sought to restrain it, especially when it involved the spending of money. Coolidge opposed the child-labor amendment; he dissolved the controls over foreign loans worked out by Hoover; he yielded most reluctantly on the Hoover Dam and other federal construction projects.

In particular he closed his mind against Hoover's pleas for timely curbs on credit inflation and the thundering catastrophe called Coolidge Prosperity. With regard to Coolidge's passivity in the face of gathering storms, Hoover was to write: "The outstanding instance was the rising boom and orgy of mad speculation which began in 1927, in respect to which he rejected or sidestepped all our anxious urgings and warnings to take action."

5

Hoover's double term as Secretary of Commerce, as we have seen, began in its initial year with a great relief job for the victims of a depression. Its final years were highlighted by a more dramatic work of rescue, in the Mississippi floods in the spring and summer of 1927. Neither of these enterprises was strictly within his official province. But Harding in the first instance and Coolidge in the second as a matter of course turned to him to take command. One can understand why Will Rogers, when an earthquake hit the Near East, thought it strange the Levantines were not calling in Hoover. "Bert was only resting between calamities," he quipped.

The calamity of the flooding was truly Hooveresque in dimension: the largest peacetime disaster in American history to that time. A congestion of waters without precedent for volume ultimately flooded the lower Mississippi for a thousand miles, from Cairo, Illinois, to the Gulf, for a width as much as 150 miles.

Two hundred people were drowned before the federal government took over in the person of its Secretary of Commerce, after which only three lives were lost. He mobilized local and state authorities, the militias of the six endangered states, the Coast Guard, the Red Cross, a naval air contingent, and Army engineers.

An expert in the economics of relief operation, Hoover by radio helped the Red Cross stage a fund-raising campaign directly from the disaster sites. It produced fifteen million dollars. The Rockefeller Foundation contributed a million dollars for after-flood sanitation work. A non-profit organization through the United States Chamber of Commerce raised ten million dollars to finance rehabilitation loans at low rates.

As the turbulent waters moved southward—a process that took about two months—rescue workers were a few safe steps ahead of them. Populations had been evacuated in ample time. Commanding the grandiose war on disaster, first from Memphis and then from other headquarters, Hoover organized the removal of some 1,500,000 men, women, and children, with such goods and animals as they could salvage; then he saw to their feeding, health, and rehabilitation.

About two million acres of crops were washed out and millions of dollars in property and livestock destroyed. Forty river steamers, each with a flotilla of small boats, worked continually at lifesaving. In ten days, at Hoover's urging, a thousand new boats were built, rough but serviceable, and thrown into the breach. About two hundred thousand people were sheltered in eighty tent colonies, under Red Cross and government supervision. Health workers plied their needles so effectively that there was no sign of the epidemics normally associated with such catastrophes; in fact, the refugees under Hoover's control were healthier than in normal times.

Bringing to a close a brilliant biography of Hoover that he published soon after this event, Will Irwin wrote:

I . . . would like to leave him as I saw him one May morning of 1927—standing on the tottering Melville levee, his aeroplanes scouting overhead, his mosquito fleet scurrying below, a group of prominent citizens about him listening to the wise, quick, terse directions which were to bring order out of chaos. It symbolizes the man, that scene—"The one tranquil among the raging floods," the transmuter of altruistic emotion into benevolent action. On that side of him his friends and intimates base their fanatical affection.

Will Irwin could not know, as he wrote those words in 1928, what history had in store for Hoover. Having talked to Irwin shortly before his death, and to many others among those "fanatical" friends, I know that they did not alter their opinion by one iota during or after Hoover's White House years. Quite the contrary, his almost singlehanded struggle with multifarious disasters as President confirmed their fanaticism. Watching in sympathetic understanding, not in bitter hostility, they continued convinced that he was "the one tranquil among the raging floods."

The frustrations of depression and another world war tended to obscure Hoover's achievements as Secretary of Commerce from 1921 through 1928. A pervasive cynicism operated to distort the very objectives which he had set himself. But history eventually made amends. The imprint of those eight years of dedication is deep on the anatomy of the American nation.

XV

1928: Nomination and Campaign

THE nomination of Herbert Hoover by the Republican party at its Kansas City convention in June 1928 was generally considered a near-certainty, despite the opposition of more conservative leaders.

Charles Michelson, Washington correspondent of the New York *World*, was right when he wrote, as the convention approached, that the Old Guard "don't like Hoover, don't understand him, and are doubtful of their ability to deal with him." It was an open secret that the finance-speculator elements, the forces broadly referred to as "Wall Street," felt affronted by his strictures on the boom and his efforts to contain the runaway credit inflation.

A close friend of Hoover who was actively involved in the pre-convention drive, David Hinshaw, would write in 1934:

Wall Street, for there was then a potent Wall Street political influence in the country, and its allied financial interests were against Mr. Hoover. With few exceptions the Republican Senate leaders opposed him. This was true in the main of Republican State Chairmen and National Committeemen as well as lesser party officials. Only the great mass of Republican voters wanted him nominated.

There was, in fact, scant enthusiasm for Hoover among the party "professionals." While admitting his towering abilities, they felt that he lacked the political flexibility, the talent for give-and-take accommodations, they expected in a party chieftain. He simply didn't fit into their preconceptions of a political leader who, if elected, would have to dispense patronage and adjust himself to the pressures of regional and group interests.

Many of them, moreover, had genuine doubts about Hoover's partisan zeal. During the war he had been prominent in the Wilson administra-

174

tion. In its aftermath he had been in the Republican minority that supported the League of Nations. Even as a top-echelon member of two Republican administrations he had often followed an independent line, putting his personal concepts of the national good above party discipline. The professionals, in short, would have been happier with former Governor Frank O. Lowden of Illinois or one of a spate of senators whose hats were in the ring. Unlike Hoover, who was starting at the top, these aspirants had come up through the ranks and were graduates of precinct and county politics. In political terms, Hoover was a maverick, unbranded and rather awe-inspiring to the herd.

As for the "Wall Street" elements, they craved a more complacent successor to Calvin Coolidge, someone less skeptical of their wishful thinking New Era of perpetual prosperity, someone less concerned with the demands of labor and farmers and problems of social equity. Indeed, Coolidge himself was their favored candidate. To the last moment they hoped that his ambiguous statement of August 2, 1927—"I do not choose to run for President in 1928"—could be construed to mean that he would yield to a draft by the convention.

Hoover, pressed from all sides to declare himself a candidate, tried several times to extract from the President a clarification of the cryptic statement and failed to get it. Aside from a brief letter to Ohio party leaders permitting his name to be entered in their February primary, written with Coolidge's consent, Hoover therefore didn't make a single pronouncement before the convention.

But support for him built up amazingly notwithstanding. It came from the grass-roots—a remarkable fact, considering that he not only did not seek popularity but tended to shrink from it. Small business and some more enlightened leaders of big business were for Hoover. So were the American Federation of Labor, the miners, the railway workers, and the mass of unaffiliated workers. Groups which had never before taken a political stand, such as the engineering societies, women's clubs, social workers, were for him. (In the actual vote in November, it was estimated, about three-quarters of all women cast their ballots for Hoover, as the man who thought unceasingly of the welfare of their children.)

He had no personal political machine. At this juncture he didn't need one. The Chicago *Daily News* did not believe its own doggerel, of course, when it rhymed in irony before the convention:

> *Who'll never win the presidential position,*
> *For he isn't a practical politician?*
> *Hoover—that's all.*

Hundreds of men and women who had worked with and for Hoover during the preceding decades, in relief enterprises and in government, now formed clubs in his behalf. They made up in zeal for what they lacked in political experience.

The Old Guard at first dismissed these amateurs as "Boy Scouts and Girl Scouts," but they were whistling in the dark. By the middle of May some four hundred delegates were pledged to the Secretary of Commerce out of a likely one thousand. The convention opened with a noisy "Stop Hoover" drive, but the bandwagon was irresistible. Hoover was nominated on the first ballot, drawing 837 of the 1084 votes cast. The selection, of course, was thereupon made unanimous.

In a eulogy of President John F. Kennedy after his assassination, the Harvard historian, Arthur M. Schlesinger, Jr. asserted that no man had ever been elected President of the United States "who had not schemed and labored to that end." Hoover was an exception to that rule: the nomination came to him without any scheming on his own part.

The telegram notifying Hoover of his nomination was so worded as to suggest that he had "earned" the right to be President. To this implication he reacted with alacrity. He wrote to the convention:

My country owes me no debt. It gave me, as it gives every boy and girl, a chance. It gave me schooling, independence of action, opportunity for service, and honor. In no other land could a boy from a country village, without inheritance or influential friends, look forward with such unbounded hope. My whole life has taught me what America means. I am indebted to my country beyond any human power to repay. . . .

During the campaign he made only seven major addresses. By this time, however, radio had attained its maturity and these sufficed to bring his ideas to the entire nation. For Hoover, refusing the comforts of ghostwriters and image-builders, even the limited speaking program meant intense effort. He was determined not only to gain votes but to project a philosophy of life and government within which his specific policies would make logic.

The first of the seven addresses was delivered in Palo Alto at the Stadium of Stanford University, where more than sixty thousand people had gathered for the ceremony. The high drama of the setting was not lost upon them or upon the country. A poor Quaker lad had come here from Oregon in the summer of 1891, one of the very first to enroll in the half-built university. He had worked his way through school. In the years that followed, as he prospered in engineering, he had played a big role in helping the institution grow in size and influence. Now, thirty-seven years later, he was being formally notified, in the great stadium he helped to build, of his nomination as Republican candidate for President!

On the turf before the speakers' stand, student bands and drum corps marched; overhead airplanes maneuvered; a battery of microphones carried the proceedings to the rest of the nation. Everyone in some measure shared the thrill of a uniquely American success story heading for its triumphant climax.

The date was August 11, one day after Hoover's fifty-fourth birthday. Through the years, his frame had filled out to a certain portliness but far this side of stoutness—six feet tall, he carried his two hundred pounds with ease. Above a high starched collar—the delight of two generations of cartoonists—his round face was austere. There were streaks of gray in his Indian-straight, sandy-brown hair. The attractive Lou Henry Hoover was on the platform behind him; she was still thin and erect, her hair now almost all gray, with a severe patrician beauty to her finely molded features.

Her husband's voice was firm and clear. Neither in what he said nor in his delivery was there any touch of heroics, any striving for mere cleverness or eloquence for the sake of eloquence. This initial address set the tone for the whole campaign as far as Hoover was concerned. He did not hesitate to present big gobs of statistics and sociological analysis. Here was an utterly serious man, incapable of either demagogic flattery of friends or demagogic derogation of adversaries.

The Democratic candidate, Alfred E. Smith, was the first Catholic to run for President, and already stirrings of bigotry were in the air. Hoover therefore sought at once to banish this issue from the campaign. It would crop up notwithstanding, but despite all that Hoover could do to stop it. He now declared:

In this land, dedicated to tolerance, we still find outbreaks of intolerance. I come of Quaker stock. My ancestors were persecuted for their beliefs. Here they sought and found religious freedom. By blood and conviction I stand for religious tolerance both in act and in spirit. The glory of our American ideals is the right of every man to worship God according to his own conscience.

And seven weeks later, on September 28, taking cognizance of episodes of religious prejudice which were causing him profound distress, he said:

Religious questions have no part in this campaign. I have repeatedly said that neither I nor the Republican Party want support on that basis. There are important and vital reasons for the return of the Republican Administration but this is not one of them.

Two candidates more different in personality, education, and experience could scarcely be imagined. Hoover was essentially the introvert: restrained, aloof, cerebral, his speeches almost academic in style and weight. Al Smith was the ebullient extrovert, a mixer and back-slapper, the colloquial man-of-the-masses unembarrassed by lapses of grammar. Smith's brown derby, worn at a cocky angle, was as much the man in one case as Hoover's starched collar in the other. For the Republican candi-

177

date campaigning was a heavy chore performed from a sense of duty, for the Democrat it was a familiar and enjoyable form of self-expression.

Al Smith had risen to the governorship of the Empire State from the slumlands of Manhattan. He was a rough-hewn, self-made man and, by all accounts, a good judge of other men under all his flamboyance. He frankly liked Hoover. They had been friends before their confrontation in a national election, and they were even better friends when the election was over. Whatever some members of their parties might do, neither man ever resorted to personal attack against the other. Never for a moment did the Democratic nominee doubt the sincerity of Hoover's constant and often angry rejection of the religious issue. Again and again, after his defeat, Smith would stand up and defend Hoover on this score, and on most other scores, when people in his presence thought to please him by attacking his successful adversary.

2

With the country riding its high tide of prosperity, there seemed little political necessity to defend the American system which had produced that tide. Yet Hoover throughout the campaign applied himself to a systematic exposition of the principles of national life which, in his view, accounted for America's high standards of living and of freedom.

"As our problems grow so do our temptations," he said in his acceptance speech, "to venture away from those principles upon which our republic was founded and upon which it has grown to greatness." It was almost as if he sensed the challenge ahead and was seeking to build ramparts of popular faith in the American system as insurance against future adversities. The candidate of a highly successful Administration, he necessarily rehearsed its blessings. But there were overtones of humility and caution, and a consistent emphasis on problems and deficiencies. Toward the close of the speech, in fact, there was a passage that, in the light of history, possibly suggests an intuition of storms to come:

No man who stands before the mighty forces which ramify American life has the right to promise solutions at his hand alone. All that an honest man can say is that, within the extent of his abilities and his authority and in co-operation with the Congress and with every element in our people, those problems will be courageously met and solution will be courageously attempted.

Hoover's most optimistic declaration on this occasion would be held against him and chanted in derision in times of trouble. "We in America," he said, "are nearer to the final triumph over poverty than ever before in the history of any land." In the context of his philosophy this was hardly the absurdity it would seem before long in the context of a great depression. He was making neither a forecast nor a promise but merely underlining a potential: the abundance made possible by the unprecedented surge of scientific and technological progress of his time.

There was drama, too, in the setting of his second address, ten days later. He spoke in his native West Branch, Iowa. Its total population was then 745; his audience counted more than 15,000. In a mood of genuine nostalgia he recalled his childhood, happy despite its hardships, and his relatives and neighbors. The grade school teacher who had tried to adopt him after he was doubly orphaned, Molly Brown (now Mrs. Carran), was in the audience and Hoover saluted her in affectionate terms.

After his victory, Hoover's campaign speeches were published in book form. In a brief foreword, Dr. Ray Lyman Wilbur, his classmate in that historic first term at Stanford and now the president of the university, wrote: "The speeches of Mr. Hoover were measured statements of a new liberalism facing new conditions with courage and with confidence in the individual human being to act wisely for himself and for his neighbors."

At Madison Square Garden in New York City on October 22, Hoover drew clear lines between his own "new liberalism"—actually the nineteenth-century liberalism adjusted to new American conditions—and what he called "collectivist" proposals being advanced under liberal labels. He repeated, verbatim, the passage from *American Individualism* warning that "you cannot extend the mastery of the government over the daily working life of a people without at the same time making it the master of the people's souls and thoughts."

Liberalism, he said, "should be found not striving to spread bureaucracy but striving to set bounds to it." This, however, "does not mean that our government should part with one iota of its national resources without complete protection to the public interest." Moreover, the government had large and legitimate functions in flood control, navigation, irrigation, scientific research, and other enterprises intended to help, rather than curtail or compete with, the free economy. Hoover's concrete proposals, in fact, included federal projects and federal financing of a magnitude which appeared to justify the misgivings of the Old Guard.

His insistent distinction between official cooperation in the national economy and government regimentation was spelled out in relation to agriculture, then as always beset by critical problems. He proposed the creation of a Federal Farm Board with "power to determine the facts, the causes, the remedies" to meet those problems. It would have large initial advances of capital from the government and broad authority to assist in the further development of cooperative marketing. He concluded:

No such far-reaching and specific proposal has ever been made by a political party on behalf of any industry in our country. It marks our desire for establishment of the farmer's stability and the same time maintains his independence and individuality. . . . It places the operation upon the farmer himself, not upon a bureaucracy. It puts government in its true relation to the citizen—that of cooperation.

For Hoover the campaign was an opportunity to explain and promote the techniques of cooperation, as he had applied them during his terms as Secretary of Commerce. There had been a great proliferation of "civic organizations, chambers of commerce, trade associations, professional associations, labor unions, trade councils, farm organizations, farm cooperatives, welfare associations." These he saw as ready-made channels for government help without the risks of government domination.

President Coolidge threw his great political weight into the scales. In one public statement he said:

Measured by accomplishment and ability, Hoover holds commanding rank. If five Americans were to be selected on the basis of merit and ability to devise remedies for the present condition of the world—Hoover's name would head the list.

Though both candidates avoided personalities and recriminations, neither could control zealous partisans at lower levels. Attempts to link Hoover to the corruptions of Harding's "Ohio gang" were inevitable. They were so patently farfetched that they merely highlighted his probity. A few of the hoary anti-Hoover libels were resuscitated. The litigation in London about Chinese mines a quarter of a century earlier was disinterred and again represented Hoover as having "robbed the Chinese." Fortunately one of the central figures in that ancient episode, Tong Shao-yi, was by this time Prime Minister of China. He issued a blistering statement in Peking denouncing the attacks as "dastardly" and praising Hoover's services to China.

Another fantastic story was freshly fabricated for the campaign and industriously circulated even after its exposure. Some years earlier, Hoover had helped a group of worthy young men to buy a ranch near Bakersfield, California. They had named it, in gratitude, the "Hoover Ranch" and proudly inscribed the name on a gatepost. Now someone hung a home-made sign under the name that read, "No White Help Wanted," the implication being that only cheap Asian labor was employed. This was photographed and disseminated throughout the country.

At the request of Samuel Gompers, head of the A. F. of L., local trade union leaders investigated the charge. They reported that the ranch, which was not Hoover's in any case, had never hired Asians. But the lie continued in circulation through the whole campaign and, indeed, was to remain in the arsenal of anti-Hoover mudgunners for many years to come.

The issue of Prohibition bulked large in the contest. As a little boy, Hoover had been taken along by his mother and then his aunts to per-fervid anti-saloon meetings. The psychological imprint of Demon Rum and his depredations was deep. Yet he had been less than enthusiastic when the Eighteenth Amendment was adopted; he had doubts about the efficacy of coercion. But now that it was the law of the land, he opposed its repeal without further attempts to obtain compliance.

The statement of this view during the campaign was at one point inept in its wording. He said of the thorny Amendment: "Our country has deliberately undertaken a great social and economic experiment, noble in motive and far-reaching in purpose. It must be worked out construc-tively." This the opposition condensed and distorted into the phrase "a noble experiment." Mocked by the extreme wets, it was resented also by the extreme drys, who refused to regard the law as still "an experiment."

On Election Day, the Republican party scored one of the biggest vic-tories in its history. Hoover carried all but eight states.

During his service in two Cabinets, the President-elect had been in-creasingly worried by the spread of hostility against "the Colossus of the North" throughout Latin America. He therefore decided to invest six of the sixteen weeks between his election and inauguration in a good-will journey to southern neighbors. On battleships put at his disposal by Presi-dent Coolidge—the *Maryland* going south and the *Utah* on the home-ward trip—he visited Honduras, El Salvador, Nicaragua, Costa Rica, Ecuador, Peru, Chile, Argentina, Uruguay, and Brazil. In addition he met with the President of Bolivia.

Hoover was accompanied by his wife, who spoke some Spanish, a num-ber of official and unofficial experts on that area, and about twenty press correspondents, among them his friends Will Irwin and Mark Sullivan. On board ship, surrounded by good friends and buoyed up by the pros-pect of great tasks ahead, he was at his best, loafing on deck, telling and enjoying stories, quite unlike the austere statesman of the public image.

He got a "good press" on the journey, both back home and in Latin America. But apparently there was one episode the press corps over-looked. A seventeen-year-old sailor on the *Maryland,* William Vance, reported it with a delay of thirty years in an article in the December 1958 issue of the *American Mercury.* He recalled "glimpses of the great man as he strode around the ship, in early morning, walking simply for the joy of being active and alive."

Then came the night when the battleship ran into a violent storm off the coast of Mexico. The storm was minutely described in the dispatches —the lifeboats lost, the tons of water that poured into Hoover's stateroom because a porthole had been left open, etc. A batch of sailors, however, saw something the correspondents missed. Young Vance was working on deck. Mountainous waves broke over the ship and a touch of panic was in the air. Then a sailor shouted, "Hey, look!" Vance looked:

Mr. Hoover was standing up above us, on the edge of the boat deck. He had on a sea-drenched overcoat and his pajamas were visible below the coat. He had his face turned to the sky and he was bare-headed. In the intermittent flashes of lightning and the light of the cargo flood, it was plain to every one of us that he was enjoying the storm! No one said anything, we just watched him. . . . Hoover was still up there when we went below. . . .

Possibly the sailor lad, writing in his middle age, romanticized the memory. But Hoover's "quality of quiet courage, the impression of which never left me through all the years," influenced his life, he said: "When I'm tempted to panic about anything, I picture him in the fury of a tropical storm, calm and unafraid, and it gives me new courage."

The good-will tour was accounted a success. In every country they visited the President-to-be was welcomed with spirited Latin hospitality, expressed in parades, receptions, and floods of oratory. The sole unfriendly event was one that didn't take place. Before reaching Buenos Aires, Hoover was shown a local newspaper which displayed on its front page a story of the arrest of an "anarchist" who supposedly had planned to blow up the American guests. Hoover quickly tore off the front page and crammed it into his pocket. "It's just as well that Lou shouldn't see it!" he muttered.

American troops were then stationed in Haiti and Nicaragua. Hoover made clear his dislike of military intervention and urged, in virtually all his formal addresses and interviews with the Latin American press, what he called "good-neighbor" policies. He referred to his visit as that of "one good neighbor to another" and looked forward to an era of "the relations of good neighbors." The phrase was destined to achieve celebrity—but was falsely credited to another President. To the victor belong the spoils, apparently including the loser's more felicitous phrases.

On his return, Hoover busied himself with the organization of his coming government. The decision of Charles Evans Hughes not to return as Secretary of State was a keen disappointment, as was the refusal of Justice Harlan Stone and former Governor Lowden to accept Cabinet posts. The final slate, however, was impressive, including Henry L. Stimson as Secretary of State; Andrew Mellon as Secretary of the Treasury; Robert P. Lamont as Secretary of Commerce; Walter F. Brown as Postmaster General; William D. Mitchell as Attorney General. Hoover induced his friend Dr. Wilbur to leave the presidency of Stanford and serve as Secretary of the Interior.

On a rainy and blustering Monday in March 1929 Herbert Clark Hoover took his oath of office as the thirty-first President of the United States. The ceremony, in accordance with tradition, took place outdoors on the east portico of the Capitol. In his Inaugural Address the new President spoke both of the strengths and the weaknesses of the national condition. "But if we hold the faith of the men in our mighty past who created these ideals," he declared, "we shall leave them heightened and strengthened for our children."

What were the ideals and aspirations of which he spoke? Hoover listed what he considered the most important of these:

The preservation of self-government and its full foundations in local government; the perfection of justice whether in economic or in social fields; the maintenance of ordered liberty; the denial of domination by any group or class; the building up and preservation of equality of opportunity; the stimulation of initiative and individuality; absolute integrity in public affairs; the choice of officials for fitness to office; the direction of economic progress toward prosperity and the further lessening of poverty; the freedom of public opinion; the sustaining of education and of the advancement of knowledge; the growth of religious spirit and the tolerance of all faiths; the strengthening of the home; the advancement of peace.

As the official party set off for the White House, the light rain turned into a downpour. In order not to disappoint the big crowds lining the route for a look at the new Chief Executive, the Hoovers rode in an open car and, of course, arrived at their new home thoroughly soaked. The new Vice President, Charles Curtis, and his sister, Mrs. Dolly Gann, also lowered the top of their car and were no less drenched. The weather remained grim during the inaugural parade in the afternoon. Among the guests on the reviewing stand was the aging West Branch school teacher, Mrs. Carran.

When the Quaker blacksmith in an Iowa village over half a century earlier announced that "another General Grant"—meaning another President of the United States—had just been born in his humble cottage, he spoke more truly than he could have suspected.

XVI

"No Politician"

W<small>E</small> pause at the doors to the White House, on the wet and chilly afternoon of March 4, 1929—on the threshold of another of Herbert Hoover's many lives. The new President, armed with an overwhelming mandate of confidence from the American people, is fifty-four, in superb health, and at the zenith of his intellectual and moral powers. Superficially all the portents are for a busy, happy, constructive reform Administration.

This climactic point in our narrative is convenient for an attempt to consider Hoover's personality and character traits, for they will have tremendous impacts, for good and ill, on the peak experience ahead of him. In the nature of such an attempt, of course, I must abandon the constrictions of chronology.

Anyone who wins the highest political prize this side of heaven, the Presidency of the United States, might reasonably be presumed to possess large, varied, and supremely effective political skills. Yet the one thing on which Hoover's devoted friends and ardent enemies were in substantial agreement was that he was "no politician." In the mouths of detractors the allegation sounded like an important item in the inventory of his shortcomings. In the mouths of admirers it sounded like clinching proof of a lofty character far removed from the political market place, beyond its vulgar trickeries, compromises, and public posturings.

One can accept the fact without necessarily accepting either set of implications. It is simply an element inseparable from Hoover's total personality; one of the defects, certainly in the operational sense, flowing from his finest qualities.

Those who placed most value on his public services had most reason to deplore a flaw that tended to limit and thwart those services by giving great advantage to more adroit and less scrupulous adversaries. Lack of political skills, even if explained by other and nobler attributes, limited the President and hurt the country in a period of terrible crises. There is little doubt that Hoover himself recognized and very likely deplored the paucity of political gifts in his over-all equipment. There is even less doubt that he would never knowingly pay the price demanded for some of these gifts in the coin of integrity as he conceived it.

The point decidedly is not that the thirty-first President was deficient in sound political judgment or in the grasp of political trends and strategies. He was a shrewd enough judge of men singly and in the mass, and of the forces of national sentiment. He dealt ably and successfully with simple miners and complex prime ministers the world over. We need only recall his remarkable capacity, in the Belgian Relief and other gigantic undertakings, to bend generals and statesmen to his will.

Where he fell short was in dexterity in manipulating people and making "deals" on the plane of democratic politics; in selling himself and his policies to the unthinking crowd; in playing on mass emotion. He understood the operation well enough but was not himself an operator in that area.

The prototype of the American politician is all too familiar in American life and literature. He is a hail-fellow extrovert, ready with the broad smile and the intimate slap on the back, more concerned with first names than first principles; with a flair for flattering the masses that is in large part contempt for their understanding. He has more in common with the showman than the statesman, the actor than the activator.

This portrait—exaggerated, admittedly, for the purposes of contrast—has no point of contact with Hoover. It is pretty much a summation of what he was not himself and what he despised in others. He would not be like them if he could, and emphatically couldn't if he would. Small wonder, therefore, that the garden-variety politicos felt out of place with him, at a loss to comprehend his moral vocabulary. They were thrown off balance by the distressing discovery that all their workaday clichés about the "public interest" and "the people," the "American way of life" and "individual freedom," had for Hoover literal and inviolate connotations.

It is no accident that among Hoover's closest friends there were few real politicians. His friends included industrialists and labor leaders, journalists and professors, engineers and diplomats, but no party bosses or political hacks. Hoover, a White House associate declared, dealt with a sure hand with genuine problems but seemed unnerved by "cheap partisan politics."

In a letter to David Hinshaw in December 1929, after the collapse of the stock market, William Allen White, the sage of Emporia, Kansas, wrote:

The President has great capacity to convince intellectuals. He has small capacity to stir people emotionally, and through the emotions one gets to the will, not through the intellect. He can plow the ground, harrow it, plant the seed, cultivate it, but he seems to lack the power to harvest it and flail it into a political merchantable product. . . . He must be what he is. What he is is important and necessary. . . .

The very calm persuasiveness of fact and knowledge which impressed a dozen men around a table not infrequently depressed a mass meeting. Inspiring blind loyalty in millions calls for histrionic arts that were no part of his native endowment. In addressing himself to the great public, Hoover appealed first, as a matter of course, to reason and only second, if at all, to feelings.

Where the born politician expands and luxuriates in the limelight, Hoover contracted and grew uneasy. His instinct was to run away from the wild applause which some other men crave and whip up artificially. He was closer to his natural element at a Quaker meeting of silent meditation than at a religious revival meeting. He had won popular admiration, of course, in surpassing measure, but it was an admiration touched with awe, the kind that did not breed familiarity. One couldn't imagine the press or the masses calling him "Herbie," as they called the New York Governor "Al."

"I have never liked the clamor of crowds," Hoover wrote. "I intensely dislike superficial social contacts. I made no pretensions to oratory and I was terrorized at the opening of every speech."

Which is not precisely a glowing recommendation for an applicant for high political office. These candid words of self-appraisal, though set down much later, harked back to 1919–20, when presidential boomlets, Democratic as well as Republican, were being launched for him without his consent and in some cases over his protest. It was a time when America was doing handsprings of adulation for Hoover. His world reputation was tall, incandescent, dazzling.

He had just returned from Europe, where he was universally regarded as a "savior," an American savior. The mechanisms of his labor might be called Commission for Relief of Belgium or American Relief Administration; to the world at large, and the beneficiaries in particular, it was simply "Hoover Relief." Every nation had its special hero, but Hoover was a hero to nearly all nations, victorious and defeated alike. President Wilson's laurels were askew. Men like Clemenceau and Lloyd George made friends at home by making enemies abroad. Even in their homelands their halos were tarnished as the victories themselves lost their magic.

Hoover was the exception, the sole exception, as popular in Germany and Austria as in Belgium and Poland. His own country went overboard in expressing an overflowing pride in the achievements of a fellow American. It was in large measure self-acclaim: America saluted in Hoover the effective agent of its own most humane impulses.

For a natural politician this would have been a setup made to order. For Hoover it was first of all a reminder that he must brace himself for the distressing "clamor of crowds" and a lot of terrifying speeches. The excitement seemed to him almost an intrusion on his privacy. In the years ahead he was able to overcome most of his terror in the face of speechmaking, but not his aversion to noisy crowds and shallow social contacts.

2

From 1929 forward, Charles Michelson, a newspaperman who was as cynical as he was shrewd, made Hoover-baiting his life's work. He studied the thirty-first President as industriously as a general studies the enemy terrain. And he classed Hoover among "the amateurs in the art of politics," as one who "did not know how to chart the process of overcoming opposition."

Another veteran Washington reporter, Herbert Corey, who in 1932 wrote a book in passionate defense of the President, remarked at one point that Hoover "seems not to have the least appreciation of the poetry, the music, and the drama of politics." He did not put on a good spectacle, that is to say, for the correspondents and the country. Instead he relied on solid fact and the presumptive patriotism of his countrymen to bring him the support he needed, precisely because he never could think of it as support for Hoover but only as support for the welfare of the nation.

Michelson had disparaged Hoover as a political figure on an earlier occasion, before he was hired to disparage the man in general. The future President was then in his second term as Secretary of Commerce and was being increasingly talked of as Republican candidate. We have already cited part of this quotation but it merits repetition in the framework of this chapter. In his Washington column for the New York *World*, Michelson wrote:

The Old Guard of the Senate, most concerned as to who is going to win the next presidential nomination, don't like Hoover, don't understand him, and are doubtful of their ability to deal with him. . . . It is bad enough to have Coolidge in the White House with his reticence and the uncertainty where his favor lies; but Coolidge at least is a politician, thinking their language, if he does not speak it much; *while Hoover revolves in a different orbit. . . .*

In other words, Hoover was no politician in the Old Guard and Coolidge sense of the word. He was not, and by reason of his whole psychological makeup never could be, "one of the boys" at the public feeding trough. The professionals could never feel at their ease with this stern amateur and his strange ethical fixations.

The Old Guard, Michelson went on to report, feared "the Hoover organization." By this he did not mean a party machine fueled by give-and-take patronage; that was an animal they could have tamed or bribed or beaten. They meant the devoted and often fanatical friends, not one of them a conventional politician, who had shared Hoover's adventures in European relief and his immense labors as Secretary of Commerce: "the small but efficient army . . . that still calls him Chief and is ready to mobilize at a word." How could political handymen deal with supporters moved not by lucre but by love?

In due time this Michelson was to become as annoyed with Hoover's rigid code of conduct, with his special orbit, as the Republican Old Guard. Alone among political leaders, Michelson would eventually complain in a candid autobiography, Hoover took "campaign asperities" and smears of his motives seriously! He was not sporting enough to brush off years of this correspondent's filth-mongering for a fee as one of democracy's little jokes. Many others were also attacked by Michelson in the line of duty and attacked him in return, but in "private" life they remained his good friends.

"In fact," he boasted, "all the Republican leaders call me by my first name, regardless of what they have been saying on the Senate or House floor as to my wickedness. We are all actors who, having wiped off their makeup, forget the villain-and-hero struggle on the stage."

Only Hoover failed in this test of political amiability. He did not play a villain-and-hero farce for the galleries; he could not wipe off the makeup because he did not wear any. The lines he spoke were not written by some Michelson of his own. Hoover's opinions, enthusiasms, worries, and indignations were not stage effects but in deadly earnest. For him politics was not a "game" for stakes of power or loot. It was a solemn obligation, a mandate for impersonal service.

All of which the authentic mummers on the stage regarded as a grievous fault—very nearly a left-handed insult, as perhaps it was. All of which, however, endeared him the more to that unprecedented "Hoover organization" which, if anything, rallied around him more faithfully in his times of trouble and defeat. They took a good deal of pride, indeed, in the man's inadequacies as an actor. This comes through in *This Man Hoover*, a book by Earl Reeves published in 1928, with only Hoover's performance as a Cabinet member to draw upon. Hoover, he wrote, "does not 'dress up' his statements or his acts; he is not on parade before correspondents. . . . A 'press agent' would say that he overlooks a million chances no politician should overlook."

I ran across supporting evidence of the no-politician verdict from another source, significant as the spontaneous impression of an impressionable lady far from the American political scene.

Secretary Hoover had addressed a banquet of the National League of Women Voters in Baltimore, to convey the greetings of President Harding. An ebullient foreign guest, Lady Nancy Astor, was moved to offer some impromptu remarks. Having aimed some pleasantries at Governor Ritchie of Maryland, she turned to—or on—Hoover. "Why, all Europe looks upon him as a sort of savior of mankind!" she announced. The fifteen hundred women in the hall thereupon exploded in applause, cheers, and a waving of napkins and handkerchiefs. The Hoover moon face blushed crimson; he was so palpably embarrassed that the demonstration was mixed with laughter.

"Look at him!" Lady Astor pursued her quarry. "He is not an ideal politician. He lacks the glad hand and the perpetual smile, thank goodness."

Plenty of more earnest and academic corroboration is at hand. In a history, *American Parties and Elections*, E. M. Sait wrote of Hoover:

Unfortunately, he had been trained as an engineer, not a politician; his contact with public life had been limited to his service as Secretary of Commerce under Harding and Coolidge; and his temperament, like his training, did not accommodate itself to the peculiar rules of the great game of politics.

Random samples, these, of the prevailing view. Most of the men most closely associated with Hoover were inclined to concur in the general judgment, though taking violent exception to this or that detail. Hoover, one of them told the writer, always seemed to him "out of character" in the political arena. Another said that "the ways of the politician were never quite clear and, on the whole, distasteful to the Chief."

3

Having conceded that he lacked popular glamor, his admirers often added in fond irritation that he would never do anything to remedy the matter. Worse, he would not allow them to do so. I am indebted to Arch W. Shaw, one of the men who could be "mobilized" by the Chief for any job at a word, for two illustrative anecdotes in this connection.

The first refers to an early stage in Hoover's political career. Some of his backers prepared for newspaper release a dramatic account of Hoover's exploits in the siege of Tientsin during the Boxer uprisings at the turn of the century. It was a true story and told, among other things, how the youthful American engineer had rescued a trapped Chinese child in the line of gunfire. They made the tactical mistake of showing it to Hoover before releasing it to the press. He read the story, frowned, slowly tore the sheets into tiny fragments, and dropped them into a wastebasket.

"You can't make a Teddy Roosevelt out of me," he said in a way that foreclosed argument.

The second anecdote refers to the preconvention campaign. Hoover's associates were chronically worried by his tendency to keep "important callers" waiting, or even to refuse to receive them, when he had what he deemed more important work on hand. Their concern came to a head when their candidate let an influential politico from a doubtful state cool his heels in an outer office and finally spared him only a few minutes on the way out to keep an appointment.

Arch Shaw was delegated to apprise the Chief of the political facts of life, tactfully. Hoover was impressed. He paced the floor for several minutes in thought. Then he turned to his friend abruptly and said, "All right! But I'll kiss no babies." Baby-kissing obviously was to him sign and symbol of the kind of clowning for votes and favor that went against the grain of his innermost nature.

On the eve of Hoover's first campaign, some Republican stalwarts met in a New York hotel to outline a program for "humanizing" their candidate. It was a good program, but in the end they decided that there was no use presenting it to Hoover—he simply would not lend himself, they knew, to their bright public-relations stunts, so they must do the "humanizing" without his consent or help.

Always he edged away in alarm from the devices of publicity buildup because, he insisted, he did not want a synthetic picture projected on the public mind. The result was to be profoundly ironical. What was in due time projected was a sort of photographic "negative," in which Hoover's whitest attributes somehow showed up black.

If he had had a better eye for personal glorification—had he been a better politician—Hoover's heroic efforts to stem the tides of calamity in the first depression years would have provided a four-ring circus for an avid press. He might easily have dramatized his almost unequaled burdens of office, his inhumanly long hours of work, his continuous struggle against political obstruction and pork-barrel demagoguery. Each of his ameliorative measures could have been launched with a fanfare of political trumpeting.

But he deliberately chose to work in semi-secrecy. Reporters had to dig hard for news which another President would have blown up for them with the help of battalions of public-relations officials at the taxpayers' expense. Anxious not to stampede an already alarmed public into a state of panic, he insisted that his colossal exertions be played down instead of up.

Doubtless there was much justice in this view. But it is also true that he naturally recoiled from the spectacular—and found plausible excuses for the recoil. At a time when Congress and the press were making him the scapegoat for tragic events not of his creation, when he had every reason in his own and in the public interest to reject the role, President Hoover told his press secretary, Theodore G. Joslin, "This is not a show-man's job. I will not step out of character."

But the Presidency is very much of a showman's job. Leadership from the White House must appeal to the heart no less than to the mind; it must generate faith and fervor and courage. In insisting that it was not a showman's job Hoover was rationalizing his distaste for showmanship and his ineptitude behind the footlights. "He has never, so far as my ob-servations have informed me," said one of the irritated newsmen, "at-tempted to add to his personal popularity by the usual methods of the guild. It would be physically impossible for him to put his right hand on the left side of his chest and repeat Fourth-of-July platitudes."

Yet it is clear in retrospect that greater personal popularity might have helped him over many a barrier when he, and the country, needed most desperately to get to the other side. It would have made the tasks of his opponents, whether honest or malevolent, more difficult. The usual methods of the political guild, however vulgar in themselves, have a democratic logic rooted in long experience.

Let me recount here succinctly a story which Joslin, in his book, *Hoover Off the Record,* told in full. On May 28, 1932, three children came to the White House door. They had hitchhiked from Detroit to the capital in childlike faith that the President could and would restore their father, Charles Feagan, to his family. Feagan, it appeared, had been jailed for stealing an automobile while in search of work. When Hoover heard of their mission he said, "Three children resourceful enough to manage to get to Washington to see me are going to see me."

By the time the youngsters, a girl of thirteen and her two younger brothers, were in Hoover's study telling their sad tale, Joslin had phoned Detroit, obtained the facts, and briefed the President. Though it was not a federal matter, Hoover risked a promise.

"I know there must be good in a man whose children are so well be-haved and who show such loyalty and devotion to him," he told his visi-tors. "I will use my good office. You may go home happy." He gave them each a little gift. "Now run along and go straight home. Dad will be wait-ing there for you."

When Joslin was summoned to the President's study, he found him standing by a window, his back to the room. In a strangely thick voice he said, "Get that father out of jail immediately." The secretary pleaded for permission to give the facts to the reporters, but Hoover would agree only to the barest announcement. "Let's not argue about it," he said. "That will be enough. That is all I will say about it. Now we will get back to work." It is easy to imagine what another kind of President would have made of the incident.

The thirty-first President represents the paradox of a great political figure who never became acclimated to the harsh and noisy world of politics and political propaganda. This limitation was summed up aptly by an editorial in the *Christian Science Monitor* many years later:

Mr. Hoover was never in his proper place as a politician. His trouble in office was not merely that he lacked political dexterity; there is in him none of that glibness, none of the superficial good fellowship, especially none of those arts of accommodation which mark the political craftsman.

It was frequently said that Hoover failed to build a personal political machine. In truth he did not fail, because he never tried. He had a fanatic, "old-fashioned" respect for the office of the Presidency, no matter who held it, that made it impossible for him to exploit it for merely political advantages. How to use the potent levers of patronage seemed to be one of the things he never learned in his engineering courses.

There was the story—typical of scores of the same sort—of two Midwestern senators who came to urge the appointment of a party worker to a vacant federal judgeship in their state. What were his qualifications, the President wanted to know. Chiefly, it appeared, that he was a Republican whose influence was badly needed in the next election. "Well, put that in writing," Hoover suggested with a straight face, and the interview was over.

In filling jobs he reached out repeatedly for experts, in blithe disregard of the political payoffs normally governing these transactions. Hoover was all but inaccessible to arguments of political expediency where his principles were affected. When a vacancy in the Supreme Court had to be filled, a number of Republican leaders and some of his close advisers counseled against the appointment of Benjamin Nathan Cardozo. Acknowledging that he was a great lawyer and a splendid man, they feared that his choice would be a political blunder. Cardozo was not only a Democrat but a devout Jew. They recalled the heated opposition to the confirmation of another Jew, Louis D. Brandeis, in 1916. Hoover brushed aside all the political considerations. Cardozo as Justice wrote some of the most distinguished pages in American jurisprudence.

On the eve of Hoover's second presidential campaign, Jeremiah Milbank and many other friends urged the candidate to make a "politically expedient" pronouncement on the issue of Prohibition. Here is his response, as recorded by Admiral Strauss:

The President of the United States takes an oath to preserve, protect and defend the Constitution. If he comes into office with the intention of changing that great instrument, it is a mental reservation which makes hypocrisy of his oath; and if, as President, he acts to advocate a change in the Constitution, it would set the most dangerous precedent I can think of. . . .

There is a constitutional procedure for changing the Constitution but the President has no part in it, and should not have. Regardless of what you believe will be the effect upon my political fortunes, and however right you may be, that is of no consequence compared with the great principle of our form of government which properly proscribes the Chief Executive from tampering with the Constitution under any circumstances.

This was the sort of rigidity on fundamentals that made more politically minded men around Hoover shrug their shoulders in despair.

The very fact that he had a deep aversion to ghostwritten speeches seemed to the conventional politician as old-fashioned as his collars. Eventually he was to discard the collars but not his allergy to literary ectoplasm. *Harper's Magazine,* having published an article in which there was an allusion to his alleged ghosts, later, after investigating the subject thoroughly, made a handsome public apology.

Louis B. Mayer, the late movie mogul, once offered to put his most expensive wordsmiths at Hoover's disposal in the hope of injecting a bit of Hollywood glitter into his campaign speeches. Nothing came of the proposal. Be it ever so unglamorous, there's no speech like your own, Hoover believed—this despite the fact that his slow, conscientious writing siphoned off so much of his time in periods when his responsibilities were staggering.

He did read suggested drafts and accept corrections of his own efforts. But his every address, article, or book (except where collaboration is acknowledged in a double by-line) was the product of his own mind and hands. Ideas to him were not externals, to be cooked to the taste of some current diners, but part and parcel of the man; though he readily conceded that his dishes lacked some of the vote-getting vitamins expert cooks might have added.

Hoover scrawled his first draft of any piece of writing in pencil, edited it laboriously, then had it copied. Then he worked on the typewritten version until it looked like a futurist design only his own practiced secretaries could decipher. The result was set up in type by a printer—not any printer, but one accustomed to his corrections upon corrections—after which he would mangle half a dozen or more successive sets of printer's proofs before the final okay. From the penciled rough to the final draft there were often a dozen or more versions.

No, Hoover was "no politician." Arch Shaw said of this aspect of the Chief's personality:

The process of politics in the sense that so many Americans envisage the word suggests opportunism, intrigue, insincerity and the use of patronage which lead by devious paths into intellectual dishonesty. In that sense he was not a politician. In the sense of being a man alert to political currents and the needs and tendencies of his time, of steadfastness to principle and of inspirational leadership, he always has been.

It should be remembered that the first and only office for which Hoover ever ran was the Presidency, and that, possibly, was the most serious error of his astounding career.

XVII

Paradox of Personality

T HERE is nearly always a wide gap between the popular image of a prominent man and his private, everyday self. It was in this sense that G. K. Chesterton once attested that almost every time he met someone he met someone else, "a private man oddly different from the public man." In the case of Herbert Hoover, the distance between the man and his shadow on the public mind has been astronomic, the contrast startling. Not until he was in his early seventies was that distance seriously narrowed down; a long overdue revision, but fortunately he was still alive to witness the gratifying change. Most of the notions about his character and personality accepted as reality by average Americans were not merely untrue but in vital respects the contrary of the truth.

Americans have thought of him as austere, monumental, and rather cold. Few of them had any inkling of the warm, friendly, and tender Hoover known to his intimates, the very human and profoundly humane Quaker behind the solemn façade.

Increasingly, in the afternoon and the evening of his long life, people said that the ex-President had "mellowed." This implied that the real man had changed. In fact, he hadn't—it was merely that the real man had become more apparent. It was mainly that, in later years, to quote Hinshaw, "he has had time to be to large numbers of men what he has always been to his close friends—gentle, mellow, kindly, whimsical and witty." With the tensions of direct responsibility in public affairs removed, the demands on his time reduced, he tended to relax. He overcame some of his inborn inhibitions, allowed himself more license for drollery in public speaking and writing. Moreover, in those riper years more and more of the veils of hostile propaganda fell away, permitting at last an unimpeded view of the man.

But from the 1920s deep into the 1940s even many of those who shared

Hoover's political and economic outlook were inclined to think of him as an unemotional engineer-statesman rather than a sentient human being. This myth happened to be a sad caricature of a sensitive, softhearted person who craved affection, enjoyed congenial company, and suffered under the slings of malice.

The caricature cannot all be blamed on misunderstandings produced by his four years in the White House. It was fairly widespread long before he became President; some of its lineaments appear even in British memories of Hoover dating back to World War I. "His personality never 'got across' in this country," an Englishman who worked with Hoover and therefore knew the falsity of the caricature was quoted by Earl Reeves as saying. "He was always too busy to talk 'sweet nothings' to society ladies; and to those who only met him occasionally he seemed preoccupied, dour, reserved."

A number of Europeans described Hoover as abrupt, stubborn, even unfriendly. "The bluntest man in Europe," Lord Curzon once said of him. What they all referred to was his manner of dispensing with amenities, when urgent matters were on the agenda, and pulling people right down to the problem under consideration. Moreover, he usually had solutions already worked out—often in succinct written form—and so skipped the polite and flattering preludes of seeming to elicit opinions.

Sometimes the picture was forbidding even when painted without malice. A friend of his has said, "Hoover isn't a stuffed shirt. But at times he can give the most convincing impersonation of a stuffed shirt you ever saw." The sculptor Gutzon Borglum offered a purely visual impression: "He looked as though a rose would wilt if you put it in his hand." And such unkind comment seemed confirmed, alas, in an initial meeting. A second and a third confrontation, a process of acquaintance, were required before the wrappings of diffidence were peeled from his character.

When his failings as a political leader are traced to their source they appear to derive from character quirks of which the general public was largely unaware. They are, in fact, quirks so rare in a successful political figure that they seemed exotic and a bit incredible. The most striking of these, everyone who knew Hoover at close range asserted, was shyness —an almost physical shrinking from strangers, crowds, demonstrations. He was ever at his best in talking informally, in a friendly setting, in his own home or among cronies at places like the Bohemian Grove. His voice then was rich, his features lighted up, and he achieved an artless kind of eloquence. Once started, he was fluent and amusing, drawing easily on a phenomenal memory for the apt anecdote and episode and funny story.

But on the platform, or in front of a radio microphone, he tended to stiffen. His voice was somehow drained of color and his features of expression. Only the intense earnestness remained and it was too rarely relieved by those sly asides and good-natured digs which seasoned his intimate conversation. The man who admitted that he was terrorized at the opening of every speech had a great relish for private talk.

Writing in the magazine *Century* in 1930, Hinshaw found the explanation for this and most other Hoover traits in Quakerism:

Hoover the Quaker, given to reticence, distinctly modest, quick in sympathy for the oppressed, with great strength and instinctive generosity and with astounding audacity of the spirit, is full of the manners and methods of his peculiar people. He does not represent Quakerism in its rigid interpretation, but the indelible impressions of his childhood have matured in a manhood concerned with things of the spirit, and the fiber of that spirit makes it pliable but unbreakable.

Doubtless his upbringing in a stern religious community that frowned on worldly pride, pomp, and pleasure did have a lot to do with it. Yet most of us know Quakers who are the opposite of dour and reticent. Hoover's father, from all reports, was a man of lively spirit and cheerful, gregarious charms. But whatever the cause, there is not much doubt of the fact. "The crown of that personality is shyness," Will Irwin said in his biography of Hoover. Lester Hinsdale, a college chum who remained a lifelong associate, in recalling his earliest impressions of the slim, aloof lad he met on the campus, declared:

"He seemed shy to the point of timidity—rarely spoke unless spoken to. It wasn't until later, when we got into politics on the same side, that I realized how much it was possible to like him." He was referring, of course, to campus politics.

"God's grace blended courage and faith and tenderness in Herbert Hoover," John Spargo, the great liberal publicist, once wrote. But those who encountered Hoover for the first time, unless they were forewarned or brought a saving insight to the experience, ran the risk of mistaking his diffidence for hardness or disinterest. There was no facile friendliness about him. He rated friendship too highly to dispense it lightly to all comers. He was likely to wait with lowered eyes for the other fellow to start the conversational ball rolling. He was not known to comment on the weather unless the information was pertinent to crop prospects or fishing.

Matters were hardly improved by his one intolerance, which was intellectual: an intolerance for beating around the bush, fuzzy thinking, and vague facts. Because he was uncompromising when he considered himself in the right, there was sometimes little room for the play of debate, and this won him a reputation for a closed mind.

What seemed a lack of cordiality was usually the result of excessive reserve. Facing people whose cooperation he needed, he preferred to appeal at once to their social conscience, if they had one, and their intelligence, if they had any. Joslin, as his press secretary, found this aspect of the President's character a serious handicap. Hoover, he would write,

either won people by the force of his arguments, or he lost them. . . . He could be a fascinating conversationalist among his friends when he put weighty matters aside, but he could not do it on demand. When advised to try, he would say: "I have other things to do when the nation is on fire."

The element of pathos in this introverted nature is evident in Joslin's further comment: "Yet few of our chief executives ever desired companionship and friendship more sincerely than did Mr. Hoover." He went on to record that the President, far from withholding himself, was always inviting people for breakfast, dinner, weekends at his Rapidan camp. "During the four years there were almost 10,000 of these guests—to be exact, 9969—most of them people who could be helpful to the country." And Joslin quoted a comment by Mrs. Hoover when he had suggested that the usual contingent of guests be omitted from one of the Rapidan trips in the interest of a better rest. "Oh no," she said, "that will not do at all. He always wants to have people around him. The more he has, the happier he is."

The greater the pity, therefore, that breaking the ice in social intercourse with Hoover could be such a chilling process. But once broken, it was "a warm and very human Hoover" who stood revealed. The quotation is from a friend who knew him for half a century or more. I have been told of instances when men and women came to seek help—and Hoover was, if anything, too accessible—and departed crestfallen, sure they had failed, only to discover later, in amazement, that he had acted quickly and generously on their particular problems.

A domestic scene in Hoover's New York residence was described to me by the late George E. Sokolsky, whose affection for the Chief bordered on adoration. George's children were paying their Uncle Hoover a holiday visit during Christmas week. The ex-President was sprawled on the floor with his young guests and their new toys, and having fun in a big, hearty way. Just then a stranger who had an appointment was announced. Instantly Hoover "froze up." The formal, stern Hoover whom the caller confronted did not seem related to the playful Hoover of a few minutes earlier.

The tableau pretty well sums up the self-consciousness that stood like a wall between the thirty-first President and the great mass of the American people. Your typical officeholder shows the new visitor his best face first, and it is often a false face. Hoover showed his worst face first, and it was always a false face.

Stories pointing up his shyness are legion. When his unexpected entry, or unsuspected presence, at some public function was discovered and evoked an ovation, he looked positively unhappy, like a guilty intruder.

Hoover accompanied President Wilson to Belgium in the course of the latter's European sojourn. A visit to the House of Parliament in Brussels was one of the incidents of that triumphal visit. The President's entry touched off a huge demonstration, of course. Hoover, according to one eyewitness, "waited until this was over and guests and members alike were preoccupied about regaining their seats; then he sidled in, turning his head away and making himself as inconspicuous as possible."

But he was observed. A second demonstration was under way, as loud and prolonged as the one for Wilson:

Hoover had no option but to turn and acknowledge the ovation, which he did with very evident embarrassment. He nodded, a bob of the head. It was the awkward, even painful, bow of a schoolboy of West Branch, Iowa. He blushed. The cheering continued. He shook his head, first at demands for a speech, and grew pinker. Then he shook his head as if to stop all this fuss, and grew red. Minute by minute he seemed to grow redder: he was the most embarrassed man anyone had seen.

It was less modesty than shyness that prompted him to avoid advance announcement when his duties as European relief head required a journey to some country. He was attempting to escape the cheers and parades and banquets. But he was not always successful. In some instances—as in his visit to Poland which I have already described—the situation demanded a publicized appearance. He suffered the acclaim as if it were a duty and sometimes, as in the Polish case, enjoyed it thoroughly despite himself.

2

Few occupants of the White House have curtained their private lives from public scrutiny as conscientiously as the Hoovers did. Lou Henry Hoover was a gracious, good-looking, highly intelligent woman. She was constantly doing useful and noble things which, in the case of other First Ladies, would have made the front pages. But except for her leadership in the Girl Scouts, which in the nature of the case involved public notice, she always remained in the background.

The two Hoover sons, Herbert, Jr. and Allan, were personable and capable young men, destined to become independently successful in mining, farming, and other fields. The Hoover grandchildren who clambered over the President were as appealing as any youngsters who ever graced the White House. Yet the private life of a Scottie named Fala in the next Administration received more press, screen, and radio attention than the private lives of the whole Hoover family and its pets combined.

When the older of the boys, Herbert, once was offered a post pretty obviously too big for him, he turned it down indignantly. "My father's name is not for sale," he said to a family friend in recounting the incident. In the mid-thirties he organized two small companies to build and operate certain seismographing instruments for mining and petroleum explorations. One of his associates in the venture told a journalist many years later: "Herb's father had a lot of important mining and oil connections that could have given us business that we needed pretty badly, but Herb would have none of that." Also, not a penny of his parents' money went into the companies. This pattern of conduct was followed no less rigidly by Allan.

Another element in Hoover's makeup that limited him as a political leader was his sensitiveness, which was in part the same shyness in another dimension. He "was always the thinnest-skinned executive in Washington," according to Michelson. Under the kind of paralyzing partisan opposition Hoover met from 1930 forward, the Democratic press agent wrote, "a stronger President would have browbeaten the politically minded Congress . . . if necessary he would have carried the fight to the people." But his "instinct in this untried field recoiled from conflict."

Here, however, an important distinction should be made. Hoover invariably defended his views and policies to the limit. His humility did not extend to intellectual and ethical judgments—he had a high estimate of his own abilities and his own litmus tests of principle, so high that it sometimes discommoded more flexible men. Even in the depths of his ordeal by abuse, he never was driven to self-doubt, let alone self-derogation.

His press secretary recalled that "it was characteristic of the President to hit back when he was attacked. Sometimes he would launch a counter-offensive himself. Frequently he would move through others, following whichever procedure seemed more desirable to him." But Joslin was writing about battles on policies. Attacks on motives or character were another matter. Once, when urged to react to personal charges, Hoover said grimly: "I cannot take time from my job to answer such stuff. No man can catch up with a lie. If the American people wish to believe such things about me, it cannot be helped."

From the beginning of his ordeal, and even when he was in his eighties, he found it difficult to comprehend the scope and ferocity of the smears and hatreds to which he was subjected. He could understand disagreement but not rank persecution, and was inclined to assign to the persecutors better motives than they deserved. You can ignore attacks "if you're right with God," according to a Quaker precept. It is scarcely a precept well suited to the profession of politics.

Naïveté is a curious word to apply to a wholly self-made and supremely successful man. Yet it is a word that obtrudes itself in appraising Hoover. Despite piled-up evidence that politicians are not exactly incorruptible, he continued to deal with them on the level of disinterested patriotism which was his own natural habitat. He stared in pained disbelief when leaders broke solemn pledges; when congressmen failed to keep confidences involving the public welfare; when reporters occasionally put a scoop above the national interest as he saw it.

"Naïve? Why, the Chief even trusted the stock-exchange boys to live up to promises to reform their practices!" a man close to Hoover exclaimed.

His basic trouble, a member of the Hoover Cabinet told me in an interview, was that he won the highest office at one big bound, without passing through the rough-and-tumble of precinct and courthouse politics. Those lusty, rowdy, "humanizing" regions and the men who inhabited them, he said, remained an alien and rather unattractive world to him. Its free-and-easy morals, the opportunism that it took for granted, its philosophy of the main chance, offended his inbred assumptions. The denizens of that untidy world, even after they reached the top rungs, sensed Hoover's squeamishness—his moral snobbery, as one phrased it —and sometimes resented it in a personal way.

The set of values to which Hoover adhered must have seemed quixotic to men acclimated to ward politics. To put duty above personal interests and rectitude above tactics must have seemed to some of them even a bit pretentious. Mark L. Requa, another devout Hooverite, once said, "I have seen Hoover at close quarters, in trying circumstances, and I have never known him to waver for a moment between right and wrong." A strange and alarming human phenomenon, surely, for most of the people who trade votes and swing states and delegations and consider compromise the most useful of all the arts.

3

In the period after Hoover's defeat for re-election he was often described—by people who did not know him—as a "lonely old man." That, like his presumed "bitterness," was unalloyed assumption by people who imagined that he was reacting as they would have reacted under equivalent conditions. The truth is that few men were so richly blessed in loyal and gregarious friendships.

During the Second World War, when extraordinary pettiness in high places kept him from contributing his special expertise to the national effort, Hoover was one of the best-informed men on public affairs notwithstanding. This was because in every department of government there were men and women, Democrats and Republicans, New Dealers and Old Dealers, who had for the former President a devotion that can only be described as filial, since it was unsullied by political motivation or any other hope of gain. Though he solicited no information and often rejected it, they kept him apprised in confidence of developments which seemed to them of special interest to a man like their Chief.

I asked several of the men who in 1947 accompanied Hoover on the globe-girdling mission to gather facts for President Truman how he managed to gather so much detailed data in such a short space of time. Part of the answer, of course, was in Hoover himself: his encyclopedic backlog of knowledge, his careful planning in advance, his unerring instinct for the relevant question in interviewing experts. But part of the answer was also in the amazing number of Hoover friends deployed throughout the world. In virtually every capital there were sure to be diplomatic, commercial, and military men, humbly placed or eminent, Americans or foreigners, for whom a request from Hoover was a sight draft on loyalty on which they never defaulted.

It is impossible to write about Hoover without writing about his friends. To have worked under Hoover once, it seemed, was to become a reserve officer in that army for life. They were (and those who survive still are) an extraordinary lot, these friends. Because of their intense devotion to the Chief, they were devoted to one another, forming a kind of loose fraternity. For each of them Hoover's suggestion had the effect of a command. On his part, he took for granted that they would drop whatever they were doing, at whatever sacrifice in time and money, to rush on some errand of mercy or public service, paying their own expenses to boot.

I became increasingly aware, in talking to many of these friends, that I was dealing with the initiates of a cult—a cult that rested solely on admiration and affection. John Spargo wrote many years ago of "This Herbert Hoover his friends love with a love that has in it some of the qualities of worship." A man who went through the Belgian experience with him—and therefore, it goes without saying, was available for Hoover jobs ever after—declared, "Attachment to Hoover tends in the end toward fanaticism."

All of which sounds exaggerated until one meets his acolytes face to face. One of them, trying to convince me how they all felt about the Chief, used the word "veneration." Another, when I alluded to Hoover's supposed coldness, all but lost his temper. "Cold?" he exclaimed. "How can anyone who inspires such loyalty and generates such warmth be cold?"

Once a year as many of these initiates as could manage it got together with him for dinner. In the earlier years, before the ranks were thinned by time, there were usually more than two hundred. It was a purely sentimental occasion, a family party, and no one recalls just how it got started. A "silver" loving cup made of high-quality tin was presented to the guest who had come the longest distance. It was won by men from Europe and China, Africa and Australia. In 1946, because the Chief was away on the Truman food mission, the dinner took place without him, an empty chair symbolizing his presence in spirit.

No President in this century, not even F.D.R., has been under such concentrated attack from many directions. But the Hoover cultists point out proudly that no attack has ever come from people close to him. A spate of vicious anti-Hoover books polluted the national air in the last year of his Presidency—they were written, without exception, by people who did not know him personally, the ugliest by men who had not even met him. Here, for the record, is a fact that should be known and savored: *Hoover had a multitude of enemies but no ex-friends.* Of the top one hundred men and women whom he appointed to office during his term in the White House, some died, a few retired for reasons of health, many were promoted; but not one resigned, not one had to be dismissed.

Hoover's gift for friendship, for inspiring associates, rates high in an accounting of his personality. Those who knew him best have loved him best. In nearly seventy years of business and public service not one major co-worker of Hoover turned against him. Whatever the general public may have thought of him at any given time, as the mercury of popularity moved up or down, the men and women closest to him have loved him constantly in all seasons. They loved him largely for those very qualities of warmth, kindness, and geniality about which the mercurial public knew almost nothing.

One discovers, too, in talking to Hoover's lifelong admirers, that their affection has had in it a large element of protectiveness, an eagerness to shield him against a heartless world. They felt that they must guard him against his willingness to credit others with his own motivations, to underrate human cussedness and greed. But when they took it upon themselves to fight the Chief's personal battles they got precious little encouragement from him.

In their unswerving loyalty to Hoover, his friends were dealing in his own native coin. Without exception they recounted examples of the Chief's quiet, unobtrusive, but vigilant concern for the men and women in his unofficial family. Not the big and dramatic things but small acts typical of the man, like the one Edgar Rickard took such relish in telling:

In the summer of 1946 Rickard was in a San Francisco hospital for an operation. Somehow Hoover surmised what his friend did not say: that he yearned to have with him his married daughter, then in Massachusetts. A few days later, on the eve of the operation, the door opened and there she was! Hoover, it appeared, had telephoned her and suggested that it would do her father good to see her. By the time she reached New York, Lucius Boomer of the Waldorf-Astoria, who was another in that circle of Hoover cultists, had arranged the transportation and at the San Francisco airport Hoover himself met her and drove her at once to her father's bedside.

Another friend told about the time when a subordinate in Hoover's Food Administration wrote an indiscreet letter in which he said something to this general effect: "To hell with the boys on Capitol Hill!" Naturally, the letter fell into the hands of a senator who immediately rushed to Hoover to demand that the man be disciplined. "When I appoint men I take responsibility—even for their mistakes," the Food Administrator told him.

And nearly all of them alluded to an aspect of Hoover's conduct that was unknown to the public until it appeared in an earlier version of this biography. As the writer expected, Hoover was not grateful for the disclosure.

There are people who practice sin in secret, but Hoover is that rarer individual who practiced virtue in secret. He went to extreme lengths to hide some of his private benevolences, especially from those who benefited through them. He avoided facing people he helped, when this was possible, as if fearing to burden them with the obligation of gratitude.

"The beginning of his extensive and well-concealed philanthropies," Will Irwin wrote, go back to college days. Much of Hoover's modest summer earnings went for "loans" to classmates poorer than himself. When he began to earn his first substantial salary, in Australia, he sent a monthly slice to his friend Lester Hinsdale for distribution among Hoover relatives and needy students. The fact was disclosed by Hinsdale; it's not the kind that Hoover would tell or admit. Forever after he ran away from questions about his personal charities as if they were clandestine vices. Will Irwin wrote in 1928:

For twenty years I have in California or New York observed men and women of our common acquaintance sliding smoothly through a crisis like a long illness or unemployment. Then, years later perhaps, I would learn by some impulsive confession or through the process of dovetailing two remote facts, that the solvent was—Hoover.

Herbert Corey, writing in *Nation's Business* nineteen years later, gave similar testimony: "Extremely generous, he has saved many of his old friends from humiliation as their earning power declined." He would wangle a loan, a job, or some other help for distressed friends or acquaintances. Only years thereafter, if ever, they might discover who was behind the miracle. One instance of this concealed helpfulness was recounted to the writer in some detail, save for the names involved. The informant was drawn into a Hoover "plot." His role was to turn over money to a person in financial straits in such a way that he would not suspect the real source of the gift!

Two of Hoover's associates told me that they had seen their Chief weeping. The occasions, more than twenty years apart, both involved his sensibility to the sufferings of children.

The first incident was after World War I, when a campaign for child famine relief was under way. More than a score of urchins called on Hoover, each clutching pennies in hot, not overly clean palms: their contribution to the fund. Hoover began to talk to the youngsters, but suddenly tears came to his eyes and he walked away to hide them. The second incident was in his New York suite, during World War II. My informant was present when a visitor was describing the ordeal of little children in Nazified countries. Suddenly Hoover walked to the window and turned his back on the room. The others looked away in embarrassment when his shoulders began to shake with sobbing.

From a much later period, here is a story told by Admiral Lewis Strauss in his book of memoirs, *Men and Decisions*. The Admiral had become the center of an ugly political battle when President Eisenhower nominated him for the post of Secretary of Commerce. In a late night session, the Senate by a paper-thin margin turned him down. In the small hours of the morning the Admiral and his wife, naturally depressed by the outcome, were walking down the corridor toward their hotel room when they heard their telephone ringing:

It was my old Chief, ex-President Hoover, calling from New York.

"How are you?" he inquired.

"Tired but well," I answered.

"Good," he said, "I have been listening to this awful business on the radio and didn't want to go to bed until I had talked with you to make sure that you are taking it the right way."

I thanked him, adding that I had his good example before me, and we said "Goodnight." Mr. Hoover was then in his eighty-fifth year. The hour was two in the morning and his regular bedtime was ten o'clock. I reflected that there indeed was a man who had no "ex-friends," and with good reason. I went to sleep, proud and not unhappy.

4

Men may be forgiven their lack of a sense of justice or decency or probity or gratitude. They may be forgiven their lack of just sense. But they cannot hope for absolution in this world and perhaps in the next if they lack a sense of humor. Which is probably as it should be: a distillation of all human experience. Consequently it is only fair to set the record straight on the most shameful of the failings imputed to Herbert Hoover. The idea that in the geology of Hoover's ample spirit there was no vein of the comic was so widespread for so many years—and persists in some degree—that it threatens to become a permanent part of the American folklore.

The idea happens to be a libel on a President whose sense of humor and ironic perceptions helped save him from the effects of souring experiences. They helped him to live through locust years of abuse without permanent damage to his love of the human animal with all its faults.

In dealing with this side of Hoover, his friend Hinshaw related it to his religious heritage. The Chief's humor, he wrote, was of the special Quaker brand:

It is unbarbed and gentle and usually comes from a turn of thought. It produces grins and smiles, almost never belly-laughs. Since it has the qualities of the rippling of a clear brook rather than the rush of the cataract, it pleases rather than pains. It is never cynical and it never discomforts the other fellow.

True enough. Yet a man's humor is not generic but as personal as his fingerprints. No two people, even among Quakers, laugh in quite the same way or about quite the same things. Hoover's brand of the jocular and his fashion in laughing are authentically Hooveresque. His cronies are familiar with Hoover's laugh. "A deep, rich chuckle which seemed to originate far down in his chest and psychology," one of them described the indescribable, "and to lose most of its force in inner mirth before it came to the surface." It is the kind of laughter that shakes a man's frame with a series of inner explosions.

Part of the new, almost guilty appreciation of Hoover in the later 1940s showed itself in belated credit for flashes of humor and drollery. Two articles about the ex-President at that time both made the same point— the same discovery, we might say—that Hoover could laugh and make others laugh.

"He can bring himself," said one, "to display the deft, highly polished sense of humor he formerly reserved for a few of his intimates." By way of illustration both of them referred to a recent Gridiron Club address which sparkled with wit, and to some amusing comments on the philosophic implications of fishing in a recent broadcast.

The joke within the jokes in that broadcast was that Hoover was largely plagiarizing some hilarious observations on matters piscatory made many years before—by Hoover. They drew laughs in their day and were forgotten, though they were on record in print. As for the Gridiron talk, his addresses under the same auspices during his four years in the White House were available in book form, under the title *Hoover after Dinner*. They made delightful reading, being quite as witty as the more recent one and in spots perhaps wittier.

Let's leaf through those earlier Gridiron addresses, eight of them delivered during his Administration. The club is composed of top Washington correspondents. Its semi-annual dinner is dedicated to sticking pins into public figures, especially the incumbent President, with lively skits and songs. As a test of a President's susceptibility to humor, both at the receiving and dispensing ends, it has few equals. We limit ourselves to a very few samples of Hoover's contributions; they may suffice to convey the general idea that the lighter style is no belated eruption.

In the first of those addresses President Hoover acknowledged that he had received "much political education from these dinners." He had found the pressmen helpful in unexpected ways, he said:

For instance, they daily assist me beyond my greatest hopes by their suspicious research work in new implications for my carefully formulated phrases. I discover by the time an idea of mine has filtered through the clear and crystal minds of one hundred different correspondents that the particular idea throbs with a sense of courage and public service, that it has sinister implications, that it spells malevolence, that it is weak and vacillating, that it is filled with political bias, that it bristles with idealism, sanity, and progress.

Kidding the correspondents gently on a propensity for making big stories out of little facts or rumors, Hoover said at another of these dinners: "One's taste for Roquefort cheese can be permanently destroyed by a microscope. And a cheese mite amplified a few thousand times is one of the most sensational and terrifying beasts exhibited to man."

Once Gridiron diners were treated to a fanciful description of the "joyous enterprise" government would become if it were revised to suit the rightful needs of the press and its reporters. Official life, Hoover said, would be limited strictly to news-producing materials; and government would be dedicated to the generation of excitement. Only officials "who start something by way of attack and combat" suitable for the front page would be tolerated. Opportunity would, of course, be given for "denial on the inside page, provided the denial is peppy enough to maintain the combat." At least two fights would have to be developed daily, "one for the afternoon papers and one for the morning . . . on a strict schedule, with advance release."

From which it must not be deduced that Hoover underrated the correspondents. He appreciated that their dinners contributed to national unity "by rubbing the salt of wit, the vinegar of hyperbole, and the iodine of satire into the raw wounds of politics." "Their streams of humor," he assured them, "refresh the political soul" and "their streams of ridicule quench the fires of ambition. I would not say that the Gridiron Club is the gyroscope of the ship of state; nor that it pours oil upon troubled waters; but it does serve to keep humility in the crew."

After the 1932 election Arthur Krock of the New York *Times* once acted as go-between in getting a message from Hoover to President-elect Roosevelt and was branded a "Hoover agent" for it. After reading Hoover's *Memoirs,* Krock asked him jokingly why his role had not been recorded. "I knew that Roosevelt had made some remarks about you," Hoover smiled, "but none as low as you mention." Besides, he added, "a conscientious political leper must be careful not to infect his friends."

The point is that Hoover's humor was not a flower that bloomed in the winter of his life. It flourished in all seasons but simply had not been sufficiently observed or appreciated. Why, then, was it so scantily recognized?

The first answer, of course, is in the fact that his public services were related overwhelmingly to serious and tragic events, to famines, wars, revolutions, economic earthquakes. His reputation, in consequence, took on some of the coloration of the events. Because the public came to expect portentious appeals, stern warnings, and solemn announcements from Hoover, it rarely caught the overtones or undertones of mirth. The second answer is provided by Hoover's deficiencies as an orator. Apparently he hadn't that special instinct for timing, pausing, and inflection without which the point of a muted witticism is blunted before a large audience.

The third and most important answer is in the special quality of Hoover's humor, which for the most part does not conform to standard patterns. It steers clear of slapstick, profanity, clowning. It does not sneer at the sacred or make fun of individuals. Hoover's wit aims at the mind and imagination of the listener, not simply at his solar plexus.

There is not exactly a bellylaugh in his discovery that "all men are equal before fish," but its flavor lasts. When the New Deal was loud in its concern for the Forgotten Man, Hoover appealed for "the Forgotten Woman—the Statue of Liberty." In the period when Secretary of Agriculture Henry Wallace was cheerfully plowing under little pigs, Hoover remarked, "It is the more abundant life—without bacon." Apropos of certain agricultural proposals he paid his respects to "politicians who live by the sweat of the farmer's brow." When the country abandoned the gold standard he summed up the event in one sentence: "We've devalued the dollar 41 percent under the hypnosis that if we reduced the length of the yard to 21.2 inches, we would have more cloth to the bolt."

His designation of Charles Evans Hughes as Chief Justice of the Supreme Court was being fought, for petty personal reasons, by Senator William E. Borah of Idaho. When word reached Hoover about that time of the birth of a granddaughter, he remarked, "Thank God she doesn't have to be confirmed by the Senate."

Not the kind of fun, one admits, that has 'em rolling in the aisles, but the kind that lingers in memory and reveals new depths on repeated savoring.

"Incidentally," Hoover once interrupted a statistical analysis, "when I comb over these accounts of the New Deal, my sympathy arises for the humble decimal point. His is a pathetic and heroic life, wandering around among regimented ciphers trying to find some of the old places he used to know." The pathos of that old-fashioned dot in the brave new world grew on one. "Those who judge progress by the size of figures will agree," he added on the same occasion, "that great improvements have taken place in the national debts. . . ."

In his second campaign President Roosevelt rebuked critics of his economic improvisations with a parable. He told of a nice old gentleman who fell off the dock in 1933 and was grateful to be rescued, but now, three years later, was complaining because he lost his hat in the process. It evoked a nationwide guffaw of laughter.

Hoover's retort went unlaughed. But without venturing into the science of comparative humor, we submit that it was at least a match for the Roosevelt story. "I have some inside information about that incident," Hoover said in Philadelphia. "The old gentleman was surreptitiously pushed off the dock in order that the hero could gain the plaudits of the crowd as a lifesaver."

Hoover's supposedly dull speeches on the New Deal were loaded with facts and figures and, dullest of all, reasoned argument. Their purpose was not to amuse or bemuse but to enlighten. In reading them, however, we strike rich veins of irony and big nuggets of humor. The intention of their wit was to make listeners wince rather than guffaw. When Hoover described "the effervescence of righteousness which bubbles through the intoxicating waters of the finer life" projected by White House theorists he could have had little expectation of shouts of glee. But there was in it a delicate ribbing of pretentious claims that rates as comic in some men's books. It reflected what Will Irwin, who knew his Hoover through and through, called "a sense of humor too delicate for anything but literal quotation."

The same delicacy could be discerned in the ex-President's discussion of certain policies which had been urged upon his own Administration: "We could have adopted the methods later adopted by the New Deal. These have proved wrong ever since they were first tried by the Emperor Diocletian. *And he was about the last of the Roman emperors.*" Or in his aphorism: "Demagoguery abhors arithmetic, except when it adds zeros to its expenditures." Or to his commentary on those who give lip service to American principles while smashing them in practice:

All this reminds me of the small girl who said, "Mother, you know that beautiful jug you said had been handed down to us from generation to generation?" Mother replied, "Yes, Ann, what of it?" And Ann answered solemnly, "This generation dropped it."

Necessarily I have resorted to published matter in refuting the libel that the thirty-first President lacked the golden gift of laughter and the silver gift of satire. Those who have known him at close range, in his relaxed moods, need none of the random proofs strung together in these pages. To Hoover life has been real and earnest, but it was a life multifarious, compounded of both smiles and tears. The portrait of him which sticks in the mind is the kind provided by John Spargo:

There is yet another Herbert Hoover . . . the genial companion and friend. . . . Singularly modest, without affectation or a trace of pomposity, he is a delightful conversationalist. To sit with him in a congenial group, with pipes or cigars, paying homage to Lady Nicotine, is to experience human fellowship of a high and rare quality. Out of a mind so amply stored that it can only be called encyclopedic, his memory draws factual information, illustration and allusion with amazing facility and precision, but with never a trace of exhibitionism or pride of intellect.

Humorous in a quaint, quiet way, he pours forth, with all the artlessness of a child, a succession of epigrams in which there is something of the whimsicalness and conceit that endeared Charles Lamb to his friends. Even when his mood is satirical, there is a generous and humane quality in the satire, as though he were flicking a whip so dexterously wielded as to be certain of his ability not to wound. To enjoy his conversation to the full, it is as necessary to watch his eyes as to listen to his voice, for in them is most of his laughter—and let me add his sadness and sympathy.

Spargo wrote these impressions in 1936, when Hoover, in the popular myth, was supposed to be an "embittered old man," and they were published three years later in his book, *The Legend of Herbert Hoover Who Did Nothing*. They still held true, I can testify, in Hoover's ninetieth year.

XVIII

Boom into Bust

In a press conference a few days before the expiration of his term, President Calvin Coolidge once more assured the American people that the nation's spectacular prosperity was "absolutely sound." John J. Raskob, the principal financial backer of the defeated Democratic candidate, announced that the zooming common stocks were still a fine buy. Franklin Delano Roosevelt, governor of the state where three-quarters of all the gambling dementia was centered, saw everything "in a healthy and prosperous condition."

No reproof attaches to such citations. They were typical for the first nine months of 1929. To censure individuals for not foreseeing depression around the corner is as futile as blaming fishermen on a sunny day for the hurricane that is sweeping down upon them. Why should politicians, in particular, be better weather prophets than the meteorologists of the big financial institutions?

The country was on a get-rich-quick binge. All the laws of economic gravity seemed suspended as America rode the towering crests of its optimism, recklessly, drunkenly, mistaking its giddiness for high spirits and the flush of fever for the color of health. The few men in business and government who foresaw the consequences of the orgy could not make themselves heard.

The incoming President's first chore was a thankless one—how thankless should be apparent to anyone who has ever tried to reason with an obstreperous drunk—and a hopeless one. The frenzy had gone too far to be arrested without an excruciating hangover. The significant fact, for a judgment of Hoover's unhappy Presidency, is that he was among those who did see the danger and did try to head it off.

He failed. Of course he failed. No mortal man could have succeeded. The avalanche had been building up for fifteen years. Millions of Ameri-

211

cans had been caught up in a debauch of fiscal gluttony. When the day of reckoning arrived they were angry, bewildered, and needed a sacrificial goat. The man in the White House was "it." He would have been "it" had his name been Smith or Roosevelt.

Hoover's had been one of the killjoy voices crying caution drowned out by the shouting of the carousers. As early as 1925 he began to issue his warnings, though he knew that they would not be appreciated or heeded. In a New Year's statement for 1926 he warned against "real estate and stock speculation and its possible extension into commodities, with inevitable inflation," and against "the overextension of installment buying." He drew attention to "the continued instability of certain foreign countries" and deplored "the fever of speculation" resting on "overoptimism" that "can only land us on the shores of overdepression."

Analogous statements on divers occasions to the day he became President, insistently repeated, mirrored Hoover's knowledge that the Federal Reserve Board was deliberately promoting credit inflation, under the delusion that the country had become immune to financial crises. Senator Irvine L. Lenroot of Wisconsin, who was fighting to prevent the Board's "regime of cheap money," obtained his most potent ammunition from the Secretary of Commerce. "The effects of the proposed policies upon the United States," Hoover wrote to the senator in 1925, "mean inflation with inevitable collapse that will bring the greatest calamities upon our farmers, our workers, and legitimate business." They succeeded in postponing those policies for nearly two years, but in 1927 the Reserve Board had its way. America was hellbent for the saturnalia.

In a long memorandum to Daniel R. Crissinger, Governor of the Board, Hoover evoked the specter of "an era of speculation and extravagance with its inevitable debacle," which Crissinger haughtily dismissed as a "parochial view." Hoover's appeals to Coolidge to take a hand in the dangerous game were equally futile. Passive by temperament and a strict legalist, Coolidge insisted that he had no authority to intervene; and his Secretary of the Treasury, Andrew Mellon, in Hoover's subsequent words, "seemed to think my anxiety was alarmist and interference unwarranted."

Hoover's fears, of course, were soon enough justified. Cheap money fueled "extravagance" and, precisely as he had foretold, led to a "debacle"—in the initial year of his own Administration, as his hard luck would have it. A telltale set of figures: Loans on stocks to New York stockbrokers and bankers skyrocketed from three and a half billion dollars in June 1927, to eight and a half billion by September 1929, and the price of common stocks almost doubled. But in the same twenty-seven months commodity prices, factory employment, freight-car loadings, and other indices rose only modestly, in a range of 2 to 5 percent—a measure of the gulf between economic realities and speculative illusions.

Looking back upon this period and the refusal of the country to see what was so obvious to a few, Hoover would write sadly:

It is difficult for the public to believe that such griefs and tragedies lay hidden in so obscure a process as credit inflation when forced on an already optimistic people. It set the stage for wicked manipulations and promotions of stock. Its collapse brought hunger and despair to millions of homes. It destroyed the savings of millions of families. It also furnished ammunition to radicals for attacks on the whole American system. The exhibition of waste, fraud, and greed which flowed from this artificial credit inflation appears in their literature as a typical phenomenon for our free civilization, whereas it was the exception. There are crimes far worse than murder for which men should be reviled and punished.

The irony of Hoover's travail as President was blotted out by its monumental tragedy. Yet a few men in public life were deeply aware of it. One of these was Adolph C. Miller, a member of the Reserve Board who had opposed its cheap-money obsessions. In an interview published in the magazine *Sphere* in July 1935, Miller's story was paraphrased in these words:

The Board knew that Mr. Hoover, from 1926 on, had been protesting that the money policy of the Reserve System was certain to bring about disaster and calamity. Mr. Hoover before and after he took office was struggling desperately to curb credit extravagance. . . . The record will show that he became the victim of a policy that was anathema to him the whole time it was in operation.

But in 1935 few as yet cared to look at that record.

The relative importance of the many causes of the depression continued to be explored and debated for decades after its advent. A New Deal economist, Dr. Mordecai Ezekiel, wrote in 1947: "The catastrophe of 1929–32 had its roots in policies we adopted, actions we took, from 1920 on." They went even deeper, those roots, into the devastations and dislocations of a world war; into the economic follies of the peace, the social upheavals in Russia and Italy. The conditions and the blunders that determined the course of our national economic spill were already history, fixed and irreversible, long before Hoover took the reins of the Presidency into his hands.

It was expedient for some politicians to pretend that the depression was made in America, then spread to the rest of the world. This tended to underline Republican culpability. The economic bubble, the Democratic candidate declared in 1932, "burst first in the land of its origin—the United States."

In truth the depression had been under way in various parts of the globe for at least two years before it hit this country. A scholarly analysis by the National Bureau of Economic Research, in 1932, found that Germany, Brazil, Australia, and other countries had entered a depression phase in 1927 and 1928. Canada, Argentina, Egypt, Belgium, Finland, even England felt the rumblings of the earthquake before Americans became conscious of it. Indeed, some four-fifths of the economic world of which America was a part (excluding, that is, China, Russia, and other areas outside the mainstream) were in deep trouble before the American stock market crashed.

Both before the depression and during the eleven years of its awesome course, Hoover believed that domestically its main cause was the inherent weakness of the American banking system, further enfeebled by unscrupulous men and methods. Recommendations for the revision of the national credit and finance structure invariably figured in his warnings against coming and then against spreading calamities. Almost continuously, as President, he pressed for radical bank reforms, only to be stymied by Congress and influential banking groups.

The Hoover view was confirmed by the startling fact that though industrial bankruptcies in the first three years of depression were 1½ percent of the total, bank failures reached almost 25 percent. The mortality rate of banks was thus about sixteen times higher than in the rest of the economy.

Most of the twenty-four thousand banks in the country were state institutions, operating under forty-eight conflicting, inadequate, and often vicious codes of law. Thousands had insufficient capital, more thousands inefficient management. They were beyond the reach of existing federal law, but state governments—including the crucial state of New York—showed scant interest in the subject. "We're doing all right, aren't we?" was the gist of their response to critics like Hoover.

In his first State of the Union message, Hoover called on Congress to create a special joint committee to examine the whole banking structure and recommend constructive legislation. His request was ignored. Repeatedly, but without avail, he returned to Congress with pleas for laws that would require every commercial bank to join the Federal Reserve System, along with foolproof machinery for continuous inspection. He wanted a separation of savings and long-term loan banks; the prohibition of long-term credits by demand deposit institutions; a ban against branch banks in areas where adequate facilities were already available. He saw the need for legislative curbs on banks which, through "affiliates," "holding companies," and other "satellites" were engaged in the very activities they were forbidden to undertake directly. Virtually all of Hoover's therapeutic measures were adopted—after he left the White House, and thus too late to ward off the heaviest blows to the economy.

President Hoover, of course, could not know that the collapse was imminent. Like the rest of the small and despised company of the sober in a time of drunken irresponsibility, he knew only that the boom was unhealthy and could not endure; that capital was being poured into unproductive speculation rather than productive investment; that the stock-market indices were galloping far ahead of the realities of prices and employment.

Finally frightened by the cyclone of speculation let loose by their own easy-money policies, Federal Reserve officials in 1928 wanted to reverse themselves but dared not act so long as the complacent Coolidge was President. Only after the election of Hoover, whose backing they could count upon, did they begin to restrict speculative credit. But it was much too late.

Even before his inauguration, Hoover conferred with the new Governor of the Federal Reserve Board, Roy A. Young. They agreed to put strong brakes on credit as soon as possible. Immediately after his inauguration, the President summoned influential editors and publishers to the White House—individually and off the record, to avoid undue alarm—and begged them to alert their public that stock prices were already too high. Many of them responded with strong editorials against the speculative fever. Again, too late.

On March 15, the eleventh day of his Presidency, Hoover induced Secretary Mellon to declare that "bonds are low in price compared to stocks." This was a direct warning, the first to come from such a source, that stocks were inflated. Governor Young followed it up next day with a public appeal to all banks to go slow on speculative loans.

The President also sent his friend Henry M. Robinson around the country, from Los Angeles to New York, to warn the bankers and promoters behind the frenzied markets. They scoffed at his requests for self-restraint; had they not found the secret of Midas? Thomas W. Lamont of the House of Morgan, as spokesman for the banking fraternity, dispatched to Hoover a long and solemn report "proving" that his doubts of the health of the New Era were unfounded and could undermine confidence. The President called the head of the New York Stock Exchange, Richard Whitney, to Washington and pleaded for preventive action. Whitney "made profuse promises but did nothing."

Largely as a result of Hoover's efforts the rates on market loans rose as high as 20 percent, but the tide of madness could no longer be stemmed by interest barriers. Housewives and millionaires alike, intent on 100 and 200 percent "killings" in a few months or even weeks, were quite willing to pay outrageous interests.

The country could not remain unaware of the President's evident in-

tention to douse its daydreams and resented it. People preferred to believe the sweet talk of bankers, brokers, and a portion of the press.
Speakers at a newspaper publishers' meeting in April gave voice to the
popular resentment of Hoover's heresy. Blistering attacks on the new
restrictive policies on money echoed through the halls of Congress.

Wall Street, the focal point of the great speculative infection, treated
the President's counsels of caution as a declaration of war. Unfortunately
the legal authority to curb the stock market rested in Albany, not Washington, and there Governor Roosevelt brushed off all pleas for moderation.
Until the day he resigned from his Wall Street law firm to run for governor, Roosevelt had been personally involved in the speculative fury as a
stock promoter. His closest associates were people who genuflected before the Stock Exchange.

In all honesty—no reflections on his public spirit are intended—
Roosevelt saw no excuse for interfering with the ticker-tape Santa Claus.
His four years in Albany were replete with bank scandals. Demands for
counteraction were made from many directions. The collapse of the City
Trust Company prompted the lieutenant governor, Herbert H. Lehman,
in the absence of the governor, to ask Robert Moses, then New York
Secretary of State, to make an investigation.

The Moses report denounced an array of deleterious practices and
cited the Bank of the United States among the culprits. The governor
then set up a commission to look into banking practices—appointing a
director and counsel of this very bank as a member of the commission. "It
was a good deal like appointing one of Al Capone's mob to make a study
of the gangster problem," John T. Flynn would remark years later. Even
the market collapse and the failure of the Bank of the United States—
affecting the life's savings of four hundred thousand depositors to the tune
of $180,000,000—did not shake Albany out of its torpor in this area. In due
time investigations disclosed fraud and gross negligence by state officials.

President Hoover had only one small-bore weapon at his disposal, and
it could reach only the lowest strata in the pyramid of greed: the tipsters
and bucket-shop operators. He instructed the Department of Justice to
go after them hard for using the mails to defraud. This was done so energetically that hundreds of the parasites were driven into hiding. The
Better Business Bureau called it the greatest cleanup of Wall Street up
to that time.

Hoover had informed Whitney, and indirectly Governor Roosevelt as
well, that the federal authorities were aware of grave abuses in the Stock
Exchange. Unless there was a genuine housecleaning, he had warned,
Congress would have to be asked to step in, much as he disliked intrud-
ing on the state's precincts. It was in pursuance of that threat, indeed,

that Hoover eventually (in March 1932) forced the Senate, over lusty partisan resistance, to investigate the New York Stock Exchange, disclosing manipulation, price-fixing, and plain thievery on a monstrous scale.

2

In October 1929 the stock market crashed. Seven months after Hoover became President his struggle against the boom was converted into a struggle against the bust.

Those old enough to remember that debacle know that one big spill was not enough to sober the joy-riders. Press and radio were flooded with cheerful reassurances. "Even in the present high market the prices of stocks have not caught up with their real value," said Professor Irving Fisher of Yale. "Yesterday's break was a shaking out of the lunatic fringe that attempts to speculate on margin." The New York *Times* reported: "Confidence in the soundness of the stock-market structure notwithstanding the upheaval of the last few days was voiced last night by bankers and other financial leaders." At a conference of governors in Salt Lake City, Franklin Roosevelt defended the soundness of the financial situation, arguing that only "gamblers" were being hurt by the collapse. His jaunty optimism left little doubt that Albany would continue to resist pressures to investigate and curb the Exchanges.

John D. Rockefeller, J. P. Morgan, Thomas Lamont, Raskob, and others in their league announced that they were buying stocks. They could afford it. Senator Carter Glass of Virginia, other top Democrats, and not a few Republicans issued cheerful forecasts. The liberal economist Stuart Chase declared that "the stock markets will not affect general prosperity." The president of the American Federation of Labor, William Green, announced that "all the factors which make for quick and speedy industrial and economic recovery are present." "Business is sound," said Alfred P. Sloan, Jr., president of General Motors.

Quotations of this character could be multiplied for pages. They came from every direction—an attempt to shoo away bad times by choral incantation. Before long these same people would be belaboring the President for allegedly promising "prosperity around the corner"—a phrase Herbert Hoover never used which was fastened upon him by political tricksters.

The President was not reassured and resisted pressures to join the chorus. He refused to utter a word in support of stock prices, limiting himself to expressions of a generalized, long-term faith in the American economy. "The fundamental business of the country, that is, production and distribution," he said, "is on a sound and prosperous basis." Not many noted how carefully he had excluded the banking, finance, and credit systems from his diagnosis. The industrial and labor leaders who conferred with him in those weeks, at his urgent invitation, knew that he spoke far more gloomily in private than in public. Editorial demands that the President encourage people to invest in stocks "notwithstanding" were steadfastly ignored.

The most worried man in the country was the man in the White House. He could draw no consolation from the fact that his dire forebodings had come true. Not once, though he must have been tempted, did he indulge in any forthright I-told-you-so reminders.

President Hoover devoted himself to action with a minimum of talk and no public posturing. He was determined, above all else, to head off panic. He began that grinding, self-lacerating labor, with only a few hours of sleep and frequently no sleep at all, which would continue until the blessed hour of release more than three years later. No galley slave of old was ever more firmly riveted to his drudgery, for he was chained by his surpassing sense of duty.

Hoover began that long regimen of unstinting exertion—physical, intellectual, and spiritual—for which he would be rewarded with the infamous legend that he "did nothing." For already, as we shall see, an efficient, well-oiled smear machine was in operation, geared to just one job, the defamation of a President.

In the judgment of one of his press secretaries, Theodore Joslin, "Mr. Hoover was peculiarly qualified for the presidency in time of adversity." Thousands of others shared that view.

Those who believe in Providence could, in fact, made a good case for the proposition that the availability of Hoover as Chief Executive during the depression was providential. This was a thought most often and feelingly expressed by people like Joslin who were intimate eyewitnesses of his Presidency. They looked in wonder and in awe upon the phenomenon of intelligence and energy, competence and dedication, combined in one man—a phenomenon of which the public at large was only dimly aware.

Hoover seemed the nearly perfect answer to a "Man Wanted" ad, had America advertised for one. Engineer, economist, humanitarian, he had grappled successfully with adversity on a gigantic scale in the past and knew its many faces. He had the experience, beyond any American in public life. He had the capacity for dealing with thousands of details under ever-shifting conditions. He was remarkably fertile in devising solutions for crowding problems; not final solutions, since the problems were for the most part insoluble, but sufficient to temper the force of each new blow. Besides, he possessed the physical vitality for immense exertions, and the moral vitality to function calmly under unexampled abuse and to resist the clamor for "easy" solutions at the price of basic principles and liberties.

Hoover was thus supremely equipped for the titanic job that was his hard fate—if only he had had talents for public relations to match. He brought to the challenge of the depression a unique blend of pragmatism and firm principle, the practical and the idealistic. He brought to them a brain to which, in the words of Bernard Baruch, "facts are as water to a sponge . . . absorbed into every tiny interstice." There was no man alive, Baruch said, to whom he would more confidently entrust a complex problem involving a vast number of details.

"He was," Joslin wrote, "a walking encyclopedia of governmental, fiscal and agricultural information, either national or international. I have seen many a conferee leave his office in a daze. And I have heard some say, 'Why, he knows more about my business than I do myself.'"

President Hoover averaged over twenty conferences, with individuals and groups, every working day. He met others at breakfast, lunch, and dinner, and on Sundays at his summer camp. The subject matter, in aggregate, covered literally every aspect of national and world affairs. Those with whom he talked—bankers, social workers, engineers, farmers, labor leaders, statesmen, military men—were usually the top people in their particular fields. Yet they all found him astonishingly knowledgeable in their own areas of expertism. Invariably he seemed able not only to diagnose their problems but ready with some plan of therapy already in his head or in his pocket.

And they never were quack remedies to conceal unpleasant symptoms. Many of Hoover's devices were denied to him altogether by hostile politicians, others were granted grudgingly and only in part. But nearly all of them were adopted in full—usually without credit to their author—when these very politicians came into power. This tribute to his ability, the flattery by imitation, certainly was not intentional.

XIX

Constructive Labors

Lou HENRY HOOVER surveyed the White House, as it had been her destiny to survey a dozen temporary homes, with a practiced eye. Her husband had always thought it a pity that Abraham Lincoln's study, so redolent of history, had since the Teddy Roosevelt administrations been used as a bedroom. Restoration of that chamber to its original grace and function, and turning the upstairs apartments into livable quarters, were her first household chores.

With the famous contemporary painting of the signing of the Emancipation Proclamation as guide, she was able to re-create the exact decor of Lincoln's time. President Hoover, especially in periods of Lincolnesque gloom, took a sentimental pride in using this room as his own study. It gave him a sense of historical continuity with the President whom he admired above all his thirty predecessors.

By searching from garret to cellar, the First Lady resurrected four of the original chairs from the study, as well as other items. Lincoln's large work-table was discovered in the headquarters of the Historical Society in Hartford, Connecticut. No one knew how it got there, but its transfer to the White House was duly negotiated. The upstairs apartments were pretty bleak. But she brought in some of her own belongings, added color and comforts, and in the end gave the place a cheerful air.

Her major job of restoration was in the spacious Red Drawing Room, which she rehabilitated in its original style, as decorated by President and Mrs. Monroe after the burning of the White House in 1812. Many of the Empire pieces acquired for Monroe by his ambassador in Paris showed up in the search of storerooms; Mrs. Hoover had them repaired. Others, which she examined in the Monroe law office in Fredericksburg, she had duplicated by master craftsmen. A copy of Mrs. Monroe's portrait, which had hung in that room, and other paintings of the period completed the decor. The costs of the restoration were paid by Mrs. Hoover out of her personal funds.

The long, unfurnished hall running the length of the White House offended her homemaker's soul. She therefore had bookcases built along both walls; they accommodated the library presented to Hoover by the Booksellers of America. Rugs were laid in this passageway, with comfortable chairs and sofas provided at convenient intervals. In a corner she arranged a collection of miniature furniture for the delight of child visitors. The once dismal hallway became a cheerful gathering place. She made other changes, and encouraged a woman friend to research and write an illustrated history of White House furnishings.

The Hoovers retained the entire domestic staff, including the cook who apprised them that she had voted for Al Smith. She kept the job, ironically, only until the advent of a Democratic administration.

Like all Presidents, Hoover felt the need for a summer camp. After some exploration he discovered a delightful spot at the headwaters of the Rapidan River, about one hundred miles from the White House. Mrs. Hoover planned and supervised the building of a series of log cabins, providing accommodations for about a dozen guests. Additional cabins were built later. At the end of the term the Rapidan camp was presented to the Shenandoah National Park, on condition that it be available to the White House or the Boy and Girl Scouts. A charge by hostile politicos that it had been built with public funds was easily refuted; every penny for the land, cabins, and furnishings had, of course, come out of the Hoovers' pockets.

On January 1, 1930, his first New Year's morning in the White House, some nine thousand people crowded the lawn to greet the President —three times the usual number on such occasions. Throughout his incumbency, in fact, Hoover attracted more tourists than any of his predecessors. The hallowed tradition of a daily reception for the general public, at 12:30 P.M., had drawn three or four hundred visitors in Coolidge's time; about a thousand came for a glimpse of Hoover.

Whether they were drawn by garden variety curiosity or admiration, the drain on an overworked President's time was a serious matter. On occasion his right hand was sore for days. Always the engineer, he soon decreed photography as a substitute for handshaking, thus saving both time and his writing hand. The visitors were deployed in groups and the President posed with each in turn for pictures, chatting with a few here and there as the cameras clicked. The results were highly satisfactory, since it enabled the callers to bring home documentary proofs of the visit.

The giant New Year's reception was abandoned after the first experience, but Mrs. Hoover's "rigid sense of duty," as her husband would report, "would not permit abolishing the other formal receptions. To her it was part of her job." There were nine or ten of these each year, aside from unscheduled receptions for eminent foreign guests.

The First Lady, of course, did the traditional entertaining on the distaff side. One of these occasions churned up a storm in the social teapot. There was one Negro Congressman at the time. As a matter of course Mrs. Hoover included his wife in a reception for legislators' wives. The Congressman himself gave the story to reporters, and instantly the Southern press yelled in near-unison that the White House was being "defiled."

The real danger was that some unpleasant incident might develop at the party itself. Press photographers, in fact, were on hand to "shoot" any snub or insult to the Negro lady. Mrs. Hoover, however, diplomatically divided the reception into several parts on different days, after hand-picking wives who were liberal on race matters for the contingent that included the Negro guest.

There were no incidents. But there were a lot of ugly editorials and speeches on the floor of Congress; a resolution condemning the "defile-ment" was passed by the Texas legislature. To divert the lightning from his wife, the President at once invited a prominent Negro educator to lunch with him at the White House. The noise thereupon grew even louder, but at least most of the brickbats were now deflected from his wife to himself.

Mrs. Hoover was brought to tears by some of the attacks. "Her tears, however, did not melt her indomitable determination," her husband fondly attested. He would write:

To Mrs. Hoover her position must be a symbol of everything wholesome in American life. She was oversensitive and the stabs of political life which, no doubt, were deserved by me hurt her greatly. She was deeply religious, and to her such actions were just plain wickedness. . . . I suggested to her one time that a good reason for holding to orthodox religious faith is that it included a hot hell, and that she should console herself that this kind of politician would find special facilities in the world to come.

Like many another husband resorting to a placating joke, he failed to draw a smile—"She was too gentle a soul to see any humor in my idea."

A woman secretary who worked in the White House through the Coolidge and part of the Hoover administrations, Mary Randolph, in a book on *Presidents and First Ladies* (1936), described Lou Henry Hoover as "tall and commanding":

Very handsome she looked . . . in winter wearing lovely, clinging velvet gowns or heavy crepes . . . in spring, soft flowered chiffons or misty floating lace, ever becoming to her with her pale clear skin, blue eyes and chiseled features. . . . Her beautifully shaped head, well set on her shoulders, boasted a mass of naturally curly silver hair . . . the admiration of all men. . . . She never fitted more perfectly into the White House picture than in her formal evening gown.

The First Lady's energy was almost a match for the President's. She entertained the distaff side of officialdom beyond the call of duty. Her presidency of the Girl Scouts was not merely honorific—she provided active and intensive leadership. "Quietly going on charitable missions," Miss Randolph recorded, "keeping in touch with many friends, riding horseback, knitting for her grandchildren, driving her own car about Washington and on longer trips through Virginia, were among the many activities of this busy First Lady."

The Hoover sons spent as much time as they could with their parents. Herbert was married by this time and had two children; a third was born while Hoover was President. No part of the White House was forbidden to the youngsters. The two older ones would barge into the President's office or the Lincoln study at will—he always had candy in a drawer for them.

In 1930, Herbert developed tuberculosis and had to spend a year in a sanitorium. His wife, Margaret, and their children came to live in the White House. The eldest of the grandchildren, Peggy Ann, made it her special assignment to see that Grandpa didn't miss his lunch. She would break in on the composition of some state paper to order him to the dining room at once. If he didn't obey she would exclaim impatiently: "I said luncheon was ready, come you lazy man!" Practically none of this engaging domestic side got into the papers—Hoover, as far as he could, discouraged stories about his family, no matter how beguiling.

2

Herbert Hoover came to the White House keyed for a supreme job of building. Instead he was obliged to patch. This is the nub of his private frustration. He was like a mariner starting off on a journey of discovery to bring home rare treasures who is forced by sudden storms to pour all his energies into just keeping the ship afloat.

It was not a nebulous do-good urge that he brought to the highest office but concrete, detailed, and ambitious blueprints impinging on virtually every aspect of national life. They embraced plans for social reforms and ameliorations in accord with his American brand of liberal individualism. They included far-reaching improvement of the country's physical "plant" through development of neglected resources, more rational transportation, measures of conservation and reclamation. They envisioned basic reformation of economic institutions, especially the credit systems and agriculture.

These intentions are amply documented in his own state papers, particularly in his messages to the Congress. They can be deduced, besides, from the myriad public enterprises he initiated or sponsored in the first few months of good weather allowed him by history; from what he attempted and in considerable part accomplished even after the storms broke.

He threw himself into the new job with the concentrated energy for which he had become famous. The record has been blurred by the piled-up troubles and blotched by systematic misrepresentation. But those who studied the Hoover administration later, more detachedly in the perspective of time, were always astonished by the magnitude of his achievements in many fields—this over and above the colossal labors directly related to meeting the depression. Vital segments, at least, of the Hoover blueprints were carried out in the midst of destruction and collapse. His imprint on physical America and American institutions was deep and endures to this day.

As Secretary of Commerce he had laid the groundwork in some areas accessible to him—home ownership, flood control, better navigation, rationalization of techniques and reduction of waste in industry, etc. He had reached out for the Presidency as a God-given opportunity to carry such tasks forward and to tackle new ones for which he had lacked authority.

Each of these things was aimed to strengthen the American system of life and to translate his philosophy into reality. But he had barely unrolled the constructive plans and assembled some of the raw materials when the world was overwhelmed by economic catastrophe. The extraordinary part of it, worth emphasizing for what it tells about the man, is that he did not discard those plans and dreams.

For fifteen years the United States had been absorbed in war, postwar adjustment, and sheer expansion. It had barely begun to digest such new forces and inventions as mass production, radio, airplanes. It had not paused to take stock of its social structure and its corroding faults. Hoover has explained:

The prolific soil of individual liberty produces not only magnificent blossoms but noxious weeds, and we have grown a lot of thistles. . . . I had come to the White House not only convinced of the necessity of easing the strains of growth and giving impulse to progress but with high hopes that I might lead in performing the task.

In some instances, of course, the economic debacle enabled President Hoover to obtain belatedly, as *curative* measures, things that he had asked for in vain in the good years as *preventive* measures. This is especially true with respect to water resources, power projects, highways, and other public works providing employment.

He had advocated a variety of public construction projects, not to boost employment but for their intrinsic and permanent value to the national "plant." The frugal, quiescent Coolidge shied clear of most of them because they were "too expensive." Now Congress quickly voted the necessary funds with a primary view to generating jobs for the jobless. Midway in his term, the President could announce that public works of some two billion dollars were under way, employing about a million workers.

Hoover was merely carrying forward ideas he had developed as Secretary when he proposed, as President, a thorough revision of the Reclamation Service to provide "the construction of great multiple-purpose water storage dams" for irrigation, flood protection, better navigation channels and, in many cases, hydroelectric power. At his request Congress authorized a program of river and harbor improvements looking to a unified trunk-line system of interior waterways. This involved large-scale, correlated projects on the Mississippi, Ohio, Tennessee, and other great rivers and a number of linking canals—to cost an estimated fifty-five million dollars annually for five years. The network was to be joined ultimately with the North Atlantic by way of the Great Lakes and the St. Lawrence River System, so that primary productive regions inland would have direct outlets to the ocean.

Parts of the construction on this monumental plan were begun after the President's Rivers and Harbors Bill was enacted in July 1930; additional appropriations were subsequently obtained. In 1931 alone the amount of material moved in connection with these water developments equaled the entire material moved in building the Panama Canal. The flood control project on the Mississippi for a thousand miles below Cairo was practically completed during Hoover's incumbency. It was estimated that the government made more progress in river works during the four Hoover years than in the preceding three decades.

As chairman of the U.S.-Canadian St. Lawrence Waterways Commission, he had played the leading role in developing this vast plan. As President he was able to negotiate a treaty with Canada for the actual construction, but the Senate withheld its ratification until after Hoover departed from the White House. Soon after he became President, the last formalities were completed on the Colorado River Compact, which he had negotiated as Secretary. He was thus able to get construction started on the Hoover Dam, the world's largest at that time.

Engineering operations were initiated, in 1930, on a project in the Northwest long close to Hoover's heart: the Grand Coulee Dam on the

Columbia River. The detailed plans were virtually completed by the end of the Hoover term, so that the succeeding Administration could at once undertake actual construction. Because Coolidge refused to approve it, a vast storage control plan for the great valley of California worked out by Hoover had languished for several years. Now the engineering work was carried forward and initial construction begun on the Sacramento, Kings, San Joaquin, and American River dams.

Development of the drainage system on the Tennessee was snarled in controversy. Hoover vetoed a bill for federal operation of Muscle Shoals, explaining again that he opposed government competition with private enterprise. Besides, he believed that such utilities should be "administered by the people upon the ground, responsible to their own communities," not by theorists in Washington panting to promote socialistic experiments. A commission which he formed together with the governors of Alabama and Tennessee recommended that Muscle Shoals power and fertilizer plants be leased to private industry under strict government regulation. In his first message to Congress and in subsequent messages he asked for a Federal Power Commission to regulate utilities in interstate business, but could not obtain the kind of effective authority he envisioned.

As relatively new industries, both radio and aviation, which he had nurtured as Secretary, now received his intensified guidance. Back in 1922, Hoover had said at a conference he called on radio regulation: "The ether is a public medium and its use must be for the public benefit. The use of radio channels is justified only if there is public benefit." The earlier law having proved inadequate for this purpose, he now obtained clarifying amendments. His objective, he made it clear, was to prevent both government ownership and private monopoly in the ether. "The price of liberty," he later summed up in this context, "thus becomes not only a matter of eternal vigilance but of a good Attorney General."

During his journey in Latin America as President-elect, he had laid the foundations for the creation of Pan American Airways. He followed this up as President by obtaining the agreement of the governments involved and by the end of 1930 air mail was being flown to a long array of Latin American countries. Hoover took many firm steps also to redeem the American merchant marine from the inefficiency and outmoded habits of the Shipping Board. Despite inadequate support in Congress, his interest was a large factor in a revitalized shipbuilding industry, with 870,000 tons built during his Administration—generating thirty thousand new jobs—as against 128,000 tons in previous Administrations.

This sort of constructive work under White House prodding could be listed in many other departments of national life. The housing of federal services and agencies, for instance, was expanded and beautified. Over

350 new buildings were completed and 460 more were contracted in all parts of the country by the time Hoover relinquished his office. Through presidential intervention, the bridge across the San Francisco Bay, long argued, was to become a reality. Construction was begun during his Administration. Federal aid to states for essential highway systems was more than doubled: from $195 million a year in 1928, to $260 million in 1930, with a corresponding increase in road-building jobs.

In agriculture, the President led the fight for fundamental reforms and obtained the organization of the Federal Farm Board, with half a billion dollars in Treasury capital. Unhappily its planned purposes were derailed by the depression, but the Board proved a useful tool in providing many types of emergency aid to the farmers.

Having as Commerce Secretary organized the "Better Homes in America" movement, to promote more and better housing, he continued this work with unabating zeal as President. His conference of over a thousand delegates from government, industry, labor, and other factors in the construction equation provided blueprints for action which have stood the tests of time ever since.

This, of course, does not complete the record. His domestic program amounted to a room-by-room overhauling not only of physical America but of its social edifice.

3

Soon after he became President, Hoover began to organize a national conference on the health and protection of children. The five hundred thousand dollars spent on the project did not come from the taxpayers; he raised all of it from private sources. At that stage a suggestion for the use of public funds for such a purpose would have horrified most Democrats and Republicans alike. Besides, Hoover continued to regard voluntary, cooperative action for great public objectives as more wholesome, more safely in the tradition of a free society.

To bring the voluminous findings and proposals of the several thousand men and women involved in the enterprise within the mental compass of the ordinary American, the President himself, in longhand, reduced them to what he called "the Children's Charter." As a succinct, practical outline of society's responsibility to its young—the fundamental social security offered by a physically and morally robust new generation—this document has never been surpassed.

Its nineteen clauses, not merely in what they say but in the goals of a perfected humanity which they envision, amount to a Magna Charta of social idealism within a framework of freedom:

For every child spiritual and moral training to help him stand firm under the pressure of life. . . . For every child understanding and the guarding of his personality as his most precious right. . . . For every child a community which recognizes and plans for his needs, protects him against physical dangers, moral hazards, and disease. . . . For every child an education which, through the discovery and development of his individual abilities, prepares him for life. . . . For every child these rights, regardless of race, or color, or situation, wherever he may live under the protection of the American flag.

Merely highlights, these, in a plan rounded and complete as an engineering graph. As an index to Hoover's concept of the good life that charter is worth tomes of research and interpretation. It may be subject to strictures only on the grounds that it is too idealistic, too ambitious, too farseeing.

Having gotten the survey on child welfare going, the President addressed himself to an even more comprehensive examination of larger problems—one of the most ambitious studies of American life ever undertaken under government aegis. This was his Committee on Social Trends, appointed on September 9, 1929, and again financed by private contributions.

The committee mobilized several hundred specialists in diverse fields —public welfare, taxation, social security, rural life, utilization of national resources, education, economic institutions, national planning (not in the coercive but the cooperative sense), crime and punishment, labor-management tensions, a score of other basic areas. Under the President's guidance they identified the problems, lined up the pertinent data, and presented alternative solutions. In issuing the report of the committee in the final months of his Administration, Hoover declared:

The significance of this report lies primarily in the fact that it is a cooperative effort on a very broad scale to project into the field of social thought the scientific mood and the scientific method as correctives to indiscriminating emotional approach; to secure the factual basis in seeking for constructive remedies of great social problems.

The survey had a profound effect on social thinking and progressive reforms in the years that followed. But Hoover's pioneering role was rarely, if ever, acknowledged—that would have impaired the stereotype of a "reactionary" President indispensable to the new Establishment.

Implementation of the ideas in the Children's Charter and the solutions in the Social Trends study was made all but impossible by the growing load of immediate problems of depression and destitution. The conduct of foreign affairs, too, was continually affected by the worldwide depression. Its guiding concepts, however, Hoover considered valid for any period.

He aimed to break through America's deepening isolationist fixations. His inaugural address underlined "the profound truth that our progress, prosperity, and peace are interlocked with the progress, prosperity, and peace of all humanity." He acted at once to implement what he had called the "good neighbor" approach to Latin American countries; adherence to the World Court; cooperation with the League of Nations in its non-political activities; a curb on the runaway naval race; first steps toward phased disarmament; agreements to give full immunity to food cargoes in time of war. He strove, above all, for joint effort with other nations to prevent or cushion economic and political disasters.

As President, Hoover carried out his pre-inauguration promises by withdrawing American marines from Haiti and Nicaragua; by pledging not to interfere in the internal affairs of neighbor nations; by enunciating the principle that Americans investing capital abroad did so at their own risk.

Except on the issue of limiting naval armaments, he was blocked in his major attempts to overcome the isolationist trend. Congress turned down his every formula for adherence to the World Court or collaboration with the League. His cherished plan for outlawing the use of civilian hunger as a war weapon was hailed by the press of the world, except the official mouthpieces of Japan and England, but it never got beyond the stage of abstract enthusiasm.

In the economic dimension he was more successful, largely because the interdependence of nations was made so grimly obvious by events. His moratorium on intergovernmental debts and the "standstill" agreement on private international debts—about which we shall have more to say later—marked the first great reversals of the supernationalist patterns set at Versailles.

The highly intricate subject of tariffs may be mentioned in this context. Hoover was not among the Republican extremists on this issue. The platform on which he was elected committed him to tariff revision in the interest of hard-pressed farmers. Mounting unemployment dictated protection in many industrial areas; but the moderation of Hoover's proposals angered protectionists. He was opposed by a united front of industrial lobbyists for his insistence on wide flexibility in tariff rates. His plan, in which he was only partially successful, called for a bipartisan tariff commission with power to make adjustments as conditions changed, after public hearings by judicial procedure. Thus he hoped to remove tariff-making from politics.

The Smoot-Hawley tariff, passed in July 1930, was unsatisfactory to the President but the best he could obtain from a protectionist majority. It suited some political critics in the next presidential campaign to blame the whole depression upon the moderate increases in this bill. They chose to ignore the fact that the crash came nine months before the law was enacted; and the further fact that some forty countries had raised their tariff walls before America did. In addition, numerous nations had set up rigid import quotas and exchange controls which made customs barriers secondary by contrast. The whole world had moved blindly toward autarchy before Hoover reached Pennsylvania Avenue; the tariff measures of his Administration were minimal defense tactics, criticized at the time for their mildness rather than for excess.

Any account of the Hoover administration which limits itself to the depression and recovery measures is clearly misleading. The President never doubted that the troubled times would pass and that time-tested American values would again be needed and honored. He found margins of time and energy, therefore, to deal with larger problems and, even in meeting immediate challenge, never flouted those values.

XX

The Big Smear

A N extraordinary factory was opened up in Washington about three
months after the inauguration of President Hoover. An understanding of the Administration and of Hoover's personal ordeal is
impossible without consideration of this unprecedented enterprise. And
the date of its organization is significant. It was not, as some people later
believed or pretended to believe, a reaction to the slump or an answer
to the President's "fumbling" of depression problems, for these things
were still in the future.

The factory might be called the Michelson Mills, although technically
it figured as the press division of the Democratic National Committee.
Its products were smear stuff, ugly rumors, verbal tar-and-feathers and
high-grade oratorical ectoplasm manufactured by Charlie Michelson and
his associated ghosts. Hoover, who should know, called Michelson and
his immediate superior, Jouett Shouse, executive secretary of the Democratic Committee, "past masters of political attack."

Their plant, occupying nearly a whole floor of the National Press
Building, specialized in "processing" every word and act of the President
—including words he never uttered and acts he never committed—into
proofs of ineptitude, callousness, and confusion. It mattered little what
went into the Michelson Mills at one end. The genius of its presiding
chemists transmuted it into evil-smelling stuff at the other end.

Hoover's pessimism in seeking to curb speculative forces before the
smashup served them as well as his restrained optimism in envisioning
recovery after the smashup. His refusal to roll out the pork barrel was
heartless parsimony; his requests for more public construction and new
economic rescue agencies was reckless extravagance. Many of these very
agencies and procedures, later dressed up as proofs of New Deal genius,
were here mocked and mauled when Hoover first proposed them.

231

No President, not even Washington and certainly not Lincoln, escaped vilification while in office and later. But in Hoover's case the practice was put on an organized, systematic, lushly financed, and almost scientific basis. It was geared for mass production and mass distribution. The techniques of smearing, after all, had been amazingly improved since Lincoln's time. Every anti-Hoover lie and innuendo was endlessly multiplied, as in repeating mirrors, through press syndication, canned speeches, quickie books, bushels of cartoons, hours of radio broadcasts. John Spargo, liberal and socialist, characterized it as "the most shamefully scurrilous machine for discrediting a public man that this or any other nation has known in my time."

There is, of course, nothing new about disloyal oppositions in American politics. The novelty of the Michelson Mills was that it functioned from the very beginning of the Hoover administration and on a daring scale. As a seasoned capital correspondent, Herbert Corey, wrote when the unholy enterprise was still young, "normally it had been the Democratic party's habit to sink into an irritated stupor during Republican administrations and only waken for the four months of its appeal to the people." This time the opposition organized for continuous attack before they had the faintest knowledge what they would be called upon to attack. Shouse and Michelson each was paid twenty-five thousand dollars a year—the equivalent in 1929 of what three or four times that amount would be today—and expenses. The financing came from Raskob ($462,000), the duPonts, Thomas Fortune Ryan, Herbert Lehman, Vincent Astor, and other men of immense wealth.

The Democratic National Committee raised nearly three million dollars after the defeat of Al Smith. Part of this went to cover campaign deficits. The rest, estimated at $2,300,000, went to oil the wheels of the mud-making mills. It was the largest partisan expenditure *between campaigns* in the history of American political life.

Two other novel features need to be mentioned. The first is that this gigantic vilification was not directed against the Republican party but specifically against one man, Herbert Hoover. The smart theory was that some Republicans, too, could be incensed against their standard-bearer who was certain to run for re-election. Ironically, the Republicans who went along were both "progressives" like Senator Borah at one end and accredited "reactionaries" at the other end.

The second novelty is that the systematic process of character assassination was not soft-pedaled, let alone abandoned, after its victim had been ousted from the White House. On the contrary, as we shall presently see, it was even stepped up and infinitely refined, until the name Hoover was turned into a synonym for all the sins and fears and hates of an unhappy passage of history.

It should be recalled that the crisis in national economy and morale in 1929–32 was as serious as war itself. Logically it demanded some measure of national unity, some relaxation of the partisan spirit, at least a moratorium on the more egregious varieties of character assassination. No President in peacetime had ever made more earnest and self-effacing proffers of bipartisan action to find solutions for problems threatening the very survival of American civilization. No President had ever been so brutally, completely, and insultingly rebuffed.

In effect Hoover found himself with the responsibilities of a wartime President but without wartime powers, wartime prestige, and most serious of all, any wartime command of patriotic nonpartisan support. Far from easing off when catastrophes such as market crashes, economic collapse, floods, drought, the repercussions of disasters in other countries, struck the United States, the Shouse-Michelson offensive went into high gear. The factory had a vested interest in calamity. Said Michelson himself, in boasting of his successes, "The table was set, all we had to do was eat." They were practiced gourmands at a feast of troubles.

Besides being well-paid propagandists, the Michelson staff were also Americans and human beings. But one would never guess this from their output. In the mountains of ghostwritten words there were few paragraphs of honestly constructive criticism; few expressions of genuine sympathy, understanding, and encouragement for the American "holding the bag." The smear mills were conducted in the spirit of high-powered shyster salesmen tearing down a competing product. It was John Nance Garner who said in a moment of candor: Michelson's job was to "whittle down Hoover *to our size*" (italics mine). The italicized words amount to a left-handed compliment to the beleaguered President.

In September 1930 the Michelson Mills had barely found their full stride. They had not yet had enough human misery to feed upon. But already in that month *Scribner's Magazine* could publish an article by a respected Washington journalist, Frank R. Kent of the Baltimore *Sun*, about "the political agency in Washington that more than any other has helped mold the public mind in regard to Mr. Hoover, magnifying his misfortunes, minimizing his achievements . . . an illuminating illustration of the power of unopposed propaganda in skillful hands." Michelson's goal, said Kent,

was to "smear" the Hoover administration. That is what he is there for and all he is there for. That is his job, and it would be hard to imagine a man with his heart more completely in it. It would have been a genuine pleasure for Mr. Michelson to "smear" the Hoover administration if he were not paid a cent. To

get $25,000 a year for doing something you yearn to do anyhow, to have the
tools furnished free of charge, to have no real opposition, to be able to hit without getting hit back, why, that is ideal. At least, so it seems to Mr. Michelson,
who has had this year, about the best time of his life. . . .

The whole aim and idea of Mr. Michelson's employment is to put Mr. Hoover
"in bad" with the American people. That is what he was hired for, and for the
first year at least he certainly has earned his money. Mr. Michelson's effort has
been to paint a picture of Hoover as an inept, weak, and unworthy man without
sense of direction, backbone or power of decision. If he has an admirable quality
it has not been mentioned among the millions of written words flowing from
Mr. Michelson's fluent typewriter in the past eighteen months. On the contrary,
Mr. Michelson has discovered more faults, failings, and flaws in Mr. Hoover
since March 4, 1929, than it seems possible for one man to have.

Frank Kent, it should be noted, stressed the fact that these massive
smears were "unopposed." This was substantially true. The Republican
National Committee had no corresponding propaganda division. Hoover,
who had raised hundreds of millions of dollars for humanitarian causes,
would have been flabbergasted by any suggestion that he raise funds for
counterpropaganda.

The succeeding Administration also came under violent attack—by
many of the same men who were now donating huge sums to the Michelson Mills. There were "Roosevelt-haters" aplenty. But Franklin Roosevelt
had a native gift for invective and a zest for feuding. More important,
he had at his disposal veritable armies of defenders and counterattackers:
not only the Democratic smear machine which he inherited but thousands, then tens of thousands, of "information" officers attached to all the
teeming New Deal agencies, whose primary job was to glorify the President and lambaste his enemies.

There was no such fighting force, offensive or defensive, under Hoover.
To make matters worse, there was Hoover's almost pathological aversion to squabbling on the plane of personalities. When associates urged
him to respond to ugly insults, he merely shrugged his shoulders in disgust. He had more important things to do, he insisted, than to deny that
he had robbed Chinese, promoted salted gold mines, exploited coolies,
made money on food relief, or remained indifferent to the misery of the
unemployed. "If the American people choose to believe such nonsense,"
he once remarked to Joslin, "there is nothing I can do about it."

Only on rare occasions did he even allude to the campaign of derogation. In December of 1930, for instance, addressing the Gridiron Club,
Hoover referred sadly to "the sordidness and gossip which oozes through
the intellectual swamps of a great political capital." But beyond that he
refused to go. He believed that it was beneath the dignity of his office to

take notice of vituperation. He believed that he could defend Hoover the man only by subjecting Hoover the President to vulgarities, and therefore chose long-suffering silence.

The unopposed propaganda hit the mark. Millions of well-meaning Americans for years thereafter carried in their minds "facts" and "opinions" about Hoover which had been artfully manufactured and planted there by the Michelson outfit and its accessory propagandists. Even now, many Americans—among them historians—still treat the falsehoods as established truth; but their number, happily, is rapidly dwindling.

What were Michelson's motives? The answer some have given is that he was so devoted to Al Smith that he could not forgive Hoover for defeating him. That explanation seems inadequate. Michelson continued the smear without Smith's approval and, somewhat later, in contempt of Smith's opposition. Perhaps he was simply the sort of twisted adult who enjoys playing with mud.

One who watched him closely declared that Michelson's qualities were "imagination, mischievousness, and a touch of malevolence." Certainly his autobiography shows no sign of self-consciousness or remorse about hitting Hoover below the belt, and a certain pride in sheer craftsmanship in his favorite trade.

In his autobiography Michelson flips off the charge that he "smeared" a President as if it were a minor accusation. But a few pages farther he alludes casually to "the gloomy occupant of the White House whom we referred to as *the author of the depression*" (italics mine). Possibly he was right: "smear" may be too mild a word for such deliberate falsification and injustice. Why he considered it somehow disreputable for a President to be "gloomy" in a time of terrible trouble is not clear.

2

The official Democratic offensive against Hoover's character, of course, was supplemented by a prodigious private campaign that was, likewise, to continue long after he was retired from the Presidency. Blaming it on Hoover became almost second nature for a country staggering under its disasters and craving a conspicuous object for its despairs and hatreds.

When a terrible drought developed in a third of the states, Hoover's friends said bitterly, "He will probably be blamed for this, too." The popular versifier, Arthur Guiterman, wrote a long satirical poem which he sent to friends who were, like himself, on Hoover's side. It opened with these lines:

If Wall Street grabbed your final cent,
That's right, impeach the President.
If Europe seethes with discontent,
Denounce the cause—our President.

And it closed with these lines:

So give your feelings proper vent
By growling at the President.
It helps us all and pays the rent
To sit and blame the President.

The shameless phrase "the Hoover depression" was injected into common usage; it was about as imbecilic as "the Teddy Roosevelt earthquake" in California or "the Truman blizzard" of 1947 would be. But once insinuated into everyday parlance by the political profiteers of the catastrophe there was scarcely any need for other issues. Why should a normal American support the monstrous "author" of a depression bearing his name? There was plenty more of this semantic strategy, none of it innocent. The country was taught to speak of "Hoover breadlines." Shanty colonies set up by footloose unemployed young people were christened "Hoovervilles." This vocabulary of abuse not only remained but was, if anything, extended after he left Washington. It became enshrined in "serious" history and sociology books.

A number of peak points in the landscape of the Great Smear are worth noting. Unlike rumor and innuendo, they were subject to checking and consequently always fizzled out in absurdity. I refer to attempts to fabricate sensational "scandals" about the Hoover administration.

The most ambitious of these had its start in the Michelson Mills and was picked up, to its ultimate distress, by the respectable New York *World,* then under the editorship of Walter Lippmann. With a great beating of drums and cymbals that newspaper announced a syndicated series of articles exposing what it actually dubbed "a second Teapot Dome" involving the President and his Cabinet. The series was widely advertised in advance, without so much as a routine inquiry about its accuracy.

The charges, it developed, were based solely on the say-so of an employee of the Department of the Interior named Kelley, who had been in charge of oil shale leases. He was paid twelve thousand dollars for his phony revelations. He claimed that shale oil lands of fabulous value were being lost to the people through contracts made by the Department; that documents relating to the outrage had been destroyed; that someone somewhere was being paid off.

The advance ballyhoo was the first that Hoover or his Secretary of the Interior, Dr. Wilbur, ever heard of the affair. An immediate inquiry revealed that Kelley had spun his fantasy out of his own confusions. The shale lands in question were without the slightest commercial value; the "destroyed" documents were all in their proper files; not a trace of misconduct or even irregularity could be found. These official findings were all subject to any reporter's confirmation, but Lippmann went ahead with the dissemination of the nonsense and it made lurid headlines from coast to coast.

Later Secretary Wilbur, by hints of a libel suit, compelled the newspaper to publish an abject apology. Though printed in small type, it was credited with speeding up the demise of the New York *World* soon thereafter. In a biography of Joseph Pulitzer, the author, J. W. Barrett, indicated his suspicion that the phony "scandal" had some part in the newspaper's death. The *World*, he wrote, "made no effort to obtain Secretary Wilbur's statement until after the series began," though "the most casual inquiry would have satisfied the *World* that there was nothing to back up Kelley's charges."

Another "scandal" that failed was initiated in 1930 by John Nance Garner, later the New Deal Vice President and still later a bitter critic of the New Deal. He accused Hoover of some shady association with sugar lobbyists. Democratic Senator Thomas J. Walsh of Montana grabbed the morsel with hungry glee and set up a Senate investigation. After having provided the press with a headline circus of insinuations, Walsh announced that there was not an atom of truth in the whole tale.

Wilbur and Hyde, in *The Hoover Policies,* have attested—as have many other students since—that "all the search of bitter partisanship" failed to locate "one particle of dishonesty . . . in the handling of over twenty-five billion dollars of income and expenditure. . . . This was because of the Hoover policy in choosing men of probity and ability and not primarily for politics. Never has the public service been raised to as high a level as during the four Hoover years."

Major libels like the shale lands and sugar lobby inventions could be met head-on and exposed, but not a thousand corrupt whispers and distortions. They came faster and traveled farther than a President burdened with momentous tasks of state could or cared to refute. The sky was the limit for malignity against Hoover.

When the nation was shocked by the kidnaping of the Lindbergh baby, ghoulish whispers had it that the President had helped Lindbergh "frame" the story for publicity!

Ivar Kreuger, the Swedish match tycoon and gambler, committed suicide on the other side of the ocean as his financial empire tumbled into a rubbish heap. At once planted stories identified him as "a friend of Hoover." The basis of this fantasy: a five-minute courtesy visit by Kreuger to the White House at the suggestion of the State Department in response to a request by the Swedish Legation.

The vilest of the smear products were packed between the covers of at least five books which Arthur Train, a first-rate lawyer as well as popular writer, took apart in the September 20, 1932 issue of *Collier's*. He indicted them as "a veritable library of scurrilous books . . . conceived in partisan animosity, in the mere lust for profit, or in a surreptitious hope of blackmail." The books were so abominable and at bottom so stupid that even the Michelson factory steered shy of them—though no one high up in the Democratic camp had the decency to repudiate them in so many words.

The most reckless of the poisoned confections, by an Englishman living in the United States ("a literary beachcomber" Hoover called him), one John Hamill, was *The Strange Career of Mr. Hoover—Under Two Flags*. Appropriately, it was published by a convicted dealer in pornographic books, who peddled it as part of a filth package called *Faro's Famous Dozen*.

A more unprincipled hodgepodge of lies, distortions, and forgeries can hardly be imagined. Soon after its publication Hamill himself repudiated his smelly handiwork in a sworn confession running to 189 pages. I have read a photostat copy of this document. Though Hamill blames the worst fabrications upon the publisher, he does not spare himself either. It was all the work of "ghouls," he says, eager for quick money through a sensational best-seller. The garbage did not achieve bestsellerdom, but its most outrageous lies took root and proliferated.

The other books derived, as Arthur Train put it, from "the same polluted source." One of them, by a small-bore Tammany hanger-on and ex-policeman, John H. (known as Constitution) O'Brien, was based on the identical "research" materials. It was O'Brien who first hatched the bright idea and raised the money to finance Hamill's work. Another book, by the socialist Clement Wood, was a straight rewrite of Hamill; a third, by a Communist fellow-traveler named Walter Liggett, likewise absorbed the worst errors and rawest lies of Hamill and O'Brien.

To add to the pretty picture, O'Brien sued Hamill, claiming he had purloined the materials and was therefore "a thief, forger and fraud." Hamill retorted no less elegantly. The malodorous details of their quarrel over the spoils that weren't there are too complicated for this writer. Reading the press reports and documents one feels that he has stumbled into a diseased swamp. Yet between them these worthies raked up the raw stuff on which anti-Hoover malice fed long after they were themselves forgotten. The liars might recant in tears, but the lies marched on and on.

In 1963 I still heard an echo of these lies. The *Reader's Digest* had published something complimentary about the former President. An incensed reader wrote me, as one of the editors, listing a few of the ex-President's "crimes"—and citing the Hamill book as her authority!

Even the President's boyhood, its Lincolnesque poverty and Quaker austerity, was treated with derision. Hamill mocked him for having "missed all the fun of childhood" and for "collecting the laundry" of his classmates. The same was true of his Quakerism. Clement Wood sagely pointed out that "Hoover, alone of all our Presidents, belonged to a sect which permitted each member to be the final judge of his own actions, his own morality," and this, he warned, "is an infinitely dangerous power to give to any man." From what sect the morality of Wood's rehash of the sordid Hamill derived was not disclosed.

All the smear artists insisted that, in his engineering career, he had been a promoter and gambler rather than an engineer. The technique of his defamers was as simple as it was dishonest. They blamed him for every mining project that went sour before, during, or after he had any connection with it. Since he had been hired to investigate, operate, or salvage hundreds of mines, they had plenty of scope for misrepresentation. Even the episode of the million-dollar defalcation by a junior partner in the London mining firm, on which Hoover and other members of the firm made good out of their own pockets, was turned into a fable of frenzied finance—with Hoover as the villain rather than the hero.

As a practical engineer, it will be recalled, Hoover wrote and spoke against coolie labor and underpaid labor generally. He regarded it as both inhumane and inefficient. Somehow the books and Michelson cohorts stood this fact on its head and painted him as a slave-driving exploiter of cheap labor. Once he had described a horrifying situation in which "the disregard for human life permits cheap mining." This quoted phrase and others in his attack on such practices were wrenched out of context and presented as if he *approved* the horrors he described and condemned.

The "two flags" part of the Hamill fabrication, endlessly flaunted during the 1932 campaign, merits mention. Echoes of it could be heard for a dozen years or more. Work abroad, wherever the exigencies of geology took him, is in the nature of the mining man's lot. It was always as an American, introducing American methods, surrounded by American associates, that Hoover worked in China, Australia, Africa, Russia, Latin America, wherever metals were stored in God's good earth.

It suited Hoover's detractors, however, to spread the two-flags myth. A few of them went so far as to allege that he had become a British citizen. Hamill offered and the rest copied "documentary evidence"—Hoover's name on a local English voters' list. They merely failed to mention that all householders and taxpayers were automatically inscribed on that list, whether they were Americans, Siamese, or Patagonians.

The scurrilities did not make their authors rich. They had carried a bad thing too far. Few in their senses could believe that one mortal being could have crowded so many crimes into one lifetime and "gotten away with it." After Hamill's repudiation of his opus, it was withdrawn from circulation; leftover copies were apparently snapped up by the Communist propaganda apparatus, for they continued to show up in Red bookshops.

3

One of the sticks for beating a President, then an ex-President, improved and embellished through the years, has a tough knob in the shape of an apple. For all the noise it has made, the matter is so trivial that one blushes in writing about it.

Suddenly, in the final Hoover months, unemployed veterans, real and bogus, appeared on city streets peddling apples. In all those cities facilities for direct relief were available. Veterans, in particular, were receiving more aid than under any previous—or succeeding—Administrations. Hoover had placed all needy and sick veterans on disability allowances. The lists of World War I veterans and dependents drawing pensions or special allowance thus expanded severalfold, to 853,800 in the last Hoover year; it would be trimmed to 462,900 in the first Roosevelt year.

But there they were, hundreds of veterans selling apples, exploiting the sympathy of bypassers. Inquiry revealed at once that it was simply a heartless sales promotion gimmick worked up by Oregon and Washington apple growers. They had mobilized salesmen for their excess wares, with lush profits for themselves and lush propaganda materials for others. The dismal business lapsed, of course, as soon as the apple growers had disposed of their surpluses.

Shrewd demagoguery, however, turned the supposedly starving veteran peddlers into a symbol of official callousness and neglect. A haggard veteran, preferably a cripple, selling apples became a set piece in tear-jerking movies, plays, and novels depicting the Hoover period. "Do you want to go back to apple-selling?" became a standard "argument" in defending the New Deal and derogating Republicans.

A more serious episode was the self-styled Bonus March. This has been so outrageously distorted that the most important fact about it should be stated at once. It is that the violence developed *before* the President intervened and ceased after his intervention. As the late General Patrick J. Hurley, then Secretary of War, put it to me in a personal letter: "Not one single shot was fired nor was any person seriously injured after the arrival of the United States troops. Law and order was established in Washington."

Hoover had opposed raids on the Treasury through veterans' bonus laws. In this he had for a time the support of the American Legion. The agitation for the immediate payment in cash of deferred bonuses continued, and a Bonus March on the capital was instigated by extremists, among them a large contingent of Communists. Some eleven thousand real and make-believe veterans encamped in Washington in June and July, 1932. They were treated with the utmost patience by local authorities, if only to prevent the violence some leaders of the demonstration were clearly eager to provoke.

At the President's request, Congress voted return fare for those willing to leave, and about six thousand availed themselves of the offer. The remaining five thousand were the diehards, including identified hoodlums, ex-convicts, and Communists. Later the government obtained the names of more than two thousand who had remained, and established that less than one-third of them had ever served in our armies and that nine hundred, nearly half of the two thousand, had criminal records.

About fifty of the "marchers" occupied some old buildings on Pennsylvania Avenue slated for demolition to make room for new public construction to give jobs to hundreds of unemployed. On July 28 the extremists had their way and the long-delayed "incident" was manufactured. That day the Washington police requested the squatters to move. Suddenly about a thousand of the men camped outside the city limits, armed with clubs, converged on the scene. They attacked the outnumbered police, many of whom were seriously injured. Two of the city policemen, beaten to the ground, fired in self-defense and two of their assailants were killed.

At that point the Commissioners of the District of Columbia and their Chief of Police appealed to the President in writing to send federal forces to maintain order. The President complied, through the War Department, which assigned six hundred troops under General Douglas MacArthur, with Colonel Dwight D. Eisenhower as second in command, to deal with the riots. As MacArthur phrased it in a statement that night: "The President played it pretty fine in waiting to the last minute; but he didn't have much margin." His point was that had Hoover refused to act, the situation, already out of hand, would have had more tragic consequences.

With the arrival of Uncle Sam's soldiers, all violence ceased. Far from "shooting down bonus marchers," as the propaganda legend has it, Hoover's action put an end to the shooting. The troops carried no deadly

weapons. Probably the military men went beyond the President's orders
in pushing all the marchers beyond the limits of the District of Columbia
instead of merely restoring order in the city as his specific orders stated.
Be that as it may, no blood was spilled after the Army took over from the
local authorities. The accusations against Hoover, repeated to this day,
were not merely untrue but the exact opposite of the truth.

Few minor episodes in American history have been so viciously misrepresented. The Michelson specialists seized upon it with great zest and
utter contempt for the facts. Some years later it was proved beyond doubt
that the Communists had a big role in the March and provided the expert leadership in the riots. Benjamin Gitlow, formerly a secretary-general
of the Communist Party, has told the ugly story in his book, *The Whole of
Their Lives*. One of the Communist leaders of the Bonus March, John T.
Pace, after breaking with the Communist Party, gave details to a Congressional committee:

I feel responsible in part for this oft-repeated lie about President Hoover and
General MacArthur. I led the left-wing or communist section of the Bonus
March. I was ordered by my Red superiors to provoke riots. I was told to use
every trick to bring about bloodshed in the hopes that President Hoover would
be forced to call out the Army. The communists didn't care how many veterans
were killed. I was told that Moscow had ordered riots and bloodshed in the
hopes that this might set off the revolution. My communist bosses were jumping
for joy on July 28 when the Washington police killed one (*sic*) veteran.

At the next Congress of the Communist International, in Moscow in
1935, the American Communists openly boasted of their initiative in the
Bonus March.

The decision the President made was under the circumstances unavoidable. He would have been criminally neglectful of his duty if he had
rejected the request of the District of Columbia government. But that
did not save him from being reviled as a "killer" nor did it deter the political opposition from using to the limit garbled versions of the affair to
rally veteran votes.

The American Legion, to its credit, did not then or ever join in the unjust campaign of abuse. When Secretary of War Hurley came to its next
convention and recounted the facts, he was accorded a warm and approving reception. During the 1932 election contest, alas, the Democrats
chose to exploit the falsified version. According to the statements of ex-
Communists under oath, the Communist Party put a special battery of
speakers into the field in the campaign months to help keep the Bonus
March legend well to the fore.

Even in 1963, thirty-one years after the event, millions of Americans
heard echoes of the Bonus March mythology on a nationwide television

news broadcast. As background for the Negro civil rights March on Washington, the speaker recalled such episodes in the past. He told about bloodshed and how Hoover sent troops against twenty thousand veterans (only five thousand were still in Washington and not all of them were involved in the rioting), leaving the impression that the President was somehow responsible for the violence.

The apple-selling, the Bonus March, a dozen other trumped-up stories were part of the Great Smear. It was in this atmosphere of unstinting personal abuse that the President had to tackle the emergencies of the depression. The very air he breathed was poisoned by exaggerations, inventions, mockery, and insult.

The principal product of the Michelson Mills was so skillfully fashioned, so continually repeated, that it persisted for years and survives, in vestigial forms, to this day. It was the myth of a President who "did nothing" in the face of calamity. Not, mind you, that he did the wrong things but that he rejected responsibility, and dawdled quiescently while his country went to hell. It infuriated those around Hoover who were pleading with him to relax from his exhausting labors and who often feared he might be crushed by the ever larger burdens he shouldered.

Of all the personal attacks hurled at him from all sides in the second election campaign, this was the only one the President deigned to answer. Speaking at Fort Wayne, Indiana, on October 12, 1932, he said:

During my public life I have believed that sportsmanship and statesmanship called for the elimination of harsh personalities between opponents. . . . I shall now say the one harsh word that I have uttered in public office. I hope it will be the last I shall have to say.

When you are told that the President of the United States, who by the most sacred trust of our nation is the President of all the people, a man of your own blood and upbringing, has sat in the White House for the last three years of your misfortune without troubling to know your burdens, without heartaches over your miseries and casualties, without summoning every avenue of skillful assistance irrespective of party or view, without using every ounce of his strength and straining his every nerve to protect and help, without using every possible agency of democracy that would bring aid, without putting aside personal ambition and humbling his pride of opinion, if that would serve—then I say to you that such statements are deliberate, intolerable falsehoods.

The "nothing" that he did, presented in bare outline, fills a closely printed book of 550 pages by Professor William Starr Myers and Walter H. Newton, *The Hoover Administration*. It fills the 640 pages of *The Hoover Policies* by Ray Lyman Wilbur and Arthur Mastic Hyde. I can touch only a few of its episodes, and that sketchily, in the pages that follow.

XXI

The "Republican New Deal"

WHEN President Hoover announced from the White House that in any major economic breakdown the Federal Government must assume responsibility—to see to it that no American willing to work should go hungry—he was establishing a new and audacious principle in federal theory and practice. Because that principle has been generally accepted since then, too few recall that it was first recognized and implemented by Hoover, and that he was assailed on this account by defenders of political and economic orthodoxy.

The country suffered serious economic depressions in the Administrations of Van Buren, Buchanan, Grant, Cleveland, Theodore Roosevelt, and Wilson. In not one of them did the central government take official action to relieve business or individual distress. It would have been considered an impermissible federal invasion. The established theory was that a depression must run its course, squeezing out the weak for a new start. The duty of the national authorities meanwhile was only to maintain law and order, protect the currency, and leave the rest to nature.

Latterday mythmakers have implied that the country from 1929 forward clamored for Washington intervention but that a President committed to "rugged individualism" stubbornly resisted public opinion. A history textbook published as late as 1961, for instance, still teaches that "Hoover was *unable to resist the agitation for farm relief*" (italics mine), thus suggesting that he acted reluctantly and only under the duress of public opinion.

The truth was the exact reverse. In projecting the government into the situation at once and on an ever-expanded scale, the thirty-first President was cutting boldly across precedent, prejudice, and honest opposition even within his own official family.

Two schools of thought, reflecting conflicting historical opinion, clashed

244

in the Cabinet. Neither of them was wicked or selfish or unpatriotic. Neither of them could claim a monopoly of human sympathy or good will. All those men had the commonweal at heart but differed on how it could best be served.

One school—a majority in political life generally but a minority in the Cabinet—was typified by Andrew Mellon, the Administration's first Secretary of the Treasury. It has been called Social Darwinist, committed to the survival of the fittest. It might be better identified as "liquidationist," the term used by Mellon himself. "Liquidate labor, liquidate stocks, liquidate farms, liquidate real estate," he advised Hoover. The panic so dreaded by the President, he said in substance, "will purge the rottenness out of the system. High costs of living and high living will come down. People will work harder, live more moral lives. Values will be adjusted, and enterprising people will pick up the wrecks from less competent people."

Those who thought like Mellon felt that after a runaway boom a sobering bust was not entirely evil. They held that it performed painful but needful services in liquidating swollen prices and wages, inflated real estate values and a gambling psychology; that if not artificially restrained, it would eliminate incompetents, misfits, parasites. There was, indeed, a touch of American puritanism in their view, in that it countenanced punishment for the wicked and prescribed a new austerity.

Mellon despised the Wall Street boom-boys and wished to see them chastised. His was at bottom the attitude of the self-made small-town banker, distrustful of the New York manipulators, disdainful of artificial financial values.

He often alluded to the great panic of the 1870s. The distress had been cruel, innocents had suffered with the guilty, but recovery came within a year. Now, Mellon and others argued, the ultimate sum total of suffering would be less if economic nature had its way unhampered, without official tinkering that would prolong the agony without curing the disease. Subsequently they were able to point to Europe, where the depression ended within three or four years, while in the United States it dragged on for eleven years, yielding finally only to the major surgery of a world war.

The other school, typified and led by Hoover, was "interventionist," convinced that the government must act to cushion the blows and to care for the victims. Hoover being President, this school prevailed, and the rest, Mellon included, loyally upheld his policies.

The President argued that this was 1929, not 1870. In our industrialized society starving city dwellers could not go back to the farm, as in the past. The farmers themselves were no longer self-sufficient. Unless the Federal Government helped to hold the depression within tolerable bounds, our complex social structure would break down entirely. The considerations, moreover, were not purely economic but political. A desperate population would then reach out for false ideologies such as were on view in Russia and Italy (and in Germany as well, before long)—paying an exorbitant price in freedom and human dignity.

This was the progressive view for its time. The President did not adopt it suddenly, for it stemmed from his natural attitudes toward life. Given his deep-seated solicitude for suffering humanity, it was inevitable. Long before, he had championed government regulation to prevent and cure social ills; his own actions as Secretary of Commerce in the 1921 slump offered points of departure for regulation now.

It was no mere token commitment that the President and his associates made. They decided to use existing powers of government, and to obtain more from Congress as needed, to prevent the kind of depositors' and credit panics that had marked past depressions; to slow down and cushion the inevitable liquidation of false values, so as to save businesses, homes, and farms from sudden bankruptcy; to organize relief for people in actual distress; and to do these things in strict compliance with the Constitution and without undercutting the basic American liberties.

The President was conscious, from the very start of his recovery efforts, that he was drawing the government into a new role—"breaking precedent to grapple directly with the depression." The quotation is from a recent appraisal by Carl N. Dengler, Professor of History at Vassar (*Yale Review*, Summer 1963). Hoover was knowingly striking out for new ground.

When he decided that it could no longer be postponed, Hoover consented to Reconstruction Finance Corporation loans to states for relief purposes. In defending this action he declared: "We used such emergency powers to win the war; we can use them to fight the depression, the misery and the suffering from which are equally great." His successor would use remarkably similar language and logic. Again and again Hoover emphasized that in obtaining "voluntary cooperation of industry with the government" for the maintenance of wages and increased construction, his Administration "inaugurated one of the greatest economic experiments in history, on the basis of nationwide cooperation, not charity." At one juncture he said:

For the first time in history, the Federal Government has taken an extensive and positive part in mitigating the effects of depression and expediting recovery. I have conceived that if we would preserve our democracy this leadership must take the part not of organizing dictatorship but of cooperation in the constructive forces of the community and of stimulating every element of initiative and self-reliance in the country.

This represented a sharp break with the theory—virtually unchallenged before him—expressed by President Cleveland in 1887, in a time of serious depression: "Though the people support the government, the government should not support the people." Hoover believed that the government *should* support the people, but always within the stringent limits set upon the federal powers by the Founding Fathers. Carried to excess, he warned, that means a paternalistic and ultimately a totalitarian state.

He was deeply convinced that disaster and distress must not be made the pretexts for risky social experiments and perversions of the American political pattern. He could not accept the cynical assumption—the point where Marx and Nietzsche, Lenin and Mussolini, intersect—that human beings were expendable raw stuff for "social engineering" by those in power. He turned away in revulsion from those who greeted mass suffering as a wonderful chance to put over this or that "revolution" while the masses, paralyzed by hunger and fear, were helpless to resist. But assuredly he rejected the Cleveland precept renouncing all responsibility. The question was not about *ends*—all decent-minded men wanted to restore normal life and relieve misery. His problem was a wise choice of *means*—not the means best for Hoover or the Republican party, but for the country.

Only fools still believe that Hoover was a fool. He knew as well as the most demagogic soap-boxer or pork-barrel impresario that he could reap applause and votes by providing sensational temporary solutions at the price of permanent impairment of American principles of life and government. Those solutions were no deep secret. He needed only to look across the Atlantic, where tyrannical regimes were "solving" fiscal problems and "abolishing" unemployment with the greatest of ease—and the help of terror machines and concentration camps.

Every one of the solutions subsequently tried, discarded, and retried until World War II came to wash them all out, from the NRA to devaluation of the currency and from make-work to pump-priming with inflated billions, was urged upon him by friend or foe. He was probably familiar with every ancient and modern trick in history's bag. Being human, he must have been under temptation to use them. But he foreswore them, deliberately, firmly, in full awareness of the political price he must pay for his restraint. In seeking re-election he would explain, though few understood him:

We have not feared to adopt unprecedented measures, [but] we have resolutely rejected the temptation, under pressure of immediate events, to resort to those panaceas and short cuts which, even if temporarily successful, would ultimately undermine and weaken what has slowly been built and molded by experience and effort through these one hundred and fifty years.

Hoover's ideas of social justice were so advanced for his time that he has himself on occasion described them as "revolutionary." But in putting them into practice he was strictly the evolutionist. His study of history, his close-up observation of postwar Europe, had convinced him that unless a people conserves its essential heritage even while refining and adding to it, social justice itself may expire in a welter of slogans and coercions.

2

In their monumental study of the Hoover administration, Myers and Newton declared:

President Hoover was the first President in our history to offer federal leadership in mobilizing the economic resources of the people, and in calling upon individual initiative to accept definite responsibility for meeting the problem of the depression. This leadership, pioneering as it was, he confined to an arena of action within the constitutional powers of the Federal Government. In some cases, where the threat to our economic or financial system came from abroad, he extended this leadership to worldwide action.

And Professor Dengler, writing in the *Yale Review* two decades later, attested:

As one reviews the actions which Hoover took it is impossible to describe him as a do-nothing President. He was unquestionably one of the truly activist Presidents of our history. . . . Hoover's conception of the depression was sophisticated, rational, and coherent; the remedies he suggested were equally so, given his assumptions. . . . To a remarkable degree one can observe in his acts those principles of individualism which he set forth so simply in his book ten years before.

Dengler questioned the general view which sees Hoover as the *opposite* of Roosevelt. When their administrations, Dengler says, "are seen against the backdrop of previous administrations and earlier social attitudes, the gulf between them shrinks appreciably. . . . Both saw big business standing in need of controls and, for a while, both believed that cooperation between business and government was the best way to achieve that control." Most important, "both Roosevelt and Hoover took the view that it was government's responsibility to do something about a depression." Hoover, he stressed, "was the first to smash the old shibboleth of government unconcern and impotence."

While Professor Dengler and others give Hoover *credit* for a pioneering role in this respect, others hold it against him. They include Hoover, that is to say, among the villains in their indictment of the New Deal. F.D.R., they charge, built on foundations laid by his Republican predecessor, carrying to devastating extremes the principle of federal intervention in the economy first introduced by Hoover.

In the mind of a *laissez-faire* economist like B. M. Anderson, Jr., for example, the tragedy of the 1930s figured as the Hoover-Roosevelt depression. He was not "just another professor." From 1920 to 1937 he was editor of the influential *Chase Economic Bulletin*. In an essay included in a book on *Financing American Prosperity*, published in 1945, Anderson wrote:

We were probably still strong enough at the end of 1929 to have gone through an orderly reaction and depression, and to have come through with an orderly revival, if the government had refrained from interference. . . .
But the New Deal was in the saddle. The President of the United States, Mr. Hoover, the back-seat driver, called in the leaders of business, railroads, and public utilities to urge upon them the policy of not cutting prices, not cutting wages, and increasing capital outlay, and called upon the states and municipalities to increase public borrowing for public works. Purchasing power must be kept up! There must be no letdown! . . .
The Republican New Deal demoralized the markets and brought about the unprecedented depression and unemployment of 1932.

This view has recently been developed to book length (*America's Great Depression*, 1963) by Dr. Murray N. Rothbard, one of the vanishing breed of classical *laissez-faire* economists. It is perhaps the best documented, most closely reasoned attack on Hoover's program from the vantage point of conservative economics as yet presented. The author seeks to demonstrate (1) that the depression itself was the cumulative consequence of state interference with free market processes, and (2) that Hoover's well-meant remedies, being essentially state interventionism, deepened the disease and made it chronic. Dr. Rothbard writes:

Mr. Hoover met the challenge of the Great Depression by acting quickly and decisively, indeed almost continuously throughout his term of office, putting into effect "the greatest program of offense and defense" against depression ever attempted in America. Bravely he used every modern economic "tool," every device of progressive and "enlightened" economics, every facet of government planning to combat the depression. For the first time, *laissez-faire* was boldly thrown overboard and every governmental weapon thrown into the breach. . . . By every "progressive" tenet of our day he should have ended his term a conquering hero; instead he left America in utter and complete ruin: a ruin unprecedented in length and intensity. . . . Hoover's new departures aggravated the Great Depression by massive measures of interference.

Strictures by business spokesmen on Hoover's use of federal prestige and power did not have to wait for historical perspective. The Guaranty

Trust Company of New York, for instance, declared soon after the market crash:

The vigorous measures undertaken by the government to combat the downward tendency in business have also injected an element of uncertainty. . . . Never before have public agencies interceded in such a direct and intensive way to alter the course of business, and the results [are] necessarily unpredictable.

The identification of Hoover with the New Deal, which one suspects annoyed him a lot, has been more widely noted with the passing of time. The Springfield, Ohio, *Sun*, of which the Democratic candidate for President in 1920, James M. Cox, was then the publisher, wrote on Hoover's birthday in 1949: "Several of the basic reforms Americans have come to associate with the New Deal were established or foreshadowed in legislation of the much-derided 'Hoover era.'" The editorial then went on to cite, among other things, the first Agricultural Marketing Act, the Reconstruction Finance Corporation, the Federal Home Loan Banks, laws prohibiting anti-labor injunctions and affirming techniques of collective bargaining.

In a history textbook published in 1955 and still in schoolrooms in 1963, *The American Nation*, by John D. Hicks, there is a chapter titled "The New Deal Begins." The reference, however, is not to the start of the Roosevelt years but to the start of the Hoover years. In explanation of the caption, Dr. Hicks writes:

In a sense, Herbert Hoover rather than Franklin D. Roosevelt inaugurated the New Deal. While the Hoover policies contrasted markedly with the Roosevelt policies, it was not Roosevelt but Hoover who first accepted as a governmental responsibility the task of defeating the depression.

He then examines the RFC, unprecedented devices for aiding farmers and houseowners, stimulation of public works, etc. to show that they were strongly New Dealish in flavor. There would have been more Hoover measures of this type, he rightly indicates, had the Congress under Hoover passed the legislation which it did enact so swiftly for his successor.

Whether they rate praise or blame, the facts themselves are clear. Hoover did face up to the challenge of depression. Without precedents to guide him (other than those in wartime), against severe opposition, he did act quickly and with determination. Those who would strip him of credit for courage have said, "But this was not an ordinary depression —any President would have been forced to intervene." They overlook the fact that in late 1929 and early 1930, when Hoover made his interventionist decisions, the magnitude of the crisis was not yet apparent. It looked at first like a repetition of past depressions. Neither he nor anyone else could know what America was in for. "Yes, we could have done better—in retrospect," President Hoover once remarked.

His intervention was many-sided: economic measures to cushion the impact and stave off panic, organization of relief to the needy, attempts to revise and strengthen economic institutions whose weaknesses were uncovered by the tragedy. Though they are really inseparable we must, for clarity's sake, deal separately with the economic and the relief phases.

3

In the weeks and months immediately after the stock market bubble burst, the White House in effect was turned into a first-aid station for emergency treatment of a nation even more shocked than burned. But few people, then or since, could see the picture whole or appreciate its stirring drama. There were no official press agents to blazon it in the press and on the airwaves. And the unofficial ones, the reporters, had to deal with a President seemingly allergic to big headlines.

Hoover did what the head of a big business organization in sudden danger of bankruptcy would do, and with the same accent on privacy to avoid alarming stockholders and creditors. He immediately called in the ablest and most responsible people in every department—agriculture, industry, labor, construction, railways, utilities—to consult on what could and must be done. In every case, like any first-rate executive, he had concrete proposals to lay before them.

It should be remembered that he had no power under the Constitution or from Congress to compel any of them to cooperate. He did not, as a matter of deep-rooted principle, want such power. The entire effort in the initial stage was voluntary—without directives or threats or penalties.

In the very first days of the market crash, Hoover set the Federal Farm Board into operation to brace marketing cooperatives. This agency, with capital of five hundred million dollars from the Treasury and wide powers to aid agriculture, had been created in the first months of the Administration. Hoover now called a conference of representatives of the leading farm organizations. They supported his plans for the Board to provide indirect support to agricultural prices by means of loans and purchase of some surplus commodities. Millions of farmers were thus helped over the marketing hump of that first depression winter.

On the morning of November 21, President Hoover conferred in the White House with top men in business, among them industrialists like Henry Ford, Owen D. Young, Julius Rosenwald, Walter Teagle, and Pierre duPont. That afternoon he conferred also with the leaders of organized labor, among them William Green, John L. Lewis, Frank Morrison, William L. Hucheson, and A. F. Whitney.

To both groups he made the same presentation, outlined the same program, appealing similarly to their patriotism, humanity, and self-interest. In past economic crises of such dimensions, he explained, labor was treated as a commodity and "liquidated." But labor could no longer be so regarded—it was human beings, homes, families. Their liquidation would simply compound the depression. The first shocks must therefore be absorbed by profits, not wages.

And amazingly, his view was substantially accepted. The result was a balanced agreement—the first on a national scale ever negotiated—to maintain prices, wages, and industrial peace. The principal decisions were: (1) To refrain from strikes and lockouts. (2) To reduce wages only as the cost of living declined. (3) For employers, within the limits of their resources, to look after the relief of their own displaced employees. (4) To share work, where this was possible, rather than lay off workers. Industry also pledged itself to undertake capital repairs and new construction. Labor actually withdrew certain wage demands already announced.

Leading railway officials, summoned to Washington, undertook not only to keep up but to expand construction. Similar pledges were made to the President by leaders of public utilities (only Samuel Insull refusing to go along), the merchant marine, home builders. Simultaneously the President instructed all federal departments to rush public works already authorized, amounting to $240,000,000; and he lined up Congressional leaders to back his request for an additional $423,000,000. This total of $663 million seemed gigantic at the time and naturally brought outcries about extravagance.

In addition Hoover sent personal messages to all governors and the mayors of the principal cities pleading for generous appropriations without delay for useful construction projects. Governor Roosevelt's response had to be filed among the more lukewarm. He agreed to recommend "a much-needed construction program . . . limited only by estimated receipts from revenues without increasing taxes."

Without ballyhoo or appeals to class antagonisms, 1930 thus witnessed an increase of $1,130,000,000 in construction activity, government and private, over the boom year of 1929. Some three billion dollars in stimulated building, most of it the direct result of White House enterprise, made up for the unavoidable construction declines, with one and a quarter billion to spare.

The early agreements reached with the various groups were in general well observed as long as Hoover was in the White House. At one time it was estimated that two million workers were being kept from becoming public charges through the spreading of available work or direct relief provided by employers to those who lost all or most of their wages. There were fewer strikes and lockouts than in any previous Administration. Enlargement of the federal employment services, working closely with state and municipal services of the same type, found jobs for more displaced workers with every year—for 1,100,000 persons in 1931; 2,175,000 in 1932.

In his first depression message to Congress on December 3, 1929, the President necessarily avoided scare talk. Yet he left no room for doubt as to the seriousness of the crisis. He asked for far-reaching banking reforms, large funds for useful construction, along with drastic economies in government to keep the budget in balance. Congress provided the construction appropriations and authorized large seed loans for farmers in drought areas, but refused to carry out the bank and other institutional reforms he recommended.

In its New Year's message at the end of 1929 the A. F. of L. official journal commended the President for his pressure on industrialists who "in earlier recessions . . . acted individually to protect their own interests." Corresponding praise for the new mood in labor appeared in business publications. Only four million man-hours were lost annually through labor-management conflicts in the first three depression years as against eighteen million annually in the three years after Hoover.

His various measures of intervention (we have mentioned only the more important of them) did not bring cure, but they decidedly brought improvement. "Indications are that the patient at the end of January has begun to recover," the New York *Times* editorialized on February 12, 1930. Six days later the President was able to announce that the Department of Labor index of employment, which had dropped from 99.3 in October to 86.0 at the end of December, had now bounced back to 92.8. By May the financial pages were reporting tangible upturn in nearly all fields. The country had reached a "point of improvement" that was "decidedly encouraging," William Green said in June.

Because of these favorable winds, Hoover allowed himself a moderately more hopeful tone. Before the United States Chamber of Commerce, on May 1, 1930, he said: "We are not through the difficulties of our situation," but "I am convinced that we have passed the worst and with continued effort we shall rapidly recover." His conviction proved mistaken. Referring to this statement in his *Memoirs,* he would write:

Presidents cannot be pessimistic in times of national difficulties. They must be encouraging. However, this bit of optimism was later distorted by our opponents to make me say, "Prosperity is just around the corner," which I never did say.

President Hoover had acted resolutely in terms of federal responsibility to keep the slump from degenerating into a panic. He did not spare himself or allow opposition to curb his zeal. He was a commander-in-chief of a war without trumpets or banners; a war fought mostly in the shadows, under continued sniping by some of the very groups he was trying to help.

He had launched what some, rightly or wrongly, have called "the Hoover New Deal." Was he "the first of the new Presidents" or "the last of the old"? This was the question with which the Emporia editor, William Allen White, concluded an appraisal of the Hoover administration in the March 4, 1933, issue of the *Saturday Evening Post*. "History stands hesitant waiting for time" to give the answer, he said.

Considering that he could not then know what the incoming Roosevelt's policies would be, the question was immensely perceptive. It pointed up the paradox of Hoover's role. The same question is also implicit in the dual character of the opposition Hoover had to contend with in Congress, from so-called progressives who thought he was not going fast enough or far enough and from conservatives who attacked him for going too far and too fast. It is a question that has not yet been answered definitively. A reasonable guess is that in time Hoover will be recognized as both the last of the old Presidents and the first of the new.

The elements that link him to the New Deal are real enough, but they are minor compared to those that distinguish him and his Administration from what followed. Hoover, unlike his successor, regarded the expansion of government as temporary and provisional, designed to meet emergencies. Most of his measures were to have terminal points, like the war measures to which he so often compared them. He was intent upon buttressing traditional institutions and ideals, where President Roosevelt, and even more so the men around him, sought to generate permanent new institutions in line with a new ideology.

One of the so-called brain-trusters closest to the throne during Roosevelt's first campaign and after his election was Professor Raymond Moley of Columbia. He was to find himself, fairly soon, out of step with the Administration's forced march to the left and thus among the first of the many defectors. Writing in *Newsweek* (June 14, 1948) more than fifteen years after the events, he declared:

When we all burst into Washington . . . we found every essential idea enacted in the 100-day Congress in the Hoover administration itself. The essentials of the NRA, the PWA, the emergency relief setup were all there. Even the AAA was known to the Department of Agriculture. Only the TVA and the Securities Act was drawn from other sources. The RFC, probably the greatest recovery agency, was of course a Hoover measure, passed long before the inauguration.

Why, then, he asked, didn't Hoover use these instrumentalities himself? His own answers were: (1) that he could not obtain the go-ahead from a Democratic House of Representatives "intent on his destruction" and (2) that he lacked "political boldness and timing." Certainly the first of these answers is valid; the second is a matter of opinion. But neither is applicable to the NRA, the AAA, and many other "instrumentalities." True, they were well known to the Hoover administration; but they had been *rejected* by the President as fascist-type measures, undesirable in themselves and impermissible under our Constitution.

Moley's basic point, however, is beyond dispute. The successor Administration did find many of its devices, hailed as evidence of the genius of President Roosevelt, ready at hand. It took them over, obtained the additional powers for their implementation which had been denied to Hoover, and continued to castigate their true author for having "done nothing."

Hoover became the ablest and most systematic critic of the New Deal, despite the fact that it had appropriated many of his own political and economic techniques. But the contradiction is more seeming than real. For one thing, his techniques did not include the NRA, AAA, and other big-government, big-spending, big vote-buying enterprises. For another, Hoover's critique was less concerned with the tools of the New Deal than with its spirit of reckless improvisation, its disdain for the historical experience of the nation, its contempt for the constitutional limitations on the executive branch of government.

XXII

Grappling with Calamity

THE Great Depression had its ups and downs, its seasons of illusory revival followed by further decline. The forty Hoover months—October 1929 to March 1933—fell into a number of fairly distinct stages, each demanding a revised approach and revised therapies.

The first and mildest stage began with the market collapse and was almost entirely domestic. The economic indices, including employment, drifted lower and lower. By February 1931, however, the press, business, labor, nearly everyone again hailed clear signs of recovery. In the first quarter, industrial output was up 5 percent, payrolls 10 percent, stock prices 11 percent. The crisis, said the New York *Times* on March 23, had passed bottom and the country was on its way up. At the end of the month 120 cities announced the closing down of relief activities because they were no longer needed.

But the joy was all too brief. Within a few months, American hopes were shattered by the reverberation of economic earthquakes in Europe. A far worse stage of depression was at hand. Matters were scarcely improved, for the President and his country, by the licking which the Administration suffered in the 1930 Congressional elections. In many ways it was the most destructive of the blows raining down on America, since it curtailed and at times paralyzed Hoover's capacity for timely counteraction.

He had contended with strong opposition in the outgoing Congress. But its successor was openly, demonstratively hostile. The midterm Democratic victory had sharpened the Democratic appetite for power. Almost automatically Congress was against anything Hoover proposed. His persistent pleas for unity in deference to common perils were brushed aside. Spearheading the obstruction was John Nance Garner, Speaker of the new House and later Vice President in the first two Roosevelt terms.

In an authorized biography by Bascom Timmons, in 1948, Garner was quoted as saying, "I fought Hoover with everything I had" under "catch-as-catch-can rules," because he (Garner) thought the Democrats "had a better program for national recovery." He went on:

I never reflected on the personal character or integrity of Herbert Hoover. In many ways he was superbly equipped for the presidency. If he had become President in 1921 or 1937 he might have ranked with the great Presidents. Today I think Hoover is the wisest statesman on world affairs in America. He may be on domestic affairs, too.

No smidgin of this admiration was in evidence when Garner in the House of Representatives led the assault on the hard-pressed President. Repeatedly he turned thumbs down on cooperation with the White House even when most other Democratic leaders were amenable. As for that "better program" cited in retrospect to explain obstruction, Garner never revealed its elements, except, as Hoover would comment acidly, "to put the Republicans out."

The Democratic Congress was bent on discrediting the Administration at any price to the economy. It blocked Hoover's proposals without offering an alternative program. Obstructionist excesses left the country almost defenseless against more and more blows from overseas, which confirmed and compounded the inherent weaknesses of the American banking system. With several bright but disappointing moments of reprieve, the course was therefore dizzily downward.

From June 1931 to June 1932 the nation suffered the year of greatest affliction and danger. But it was also the year of President Hoover's most memorable political and economic innovations: the moratorium on intergovernmental debts, the "standstill" on billions of short-term private international indebtedness, the Reconstruction Finance Corporation, the National Credit Association, the World Monetary and Economic Conference, Federal Land Banks, Mortgage Discount and Home Loan Banks, and a score more that could be listed. The Administration forced a good deal of vital legislation through the recalcitrant Congress, though invariably in inadequate or mangled forms and with tragically costly delays.

Then, in July 1932, came the most clean-cut improvement, not only in America but in most of Europe. The nation, it seemed, had been brought safely through the valley of shadows—without a panic, with a sound currency, with heightened world prestige and without crippling the accustomed American freedoms. The hoarding of currency at home and the runs on gold from abroad were sharply reduced.

On the other side of the Atlantic the improvement continued to the point of genuine recovery. In the United States, alas, it was violently arrested, as we shall see, and then turned into a nearly complete rout, primarily because of the outcome of the presidential election in November and the character of the man elected.

The final stage covered the short interval between the defeat of Hoover and the inauguration of Roosevelt. The ship of state was then in effect without a pilot. In the interregnum the defeated President was shorn of effective authority. Not in law but in fact, the incoming President had the decisive power and command of the legislature, but for reasons of his own chose to "do nothing."

Writing on July 16, 1934, when the Democratic New Deal had been under way for sixteen months, the New York *Times* declared: "The change for the better in the last half of 1932 is beyond dispute. That this evident revival of confidence was suddenly reversed in February 1933 is equally true." The crisis in confidence—that was at the core of the sudden collapse—coincided with the approach of the new regime, and grew more acute as time ran out for the incumbent. Newton and Myers were to record:

During the administration of Hoover the country was five times turned back from a like number of crises, any one of which threatened to produce the destruction which can come from an acute public and banking panic. . . . On each of these occasions the tide was turned almost wholly through the battles fought by President Hoover and his associates. The country gradually gained strength after each crisis was passed—only to be swept by new hurricanes of economic trouble.

The sixth of these hurricanes, sweeping down on the country as a reaction to his defeat, the President was powerless to turn back. That was when the panic he had staved off for more than three years finally inundated the land. It was in the Hoover portion of the depression by the calendar; in simple justice as well as historical accuracy it belongs in his successor's portion.

Such, in summary, was the course of the depression in its first three and a half years, its Hoover years. Its main elements will be examined in some detail in the pages that follow.

2

Few American Presidents before or since Hoover worked as long and as hard as he did. "Work" is a feeble word for his unrelenting labors; it suggests only the physical drudgery, not the greater and more lacerating emotional strains.

Even when billed as vacations, his brief absences from the executive offices were devoted to conferring, studying reports, drafting messages

and addresses. Sometimes, indeed, a "vacation" was deliberately contrived to camouflage long days and sleepless nights of activity to meet
a new emergency which, he felt, required absolute privacy.

In his own voluminous *Memoirs* we find few references to the cruelly
heavy loads Hoover carried. He organized that record, with an engineer's
rather than a literary man's skill, by subject matter and "stages." The
reader therefore tends to forget that the stages overlapped; that subjects
neatly examined in separate chapters, in actuality had to be dealt with
simultaneously. Besides, it was scarcely in Hoover's nature to complain.
Having described a particularly wearing period in his struggle with legislative opposition, he added hastily: "I am making no complaints. I accepted the job of my own free will."

Time being his most precious commodity, he budgeted it with miserly
care. This left lamentably little to spare for his family and cherished
friends. There were no margins for recreation, except the early morning
medicine-ball game with hardy associates for half an hour or so on a dirt
court in the South Grounds. This was almost a ritual, observed every
morning, summer and winter, rain or snow. Though he enjoyed the break,
it was strictly for physical fitness rather than recreation. Tossing and running after the heavy ball, he figured, offered maximum exercise for the
least investment of time.

The regulars who participated in the game, from six to eighteen men
—officials, male secretaries, a few friends, a journalist or two—were inevitably dubbed a "kitchen cabinet" by the press. It was no such thing.
After the game the players went indoors for fruit juice and coffee, but
by common consent the talk was held on the light side.

The best descriptions of President Hoover's arduous schedule that I
could find are scattered through Theodore Joslin's memoirs:

> Pressed and harassed, he labored early and late in an effort to bring order
> out of chaos. . . . Words fail to give an understanding of the pressures center-
> ing upon the White House. Crowded hours became more crowded. Long days
> became longer. No sooner did the President attend to one crisis than another
> swept down upon him. Indeed, crisis piled on crisis. The greatest strain, the
> most ticklish situation, invariably came on a Saturday or Sunday, when humans,
> even Presidents, are supposed to have at least some rest.
>
> There was no rest for President Hoover. There was no relief whatsoever.
> There was nothing but trouble, complaint. If he could only have told the people
> what he was doing, if he could only have had the encouragement of an occa-
> sional commendatory word, there would have been an atom of consolation for
> him. But the nature of the impending disasters did not permit confidences. Any
> revelations would have accentuated panic. This he prevented. . . .
>
> Day by day, night by night, he summoned experts, government officials,
> masters of finance, captains of industry and leaders of labor to the White House.

He consulted earnestly with them, seeking to bulwark business, rehabilitate banking, lift farm prices, and lay the groundwork for relief. With these advisers he talked in mighty plain language of the problems confronting the nation. He sought advice. He commandeered their assistance.

Hoover's "normal" day began at six in the morning and, if he was lucky, ended at eleven at night. Often it was prolonged beyond midnight and into the early morning hours. After a few hours' sleep, he would get up to read and write for an hour or two, then return to bed. Arising again at six, he usually resumed some urgent task—perhaps briefing for an important meeting that day—until the medicine-ball claimed him at 7:30. Before 8:30 he was at his desk. The first half hour he gave to dictating letters and to writing. Since he composed and edited all his own speeches, messages, and statements with meticulous concentration, he was rarely without a manuscript-in-progress at hand. Often he would scribble a few sentences in the thirty seconds between the departure of one guest and the arrival of another.

In order to save time, Hoover had installed a telephone on his desk, the first President to do so. This enabled him to consult key officials and experts and transact other business by phone, and it had the additional advantage of avoiding the notoriety attending a personal visit. Because of the abnormal conditions and clamoring problems, his conference schedule was heavier than it had been for any previous President. But by 12:30 he was out on the grounds greeting the daily quota of anonymous citizens. To quote Joslin again:

The afternoons were as crowded as the mornings, people surging in and out with ideas for this and schemes for that. They emphasized, argued, pleaded, squabbled. I often thought that the only difference between the executive offices and an insane asylum was that we went home at night.

Dinner was normally at 8 P.M. It was Hoover's custom to snatch a half-hour or even an hour of sleep before dinner. He had the happy gift of falling asleep instantly and always awoke refreshed, ready for a long night of work. Always there were guests at dinner. After the meal, while Mrs. Hoover took the ladies to an upstairs living room, the men joined the President in the Lincoln study. These after-dinner conferences on vital issues frequently went on for hours.

"The public," said Joslin, "had the impression that he was indifferent, cold. Not those who assembled in the Lincoln study. They marveled at the warmth of his personality, the simplicity of his character, and the freedom with which he discussed subjects of the greatest moment." Fortunately, he added, the President's confidences were very rarely violated —he chose his guests with care.

One example out of hundreds of the President's staggering burdens:

Joslin tells of a Saturday evening in early 1932 when Hoover returned to the White House after a brief absence. An updated report on hoarding of currency and flight of gold which he had been expecting was waiting on his desk. It left no room for doubt that this problem was heading for a disastrous climax. The President stayed with the report until three o'clock on Sunday morning. Up again at six, he "worked ceaselessly until midnight, financial advisers coming and going and others being consulted by telephone":

From then on, he became the "workingest" man I have ever known. He had just been practicing before. Three hours' sleep did for him what eight or ten hours would do for the average person. His rebound from a little rest was almost unbelievable. He worked those about him until they could hardly drag one foot after the other. He brought in fresh talent from the outside and soon had it fagged and groggy.

He maintained an almost killing pace. None of us fooled ourselves into believing he could keep it up indefinitely. We speculated, when we had the time, how long it would be before he would "crack." The amazing fact is he never really broke, although he continued it, except for brief spells, until the last day he was in the White House.

In the hoarding crisis which had thrown the President into a burst of exertion spectacular even for Hoover, the country came close to being forced off the gold standard; so close that, had the public been aware of the danger, the long-delayed panic would assuredly have exploded. Hoover had only a fortnight, and then only a day or two, to head off this new catastrophe. His arduous work paid off: the nation's credit structure, though perilously shaken, did not topple.

3

Anyone interested in the detailed picture, at once heroic and heartrending, of a President who ate, slept, and lived with his work, driving those around him and especially himself to superhuman efforts, should read Joslin's *Hoover Off the Record*. Much of it, unfortunately, was off the record.

Activities in progress which, by the test of newsworthiness, rated the front pages Hoover from time to time deliberately muffled in silence and even in secrecy. Important visitors were smuggled into and out of the White House through back doors to evade publicity. At a number of grave junctures the President betook himself to a rendezvous outside the White House to keep news hounds off the trail of some important scheme of salvage under consideration.

In the years when he was Secretary of Commerce, he had been considered a prime source of news and had won the heart of the Washington press corps. His accessibility and candor contrasted with the taciturnity of Coolidge. It was taken for granted, by himself as well as the reporters, that this fine rapport would continue in the White House. And it did during the first seven or eight months—until depression came.

Thereafter, his relations with the reporters became ever more strained. That, too, helped to shape the unfavorable portrait of the Chief Executive being projected on the public mind. Even Herbert Corey, one of the correspondents whose admiration for the President never wavered, could write in a magazine article some fifteen years later: "In plain words, the reporters didn't like him. He was never at ease. . . . The bar of his innate diffidence and his acquired caution was always up. Most of all . . . his reverence for the Office of the Presidency . . . made him appear stiff and almost hostile."

But Corey overlooked the most important element in the equation. Too many of the vital things Hoover did during his bleak years, he felt, might be wrecked if exposed prematurely to the limelight. The spectacle of a President continually patching, pleading, conferring, pressing for action, he feared, might have stimulated dangerous alarm.

He was much like the head of a family who keeps disturbing news from his loved ones. Because he had no stomach for white lies and little deftness in witty evasions, Hoover repeatedly called off scheduled press conferences, though he knew some correspondents would be bitter. The crises in public affairs were far too tragic to risk free and easy, spontaneous press gatherings. Reluctantly he ruled that questions be submitted in writing in advance.

Speaking in Des Moines during his second campaign, and referring to the entire depression struggle, Hoover said:

Many of these battles had to be fought in silence, without the cheers of the limelight or the encouragement of public support, because the very disclosure of the forces opposed to us would have undermined the courage of the weak and induced panic in the timid, which would have destroyed the very basis of success.

Hideous misrepresentation and unjustified complaint had to be accepted in silence. It was as if a great battle in war should be fought without public knowledge of any incident except the stream of dead and wounded from the front.

From where he sat, the appalling facts of life were too clear for optimism. Yet it was his plain duty to bolster public morale and block the descent into defeatism. He knew that a depression feeds on bad news. On occasion the only road open to him was a retreat into silence, which was sometimes misunderstood by friends and always exploited by enemies.

"It was Roosevelt," according to Professor Dengler, "during the campaign of 1932, who created the erroneous image of Hoover as a man without faith or hope in the future." This did not deter the Democratic campaigners from harping simultaneously on the wholly contrary image of a man recklessly overoptimistic. The very tricksters who manufactured the prosperity-around-the-corner phrase repeated it *ad nauseam*.

But supposing he had said it, what, in all conscience, was the crime imputed to him? Simply that he had taken advantage of symptoms of improvement to inject some starch into a wilting people. Did his detractors expect a President of the United States to pronounce funeral orations over the living body of America? With so many others eager to assure the American people that faith in recuperation was an imbecilic delusion—that the time was ripe for descent to some version of totalitarianism—should the Chief Executive have joined the Cassandra chorus?

There has never been a President, before or after Hoover, who did not in time of stress invoke the nation's tradition of faith in recovery. Franklin Roosevelt, year after year, inveighed against defeatism. His very smile and the tilt of his cigarette holder were banners of all-out optimism. The ringing formula, "There is nothing to fear but fear itself," which ghosts had written into his Inaugural Address, was a call to faith; and he played variations on this theme continually in the face of ten million unemployed and ever-growing relief rolls. "Now that we are definitely in the process of recovery," he said in his annual State of the Union message to Congress on January 4, 1934, by way of prelude to a proposal. For nearly eight years he announced recovery around a corner that was not turned. "In declaring that there was nothing to fear but fear," Professor William E. Leuchtenburg wrote in a book about the New Deal, "Roosevelt had minted no new platitudes; Hoover had said the same thing for three years."

Besides—and this is the central truth—Hoover did believe deeply in America. In the larger, historical sense he remained optimistic always. "No one can occupy the high office of President and be other than completely confident of the future of the United States," he said in October 1930. "Perhaps as to no other place does the cheerful courage and power of a confident people reflect as to his office." And he added:

There are a few folks in business and several folks in the political world who resent the notion that things will ever get better and who wish to enjoy our temporary misery. To account to these persons the progress of cooperation between the people and the government in amelioration of this situation . . . only inspires the unkind retort that we should fix our gaze upon the unhappy features of the decline. . . . This is no time to talk of any surrender . . . the spirit of the people will never brook defeat.

None of this was a pose. Hoover could not pose falsely if he tried. He said in his Inaugural, "I have no fears for the future of our country. It is bright with hope." He never relinquished that hope and the faith it connoted. Constantly he sought to restore confidence because he truly believed, as he said to staff officers in the battle again and again, that "our country is fundamentally sound."

In a period of black reverses he told a gathering of bankers that he could not go along with the idea, voiced by other speakers, that American standards of living should be lowered:

Any retreat—and this should be underscored—from our American philosophy of constantly increasing standards of living becomes a retreat into perpetual unemployment and the acceptance of a cesspool of poverty for some large part of our people.

Hoover was a knowing engineer assuring a frightened public that the dikes and the bridges will hold. He was honestly trying to sustain the morale of a hard-hit people; not with optimistic lies but with proofs that the free economy was basically strong and resilient, that given a chance it would weather the heavy storms. The "image" of the depression he deliberately set himself to convey was that of a passing trial from which would come greater knowledge of the faults of our system and the ways to correct them. From the travail, he said, we must draw "courage and wisdom to improve and strengthen us for the future."

4

As if nature itself were conspiring to undo Hoover's work, one of the worst droughts in American history hit huge areas of the Midwest and the South in the late summer of 1930. Over a million farm families and twenty million animals, in about three-quarters of the states, were affected. The sad jest of Hoover's friends, to the effect that he would be blamed for that calamity too, nearly came true. He was blamed, if not for the drought itself, for its consequences in worsening the general depression.

The President acted at once to meet the new emergency. He induced the railroads to haul feed to drought sufferers at half the normal rates. Surpluses held by the Federal Farm Board were thrown into the breach. He instructed the Department of Justice to report publicly any attempts to profiteer on food. In concert with the governors of the stricken states, quickly summoned to Washington, he worked out plans for swift relief. White House orders went out to all federal departments to accelerate construction on highways, waterways, and flood control in the afflicted regions to generate emergency employment. Hoover asked and got from Congress an appropriation for seed loans to the farmers.

At the President's request, the Red Cross assumed responsibility for a comprehensive job of direct relief. It earmarked five million dollars for the task and launched a successful public appeal for more.

Never before had Washington dealt with a great drought so promptly and effectively. Yet even this new disaster superimposed on the old was grist for the Michelson Mills. Senator Pat Harrison of Mississippi introduced a bill granting twenty million dollars to the Red Cross, although Judge Payne, its chairman, and then its entire board, assured Congress that the public response was sufficient and government gifts were not needed. The very proposal had the effect of slowing down private contributions, which are the lifeblood of the Red Cross.

Under its humane habiliments, the Harrison measure was of course strictly political. After two months of acrimonious debate it was defeated. For opposing it firmly, however, the President was pilloried from coast to coast as "heartless" and impervious to cries for help. The episode was used to the limit to fortify the fable of a callous Chief Executive; it continued to show up in anti-Hoover polemics long after the essential background had been completely forgotten.

The Red Cross, in the final checkup, could use for drought relief only twelve of the fifteen million dollars it raised privately. Had Congress drawn on the taxpayers' money, few of those millions would have been forthcoming on the age-old basis of human sympathy. Incidentally, while the Senate debate was under way, a hue and cry was suddenly raised about "hunger riots" in Arkansas. Army investigators rushed to the scene found that it was a cruel hoax intended to discommode the occupant of the White House.

The "easy" solution of every problem was to take a billion or two out of the Treasury, even if the billions weren't there and had to be created by the magic of "fiat" and "rubber" dollars. In December 1930 depression appropriations in bills before Congress—above those requested by the President—totaled nearly four and a half billions: more than the whole pre-depression budget! In later sessions the total was raised. Hoover set his face against these assaults on the taxpayer.

The very fact that the bills were nearly all on a purely geographical basis, rather than on the basis of clear need, supported the general suspicion that they were of the pork-barrel, vote-getting variety. The President did not hesitate to charge that some men were "playing politics at the expense of human misery." In a statement to the public at the end of 1930 he declared:

Prosperity cannot be restored by raids on the Treasury. . . . Some of these schemes are ill-considered; some represent the desire of individuals to show that they are more generous . . . than even the leaders of their own parties.

In terms of the gigantic trust in his hands—the conservation of liberty —the juggling of billions and the juggling of executive powers seemed to him equally reprehensible. "Never was the lure of the rosy path to every panacea and of easy ways to imagined security more tempting," he told the country in a difficult period, when miracle cures were being peddled on a thousand political corners.

At every turn he warned against the "specious claim that hired representatives of a hundred million people can do better than the people themselves in thinking and planning their daily life." It was precisely because he understood so well the fatal allure of the siren song of the "easy way for the moment of difficulty" that he begged his fellow countrymen to close their ears to it. Instead, and in full awareness that the advice was not good politics, he urged "the part of self-reliance, independence, and steadfastness in time of trial and stress."

By firm resistance and when necessary the use of his veto, Hoover defeated nearly all of the panacea-type proposals. He sought instead to provide jobs through expansion of useful public works. More was spent for this purpose in his Administration than in the preceding thirty-six years, including the building of the Panama Canal. Soon after its formation, the Reconstruction Finance Corporation was authorized to loan up to $1,800,000,000 for public works in addition to specific appropriations. Hoover, moreover, held himself ready and pledged to recommend as much federal aid as necessary for direct relief—to be administered through the states—as soon as the need arose. He lived up to this pledge. But he would not yield to colossal pressures for mere political spending.

Which repeatedly made Roman holidays for those who accused him of excessive caution and unfeeling parsimony. But this did not inhibit charges—by the same people, in many cases—of excessive spending and failure to balance the budget.

Most of the funny-money bills were defeated. Fiscal sanity still held a narrow margin of advantage in the halls of Congress and in public opinion. The great exception was with respect to cash handouts to 3,500,000 veterans: not only to the needy veterans but to all of them. The gimmick had too much political sex appeal as a vote-getter for Congressmen to resist.

Agitation for a bonus had begun back in Harding's days. It was granted, but payment was deferred for twenty-five years, the veterans receiving a "bonus certificate" for future collection. The arrangement was a species of endowment policy, with the government earmarking about $112,000,-000 a year toward the due date.

Now the cry was raised for immediate payment, in the form of cash "loans" against the certificates. Hoover was in favor of lending reasonable amounts to the estimated 15 percent of destitute veterans. He had already extended the rolls of veterans and dependents receiving special care and pensions. The bill introduced, however, was for an across-the-board payment of 50 percent of the face value to all veterans, involving an immediate drain on the Treasury of $1,700,000,000. It was passed in February 1931, over a presidential veto.

In the midst of the nightmare churned up by the European collapse, while the President was struggling to safeguard the American dollar, the American Legion announced that it would demand the other half of the bonus now. A resolution to this effect was coming up at the Legion convention in Detroit. For once Hoover chose to make a "grandstand play" to dramatize the seriousness of the proposed blow. There was some doubt whether he would go to the convention, to which he had been invited. At the last moment, however, on September 21, 1931, he suddenly boarded a train to Detroit, took the rostrum at once, made a strong eleven-minute speech, and immediately returned to the capital.

The convention evidently was impressed and convinced. It turned down the bonus resolution. What he looked upon as a major threat to the national fiscal structure was staved off for about six months. But the politicians were not dissuaded. In the spring of 1932 the President was obliged to stop a second bonus bill for $2,400,000,000. It was this action that prompted the Bonus March, the story of which has already been told in another context.

The anxiety to balance the national budget, or at worst to hold down the deficits, was central to Hoover's policies. Whether this was wise, whether the alternative of more taxes was not the greater evil, I am not enough of an economist to judge. What needs to be remembered, in retrospect, is that the Democrats were at this time as firmly committed to a balanced budget as the Republicans. As yet only a handful of Keynesians on the fringes of both parties raised questions on this score. There were few to challenge him in his own party or in the opposition, when Hoover declared: "The Government, no more than individual families, can continue to expend more than it receives without inviting serious consequences."

When the deficit reached half a billion dollars, on July 1, 1931, the cries of dismay were bipartisan. With a heavy heart, the President called for higher taxes. On this even Speaker Garner backed up the Administration. The press, too, was almost unanimous on the importance of balancing the budget. The long debate that ensued was largely about the kind of new taxes to be imposed. Hoover's recommendation for a manufacturers' sales tax was defeated, but the tax increases voted by Congress were large for their time.

Years later, with the wisdom—if wisdom it was—of hindsight, Hoover was pilloried for his insistence, while President, on a pay-as-you-go budget. His critics conveniently forgot that he was not challenged on this account during the 1932 campaign; that, on the contrary, the modest deficits were held against him; and that the Democratic candidate was, if anything, more emphatic in pledging a balanced budget than the incumbent.

XXIII

In the Valley of Shadows

I N his year-end message to Congress in December 1930, President Hoover had said: "In the larger view, the forces of depression now lie
outside the United States."

Because of the sense of relief produced by substantial improvement in
the domestic picture in February and March of 1931, not many Americans
remembered his warning of a few months earlier. But Hoover had not
spoken casually. Knowing how deeply American finance and business
were implicated in Europe, he was keeping a worried eye on that continent. The U.S. diplomatic corps and other sources were under instructions to keep the White House informed continually and in detail.

By May, Hoover realized that his forebodings were about to be brutally
confirmed. The largest bank in Austria, the *Kreditanstalt* of Vienna, was
suddenly besieged by rioting depositors. There were more and more runs
on banks in Austria, Germany, and other countries. The whole continent
shook with the tremors of earthquakes to come. European currencies
were rapidly being demoralized, securities plummeted, gold fled from
one country to another in the futile search for a safe haven.

American banks, loaded to the gills with European obligations, began
to feel the pinch. Europeans were hastening to dispose of their U.S. securities. Foreign orders for wheat and cotton were drying up. The green
shoots of recovery which Hoover had coaxed into life were turning brown.
The President had been reproved for his occasional notes of optimism. Yet
when he called in American financiers to alert them that they would soon
feel the full impact of overseas cyclones, most of them—including the
Governor of the Federal Reserve Board, Eugene Meyer—denied that the
menace was as grave as he claimed. Some of them charged him with
"seeing ghosts."

They turned out to be such lusty and mischievous ghosts that they all but pushed the United States over the edge of the precipice. Average Americans, reading about the faraway troubles, could not grasp the implications of those events for themselves, and Hoover, anxious to prevent runs on American banks and to gain time for counteraction, did not dare as yet to enlighten them. First he was determined to find some means for helping Europe and thus helping his own country. As on many previous occasions, he had to live with his dread knowledge in painful silence.

The world, he knew by June 1931, was plunging into the deepest slough of the depression. The United States was entering the valley of shadows, where it would wander in near-despair for a full year. This was the year in which Hoover conducted not one but a series of desperate, soul-searing campaigns to save the nation from total economic collapse. He conducted them almost alone, handicapped by a bewildered and partisan Congress, under a barrage of ever uglier personal vituperation, amidst demagogic appeals to mob angers. Communists and other assorted heralds of glittering utopias around the corner were licking their chops in anticipation of the red meat of revolution.

"These events," Hoover later said, "were not as children playing with blocks. They brought revolutions, mutinies, riots, downfall of governments and a seething of despair which threatened civilization."

Germany was then the weakest link in the European economic chain. In a long personal letter to Hoover, President Paul von Hindenburg said that his country's economy was on the brink of dissolution and appealed for swift American intervention.

Even before receipt of the German S.O.S., the American President had decided upon a bold course. In talks with his Ambassador in Berlin, on May 6, he had sketched his plan for a year's moratorium on all intergovernmental debts. He did not, of course, regard the device as a "cure" but merely as a palliative to slow up the debacle. The payments involved came to $1,200,000,000—about a quarter of the amount being due to the United States. Their postponement was intended to remove some of the immediate fiscal pressures.

The six weeks between the conception of the moratorium and its publication on July 20 were among the most harrowing Hoover had as yet faced. He had to persuade an array of foreign governments, international bankers, and key Congressmen at home to go along with the plan, and to do so without fatally premature publicity. Secretary Mellon at first objected to the whole scheme. Europe's mess, he said, was no concern of ours. But having inspected the European picture personally, at Hoover's behest, he was soon frantically telephoning the President across the Atlantic for accelerated action.

Long before the advent of the European crisis, Hoover had agreed to make a swing of the Middle West. He was slated to speak in the principal cities. Now he had neither the time nor the peace of mind for such a chore, but he feared that its cancellation would stir up a hornet's nest of jittery speculation. So he went through with it: four days of outward calm and confidence while inwardly torn by anxieties.

The President spoke from the rear platform of his train, conferred with local political leaders, and delivered the addresses he had prepared, though constantly preoccupied by the vision of looming calamity. The press had as yet no inkling of the story and he had to keep it that way. In consequence he had to resort to various stratagems to maintain continuous touch with negotiations in progress, yet prevent a "leak." Back in the White House, he called batches of influential congressmen to his chambers, took them fully into his confidence, and exacted pledges of secrecy. One senator, of course, spilled the story "off the record" to favorite reporters who promptly spread it on the front pages. Luckily the "leak" came late enough not to wreck the plan.

Rarely had any depression move evoked such nearly unanimous acclaim. A British editor was quoted as saying: "We look upon it as the greatest thing since the signing of the armistice." Prime Minister Ramsay MacDonald called the moratorium "an action of great wisdom, courage and deep insight." The New York *Times* said editorially: "We cannot but wonder with the rest of the world at the happy revulsion of feeling which everywhere followed."

At once the price of securities and farm products rose, retail trade increased, thousands of men were called back to work. Only nine days after the announcement, the New York *Times* spoke of "great results already achieved" and expressed the belief that the danger "not only to Germany but all of Europe and the United States was removed." In all the enthusiasm, however, little mention was made of Hoover's gargantuan labors, his multifarious negotiations, the anguished fluctuations of his hopes, behind the moratorium.

It was no more Hoover's fault than yours or mine that the effects of the moratorium were quickly dissipated. Europe was much too sick for one dose of medicine to cure. It was paying the price of seventeen years of troubles postponed and compounded: of new loans used to head off default on old loans, in an endless progression at always higher interest. And the American financial community was organically linked to the stricken continent.

Too soon, central European banks again began to cave in. The White House demanded information on the amount of short-term paper from Europe held by American institutions. It was given figures from four hundred to five hundred millions. But the bookkeeping, like the transactions it shielded, was misleading. Pressing his inquiries, the President was appalled by the realization that if the German and Austrian banks, already staggering, collapsed they would wipe out $1,700,000,000 in private obligations to American creditors; this in addition to billions in other uncollectable debts about which he had already been aware.

A German default would have tumbled most of Europe and a large part of America into a common pauper's grave. Matters were again made more galling by the absolute need to conceal the real dimensions of the approaching new catastrophe. "The haunting prospect of wholesale bank failures," Hoover recorded, "and the necessity of not saying a word to the American people as to the cause of the danger, lest I precipitate runs on banks, left me little sleep."

The cause to which he referred was garden variety greed: "Some of our banks had been yielding to sheer greed for six or seven percent interest offered by banks in the European panic area." The four or five hundred millions in short-term notes taken up by Americans had been "kited" more than threefold. And this, it eventually appeared, was only the American share of an estimated ten billion dollars in German and Austrian paper afloat throughout the world.

Hoover saved the situation once more, and again in the nick of time, by what came to be known as his "standstill" agreement. To safeguard American interests he had to assume firm world leadership. This he did. He had to bludgeon the principal financial elements both abroad and at home into conceding a year's leeway on the mountains of indebtedness falling due.

The bankers, foreign and domestic, had other ideas. In effect they wanted the U. S. Government to bail them out with a five hundred million dollar loan. When top financiers whom he summoned to discuss the matter refused to agree to the standstill, they saw the rare spectacle of Hoover in a towering rage. It took the form of a brusque ultimatum: if they did not accept his proposal in twenty-four hours, he would *expose their banking conduct to the American people*. The acceptance came through before the twenty-four hours were up. The futility of the Treasury loan asked for by the bankers became sufficiently clear when the true magnitude of the "kited" paper became known; it would have been only a drop in a ten-billion-dollar bucket.

Through the moratorium and the standstill, the American public was being educated in the facts of life in an interdependent economic world. Bad economic news from other parts of the world were no longer accepted so complacently—and unhappily there was no dearth of it. Conditions in central Europe had barely been stabilized when the cyclones moved into Great Britain. Since England was then banker for the world, the resultant wreckage was scattered across the six continents. Resolutions touched off by economic shock took place in several Latin American countries. In Germany both the Communists and the Hitler Nazis, sometimes working together, gained a lot of ground.

The Bank of England, once a synonym for strength and reliability, defaulted on payments to foreigners and on September 21, 1931, England went off the gold standard. Fifty to twenty other countries followed suit. In a last-ditch effort against default on gold, the President had authorized two loans to Britain, totaling $625,000,000, but it could no longer be prevented. For the first time in a century the expression "safe as the Bank of England" became a sour joke.

The impact on America was stunning. Convinced that the United States was next, foreigners began to withdraw gold as fast as boats could be found to ship it. American payrolls again declined, placing more millions on relief. Dozens of banks closed their doors. It was into this maelstrom of disaster, let it be recalled, that calculated demagogy tossed a three-billion-dollar bonus time bomb.

In off-the-record meetings with publishers and other groups of opinion-makers, the President of the United States appealed for cooperation in buttressing morale and keeping the boat steady. The reduction of fear was as important as any of the tangible economic goals.

By a score of devices (a few of which I will touch on summarily) the President was able, for a third time, to avert an all-out panic. Given the circumstances, this was assuredly a great accomplishment, especially when he was obliged to work under the pelting of the ever more odious smear campaign. He could scarcely open a newspaper or turn on a radio without being taunted by the cruel implications of a "Hoover depression . . . Hoovervilles . . . Hoover bread lines." He was compelled by his conscience and his nature to deal moderately in a time of extremist counsel; in a time when instant salvation was being preached by political quacks, a few of them in the chambers of Congress itself.

2

The central problem, now as always, was to revive the flow of credit. Loans must be made available to keep factories from closing down; to obviate needless dispossession from farms and homes; to save businesses in temporary difficulties; to enable country banks to tide farmers over the next crop season; to finance private home-building and other construction; to help closed but basically sound banks to unfreeze their assets.

Even before the British debacle reached its climax, the President met with the Advisory Council of the Federal Reserve Board. He persuaded its twenty-four members to organize the banks in each Reserve District to make pooled loans against the assets of closed banks. Tens of thousands of depositors were the immediate beneficiaries. At this confidential meeting, furthermore, Hoover outlined a more ambitious central credit pool,

273

capitalized and administered jointly by the leading banks. His plan, how-ever, had to wait for the shattering blow of Britain's renunciation of the gold standard before he could get action.

On the evening of October 4, 1931, an extraordinary emergency meet-ing was held in Washington, at Secretary Mellon's home to avoid alerting the press. As a further precaution, the President was "sneaked" out of the White House. The forty or so men in attendance were virtually a who's who of the nation's leadership in banking, insurance, real estate, and loan companies.

Hoover did not spare their feelings. It was the last chance, he said, for "American private enterprise to demonstrate its ability to protect the country and itself." If they failed to cooperate, the government for the first time would have to intervene on a major scale to rescue the free economy. This was not rhetoric, he revealed, for he had already sched-uled a meeting with ranking legislators (Congress was in recess) for October 6, two days later. If necessary, he was prepared to call a special session of Congress. He laid before the men in the Mellon living room a program in two parts, one for the bankers, the other for the insurance and loan institutions.

He concentrated that night on the first of these, as the one that had more chance of quick acceptance. It was the aforementioned credit pool, now christened the National Credit Association: a corporation with five hundred million dollars paid-in private capital and authority to borrow an additional billion. Its basic objectives would be to thaw out huge amounts of frozen deposits in thousands of the sturdier banks already closed down, to salvage banks now at the brink, and to supply emergency credit to industrial concerns.

A number of the participants were enthusiastically for the idea, but the majority preferred that the government itself set up the credit reservoir. Several of them, Hoover would recall wryly, "in courteous terms gave me some unnecessary instruction in the principles of banking and insurance." The spectacle was ironic: the head of the government trying to convince two score top-shelf capitalists to rely on fairly familiar capitalist tech-niques rather than on the government. The agreement reached was that an emergency conference of New York bankers on the following day would make the crucial decision, on the basis of a written memorandum to be submitted by the President.

Hoover dictated and signed the memorandum next day on a train en route to Philadelphia, to attend a World Series game. He was keeping the engagement, despite the crisis on which his mind and energies were cen-tered, as a tranquilizing public gesture. To fill his cup of secret sorrows, he received during the game the shocking news that Senator Dwight W.

Morrow of New Jersey, an intimate friend and one of his main supports on Capitol Hill, had just died.

As Hoover left the ball park—burdened by bleak and secret knowledge, worried about the critical decision being made in New York—he was followed by cries of "We want beer! We want beer!" One must pause to savor this scene, as a measure of the astronomical distance between the Job-like preoccupations of a dedicated President and the frivolous preoccupations of the citizenry. Fortunately, on returning to the White House after midnight, he found an item of cheer—news that the reluctant bankers had decided to form the National Credit Association, and precisely as he had formulated it.

The congressional contingent which met him on the sixth heard another candid briefing, as prelude to another plea for patriotic collaboration divorced from politics. The private Credit Association would be helpful, but bold and swift government action would still be required. Only Speaker Garner and Senator Borah refused to join in "approval in principle" of the President's blueprint, as summed up in a statement to the press which he read to them.

It was in this statement that Hoover first alluded publicly to his plans for a Reconstruction Finance Corporation (RFC), although he did not as yet use the name. He announced:

If necessity requires, I will recommend the creation of a finance corporation similar in character and purpose to the War Finance Corporation, with available funds sufficient for any legitimate call in support of credit.

The businessmen at the October fourth meeting most directly concerned with mortgage problems gathered again in the White House the day after the congressional conference. They heard Hoover prescribe drastic medicine, including the suspension of further foreclosures on the homes and farms of responsible owners—a sort of domestic standstill; more generous new mortgages at lower rates; a network of well-capitalized Mortgage Discount Banks. The last item was something Hoover had already proposed when he was in the Coolidge Cabinet; had he then been heeded, literally millions of farm and home owners would not have lost their properties in the years of the locusts. The insurance tycoons, who held the key to the mortgage complex, spurned the bitter medicines. Their only job, they explained, was to protect the income of policyholders!

The President had to wait for the new session of the Seventy-second Congress, convened December 7, to push his plan on the government level. In the end, because the mortgage lobbyists were too influential with a Congress too willing to be influenced, he was forced to trim down his concept in this area to the Home Loan Banks to obtain its passage. The availability of easy financing for home-building, as Hoover saw it, offered the best single opportunity for aid to the unemployed. This was a primary provision in the Home Loan setup. Congress took nine months to act on it and even then it hobbled the home-building powers.

There were many other White House moves and plans. Those that could be implemented without new legislation were quickly put into effect. The rest had to wait on Congress. But the mere publication of sensible proposals, as indications that the woes might be cushioned if not removed, had a salutary impact on the public mood. The initial conduct of the National Credit Association, too, lifted some spirits. The press could again report zephyrs of renewed confidence. Foreigners were increasingly convinced that the United States would not devalue its dollar after all. Thus in November, currency hoarding and gold outflow practically ceased, and bank failures declined sharply to the pre-depression rate of mortality.

The crisis galloping to a climax was headed off this side of the panic line.

The slight recuperation, however, soon gave way to new fevers. The opening of Congress acted as a wet blanket on the nation's spirits. It became plainly apparent that the Hoover proposals, though they had been "approved in principle," would run into know-nothing political resistance, with no plausible alternatives forthcoming from his opponents. In describing the succeeding six months, Hoover was understating reality when he wrote:

At this time I was faced with a practical Democratic control of the Congress, whose antagonism no man could measure or conciliate. The skirmishing preliminary to the presidential campaign of 1932 had begun. Out of power for three administrations, the Democrats saw a chance for victory. They were hot with partisanship, and many of them would not have regretted if demoralization extended through the election.

Legislative tactics of delay and sabotage, according to historians of the Administration, prolonged and deepened the depression. True, these were historians friendly to Hoover, but their charge is too easily documented to be dismissed. An immense amount of time and effort which the Chief Executive could have invested constructively were siphoned off by his incessant battles with the legislative branch.

3

Hoover laid before this congressional session a many-faceted program for amelioration and recovery—parts of it, of course, repetitions of previous proposals. In the following months he supplemented the annual message with a stream of urgent, often desperate, messages making additional suggestions or pleading for restoration of vital elements in bills enacted in mutilated versions. All this stands on the record, and it adds up to one of the most farsighted and comprehensive programs ever formulated to deal with economic misfortune. In substance it would not only be adopted *after Hoover's departure,* but would be carried to self-defeating excess, by the very men who now blocked it.

Most of the President's plans were defeated. Those enacted were first mangled in committee rooms. Some were deliberately delayed so that the political credit for their beneficent effects might not accrue to the party of the man who had devised them.

Among other things, Hoover asked for the legislation establishing the RFC, with an initial capital of half a billion dollars and authority to borrow up to three billion more from the Treasury and private sources. He set forth his minimal suggestions with respect to mortgage finance through a system of Home Loan banks. He proposed revision of bankruptcy laws to give a bigger chance of survival to firms in temporary difficulties. Over and over again, now for the third year running, he demanded reform of the banking structure and practices. At the same time he urged reform and regulation of the Stock Exchanges and rigid curbs on stock promotion practices; federal regulation of interstate electric power rates and utility finances; the reconstitution of the former World War Debt Commission to deal promptly with the problems that would arise when the moratorium expired. And this, of course, is only a partial inventory.

In the version submitted by the President, the RFC was to be empowered to channel its capital, as needed, wherever normal credit facilities were inadequate. The bill was enacted on January 22, 1932, after a six weeks' delay that spelled ruin to myriad individuals and firms. Since the top legislators had approved the organization in principle back in October, the politically inspired procrastination was hardly excusable. And the President's plan was whittled down to restrict its operations.

Congress could not reject the RFC but its more intransigent members managed to cut down its usefulness. The bill as passed struck out many of Hoover's most important provisions. For instance, it eliminated agricultural credits to support exports, loans for plant improvements, loans to closed banks, loans to public bodies for additional public works; it denied other credit authority the President considered vital.

To make matters worse, the bill, on the initiative of Speaker Garner, ordered monthly publication of the names of all borrowers. This, the President and others protested, would defeat the very purpose of the loans by alarming depositors and creditors of the borrowing institutions. Hoover threatened a veto unless this provision was deleted. The Senate then modified the clause to require only a confidential report of loans to be filed with the clerks of the House and Senate. Hoover signed the Act, as the best he could obtain, but only after man-of-honor assurances that the loans would not be publicized.

Under the energetic presidency of Charles G. Dawes, even the curtailed RFC was able to ease pressures in many economic areas. Hoover, said the New York *Times* (February 7, 1932), "is putting into operation the most revolutionary measures ever passed in peacetime, to bolster private credit with government credit and thus thaw out the hidden assets of the nation." In the month before the RFC went into action, bank failures, measured by deposits, ran to two hundred million dollars. In the next six months the total was steadily reduced until it reached the pre-depression monthly level of ten million dollars.

The limited victory scored by the Administration on the RFC was extended by its success one month later in forcing through the Glass-Steagall Bill. This, by increasing the bases for Federal Reserve System reserves, broadened credit and helped conserve gold.

As legislative confusion and opposition on other important proposals built up, the President sought to take Democratic leaders and recalcitrant Republicans into fullest confidence on his every move. If they preferred to act on a program of their own, he promised his unstinting cooperation. He suggested that certain measures be sponsored by Democrats, so that no political profit would redound to his own party. The need was urgent for prompt remedial action in a dozen imperiled fields.

Those in control of the Congress would neither go along with Hoover nor offer a program of their own. Their job, they informed the White House, was only to "scrutinize" recovery suggestions, not to initiate them. Hoover asked respected Republicans in both Houses to meet with Garner and other key Democrats in a further attempt to win their support. It failed, utterly. One of those present, the Democratic floor leader, Henry T. Rainey of Illinois, declared, "We intend to beat him—Hoover," then repeated it in unprintable language.

Congress took seven weeks to authorize additional funds for the Federal Loan Bank, and even then postponed action on amendments requested by the Administration that would have allowed this agency wider latitude in aiding hard-pressed farmers. The amendments eventually were enacted—fourteen months later.

At the President's suggestion, building and loan association leaders promised to bring pressure on Congress in behalf of the Home Loan Banks. Then they promptly stepped up their lobbying against the plan. The banks were legislated into being—nine months later and with hamstringing provisions to hobble its operations. One of the delays was caused by Senator Borah's attempt to tack on an amendment for a billion dollars in fiat money. Meanwhile thousands of the families the bill was designed to help lost their homes. One of the obstructionists stated with cynical candor that these banks *had* to be delayed in order that the Administration might not draw any political benefits from them in the coming election.

On March 4, 1932, the Senate yielded to the President's long-standing call for a public investigation of the Stock Exchanges. There was doubt about the constitutionality of federal laws in this area. "But I hoped," Hoover presently would explain, "that at least when we exposed the situation the Governor of New York would recognize his fundamental responsibility and act accordingly. That hope, however, proved to be little more than wishful thinking."

The top New York bankers, with Thomas Lamont as spokesman, protested the President's strictures on Exchange practices. In his reply Hoover said simply, "Men are not justified in deliberately making a profit on the losses of other people." It was hardly the kind of argument that carried weight at that time with the House of Morgan. The Senate hearings confirmed the worst suspicions of the President and the public. Some of the most glittering names in finance were implicated in shady and unethical transactions.

On his cherished plans for a reorganization of the national banking system, Hoover got nowhere. The drastic reforms he demanded included compulsory membership in the Federal Reserve System, elimination of promotion affiliates, limitations on branch banking. The failure to achieve the reorganization early in the depression, Hoover repeatedly stated, "was one of the reasons why we were compelled to put props under the structure to save it from collapse."

The opposition of the interests roughly implied by "Wall Street" prevailed in the Congress. Not until January 22, 1932, more than two years after he submitted it, was legislation on banking reported out of committee—only to be sent back there, time and again. In his message to Congress in December 1931, Hoover said: "Our people have a right to a banking system in which their deposits shall be safeguarded and the flow of credit less subject to storms." He was obliged to return to this theme in December 1932, in his last annual message.

On January 26, 1933, finally, a bill embodying some of Hoover's proposals was passed by the Senate. The House refused to act on it—on hints from the President-elect! Apparently nothing so substantial must be entered on the credit side of the Republican ledger, even after his defeat at the polls.

The shock administered to public opinion by the Senate investigation of the Exchanges, of course, paved the way for remedial legislation in

the Roosevelt period. Nor was the struggle for bank reform wholly in
vain. Subsequently Senator Frederic C. Walcott of Connecticut would
write to the ex-President: "You, more than anyone else, were responsible
for the constructive reforms eventually adopted."

To ward off popular wrath, the obstructionist coalition on Capitol Hill
indulged in oratorical flights about the sufferings of the people. But Congress continued to back and stall and play politics until its procrastination
became a scandal. A large part of the press, Democratic as well as Republican, spoke out more and more sharply in criticism.

On May 31, 1932, the President took what was for him the unusual step
of addressing the Senate in person. He demanded an end to the impasse,
particularly with respect to retrenchment in federal expenses and balancing of the budget. Any doubt that this Quaker could speak out vigorously
when he wished was removed by this address.

"Despite our national wealth and resources, and our unparalleled gold
reserves," he said, "our dollar stands at a serious discount in the markets
of the world for the first time in half a century." This he blamed in largest
measure upon temporizing by the Congress. He rehearsed the basic proposals which he had submitted and their sad fate at the hands of the
legislature. "The inherent abilities of our people to meet their problems
are being restrained by the failure of the government to act," he said, and
"every day's delay makes new wounds and extends them."

The press reaction was all that Hoover had reasonably hoped for. An
editorial in the Democratic Baltimore *Sun* declared:

Congress deserves what it has been given. It asked for all it has been given.
Mr. Hoover's message is an unanswerable indictment. Bitter and savage as it is,
in substance it is no more than a summary of the proceedings of Congress in the
last two months. . . . Congress has flagrantly and disgracefully deserted its own
standards. . . . Congress has missed no opportunity to disembowel the policy
of orthodox finance.

The New York *Times* pointed out:

On the importance of federal retrenchment and the necessity of balancing
the budget he [Hoover] has spoken in no less than twenty-one messages, statements, and addresses. . . . Responsibility for the chaos which now exists in
Washington rests upon those members of Congress who have blocked the
President at every turn and bolted their own party leadership.

Such evidence of growing popular disgust with the whole sorry performance on Capitol Hill enabled Hoover to crash through at least on the
budgetary issue. A momentarily sobered Senate remained in session until
midnight and passed the revenue bill which had gathered dust since the
beginning of its term. The tax bill was signed on June 6. But the sorely
needed additional revenue, having been held up for six months, came

too late to affect the current fiscal year—Hoover's last. It was harvested by the next Administration, as the procrastinators had intended.

As a result of its conduct, the prestige of Congress was perhaps at its lowest ebb in this century. This was doubtless a factor in making it possible for Hoover's successor to turn the legislative arm of government into little more than a rubber stamp for the executive.

A premonitory betterment in economic conditions could be discerned in the middle of March 1932. It was drowned in a flood of inflationary bills and buried by tactics of delay. Soon after Congress adjourned, however, the situation began to look up again. In July a truly remarkable turn for the better became manifest, both in the United States and in Europe. Across the Atlantic the improvement marked the beginning of the end of the depression. But in this country progress continued encouragingly until the election in early November, then began to decline at an ever faster rate.

Shortly before he departed from the White House, the President summed up his dilemma, the dilemma of every President unlucky enough to serve during a major depression. In talking to Joslin, who recorded his words, Hoover said:

What I have tried to do during these years has been to save the American people from disaster. They do not know what they have missed. Because they don't know what they have missed, they are dissatisfied with what has been done. In such circumstances, they turn to other leaders.

A former European official recently observed that statesmen, in trying to prevent disaster, kill themselves off. He might say that my tactics have been wrong, that I should have waited until the American people were half-drowned and then have waded in and tried to save them. In such an event, they would, of course, have known what it was all about. But it would have meant catastrophe!

President Hoover's was the heartbreaking task of plugging leaks to keep the ship from sinking. The mean of spirit castigated the captain for failing to make port, instead of cheering him for keeping the battered vessel afloat.

XXIV

Direct Relief

IN the 1932 presidential campaign the Democrats fought the incumbent Administration fiercely, without inhibiting scruples. Every real and fancied popular grievance was exploited to the utmost limits. Yet one presumably hot issue was strangely, inexplicably, neglected. This is the more curious in view of the fact that after the election it was discovered and promoted to the head of the list in the indictments of President Hoover.

The Republican candidate took public notice of the omission during the campaign: "Roosevelt," he said, "made no attack upon our measures of direct relief. It is certain that if these measures had not been successful, every molehill would have become a mountain." And he had plenty of reason to refer to it in retrospect, when completely different relief doctrines and techniques were in vogue. Thus, looking back from a decade's distance, he would declare:

Upon coming into office the New Deal administration claimed that millions of people were starving and that nothing had been done in the way of real relief. *Had that been true, they would not have failed to say so during the presidential campaign.* It would have been the best possible vote getter. But since it was manifestly not true, the charge would have antagonized the great body of devoted people who were carrying on the work efficiently in the spirit of neighborliness and patriotism.

In that "great body of devoted people" there were as many Democrats as Republicans, possibly more. They were there not under party labels but as Americans and as human beings, overwhelmingly on a volunteer basis and with a sense of participating in a humanitarian crusade.

In the literature of the 1932 campaign one finds few traces of the later fairy tale of mass starvation. That charge made a timid debut in the invective of more extreme left-wing propaganda (some of it directed against *both* candidates) but it did not figure in the basic Democratic thesis. Every community knew that its own needy were being cared for by committees of local citizens; that private and public agencies in unexampled cooperation on a nonpartisan basis were proving themselves effective.

Throughout the Hoover segment of the depression, of course, wild statements were continually being made by advocates of a federal "dole" that millions of the unemployed were going hungry. In the grim winter of 1931–32 the figure sometimes used was six million families, or thirty million people, reduced to starvation. What was the truth?

There was good reason for viewing the advent of that winter with sinking spirits. In September our economy had been staggered anew by the British devaluation of the pound. A special note of anxiety could be detected in the seasonal fund-raising drive for relief, this time headed by Owen D. Young. In formally opening the drive on October 18, the President said in part:

The depression has been deepened by events from abroad which are beyond the control either of our citizens or of our government. . . . This organized effort is our opportunity to express our sympathy, to lighten the burden of the heavy-laden, and to cast sunshine into the habitation of despair. . . . The possible misery of helpless people gives me more concern than any other trouble this depression has brought us. . . . I would that I possessed the art of words to fix the real issue with which the troubled world is faced into the mind and heart of every American. . . . This civilization and this great complex, which we call American life, is builded and can alone survive upon the translation into individual action of that fundamental philosophy announced by the Savior nineteen centuries ago. . . . Modern society cannot survive with the defense of Cain, "Am I my brother's keeper?"

The undertaking was thus pitched on a lofty level of appeal to the individual conscience. And it proved completely successful, not only in raising the required funds but, in Hoover's words, "in awakening the national responsibility for being 'my brother's keeper.'"

Repeatedly that winter, surveys were made through state committees and state governments on the actual needs and the available relief. Forty-seven of the forty-eight governors—including Governor Roosevelt of New York—attested that they did not require or want federal grants-in-aid. The one exception was Governor Gifford Pinchot of Pennsylvania, but the relief committee in that state denied that his demand for a Washington handout was justified by the facts. In 277 of the largest cities, the Community Chests advised the President that they were confident that their local problems would be met without direct federal aid.

As a further test, the Surgeon-General, Dr. Hugh S. Cumming, was instructed to report on the health of the population. He found that the death rate was lower than in the last full prosperity year of 1928 and that infant mortality, the most sensitive test of living conditions, was lower than ever in the past. Hoover obtained congressional authority to draw seventy-five million bushels of wheat and five hundred thousand bales of cotton from Farm Board surpluses, their distribution through the relief committees being handled by the Red Cross. The milled wheat thus provided was sufficient to supply bread to all relief applicants for at least nine months.

At the winter's end, the evidence of success was beyond doubt: only two million families, not the six million of the scare propaganda, had applied for help and all of them had received it. There were privations, inevitably, but remarkably few authenticated cases of people without food, heat, or shelter.

The great debate on relief related only to the methods of providing it. Essentially it was a running dispute between those who demanded and those who opposed a handout or "dole" by the central government. The great majority of Democratic leaders, including Roosevelt, firmly sided with the Administration against the dole; so did the 1932 Democratic platform. The history of the Hoover administration has been so distorted that after a while this fact—that the country was overwhelmingly against the federal dole type of relief—came to sound incredible. But it *was* a fact. A bill sponsored by Senator Robert LaFollette of Wisconsin and other "progressives," making large federal appropriations for relief, was defeated, 48 to 35; and 40 percent of those opposing the bill were Democrats.

The economic smashup of 1929 found at the helm in Washington the American who was unquestionably the world's leading expert on large-scale relief of human privation. In that circumstance one is tempted to trace a divine intention. Hoover had raised mass benevolence to a science. The premise that this man refused to use his rare expertise to the fullest when his own flesh and blood faced destitution simply makes no sense. It was the kind of falsehood to which only a generation dizzied by propaganda could have given a moment's credence.

There is, of course, ample room for argument as to the relative efficacy of the theory and methods of relief applied by President Hoover and by his successor. The two systems were universes apart in spirit and substance. Hoover relied primarily (though not exclusively) on local, volunteer, non-political forces; the New Deal came to rely on a rapidly expanded and exorbitantly costly federal bureaucracy. The first system rested on the alerted neighborhood, the second on the welfare state. The first was an emergency setup; it did not accept the assumption that relief would be a permanent function of government with its own gigantic civil service. The second was geared more and more to the acceptance of permanent, systematized destitution and a new millionfold pauper class in the population.

Under both dispensations there were hardships, failures, injustices, and for the victims physical suffering and anguish of spirit. No enterprise of such vast dimensions is without its faults and fumblings.

Actually, the President thought of most of his efforts to cushion the depression and speed up recovery as "relief" measures. He considered direct relief—aid in cash or in kind to the destitute—as supplementing *indirect* relief: the sort that helps people keep their jobs or obtain new ones. For example, public utilities, railways, and other industries, with government credit and encouragement, were able not merely to maintain their pre-depression rate of construction but to enlarge it. According to Department of Commerce data, their 1929 construction totaled $6,500,000,000; in 1931–32 it stood at $7,000,000,000. At the government end, indirect relief was provided by an aggregate of $2,358,000,000 in public works in the four Hoover years. In addition, under the prodding of the Administration, state and local governments chalked up an estimated additional $1,500,000,000 in public works above their normal appropriations.

Besides, there were the massive credits through the RFC and other federal sources for "self-liquidating" public works not encompassed by the above figures. Those were the type that repaid the funds advanced, plus interest. More than a hundred federally supported projects in this category in the Hoover administration included the San Francisco-Oakland Bay Bridge, the Los Angeles water supply system from the Colorado River, Jones Beach in New York, and the Mississippi River Bridge in New Orleans. Hoover also sought to initiate slum-clearance projects—probably the first time that this had been proposed at the Washington level—but failed to get the necessary authority.

Indirect relief, obviously, was not enough. Unemployment grew apace. Hoover made sure, therefore, that direct relief would be available to those in want. At frequent intervals he made detailed studies of the needs, the resources available, and the additional funds required.

Hoover had learned in Europe that the most reliable measure of the effectiveness of relief was the health of the population. There is, indeed, no other way to gauge the ravages of undernourishment. The reports of social workers "on the spot" may be subjective, colored by irritation, the hope of larger subsidies, and political pressures. Death and health statistics are matters of objective record. Periodically, therefore, the President had Surgeon-General Cumming provide him with detailed surveys.

They showed a declining death rate, especially among infants under one year. On January 2, 1932, as already noted, Dr. Cumming reported that "infant mortality during the past year was definitely lower than in any preceding year on record"; lower, that is to say, than in 1929 or any pre-depression year. The president of the American Public Health Association in October 1932 declared in a formal statement that "By and large the health of the people as measured in sickness and death has never been better despite the depression."

Advocates of the relief theories subsequently embraced by President Roosevelt were sufficiently vocal from the start. They wanted centralized distribution of billions of dollars in taxpayers' money. There were among them Republicans as well as Democrats. No doubt their system would have "simplified" matters for the President. There would have been no fund drives, no appeals to local communities to pitch in—and a vote dividend for the politicians commanding the largest slices of those billions.

President Hoover was profoundly convinced that such dependence on the Federal Treasury "would bring an inevitable train of corruption and waste," and partisan exploitation of a people's misery, along with intolerable strains on the nation's monetary structure. The alternative, his own conception, was not improvised. It was a strategy carefully developed through his long years of practical experience. Its essence can be summarized in four paragraphs:

1. Local resources—the neighbor, the existing social agencies, the municipality, the state—represent the first lines of defense against distress. Being in lifelong contact with the victims of the depression, local volunteers would bring their hearts, not merely red tape and badges, to their work. They would not so easily be imposed upon by chiselers and malingerers, thus leaving more for the families in real trouble.

2. The Federal Government is the last line of defense, in constant readiness to provide help if and when the first lines weaken. Meanwhile, however, it is not inert. It seeks to reduce the size of the problem by generating jobs, stimulating capital investment, providing credits for endangered farms and businesses, spreading available work and other methods.

3. When it becomes necessary for the U. S. Treasury to make grants, the funds are not divided indiscriminately on a population basis but strictly in relation to concrete needs, and their administration is left with the states through their local committees. This has at least three vital advantages: it keeps down the incidence of patronage and pork-barrel diversions; it removes the need for an immense federal bureaucracy; and it continues to utilize to the maximum the leverage of human good will.

4. The effort as a whole is treated as an "emergency program" for meeting specific needs in specific places, not as an excuse "to implant a new social philosophy in American life in conflict with the primary concepts of American liberty." The quoted words are Hoover's. "It is not the function of the government," he argued, "to relieve individuals of their responsibilities to their neighbors, or to relieve private institutions of their responsibilities to the public."

Direct federal handouts, Hoover said in 1931, must be ruled out because "the net results of governmental doles are to lower wages toward bare subsistence level and to endow the slacker." Beyond this and other economic objections, he regarded the self-respect and self-reliance of the local community as values to be cherished for their own sake. He saw only grief and moral debility from "a cold and distant charity which puts out its sympathy only through the tax collector" and "yields a very meager dole of unloving and perfunctory relief."

2

In pursuance of that strategy Hoover in October 1930 set up the President's Emergency Relief Organization, with Colonel Arthur Woods as chairman. He later was succeeded by Walter S. Gifford, head of the A. T. & T. This organization, in turn, formed State Unemployment Relief Committees, whose work was decentralized through thousands of county and city committees run by respected local people. The Washington staff, except for purely secretarial work, was almost entirely voluntary. Several dozen inspectors crisscrossed the country continually to check complaints and make sure there were no failures. The great majority of local staffs, too, were unpaid volunteers.

At intervals until the end of his term, the President enlarged the organization to meet new demands, raising money from many sources as required. At his request, the Friends' Service (the Quaker agency) assumed the responsibility for feeding children in coal regions. The Red Cross and other such private groups were assigned to solve problems within their special capacities.

No purely bookkeeping total of the Hoover species of relief is possible, since it did not flow from one source and was not managed by a single agency. There is no arithmetic to encompass the varieties of aid evoked by the continuous appeals to self-help and community spirit. It came abundantly from neighbors, employers, trade unions, religious groups, social organizations, regional and state treasuries. In later years these sources were for the most part choked off, as the government undertook to do it all by taxing and borrowing and taxing some more.

The overhead for relief administration under Hoover rarely exceeded 3 percent. After his departure it came to consume 25 and in some places as high as 50 percent of the relief funds. Despite the launching of many new agencies, there were ten thousand *fewer* federal employees at the end of Hoover's term than at its start. In 1935, at the end of the first New Deal term, their number grew by 335,000. "In his Jackson Day speech," Hoover said at that later date, "the President urged committees of one to support the New Deal. He has a good start with 335,000 committees —and their wives."

Looking over the New Deal landscape after a few years, he felt justified in speaking of politicians as miners digging for votes:

They extracted this precious ore not only from the families dependent on the WPA, the CCC, and similar alphabetical organizations but from their relatives to the third and fourth degrees, from employees of the local bureaucracy formed to bestow these benefits. And they mined it in great nuggets from communities—preferably those on the doubtful list of political managers—on which they bestowed special favors at the expense of the government. Votes are the professional politicians' idea of the food of gods, which is kept in pork barrels.

Hoover's obstinacy in barring the way to those barrels was resented and the resentment now and then took startlingly petty forms. Thus on July 15, 1932, the President applied to Congress for an emergency appropriation of $120,000—thousands, not millions—to help pay purely clerical expenses of his nationwide relief organization. He pointed out that the effort was rigidly nonpartisan and that its members received no pay. Congress—the same Congress which a year or two later was shelling out billions and no questions asked—refused the appropriation. The President had to raise the money from private sources, including his own pocket.

Each time he warded off another assault on the Treasury, Hoover touched off new cries of "heartlessness." On one such occasion he felt it necessary to address the American people:

This is not an issue as to whether people shall go hungry and cold in the United States. It is solely a question of the best method by which hunger and cold shall be prevented. . . . I am willing to pledge myself that if the time should ever come that the voluntary agencies of the country together with the local and state governments are unable to find resources with which to prevent hunger and suffering in my country, I will ask the aid of every resource of the Federal Government, because I would no more see starvation amongst my countrymen than any Senator or Congressman.

In his last year in office he made good on that pledge. Until then forty-seven of the forty-eight states (as already noted) had indicated officially that Washington grants-in-aid were not yet required. Then the growing stringency of local resources made federal help necessary. Hoover obtained legislative consent for three hundred million dollars in loans to states, to be supplied according to need and to be administered through existing committees. He made it clear that more would be forthcoming if and when it was needed. He also authorized the RFC to lend more than a billion dollars for relief purposes.

In March 1932, unemployment had topped the ten million mark and the outcries for direct federal relief were gaining in strength. The President called a group of leading Democratic and Republican senators and representatives into conference. He asked for their frank advice on one simple question: should the government go in for the dole? The answer was unanimously in the negative. Those in Congress and in left-wing organizations who wanted the dole and abused Hoover as "stony-hearted" for not granting it, could cite no genuine failure of the voluntary system.

Hoover took no satisfaction in later years when the worst of his forebodings about waste and political corruption under a federalized relief system came true. But he could not ignore the facts. They helped to explain why, as President, he was so determined to keep relief out of the political arena and to deny politicians access to the Treasury under the convenient banners of concern for suffering people. And during his tenure he had, at least on this score, the support of many of those who later invented and disseminated the legend of his callousness.

Let me quote a few significant sentences. They date back to the time when Hoover was still President:

I am opposed to any dole. I do not believe that the state has any right merely to hand out money. . . . People suggest that a huge expenditure of public funds by the Federal Government and by state and local governments will completely solve unemployment. . . . Let us admit frankly that it would only be a stopgap. . . . Under no circumstance shall any money be paid in the form of a dole or any other form by the local welfare officer to any unemployed or his family. . . . Revenues must cover expenditures by one means or another. Any government, like any family, can for a year spend a little more than it earns, but you and I know that a continuation of that habit means the poorhouse. . . . High-sounding, newly invented phrases cannot sugar-coat the pill. Let us have the courage to stop borrowing to meet continuing deficits. Stop the deficits!

The man who spoke in this vein was not Herbert Hoover but Franklin D. Roosevelt during his successful campaign to replace Hoover. Before that, at a conference of governors in Salt Lake City, he denounced the dole as a "character-destroying" device. Nor did he at any time as governor during the depression complain about his own state and municipalities being burdened with relief responsibilities that should have been shouldered by the Washington government. Only after attaining the Presidency did he bring into the Federal Government the authors of those "high-sounding, newly invented phrases" he had earlier denounced.

Yet the stick with which Hoover's character was so mercilessly belabored in subsequent years was the charge of his failure to give relief. It was fashioned, let it be clear, after he left the White House. If there be doubts as to whether President Hoover's system of relief through local and self-help, from the bottom up instead of the top down, was good public policy, there is no doubt at all that it was wretched politics. It had none of the vote-getting magic of openhandedness with public funds. It did not produce armies of jobholders with a personal stake in perpetuating the Administration in power. Indeed, it guaranteed that the Administration would garner the most blame and the least appreciation.

The vote potential in food and funds to the needy would be demonstrated before long on an overwhelming scale. But Hoover fixed it so that all largesse, the federal guidance and cash contributions included, came through the city, county, and state, and through private channels like the Community Chests. A seemingly passive Federal Government reaped all the odium of relief failure and confusion where these occurred, but garnered none of the credit where relief was provided adequately and without incident. A billion dollars handed out by officials of a welfare state is one thing; the same billion raised from many sources and administered by volunteer committees is quite another thing.

One of the most harmful facts about the Hoover system, *judged as politics,* is that it provided maximum visibility for the grimmest side of depression and unemployment. It could not sugarcoat or conceal unpleasant realities. On the contrary, Hoover's repeated appeals to the nation's charitable instincts kept the consciousness of privation always to the fore. Every new fund drive naturally played up the grave sufferings and the danger of more suffering.

Hoover did not set millions to raking leaves, flailing water, daubing walls, writing guidebooks and gibberish to gloss the facts of joblessness. His system left the unpleasant truth starkly exposed. Average annual unemployment during the Hoover administration was 6.2 millions; in the first two Roosevelt administrations, that is to say until the war came, the average was 10 millions. But the general impression was the exact reverse.

The impression that the country was "better off" during the New Deal era had little reference to economic fact. In largest part it was the product of superb showmanship. It is exhilarating to watch rabbits being pulled out of hats even if they are papier-mâché rabbits and inedible. Moreover, the mere passage of time, after Hoover, would help create a growing sense of well-being. The man who loses a fortune or a limb is at first tragic and embittered, but in time adjusts himself to the loss. In the early depression years the awareness of disaster, the contrast with the prosperity just lost, was painfully deep. Then, as the depression continued, it gradually lost its sting; idleness and want became almost a way of life; dependence on the government became for thousands a preferred way of life.

As the 1932 campaign shaped up, Hoover relief was effective but, I repeat, wretched politics. The angers and frustrations of the slump were at peak points, despite improvements in all key economic indices in the preceding few months. The American people ached for a scapegoat. Their President had been widely heralded—by others, never by himself— as a "miracle man." But no miracles that the electorate could identify had been forthcoming.

The many true economic miracles he had performed, through unprecedented credit and banking devices, were not of the sort ordinary citizens could see or comprehend. In the emotional shorthand of political folklore, which has nothing in common with logic or fact, the period of his Presidency and therefore Hoover himself came to mean hardship and despair. A President had become the whipping-boy of the country as he entered the lists for re-election.

It was in an atmosphere polluted by smears and lies, fevered with the rantings of snake-oil schools of economy, shadowed by terrible fears, that the 1932 campaign got under way. Hoover had no real hope of winning. He made the best fight he could, in deference to duty.

XXV

1932: Hoover is Defeated

As the 1932 election campaign loomed on the horizons of his crowded, harried, sleep-starved life, President Hoover instructed his staff and associates that in the months ahead first priority must go to the duties of his office. He planned to confine himself to three or four policy addresses, while Cabinet officers and Republican stalwarts would carry the brunt of the battle.

But he was forced to make a far more strenuous fight. The nature of the Democratic attacks and the limitations of the Republican party mechanism left him no alternative. He had given little enough time to party affairs, for which he had no natural relish anyhow. Now, though thousands of men and women labored for his re-election with unlimited enthusiasm, the party showed itself deficient in organization, planning, and preparation.

Early in the game the Republican National Committee went stonebroke, so that Hoover had to add party fund-raising to his other burdens. He was obliged also to assume much of the responsibility for providing the data and arguments to counter accusations and distortions. One Sunday in August, for example, after a radio address by his adversary, the President telephoned sixty-one Republican leaders throughout the country to feed them the facts in refutation.

During the campaign he made nine major and a dozen secondary addresses. Since many days and nights of writing and editing went into his every text, the drain on his time and stamina was serious. The scores of talks at "tank-stops" from the rear platforms of trains were extempore and, by all accounts, effective.

His obligations as President took precedence over everything else notwithstanding. There had been, since the Congress recessed, an unmistakable upturn in the economy and he was determined not to allow it to slip back. To those around him it seemed impossible that one mortal man could survive the multiple strains of the Presidency and the campaign. The question, as they discussed it in fearful whispers, was not *whether* but *when* he would collapse. His eyes were now chronically bloodshot, the lines in his face appeared to deepen by the day. Only once, however, did it seem that his extraordinary reserves of strength had been drained to the bottom. That was in St. Paul, three days before the election. That night, even radio listeners sensed, he was staggering on the brink. But next morning he seemed to be in fair form again.

There is substantial agreement among historians, regardless of their political bias, that the domestic and world depression had been arrested by the middle of 1932. A million American workers returned to their jobs and more were streaming back at the rate of five hundred thousand a month. The values of bonds rose by 20 percent in a couple of months, factory output by 10 percent, and in selected industries, such as textiles, by 50 percent. The farmers, reliable statistics showed, would be a billion dollars better off that year.

This was for the Republicans the most hopeful element at the start of the campaign. The President was not whistling in the dark when he apprised voters that recovery was at last within sight. Even as he spoke, however, the election struggle itself began to slow up and in the end halted the processes of progress. "As Maine goes so goes the nation"—and in late September Maine went emphatically for Governor Roosevelt.

The increasing Democratic talk of "a new social order" and of startling experiments in "economic planning" to come doubtless rallied votes. But they raised misgivings among those who had to make decisions on immediate investments and future enterprise. The fact is that the new-born and fragile confidence ebbed as the campaign proceeded, and dried up when the returns came in.

The strange and ambiguous stance of big and middling businessmen should be noted. They feared the coming regime—yet connived in its coming. They drew comfort from the Democratic candidate's unending assurances of economic and monetary orthodoxy—and discounted the lusty radicalism of his supporters and his failure to repudiate even the wildest of their doctrines.

The scheme which would in due time proliferate as the National Recovery Administration (NRA) and be hailed as a noble common-man invention was brought to President Hoover a year earlier, at the end of 1931. Not by "common men" but by spokesmen for business. Actually, it had its genesis in a speech on September 17 that year by Gerard Swope, president of General Electric. He proposed to "stabilize prices and distribution" through industry agreements under government supervision. It would in effect suspend the Sherman and Clayton anti-trust laws.

The President forwarded the Swope plan to his Attorney General for an opinion on its constitutionality. In a covering memorandum, he recorded his own immediate reaction. Hoover saw it as "the creation of a series of complete monopolies over the American people" which would guarantee "the decay of American industry . . . the most gigantic proposal of monopoly ever made in our history." Elsewhere Hoover castigated it as a fascist-type vision. The parallel with Mussolini's "corporate state" resting on a series of industry corporations was, as a matter of fact, all too apparent. The Attorney General advised that the plan was wholly unconstitutional.

But amazingly, the idea was taken up by the United States Chamber of Commerce and endorsed in a referendum of its members. Those who argue that the capitalists were then gripped by an impulse to suicide have plausible proof in this astonishing event.

The head of the Chamber, Henry I. Harriman, called on the President to urge him to recommend the plan to Congress. Hoover patiently explained to him that it amounted to a shortcut to fascism and socialism and could be the deathblow to America's free economy. Eight months later, with the campaign in progress, Harriman returned to the White House. He wanted a pledge that the President, if re-elected, would support the NRA scheme. Hoover would have none of it. He wanted it inscribed on his tombstone, he said with some heat, that he had stood firm against an unconstitutional attempt to smuggle fascism into America through a back door.

His guest, according to the President's notes on the interview, thereupon disclosed that Franklin D. Roosevelt had already accepted the idea, and warned that if Hoover remained obdurate the cash and influence of the business community would be thrown to the Democrats. Hoover did remain obdurate and Roosevelt did, in consequence, reap immense business backing.

In their book *America in Midpassage*, Professors Charles A. Beard and Mary Beard pointed out that "Hoover had few ardent friends in Wall Street, which was supposed to be the nerve center of the economic system he was trying to resuscitate." They explained this by the fact of Hoover's long record of attacks on market manipulations. Rejection of the NRA idea further forfeited business support. One of the results was the aforementioned shortage of Republican campaign funds.

The Hoover forces disposed of only about a third as much money as their opponents. The public was not aware that the nationwide radio broadcast of one of the President's most important addresses, the one in Detroit, was in doubt until the last moment for lack of funds. Perhaps the Republicans are not to be blamed for saving their cash in what they appraised as a hopeless contest, although many of them in time recognized the blunder of allowing their party to be crushed so decisively. Their candidate paid his own heavy traveling expenses and for much of his radio time.

In the defection of big business to the radical camp, Freudians might detect a death wish. The Shouse-Michelson strategy of relentless Hoover-baiting accomplished what John J. Raskob, the duPonts, and the other moneyed gentry who paid the bill could scarcely have wanted. They helped build a Frankenstein that has tormented them to this day. By stimulating radical and revolutionary movements far beyond the natural leftward trend in hard times, they defeated their own preferred Democratic party candidate, Alfred E. Smith. He came to the Democratic convention with the tag of "reactionary" around his neck, giving the nomination to Roosevelt virtually by default.

The governor of New York and his Texas running mate, John Nance Garner, concentrated their fire on allegedly excessive spending and deficits in the Hoover administration. In specific, unambiguous terms they pledged "to accomplish a saving of not less than 25 percent in the cost of federal government," to trim down debts and balance the budget. "On my part," said Roosevelt, "I ask you very simply to assign to me the task of reducing the annual expenses of your national government. . . . Rigid governmental economy shall be enforced by a stern and unremitting policy of living within our income." And Garner promised: "When we come into power we'll give the country a demonstration in real economy."

The galleries echoed the Democratic slogan: "Throw the spenders out!" Year after year, the Democrats had tried to spend billions in printing-press money. Only a few months earlier Hoover was forced to make a personal appearance in the Senate to demand action to balance the budget. He had stopped dozens of pork-barrel raids on the Treasury—but what are mere facts in a campaign of slogans?

Too much spending and borrowing by Hoover, Democratic orators repeated a thousand times, were responsible for the country's continuing ills. Said Garner: "Their failure to balance the budget of a family of 120,000,000 people is at the very bottom of the economic trouble we are suffering." Said Roosevelt: "Let us have the courage to stop borrowing to meet continuing deficits. . . . Let us have equal courage to reverse the policy of the Republican leaders and insist on a sound currency." Also:

I accuse the present administration of being the greatest spending administration in peacetime in all our history. It is an administration that has piled bureau on bureau, commission on commission, and has failed to anticipate the dire needs of and the reduced earning power of the people. Bureaus and bureaucrats, commissions and commissioners, have been retained at the expense of the taxpayer.

Three weeks before the balloting, Governor Roosevelt was still talking in the same vein: "I regard reduction of federal spending as one of the most important issues in this campaign." And four days before the election he riveted down the promise: "The Democratic platform specifically declares, 'We advocate a sound currency to be preserved at all hazards.' This is plain English."

Could anything be more sensible and orthodox? Could anyone ask for more specific pledges against big government and rash experiments? The views of the people around Roosevelt might alarm his business backers, but clearly the candidate was sound. After all, many of the targets of his oratory were precisely those elements in the Hoover policies which would be identified, in the perspective of a few years, as the precursors of the New Deal.

How were the voters to surmise that Hoover would be the last President in twenty years who would even attempt to balance the budget? How were they to guess that in "throwing the spenders out" they were bringing in the philosophy that government deficits were a healthy thing? "It certainly makes life more easy and governing more popular for Presidents," Hoover would remark in retrospect about the new fiscal doctrines.

Governor Roosevelt, there is ground for conjecture, tried to keep himself on a plane of reason above the economic extremists who made up a large part of his entourage. We have testimony of Professor Raymond Moley to this effect. In preparing for the campaign, Moley revealed in his memoirs of disillusionment, Professor Rexford Guy Tugwell and other left-wingers urged Roosevelt to come out for a huge program of public works. But the candidate "repeatedly shied away from this proposal," partly because Hoover had found it so hard to think up "good" projects, but "also because Roosevelt certainly did not, at that time, subscribe to the pump-priming theory."

His doubts, however, did not carry the candidate to the point of disowning the pump-primers and assorted experimenters orating in his behalf. Besides, Roosevelt was in some measure the prisoner of his brilliant but doctrinaire ghost-writers. Believing as they did in a "new social order," they could not fail to weave their own convictions into his addresses. Moley was especially conscious of the risk of putting ideas and words into the mouth of a man who was not always intellectually discriminating. Roosevelt's mind, he has written, "was neither exact nor orderly. . . . He seldom trusted himself to say in public more than a few sentences extemporaneously. . . . I labored with the tormenting knowledge that I could not afford to be wrong."

2

Some years after the campaign, Herbert Hoover wrote that "the whole Democratic performance was far below the level of any previous campaign in modern times. . . . My defeat would no doubt have taken place anyway. But it might have taken place without such defilement of American life." Roosevelt, he said, "delivered a multitude of ghost-written speeches, some written by irresponsible or ignorant men," and among the brain-trusters were men "expert in semantics but grievously undernourished on truth."

These harsh judgments did not refer primarily to the personal slanders, though these were extensive and venomous. Somewhere in the strategic high command a decision evidently was made to focus the fire on Hoover the man, not merely his policies and his party. The whole reservoir of anti-Hoover inventions and innuendo was unloaded on the electorate. Some of the contents of the scurrilous books repudiated by the authors themselves were disseminated in "fact-sheets."

The President ignored this aspect of the offensive. He felt it demeaning, not only to himself but to the office he occupied, to dignify the absurdities with rebuttals. The "defilement," as he saw it, was in the nonchalant disregard of clear facts, the avoidance of national debate on real issues.

Governor Roosevelt and John Garner did not descend to charging Hoover with robbing coolies or stealing Belgian relief money. That was left to authenticated "progressives" on the fringes and beyond. But their own charges, to a man like Hoover, were even more insulting and cruel, for they painted a President devoid of compassion, indifferent to the agony of his countrymen. This accusation was implicit every time they alluded to the "Hoover depression" or "Hoovervilles." It was explicit in the claim —the heart and substance of the Democratic case—that Hoover was "responsible" for the depression, "did nothing" to allay its tragedy, and squandered billions on this "nothing."

The President's frustration in the face of such tactics came through now and then in his speeches: "So few of the statements made by the Democratic candidate are in accord with the records of fact, that it leaves me nonplussed where to begin." What, in truth, could Hoover do when confronted with a Rooseveltian whopper like this: "The only efforts made by the national administration to cope with the distress of unemployment were to deny its existence."

Roosevelt placed the aggregate budget deficit in the Hoover period at five billion dollars. Actually the apparent deficit was $3,347,000,000. But this included two and a half billion of recoverable loans by the RFC and other agencies. The true deficit amounted to a little over one billion. In view of the sharp decline in tax receipts, this was a negligible amount and reflected the President's desperate struggle against Treasury raids. But Roosevelt continued to cite the erroneous five-billion figure, as if he hadn't heard the correction. (Aggregate deficits in the first Roosevelt administration came to fourteen billion.)

"We cannot go back to children working in factories," the Democratic candidate exclaimed. This was hitting below the belt. Whoever wrote it into his text could not have been ignorant of the fact that Hoover inspired a Constitutional Amendment prohibiting child labor and had been pressing the states to act favorably on it. New York was among those that had refused to act.

Roosevelt charged that "over 6,000,000 of our school children have not enough to eat," and that they were fainting in classrooms. He gave the United States Public Health Service as his authority. The head of that service immediately denied both the source and the allegations. The President cited official health statistics refuting the charge. A number of Community Chests made angry denials. But Roosevelt's campaigners, if not the governor himself, persisted in repeating the falsehood.

In pursuance of the do-nothing theme, Roosevelt declared: "My friends, all that I can tell you is that I deplore, I regret the inexcusable, the reprehensible *delay* of Washington, not for months alone, but for years. . . ." There had, indeed, been reprehensible delays of months and years, caused in every instance by a politically minded Congress.

We have seen how persistently the President fought, in Congress and with private interests concerned, to liberalize mortgage procedures and curb unjustified foreclosures. Yet his opponent found it possible to say that in this campaign Hoover *for the first time* "has discovered the fact that there is such a thing as a farm or a home mortgage." Small wonder that the President declared himself "nonplussed."

The Democrats barely mentioned the RFC and sneered at the Federal Land Banks, the Intermediate Credit Banks, the Agricultural Production Banks, the Home Loan Banks, the expanded powers of the Federal Reserve System to help industry and agriculture. These extensions of credit facilities were lumped in their indictment of the Administration's "extravagance."

And, in the nature of the case, such new institutions were ignored in the over-all do-nothing fable. "I want to say with all the emphasis I can command," the governor declared, "that this administration did nothing and their leaders are, I am told, still doing nothing." From the day of the market crash until the end of 1931, he said, the President "did absolutely nothing to remedy the situation. Not only did he do nothing himself but he took the position that Congress could do nothing." Variations on the theme were played by the whole orchestra from Garner to the far Left.

The President and his supporters could only recite, day after day, the long litany of "somethings" done, of other "somethings" stymied by Democratic obstruction. Said Hoover:

It is now taken for granted that this Republican program has come of its natural self because in retrospect there is such universal recognition of the necessity. On the contrary, it has been wrought out of the fiery ordeal of hard and honest thought, the facing of facts when loose-thinking or frightened men offered every temptation of specious panaceas. It was wrought against the heart-breaking obstructions and delays of the Democratic House.

He called attention to the fact that "with the Democratic victory in the Congressional elections of 1930 their leaders promised to produce a program which would redeem this country from the depression. No such program was produced." He asked his adversary to be frank enough

to recognize the successful care of the distressed in the United States; that the savings of more than 95 percent of the depositors in our banks have been held secure; that the 20,000,000 borrowers who otherwise would have been bankrupt by forced selling of their assets in order to pay their debts have been protected; that the 70,000,000 life-insurance policies which represent the greatest act of self-denial of our people in provision for the future of their loved ones have been sustained in their validity; that the foreclosure of hundreds of thousands of home and farm mortgages has been prevented.

But the do-nothing slogan kept growing in decibel count. With it went the charge that the Republicans, and Hoover personally, were directly responsible for the depression. They had "overbuilt industry" and unduly enlarged farm output. They had countenanced unproductive investment and unwise loans to foreign borrowers. In short, theirs was the blame for the runaway prosperity.

Any high school boy knew that Democrats had been as drugged by the myth of perpetual-motion prosperity as the Republicans. The smarter ones knew that Hoover was one of the few who refused to join the zombie parade from boom to bust. Apparently, said the President, "the leading Democrats did not discover the Republican responsibility of this depression until it reached a vote getting state. . . . They should, as a responsible political party, cease to appeal to unthinking people for votes based upon their suffering by misleading them as to its causes." He might as well have tried to stop a cyclone with bare hands. A piece of doggerel popularized by his enemies went:

299

Mellon pulled the whistle,
Hoover rang the bell,
Wall Street gave the signal
And the country went to hell

Roosevelt's vehemence in condemning the sale of foreign bonds to American investors seemed ironic to those who remembered the nature of Roosevelt's business career before he became governor. "The Governor has the advantage of me in experience in that particular," Hoover said in a major address. "As late as 1928 the Governor was engaged in that business for profit and actively occupied in promoting such loans." Roosevelt, of course, was then chairman of the Federal International Banking Company, a private outfit specializing in pushing foreign securities in the American market. He had personally signed the company's extravagant sales promotion prospectus.

The atmosphere of the campaign, however, was too torrid for cold facts.

3

The President devoted himself largely to a reasoned, factual analysis and defense of his Administration. In his acceptance address on August 11, in Washington, he traced the fluctuations of the depression; the impact of the European collapse on America; the improved prospects for recovery at the moment:

Two courses were open. We might have done nothing. This would have been utter ruin. Instead, we met the situation with proposals to private business and the Congress of the most gigantic program of economic defense ever evolved in the history of the Republic. We put it into action. . . .

Our measures have repelled these attacks of fear and panic. We have maintained the financial integrity of our government. We have cooperated to restore and stabilize the situation abroad. As a nation we have paid every dollar demanded of us. We have used the credit of the government to aid and protect our institutions, public and private.

We have provided methods and assurances that there shall be none to suffer from hunger and cold. We have instituted measures to assist farmers and homeowners. We have created vast agencies for employment. Above all, we have maintained the sanctity of the principles upon which this Republic has grown great.

In a large sense the test of success of our program is simple. Our people, while suffering great hardships, have been and will be cared for. In the long view our institutions have been sustained intact and are now functioning with increasing confidence of the future. As a nation we are undefeated and unafraid. Government by the people has not been defiled.

Having outlined the doctrines of American individualism and the futility of magical cures, he proceeded to list the practical devices which he had utilized to meet the shifting challenges, and his plans for the future. He concluded:

Through it all, our first duty is to preserve unfettered that dominant American spirit which has produced our enterprise and individual character. That is the bedrock of the past, and that is the guaranty of the future. Not regimented mechanisms but free men is our goal. A representative democracy, progressive and unafraid to meet its problems, but meeting them upon the foundations of experience and not upon the wave of emotion or the insensate demands of a radicalism which grasps at every opportunity to exploit the sufferings of a people.

The plainly demagogic retort, in a hundred variations, was that his Administration had helped business, the banks, the insurance companies —not "the people." The President therefore found the occasion to say of Roosevelt:

He knows full well that the only purpose of helping an insurance company is to protect the policyholder. He knows full well that the only purpose in helping a bank is to protect the depositors and the borrower. He knows full well that the only purpose of helping a farm-mortgage company is to enable the farmer to hold his farm. He knows full well that the only purpose of helping the building and loan associations is to protect savings and homes. He knows full well that in sustaining the businessman it maintains the worker in his job.

On two issues the Republicans had no call to defend themselves. One was foreign affairs. Roosevelt made practically no reference to this. "Let's not do anything on foreign policy," he told Moley. "Hoover's all right on that." In the initial period of the campaign the Democrats assailed the tariff enacted during Hoover's tenure as too protectionist. But this touched off such vast protest from farmers, industry, and labor that Roosevelt, speech by speech, amended his views until he ended by promising steep duties and trade barriers around the country.

The other issue, as already indicated, was the Hoover system of providing and administering direct relief. Roosevelt matched him in denunciation of "doles." At the same time, however, and without seeming to be aware of the contradiction, those around him advocated—and wrote into his speeches—a hundred varieties of what would come to be known as "made-work" gadgets that were simply doles in transparent and humiliating disguises. Among the more remarkable gadgets, seriously pledged by Roosevelt, was the immediate planting of a million trees to employ a million men—one man per tree. Secretary of Agriculture Arthur M. Hyde produced the statistics proving that all the trees then available for planting would give a million men less than three days' work.

The liquor question bedeviled both parties. President Hoover, at a private luncheon in May with Senator Borah, who led the drys, told him that the Eighteenth Amendment could not be enforced and therefore should be repealed. The Republican plank formulated by Hoover said that "an amendment should be promptly submitted that shall allow the states to deal with Prohibition as their citizens may determine," but with "a safeguard against the return of the saloon and its attendant abuses." At the convention this was watered down by the drys and liquored up by the wets into an impossible straddle.

The Democratic plank was almost equally straddling. It advocated repeal, subject to federal safeguards for states choosing Prohibition. Roosevelt began by putting his stress on full repeal. As the campaign proceeded, however, he switched the emphasis to preventing "the return of the old-time saloon." Hoover adhered to the purport of his original plank proposal: "that each state shall be given the right to deal with the problem as it may determine" under conditions which would rule out the saloon and its corruptions.

In many ways the most significant aspect of the Democratic campaign, a key to its thinking, was something most Americans underrated at the time. It was the brand-new doctrine that the American economy was now "mature," completed, that the time had come to jettison dreams of further growth. In later years this theory became the justification of a cheerful defeatism that regarded ten million jobless and twenty million on relief rolls as natural and permanent: we must batten down the hatches for a century of stagnation.

The origins of this theory could readily be traced in the writings of some of the professors drawn into the Brain Trust. Their candidate embraced it without reservation. Speaking in San Francisco, on September 23, he said:

Our industrial plant is built; the problem just now is whether under existing conditions it is not overbuilt. Our last frontier has long been reached, and there is practically no more free land. . . . A mere builder of more industrial plants, a creator of more railroad systems, an organizer of more corporations, is as likely to be a danger as a help. The day of the great promoter or the financial titan, to whom we granted anything if only he would build, or develop, is over.

Our task now is not the discovery or exploitation of natural resources, or necessarily producing more goods. It is the soberer, less dramatic business of administering resources and plants already in hand, of seeking to re-establish foreign markets for our surplus production, of meeting the problem of underconsumption, of adjusting production to consumption, of distributing wealth and products more equitably, of adapting existing economic organization to the service of the people. The day of enlightened administration has come.

This was not a view suddenly improvised. It fitted into all the marvels of "economic planning," including the NRA, being excitedly elucidated by men like Tugwell and Felix Frankfurter, and beyond them spokesmen like Huey Long, LaFollette, Norris, Wheeler.

The rising enthusiasm for total planning in some quarters of American life was frankly related to the Five-Year Plan in Soviet Russia. Despite its attendant horrors, the Soviet Plan was getting a good press here. It had become a test of the new tough Liberalism, a hard-boiled Liberalism no longer squeamish about blood and death, to be able to shout hurrah for Stalin "despite everything." *A New Deal,* a book by Stuart Chase published in late 1932, concluded with the cry: "Why should the Russians have all the fun of remaking a world?" I was in Russia then, reporting the "fun" the lucky Russians were having in the nightmare of slave camps, famine, torture chambers, and the rest. But the economist's rhetorical question was not irony, it was genuine envy.

The presumed Soviet "miracle" provided the backdrop for the many brands of "planning" featured in Democratic oratory this campaign season. But Hoover, the engineer, warned against such "human engineering." He insisted that colossal centralized control of all production and distribution could not be accomplished without regimentation of the people, their submission to an immense bureaucracy, and the end of American freedoms.

In Soviet Russia the planning was intended to industrialize a backward country. In the United States the proposed planning was at the other extreme: a technique for managing a country "overindustrialized" to the point of maturity. The paradox went unnoticed.

Hoover rejected the economic gibberish in a tone that went beyond mere partisan emotion. Roosevelt and his academic mentors, he said, were mistaking an *effect* of the slump—namely the temporary excess of productive capacity—for its *cause.* In Madison Square Garden he exclaimed:

I challenge the whole idea that we have ended the advance of America, that this country has reached the zenith of its power, the height of its development. . . . I deny that the promise of American life has been fulfilled, for that means we have begun to decline and fall. No nation can cease to move forward without degeneration of the spirit. It is the philosophy of stagnation. It is the end of hope. . . . It would be the end of the American system.

Roosevelt, he said, "overlooked the fact that we are yet but on the frontiers of development of science and invention." Let not the temporary difficulties, he pleaded, destroy faith in the youth and fertility and growth potentials of our country. About a quarter of a century later Hoover could point out, in a footnote, that American plant capacity and manufacturing

303

had doubled over 1928 in the five years after Roosevelt's death. Still later, another Democratic President made the New Frontier the central tenet of his Administration's philosophy.

4

Neither the 1932 Democratic platform nor the oratory of its standard-bearers offered a forthright statement of the New Deal pertinent to its future shape. The phrase was bandied about but none of its lineaments were exposed. The most emphatic pronouncements of the Democratic candidates, in point of fact, sound like a preview of the *anti*-New Deal polemics in years to come. The electorate voted against Hoover and for Roosevelt, but they certainly did not vote for the New Deal. More: if words have any meaning, they voted *against* the New Deal.

And yet, though the substance was not manifest, the spirit of the coming New Deal, its mood, was very much in evidence. The Democratic campaign was marked by a high-pitched optimism, a flamboyancy, a tumult of amorphous slogans and outsized promises that foreshadowed the future. There was an aura of circus and vaudeville, of professors doing mental handstands, of new theories by the dozen. Along with the pledges of economy and sound money were projects for artificial employment regardless of the costs. A motley crew of brain-trusters around the throne panting to turn a suffering nation into a wonderful experimental laboratory. A welter of catch-phrases: Economic Planning, the New Social Order, Production for Use, Redistribution of Wealth—and the catch-all catch-phrase New Deal itself. Change, brothers, any change! What have we to lose? They would have their answer soon enough.

By the fall of 1932 the country was clamorous with movements for displacing the American way of life. Self-appointed saviors were peddling instant salvations, most of them variants of European totalitarian ideas. Private enterprise was derided. If allowed to survive, it would be amputated into a basket-case, fed and medicated by planning officials. Already the first of the Communist "study groups"—which in a few years would produce a sinister crop of self-righteous traitors deployed throughout the government—were meeting in Washington and on university campuses.

The political climate was affected by the loud socialist and Communist campaigns. Both groups had their own candidates and necessarily, therefore, lambasted the major parties. But their main target was Hoover. Psychologically, at least, their "planning" slogans, under flags of revolt, were a link with the milder versions under the Democratic party banners.

The Socialist party rolled up 884,781 votes for Norman Thomas, more than it would ever again muster.

The atmosphere of the time is pertinent to the Hoover story. The misgivings and fears of the depression were driving a portion of the middle classes into more or less fascist movements at one extreme, more or less socialistic movements at the other extreme. It became the fashion to sneer at democracy as "doddering . . . hypocrisy . . . sham." In *The Red Decade*, a book written when the memory was still fresh, I said in part:

Thus it happened in the years that followed the market crash that the Communist Party of the United States became the magnetic center for a large and fast-growing mass of near-communists, sympathizers, fellow-travelers, spare-time insurgents, frightened liberals and masochistic capitalists. It was the dawn of a Red Decade. Many a bankrupt broker hesitated between jumping out of his skyscraper window and jumping out of his class. Intellectuals, so-called, hesitated between joining the Catholic Church and joining the Communist Party—they yearned for a faith and surcease from thinking. . . .

Professors and financiers and clergymen argued earnestly when, precisely, the revolution would break out. If the very poor didn't believe in the promised upheaval, a good many of the very rich did. They bought themselves farms or Caribbean islands against the dire moment. Others associated themselves with the revolution by way of psychological insurance; not in the front trenches, of course, but somewhere far back in the intellectual and emotional commissary departments. A good many, I happen to know, did both, hurrahing for the revolution and buying an island to escape it.

The American Communist Party was still very small:

But around it was that solar system of "mass organizations," a mushrooming universe of interlocking causes, unions, committees, leagues, centers, etc. Around these, in turn, were agitated clouds of Depression Bolsheviks, and beyond them thinnish vapors of tentative sympathizers, admirers of the Soviet "experiment," innocent trailers of fashionable phobias, mobs of intellectuals without intelligence, half-literate proletarian *litterateurs* and unassorted proletarian social climbers.

It was, therefore, not solely the Democratic opponents whom the President had in mind when he warned, in his first speech and in his last, that: "This campaign is more than a contest between two men. It is more than a contest between two parties. It is a contest between two philosophies of government." He was responding to the whole climate of those years.

With a sure instinct, as confirmed by subsequent history, Hoover selected "collectivism" as the central issue. He could not pin his fears in this connection directly on the orthodox-speaking candidate. He was relying on his intuitions. That they served him remarkably well is suggested by one warning.

Governor Roosevelt had said at one point that the Republicans were in control of the government—"and I may add for good measure of the Supreme Court as well." Few paid much attention to the charge, but the President reacted as if he had touched a live electric wire. "There are many things revealed by the campaign of our opponents that should give Americans concern for the future," he said. "One of the gravest is the state of mind revealed by my opponent in that statement. He implies that it is the function of the party in power to control the Supreme Court." If that were the case, he added later, "he is proposing the most revolutionary new deal, the most stupendous breaking of precedent, the most destructive undermining of our form of government yet proposed by a presidential candidate."

Hoover's guess that even the Supreme Court might be tampered with was denounced as a "splenetic libel." Even some of his supporters thought it was a farfetched and unfair deduction from a casual remark by a candidate. But the "court-packing" episode a few years later showed that Hoover's sixth sense in such matters had not betrayed him. Though the New Deal was not being defined by its authors, Hoover sensed it, smelled it, and had no doubt as to its essential nature. In judging the total mood of the campaign he was conscious of the difficulty of documenting the menace as he saw it. But this did not deter him from expressing fears of "this inchoate new deal":

My countrymen, the proposals of our opponents represent a profound change in American life—less in concrete proposal, bad as that may be, than by implication and by evasion. . . . This election is not a mere shift from the ins to the outs. It means deciding the direction our nation will take over a century to come.

The address in which he dealt most sharply with the issue of "collectivism," without using the word itself, was delivered a week before Election Day, in New York's Madison Square Garden. His advisers had urged against it, as too academic, but in the light of history it turned out to be perhaps the most meaningful of Hoover's speeches. He took note of the new vocabulary of radicalism:

The expressions our opponents use must refer to important changes in our economic and social system and our system of government, otherwise they are nothing but vacuous words. . . . I may say at once that the changes proposed by all these Democratic principals and allies are of the most profound and penetrating character. If they are brought about this will not be the America we have known in the past. . . . If these measures, these promises, which I have discussed; or these failures to disavow these projects; this attitude of mind, mean anything, they mean the enormous expansion of the Federal Government; they mean the growth of bureaucracy such as we have never seen in our history.

The speech is memorable, too, for its exposure of the strange devolution suffered by the majority of liberals under the dual impacts of the Russian Revolution and the American depression. Hoover said that he "can respect the sincerity of these men in their desire to change our form of government and our social and economic system." He insisted, however, that they had forfeited the right to call themselves liberals:

True liberalism seeks all legitimate freedom first in the confident belief that without such freedoms the pursuit of blessings is in vain. Liberalism is a force truly of the spirit proceeding from the deep realization that economic freedom cannot be sacrificed if political freedom is to be preserved. . . . Men who are going about the country announcing that they are liberals because of their promises to extend the government in business are not liberals, they are reactionaries of the United States.

This was, in a sense, the last stand of the "old-fashioned" liberalism which Hoover had championed all his life. His conviction that the nation was on the borderline between two eras explains Hoover's anxiety to lift the contest to a higher dimension of the moral and the spiritual. From the first he declared:

The present check to our material success must deeply stir our national conscience upon the purposes of life itself. It must cause us to revalue and reshape our drift from materialism to a higher note of individual and national ideals. Underlying every purpose is the spiritual application of moral ideals which are the fundamental basis of happiness in a people.

The opposition would not follow him into the rarefied dimension. A decisive majority of the people was apparently bored by talk of spiritual values, and crowded into the gayer, more self-confident, less preachy opposition camp. On Election Day, 22,821,857 citizens, about 57 percent of those who cast a ballot, voted for Roosevelt, who obtained an Electoral College score larger than Hoover's in 1928. The minority, represented by the 15,761,841 citizens in Hoover's column, was also vast and would in the long run exert a restraining influence on the New Deal.

One of the curious facts is that Hoover drew phenomenally large and enthusiastic crowds in his swings through the country. Joslin, as a newspaper correspondent, had traveled in campaigns with Taft, Wilson, Hughes, Harding, Cox, Coolidge, and LaFollette. After a trip in which the President made sixteen stops between Chicago and Altoona, Pa., he recorded that he had "never seen anything like the ovations" given to Hoover. At Altoona, it looked as if the whole population had turned out to greet him. And at the destination on that trip, Des Moines, the press estimated the crowds lining the streets at 125,000. Repeatedly Hoover was obliged to say a few words to overflow meetings in the streets outside the halls where he spoke.

There had been rumors of possible crackpot attacks on Hoover which kept the Secret Service men worried and alert. But only one hostile demonstration actually developed. That was in Detroit, where about a hundred Communists, massed beyond the police lines, indulged in booing and catcalls. The Detroit crowds were record-breaking and friendly notwithstanding.

On the evening of November 8, 1932, the President of the United States, surrounded by his family and many friends, received the election returns by radio at his Palo Alto home. Neither he nor those with him had counted on his being re-elected, but the size of his defeat left them mute with sorrow. Having drafted the traditional message congratulating the winner, Hoover passed it among his guests for comment.

Admiral Joel T. Boone, the White House physician—and therefore, like all those who ever lived close to Hoover, a committed admirer—was in the company. A quarter of a century later he recalled the scene in a letter to Neil MacNeil:

Mrs. Hoover entered the room and told the President that it was time to retire for the night. He did an unusual thing by shaking each of our hands as he walked around the room from his desk to the door where Mrs. Hoover was standing. Putting his arm in hers, he looked across the room at us, smiled broadly and said, "Good-night, my friends, that's that!" and went off to bed. Here in defeat stood the every inch of the man the world knows as one of history's most heroic figures.

Hoover slept for eleven hours. The bitterest four months of his incumbency, for the country and its rejected President, were still ahead of him.

XXVI

Interregnum—and Panic

T HE American people, as represented by those who voted, chose Franklin D. Roosevelt by a handsome majority; the business community, for the most part, had backed and financed his campaign. Logically, therefore, they should have been elated by their success and confident of the future. Instead, the clammy hand of fear, beyond anything in the preceding three years, gripped the nation. The people hastened to withdraw their savings from the banks and business was frightened almost to the point of paralysis.

An oversimplified statement of the facts—but close enough to what occurred to pose a paradox and a mystery of democracy in action. We can leave the enigma to the political scientists in the certainty that they can't solve it.

The beginnings of genuine recovery had been clearly in evidence in mid-1932. Except for some faltering in September, after Maine went Democratic, the national economy moved steadily to higher ground until Election Day. Then it turned tail and rushed headlong toward the abyss. Some of the concrete evidence of the upsurge was set forth by Wilbur and Hyde in their scholarly study of the Hoover administration, in which they had served, respectively, as Secretary of Interior and Secretary of Agriculture:

In the months of August, September and October 1932, bank failures had almost ceased while banks reopened were more than suspensions. The great flow of gold in the months previous to July reversed itself into an enormous inflow. The whole banking structure greatly strengthened. Wholesale commodity prices and farm prices advanced steadily through July, August and September. Cotton and wheat advanced over 20 percent. United States cotton-manufacturing advanced from 51.5 percent of mill capacity in July to 97 percent in October. Domestic wool consumption advanced from 16,500,000 pounds in

309

May to 46,100,000 pounds in September. The Federal Reserve Board's index of industrial production swept upward from 56 in July to 68 for both September and October.

The Department of Commerce review for 1933, though understandably cautious in formulating judgments under a new Administration, reported that in 1932:

business in the more important commercial nations of the world was showing a tendency to recovery. . . . In the United States business improved substantially from July until September and held firm without much definite tendency either way in October and November. . . . The relatively long interval between the election and the inauguration proved unsettling to business and was a factor in mitigating against further improvement.

In a speech on December 28, 1933, Professor Irving Fisher of Yale declared: "We should have been further on the road to recovery today had there been no election last year. Recovery started under Mr. Hoover but . . . a recession [came] because of the fear over political uncertainties." Leonard P. Ayers, in *Economics of Recovery,* stated that "the corner was turned in the country in the summer of 1932"; the most important factor in reversing the trend in America while it pushed forward abroad, he added, "was political in nature."

Said the National Industrial Board, on November 10, 1934: "The facts presented in the chart bring out clearly that the first steps toward recovery were taken in the year 1932." Edmund Platt, former vice-governor of the Federal Reserve, declared (New York *Times,* July 4, 1933): "If 1932 had not happened to be a presidential year, the recovery begun then might have continued without any serious interruption."

Walter Lippmann in 1936 wrote that Hoover and his associates "had hold of the essence of the matter in the spring of 1932 when . . . they arrested the depression." David Lawrence, many years later, wrote that "Hoover's courageous fight against the depression was virtually won by the time he was leaving office," but that between his defeat and Roosevelt's induction panic finally overwhelmed the country—"because of the uncertainty of what the new administration would do."

Similar verdicts could be quoted for pages. The recovery coaxed into being by long and patient effort was canceled out by the election of Roosevelt. Until March 4 Hoover was President in name only, his word worth little more than that of any private citizen. The outgoing Administration, in Hoover's graphic words, was helplessly "handcuffed by a hostile Congress and an uncooperative President-elect."

Within a week after Election Day, the President was back in Washington, laboring at his usual unsparing pace. On his first day in the White House, he held nineteen conferences. The news was increasingly bad, the tempo of deterioration staggering. The things that needed to be done quickly to restore some confidence depended primarily on a Congress which looked for inspiration to Albany rather than the White House.

Not only Congress but the American people and the world listened only to the President-elect. They heard nothing to still their suspicions—quickly turned into a conviction—that the country was hell-bent for alarming monetary and social experiments, orthodox campaign pledges notwithstanding. Men close to Roosevelt spoke openly of vast make-work projects to cost billions. Men with a record for currency tinkering in the previous Congress were known to be *persona grata* with the incoming Administration.

As signs of jitters multiplied, as the hard-won margins of improvement crumbled, the press, economic organizations, many legislators, prominent individuals, and the outside world pleaded with Roosevelt to do one simple thing: *merely to assure the country that he would abide by his campaign promises and by the platform on which he was elected.* This he refused to do. He was jovial, high-spirited, bubbling with flippancies, but stubbornly silent about his intentions.

Hoover had assumed that the President-elect would cooperate with him on problems self-evidently too critical to be kept on ice for the four months of interregnum. Immediately after the election he asked publicly for Roosevelt's help in the name of unity above partisanship to meet a growing emergency. The realization that his assumption was in error came quickly. It left him stunned.

Roosevelt had not criticized the Administration's foreign policies. Hoover therefore took it for granted that, at the very least, he could count on cooperation with respect to pressing items of foreign affairs—the Japanese invasion of Manchuria, the imminent expiration of the intergovernmental debts moratorium, the World Economic Conference scheduled to open in London. Even in this expectation Hoover was disappointed. The President-elect insisted that these were all "a responsibility which rests upon those now vested with executive and legislative power." This, of course, was technically true. No one, least of all the lame-duck President, denied it.

Roosevelt came to the White House, on the President's invitation, on November 22, accompanied by Ray Moley. Hoover sought to convince them that decisions on matters such as the war debts and the impending London Conference would be worthless without assurances that they would be honored after March 4. He pointed to historic precedents for intervention by a President-elect.

Moley in subsequent years recalled how profoundly he had been impressed by the defeated President's grasp of the economic facts and the cogency of his presentation. Hoover, he wrote, "spoke without interruption for nearly an hour. . . . Before he finished it was clear that we were in the presence of the best-informed individual on the question of the debts. His mastery of detail and clarity of arrangement compelled admiration." When Roosevelt signaled his associates to leave, Hoover reminded them icily, "Nobody leaves before the President."

Pressed by newspapermen on the issue of international debts, Governor Roosevelt laughed and wisecracked, "That's not my baby." Editorial comment expressed shocked disbelief. Roosevelt, said the New York *Times*, "obviously displayed more tact than courage." The Detroit *Free Press* said, "It is highly unfortunate that Governor Roosevelt was unable to bring himself to meet the President halfway. . . . Mr. Roosevelt had an opportunity unique in the history of the American presidency and he failed to grasp it." The Baltimore *Sun* warned that though "the baby" is not Roosevelt's it "may soon develop into an unruly stepchild lodged permanently under his roof and disposed to play with matches."

In instructing the Democratic Congress what to do and what not to do, Roosevelt acted the role of Chief Executive from the day of his election. On December 29, for instance, he advised the Congress to oppose measures for balancing the budget. In January, his Congress refused to act on a bank-conservator bill Hoover had drafted to prevent more bank closings —the same bill, with hardly a change in wording, that was adopted within days after the inauguration. In line with Roosevelt's view, the Senate failed to confirm a long array of presidential nominations. But when the need to quiet public apprehensions, sustain national morale, and reassure foreign governments was involved, the President-elect adopted the legalistic position that until inauguration he was just another private citizen.

There were those who asked why even a patriotic private citizen, having the prestige to allay careening fears, did not use it. Could it be that he shared the belief, voiced indiscreetly on his left flank, that "the worse the better"? Could it be that he approved the cynical political logic which held that the lower the base at which a new regime started, the brighter its record would seem—and the readier a despairing people would be to countenance broken campaign covenants and swallow extreme innovations?

Roosevelt's refusal to touch the very questions which he had stressed during the campaign—sound money, economy in government, budgetary responsibility—now naturally nurtured rumors of inflation, devaluation, big spending—in short, repudiation of his campaign pledges. Charles Michelson has written:

The President-elect told me on one occasion that the bank crisis was due to culminate just about inauguration day. . . . *Naturally he did not care to have the dramatic effect of his intended proposals spoiled by a premature discussion of them in advance of their delivery.*

The italics are mine. One hopes that Michelson misquoted his friend. It is hard to believe that any American, and a President-to-be in particular, would put "dramatic effect" above an opportunity to halt his country's dizzy plunge into the lowest depths. We know that the plunge did enhance the drama of the inaugural, whether or not it was intended that way by the one man who might have stopped it and didn't even try.

According to Michelson, Roosevelt was a three-in-one personality: a fanatic idealist, a stubborn Dutchman, and a practical politician. "The practical politician was on the job when the Hoover proposition was broached," he concluded. What was the proposition? Nothing more than a plea that Roosevelt deny rumors which were sending hordes of depositors to draw their money out of banks and prompting smart insiders to send their cash out of the country—foresight which before long would net them 60 percent profits through devaluation of the dollar. If Michelson was right, "practical politics" has rarely taken such cynical forms.

"The panic and setbacks of the last period could have been easily prevented," Hoover would write as ex-President. They were not due to new economic factors but the result of a sudden crisis in confidence. Possibly even promises by the President-elect to make good on his orthodox campaign pledges would not have arrested the panic touched off by his election. It is one of those things that can never be proved. But one thing is certain: If Roosevelt and his brain-trusters had *planned* to push the country over the brink by March 4, in order to dramatize the transfer of power, they would have behaved exactly as they did behave.

Individuals and business organizations rushed to protect themselves as best they could against what his associates were already celebrating as "the Roosevelt Revolution." Billions of dollars were hastily transferred abroad. Thousands of depositors demanded payment in gold: proof that they were not merely doubting the stability of the banks but the stability of the American dollar. Business orders running to hundreds of millions, placed before the election, were now canceled. The discouraging news got around, without effective denial, that prominent Democrats were sending large sums abroad; these insiders, of course, would share in the 60 percent bonanza for the foresighted. Unemployment rose by 1,500,000 to the terrifying total of nearly thirteen million.

Meanwhile, in most of Europe, business indices were improving, unemployment was declining, confidence kept rising.

2

Reluctant to believe that minimal cooperation between the outgoing and incoming Administrations could not be worked out, the President suggested to Roosevelt ever new plans, new formulas. He was willing to settle on any statement that would help calm the country. For him there could be no thought of personal pride, or politics, or appearances. Through intermediaries he offered to transmit to Congress any proposals Roosevelt himself might wish enacted; bad news might be better than the prolonged uncertainty which bred panic.

If the President-elect was jovially tightlipped, the aggregation of panacea-peddlers around him was not. Moley, then in the very thick of the Roosevelt entourage, would in due time list some of its ingredients: "There were old socialists, municipal reformers, greenbackers, free silverites, public ownership zealots, together with a large number of Wilsonian Democrats whose administrative skills had rusted during twelve years of Republicanism and, as we learned later, a handful of communists." Their hints of new currencies and unlimited spending fed the swollen fears, as they may have intended. Not once did Roosevelt disown them. Even when the press quoted him personally on plans for "managing" the currency, and the dispatch was read into the Congressional Record, he could not be induced to issue a denial.

It was a time of hysterical rumor and demagogic incitation. Father Coughlin was holding forth on the radio. The Communists announced a march on Washington. The magazines and the airwaves were filled with wild talk about "revolution" and the need for a "dictator" to save the nation. Not since the War between the States had there been more urgent need for counsels of faith in America. A message of reassurance from the newly elected President might have cleared the air.

A bombshell was tossed into this unsettled post-election period when Congress, on the initiative of Vice President-elect Garner, proceeded to make public lists of loans extended by the Reconstruction Finance Corporation. President Hoover, it will be recalled, signed the bill creating the RFC on explicit promises by Garner and others that this would not be done. Business and labor leaders rushed to Capitol Hill to demand that the disastrous practice be stopped. Congress did later bar such publicity —after Roosevelt took office.

In retrospect nobody, not even Garner, could defend that act of economic vandalism. In that fevered time publication of the fact that a bank had sought and obtained an RFC loan was treated by jittery depositors as *prima facie* proof of weakness, precipitating a run. At least a thousand banks closed solely because of this publicity. The loans which aimed to keep institutions solvent were turned into instruments for their demolition. Many banks which could have weathered the storm with RFC help feared to apply for it. After he resigned as vice-chairman of the Federal Reserve Board, Atlee Pomerene told the Associated Press: "It was the most damnable and vicious thing that was ever done." For it operated to turn the danger of a bank panic into a certainty. Again, could it be that this was the covert purpose of the action?

In his last annual message to Congress, in December, President Hoover again urged legislation on bank reform, on bankruptcy, and other immediate measures to restore faith and cushion disaster. Once more he proposed basic reorganization of the operations of government that would save as much as seven hundred million dollars a year. He returned to these subjects in special messages. But the Democratic Congress did virtually nothing; it was marking time until the new boss took over.

The last sixty days were the most desperate. By January 23 the financial editor of the New York *Times* was pleading with Roosevelt to deny the proliferating rumors about his New Deal fiscal plans. Instead came the news that he was considering "controlled inflation," generating a new and bigger flight of the dollar. On January 31 Henry A. Wallace, slated to be a member of the new Cabinet, remarked almost casually: "The smart thing would be to go off the gold standard a little further than England has." Then, in mid-February, Senator Carter Glass announced his refusal of the post of Secretary of the Treasury in the new Administration. Because Glass was a "sound money" man, this amounted to confirmation of the country's worst fears. The jitters turned to near-hysteria.

Melvin A. Traylor, a prominent Chicago banker who had supported Roosevelt during the campaign, told a Senate committee: "Nothing but a declaration from Mr. Roosevelt that there will be no devaluation will save the situation from a general panic." Another financier who had worked for Roosevelt's election, Bernard Baruch, went before the Senate committee to warn that inflation was "the road to ruin." Appeals for a few reassuring words also came from London, Paris, and other capitals. Roosevelt smiled knowingly and cocked his cigarette holder at a jauntier angle.

President Hoover continued, without avail, to beseech his successor for some magic words, and to press Congress for remedial action. In a Lincoln's Day address he said that three roads were open to the country. The first was international cooperation to stabilize currency and trade; the second was a policy of "self-containment" or autarchy; the third was to cheapen our money, raise tariffs, and drive the world to a debilitating trade war. He analyzed them all to show that only the first of these choices, which had led him to initiate the London Economic Conference, held hope. The President-elect grinned: "No comment."

The incoming crowd was cheerful and cocky about the cumulative troubles. What some of the men around Roosevelt said among themselves inevitably reached the White House and the press. Their jubilant chatter played variations on the shocking, the incredible theme, "the worse the better." However impractical their economics might be, they were apparently all "practical politicians."

Several weeks before the inauguration, for example, Professor Tugwell was lunching with James H. Rand, Jr., a prominent Roosevelt man. According to Rand's later account, Tugwell told him cheerfully that the banking structure would soon collapse and added, "We should worry about anything but rehabilitating the country after March 4."

With banks folding up and one state after another declaring "bank holidays," Hoover on February 17 sent a final plea to Roosevelt, in a handwritten letter delivered the next day. It began with these words:

A most critical situation has arisen in the country of which I feel it my duty to advise you confidentially. I am therefore taking this course of writing you myself and sending it to you through the Secret Service for your hand direct, as obviously its misplacement would only feed the fire and increase the dangers.

The major difficulty is the state of the public mind, for there is a steadily degenerating confidence in the future which has reached the height of a general alarm. I am convinced that a very early statement by you upon two or three policies of your administration would greatly restore confidence and cause a resumption of the march of recovery.

Roosevelt did not acknowledge the communication until March 1, for twelve days, that is—twelve days that shook the national economy almost beyond repair—and his answer was one more No. Later he claimed that he had replied at once but that his missive had been "mislaid." There were discrepancies in the claim which opened the alibi to doubt. Since the answer was in the negative, however, the excuse made no practical difference.

We know, from Moley's memoirs, that Roosevelt had the letter in his pocket on the evening of February 18. He was on the dais in the ballroom of the Hotel Astor at a banquet of the Inner Circle, an organization of New York political reporters. Moley sat opposite him. After midnight, while a stage show was in progress, F.D.R. passed a piece of paper to him. He opened it cautiously and began to read: "A most critical situation has arisen in the country . . ." It was from the President of the United States, in his own handwriting.

Moley saw in the letter nothing less than "the bony hand of death stretched out over every bank in the country." But his boss was roaring in laughter at the show and bantering his neighbors. Clearly the bony hand did not affect his spirits. He seemed utterly disinterested in the approaching catastrophe. As things went from bad to worse, he was vacationing on Vincent Astor's yacht. In this, assuredly, there was nothing sinful; but it is easy to imagine what the "champions of the common man" and enemies of "economic royalists" around Roosevelt would have made of such a fact in the midst of disaster if the culprit had been Hoover.

The personal appeals by President Hoover, the discomfiture of Moley and a few others in the Roosevelt circle, were all part of a grisly comedy of errors. The fact is that while Hoover was bending all his strength to avert the panic, Roosevelt and most of his advisers watched its coming with delight. For it meant that Hoover would leave the White House amidst utter ruin just as the saviors took power.

The President did everything he could to stop the banking disaster. Early in February he proposed to the Federal Reserve Board that all banks suspend operations for a single day. Every bank would then submit a statement of its assets and liabilities. The next day the solvent banks—and they were in the overwhelming majority—would reopen with federal guarantees of their solvency. This doubtless was the plan Hoover wanted to lay before his successor had he responded to the historic letter. The Attorney General had ruled that the Executive could not put it into effect without absolute assurance that Congress would confirm it—and only Roosevelt could offer this assurance.

The President badgered Congress to act. In vain he sought its authority for immediate enlargement of RFC lending capacity, including funds to states and municipalities now staggering under a growing relief load. The legislature waited for signals from the new boss, and they didn't come. Hoover was in almost continuous day and night sessions with Treasury officials, finance experts, and banking heads. The Advisory Council of the Federal Reserve and some influential newspapers joined him in last-minute appeals to Roosevelt to cooperate.

In the final days, Secretary of the Interior Wilbur remarked that in view of Roosevelt's attitude the battle was lost anyhow, so why not relax a little? The President exclaimed:

"We will fight until 10:49 A.M. March fourth, when I leave for the Capitol. We must try everything, not once but a dozen times."

Whether the new regime planned it that way or not, the great cave-in came with miraculous exactitude on the last morning of Hoover's term. Those who wished to take over at the lowest point had their way with a vengeance, at incalculable cost in substance and suffering for the whole population. Those who wanted the most catastrophic base possible for future political bookkeeping had their wish fulfilled. And always thereafter, as a matter of fact, they used March 4, when Roosevelt was sworn

317

in—not November 8, when he was elected—as their base in making invidious comparisons. Most historians, for years to come, meekly followed their lead on this statistical hoax.

The panic which Hoover had repeatedly warded off thus came at last, when he no longer had the authority to avert it. Whatever may be said of the preceding years, certainly the final catastrophe had more to do with the incoming than the outgoing Administration. But the blame for that debacle, too—for that debacle especially—was thrown on Hoover's shoulders.

3

I have not done full justice to those terrifying four final months. A correspondent who covered the grim events, Lawrence Sullivan, wrote a book about them which he called *Prelude to Panic*. Anyone who doubts where responsibility for the climactic tragedy really belongs will find in its pages a clear answer. The public could not know all the facts at the time. In the great glad din of the dawning New Deal era those who tried to tell the facts—and that included Hoover—could not make themselves heard.

The ex-President once asked Ray Moley why Roosevelt had refused to cooperate in the banking crisis. Moley replied, in writing, that Roosevelt

either did not realize how serious the situation was or that he preferred to have conditions deteriorate and gain for himself the entire credit for the rescue operation. In any case, his actions during the period of February 18 to March 3 could conform to any such motive on his part.

To suppose that the President-elect "did not realize" what the country at large knew is a strain on plausibility. Only the second of the alternatives mentioned by Moley makes sense. In retrospect Hoover wrote:

Roosevelt did not need to *close* the banks. All he needed to do, until bank depositors got over their panic, was to restrict bank payments to necessary business and limit foreign exchange likewise. But closing the banks would be a sign the country was in a ditch. It was the American equivalent of the burning of the Reichstag to create an "emergency."

He pointed out a telltale fact:

After the storm had blown over, institutions representing more than 98 percent of deposits ultimately paid off their depositors. They should never have been closed. The two percent of insolvent banks at depression values at the time of the panic could have recovered their position with the inevitable restoration of values. . . .

318

We had successfully fought off four far greater crises during the three preceding years. We had no panic after the stock market collapsed in October 1929. We had no panic when the financial crash of Europe culminated in the British collapse in September, 1931, nor when we were nearly forced off the gold standard in February, 1932, nor at the bottom of the depression in June, 1932, when our structure was greatly weakened by Congressional obstruction and foreign pressures. At any of these periods panic could have risen.

It is not difficult to explain why we had a panic of bank depositors during the few days before March 4, 1933. It was simply because the bank depositors were frightened. Their fright had mounted steadily for two months. What were they afraid of? Surely not an outgoing administration with but a few days to run. Certainly not of the foreign countries, for they were steadily recovering. . . . The United States alone had deserted the world recovery which began in the previous July. We alone slipped backward. . . . All the countries free of New Deals or collectivism progressed uninterruptedly to full employment and prosperity within two years.

Elsewhere, on December 16, 1935, about three years after the cruel events, he summed them up thus:

It was the most political and most unnecessary bank panic in all our history. It could have been prevented. It could have been cured by simple cooperation.

This was a serious charge the ex-President made—perhaps the most sensational that a former President had ever made against a succeeding Administration. But it did not make news. Ten thousand official and voluntary press agents shouting hallelujah for the new dispensation drowned him out.

It is as well to wind up the panic story here. Immediately after his inauguration President Roosevelt issued his proclamation closing all banks. In preparing this document his associates adapted a draft already prepared by Hoover's Secretary and Under Secretary of the Treasury, Ogden L. Mills and Arthur A. Ballantine. These two men, from a sense of duty, remained in the Department to help their successors steer the country through the crisis period. Their testimony, and that of Roosevelt men who in the fullness of time told tales out of school, leave little doubt that the new President, having closed the banks, had not the foggiest idea of how to reopen them.

The plan for reopening finally adopted was close to the one which Hoover had worked out. It was substantially this that Roosevelt announced in his first fireside chat, on March 12. To cap the irony of the business, the speech he delivered at the "fireside" had been written by a Hoover official, Ballantine. For "a plan he didn't construct, announced in a speech he didn't write," to quote the late John F. Flynn, he was universally hailed as a financial magician.

In 1947, fourteen years after he ceased to be President, I asked Hoover this question: "In the perspective of time, if you knew then what you know now, would you have changed any of your major policies as President?"

He did not need to ponder that one. Evidently he had answered it in his own mind innumerable times.

"No," he said. "I am convinced of the essential correctness of my Administration's policies. We definitely had the depression licked, but the election of the New Deal reversed the trend and perpetuated the depression. It was to be many years before conditions approximating the summer and early autumn of 1932 would be attained again. The processes of liquidation had been about completed at that time. Other nations continued their march to recovery. Ours was forced back by fear of the unknown and suspicions which quickly materialized after March."

"How about relief?" I asked. "You've been attacked more on that probably than any other side of your Administration."

"As to relief policies," he replied, "I believed then and even more so now, after the experience of the New Deal years, that we were right in keeping it on a local basis and keeping it out of politics. Centralized federal monopoly of relief brought with it bureaucracy, waste and political trading on human misery. The cost of relief went up twice and threefold per person as soon as it was made a football of politics. The instincts of charity and mutual help, all the vast local resources and spiritual leverages, were never used again."

Wilbur and Hyde, in concluding their detailed, blow-by-blow story of *The Hoover Policies,* summed up the 1928–33 Administration in these words:

History will record that despite many handicaps President Hoover guided the nation safely through perilous times and placed it on the road to recovery in 1932. It will also record the effective care of distress, the unparalleled industrial peace of the times and the fidelity to national obligations.

It will record that Hoover originated and developed more new government policies for the correction of business abuse and the advancement of economic life than any President up to his time. It will record that it was Hoover who laid the foundations for an era of social progress in this country. It will record that with these great accomplishments he held to Constitutional Government and to the fundamental ideals of free men. Above all, it will record him as the American leader of these principles in his time.

Washington, on March 4, 1933, was like a conquered city. G.O.P. officials and their families were packing to evacuate, while thousands of those hoping to succeed them were arriving from all corners of the country. "The happy hosts of the conquering Democrats poured into the city, hastening to take over after so many hungry years in the wilderness," in Flynn's words. In the White House, a weary and worn President, "spent with the vigil of long sleepless nights as he struggled to hold back the tide of the onrushing crisis, was at his desk early for the last dreary duties before laying down his intolerable burden."

The two central figures on the inaugural platform in front of the Capitol that day presented a contrast to gladden the hearts of New Deal zealots. Hoover was solemn and silent and showed the signs of his fatigue. Roosevelt was gay, debonnaire, brimming with pleasantries. About one hundred thousand people crowded around the reviewing stand, the largest throng ever gathered for the ritual of changing Presidents.

The band, mysteriously, failed to accord the departing President the usual final salute of respect—if not for the man, at least for the office. Other strange and unprecedented things happened that day.

Traditionally the outgoing President continues to be guarded by Secret Service men as long as he deems it necessary. The tradition was now shattered. Anti-Hoover sentiment was then inflamed and some act of crackpot violence wholly conceivable; an attempt on Roosevelt's life had been made in Florida not long before. But when Hoover's staff, as a matter of routine, asked for the guards to be assigned, the request was denied! There were orders to the contrary from the new Administration, much to the chagrin of the Secret Service officials themselves.

The thirty-first President of the United States was not treated as a Chief Executive who had laid down heavy burdens but a felon driven from the scene of his misdoings. On the ship of state, normal amenities were lightheartedly tossed overboard. Roosevelt's incredible vendetta against his predecessor, which was to continue unrelentingly to the day of his death, had been launched. It was a ruthless enterprise, without precedent in the relations between two American Presidents. In the end it embarrassed and in some cases deeply wounded many of President Roosevelt's own followers. It was too emotional and consistent to be wholly explained even by "practical politics," though the political advantages of an authenticated villain in the drama soon to be staged are apparent.

At the Washington end, on inauguration day, the railroad police took on the job of protecting Hoover. At the New York end, the Chief of Police, having been informed of the curious state of affairs, showed up personally to greet the ex-President and to inform him that adequate police forces had been assigned for his safety.

As he left Washington, Herbert Hoover was outwardly stoical. Then, as Joslin recorded the scene:

From the observation platform of his private car, he looked down upon the tense, upturned faces of the thousands who had gathered to bid him farewell.

The evidence of enduring friendship thus shown stirred him to the depths. With the first movement of the train, he turned abruptly from the platform and disappeared into his private car. The train had started none too soon for him.

To some of those who watched the train pull out of the station, he was a most tragic figure. But to those of us who truly knew him through close association behind the wall of silence he had erected for the public good, he was the man who had served his country devotedly through unparalleled disaster and under unexampled handicaps, and who could await unafraid and with a clear conscience the evaluation of his acts by history.

XXVII

Scapegoat for Cataclysm

LITTLE has been said about the private life of Herbert Hoover as President, but in truth he had allowed himself neither time nor thought for a personal existence. Again and again eager plans for a family vacation in California were washed out by a new inundation of trouble.

His two sons, now grown to tall, attractive, intelligent manhood, his lovely daughter-in-law, the lively grandchildren whom he adored, the First Lady—all of them respected the heaped-up anxieties under which he labored. In addition they had to conceal from him their own special anxiety, which was for his health under the punishing pressures.

Because they had no relish for the glitter and pageantry of the great office, residence in the White House—aside from the joy they took in one another—was more of a discipline than a thrill. As a matter of principle they evaded publicity, or even the innocent semblance of exploiting their name and address.

Lou Hoover was one of the ablest, handsomest, and most keen-minded First Ladies in the annals of the Presidency. If she did not register sharply on the country's mind, it was because she willed it that way. She ran the household, and her myriad social obligations, with grace and tact and wisdom. Knowing her husband's need for affection and companionship, she saw to it that a few of the men whose lives were woven into his own were frequently at the White House and at Rapidan. They were less a brain trust than a heart trust, bringing the President the generosity of spirit he received so scantily from the country or even his own party.

To all the Hoovers the exodus from the White House was a species of liberation, despite its tragic overtones. "There was a great sense of release —a revolution back to freedom," Hoover himself recalled. The glowing vision of a normal life in their Palo Alto dream house, so long postponed, was coming true. The slump had worked havoc with the family fortune, but they were still wealthy in relation to their modest needs and tastes, especially now that Herbert and Allan were prospering financially on their own.

For the first time in almost thirty years, the ex-President and Mrs. Hoover could sleep as late as they wished. It was good to be able to read the papers and listen to the radio after breakfast, not between bites. Again the Hoovers were able to enjoy fishing, camping, and motoring to their hearts' content. Their home became a warm haven for close friends living in or passing through the area.

Home was not only the lovely house Lou Hoover had planned and built but the entire campus on which it stood. When she and her husband arrived at Palo Alto after the inauguration, private citizens for the first time since 1917, the entire Stanford student body gave them a fervent reception. Hoover found some twenty thousand letters waiting for him, and thousands more poured in during the next months. They conveyed not only gratitude and loyalty but, more important, plain human affection. He was touched in particular by the fact that about a third of these messages were "handwritten on the blue-lined paper of lowly homes."

Knowing the Hoovers' love of the outdoors, friends all over the country with fishing camps or boats pressed invitations upon them. The ex-President fished for trout and bass from California and British Columbia to New England; for salmon in the state of Washington and New Brunswick; for big-game fish in Florida, Texas, and Lower California.

Hoover would write in a nostalgic magazine article:

Fishermen are always good company. They are optimistic or they would not be fishermen. They are patient of the weaknesses of men and fish alike. The only drawback was the local political leader who insisted on sitting on the bank or getting into the boat and pouring out local frictions or the wastes and injustices of "Planned Economy." . . . Stopping overnight in auto camps brought contact with the carpenter, the plumber and the grocer on holiday with their wives and children. One learned again the depths of real patriotism in this America.

But if the Hoovers, with political office behind them, counted on real seclusion, they were at once disillusioned. Immense effort and cost had gone into the job of turning Hoover into a symbol of inequity. The investors had no intention of discarding their masterpiece. Propaganda in a carnival mood, complete with angels and devils, from the outset emerged as one of the main skills of the new government. Droves of information officers, disguised under a variety of titles, became regulation equipment in every department and agency—thirty thousand of them by 1939, according to Senator Byrd's estimate. Hoover was too valuable a stage property at the demoniac end to be retired to the lumberroom.

Attacks on the ex-President were pressed with new fervor, new financing, new vengefulness. Routine references to "the mess left by Hoover" were among the earmarks of the new statesmanship. The do-nothing myth was improved, enlarged, and embellished; new wings were constantly added to the old structure and stocked with fresh horrors. The foulness washed up to Hoover's very doorstep; the mockery and misrepresentation overflowed his years. Day after day the shyness and sensibility that were the marks of his nature were outraged by name-calling and garish accusations.

It reached beyond political attack to become a persecution. Every time he opened a paper or turned on the radio he ran the risk of facing routine vilification. He saw his words and acts and intentions turned into caricatures. Most distressing to a man with a strong historical sense, he saw the lava of abuse congealing into unquestioned "facts" and, before long, being handed on to innocent school children as "history."

The anti-Hoover legend appeared to be hardening into folklore. It embraced the "fact" that Hoover somehow had "caused" the depression—"a great compliment to the energies and capacities of one man," he told an audience in 1936; the "fact" that he abandoned millions to starvation; that he shot down veterans begging for a bonus; that hungry heroes had to peddle apples to keep alive—the trivial incident was stretched to cover the entire Hoover period.

Fortunately the ex-President was psychologically prepared for the worst even in his best days. Referring to the years just after the war, when he was generally idolized, he now wrote to a former secretary:

I could establish by contemporaneous documents that I was not fooled by all this adulation. While my period of popularity lasted for nearly twelve years, and my real friends never deserted me, I was at no time under any delusions. I knew that if a man continued in public life he was bound to create opposition . . . that he was fated to accumulate enemies; that in the United States the laws of libel and slander had little potency, and that the customary form of reply to sober argument was aspersions on one's parentage or assumption of corrupt motives.

I knew from the bitter experience of all public men from George Washington down that democracies are fickle and heartless. When the ultimate bump came, I was well fortified to accept it philosophically and, in fact, to welcome it, for democracy is a harsh employer.

He was hurt and saddened but not surprised. If he was "bitter," as asserted by people who didn't know him, he did an amazing job of dissimulation.

There were many in Hoover's intimate circle—more politically minded than himself, or simply burning with indignation—who wanted him to strike out at once against the new Administration. Certainly the occasions for hot retort and acid comment came thick and fast, both on the personal and the public level. One after another Hoover's campaign warnings of big government, big spending, inflated dollars, runaway bureaucracy, politicized relief, were being justified much sooner than he had foreseen. Congress turned into a passive tool of the White House and executive decrees by the hundred were encroaching on the domain of ordered law.

But Hoover informed his friends that he intended to hold his tongue, publicly at any rate, for at least twelve months. Actually he observed this self-imposed silence (with only minor and unavoidable exceptions) for over two years. Firmly he turned down the many pleading, flattering invitations to speak. No less firmly he refused to identify himself with any of the anti-New Deal organizations that soon were being launched, with howls of pain, as the physiognomy of the Roosevelt administration came into clearer focus.

The most prominent of these was the Liberty League. Among its founders, ironically, were the self-same Raskobs, duPonts, and others who had helped finance the attacks on President Hoover. The job had been done so expertly that these men now had to put up more money to *undo their own handiwork*—with Jouett Shouse, of the Michelson enterprise, as director! Michelson himself, who did not much care whether his salary and expenses came through a Shouse or a Farley, remained with Roosevelt after most of his original financial angels had disavowed the new epoch.

An amusing—or perhaps not so amusing—sidelight: When the Liberty League was organized, Raskob had the astonishing gall to invite ex-President Hoover to enter its ranks. Hoover's opinion of the League is on record, in a letter to a friend who asked for advice about joining it. Some of the organizers, Hoover wrote, "are hardly the type of men to lead the cause of Liberty. . . . I may state emphatically that I have no more confidence in the Wall Street model of human liberty, which this group so well represents, than I have in the Pennsylvania Avenue model which the country now rides."

While abstention from public debate was a painful test of patience, it rewarded Hoover with relative leisure to refresh not only his physical but his spiritual vitality. He now had precious time for reading, studying, thinking, and for helping men and women dear to him with their assorted problems. He could re-examine his record as President in the light of the activities and professions of the new Administration.

2

Being Hoover, leisure meant work in other, if less exhausting, directions. He began writing another book on his philosophy, *The Challenge to Liberty,* and organized the materials for his *Memoirs.* He resumed active participation—as trustee, director, or chairman—in the work of Stanford University, the American Children's Fund, the Belgian-American Educational Foundation, and "a host of other boards and committees." Much of his time went to fund-raising for good causes; he took part, he estimated, in raising from fifty to seventy-five million dollars in the next fifteen years or so.

Because these activities, and Mrs. Hoover's duties with the Girl Scouts, took them to New York a great deal, they rented a spacious apartment, with a suite of offices attached, on the thirty-first floor of the Waldorf Towers. In time they made New York their legal voting residence.

On leaving the White House, Hoover had relinquished the many honorific posts that accrue to a President. But he remained on boards which involved the well-being of youth. One of these was the Boys' Clubs of America. In 1936 he agreed to serve as Chairman of the Board and thereafter was drawn ever more deeply into its affairs. In the process he became the idol of hundreds of thousands of "pavement boys," as he called them, enrolled in the clubs.

Although not normally given to boasting, Hoover boasted unabashedly of the dynamic expansion of the organization and of the benefits it dispensed. He took a genuine pleasure in attending the opening of another club in another city. Under his tutelage the organization was to grow fourfold by 1963—to 625 clubs in four hundred cities. He never wearied of proclaiming, however, that "there are millions more of these pavement boys whom we should reach."

Once, at his White House conference on child welfare, Hoover had said: "If we could have but one generation of properly born, trained, educated and healthy children, a thousand other problems of government would vanish." Now he was zealous in providing well-equipped clubs where boys could find antidotes to gang life and juvenile delinquency in sports, crafts, books, fun, and comradeship. A fragment from one of his myriad Boys' Clubs speeches has been extensively reprinted and quoted. It answered the question, "What Is a Boy?":

Together with his sister, the boy is our most precious possession. But he represents not only joys and hopes but also paradoxes. He strains our nerves, yet he is a complex of cells teeming with affection. He is a periodic nuisance, yet he is a joy forever. He is a part-time incarnation of destruction, yet he radiates sunlight to all the world. He gives evidence of being the child of iniquity, yet he makes a great nation. He is filled with curiosity as to every mortal thing, he is an illuminated interrogation point, yet he is the most entertaining animal that is.

The whole world is new to him. Therefore his should be a life of adventure, of discovery, of great undertakings. He must spend much time, if he is to expand, in the land of make-believe. One of the sad things in the world is that he must grow up into the land of realities.

He is endowed with a dynamic energy and an impelling desire to take exercise on all occasions. His primary instinct is to hunt in a pack and that multiplies his devices. He is a complete self-starter, and therefore wisdom in dealing with him consists mostly in what to do next. He and his pack can go on this hunt for happiness either constructively or destructively. Our first problem is to find him constructive joy, instead of destructive glee.

It would be a mistake to suppose that Hoover's designated role as the nation's house-demon was universally accepted. Doubtless millions of Americans were ashamed of the endless smearing of the then only living ex-President. Voices in his defense were raised in the press. Wherever he went he met with kind and often admiring attention. More and more, as the New Deal unfolded, his heavy correspondence was "studded with touching man-to-man apologies from complete strangers, who said they had been misled, had taken part in campaigns of lies." Some of them asked for a letter of forgiveness to ease their conscience. Then, one by one and later in droves, embittered defectors from the New Deal began to convey to Hoover their sorrow and remorse for what they had said about and done to the ex-President.

There were times for laughter, too. Recently, in the New York *Times* (September 7, 1962), Robert T. Hartman wrote of the time, after their return to California, when the Hoovers were hosts to a debating team from an Australian university:

One young guest—not too familiar with U.S. electoral processes—said, "Really, Mr. Hoover, we Australians were dreadfully sorry to hear of your defeat in the last election. Tell me, sir, did you keep your seat?" At that the icy image melted. Hoover roared like a buffalo, slapping his knee, and retorted, between mirth and tears, "Yes, indeed, young man, but that's about all I kept."

An ex-President, no matter how denigrated, was still normal quarry for the tribes of autograph hunters. If he were minded to overrate this token of interest, there was an amusing experience to keep him humble. He loved to recount it. A youngster one day asked him for three autographs. "Why three?" asked Hoover smilingly. And the boy told him that in swapping signatures, he said, it took two Hoovers for one Babe Ruth. He got the three.

On his way from California to Washington in November 1932 President Hoover had paused in Boulder City to inspect the great dam bearing his name then going up on the Colorado River.

It was only a few days after his decisive defeat. The sight of the structure in progress—"the greatest engineering work of its character ever attempted by the hand of man," as he described it the next day—must have been balm for his battered spirit. Here was a solid, indestructible achievement, symbol of a hundred other visions he had translated into reality in the preceding dozen years. Here was something that the snipers and vilifiers could not easily soil with mockery and slander. So it was good to look at the huge skeleton of the Hoover Dam upon which flesh was being put. If there was one project in all the land that was clearly the product of his mind and energies, this was it. He had planned it, fought for it, from his first day as Secretary of Commerce.

For many years, as chairman of the Colorado River Commission, he labored as an engineer and a political leader to clear away the tangled underbrush of legal and technical obstructions, to obtain the necessary money, to adjust the conflicting claims of six states to water rights. He helped to draft the legislation authorizing the construction. He provided the basic plan, embodied in the Sante Fe compact after three years of negotiation, apportioning the interests of the six states along the harnessed river. As the first engineer in the White House, he even passed on the technical plans. The project, when completed, would cost more than four hundred million and Hoover had so managed it that every dollar was eventually returned to the Treasury. His Secretary of the Interior, Dr. Wilbur, negotiated the power contract, the largest of its kind in all history, to govern the use of the dam.

It was against this background that President Hoover spoke next day to a gathering in Boulder City. "This is not the first time I have visited the site of this great dam," he said. "And it does give me extraordinary pleasure to see the great dream I have long held taking form in actual reality of stone and cement." He traced a little of the history of the undertaking and summarized its purposes. Then he added:

But the whole of this translates itself into something infinitely more important. It translates itself into millions of happy homes for Americans out under the blue sky of the West. . . . *I hope to be present at its final completion as a bystander. Even so I shall feel a special personal satisfaction* [italics mine].

It had long been the custom to name such works of man for Presidents. There was the Roosevelt Dam for Theodore Roosevelt, the Wilson Dam, the Coolidge Dam. In those instances the use of their names was a gesture of courtesy. In the case of Hoover, who had fathered and nurtured the project, it was vastly more. In accordance with precedent, Secretary Wilbur therefore named the Colorado dam for his chief on September 8, 1930. Congress confirmed and legalized the christening when it appropriated funds explicitly for the "Hoover Dam."

But early in the term of Hoover's successor an almost incredible thing happened. The Secretary of the Interior, Harold L. Ickes, arbitrarily changed the name to Boulder Dam! Legalities aside, viewed in its purely human aspects, it was a piece of pettiness to make normal people cringe. Having attached the ex-President's name to the Hoover depression, Hoover breadlines, Hoovervilles, certain men now tried to erase it from the Colorado River and other products of Hoover's efforts. In some cases the ex-President's name, engraved on the cornerstone of post offices and other public buildings begun during the Hoover administration, was actually chiseled out and the name of Roosevelt inscribed in its place.

Secretary Ickes was a man of many gifts, the most conspicuous of which, alas, was his talent for bitter and long-sustained personal animosities. Having dug his fingernails into a victim, he did not let go for months, for years, forever. The very syllables of Hoover Dam seemed to upset him. One of his first acts in office, in May 1933, was to instruct the Commissioner of Reclamation that the Colorado structure thereafter be referred to as Boulder Dam in his publications.

This he followed up with two years of campaigning to maneuver the United States Board on Geographical Names into formally rechristening the dam. According to the New York *Sun*, this board deserved "a delayed citation for deft broken-field running" in evading Ickes' pressures. Ickes then simply decided on his own authority that Boulder Dam was a more suitable designation; he attested the decision in a letter dated May 7, 1935.

When the dam was finally completed, Hoover was not invited to the dedication ceremonies presided over by Roosevelt. His hope "to be present at its final completion as a bystander" apparently was adjudged presumptuous by those who chose the guests. The embarrassed mayor of Boulder City asked Hoover to come anyhow, but the former President decided to stay away. "I somehow did not feel like making myself so public an exhibit of vindictiveness," he explained.

Hoover had a Quaker-bred disinterest in worldly honors. He had watched the struggle over the name of the dam more in sorrow than in anger. In the aggregate of insults it was just one more item. But to his friends the erasure of his name seemed, by the very childishness of its malice, a crowning crime. It meant a lot to them, therefore, when in 1947 a Republican Congress and a Democratic President moved to wipe out that piece of vendetta of which no one—including, one prays, its authors—were too proud. Congress passed and President Truman signed a bill restoring the original name of the Hoover Dam.

3

Hoover, who knew more about many of the problems confronting Congress than any man alive, was not invited to testify at hearings. (Individual legislators did turn to him for counsel and guidance.) Other Republicans, among them some from his own official circle, were drawn into government work again, but not the former President. Not once, as long as Roosevelt was alive, did Hoover set foot in the White House. The only living ex-President was not invited to his successor's inaugural ceremonies. He was even denied the courtesy, until then customary for ex-Presidents, of an invitation to the Army-Navy football game! The very pettiness tells the squalid story.

A special section was set up in the Justice Department to explore the Hoover term for corruptions. The energetic treasure-hunt netted exactly nothing.

A few pathetic reports of scandal under Hoover ballooned skyward and were deflated with a bass whistle. One of these referred to an RFC loan to a Chicago bank in which General Dawes had a large interest. It made a sputtering noise and collapsed in nothingness. The loan, it turned out, was not only wholly legitimate but highly commendable; it had been urged and endorsed by Democratic members of the RFC in behalf of the whole Chicago banking community; Dawes had resigned from the RFC before the loan was negotiated. And every dollar of it had been returned with interest.

Another of the attempts was scandalous enough, and tragic in its consequences, but not in the way the balloonists had planned.

In 1930 the Postmaster General, Walter F. Brown, negotiated airmail contracts with aviation companies, to standardize rates and procedures. Costs to the department were reduced, routes were consolidated, and other overdue reforms effected.

But suddenly, more than three years later, the public was apprised that its interests had been traduced by Hoover's Postmaster. At Washington cocktail parties there was happy talk of the "graft, profiteering, collusion and lawlessness" charged by the Roosevelt administration. In February 1934 President Roosevelt canceled all airmail contracts without the formality of hearings or investigation and ordered the Army to fly the mails. When Colonel Charles Lindbergh, among others, warned the President that the Army was not equipped for the job, the White House denounced him as "just a publicity seeker." Unfortunately Lindbergh and the other aviation experts who protested were right. Twelve Army officers were killed in those flights.

A Senate investigation of the contracts—not *before* but *after* their abrogation—could find no trace of malfeasance, for all its eagerness to justify Roosevelt and embarrass Hoover. Meanwhile Postmaster General James A. Farley was made the "goat" for the twelve deaths. Years later he revealed that he had advised Roosevelt against the investigation and protested against the issuance of statements in his name without his consent.

The last mistake of that Senate committee was to announce a foray on the character of the ex-President's older son. Young Herbert had helped develop a system of ground-to-plane radio communication, as a result of which he was hired at one hundred dollars a week as chief engineer of a small air transport company which, like all such companies, flew some mail. His father did not even know about this until the Michelson Mills began to circulate innuendos. The young man thereupon tried to resign but was dissuaded by his father and the company.

When the Senate committee announced plans to summon Herbert, Jr., he released to the press a copy of his letter of resignation. There the true facts were so clearly set forth that the committee changed its mind about calling him. A wave of popular resentment against the whole show forced the Administration to reinstate the airmail contracts. The smear that failed had cost twelve innocent lives.

Another attempt to strike the ex-President through his sons was made later. Allan Hoover was then engaged in farming in the San Joaquin Valley. The law prohibited disclosures by government officials of subsidies to individuals under the AAA. But one day Secretary Wallace informed reporters "off the record" that while the former President was attacking the AAA, his own son, through the Kern County Land Company, was receiving twenty thousand dollars for curtailing crops, and hinted that the press ought to expose the facts.

It did. Allan, it developed, owned only a few shares in the Kern company, which entitled him to draw, not twenty thousand dollars, but two dollars, which he rejected. What's more, the younger Hoover said, "Wallace's farm regimentation was depriving him of the right to buy feeder cattles and calves that he needed" for his operation. His father was good and sore about what he called "a pretty immoral attempt to smear me over the shoulder of a decent boy."

Hoover advised his son to "charge the Secretary with unconstitutionally robbing him of his honest earnings, violating the law as to exposure" and trying to smear his father. "Allan did so in language that echoed all over the country. The New Deal let him alone thereafter."

A further effort to get Hoover was made in 1935, this time over the shoulder of his first Secretary of the Treasury, Andrew Mellon, whom the Department of Justice tried to indict for allegedly fraudulent income tax returns. The New Deal, naturally, made a Roman holiday of the charge against an authenticated "economic royalist." Hoover would write:

Not only was he [Mellon] a man of the most scrupulous integrity, but I knew that in the period when he was supposed to have defrauded the taxpayers, he was the backbone of support for the unemployed in the Pittsburgh area. His expenditures on this and other charities during the time far exceeded his purported gain from evasion of income taxes.

President Roosevelt knew that Mellon was preparing a gigantic gift to the nation: one of the greatest art collections extant. The new Administration had confirmed the site of the National Gallery to house the collection. Despite the attempted indictment, Mellon went ahead with this and other gifts totaling around one hundred million dollars—the larger part of his fortune.

A grand jury, having heard testimony on the complicated allegations, refused to bring in an indictment. The drive to "get" Mellon, however, was not abandoned. The former Tax Commissioner, Elmer Irey, subsequently told a well-known reporter, William J. Slocum: "The Roosevelt administration made me go after Andy Mellon. I liked Mr. Mellon and they knew it, so the FBI took the first crack and got tossed out of the Grand Jury room." Then Roosevelt's Secretary of the Treasury, Henry Morgenthau, Jr., ordered Irey to take another crack at it. Again the Administration failed. For a time, however, it looked as if Mellon—by that time a very old and very feeble man—would have to stand trial for defrauding the government to which he had given many years of devoted service.

There was a moment when New Deal probers thought they had found the elusive object of their search. Charles F. Adams had been Secretary of the Navy under Hoover. One day the Democratic chairman of a House committee announced in happy excitement that Adams held stock in ten firms doing business with the Navy. The legislator might have spared himself and his party a load of humiliation had he done what Hoover did when the story was released to the press. He simply phoned the ex-Secretary and learned that he had never owned a share in those firms—it was another Charles F. Adams, neither known nor related to him. The ex-President and the ex-Secretary decided to have their little joke. They let the New Deal proceed with the attack one more day before exposing the silly blunder.

In the end the staff of the special section of the Department of Justice conceded that it could strike no paydirt. The Hoover administration had collected and disbursed some twenty-five billion dollars. The extraordinary, possibly unprecedented fact is that not one true case of malfeasance in office, large or small, was turned up by the industrious diggers.

4

Hoover left the White House in a time of sorrow and anguish. The fates, with some hefty mortal help, had contrived to bring the depression to its nadir precisely at the moment of his departure. Why shouldn't the cheerful newcomers, dangling their bag of tricks, show contempt for his trivial person? The Michelson Mills pushed the old lines of anti-Hoover goods and added bright new numbers. But the outfit now lost its near-monopoly. Dozens of new propaganda mills, inside and outside the government, came into being. And in 1935 the Communists and their graded fellow travelers pitched into the job.

We should not underestimate the role of the Communists in Hoover's ordeal by abuse. Their party had grown from about eight thousand in the Republican period to a claimed one hundred thousand in the first two or three years of the New Deal. This was only the hard core of a periphery of fellow travelers and innocent camp-followers running into millions. Moreover, the Communists had been past masters in the science of character murder when the brain-trusters were still apprentices.

This was the Red Decade. It was smart to be Red. It was liberal to be illiberal the Communist way. Comrades infiltrated the schools, the churches, the press, the labor movement, every corner of American life, including the government. They could pulverize a reputation more swiftly and deftly than any other group in the past.

For a while they lambasted the Roosevelt administration almost as fiercely as its predecessor. F.D.R. figured in their poison-pen literature as a "fascist . . . financial dictator . . . imperialist" given to "shameful demagogy" and "drastic attacks upon the living standards of the masses . . . terrorization of the Negro . . . systematic denials of civil rights." About the middle of 1935, however, everything changed. The heat was off Roosevelt. Hoover was their number one whipping-boy.

Moscow had adopted its united-front, Trojan horse line. In France and other countries this was bodied forth in Popular Front governments. In the United States, where political Communism was too weak to demand a place in a coalition regime, it operated indirectly through stooges and sympathizers and the new breed of totalitarian liberals. What unfolded in this country was an amazing *unofficial Popular Front government*— unacknowledged, independent of the Administration, yet operating energetically within the New Deal empire. It added up to the most potent and ubiquitous single influence in Washington, a half-clandestine government-within-the-government, arrogantly open on some occasions but conspiratorial in essence.

Let me quote the late George Creel on this subject. An eminent journalist and a Wilsonian Democrat, he had during World War I headed the information service, generally referred to as the Creel Bureau. For some twenty years he had been a close friend of Franklin Roosevelt and in its first four years an insider in his Administration. After his disillusionment, Creel wrote his autobiographical *Rebel at Large*, in which he tongue-lashed the Communists and their New Deal associates:

Present-day "liberalism," as it has the impudence to call itself, is anti-American; for at its back, as cunning as secret, are men and women who give their allegiance to a foreign power. And what of their following? Dancing to the strings pulled by hidden hands is as motley a crew as ever gathered under one banner.

Shoulder to shoulder with avowed communists and subversive aliens is the weird conglomeration known as "fellow travelers" made up of embittered failures, discredited politicians, crystal-gazers, venal labor leaders, underpaid professors and overpaid actors, feminized preachers eager to gain an effect of virility, perennial sophomores, frustrated incompetents, idle wealth seeking protective coloration, motion picture stars hopeful of a smoke screen to hide inanity and illiteracy, scatterbrains rejoicing in an emotional experience and cowardly Esaus willing to trade freedom for a bogus security.

And I venture to quote again from *The Red Decade* on that "weird conglomeration":

The Stalinist slogans of the period were so beguiling that the more befuddled officials—like the professors and literati and penthouse rebels—saw no harm in tagging along. The New Deal doors, politically and socially, were thus opened wide to the temporary Kremlin democrats. . . .

The Popular Front prospered in Washington through the snob appeal of the New Deal intelligentsia, and subcontractor brain-trusters and pseudo-intellectual lawyers and writers-turned-politician. Certain Congressmen and especially the bored wives of politicians were thrilled and flattered by friendship with the polysyllabic sophisticates scattered through all the new bureaus, agencies, projects. It all fitted into the amorphous crusading fervor of the New Deal era. Political patronage was being lapped up greedily by boys and girls who talked Veblen, Spengler, Marx, and the Party line as glibly as the morning's news.

Mention of Hoover in that environment was always good for a sneer and a laugh.

President Roosevelt sent eulogistic messages to Stalinist "front" conferences. His wife served as patron saint of the Communist-controlled American Youth Congress. His Cabinet members presided at Red front meetings. The easiest road to a New Deal job—especially in the lush fields of federal relief setups—was through friendly fellow-travelers.

This grotesquerie cost our country more than it realizes even today. Congressional committees belatedly exposed hundreds of fanatic New Dealers as fellow-travelers or members of Red front outfits. Still later inquiries showed that over fifty men and women in important policy-making positions were members of the Communist Party. Eight persons who occupied vital positions of trust, in the White House, the Treasury Department, the Department of Justice, and elsewhere, were convicted as traitors or perjurers in relation to traitorous actions. Dozens of others evaded exposure and conviction only because of statutes of limitation and resort to the Fifth Amendment. Those who attempted to alert the country to this incredible condition were castigated as Red-baiters and ostracized from decent "liberal" society.

The government was neither more nor less blameworthy than the colleges, the magazines, the movie industry, and other areas of national life. Each of these had its contingents of open and camouflaged comrades who helped set the intellectual fashions. And the habitual defaming of Herbert Hoover was one fashion that endured while others were amended or displaced.

"We'll hang Herbert Hoover on a sour apple tree," the comrades sang to the tune of "John Brown's Body." "We'll hang Herbert Hoover on a sour apple tree, when the revolution comes." Insulting cartoons of the ex-President became as standardized in the "liberal" press as any of the Party-line slogans. The vile fabrications of the discredited Hamill and his pornographic publisher were treated as indisputable fact. As late as October 12, 1947, Hedda Hopper could report that a Hollywood actress "turned down *B.F.'s Daughter* because the script called for her to read a line praising Hoover."

The July 10, 1944, issue of a Party-line smear sheet called *In Fact,* edited by an unhappy little man who worked off his inferiorities by throwing mud at his betters, was devoted to "Hoover, Merchant of Death." It presented as "inside news," the supposed specialty of the sheet, shovelfuls of the decayed lies which Hamill had confessed to fabricating twelve years earlier. Hoover, the little man recorded, called out the Army "to shoot down the American Legionnaires at Anacosta." He "started hating Russia when his oil, gold and other mines were confiscated and he lost a billion dollars." He was "making millions out of coolie labor" and "believed that the disregard for human life permits cheap mining."

Column after column of this putrescence—all of it typical of the anti-Hoover campaign from 1929 forward. In Party-line publications it could be presented crudely. In higher echelons of the American press, movies, radio, wherever the New Deal and its camp followers were deployed, Hoover-baiting was a shade or two more decorous and came seasoned with satire. But taken together, the attack convinced a whole new generation of Americans—the new voters among them—that their thirty-first President had been a monstrous exploiter, a sharp promoter, a hard-hearted plutocrat, and an enemy of the people. The slanders were enshrined in classroom textbooks.

A widely used American history book, published in 1953, is before me as I write. On the whole it is rather friendly to Hoover, and certainly not intentionally malicious. Yet it says of the former President, as though setting down unquestioned truth: "Trained in business, he was an ardent advocate of 'rugged individualism' without government interference. He continued to talk about prosperity being just around the corner."

Such was—and to some extent still remains—the denigration of a President transmuted by gigantic propaganda into "history" and imposed upon young minds.

The Hoovers, nevertheless, did not tolerate personal vilification of the Roosevelts in their home or their presence. One night a guest at dinner became heated and picturesque in assailing the character of the Roosevelts. He thought he was pleasing his hosts. Mrs. Hoover turned to her neighbor (on whose authority I have the story) and whispered, "Please, please talk loud and fast about something else, anything else!" He did, and his stentorian voice drowned out the Roosevelt hater.

The following is from Raymond Moley's memoirs:

I'm reminded of an incident that took place in 1938, when accidentally I happened to meet Herbert Hoover traveling to New York from California. We were sitting in a dining car together when the steward, who was not only an entrepreneur of food but of gossip, stopped by the table.

"Do you think," he said, "that Mr. Hoover would like to hear the latest story about Mr. Roosevelt?"

Hoover then gave expression to one of the most brilliant pieces of unconscious humor that I have ever heard. Glowering at the menu, he rumbled, "I don't like stories about Presidents."

It was not humor, unconscious or otherwise. It was genuine and in character for the man who before he became Chief Executive himself once declared: "The presidency is more than an executive responsibility. It is the inspiring symbol of all that is highest in American purpose and ideals."

5

The Republicans for the most part showed little courage in the face of the massive assault on the titular head of their party. Few of them believed the unclean absurdities about Hoover, but even fewer had the gallantry—and the good political sense—to defend him without reserve.

Evidently they had suffered a loss of nerve and with it a blackout of self-esteem. It has been reported that in Nazi Germany many Jews, after years of cruel defamation, themselves turned into anti-Semites. In America in the 1930s many Republicans by the same psychological process succumbed to anti-Hoover propaganda. Some of them, though not persuaded of his villainy, were too intimidated by the sheer magnitude of the attacks to react with normal self-respect.

A distinction must be made here, however, between the rank-and-file, millions of whom admired the ex-President "despite everything," and the professional Republican politicians and leaders. The more unfairly Hoover was besmirched, the more eager the latter seemed to disavow him. The more cynically the facts about the last Republican administration were misrepresented, the more eager ambitious chieftains were to behave as if their party did not exist before 1933.

In a *Collier's* article in October 1935, on the eve of another presidential year, George Creel quoted top Republicans as saying in substance, "Lord, if only Hoover would get out and leave us alone!" The anxiety to dissociate themselves from Hoover may have reflected only political expediency, but it looked like a plea of guilty on all counts to every libel and lie about the Republican party. In the last analysis, therefore, their desertion of Hoover was not only morally reprobate but politically stupid. In the measure that they left their last Administration undefended, they guaranteed the victory of the attackers by default. The assault on Hoover was thus more effective than the New Deal itself had expected, in that it psychologically disarmed the Republicans.

As the Roosevelt vendetta against his predecessor persisted, year after year, it became a subject of spirited discussion in political circles. The President's motivations were not easy to appraise. But Moley, and he was not the only one, disagreed with the majority who attributed it "entirely to ungenerous and vindictive caprice."

In his book, *Twenty-seven Masters of Politics*, published in 1949, Moley wrote that it had been "the result of political prudence, for Roosevelt entertained a view that only Hoover among the notables of the Republican party possessed the massive convictions and intelligence to provide an alternative to the New Deal. Roosevelt actually believed that Hoover might emerge once more as the leader and candidate of the party." A singular belief, if true, considering that Hoover was sixty-two years old in 1936, sixty-six in 1940, seventy in 1944.

Whether prompted by vindictive caprice or political prudence, the vendetta was carried out with extraordinary success as long as the generalissimo was alive to direct and fuel it. At one extreme the smear campaign had the open collaboration of the Communists. At the other it was unwittingly abetted, through timidity and confusion, by Republican failure to stand up like men for their last Administration and the titular head of their party. In contempt of common sense, Herbert Hoover was made the scapegoat for a global cataclysm.

XXVIII

Critique of the New Deal

THE idea that the New Deal "ended" the depression is as spurious
as the idea that Hoover "caused" it. Despite the colossal injections
of public funds, tax money, and borrowings, the 1930s wound up
with some eleven million unemployed, twenty million on relief, production still below the pre-depression levels. The building industries were
stagnant, private financing inadequate and timorous. Millions of those
counted as employed in the official statistics were engaged on useless,
make-believe projects. The economic picture remained for nearly eight
Roosevelt years as bleak as it had been in the preceding three Hoover
years—until the advent of war, and the country's conversion into the
"arsenal of democracy."

There was a period of improvement in late 1936 and early 1937, reflecting transfusions of greater doses of government money. The sick
economy was thus periodically kept on its feet with billions in pep pills.
The end of 1937 witnessed another market panic described by Henry
Morgenthau as "a hysteria resembling a mob in a theatre fire." The employment census for November 1937—just five years after Roosevelt's
election—showed eleven million out of work and three million more only
partly employed.

Yet the semantic nonsense about how the New Deal liquidated the
depression was widely believed in its own time, when the contrary was
evident to the naked eye. Thereafter it hardened into an article of faith.
One still finds people who are shocked by sudden realization that the
Great Depression lasted not for three but for eleven years.

Elliott V. Bell, editor of *Business Week* and a member of the late
President Kennedy's Advisory Committee on Labor-Management, addressed himself to this curious fact in a speech at the University of Iowa
on February 19, 1963. Having listed some of the New Deal measures, he

339

said: "What all this busy improvisation did *not* do was end the depression. . . ." Yet, he said, "for a long time, Democratic politicians sought to perpetuate the myth that the New Deal had succeeded in ending the depression." Myths die hard.

The New Deal's continued failure to solve economic problems put a premium on Hoover's value as a certified whipping-boy. The new officialdom could prove that things were now tolerable chiefly by convincing the country that they were intolerable under the previous regime. The horrors of the first three years of depression had to be magnified and painted in the most gruesome colors. Droves of satraps in the expanding empire of federal relief, if only to justify demands for yet more billions, had to exaggerate the distress that prevailed before their own arrival on the scene.

The central failure had to be blamed on capitalists, economic royalists, plutocrats, Liberty Leaguers, Republicans, reactionary Democrats, old and new species of reprobates—and of course on the king demon of them all, Herbert Hoover.

There was no American so humble that he was not provided with someone or something to hate. Every fireside chat set up a few more lightning rods to deflect popular wrath from the government to some group of citizens. There might be no more jobs now than before—but there were more excitements, slogans, schemes, accusations. A hundred new agencies flourished flamboyantly where one had bloomed unseen and unheard. New legions of office-holders tossed confetti billions into the air and everyone, the rich included, scrambled for the gaudy stuff. There was no end of "must" orders to a supine Congress and of "directives" to a dizzied citizenry. A new industry grew up: the sorting and interpretation of Washington edicts, exegesis on Official Writ.

The White House, once a place of work and a home, came to resemble a five-ring circus. "It lacked nothing but a merry-go-round and a roller coaster to be a Coney Island," George Creel reported. Its denizens, from the family dog up, made headlines and newsreels and radio skits. They sold soap, insurance, gossip, newspaper columns, articles, airplanes. The First Lady did radio commercials at a thousand or several thousand dollars a throw.

Never had such a barking and screeching and cooing issued from Washington to delight a fun-starved citizenry. Never had court favorites reigned in glory and resigned in disgust with such syncopated publicity. There were Tommy the Cork, Harry the Morgue, Sammie the Rose, Harry the Hop, and a hundred others to give a continuing depression the look and feel of a national mardi gras. Showmanship outranked statesmanship. On Madison Avenue in New York there were high-priced public relations firms whose prosperity rested on their "inside track" with White House poo-bahs.

The previous Administration—for that matter all previous Administrations—seemed drab and stodgy and stingy by contrast. Old-fashioned concern for constitutional limitations seemed pettifogging and timid. Now the old restraints were off. The sky was the limit. Everything was bigger and more openhanded—the appropriations, the federal payrolls, the relief scandals, the national debts, the political promises. And the budgets were kept from being *too* unbalanced by the elementary trick of listing new expenditures in a separate "emergency" column.

Thus everyone joined heartily in "Happy Days Are Here Again." Many Americans, looking back, could not forgive the austerity of the Hoover administration, its constant beefing about costs, its high-collar appeals to moldy ethics, its sentimental calls to neighborly sympathy and outmoded charity. Poor Hoover was a Gloomy Gus who treated disasters as if they were disastrous when in fact, as was now being made manifest, depression could be barrels of fun.

2

In a speech on December 16, 1935, Herbert Hoover alluded to "dark alleys of inspired propaganda" where "ideals and men are assassinated with poisonous whisperings." But there are few such allusions to his personal trials in the record of his decades as ex-President. He shrank from making a public spectacle of his private dismay.

His duty, he believed, was to elucidate his concepts of public affairs, rather than defend the private Hoover. His conduct in the White House had not been conditioned by politics but by convictions. It was fitting, therefore, that he should devote himself, immediately upon retirement from the Presidency, to re-examining those convictions. The product of this effort was *The Challenge to Liberty*, published in 1934. The book was an elaboration of his *American Individualism* (described in an earlier chapter), enriched by his wide-ranging experience in the intervening twelve years.

In the first book he had drawn upon developments in postwar Europe to point up the perils of an erosion of freedom under the pounding of economic storms. In the second he was able to draw on what he considered similar erosive processes in his own country. Read in awareness of the slanders to which he was at the time being subjected, the book seems remarkable for its calm, its charity, and particularly its undiminished confidence in America's destiny.

The abridgement of individual rights in the name of collective good, he emphasized, was the American expression of a worldwide crisis of the human spirit. In furious haste to bring about change, "people and governments are blindly wounding, even destroying, those fundamental human liberties which have been the foundation and inspiration of progress since the Middle Ages." He did not accuse the New Deal of being consciously either fascist or communist, but he identified elements in its conduct and policies running parallel with the early stages of totalitarianism.

The most alarming of many symptoms in the United States of the disease tormenting half of Europe, as Hoover saw it, was regimentation by a self-willed bureaucracy—"a vast centralization of power in the Executive. "The hope of America and the world," he wrote, "is to regenerate Liberty and its responsibilities—not to abandon it. . . . I should be untrue to that service if I did not raise my voice in protest, not at reform but at the threat of the eclipse of liberty."

There are in his pages no disparagements, no mocking of men's motives. Some of the measures hailed as unique New Deal inventions, he noted, were launched in his own Administration and "many additional measures undertaken in these directions during the past months are admirable if properly administered." His criticism referred to means, not to ends: "Cooperation appraises its methods and consequences step by step and pays its bills as it goes. Bureaucracy rushes headlong into visions of the millennium and sends the bills to the Treasury."

In troubled times people clamor for drastic change, he explained, impelling governments to experiment with "miracle cures" and in the process expanding their own power. But the ills of society "must often be cured by building up the cells of the economic body under careful nursing, rather than by surgery or patent medicines." There are evils, but "we do not need to burn down the house to kill the rats."

To those enamored of the slogans of "revolution," he tendered the reminder that true American liberalism, geared to respect for the individual entity, is the most revolutionary concept in two thousand years.

The closing words of his book were these: "The spark of liberty in the mind and spirit of man cannot be long extinguished; it will break into flames that will destroy every coercion which seeks to limit it." This underlying confidence in the future sustained ex-President Hoover as he observed and analyzed the course of the nation.

While maintaining his self-imposed silence, he was studying not only the operations of the new regime but their impact on people at the grassroots. Letters by the thousands came to him, nearly all complaining of New Deal invasions of their private rights. Simple people, recognizing the ex-President in fishing villages or at gas stations on the road, confided their griefs under the NRA, the AAA, and other alphabetical visitations.

But Hoover waited, Quaker fashion, for the spirit to move him to bear Witness. Besides, he did not consider it seemly or proper for a retired President to criticize his successor too soon after handing over the reins.

This political asceticism was not always easy to sustain. The provocations were many and continuous. For within months the "Roosevelt Revolution" littered the national landscape with broken platform planks, the debris of shattered campaign pledges, and the wreckage of new enterprises tried and discarded—willingly or with the help of the Supreme Court. A compliant Congress, called into session by President Roosevelt at once after the inauguration, ground out laws and appropriations wholesale. Those were the "heroic" Hundred Days. They produced a deficit in three months larger than Hoover's in two full years, including a $3,300,000,000 "blank check" for President Roosevelt to disburse as he pleased.

Roosevelt had repeatedly accused Hoover of attempting "too many functions" and of "piling bureaus on bureaus, commissions on commissions." Now Roosevelt himself was creating new commissions and bureaus at an astonishing rate. The bureaucracy was growing with cancerous speed: 265,000 added to the payrolls in those two years; by 1949 there would be 2,100,000 federal employees. The growth, moreover, largely bypassed the Civil Service system in favor of crudely political appointments.

The noise and drama of crowding new activities, the daily tom-tom of exciting headlines, the hailstorm of startling laws, decrees, directives, and fireside lectures—these created an illusion of accomplishment in the first months. Much of it soon proved empty of real content, in meaningful terms of economic betterment. Some of the more softheaded businessmen and seers of Wall Street actually began to talk of the coming "Roosevelt boom." But there was no boom around the corner.

The former President watched in despair as endless "emergencies" were invoked to explain administrative acts. In 1933–34 alone over two hundred Executive Decrees were justified in terms of emergency. With his penchant for statistics, Hoover calculated that the President used the word "emergency" at least four hundred times in public pronouncement in those two years. But what was an emergency? Anything that the White House designated as such.

Since he looked upon the constitutional separation of powers as an indispensable safeguard of democratic freedom, Hoover was particularly alarmed by the downgrading of Congress. Day after day bills slugged "Must" or "Priority" by the Administration were enacted automatically, with barely the pretense of study and debate. The veteran New York *Times* correspondent, Arthur Krock, would ultimately report (May 10, 1938): "Often the leaders introduced the bill without reading it. . . .

Always the rank and file of Congress knew nothing of the bill's contents until they had read it in the newspapers. Sometimes they did not trouble to do that." The hackneyed term "rubber stamp" had rarely been applied to a legislature more accurately and never for such a protracted time. The Securities Act of 1933 was passed by the House without bothering to hold hearings. The NRA and the AAA, the two foundation schemes which in effect set up a new social system, were rubber-stamped on Capitol Hill in six and eight hours respectively. Substantially, Congress surrendered its functions to the Executive.

In his last year of tenure Hoover had carefully prepared a World Monetary and Economic Conference to stabilize currencies and credit and to remove other barriers to international trade. He had invested a lot of hope in the undertaking. Sixty-six nations were represented when the conference foregathered in London after Roosevelt's accession. The President allowed the conference to run along for many weeks and then, in July 1933, deliberately wrecked it with a neatly placed "bombshell." He ruled that currency was not on the agenda, though it had been identified as the principal subject in the very name of the conference. Neither Hull nor Moley, who headed the U.S. contingent, were consulted or notified in advance. The conference, of course, collapsed at once. Only J. Maynard Keynes proclaimed that Roosevelt was "magnificently right," to which Moley in due time quipped, "magnificently left, Keynes means." However that may be, the United States had opted for autarchy and economic isolationism.

In his campaign oratory, Roosevelt had described the gold backing of the dollar as a sacred "covenant" between the government and the people. He was no sooner in the White House, however, than he moved to abandon gold, devalue the dollar, and open wide the doors to inflation. In his first month in office he obtained authority, in case of "emergency," to assume dictatorial control of all "transactions in foreign exchange" and "transfers of credit between, or payments by, banking institutions." On April 5, 1933, he issued an Executive Order requiring all persons— on pain of imprisonment and fines up to ten thousand dollars—to surrender their gold coin, gold certificates, and gold bullion to the government.

"To me," the sound-money Democratic Senator Glass exclaimed, "the suggestion that we devalue the gold dollar 50 percent means national repudiation. To me it means dishonor; in my conception of it, it is immoral."

The suggestion became a reality in May. With his Puckish relish for the swift, unexpected blow, President Roosevelt invited a group of Cabinet members and advisers to dinner and, along with the dessert, casually handed them the text of the Thomas Amendment to the proposed

AAA law. This gave the President, in Hoover's words, "legal authority over money as absolute as that of Tiberius Caesar or Henry VIII, Stalin or Hitler." He was empowered to issue three billion dollars in greenbacks, to permit free coinage of silver, to devalue gold up to 50 percent.

Moley, who was among the guests summoned for that shock treatment, presently recorded that "hell broke loose in the room." Budget Director Lewis Douglas, Herbert Feis, and others "were so horrified that they began to scold Mr. Roosevelt as though he were a perverse and particularly backward schoolboy." But the Amendment was quickly rubberstamped along with the rest of the agricultural act. Some years later Secretary of the Treasury Morgenthau revealed that Roosevelt fixed the price of gold, devaluating the dollar by 41 percent, through the scientific process of flipping a coin. Endless billions were now available, in unsecured currency and credits, "to end the depression," which, however, stubbornly refused to die. The Administration lost thousands of its more conservative supporters, but for each one of them a thousand lined up hurriedly for the juicier government handouts now available.

The cornerstones of the New Deal edifice in the first few years, of course, were the NRA and the AAA, both of which were ultimately thrown out by the Supreme Court. But while they lasted they worked havoc upon a bewildered population. Said Hoover: "The New Deal method of testing poison apparently is to make the nation swallow it."

The NRA compelled every industry and trade to combine in associations and adopt a code satisfactory to the government. Its operation was then controlled by the large staffs of federal "authorities" with law-making and law-enforcing powers. The NRA retained capitalist forms, stripped of anti-trust impediments, within a system of government stewardship: a pattern remarkably close to those imposed in Mussolini's Italy and Hitler's Germany. Because wage-earners got the short end of the stick, and a soaring cost of living to boot, there were waves of strikes. The Blue Eagle, symbol of the regimented industries, soon became the butt of radio and vaudeville humor and derisive cartoons that mirrored the popular confusions and dismays.

The AAA, with Henry Agard Wallace in charge, turned the farmers into unhappy wards of the central government. Though vast quantities of grains, lard, and other foodstuffs were being imported and foreign markets for American farm produce were fading out, the government paid out hundreds of millions of tax dollars to burn oats, kill pigs, plow under corn and cotton. The magic word was Scarcity, on the theory that it would raise prices—that, at least, it accomplished in full measure. In two years, over seven hundred million dollars was paid out to farmers for *not* raising crops and livestock. Naturally the largest agricultural enterprises, possessing more land on which *not* to plant and *not* to graze, received the biggest subsidies—some of them a million dollars and more.

The NRA in particular was drawing ever louder shrieks of protest, even within the President's political family. Hoping to contain the clamor with an independent appraisal, the President assigned his friend Clarence Darrow, the liberal lawyer, to the job. To his astonishment, Darrow in May 1934 brought in a verdict of guilty on all counts. He damned the whole business with words like "monopolistic . . . grotesque . . . ghastly . . . oppressive . . . savage."

But the grotesque system continued for another year. Voracious Blue Eagles nested in hundreds of Code offices and government authorities, consuming billions of the people's money. Alfred E. Smith, whose original sponsorship of Roosevelt for governor of New York led him to the White House, denounced the NRA as "a vast octopus set up by government that wound its arms around all the business of the country, paralyzed big business and choked little business to death." George Creel, himself for a time the director of the West Coast division of the organization, declared:

All but the cockeyed could see that the NRA was headed hellbent for a bust. . . . Going back to Washington was like a journey into bedlam, for all touch with the sane and simple had been lost. . . . The spread of the bureaucratic mania had the sweep of a pestilence. Instead of holding to a comparatively small number of basic codes, the administration went crazy, and soon some six hundred were in active operation with more in process of preparation. As one instance out of scores, the manufacture of egg beaters and bird cages were not put under the Wire Code but had separate codes of their own.

Hundreds of men and women, tangled in the meshes of red tape and injustice, turned to the ex-President for advice, or at least sympathy. Convinced that the major New Deal acts would not survive constitutional test, he suggested that they seek recourse through the courts. Characteristically, he drew lawyers among his old friends into an informal legal first-aid task force on a voluntary basis, to help such people without payment. He was able to write in retrospect that "in no case did the authorities persevere against a threat of exposure" through judicial process.

Another development, in foreign affairs, that went against Hoover's grain was the establishment of diplomatic relations with Soviet Russia in November 1933. Four Presidents and five Secretaries of State had refused the American recognition, long and ardently sought by Moscow as a token of respectability. Hoover could discern no genuine excuse for the reversal of the sixteen-year-old policy, except the curious notion that it was somehow "liberal" to do business with one of history's most illiberal tyrannies. The official alibi was the expectation of immense job-making exports to Russia; ironically Soviet-American trade *declined* by 60 percent after the recognition.

The Soviets promised in writing to discontinue their vicious anti-American campaigns. Instead, Communist propaganda, infiltration, and subversion soon reached new heights and depths. The Soviet Embassy and consulates themselves became centers of anti-American activity. Within forty-eight hours after signing the diplomatic-relations agreement, the Soviet Commissar of Foreign Affairs, Maxim Litvinov, met secretly with American Communist leaders in New York to reassure them that their work would not be restricted by the agreement.

What concerned Hoover most, as he observed the gaudy spectacle of improvisation and unlimited spending, was the deterioration of the moral tone in government and its inevitable reflection in the daily life of the country. "You can't beat Santa Claus!" the politicos boasted. Worsening economic conditions were blamed by the President on imaginary "plots" by Wall Street and "economic royalists." The people's money was openly dispensed to fuel corrupt city machines. And doles thinly camouflaged as "work" made a sorry joke of the dignity of labor.

More level-headed Democratic leaders—men like Senator Glass, Lewis Douglas, Al Smith—pulled no punches in their outcries against the federal relief system. But the runaway machine could not be put into reverse. At one time Harry Hopkins, chief dispenser of money, said that twenty-five million Americans drew their livelihoods from the government. Burdened with billions that had to be disbursed somehow, the resourceful Harry the Hop invented ever new varieties of artificial employment. In the end, however, even Harry ran out of plausible projects to absorb the pump-priming largesse at his disposal.

The government's fantastic experiments with money and men nurtured a sort of chain reaction of crackpottery. There was Huey Long's "Every Man a King" movement, with himself as the Kingfish. There were Dr. Townsend's Old Age Revolving Pension Plan; Upton Sinclair's EPIC; the Technocracy craze; the Ham-and-Eggs movement. A contagion of snake-oil utopianism assured every scheme for instant abundance a hearing and a following. Meanwhile the Communists—enjoying the advantages of a disciplined party, a consistent ideology, and the support of a foreign despotism—could burrow ever deeper into government.

The Administration, to be sure, was not directly responsible for the whole pestilence of panaceas. Hucksters of utopia inevitably set up their soapboxes in times of distress. They had been active from 1929 forward. Not until Roosevelt and his crowds of assorted theorists were in Washington, however, did they achieve formidable success—in organization, popular followings, political power. At times the New Deal was embarrassed by the more crackpot by-products of its fabulous era, as in the case of Huey Long. At other times it took the monstrosities right into the family, as in the case of Sinclair's EPIC.

But the Administration could not slough off indirect responsibility. For it set the tone of the time by its disdain for orthodox finance and sound currency, for traditional American values and constitutional restraints. The circus climate was congenial to the growth of daft ideas and know-nothing movements. Soon the boundaries between the rational and irrational, the practical and the utopian, were so blurred that prudent men seemed out of place. Crackpottery, especially if presented in recondite academic verbiage, achieved not only respectability but ready access to the fountainheads of political power.

All of which provides the measure of Hoover's self-control in waiting two years before he spoke out publicly.

3

Beginning with an address in Sacramento in March 1935, the ex-President made up for lost time. He dealt unsparingly with the phenomenon—incommensurable with the American past, as he saw it, and in large part with the Constitution, as the Supreme Court saw it—called the New Deal. More and more speeches and articles followed at frequent intervals. Taken together, this running commentary added up to an earnest, penetrating critique of the New Deal.

The Sacramento speech and a Commencement Address at his alma mater in June were keynote statements. These were followed, into the middle of 1936, by declarations focused on specific aspects of the new government: fiscal policies, Economic Planning, relief policies, agricultural devices, the impacts on labor and industry. He dealt not only with tangible policies but with the ethics of the New Deal, as mirrored in a vengeful attitude toward honest disagreement, a zest for defamatory rhetoric, and the scarcely concealed use of tax funds for political purposes: "buying the people with their own money," in Hoover's phrase.

Many of his speeches were broadcast on coast-to-coast radio and sometimes they were well reported in the press. By the time the Republican National Convention met in Cleveland in June 1936, Hoover was once more in the limelight of national attention. Reasoned opposition to the New Deal, as distinct from emotional harangues and name-calling, had found its most impressive voice.

"This country is in need of a rejuvenated and vigorous Republican party," Hoover said in Sacramento. And in Philadelphia, a few weeks before the convention: *It would be better that the party go down in defeat, the banner of principle flying, than to win by pussyfooting* (italics mine). Cleveland was the test—and it chose pussyfooting.

The nomination of Hoover was rated by political pulse-takers as unlikely but not impossible. I am indebted to the book by Hinshaw, who was an eyewitness, for a summary of what happened. Millions of Republicans, he believed, regarded the ex-President as the one man who could "save the soul" of their party, win or lose. There was little hope of unseating Roosevelt in any case, but there was hope that the party might redeem its reputation and salvage its historic character.

The convention received Hoover with great warmth. He looked fit and almost as young, at sixty-two, as he had looked when he started his term in the White House seven years before. The address he delivered was the high point of the proceedings, felicitous in formulation and charged with deep feeling—almost as if this were a "new Hoover," some reporters said. He reviewed the twenty-eight New Deal months in searing words:

To some people it appears to be a strange interlude in American history in that it has no philosophy, that it is sheer opportunism, that it is a muddle of a spoils system, of emotional economics, of reckless adventure, of unctuous claims to a monopoly of human sympathy, of greed for power, of a desire for popular acclaim and an inspiration to make the front pages of the newspapers. That is the most charitable view. To other people it appears to be a cold-blooded attempt by starry-eyed boys to infect the American people by a mixture of European ideas, flavored with our native predilection to get something for nothing.

Both views were right, he believed, since the Administration, composed of widely disparate elements, had few consistent guiding lines. But it could be judged by its works: "We have spent fifteen billion dollars more than the last Republican administration. We have a debt ten billions greater than even the great war debt. After three years we still have the same number of unemployed that we had at the election of November 1932." Hoover pointed to "the repudiation of obligations, the clipping of the coin, the violation of trust to guard the Constitution, and the coercion of the voter." He indicted the eight or ten major enterprises canceled out by the Supreme Court as a massive and deliberate effort to bypass the Constitution and denounced the misuse of relief by political machines to buy votes. And he wound up with a spirited appeal for the return to morality in government:

Here in America, where the tablets of human freedom were first handed down, their sacred word has been flouted. Today the stern task is before the Republican party to restore the Ark of that Covenant to the temple in Washington.

With almost prophetic insight, in this first quadrennial convention in the wilderness of defeat, Hoover warned the Republicans against the temptations of what would in time be called a "me-too" strategy. "Will you," he exclaimed, "for expediency's sake also offer will-o'-the-wisps which beguile the people? Or have you determined to enter in a holy crusade for liberty which shall determine the future and the perpetuity of a nation of free men?"

He held the audience spellbound. And when he finished, the convention exploded in wild applause and cheers. State standards fell in line and marching began. "I was standing on the convention floor at the time and watching the swift growth of a stampede," Hinshaw has recorded. The managers on the rostrum, however, had other plans. They acted to douse the enthusiasm. In a lull, Hinshaw charged, the chairman announced that Hoover had left to catch a train to New York—actually the former President was resting in a nearby room. After its one great outburst the convention returned to drabness and defeatist gloom and nominated Kansas Governor Alfred Landon.

On the candidate's invitation, Hoover agreed to participate in the campaign. But mysteriously, party headquarters delayed bookings; local officials, it claimed, were reluctant to invite him to speak. Refusing to be deflected from what he considered his duty, Hoover independently made his own schedule of addresses and broadcasts as an independent unit. The Democratic President, that year, debated Hoover, not Landon. That, indeed, was to be the pattern of Roosevelt's third and fourth campaigns, in which attacks on Hoover bulked larger than those on Willkie or Dewey. Even in 1956, though the former President was an octogenarian and again in high popular favor above parties, Adlai Stevenson still tilted at windmills he called "Hooverism."

No, the Republican leadership in Cleveland was not in a heroic mood. The 1936 campaign and those that followed did present those "will-o'-the-wisps which beguile the people" against which Hoover had cautioned, and it brought them neither victory nor honor. As Moley put it in 1949:

The concentration of Democratic policy against Hoover succeeded even beyond the expectations of its progenitors. For the Republican party itself caught the malicious infection. . . . Undefended by Republicans, the Hoover history as it was learned by millions of new voters was exactly what Democratic bias and vindictiveness wanted it to be. And this distortion proved in large measure to be a decisive factor in five successive Republican defeats.

4

Hoover's principal pronouncements on the New Deal and related issues fill some five hundred pages in three volumes of his *Addresses upon the American Road*. In addition, a succinct, point-by-point analysis of the New Deal required about 135 pages in the last volume of his *Memoirs*.

The materials are too vast to be encompassed in this one-volume biography. Necessarily I shall limit myself to a handful of citations, almost at random, merely to convey the flavor and temper of his critique. But it should be remembered that its unfoldment was his chief occupation and preoccupation during the eight years of what, in semantic retribution, should be called the "Roosevelt Depression."

From his first indictment of the New Deal to the last, Herbert Hoover focused his criticism on "the newly created system of regimentation and bureaucratic domination, in which men and women are not masters of government but are the pawns and dependents of a centralized and potentially self-perpetuating government." He said:

Eight days before that election [1932] I stated that the real intention of these men was to tinker with the currency. I said their program would expand government expenditures to nine billion a year. I said it was their intention to undermine state and local government by centralization in Washington. I said it was their intention to regiment our people and undermine the American System with imported European philosophies. That was all vociferously denied. All those interpretations have come true, except as to that nine billion—it was only 95 percent correct.

Once the process of enlarging government is begun, he believed, it could not be stopped from within:

Whenever you increase the numbers of political bureaucracy you not only have to pay them but they are veritable research laboratories for new inventions in spending money. . . . There are three implacable spirits in bureaucracy —self-perpetuation, expansion and demand for more power.

In the third year of the New Deal, he summed up the course of the successor Administration thus:

The most solemn government obligations have been repudiated. The nation is faced with the greatest debt ever known to our country. The currency has been rendered uncertain. The government has been centralized under an enormous bureaucracy in Washington which has dictated and limited the production of our industries, increasing the costs and prices of their products with inevitable decreased consumption. Monopolistic practices have been organized on a gigantic scale. Small businessmen have been disabled and crushed. Class conflicts have been created and embittered. The government has gone into business in competition with its citizens. Citizens have been coerced, threatened and penalized for offenses unknown to all our concepts of liberty.

Economic Planning on a nationwide scale naturally was among Hoover's constant targets. Repeatedly he stressed the sheer confusions of the enterprise:

I need only recall the first two builders of confusion, the NRA and the AAA. These two Towers of Babel which the children of men built were also to reach

351

to Heaven. The headlines tell us of the character of the bricks and mortar. Must Legislation. No Debate. Personal Government by Proclamation. Ballyhoo. Codes. Factory Production Restricted. Competition Limited. Monopolies Created. Government Price Fixing. Increasing Costs. Increased Prices. Decreased Consumption. Strikes. Lockouts. Boycotts. Coercion. Crackdown. Jail. Small Business Men Washed Out. Crops Plowed Under. Animals Slaughtered. Housewife Strikes. Economy of Scarcity. Nation Gets Richer by Producing Less at Higher Costs.

Hoover cited this perhaps too candid statement on National Planning made by Professor Tugwell:

It is . . . a logical impossibility to have a planned economy and to have business operating in industries, just as it is also impossible to have one within our present constitutional and statutory structure. *Modification in both, so serious as to mean destruction and rebuilding* [italics mine], are required.

Hoover's comment:

This is involved language but if it means anything it means that both private business and the Constitution must be modified so seriously as to mean destruction and rebeginning. The President, far from repudiating these ideas, has continuously supported Planned Economy.

The overriding threat posed by this commitment, in Hoover's view, was not in this or that component scheme, but in the continued "weakening of the structure of liberty in our nation." In his address to the Republican convention in 1940 he underlined that totalitarianism was not a cause but an effect. Pointing to European experience, he said:

In every single case before the rise of totalitarian governments there had been *a period dominated by economic planners* . . . [italics mine]. They exalted the State as the solvent of all economic problems. These men thought they were liberals. But they also thought they could have economic dictatorship by bureaucracy and at the same time preserve free speech, orderly justice and free government. They might be called the totalitarian liberals. They were the spiritual fathers of the New Deal.

At another time he said:

Regulation to prevent abuse has been stretched into instruments of dictation. The policeman on the streets of commerce to expedite the traffic, to keep order and stop robbery, now orders our destination and tells us what to do when we get there. . . . The forces of Planned Economy involve constantly increasing delegation of discretionary power to officials. They involve constantly greater centralization of government. They involve conflicts with the Constitution. They involve minimizing the independence of the Judiciary. Certainly there is a gigantic shift of government from the function of umpire to the function of directing, dictating, and competing in our economic life. We have had nearly five years' experience with these ideas. They were put forward only for an emergency. And yet every session of Congress faces demands for more and more.

By 1936 relief scandals, evidence of manipulation of projects for vote-getting, exploitation of distress by a swollen bureaucracy to enhance its own power, were matters of common knowledge.

Charges of extravagance and corruption had become almost routine under federalized relief. Hoover often cited examples of the waste inherent in the new system:

Recently I had the opportunity to observe comparative morals in the spoils system by a contrast between Tammany Hall and the New Deal. In a Tammany-dominated borough in New York in early 1933, before the New Deal, there were about 11,000 persons on relief. Tammany had appointed about 270 additional officials under their particular spoils system to manage relief at a cost of $30,000 a month for the officials. This job was taken away from wicked Tammany influence and directly administered by the New Deal.

At a recent date there were in the same borough 2000 federal officials appointed under the New Deal spoils system at a cost of $300,000 per month for salaries to manage 16,000 persons on relief. Tammany may learn something new in this spoils system. It was only 10 percent efficient. And the same thing is going on all over the country.

For further concrete exemplification, Hoover turned to figures provided by the New York *Times* with respect to the Resettlement Administration. That agency, the newspaper claimed, employed 12,089 federal officials and was giving relief to 5012 persons or families. The monthly cost for officials was $1,750,000 and the relief cost $300,000. Each family, in other words, enjoyed $350 worth of official supervision with its $60 of relief!

To conceal this profligacy, the ex-President repeatedly charged, the Roosevelt administration was resorting to fiscal legerdemain of a type he denounced as shockingly immoral—in effect "government by deception":

The New Deal quickly introduced an entirely new system of double book-keeping. "Emergency" or "recovery and relief" expenditures on one side were separated from "general" or "ordinary" or "routine" expenditures on the other. Such double bookkeeping never has been used for honest purposes by government. Its very motive is intellectual dishonesty. That is pernicious deceit. . . . You may be surprised to know that a large part of the burden the people have willingly assumed *for relief* during the past four years was used in hundreds of millions of reckless increase of ordinary routine expenses of government.

The high cost of relief and other government functions in billions, however, seemed to Hoover less important than its high cost in political ethics:

It is not by violation of the Constitution that they are making headway today. It is through taking vast sums of the people's money and then manipulating its spending to build up personal power. By this route relief has been centralized in their hands. . . . In this way a score of new instruments of public power have been created. . . . Public funds are used right and left to subsidize special groups of our citizens and special regions of the country. At public expense there is a steady drip of propaganda to poison the public mind. . . . There can be no device by which the people can escape paying for this spending.

More on the new morals:

The most dangerous invasions of liberty by the New Deal have not been in the economic field, violent as they are. The Supreme Court can check that. The corruption of clear thinking is in the long view far more insidious and destructive to the safeguards of America. . . . The New Deal has developed a new technique in debate. They set up a glorious ideal to which we all agree unanimously. Then they go somewhere else or into the ditch. When we protest they blackguard us for opposing the glorious ideal. And they announce that the protestors are all tools of Satan or Wall Street. . . . Some of the rugged prima donnas who have directed these policies have resigned and said worse things than I would say.

The Administration's attempt to "pack" the Supreme Court naturally drew Hoover's fire—and for once he was on the side of the majority opinion even in the New Deal Congress:

The Supreme Court has proved many of the New Deal proposals unconstitutional. Instead of the ample alternatives of the Constitution by which these proposals could be submitted to the people through constitutional amendment, it is now proposed to make changes by "packing" the Supreme Court. It has the implication of subordination of the court to the personal power of the Executive. Because all this reaches to the very depth of our form of government, it far transcends any questions of partisanship.

The Republican convention, in 1940, heard but scarcely heeded another Hoover demand for firmed-up principle:

The crisis in America is not to be obscured by any events abroad. We have witnessed a steady sapping of our system of liberty and the mismanagement of government for the last seven years. During all this time we have had ten million chronically unemployed, eighteen million of our fellow Americans have been continually on relief. Agriculture has been held afloat by government subsidies. Unending deficits and huge increases in debt threaten the financial stability of the government. Our industry and business are hesitant and afraid. In this decade, we have actually decreased in national income and national wealth for the first time in 150 years. America has gone backward. The human consequence is that one-third of our people are frozen to poverty. . . .

Unemployment is not a chronic disease of a free system. It is a disease of governmental interference with that system. These jobs can be restored alone by the restoration of the vitality of free enterprise. . . . I am not interested in free enterprise because it is a property system. I am interested in it because intellectual and spiritual liberty can best be sustained by economic liberty. They are indissolubly bound in a common fate. I am interested in free enterprise because it is the one dynamic force by which we can restore productive jobs to the people. . . . Is this nation to be a great eleemosynary institution? We cannot exist two-thirds workers and one-third dependents.

Hoover, of course, did not condemn the New Deal innovations wholesale. He hardly could, since he had himself initiated many of them. In his *Memoirs* he devoted a chapter to "Some Good Actions" of the Administration:

The New Deal has brought into being a number of long needed reforms and some constructive actions. Some were completion of efforts started in the previous administration, and many were possible only because the President and the Congress were of the same party. However, the patterns and principles set up often defeated the full measure of these reforms.

Evidently he made a generous effort to give as long a list of the "good actions" as he could, but it proved pretty skimpy despite padding. His conscience forced him in almost every case to criticize the methods used even for worthwhile purposes and the distortions due to bureaucratic implementation.

Despite his vigorous strictures on the course of affairs, Herbert Hoover did not embrace despair:

Our failures give no ground for defeatism. So long as the soul of a people holds, with its hopes, its courage, its aspirations, and its ideals, then the Spirit of America will live. And it lives in every cottage fireside.

I am all too conscious that a disordered collection of quotations out of context is not always just to the man quoted. Hoover's analytical criticism of the New Deal, during six years, had organization and logical structure. Moreover, it was not as negative as my selections in this chapter might suggest; it was always accompanied by positive recommendations and it was given coherence by the framework of his lifelong philosophy. His guiding purpose was constructive: to summon his countrymen to restore and defend those rock-bottom political and economic principles which had made the nation great.

XXIX

Another World War

FOR the first time since he had departed from Europe in a blaze of personal glory nineteen years before, Herbert Hoover returned to that continent early in 1938.

The precipitous decline of his popularity at home had no effect on his shining reputation overseas. In Europe he was still the best-known and perhaps the most admired American. Year after year, he had declined dozens of invitations from governments, universities, scientific and philanthropic bodies eager to extend their hospitality and homage. Finally he decided to make the trip.

A "sentimental journey," he called it, and that it was in large measure. His visits to fourteen countries—among them Belgium, France, Austria, Czechoslovakia, Germany, Poland, and Finland—were for him replete with memories of stirring battles against famine and plague. But his overriding purpose went far beyond sentiment. It was a desire to assay the piled-up political and ideological conflicts that clearly held the threat of a terrible war. Hoover discussed local and world affairs with about a hundred leaders whose friendship he had enjoyed in the past, and with as many more whom he now met for the first time—including twenty-two Presidents, Kings, and Prime Ministers, fifteen Foreign Ministers, many Cabinet officers, industrial captains, labor leaders, professors, and journalists.

Everywhere except in Nazi Germany, Hoover's arrival drew popular and press ovations, over and above the official receptions and eulogies. He was loaded with doctorates and medals from leading universities, illumined "addresses" from distinguished societies. Streets were named for him in Brussels, Lille, Prague, and Valenciennes. Even an asteroid, newly discovered by the Brussels Observatory, was named "Herberta" in his honor, only to have the name annulled by an International Astronomical

Union ruling that asteroids must be named for Greek gods. This was the second time he failed to make the grade of Greek godhood; nearly a generation earlier a new asteroid christened "Hoovera" by European astronomers was similarly canceled out by the International Union. So, Hoover remarked dryly, "I lost two planets and had to move off of Olympus."

At a large welcome-home gathering in San Francisco on April 8, 1938, Hoover expressed appreciation of the warmth of his reception in Europe. He called it "a unique hospitality which seldom comes to men," expressed in "great demonstrations of affection and respect for America":

> No American can remain unmoved when tens of thousands of school children line the streets with their cheerful yells of "Long live America!" with the frantic waving of thousands of American flags. No American can remain unmoved when tens of thousands of the common people gather in city squares and remove their hats to the American National Anthem.

His meeting with Adolph Hitler, understandably, was the one that provoked most press excitement back home. Actually Germany had not been on the planned itinerary, except as a railway stopover in Berlin. But the American Ambassador, Hugh R. Wilson, informed Hoover at the station that the Führer wished to see him and urged that he accede to the request. The ambassador, having arrived at the Berlin post only recently, was delighted by his own opportunity to meet Hitler for the first time.

The meeting took place on March 8. Although scheduled as merely a brief courtesy visit, the Führer prolonged it to nearly an hour. In a *Collier's* article many years later, adapted from notes made the same day in Berlin, Hoover said that the Nazi dictator "was forceful, highly intelligent, had a remarkable and accurate memory, a wide range of information and a capacity for lucid exposition." All of which, he indicated, was contrary to his "preconceptions based on books which tried to make him out a dummy."

In discussing most subjects, Hitler seemed entirely rational and self-controlled, but, Hoover wrote, he had "trigger spots in his mind which, when touched, set him off like a man in furious anger." One of these, of course, was Communism. Another fury button was democracy, which Hoover defended with quiet vigor. He did not know then "that Hitler had already determined upon his barbarous invasion of Austria four days later," the ex-President wrote. "He certainly did not confide in me."

A considerably exaggerated version of the argument on democracy reached the American press. Nazi officials thereupon pressed the visitor to issue a denial or, at least, to say a cordial word about Hitler. Hoover withheld all comment. When the University of Berlin offered to confer a degree, he politely declined the honor.

The following day Hoover, again accompanied by the American Ambassador, called on the number two Nazi, Hermann Goering, at his urgent invitation. The scene was Karin Hall, the Nazi leader's fabulous residence-*cum*-museum outside Berlin. This so-called hunting lodge would have humbled the wildest Hollywood imagination, with its outsize splendors, medieval costumes, gaudy trumpeters, and vast art treasures.

Among other things, in talking to the best-informed men in Europe, Hoover sought information on the origins of the depression in their countries. Views differed but not one of these men, Hoover could report, thought that the United States was to blame, as was still being charged by his detractors. "There has been general recovery in Europe from that depression," he told his San Francisco audience. "In the democracies there is no unemployment. They are indeed prosperous. France is, of course, having trouble because she adopted the New Deal two years ago." He was referring to Léon Blum's Popular Front government.

Hoover returned to New York on March 19. In a newsreel interview ten days later he stated his conviction that American policy should be one of "inflexible determination to keep out of other people's wars and Europe's age-old quarrels." He had, probably knowingly, struck the keynote of his consistent campaign, from then until Pearl Harbor, to keep his country out of war.

In several speeches, he summed up the impressions he had gleaned in his "sentimental journey." His condemnation of Nazism, of course, was unqualified. Germany's material accomplishments were considerable: reborn military might, nearly full employment, a degree of security for the masses. But none of this, he cautioned, should influence "a lover of human liberty." The democracies, except France and the United States, had made even larger and certainly sounder economic progress. "The darkest picture" in Germany, he said, is presented "in the heart-breaking persecution of helpless Jews." The inevitable results of the system were "intellectual sterility and deadened initiative and individuality."

His over-all conclusion was that America must remain supremely strong, and clear-headed enough to help the free peoples without becoming embroiled in wars. We must maintain, he said, "absolute independence of political action." We must "cooperate in every sane international effort to advance the economic and social welfare of the world," while concentrating on making the Western Hemisphere invulnerable—the "Fortress America" concept that was to bring him, deservedly in the opinion of most military experts, a continuing hail of brickbats.

Hoover had found in Europe, as of the spring of 1938, "an alarming and disheartening picture." Yet he denied that a general war was imminent. Later he, too, went along with the peace-in-our-time position brought back by Chamberlain from Munich. To recall the climate of the time, it should be noted that President Roosevelt received a thank-you letter from King George VI of England for his role in making the Munich settlement possible. "War is today more remote," Hoover said after the Munich appeasement. But if it comes, he repeated, the United States should remain on the sidelines: "We can make war but we do not and cannot make peace in Europe." As late as February 1939, though conceding that the dangers had increased, he insisted that war was not close.

Germany invaded Poland on September 1. Along with most Americans, Hoover had been too optimistic.

2

As one country after another was conquered by the Nazis and then the Fascists, it again turned as a matter of course to Hoover for help. Each of them appealed to him to organize emergency feeding of hungry and destitute civilians. He shouldered the responsibility and carried it, despite heartbreaking opposition and frustration, through all the cruel years of conflict.

Better than most Americans, Hoover knew what war could do to beleaguered populations. As President he had sought, without success, to obtain international agreements to provide safe passage in time of war for ships carrying only food cargoes. Less than two months before Hitler launched the war, Hoover, addressing a convention of Christian Endeavor Societies, again urged that nations extend to food transport the immunities normally granted to hospital ships.

But war came and belligerents were again treating food as a strategic weapon. Compassion seemed even more alien to this ideological war than it had been a generation earlier. This time Hoover was, in general, unsuccessful in breaking through obstructions to feed the starving. Once more the United States was formally neutral and emotionally aligned with England and her allies. But where the Wilson administration had used its great influence to facilitate the relief of Belgium and northern France, the Roosevelt administration remained adamantly opposed to an equivalent effort.

Within weeks after the Hitler-Stalin invasion of Poland, Hoover, at the request of its government-in-exile, established the Polish Relief Commission. Most of the necessary funds were raised by the exile regime itself. The Germans, with an eye to American public opinion, guaranteed non-interference with relief work and the British, at this stage, allowed relief ships through its blockade. Some three hundred thousand children in the German-occupied part of Poland were thus supplied. When Britain rescinded its cooperation, the American organization managed to buy enough food in the Baltic and Balkan countries to continue the child-feeding. But with the German drive to the east in June 1941, all sources of supply were closed and Polish children were left to the ravages of malnutrition.

After the Soviet attack on Finland, Hoover responded to a call by its government to set up a Finnish Relief Fund. He was able to raise about four million dollars and sent food, medicines, and other supplies to the doughty little country.

Then, when the Nazis invaded western Europe, in May and June of 1940, the whole picture changed. One after another, Belgium, Holland, and Norway were overrun. Their governments-in-exile, each in turn, appealed to Hoover to revive the measures of succor he had used in World War I. Humanitarian bodies inside the countries joined in the appeal.

With the help of friends, many of them veterans of the earlier life-saving efforts, Hoover created a National Committee on Food for Small Democracies. Its membership of about fourteen hundred included five hundred religious leaders, hundreds of publishers, editors, and writers, hundreds of prominent Americans of the stature of General Pershing, former Vice President Dawes, Theodore Roosevelt, Jr., and Admiral William V. Pratt, who had dealt with blockade problems in the First World War. The Committee's mantle of dedication was stretched also to cover Finland, where distress continued, and Poland. In all, the survival of at least thirty-seven million people was at stake.

The Committee needed the leverage of its large and impressive roster of supporters not primarily to raise money—most of the nations involved still had funds on deposit in neutral countries—but to overcome the opposition of the British and American governments. What came to be called the Hoover Plan was modeled on the Belgian Relief Commission of 1914. It required, that is to say, the cooperation of the belligerents—Germany to permit distribution of food under neutral auspices, while pledging not to requisition native food; Britain to open its blockade to relief ships.

Again, as in the past, Hoover sent experts into the occupied countries to ascertain the needs, while he negotiated with the belligerents. By February 1941, what was thought to be the biggest hurdle had been taken—the Germans agreed to allow neutral relief and to keep hands off local crops. But this time it was the British who proved inflexible. Only official American pressure, of the kind that President Wilson had brought to bear, might have budged the British from their rooted position. But Washington, itself soon deeply committed to the war effort in everything but name, simply followed London's policies on denial of relief to the people in occupied areas.

Hoover and many of his eminent colleagues took their case to the American people. By radio and in the press, they implored the country to give the benefit of the doubt to the cause of humanity. Resolutions backing the Hoover Plan were endorsed by a majority of the Senate and a substantial part of the House. Some six thousand churches and public bodies, representing an estimated twenty million Americans, petitioned the government to relent.

Every expression of mercy, however, was brushed aside by Roosevelt's State Department. Hoover then proposed a modest "pilot plant" experiment in Belgium only, limited to providing one meal a day to a million adults and two million children through public soup kitchens; if it proved successful, this restricted and readily inspected type of relief could then be extended on a larger scale to Holland and Norway. Even this compromise was rejected.

The Committee did not hesitate to lay the blame for the spreading hunger and disease in the small democracies at the doorstep of the American Government. "Can you believe," Hoover said to his countrymen, "that American public opinion or the spiritual leadership of America has so lost its bearings as to be opposed even to an effort to help those who lie in the ditch?" The answer was Yes, decidedly. But his Committee never gave up. It succeeded in getting some food into the stricken countries through the Red Cross, church organizations, and other such groups. Also, it organized large-scale delivery of American food packages to Allied prisoners-of-war.

Said Hoover in Poughkeepsie, N.Y., toward the end of 1940:

There are things in the world that are not silenced by ideological argument or armchair strategists or declamations as to who is responsible. They are not settled that way because of the teachings of Christ which have resounded down these two thousand years. . . . The greatest Teacher of mankind did not argue and debate over the ideology and the sins of the two thieves. And He thundered scorn at the priest and the Levite who passed by.

Meanwhile more countries fell to the Nazis and their Fascist allies. The toll of misery and death among civilian victims kept growing. Suffering was particularly acute in Greece. In June 1942 the Turkish government insisted on sending in food. The British and American governments regularized this Greek relief, since they could not stop the Turks in any case, by placing it under Swedish, Swiss, and Red Cross supervision. The State Department in due time formally acknowledged that the arrangement was working—that neither native food nor the relief shipments were being diverted to German uses. This amounted to a belated admission that the Hoover Plan would have worked, yet the barriers against systematic relief for Belgium and the other small democracies were not removed.

The former President took it hard. All the lofty rhetoric of democracy and freedom seemed to him clouded by the freezing of hearts against hungry little children. With America's entry into the war, Hoover stopped his campaign against intervention. But he did not stop his crusade for compassion.

3

Between the outbreak of World War II in September 1939 and Pearl Harbor on December 7, 1941, a great debate on the issue of actively joining the war agitated America. It was never resolved by the people or their Congress, being settled by the bombs that fell on Pearl Harbor. Immediately Herbert Hoover, like thousands of others resolutely opposed to intervention in the world struggle, announced that the debate was closed. We were at war and must unite for victory.

While the debate was in progress, emotions ran high on both sides. Among the most forthright and articulate opponents of direct participation in the war was the former President. Even in the sharply reduced state of his personal prestige, he still exercised a substantial influence on public opinion. Only the lunatic fringe of pro-war hysterics dared dismiss his logic with smear words, or confused his reasoned, patriotic position with that of Communists chanting "The Yanks aren't coming!" or with Nazi-oriented Americans.

No one in his right mind doubted that Hoover's sympathies were with the democratic belligerents. But he held that America should limit its role to producing the sinews of victory; that a diversion of our manpower to military action and of our industrial capacity to equipping our own forces would prolong the war. Most important, he believed that if America remained technically neutral, with its military and economic power at the peak, it could be decisive in promoting a just and durable peace when the war ended.

At the Republican National Convention in Philadelphia on June 25, 1940, Hoover declared:

The immense task now is to shape our foreign policies to protect us from the conflagration in Europe and Asia. . . . The most vital realism in our relations with the world today requires that we keep out of wars unless the Western Hemisphere is attacked.

These sentiments hardly startled the delegates; these were the views of the overwhelming majority of the American people. At the Democratic convention, too, similar sentiments were voiced and endorsed. Both party platforms promised to keep the country out of the war, while generating the tools of victory for the democracies.

During the campaign, Roosevelt was no less emphatic than the Republican candidate, Wendell Willkie, in his no-war pledges. "We will not participate in foreign wars and will not send our Army, Navy or air forces to fight in foreign lands outside the Americas," the President promised "again and again and again." On one occasion he said:

And while I am talking to you mothers and fathers, I give you one more assurance. I have said this before and I shall say it again and again: Your boys are not going to be sent into any foreign wars.

The principal difference between the President and the ex-President, on this issue, was that Hoover's sincerity was beyond question whereas serious doubts existed whether Roosevelt meant what he was promising. A number of historians, and not all "Roosevelt haters," have since then concluded that the doubts were justified; that by late 1940 Roosevelt had already decided to draw the country into the conflict.

One of them, Professor Thomas A. Bailey, would write in *The Man on the Street:* "Roosevelt repeatedly deceived the American people in the period before Pearl Harbor." This judgment he made not in derogation but in admiration of the President's courageous statesmanship. He considered the deception necessary, because Roosevelt would have been defeated had the voters known his real intentions. A younger historian, Arthur M. Schlesinger, Jr., would then cite Bailey approvingly: "If he [Roosevelt] was going to induce the people to move at all, Professor Bailey concludes, he had no choice but to trick them into acting for what he conceived to be their best interests."

In the time of the hot debate the term "warmonger" applied to interventionists packed, if anything, more opprobrium than the term "isolationist" applied to non-interventionists. However, the decision was won by the "warmongers," after which only isolationism retained its sting of insult. It was added to the long list of sins imputed to the former President. And it was, in truth, as false as most of the rest of the vocabulary of abuse employed against him. Hoover had always been classed among the "internationalists," in the sense that he was keenly aware of the interdependence of the current world.

From the outset Hoover supported the idea of turning the United States into the "arsenal of democracy." He went as far, and in some respects farther, than many of the loud interventionists in demanding stepped-up production and expanded shipping to keep the democracies maximally supplied. Among other things, he proposed that a Munitions Administration be created in Washington at once in the interests of increased output. Remembering the "snafus" and inefficiency in World

War I, he urged a single Administrator, not a politician but an industrialist, armed with adequate authority.

Rightly or wrongly, Hoover believed that America, if it avoided entry into the war, would hold the key to a democratic peace. If embroiled in the conflict, he warned, "far from standing on the side of liberty, we should be standing on the side of communism. . . . I am convinced that if Americans stay out of European wars it will best serve the world. It will serve liberty itself." And he denied that this view was "isolationist." The American "arsenal," he insisted, must not be turned into a device for involving the country in the war. "Our greatest service to civilization," he wrote (*Saturday Evening Post,* October 27, 1939), "is to put our own house in order and maintain true liberty upon this continent. For it may be that otherwise liberty will sink for centuries in the night of despair."

The Communist element in the equation of Europe always figured in Hoover's calculations. Some months after the invasion of Poland by both Germany and Russia, he pointed with distress to a "contradiction" in Administration pronouncements: while they "tilted at the windmills of lawless and obnoxious ideologies" in Fascism and Nazism, they had "studiously overlooked communism until the Hitler-Nazi Pact." He also drew attention to the fact that Roosevelt, in the 1940 campaign, often denounced Hitler but failed to include Stalin in the indictment. If our purpose is to "clean up noxious ideologies," Hoover said, Red Russia cannot and must not be omitted from that category.

He protested against the sort of hysteria which might preclude a rational policy. He was referring to statements such as the President's that "We are next on Hitler's list." One congressman exclaimed that "we may be attacked within hours, perhaps in a few days." Another rose to say: "Hitler may be coming any moment."

Hoover summed up his program tersely on October 31, 1940:

Furnish all the support to England that we can within the law. . . . Stop cultivating hysteria at home and sticking pins in the tiger abroad. . . . Make one more talk and stop talking. . . . That one talk should make clear that we're arming to the teeth, organizing our economic strength to the limit, and that we shall use our power to demand a just peace.

4

The most potent argument for intervention was that England was in imminent danger of invasion and conquest. But Hoover was convinced that England could not be beaten. "I do not believe—and most of our military authorities do not believe—that the British are going to be defeated in their heroic defense," he said on October 31, 1940. Britain would come through safely, he insisted, "especially . . . if our industry furnishes them with all the guns and planes it is capable of producing."

The propaganda of the war party misrepresented this conviction to make it look heinous. There were know-nothing zealots who called it "pro-Nazi." Yet we find the Secretary of State at the time, Cordell Hull, attesting in his reminiscences: "The President and I believe that Britain could and would resist the Nazi attack successfully. . . ." Alluding to the fear of a British defeat, Hull stated that "neither Lothian [the British ambassador] nor I contemplated this at all."

In any event, when the Nazis invaded Russia on June 22, 1941, the argument was washed out. With the major German forces pinned down in the East, any immediate threat to the survival of Britain was removed. Confidence in British victory was raised to a certainty. There seemed less reason, therefore, for our military involvement. Moreover, as far as Hoover was concerned, the purely ideological aspect of the struggle ceased to have any reality. He refused to credit the absurdity that Hitler, by violating his deal with Stalin, had magically converted the Soviet despotism into a "freedom-loving democracy."

As early as February 1941, the American Government was aware of the Nazi deployments for an attack on Soviet Russia. The knowledge was kept from the American people, Hoover surmised, because it would weaken the argument of England's great peril. Secretary Hull informed him, in a friendly meeting on February 20, that Hitler had concentrated 1,500,000 troops on his eastern frontiers and at least 300,000 more on the Hungarian border. In that case, Hoover remarked, Britain was safe. The course of wisdom, he told the Secretary, was for the United States to desist from further warlike provocations *and wait for the Great Dictators to destroy each other.*

The former President was scarcely alone in this deduction. Harry S. Truman, then a senator, said publicly the day after the invasion of Russia: "If we see that Germany is winning we ought to help Russia and if Russia is winning we ought to help Germany. . . ." The other Democratic senator from Missouri, Bennett Champ Clark, said that same day:

It's a case of dog eat dog. Stalin is as bloody-handed as Hitler. I don't think we should help either one. . . . If the United States should accept Josef Stalin as a virtual ally we can do no less than take communism to our bosom and release Earl Browder from the penitentiary and make him an honored guest at the White House. [Browder *was* released; though not invited to the White House, he kept in intimate touch with President Roosevelt through intermediaries.]

Possibly the most perceptive observation was made that day by Senator LaFollette, Jr., who forecast:

In the next few weeks the American people will witness the greatest white-wash act in all history. They will be told to forget the purges in Russia by the OGPU, the persecution of religion, the confiscation of property, the invasion of Finland and the vulture role Stalin played in seizing half of Poland, all of Latvia, Estonia and Lithuania. These will be made to seem the acts of a "democracy" preparing to fight Nazism.

President Roosevelt felt no call to consistency by such points of view. During the aggression against Finland he had denounced Soviet Russia as a dictatorship no better than Germany's. Now he embraced Stalin forthwith and unconditionally, assuring unlimited lend-lease aid with no strings attached. Hoover was so distressed by the new situation that he bought radio time for a nationwide broadcast. He said:

In the last seven days, that call to sacrifice American boys for an ideal has been made as a sounding brass and a tinkling cymbal. For now we find ourselves promising aid to Stalin and his militant communist conspiracy against the whole democratic ideals of the world. Collaboration between Britain and Russia will bring them military values, but it makes the whole argument of our joining the war to bring the four freedoms to mankind a gargantuan joke.

He recalled the partnership between the two tyrants; how Soviet Russia destroyed the freedoms of an array of democracies; how it unleashed an unprovoked attack on Finland, adding:

Stalin has taken advantage of the very freedoms of democracy to destroy them with the most potent Fifth Column in all history. He contributed to the destruction of France. He has daily implanted class hate in America and a stealthy war against our institutions. In these last weeks it is declared not only by public officials but by labor leaders themselves that the strikes which hamstring the defense of the United States have been communist conspiracies. Thus Russia has continued her mission of destroying our democracy down to the last week. . . .

If we go further and join the war and we win, then we have won for Stalin the grip of communism on Russia and more opportunity for it to extend in the world [italics mine]. We should at least cease to tell our sons that they would be giving their lives to restore democracy in the world. . . . These two dictators, Stalin and Hitler, are in deadly combat. One of the two hideous ideologists will disappear in this fratricidal war. In any event, both will be weakened. Statesmanship demands that the United States stand aside in watchful waiting, armed to the teeth, while these men exhaust themselves. Then the most powerful nation in the world can talk with mankind with a voice that will be heard. . . . To align American ideals alongside Stalin will be as great a violation of everything American as to align ourselves with Hitler.

At the very least, Hoover insisted publicly, as American guns and planes began to move toward Russia, we should demand that Stalin give ironclad guarantees, in the event of victory, to restore freedom to the countries he had crushed as Hitler's partner in crime. He made this point in a private letter to Secretary of War Stimson on July 30:

We should make agreements with him [Stalin] now to restore the independence of these many despoiled peoples as a condition of our assistance. . . . I fear the administration will not approach this situation in the light of grim reality but in the glow of our left-wing lamps.

The great whitewash of Soviet Russia and its blood-soaked tyrant prophesied by LaFollette quickly came to pass. Never before had the power of concentrated propaganda been so dramatically demonstrated. Within months a miracle of amnesia was induced, so that the black crimes of Communism were forgotten. Before long it called for courage openly to mention Stalin's hideous blood-lettings at home and aggressions abroad, or to question his devotion to "peace," or to doubt the Kremlin's good faith. These are some of the things Hoover dared to do.

The ex-President, moreover, felt deeply the need to block the spread of the war to the Far East. He was certain in his own mind—on the basis of intimate information from Administration sources—that Japan was eager to avoid conflict with America and that almost to the last moment an amicable settlement was possible. Ten days before Pearl Harbor, Secretary Stimson wrote in his diary that Roosevelt had told him that it was American policy to maneuver Japan into attacking us. Had he been looking over his shoulder, this startling information would not have surprised Hoover.

A war with Japan, by siphoning American industrial and naval might from the Atlantic to the Pacific, seemed to him a risky weakening of the British potential. This view was shared by many British war leaders. They feared that extension of the war to the Pacific could postpone victory for years and that, win or lose, it would strip England of her Pacific empire.

5

In the ninetieth year of his life—surely a commentary on his amazing intellectual vitality—Hoover was at work on a three-volume history of Soviet-American relations, tentatively titled *Freedom Betrayed*. I was privileged to read his manuscript of the first two volumes. In form, I found, they were more "documentaries" than conventional books. He let documents and quotations tell their own story with a minimum of his own comment.

Necessarily the work deals chiefly with the origins of the war, its political content, the ambiguous peace, and the cold war that followed. Hoover had been collecting these materials ever since he left the White House. Some of them had not been available to the general public; the implications of others would have been hard for the uninitiated to grasp in any case. During the war many disturbed high officials came to Hoover secretly to report in confidence what was occurring and to seek his advice.

It is useful to remember, in order to understand Hoover's relation to the war, that this massive knowledge was in his files and in his mind as events unfolded. He was able to see far beneath the surface of official claims and postures. What he saw and pondered convinced him: (1) That though President Roosevelt had encouraged and applauded the Munich appeasement, he was from the start of hostilities determined to bring the United States into the war. (2) That this country was neck-deep in the war *de facto* long before Pearl Harbor made it *de jure*. (3) That a commitment to draw the United States into the war was made to Churchill early in the game. (4) That Roosevelt's principal problem was his certainty that Congress, reflecting popular sentiment, would not declare war short of some major overt action by the enemy. (5) That a peaceable settlement with Japan was possible to the last, had the will to make it existed in Washington.

Some of these conclusions have been confirmed by time, through revelations by many of the main actors in the great drama and the unfreezing of confidential records. Others are still the object of dispute among scholars and journalists. These, in any event, are the things a closely informed ex-President believed. They help explain not only the vehemence of his campaign against intervention but some of its elements. Running through all his writings and speeches at the time, for example, is the warning that the American people should not permit their Congress to be bypassed in the peace-or-war decision.

Central in Hoover's thinking was the belief that a triumph of American arms could not bring true peace or enlarge the area of genuine democracy. A victory, if we joined the war, would only shift the center of gravity of totalitarianism from Berlin to Moscow. The mere avoidance of an alliance with Communism, he argued, would enhance our moral leverage in the postwar settlements. These opinions he expressed explicitly and forcefully as long as we were technically neutral.

Roosevelt said of Stalin at the end of 1943, after the Teheran Conference: "I believe he is truly representative of the heart and soul of Russia; and I believe that we are going to get along very well with him and the Russian people—very well indeed." A few months later he added that the Russians "haven't got any ideas of conquest." On the trip home from Yalta, according to the notes of Harry Hopkins, Roosevelt appeared convinced "that the United States and the Soviet Union could work together in peace as they had in war," and spoke often of his "respect and admiration . . . for Marshal Stalin."

This extraordinary misjudgment of the dictator worried Hoover throughout the war years because of its possible effects on the postwar settlements. Eventually even his henchman and successor, Nikita Khrushchev, denounced Stalin as a faithless criminal.

Surely no one can survey the present world—with half of Europe, all of mainland China, and other portions of the globe in totalitarian bondage; with the nightmare of a nuclear Third World War obsessing men's thoughts everywhere; with the ideals set up in the Atlantic Charter and in wartime propaganda trampled underfoot—no one can see these tragedies and not feel an inner nudge of doubt about the wisdom of America's intervention. Suppose Japan's minimum condition for peace—presumably continued mastery in Manchuria—had been accepted. Suppose that the total American industrial potential had been thrown into the scales in the European war. Suppose the war had been won under those conditions. Could the world picture conceivably have been any uglier, any more menacing, than it is today?

If there is any merit in honesty and courage, therefore, Hoover must be credited with both. Certainly all the pressures were on the side of conformity with the official line.

Consider his personal position on the eve of Pearl Harbor. For more than a decade Hoover had been so persistently maligned, so expertly misrepresented and lampooned, that a further decline in his personal stock seemed impossible. But the impossible did occur: his stock reached a new low. Hoover was indifferent to prevailing intellectual fashions. In this there was no snobbishness, no nose-thumbing defiance. He was no more capable of improvising or trimming opinions to shock herd prejudices than to flatter them. In his moral makeup there was no trace of the perverse or paradoxical. Right or wrong, his views flowed from the depths of his nature; they were integral with his philosophy of life. But had he chosen perversely to make himself the focus of the major irritations of the moment, he could scarcely have done better.

With war fevers mounting, he remained stanchly opposed not only to military intervention but to those measures "short of war" which made military involvement unavoidable. With the Administration reaping credit for the first signs of wartime prosperity, he continued to denounce New Deal methods. A new tolerance of Soviet Russia was sweeping the country, but Hoover felt it necessary to underscore the totalitarian antidemocratic essence of the Kremlin regime. Contrary to the most clamorous of the competing public opinions of the time, he was demanding that America feed the starving in Hitler-held countries.

As a bid for unpopularity, his stance was a masterpiece. He seemed on the "wrong" side of so many issues and wrongheaded in proclaiming the fact. At that low ebb perhaps only a journal specializing in faith and rectitude, I suppose, could have risked the prophecy that Hoover "is now approaching the summit of his career." This is precisely what the *Christian Century* did. It referred, of course, to a moral rather than a political summit. Its editors had been moved by the former President's tireless accent on compassion and charity in a world riven by hatreds. On October 29, 1941, they wrote:

Out of the agony and bitterness of these days one great humanitarian figure is emerging in America. That is Herbert Hoover. . . . This American has moved straight forward, refusing to give up his struggle to carry mercy and pity to the most hopeless victims of the war. . . . We believe that he is only now approaching the summit of his career.

6

Immediately after the attack on Pearl Harbor, the former President released an unambiguous statement:

American soil has been treacherously attacked by Japan. Our decision is clear. It is forced upon us. We must fight with everything we have.

I have opposed the foreign policies of our government. I have believed alternative policies would have been better. But whatever our differences of view may be as to the causes which have led to this situation, those are matters to be threshed out by history. Today there is just one job before the American people. We must defeat this invasion by Japan and we must fight it in any place that will defeat it. Upon this job we must and will have unity in America. We must have and will have full support for the President of the United States in this war to defend America. We will have victory.

It is worth noting that even in the hour of total eclipse of his viewpoint, Hoover did not foreswear what he considered the truth. The debate was suspended, but the differences of view would eventually be "threshed out by history." The time for threshing came with victory and is still under way.

Hoover's statement on the morning after Pearl Harbor was a pledge of unstinting cooperation, offered by a man who had never broken one. His total exclusion from the war effort therefore seemed at the time, and more so as the years passed, petty and ignoble. Thousands of others who had been no less outspoken against intervention before Pearl Harbor were welcomed for active service. Indeed, men and women who had been anti-war not through conviction but simply on orders from a foreign power—who had changed their attitude only when the orders changed, with Hitler's attack on Soviet Russia—were assigned to responsible war jobs. No such forgiveness or trust could be found by the White House for a man with Hoover's record of service to his fellow men.

Many people close to the Commander-in-Chief, among them members of his Cabinet, importuned him to use Hoover's great abilities. The food situation quickly deteriorated; the ration system produced widespread black-marketeering and other corruptions; farm production was choked in a jungle of red tape. Here, at least, was an area where the former President's expertise was universally acknowledged. Besides, if only as a symbol of national unity, the employment of the only living ex-President seemed indispensable.

But whatever the basis of Roosevelt's psychosis on Hoover may have been, it was not affected even by the war. Hoover, nonetheless, did what his conscience dictated. Without official sanction, frequently in the face of official attacks, he persevered in three major activities.

First, he continued his work of relief, through his own Committee for Small Democracies; through cooperation with new groups organized by Americans of Greek, Polish, Scandinavian, and other origins; and through the facilities of the Red Cross, Quaker, and other humane organizations.

Second, in speeches and articles, he systematically analyzed the domestic techniques of food conservation and distribution. He helped to arouse public opinion in this area, specifically by explaining the advantages of cooperation as against coercion, and his influence was credited with obtaining wholesome changes.

Third, he addressed himself vigorously to the problems of the peace to come. It was not too early, Hoover believed, to lay the groundwork for settlements based on justice and democratic freedom. Now, when American aid was so desperately needed, seemed to him the time to exact commitments to justice from Stalin, Churchill, and other leaders.

In collaboration with former Ambassador Hugh Gibson (who was also denied a role in war work), Hoover in 1942 published a book on *The Problems of Lasting Peace*. They wrote:

The purpose of this war, the most terrible in three centuries, is to make a lasting peace. We must first win the war. But we will not win the peace unless we prepare for it. And we can prepare only by a full and free public discussion, by the cold surgery of analysis.

The book was widely acclaimed. "The only intelligent answer to *Mein Kampf!*" one commentator called it. "Indispensable to anybody who hopes to think intelligently about postwar problems," said *Collier's* editorially. A noted Washington journalist, William Philip Simms, declared: "So objective and thorough is this work that what they have produced is nothing less than a state paper and will be so regarded here." He was wrong: although some twenty government agencies were working on blueprints for the future world order, none of them consulted either Hoover or Gibson.

In an address before the Republican National Convention in Chicago on June 27, 1944, broadcast to the public, Hoover said:

It is obvious the American people have but one purpose in this war. We want to live in peace. We do not want these horrors again. We want no territory except some Pacific island bases that will protect the United States. We want no domination over any nation. We want no indemnities. We want no special privileges. *But we do want the freedom of nations from the domination of others, call it by whatever name we will—liberation of peoples, self-government or just restored sovereignty. We want it both in the cause of freedom and we want it because we know that there can be no lasting peace if enslaved peoples must ceaselessly strive and fight for freedom* [italics mine].

The war was still going on when Herbert Hoover suffered the greatest personal blow of his life. On January 7, 1944, his wife died in their apartment at the Waldorf.

Mrs. Hoover and her husband's secretary, Bernice Miller, were at a concert that afternoon. They walked back part of the way. When Mrs. Hoover admitted to a little fatigue, they took a cab and reached home around six-thirty. Lou Henry came to the room where her husband was working, waved to him with a smile, and went to her own room. A bit later, friends having arrived to take him to a public stag dinner, Hoover went to her room to bid her good-bye. He found his wife on the floor unconscious. It was heart failure. She passed away at seven P.M.

Hoover wrote of his incalculable loss in an autobiographical article more than seven years later:

I had lived with the loyalty and tender affection of an indomitable soul almost fifty years. Hers were those qualities which make a real lady: loyalty and gentle consideration for the rights and needs of others, no matter who. And these qualities brought her great loyalty in return.

These loyalties came from, among others, servants over many years and of many nationalities. Their very names make up a League of Nations. Quah and Troi, who stayed with us during the siege of Tientsin when most other servants fled the settlement, and who during their lives afterward never failed to send some trifle and inquiry to her every Chinese New Year. "Lovell the Parlor Maid," "Judith the Cook," "Amy the Nurse," "Player the Chauffeur," and "Jenkins the Gardener," who were fixed parts of the London House—which they kept open for our periodic sojourns for fifteen years.

Abdul the Arab and his multitudinous family in Burma were always inquiring when she would be coming back. In Washington we had the same Negro servants for fourteen years. One of the touching scenes at her funeral was the fact that Ellis and Leon came up from Washington to New York to attend the services. And in California there were Kosta Boris, the Serbian; Mary Gianelli, the Italian; Marie and Frank Franquet, the Belgians; Perry, the gardener, and Lee, the Chinese cook.

With World War I, we had divided our accumulated savings in order to simplify things that might result from her and my dangerous occupations. I knew little—and wanted to know nothing—of her expenditures. But in settling the taxes for her estate, we had to go back over many years of her carefully-kept accounts. And there we learned that she had given away most of her possessions, largely in helping out individuals in trouble or in aiding the education of a multitude of boys and girls.

There were in her files many thousand dollars' worth of checks to her order which she had never cashed. They were all repayments of "loans" which she had turned into gifts by so simple a device as not depositing them in a bank. Not even I knew many of the persons who had been the beneficiaries.

She left the sweetest compliment ever given to men when, in her simple letter of a will addressed to her sons, she wrote: "You have been lucky boys to have had such a father and I am a lucky woman to have had my life's trail alongside the path of three such men and boys."

Ever reticent on personal feelings, Hoover rarely referred to his loss and his undying love for the "great lady." But sometimes those feelings were made manifest indirectly. Dr. Felix Morley, for instance, has told of the time when his daughter was about to be married, in May 1953. A gift package from Hoover arrived before the wedding, the three volumes of his *Memoirs*. The inscription read: "You are about to undertake the greatest adventure of your life. I wish you the same success in married life that came to me."

XXX

The Tide of Slander Recedes

HERBERT HOOVER'S popular prestige, we have seen, declined
again just before and after the United States entered the Second
World War. In a time of universal killing, his unflagging concern
with *saving* lives—even the lives of children in enemy lands—seemed
quixotic and vaguely "unpatriotic" to the unthinking. Casualty lists understandably took precedence over conscience. The fact that he was until
the very last minute opposed to joining the conflict, though ostensibly this
was official policy, continued to be held against him. Nor did his forthright criticism of some aspects of wartime policy, especially in the administration of food resources, sit well with some elements in public opinion.

This kind of generalization, however, can be misleading. For in truth
Hoover was never without an ardent following. At the lowest ebb, there
was still a loyal minority who esteemed his humanism and considered
him unfairly used—and dissident minorities usually make up in emotion
what they lack in numbers. There were the contingents of those whose
trust in the Chief never wilted in any weather, their enthusiasm now
heightened by indignation over his total exclusion from the war effort.
And beyond these were growing ranks of new admirers.

Disillusionment with the New Deal, if nothing else, impelled more
and more people to reappraise Hoover or, more accurately, their feelings
about Hoover. They tended to make amends for past neglect or calumny
with an excess of praise. It was, as one journalist put it, "as though they
had rediscovered rather than remembered him." For those disturbed by
the moral climate of an exuberant, boastful, big-spending political period,
his ethical austerity seemed to shine with a new luster.

Three or four years after the advent of the Roosevelt era, the popular
writer Irvin S. Cobb was addressing a group that included the former
President. "Mr. Hoover," he said, "twice in bygone presidential campaigns

374

I voted against you. The first time was a petty gesture, I being then, as now, a survivor of that well-nigh vanished species known as Old-Line Democrats. The second time was a grievous error which I have since repented in sackcloth and ashes. . . . Merely let me say, sir, that we are grateful because in your occupancy of the White House you never got the idea of burning down the temple in order to destroy a few cockroaches in the basement."

This combination of repentance and a jab at the New Deal was by then quite familiar to Hoover. Nearly every mail brought him letters from complete strangers, expressing contrition for former attitudes. So many of President Roosevelt's associates and public champions turned against him that it almost ceased to be news, and the defectors usually looked to the former President for solace. A new appreciation of Hoover, in fact, was one of the hallmarks of New Deal apostasy.

Much later, Americans would find it possible to admire or reject both Presidents simultaneously. But as yet approval of Roosevelt—certainly as long as he was alive—by definition included disparagement of his predecessor. In people's minds the two men seemed inseparable.

No one, so far as I know, has come up with a wholly satisfying explanation of Roosevelt's animus toward his predecessor, climaxed by the implacable banishment of Hoover from the war effort. The late Fulton Oursler, who was a frequent guest at the White House, told his son Will (who reports it in his recent book, *Family Story*) that "the Roosevelts were bitter about Hoover" and that "it was an unreasoning kind of hatred they felt for him and everything he stood for." What baffles one is precisely that irrational element in the hatred.

The motives could hardly have been ideological. The President found it possible to work in tandem and maintain friendships with men much farther to the right than Hoover. Besides, Roosevelt was never passionate about ideas—he easily switched from one to its opposite as political considerations prompted. Political explanations, such as the one advanced by Raymond Moley, fell short of explaining a hostility far beyond the call of political considerations.

And there seemed little purely personal grounds for the largely one-sided feud. The two men had been friends on the same team in the Wilson administration. Back in 1920, as we have seen, Roosevelt had considered Hoover the best presidential material. No matter how immoderate in attacks on the New Deal, Hoover in general avoided personal slurs on its generalissimo.

There were exceptions, of course. In the heat of the 1940 presidential campaign, after Roosevelt in speech after speech had concentrated his fire on Hoover, the former President struck back. He must raise questions that lay, he said, "in the field of intellectual honesty" and he accused

Roosevelt of a "lively crusade for bigger and better production of falsifications." Considering the volume and acerbity of the years-long attacks on Hoover, this sort of rare retort hardly evened the score.

In any event, the Hoover-Roosevelt syndrome affected the thinking and emotions of millions. The contrast between the two men as human beings, quite aside from their political-economic disagreements, was too striking to be evaded.

Hoover was "no politician," Roosevelt was all politician—this was the most obvious difference. One was an actor and manipulator, the other looked down on both these arts in a public servant. But that was only the beginning of the antitheses. Roosevelt, to the manor born, could not conceal an edge of the patronizing in his belated interest in the Common Man. Hoover was born to poverty, had rubbed shoulders with the lowly, and there was nothing contrived or histrionic about his compassion for all men. On the intellectual level, Roosevelt was the lowbrow who never voluntarily read a serious book, except about ships and navies, which were his hobby. Hoover was avid for scholarly knowledge in all fields and himself the author of thoughtful books. Whether one agreed with him or not, Hoover had a rounded philosophy and traveled by a compass aligned to principle. Roosevelt was a blank slate on which others chalked their ideas, which he tasted, tested, then imbued with his own dynamic spirit—and dropped when they had served his purpose.

We are all prisoners of our prejudices. Yet one finds estimates of the two Presidents by distinctly "progressive" historians, even champions of the New Deal, not too different from my own.

Professor Arthur S. Link, for example, in his *American Epoch*, published in 1955, concludes that the New Deal era marked "the full flowering of the humanitarian-progressive movement." He declares, though, that Roosevelt "often gave the impression of duplicity, because he found it difficult to disagree with a good friend. . . . Toward his enemies, on the other hand, he could appear vain, deceptive and vindictive." (The alibi for the "impression of duplicity" is curious, since Roosevelt made the identical impression on people who were not his "good friends" and with whom he did disagree. Nor was it that he seemed "vain, deceptive and vindictive" to his enemies—often they became his enemies because they discovered these qualities.) Professor Link continues:

Intellectually, Roosevelt was narrow—poorly read, averse to hard, logical thinking, preferring intuition to reason in solving difficult problems. He was not an original thinker, but he had a great capacity for learning and for thinking in broad terms and a willingness to try almost any experiment in order to achieve his goals. In economic matters Roosevelt was almost totally deficient. Ignorant himself on economic theory and history, he was at the mercy of his advisers in formulating policies and often approved inconsistent measures.

376

This Rooseveltian readiness to "try almost any experiment" is more of an indictment than Professor Link realizes. After all, the laboratory was a nation in distress and the guinea-pigs were the American people. Unwittingly the historian gives substance to Hoover's remark that the New Deal method of testing poison was to make the country swallow it.

Of Hoover, Professor Link writes: "In his rigorously honest and orderly mind he probably had contempt for mere politicians, for men who consulted only the popular will. . . . He could command men's respect in times of prosperity but not in times of adversity." (Of course, he did command the love and devotion of multitudes of men in times of almost unprecedented adversity during and after World War I.) Though no *laissez-faire* economist, this historian says, Hoover "opposed all measures, like federal operation of Muscle Shoals, that would diminish private energies or impede private investment or enterprise." Hoover was forced to invoke federal powers, but "he never lost confidence in the inherent soundness of American economic institutions or in the altruism of businessmen and bankers. . . . Hoover was not callous to the suffering of the unemployed; but he insisted that relief was a local problem and that the Federal Government could serve the people best by working through the cities and states."

The strictures, in brief, are not on the man's character but on his policies. Professor Link rejects "the generally accepted theory that Hoover fiddled while the country burned" as pure "mythology." Hoover, he says, "was obviously no old-fashioned conservative, no social Darwinist, willing to allow the depression to run its full course. . . . On the contrary, he was a cautious progressive. . . ."

Link credits Hoover with "saving the capitalist structure" at the price of losing "the confidence of a large majority of the American people." The result was that he "left office . . . despised and rejected as few Presidents have been, his name an article of common sneering and associated with horse-drawn carts and assemblages of human misery." By contrast, Roosevelt "in spite of all his shortcomings . . . won such affection and loyalty from the American people as few Presidents have earned."

In human terms, the surpassing injustice of the popular verdict on Hoover is matched by the surpassing illogic of the popular verdict on Roosevelt. It would take a long time to redress the balance and the process is not yet completed.

What obtrudes is that, except on the lunatic fringes, it occurred to no one to question Hoover's honesty. He was assailed on his economics, the rigidity of his ideas, the validity of his decisions, but he was never charged with "duplicity." Serious historical writers, regardless of their political vantage points, rarely if ever credit Roosevelt with integrity, while the word or its equivalents are invariably attached to Hoover's character.

377

That, in my view, is the heart of the contrast, which seems to me essentially on the moral level. And this, I suspect, may hold the key to the psychological enigma of President Roosevelt's otherwise inexplicable bitterness.

2

One cannot put a date on the time when the tide of public sentiment on Hoover turned. Obviously such changes do not take place overnight. It was a process of thawing. But by the time the first version of this biography was being written, in 1947–48, the ice had broken and rivers of revived or rediscovered good-will for the ex-President were running strong. In the seventy-fourth year of his life and the sixteenth year since he went directly from the White House to the doghouse, Hoover again enjoyed great public prestige and a rapidly growing influence on public affairs. As a matter of course he was suddenly being referred to as our First Citizen and outstanding Elder Statesman.

Fragments of my book having been published in advance in the *Reader's Digest,* resulted in a large number of letters from all parts of the country and from all kinds of people. Nearly all of them offered variants on the same theme: "Thank God the truth about Hoover is coming out at last. . . . About time someone spoke up for a great man and a great American." One felt, reading those letters, that many of his countrymen had a sense of guilt about the ordeal of their thirty-first President. The tone of the press and radio began to turn more and more deferential. Democratic politicians seemed able, at last, to carry on their professional bickering with Republicans without sideswipes at Hoover. Except in the far-Left propaganda, where he remained the reigning demon, slander gave way to respectful disagreement.

A liberal columnist at that time prefaced an attack on certain Hoover proposals with this revealing comment: "I wonder why I stick my neck out in this way, for I realize that Mr. Hoover is one of the three or four elder statesmen before whom we customarily abdicate our function of criticism." Customarily? Decidedly a new custom, though it was catching on fast. Only a year or two earlier, writers of that columnist's political coloration would have felt it necessary to apologize for agreeing with Hoover, not for lambasting him. Dr. Alvin Johnson of the New School for Social Research, a ranking liberal, in an open letter to the ex-President in June 1947 declared:

The place of Hoover in history, a most honored place, is that of the man who extended American neighborliness to the world. . . . I do recognize that among the Americans of my time you have been the greatest, by virtue of your extending the concern of Americans for the whole world.

Trivial in themselves, these and a thousand other expressions and incidents reflected the changing mood of the nation in relation to Hoover. They signalized the fact that he was out of the doghouse. His virtual ostracism from public life, roughly coinciding with the New Deal era, was ended. Let me cite a few bits of symptomatic import:

In May 1947 Hoover attended the Gridiron Club dinner in Washington for the first time since he moved out of the White House. Charles L. Lucey of the Scripps-Howard chain wrote: "It violates no rule to report that his presence here brought him acclaim among today's national leaders such as he has not known in many years. Party leaders on both sides paid him tributes."

In the course of the newspaper publishers' annual convention in New York, some time later, Hoover was the guest of honor at its official dinner. His arrival evoked a thunderous and spontaneous ovation. "So spontaneous," George Sokolsky reported, "that he could not and did not respond to it except in an expression on his face that might have been the struggle to withhold a tear." The publishers gathered in the Waldorf ballroom rose, and cheered and cheered. It was the established custom of the convention dinner to toast only the President of the United States. That night the custom was broken; an ex-President, too, was toasted.

For fifteen years Hoover's birthday had been ignored, or at most, mentioned briefly and grudgingly. But when he reached seventy-two, on August 10, 1946, it was front-page news for many leading newspapers and the occasion for warm and even sentimental editorial tributes across the nation. Running through them all was the same pleased awareness of a wrong being redressed that ran through the letters to the *Reader's Digest*. Again, I had the feeling that America bore an uneasy conscience. Never again was a Hoover birthday allowed to pass without nationwide editorial bouquets.

Republicans increasingly sought his opinions and guidance, on domestic and foreign affairs. And not only Republicans. There was hardly a week during the sessions of Congress when its members, of both parties, did not solicit Hoover's counsel. Individually or in groups they wrote to him or came to consult him at his apartment in New York. A dozen House and Senate committees invited him to give his views on as many issues.

The ex-President, a Washington *Post* special writer reported in 1947, "packs more weight on legislation today than any Republican leader outside Congress." By way of example, he cited the $350,000,000 foreign relief bill that had just been enacted. "It was Hoover's word that saved the President's relief bill from defeat," he showed, and "most of the safeguards written into the bill by the House were Hoover's." An Associated Press dispatch similarly declared that the former President "is emerging as one of the top economic counselors" of that Republican Congress.

How account for the change? The healment worked by time is perhaps the basic answer. In addition, certainly, there was a growing sentiment against the collectivist trends which Hoover had been exposing. The New Deal had lost much of its mystique. In 1946, for the first time in sixteen years, the country elected a Republican Congress.

A Democrat was still President—and in 1948 he would be elected to a full term, though by a paper-thin margin. But Harry S. Truman bore none of the unreasoning personal bitterness of Roosevelt against Hoover. The anti-Hoover vendetta had been interred with its author. A new generation was reaching maturity. True, it had been indoctrinated against Hoover in the schoolrooms and in the press, but its grievances were not as intensely personalized as those of their fathers. It was a generation more open to reason and evidence. And there was another factor: as relations with the Soviets worsened and the Cold War took shape, the country suddenly remembered that Hoover had been among the relatively few who had foreseen it all and been stoned for their prescience.

It soon ceased to be a secret that in his second month in office President Truman invited Hoover to the White House and that their meeting was mutually heartwarming. The two men were worlds apart in experience, mental scope, and grasp of world affairs. But they had in common essential human qualities and a certain guilelessness and it sufficed to make them friends. At the aforementioned Gridiron dinner, Hoover's neighbor on the dais reached over impulsively and inscribed Hoover's speech manuscript: "With regards to a great American." It was signed Harry S. Truman.

Admiral Strauss has recounted, in his memoirs, that he was Hoover's guest at the Bohemian Grove in California when he was summoned by Truman and offered the post of chairman of the newly authorized Atomic Energy Commission. At the White House, Strauss said:

"Mr. President, before attempting to answer, may I ask why you have chosen me? Do you know that I am a black Hoover Republican?"

Truman smiled. Of course, he said, he knew his guest's politics. Then he added, earnestly:

"As for Mr. Hoover—you may not know it, but I hold him in very high regard. I think he is a great American and will someday be so recognized even by the people who have defamed him."

The zooming spiral of the ex-President's revived popularity was accelerated by Truman's action in asking him to make an intensive survey of world food stocks and relief requirements. We shall deal with that in some detail in the next chapter. Suffice that it entailed a globe-girdling journey by air and considerable physical hardship. Less than a year later Hoover, again at the President's request, made a broader study of German, Austrian, and all-European economic conditions.

The very gallantry of such undertakings by an aging man somehow bridged three decades. It helped restore Hoover to his essential historical role as the most effective instrument of America's conscience and humanitarian impulses. Again he became, in the words of *Newsweek*, "the symbol of hope and sympathy for a distracted world." Benevolence, rather than party politics, seemed to be the major sphere of Hoover's genius.

3

It was said then, inevitably, and was repeated endlessly thereafter, that Hoover had made a "comeback." It was not true. He was not a forgotten vaudeville artist once again recognized and getting bookings. Hoover could not come back because he had never gone away. It would be more accurate to say that the country came back, and found Hoover where he had always been, too securely planted in his moral soil to be uprooted by hurricanes of slander. A magazine said it simply at the time: "The essential Hoover has not changed, except to mellow a bit with age."

He would have been less than human if he had not been gratified by the conspicuous reversal of sentiment in the years after the war. Man's hunger for understanding and affection is the most human of our appetites, in which vanity is not necessarily implicated. Besides, as many men have learned the hard way, uninterrupted abuse can become more boring than offensive; it tends to become so repetitive, standardized, banal. None of his detractors had thought of any really new accusations or devised any new sneering adjectives in years.

The increased flow of friendly correspondence; editorials which "thank God that the nation and the world begin to see in him a shelter in time of storm" (the quotation is from a newspaper editorial); the cordiality of Republicans who used to think him "poison"—such things were naturally welcome to Hoover after a steady diet of contumely.

He had a humility that was inborn, Quakerish—a humility that was not proud of itself. It was genuine, and therefore without alloy of mock modesty. He had an engineer's respect for facts—including the obvious facts of his own exceptional abilities. No man could have commanded the colossal jobs he did with the confidence he always brought to them if he doubted his own abilities and judgments. Yet the implied vindication seemed to have given a visible lift to his mood, an unwonted springiness to his personality. He had, perhaps with a sigh, jettisoned the high collars and adopted some of the easier manners of the new times. He radiated again the self-assurance of his most active periods. Meeting him, as I did, after an interval of several years, he seemed actually younger looking, more buoyant.

He was erect, robust, vigorous in appearance, his face remarkably unlined, his eyes clear and bright. He carried his seventy-odd years easily, as the expression goes. And they seemed to have deepened his clarity of perception and analysis.

To hear Hoover discuss a subject to which he had given thought—and he was reluctant to enlarge on subjects where his knowledge was sketchy —was an experience. It was like watching a precision instrument in the hands of an expert. He cut through non-essentials, avoided tempting tangents, and was almost at once at the heart of the issue.

When I pressed him to explain the kindlier winds of opinion playing around his head, he shrugged and said with a characteristic chuckle, "Look at the election—there's your answer." He was referring, of course, to the election of 1946, when America went Republican for the first time since the stock market crash of 1929 and the Democratic party itself sloughed off some of its more disfiguring barnacles on the Left.

No doubt he was correct. The change was, as he meant to suggest, primarily in the country, not in himself. Certainly he had not run away in panic from any of the reasoned and instinctive attitudes which had contributed to his loss of popularity. At no point had he adjusted himself to propaganda pressures. Neither had he—and this is the greater temptation for men under political assault—taken up the role assigned to him by opponents yelling "Reactionary!"

The New Deal and Communist propaganda, he said in effect—I am not quoting his exact words—had made him the symbol of depression, hunger, reaction. It made a kind of convenient political shorthand. Why bother to deal with these things rationally when you can personify them in the few tiny syllables of a man's name? Then, roughly around 1946, the symbolism ceased to make much sense. On the whole, he said, there was no more logic in the credit that was being given to him today than in the debits that were loaded on him yesterday. He did not catch up with the people; the people were streaming back to him after some hectic wanderings.

Hoover never believed in what is called the middle way. He saw no special merit in a cautious centralism. You cannot compromise with evil and error and thereby achieve approximate virtue or approximate truth. The logic of the modern tendency to strike an average between extremes, Left and Right, revolution and reaction, may make good politics but rarely makes good sense. A point equidistant from two admitted horrors may be as horrible as either of them.

True, the change we were talking about was less in Hoover than in the times. It was still a fact, however, that there was a notable mellowing of his personality, a certain easing of his manner. Some of the reserve and stiffness had crumbled. More of the affectionate, often droll, and always sympathetic Hoover known to his immediate circle was getting through to the American public.

In June 1948, in Philadelphia, the Republican National Convention accorded Hoover a stormy reception which old-timers said had few precedents for joyous spontaneity. In the galleries—where I was sitting—the enthusiasm was as great as on the floor. The cheering would subside, only to be resumed, again and again. The ex-President, solemn and embarrassed, tried to begin his prepared address, only to be drowned out by a new outburst.

Though his eyes were clouded, they did not miss some details. A few days later, in discussing the ovation, I mentioned the fact that the whole press corps had stood up and joined in the applause. No, he said, there was one exception. A lady publisher of a Republican paper with "liberal" persuasions, he observed, sat grimly, unsmilingly, through the excitement.

When he remarked in the course of his speech that, in the natural order of life, this was probably his last appearance at his party's convention, there were shouts of "No, no!" from the galleries and the delegates. Three times more, at intervals of four years, the last time in 1960, he was destined to make the same gesture of farewell.

The address he delivered at the convention was essentially "inspirational." He summoned Republicans to champion "the cause of human liberty," for only America could prevent "the annihilation of freedom." America, too, had "been infected with the European intermittent fever of creeping totalitarianism," promoted by "fuzzy-minded" men and women who, though they claimed to be liberals and middle-of-the-roaders, were in fact "a half-way house to totalitarianism." He warned the party against compromising with collectivist tendencies. It must defend traditional American ideals, inspiring in the people a love of their country and their civilization. There must, he concluded, "issue from this hall a clarion call, in as full a tone as that call to arms which your ancestors issued at Ripon, Wisconsin, when this party was born to make all men free. And so I bespeak you tonight to make yourselves worthy of victory."

When he finished speaking, there was another spirited ovation. There was no longer room for doubt that the Republican party again regarded Hoover as an asset. Because he was then deeply engaged in the Hoover Commission study of government operations, however, he took only a minor part in the campaign.

XXXI

Fighting Another World Famine

THE most helpful tonic for Herbert Hoover's spirits was always big and vital work. The end of his ostracism from government affairs restored to the service of the nation and the world his special blend of effective organization and idealism.

He had, of course, been thoroughly occupied with domestic philanthropies: Stanford University and its Hoover Library, the Boys' Clubs of America, a score of other commitments. His unique talents for organizing fund-raising campaigns, honed by long experience, had been enlisted for one humane or educational task after another. But it was the renewal of the tonic of significant involvement in public undertakings—on a scale to challenge him to the utmost—that accounted for the new buoyancy now noted by those in contact with him.

The ravages of the Second World War left many countries in Europe and Asia exposed to famine, pestilence, and the social chaos bred by hunger. The defeated nations on both sides of the globe were hardest hit, but others were affected in varying degrees. The UNRRA operation, largely financed by the United States, beneficial as far as it went, was limited chiefly to Eastern Europe and, even there, was not adequate for the rising needs.

There was scant understanding among the American people of the onerous burdens assumed by their country with the military occupation of wrecked and festering Germany, Japan, and Korea. Feelings of humanity aside, large-scale famine under the American flag would be politically baleful. The small countries liberated from Nazism were as badly off as Germany itself. The Iron Curtain cut off farming areas upon which Western Germany in the past had depended for most of its supplies. The influx of refugees and displaced persons deepened the distress. Japan, already close to the starvation line, had to accommodate some six million Japanese shipped back to the homeland.

If tens of millions were to be saved from death and hundreds of millions from devastating undernourishment, food resources in the world, in particular grains, rice, and fats, had to be located and redeployed. Only one man had the expertise and the worldwide prestige to tackle the task —Hoover. While the war was under way and in its immediate aftermath he had kept himself intimately informed on the global food equations. Indeed, had his repeated proposals for advance organization to deal with them at the war's end not been ignored, many lives would have been spared.

Speaking in New York before the Annual Assembly of the National Industrial Conference Board on May 20, 1942, for example, he had warned:

Unless we are to see again the aftermath of the Thirty Years' War, when one-third of the people of Europe fell before the Horsemen of Famine and Pestilence, we must have preparedness, not alone in America, but in every surplus food producing country, and unless there be food there will be no foundation for peace.

His warning, often reiterated, went unheeded. Now, a year after the war, the shadow of the dread Horsemen deepened over both Europe and Asia. The immediate problem was not primarily financial. Most of the food-short nations had money or credits, if only the necessary supplies could be found and made available without delays. Early in 1946 President Truman appealed to the American people to cut down drastically their consumption of grain and fats, to provide surpluses for stricken areas. Hoover went to the press and on the air in support of the appeal. Working closely with Washington officials, he made a series of recommendations, all but one of which were adopted.

The political hurdle, for the White House, would be to obtain large relief appropriations from a Congress still under the hypnosis of wartime hatreds. Only Hoover, President Truman and his advisers decided, could establish realistically the dimensions of the need and present the facts to the country in concrete and persuasive terms.

Hoover was designated to head a Famine Emergency Commission, with an on-the-spot study of the world crisis as his assignment. In a coast-to-coast broadcast on March 16, the ex-President announced that he was flying the next morning on a fact-finding mission clear around the globe. He was accompanied by four veterans of his World War I life-saving crusades—Hugh Gibson, Perrin Galpin, Maurice Pate, and Hallam Tuck —along with Dennis A. FitzGerald of the Department of Agriculture and a top-flight journalist, Frank E. Mason, as public relations officer. A U. S. Transport Service C-54 plane was to be their workshop and, in large part, their home in an epic thirty-five-thousand-mile journey. Because the wing-flaps made a mooing sound when lowered, the Chief kept referring to the plane as "our Faithful Cow"—a winking allusion to the *Sacred Cow* which had flown another President—and the name stuck.

The world-girdling mission of the seventy-two-year-old ex-President and his little band caught the imagination and engaged the sympathy of the public. It was well reported. In most key cities—Rome, Berlin, Cairo, Bombay, Tokyo, etc.—a large corps of American pressmen and photographers was on hand. In fifty-seven days the group visited twenty-two countries and gathered information on a dozen others.

Basic data had been lined up in advance. Now they were evaluated in the light of information provided by governments, charitable bodies, resident American military and diplomatic personnel, and scores of knowledgeable individuals with whom Hoover had maintained relations through the years. U.S. occupation heads like Generals Mark Clark, Lucius Clay, and Douglas MacArthur gave unstinting help.

The job involved conferences with hundreds of people, from Prime Ministers down, netting mountains of information, which Hoover analyzed and organized as he went along. Much of the work had to be done while in flight, with narrow margins for sleep and none for sightseeing and entertainment—aside from the absolute minimum imposed by diplomatic protocol. Never before, it was generally said, had such an intensive and extensive survey been made in so brief a time.

The "gap" between cereals available in producing countries and the minimal requirements for survival in deficit areas until the autumn harvests had been estimated at eleven million tons. In the nature of the situation, the hungry nations tended to exaggerate their rock-bottom needs, and surplus nations were reluctant to reduce their diets or dig into reserves.

Formally his authority was limited to fact-finding, but Hoover went far beyond these limits. He used his position as the President's spokesman and his great personal prestige to trim demands of food-deficit countries to the bare necessity. He persuaded surplus countries to reduce domestic consumption, on the American model, and others to cut down normal grain imports. Time and logistics being of the essence, he induced some importers to reroute wheat and rice already committed or in transit to closer and more hard-pressed destinations. In a few places he was able to unfreeze grain reserves earmarked for future use. In India, Siam, Japan, and elsewhere he encouraged revision of rations to relax dependence on rice.

Thus, through pressures and devices suggested by his engineering brain and past experience, Hoover was able to reduce the world "gap" from eleven to only five million tons in the European stage of the mission, and then to about three and a half million at the end of the journey. While this meant only fifteen hundred calories a day—and in a few areas as little as one thousand calories—for several hundred million people, it sufficed to sustain life until the next harvest and avert the looming famine. His achievement, in sum, was to bring the vast problem within the compass of realistic solutions.

"I admit," he would say of this mission about eight years later, "that I was frightfully concerned in those days that we would not succeed in preventing the death of three hundred to five hundred million people." By redeployment of foods available and spreading them as thinly as possible, however, the calamity was headed off.

2

Italy, Hoover found, had barely enough cereals to stave off mass starvation for thirty days. Yugoslavia was equally short. In Germany, by the time he reached Berlin, daily rations were down to a thousand calories. Poland, as Frank Mason wrote in airmailed letters to friends, presented "the worst situation we have seen so far . . . lightened only by the gallantry of the Polish people." Because of the destruction of housing—some 90 percent of it in Warsaw—millions of Poles were homeless as well as hungry. In Greece, mass distress was so great that Hoover at once asked the British authorities to divert to Greece part of the grain cargoes then in transit to England.

Infant mortality rates were staggering: from 20 percent in central Europe to 50 percent in a few East European cities. Hoover estimated that between twenty and thirty million children on the continent were already physically subnormal. "The reconstruction of the children," he told his own country in a broadcast from Egypt, "is more precious than factories and bridges." And on his return to America: "Civilization marches forward upon the feet of healthy children. It is not too late to stop this costly retreat and its debacle of endless evil." Wherever possible, he obtained agreements for extra calories for children.

Russia, for the moment, was potentially a surplus grain country, having enjoyed fair harvests since the Germans were driven from its soil. Stalin, in fact, had demonstratively sold seventy-five thousand tons to France. Hoover therefore appealed to the Soviets to expand their exports to three hundred thousand tons a month in the critical period ahead, and offered to fly to Moscow to arrange it. He did not receive so much as a polite reply. The Soviets—and Communists throughout the world, including those in the United States—were denouncing the Hoover mission as "American imperialism."

Disturbing news awaited the party when the *Faithful Cow* reached Cairo. The press had reports that the mission was being summoned home at once, though its announced itinerary called for two weeks in Asia. A belated cable from the President confirmed the news. Truman, it appeared, thought the crisis so desperate that it would be well for Hoover to get back and "awaken the conscience of the American people."

He was ready to comply, Hoover cabled back, but he considered the interruption a mistake: the Asian countries would interpret it as proof that America was interested in helping only Europeans. He then telephoned the President, who yielded to Hoover's judgment.

In a half-hour broadcast to the United States from Cairo, Hoover summarized his findings on Europe. At least 150,000,000 people must be provided with grain until the autumn harvest. Unless an immediate beginning was made in closing the "gap," vast numbers of men, women, and especially children would die or would be crippled by the ravages of undernourishment.

He offered an array of concrete proposals. Americans, he said, must voluntarily reduce their consumption of wheat by 40 percent and fats by 20 percent. Latin American countries must cut their imports of wheat and flour from the United States, Canada, and Argentina by 40 percent during the next four months. Since these Latin American countries were largely Catholic, he reminded them that "it would be a translation into action of the eloquent appeal of His Holiness, Pope Pius XII, a few days ago." He concluded:

If every source of supplies will do its utmost, we can pull the world through this most dangerous crisis. The saving of these human lives is far more than an economic necessity for the recovery of the world. . . . Such action marks the return of the lamp of compassion to the world. And that is a part of the moral and spiritual reconstruction in the world.

Rousing popular demonstrations had greeted Hoover in Belgium and Finland. Unavoidably he submitted himself to official receptions in a number of capitals, such as the magnificent luncheon banquet for a hundred guests given by the King of Egypt—"an experience out of the Arabian nights none of us will ever forget," in Mason's account to his friends. But with Hugh Gibson, the seasoned diplomat, handling the amenities, they were kept to a minimum. From Berlin, the Associated Press bureau chief there, Louis Lochner, cabled:

Hoover after one glance at the program tentatively outlined for him decided to eliminate sight-seeing tours arranged for 12:30 tomorrow and also an extended rest period which was to follow. Instead he asked to be enabled to go to work immediately.

His companions marveled at Hoover's physical vitality. Something they ate or drank at a luncheon tendered by the Viceroy of India apparently did not set well with the American guests. Most of them took ill in different measure; even the doctor was laid up for a day. "Through it all," Mason wrote en route from Bombay to Bangalore, "the Chief goes imperturbably on, writing his talks with a pencil, and handing them over to be copied. He stood up under this terrific pace in a miraculous manner."

Among the highlights of the Bombay stopover were a call upon the Chief by Mahatma Gandhi, attired only in a loincloth, and a visit an hour later by Jawaharlal Nehru. Hoover told his group after the Mahatma departed: "Mr. Gandhi and I have one thing in common. As a common mark of our humility, we each carry a dollar watch."

Typical of the Hoover mind is the fact that, in Baghdad, he found time to help a construction project by the American School there. He cabled Lowell Thomas in New York authorizing him to arrange for an article by Hoover, as suggested by a major magazine, with the five-thousand-dollar honorarium going to the Baghdad School for Boys. Also, he personally set the plane's course so that he could have an aerial view of the Tigris and its valley. For already he had in mind plans for systems of dams and irrigation projects to help solve the problems of Arab refugees. His proposals along these lines, alas, were not acted upon.

Hoover's report to the President was well formulated by the time the *Faithful Cow* touched American soil in California. The completed document, dated May 13, probably set a record for brevity on an enterprise of such scope. The text ran only a few pages, with the meat of his findings set forth in five succinct statistical tables. It amounted to a blueprint which every cooperating nation could easily read and follow.

He saved the rhetoric of heart appeal for his interviews with the press and radio broadcasts. In a speech in Chicago soon after his return, Hoover said in part:

Hunger hangs over the homes of more than 800,000,000 people—over one-third of the people of the earth. Hunger is a silent visitor who comes like a shadow. He sits beside every anxious mother three times each day. He brings not alone suffering and sorrow but fear and terror. He carries disorder and the paralysis of government, and even its downfall. He is more destructive than armies, not only in human life, but in morals. All the values of right living melt before his invasions, and every gain of civilization crumbles. But we can save these people from the worst, if we will.

Before the month was over, again at the President's request, Hoover and his *Faithful Cow* were off for a swing through Mexico, Venezuela, Brazil, Argentina, Peru, Chile, and five other Latin American countries. The aggregate distance covered by the mission was thus raised to over fifty thousand miles. Though again billed simply as a fact-finding trip, Hoover was able to activate Latin American governments to do their appointed parts in the global anti-famine plans.

The months after his return Hoover devoted to conferences with key legislators, work with federal departments involved in the feeding programs, and above all, to "awakening the conscience of the American people." Now, as in the First World War and its aftermath, he looked upon a vigorous follow-up as intrinsically a part of any assignment. His intervention played a clinching role in getting a $425,000,000 appropriation asked by President Truman for food in fiscal 1947 for defeated peoples under American occupation.

It had been a short-term mission to tide over an immediate emergency and was in largest measure, the world press attested, successful. The underlying problem, of course, still remained to be solved.

3

By the end of 1946 it was becoming obvious that more drastic measures were called for if the heavy drain of our occupation costs were eventually to be reduced. Once more Truman turned to the ex-President. He invited Hoover to head up a President's Economic Mission to Germany and Austria. At a White House conference in January 1947 Hoover spelled out his conviction that the feeding problem would remain chronic if treated in isolation from the entire economic picture, not alone in Germany but in all of Western Europe. He readily obtained authority to broaden the new survey accordingly.

Apparently the State Department was not informed of the expanded scope of the enterprise. The day before the scheduled departure on February 2, a set of "directives" was delivered to Hoover at his New York home, setting various restrictions on the activities of the mission. It was an angry Hoover, prepared to resign, who telephoned the White House. The President heard him out, then instructed him to tear up the State Department document and do things his own way.

Three of the men who had taken part in the previous mission—Hugh Gibson, Dennis FitzGerald, and Frank Mason—were in the repeat performance, along with Dr. William H. Sebrell, Jr., medical director of the U. S. Public Health Service; Dr. Gustav Stolper, an economist; and Tracy S. Voorhees, Special Assistant to the Secretary of War. Louis Lochner, having in the meantime retired from the Associated Press after twenty years' service, joined the party—a welcome addition because of his profound knowledge of Germany and its people.

Again and again in his many careers, men who came into contact with Hoover found themselves caught and held by the man, and were gradually engulfed in the Hoover cult. Before long they were referring to him as the Chief in that tone of affection, a little proprietary, that marked its initiates. They might have been members of some Hoover undertaking, officials assigned to work with him, or as in Lochner's case, newspapermen. Having cooperated with the previous mission while reporting it, the veteran A.P. man remained forever enlisted in the company of devotees, available for public service at the Chief's call. In 1960 Lochner would write a splendid book on *Herbert Hoover and Germany.*

The new mission made its first stop in Frankfurt, the seat of the U. S. Military Government, then flew to Berlin, Hamburg, Stuttgart, and Vienna. Accompanied by Gibson, Hoover made a special trip to Rome to pay his respects to Pope Pius XII. On the return flight, in addition, he stopped in London to brief Prime Minister Clement Attlee on his findings and the recommendations he intended to submit to Washington.

Since the end of the war the belief had been maturing in Hoover's mind that a totally new approach to the challenge of wartorn Europe was indispensable. Now, as nearly two decades earlier, he rejected hatred and vengeance as guides to rehabilitation. "Not a hard or a soft peace, but a just peace," was his formula. The so-called Morgenthau Plan for dismantling German industry and turning the country into farmland had seemed to him a prescription for crippling, not only Germany, but Europe.

Twenty days of crowded, high-powered investigation gave him ample confirmation of his views. Once more he conferred with dozens of German and Austrian officials as well as top men in the American and British occupation governments. "We, his associates, marveled at the robust health of our then seventy-three-year-old Chief," Lochner would write in retrospect. "We could not but be deeply impressed by the stamina evinced by his sitting for a whole day in an ice-cold room in Hamburg to preside over a meeting." He cited a United Press dispatch from that city on this point: "Former President Hoover, swathed in a blanket and wearing a heavy overcoat, today conferred with British regional commissioners on the critical German food problem." Lochner has reported:

We envied him for his tireless energy displayed not only in listening patiently for hours to the testimony taken but also following full days of work with long nights devoted to the study of documents submitted. One night I heard him get up at four o'clock in the morning and turn page after page of voluminous data submitted to him.

Checking on possible food reserves, Tracy Voorhees discovered nineteen million dollars' worth stockpiled by the Military Government for other purposes and arranged to have it released to Hoover. This windfall enabled the Chief to launch at once his priority project: "a school lunch program which helped save a whole generation of German youngsters," as Lochner described it. With General Clay's enthusiastic collaboration, the Children's Feeding Program was soon providing one hot meal a day for some 3,500,000 school children in the main cities of the American and British zones, by this time under unified administration. There would be considerable evidence in the following years that the generation thus favored with additional nourishment emerged in a healthier state, physically and politically, than the one that preceded.

One sad consequence of the mission was not reported in the press at the time. Because of the deplorable working conditions, Hoover had contracted a cold which grew worse on the return flight. A refueling stop was being made at Stephenville, Newfoundland, where a raging blizzard caused zero-zero visibility. The weather and topography forced the pilot to maintain a high altitude until the plane was almost over the airport, where it descended abruptly for some ten thousand feet. Hoover's ear passages being clogged by the cold, one of the eardrums was ruptured during the landing operation, leaving his hearing impaired for the rest of his life. Not long afterward he began using a hearing aid—of which he spoke almost fondly as the "decoration" won in his 1947 mission to Europe.

Back home, Hoover discussed his findings and conclusions at length with the President, Secretary of State George C. Marshall, and legislative leaders. His formal reports, two on Germany and one on Austria, have been widely credited, both in the United States and in central Europe, with helping alter the climate of American opinion on relations with the defeated nations.

The first report, on *German Agriculture and Food Requirements,* was made public on February 28, within five days after his return. Its concluding paragraphs read:

[Even] those who believe in vengeance and punishment of a great mass of Germans not concerned in the Nazi conspiracy can now have no misgivings, for all of them—in food, warmth and shelter—have sunk to the lowest level known in a hundred years of Western history.

If Western civilization is to survive in Europe, it must also survive in Germany. And it must be built into a cooperative member of that civilization. That, indeed, is the hope of any lasting peace. After all, our flag flies over these people. That flag means something besides military power.

The second report carried what was perhaps the most argumentative title on record: *The Necessary Steps for Promotion of German Exports, so as to Relieve the American Taxpayers of the Burdens of Relief, and*

for the Economic Recovery of Europe. Evidently its author had decided
to pay the price of inelegant wording in order to compress his basic message into the very title. In the text he explained that "the productivity of
Europe cannot be restored without the restoration of Germany as a con-
tributor to that productivity." He called for canceling out "the delusion
that the New Germany after the annexations can be reduced to a 'pastoral
state'" and "the further delusion that Europe as a whole can recover
without the economic recovery of Germany."

The truncated country, Hoover urged, must be freed, under proper
supervision, to revive industry and exports. Only in that way, he believed,
could we promote "regeneration" instead of "further degeneration of
Europe." He demanded complete cessation of the removal or destruction
of German plants, except those producing arms. In short, he focused
official and popular American opinion on the wisdom of renouncing
vengeance in favor of realistic measures of rehabilitation. "We can keep
Germany in chains," he said, "but it will also keep Europe in rags."

Hoover dedicated himself in the following months in what amounted
to a one-man crusade for the translation of his proposals into action as
soon as possible. The Morgenthau school of thought, calling for the reduction of Germany to an agricultural pasture, still had substantial influence. Directly through interviews, radio speeches, and articles, and
indirectly through leaders in Congress sharing his views, Hoover labored
to counteract that influence.

The White House supported him from the start. Many restrictions on
the German economy were quickly relaxed or lifted. Congressional backing came only after vociferous debates in which the weight of the ex-
President's opinions undoubtedly was decisive. The appropriation of
$725,000,000 for food and other relief supplies for Germany, Japan, and
Korea requested by the War Department was granted.

More important, the new atmosphere made possible the formulation
and acceptance of the Marshall Plan. While the extent of Hoover's contribution to that policy can only be estimated, there is little doubt that it
was substantial. Thus Raymond Moley, in a magazine article in late 1948,
could say flatly: "It was Hoover's report on his surveillance of the food
situation in Europe for Truman, plus confidential information he gave
Truman and Marshall, that formed the basis . . . for the Truman-Marshall
Doctrine."

On a wall in Hoover's apartment there is a framed letter he received
soon after the release of his three-part report. It bears forty-eight signatures remarkable for the diversity of political allegiances represented.
The letter commends Hoover's "refusal to yield to hate or bitterness," his
stress on "the indubitable fact that if Western civilization is to survive in

Europe it must survive in Germany," and in general for a report "in the finest American spirit of benevolence and justice."

Among the signers were Oswald Garrison Villard, Dorothy Thompson, Henry Luce, Clare Boothe Luce, Winthrop W. Aldrich, Adolph A. Berle, Jr., the Rev. John Haynes Holmes, Dr. James T. Shotwell, the Rev. Harry Emerson Fosdick, Dr. Nicholas Murray Butler, Roger Baldwin, Norman Thomas, Dr. George N. Schuster, Christopher Emmet, Allen Dulles, Arthur Dean, Jeremiah Milbank, General William J. Donovan, Vincent Sheean, and Thomas J. Watson. It is not often that spontaneous praise comes from men and women spanning the whole spectrum of political and social opinion between Democrats and Republicans, liberals and conservatives.

"Summing it up," Louis Lochner was to write, "it is no exaggeration to say that what was done under Mr. Hoover's continuing guidance to feed Germany averted Germany's going communist."

He used the phrase "continuing guidance" because he knew how intently Hoover labored, both openly and behind the political scenes in Washington, to make sure that his recommendations would be translated into policy and action. Nor were the effects of this labor limited to Germany. During the years of the child-feeding program, thousands of German children wrote to *Onkel Hoover* across the seas. They could not know that the hot meal for which they thanked him was the starting point of a Hoover campaign in behalf of twenty million children throughout the world, which in due time came to fruition as the United Nations International Children's Emergency Fund.

4

To round out the German story:

When Dr. Konrad Adenauer, the Chancellor of the Federal Republic of Germany, arrived in New York in the spring of 1953 for his first visit to the United States, he went directly from the ship to the Waldorf Towers on Park Avenue. As a feature story in the German press reported it:

Before meeting any representatives of official America, he stood face to face with a man with whom he considered it his first duty as guest of the American people to shake hands in gratitude. That man was Herbert Hoover.

During his second American visit, the Chancellor pressed Hoover to come to Germany as the nation's guest. Although it meant a week's absence from the Government Reorganization work, Hoover accepted, with the full approval of President Eisenhower and Secretary of State

Dulles. The President put his personal plane, the *Columbine,* at his predecessor's disposal for the journey.

Hoover was universally regarded by Germans as a benefactor without blemish. The news of his impending arrival created national excitement. In response to an invitation, General Clay wrote a long article about the former President's role in the recovery of Germany that was published throughout West Germany. It said in part:

As he did not seek publicity from his two visits to Germany, neither Germans nor Americans fully realize what he did to revive hope in Germany and to make possible its eventual entry into the Atlantic group of nations. . . . Our efforts to obtain food and economic assistance from the United States succeeded only because of the strong support which we received from former President Hoover. . . . Mr. Hoover did much to change thinking at home, so that it would become possible for us to reform and stabilize currency, to stop the dismantling of German industry, and to permit free competitive enterprise to begin the rebuilding of Germany.

Accompanied by a few friends, mostly co-workers in international relief, the eighty-year-old Hoover landed in Bonn on September 22, 1954. They were met at the airport by the Chancellor and other top officials. While in Bonn, Hoover lived with James B. Conant, U. S. High Commissioner for Germany, in the U.S. headquarters residence. His six days were crowded with receptions, awards, and every token of a people's gratitude that the Germans could devise. The press pulled out all stops in compounding tributes.

At a state dinner on the night of arrival in his official residence, the Palais Schaumburg, Dr. Adenauer spoke with emotion unusual for him. At one point he said:

Mr. President, for us Germans your name is an epitome of the most striking qualities of the American people. It personifies for us the pluck of your pioneers who opened up the great wide spaces of your country, the faith in creative power of the free human personality, the respect for the rights of every individual, and the truly Christian love of fellowmen. . . . We owe it to your political far-sightedness, to your comprehensive knowledge of economic life, that we could again build up our country and our economy after the ravages of the Second World War.

The other cities Hoover visited were Stuttgart—where he was given a degree by Tübingen, one of the most ancient universities on the continent —and Berlin. In all three cities, thousands of school children turned out to greet the American guest. In all of them he was reminded that the child-feeding program he had started was still functioning. A syndicated German news story summed up the popular feelings:

For millions the name of Hoover recalls to memory the relief work which rescued countless compatriots from hunger's merciless onslaught during Germany's hard times after the first and second world wars. Twice in his life of eighty years the white-haired former President of the United States mobilized the hearts of his contemporaries for his campaigns against the nutritional catastrophies of the world.

About fifteen months later Hoover received the kind of compliment he prized above gold medals and degrees. It was minor in itself—a technical school in Wedding, a working-class district of Berlin, was renamed the Herbert Hoover Schule. His son, Herbert, Jr., was present at the christening ceremony and read a message from his father:

There is no greater honor that can come to a man than to have a school named for him; there is no part of our life with which I would rather be associated than the education of our young, for within it lies the basis of the future.

XXXII

Reform of Government Operations

FROM his earliest years in public life, Herbert Hoover had been appalled by the waste and confusions in government. While private business was being constantly modernized and streamlined, public business remained extravagant, slow, and chaotic. "Our federal machinery," he said in October 1920, "is the result of a hundred years of patchwork and has lagged lamentably behind the skill in organization of our people."

As Secretary of Commerce he had dealt with aspects of the problem and succeeded in improving many operations. He addressed himself to the challenge again in his first State of the Union message as President. But then came the great economic debacle, and after Hoover the deluge of spending and bureaucratic empire-building.

At the war's end the government leveled off to some eighteen hundred agencies employing 3,500,000 persons, housed in five thousand office buildings in the country (not including post offices), with expenditures by the executive branch of over forty billion dollars annually. Somewhere between seventy and a hundred agencies, boards, and commissions, in theory reported directly to the President, others were accountable to Congress, yet more to various Cabinet heads; not a few apparently accounted to no one, the line of authority having been blurred or broken. The government owned more than a million cars and trucks. It was spending a billion dollars a year just to maintain its records. Different bodies in the government doing the same or similar work were competing for the tax dollar in a welter of duplicating activities.

Congress had concerned itself with the problem repeatedly in the past, most recently in the Teddy Roosevelt and Taft administrations, but little had been accomplished. Two world wars and eleven years of depression had compounded the confusions. Congress again began to worry about the tangle of snowballing executive agencies, some of them "temporary" bodies tottering with old age.

Consulted by legislative leaders in the spring of 1947, Hoover outlined a project for a twelve-man bipartisan commission with wide powers to examine the tangle and propose methods for unknotting it. He hoped that the job wouldn't end in his lap and feared that it would. He was then suffering from infections contracted on his missions to Germany and was being instructed by physicians to slow down. He could have no illusions about the magnitude of the project he had sketched.

In July, Congress adopted his proposal and everyone took it for granted that it would be Hoover's "baby." The summons came to him while he was resting in California. So he quit sea and sun, "packed up his staff of secretaries," and went off to Washington for another titanic job. Reluctantly, as a matter of inescapable duty, the ex-President accepted the appointment to organize and head the Commission on Organization of the Executive Branch of the Government, and at once set to work. He could not guess that what he called his "last public assignment" would engage him, with one interval, until he was eighty-one years old. From the first the formal name of the undertaking was all but forgotten —it became simply the Hoover Commission.

Its membership was evenly divided between Democrats and Republicans, four each being named by the President, the Speaker of the House, and the President pro tempore of the Senate. With Hoover as chairman and Dean Acheson as vice-chairman, the other commissioners were Secretary of Defense James Forrestal; former ambassador Joseph P. Kennedy (father of a future President); Arthur S. Flemming; James K. Pollock; Representative Carter Manasco; James H. Rowe, Jr.; Senator George D. Aiken; Senator John L. McClellan; Representative Clarence J. Brown; and George H. Mead. These men were not mere letterhead decorations; they all participated actively. But the lion's share of the toil fell to Hoover.

The techniques he put into effect provided a blueprint for large-scale government studies ever after. Hoover set up nineteen task forces to concentrate on delimited areas such as accounting, budgeting, personnel, transportation, real estate, purchasing, medical and veterans' affairs, natural resources, etc. and the machinery of the principal Cabinet departments. Over three hundred specialists were personally selected by Hoover, with the consent of the other commissioners, and attached to appropriate task forces. Many of them had worked under the Chief before, and his invitation was tantamount to an order; but remarkably few of the others whom he "tapped" refused to serve, though it entailed sacrifices of personal interests.

The quality of the army thus lined up for the big battle against sloth, confusion, and waste is indicated by the fact that it included two former

Cabinet members, three ex-senators, five former governors, ten university presidents, and leaders in many fields of the caliber of Owen D. Young, Robert Moses, Ferdinand Eberstadt, Joseph P. Binns, and Dr. William C. Menninger. Like Hoover himself, most of the commissioners and task force members served without pay, only those who could not afford it being compensated. Congress had appropriated two million dollars for the Commission—Hoover was able to turn back a surplus of unspent funds when the job was completed.

The apparatus had already been largely organized by the time the commission was officially launched at a meeting with President Truman in the White House on September 27, 1947. To all the men involved, Hoover's directive was plain enough: "Stay open-minded, forthright, non-political. Just bring back the most honest findings you can get and don't worry whom it might or might not please."

For some twenty months, Chairman Hoover and his high-powered team painstakingly gathered and analyzed basic facts, delving into the incredibly complex and overlapping mechanisms of government operations. Members of the force roamed the length and breadth of the land in field trips, examining files, asking questions. With few exceptions they had the cooperation of officialdom. The raw notes compiled, mountains of them, eventually ended up on Hoover's desk. He supervised a staff of hundreds, sat in on task force meetings, and presided over sixty-nine of the seventy commission meetings. Almost daily he settled disputes within the forces, guided associates through the labyrinths of their areas of inquiry, and reduced long, complicated reports to short, clear dimensions.

Because the conference and much of the collation of information were centered in Washington, Hoover and his immediate staff practically commuted between New York and Washington. Since they worked while traveling, however, little time was lost.

Less than a month after he assumed the job, Hoover developed a case of shingles, a viral disease that caused painful itching and blisters. So severely did it run its course that there was a temporary paralysis of his right arm and shoulder. Despite the discomfort and the excruciating pain, he waved off every suggestion that he put the work aside until he recuperated.

On a typical Hoover day, as recalled by his executive secretary, Bernice (Bunny) Miller, he would take a mile walk before breakfast, returning in good appetite and complexion. Usually there were breakfast guests, followed by other task forcers reporting on their assignments.

"Then," Miss Miller said, "Mr. Hoover, Larry Ritchie (an old friend and administrative assistant), myself and other secretaries would often board a 10 or 11 A.M. plane or train for Washington, usually in time for a luncheon conference at our Mayflower Hotel headquarters. Ten P.M. we considered an early quitting time. Most of us worked alongside him as long as he did, which was usually midnight. Sometimes he rewrote a draft five or six times before he was satisfied."

Joseph Binns, manager of the Waldorf Astoria and all Hilton hotels in the East, headed the Subsistence Task Force. Its job was to evaluate government operations in food, lodging, housing—in short, the housekeeping services of government. A fellow Quaker as well as his "landlord" at the Waldorf, he had known the ex-President long and intimately. Hoover, he said recently, did manage to steal a little relaxation now and then, during the commission period:

"After a long day, the Chief sometimes enjoyed a few hands of canasta with his closest associates. He was the greatest story teller all through the game, drawing on a fabulous memory for amusing tales sometimes going back fifty years or more. Yet with all his love of people, he had an innate reserve, a dislike of gushiness or sentimentality. Those who worked with him as volunteers all came to admire and love him. One of the reasons I accepted the mammoth job of handling a task force was my deep affection for Hoover, despite his reserve, and frankly, I did not regret that he was not more of a back-slapper."

The first of the nineteen sections of the Hoover Commission Report was submitted to Congress on February 7, 1949, and thereafter came in at the rate of about three a week. Hoover had written sixteen of the reports and, of course, the over-all covering report, and had edited the other three. The very first report submitted set the tone of bold criticism where it was called for. It said in part:

Definite authority at the top, a clear line of authority from top to bottom, and adequate staff aides to the exercise of authority do not exist. Authority is diffused, lines of authority are confused, staff services are insufficient. Consequently, responsibility and accountability are impaired.

The commission produced the most comprehensive survey in the history of government—surpassed only by a second Hoover Commission some five years later. What they provided was, in David Hinshaw's words, "a panoramic picture of the world's largest business, that of our Federal Government today."

Congress now had before it, in some two and a half million words of concrete data, the most imposing collection of information and opinions on government ever assembled, all superbly organized for easy understanding and action. The commission offered 280 individual recommendations, each of them spelled out in detail. It asked, to mention only a few at random:

That competition between two or more agencies in the same area of operation be eliminated—the kind of competition between the Bureau of Reclamation and the Army Corps of Engineers, the Forest Service and the Soil Conservation Service in the same Department of Agriculture.

That responsibility for land-management activities, spread through many agencies, be concentrated in one department.

That the building of duplicated hospital facilities by the Army, the Navy, the Public Health Service, and the Veterans Administration be obviated through unified planning and responsibility.

That the purchasing, inventory controls, and other so-called housekeeping functions of government be simplified and consolidated.

That a new Department of Health, Education, and Welfare be formed to take over work spread through a congeries of bureaus.

That more money be spent on preventive medicine and basic medical research but less on medical benefits to non-service veterans.

That the Post Office be removed completely from politics.

That a large number of agencies reporting to the President be reassigned to various Departments for more rigid accountability.

Savings of up to three billion dollars a year were envisioned in the recommendations, with a reduction of federal payrolls by three hundred million dollars. More important, provisions were suggested for raising efficiency right down the line.

Inevitably, there were loud cries of pain from entrenched officeholders, most of them honestly convinced that the sky would fall in if their time-honored jobs were curtailed or ended. But public opinion was overwhelmingly on the side of the commission. The final report, published in book form, became a best-seller, certainly a rarity for government documents.

Typical of the press reaction was an editorial in *Collier's*:

Thanks to Herbert Hoover and the Commission he has headed, we have the best opportunity to simplify and make more efficient our Federal Government. This is a remarkable partnership: the President of the United States and the only living ex-President combined with the Joint Congressional Committee to improve the effectiveness of governmental organization. The country owes a debt of gratitude to Herbert Hoover who has been performing what he calls his last public service. Mr. Hoover has been working ten, twelve, eighteen hours a day to get this work done . . . a great achievement for a man who will be seventy-five years old on August 10.

Truman's enthusiasm for the job done was unlimited; he would point to it in the future as one of the accomplishments in his Administration in which he took particular pride. On February 7, 1949, the very day when it received the initial report, the House of Representatives, by a vote of 356–9, gave the President broad powers to carry out administrative reforms indicated by the commission. Some of the changes could be made by Executive Order under existing authority over agencies directly accountable to him. Others were authorized by Congress on his initiative.

Once more Hoover assumed the responsibility for an effective follow-up. "Our field of inquiry," he had told the public at the outset, "not only concerns every citizen, it concerns the very strength of democracy." It would take persistent pressures from the people, he now declared, to overcome bureaucratic inertias. Accordingly he organized a Citizens Committee to press for adoption of the commission's recommendations—a kind of people's lobby against waste in government. Thousands of Americans joined the committee for what Hoover called "a crusade to clear the track for competency . . . a job for citizenship rather than partisanship."

Despite loud opposition, an estimated 70 percent of the recommendations had been adopted by the end of the Truman term and in the first Eisenhower year. "Even the least of the Hoover recommendations," the *Saturday Evening Post* wrote, "has been enacted over the dead body of some bureaucrat who screamed that any change in his agency would result in a national calamity. No calamities and a great deal of good has resulted."

2

By 1953 the intensifying cold war, the Korean struggle, and massive rearmament had again expanded government and its costs. The budget stood at seventy-two billions and the federal payroll had increased by half a billion. Congress therefore re-established the commission and Hoover was once more entrusted with its command, this time by a Republican President, Dwight D. Eisenhower. Though he was now approaching eighty, Hoover disregarded medical admonitions to reduce his work load.

The second commission turned out to be more difficult and demanding than the first. Besides, it proved far more controversial and thus involved the former President in debate on many of its issues. Whereas the first commission dealt with governmental practices, its successor examined also policies and functions. Neil MacNeil, a former editor of the New York *Times*, who joined the commission as Editorial Director, recently explained to me:

"The first job was vertical, concerned with the structure of government. The second was horizontal, concerned with functions. It therefore raised fundamental questions of the philosophy of government, including its impact on the free enterprise system."

On September 29, 1953, the initial meeting of the second commission, its membership mostly new, was held in the White House with the President attending. Hoover had already laid the groundwork, having set up a new array of over twenty task forces. Actual work was begun by mid-November. To overcome obstructions met in the first round, he had now obtained from Congress the authority to subpoena witnesses and administer oaths.

This time the commission dealt not only with *how* things were done but *whether* they should be done at all by government. Budgeting and accounting, lending and insurance, water resources and power, for example, would be examined to ascertain the extent to which they were preempting activities that were not necessarily within the competence of government. Inevitably, under these circumstances, there could be no unanimity within the commission; eventually a number of minority findings were appended to the Hoover Report.

Again there were six Republicans and six Democrats, but virtually all of them came from the more conservative wings of the two parties. The selection of experts for the task forces was left entirely to Hoover. Representative Wright Patman polled the members of the commission to learn why no vice-chairman had been designated. The concensus: "We don't need one. Hoover spends so much time on the job himself that there's just nothing a vice-chairman could do."

The commission, besides Hoover, consisted of Attorney General Herbert Brownell; Director of Defense Mobilization Arthur S. Flemming; Senator Styles Bridges; Representative Clarence J. Brown; Senator John L. McClellan; Representative Chet Holifield; James A. Farley; Joseph P. Kennedy; Robert G. Storey; Solomon C. Hollister; and Sidney A. Mitchell (who had been executive director of the first commission). The executive director of the new commission was Representative John Hollister.

General Mark Clark headed the task force on Intelligence activities. Personnel and Civil Service came under Harold W. Dodds. General Robert E. Wood led the task force on Surplus Property. Admiral Ben Moreell headed the group studying Water Resources and Power, whose findings were to touch off the bitterest of the controversies on public versus private power.

The vigor of their octogenarian chairman was a source of endless astonishment to his associates. He not only personally recruited the staff of some five hundred but kept continually abreast of their manifold activities. Again he and his secretaries lived out of suitcases, shuttling between the Waldorf Towers and a suite in the Sheraton-Park Hotel in Washington. Again he attended dozens of task force meetings and presided at nearly all the commission conferences. Again he wrote or rewrote all but two of the twenty reports on sixty government agencies turned over to Congress and made available to the public.

According to insiders, Hoover labored nearly thirty days on bringing one of the reports into shape. On Water Resources and Power, he boiled down 1783 pages of findings and suggestions to 124 lucid pages.

"His knowledge of the functioning of the government," said Neil Mac-Neil, "was a constant source of amazement. At task force conferences he was usually the one who reconciled differences. Often he astonished task force experts who had been wrestling with a problem for months by pin-pointing elements in their reports that they themselves did not remember. Through it all he was a model of patience and thoroughness."

When the commission had been at work for more than a year Hoover outlined the dimensions of the enterprise and the multiplicity of problems involved. Speaking in New York to the West Side Association of Commerce, he said:

That job is a fantastic nightmare, whose other name is bureaucracy. The nightmare was bred from Organized Confusion out of Regimented Chaos. . . . I may relate that the Federal Government has made loans, guarantees of loans, of insurance of various kinds for which it has either financial or moral obligations exceeding 230 billion dollars. And that does not include the national debt or the currency.

The government holds issuable personal property which costs about $66 billions and this does not include buildings, naval and other vessels, airplanes, weapons, industrial establishments or vehicles or furniture in use. Many of the articles on hand are obsolete as a result of new inventions or wear, costing about $30 billions, which need to be disposed of.

The Army and the Air Force are now trying to make an inventory of their possessions. The magnitude of that job is indicated by the fact that something like five million different items are in their records. Until they get an inventory and simplify the number of items, the huge losses come out of duplicate buying and other wastes.

The government is also engaged in about one thousand business enterprises competitive with private enterprise, and there is probably $15 billions invested in it.

In the end this estimate of business enterprises had to be almost tripled. In public remarks somewhat later he pointed to the multitude of government warehouses for surplus and obsolete possessions, penalizing the taxpayer by many billions in rent and maintenance. The extent of government holdings in valuable real estate, he showed, was staggering—yet more was constantly being acquired, though usable sites belonging to Uncle Sam stood idle. In addition, Hoover said:

We have undertaken a study also in paper work of the government. Now that doesn't sound like very much. You would understand it better if it were called "The Birth Control of Federal Documents." The fact is that aside from some hundreds of tons of printed matter, the Federal Government circulates about twenty-five billion pieces of paper each year, at a cost of about four billion dollars. That is the cost of preparing them and sending them out and filing them when you get them back. Some eighteen million of these are forms— mostly questionnaires by which the government tries to discover your inner life.

As part of his study, he indicated, he hoped to ascertain how much the citizenry paid directly for replying to government inquiries, in clerical services, lawyers, accountants—and "loss of sleep."

3

Release of the second round of reports began in March 1955 and continued at brief intervals thereafter until May. They embraced over three hundred specific recommendations, looking to an estimated annual saving of six billion dollars. Beyond that the commission pointed to ways and means of recovering billions by the Treasury through liquidation of useless functions and withdrawal from enterprises in flagrant competition with private business. Incidentally, the second commission, like the first, had to admit one failure: it had failed to spend all the money assigned for its work by Congress and returned a surplus to the Treasury —"a rarity, I regret to say, in Washington today," Senator McClellan commented.

"Some people will not like the second commission report," Hoover predicted—surely an understatement. "But," he added, "I manage to console myself with the thought: 'Old reformers never die; they get thrown out.'" He was on less dependable prophetic grounds when he said: "I think the final score box on this commission's recommendations will be as good as the last—over 70 percent of them adopted and put into effect."

His forecast of opposition came true, in full measure, but the one on the box score did not. A generous estimate several years later put the acceptance at around 30 percent, and possibly it was not that high—the medicine prescribed was far too bitter for the bureaucratic palate.

The definitive report on government-in-business was the last in the series, made public in May 1955. Addressing the National Conference Board a few days later, Hoover spoke of two to three thousand functions that were in competition with American business:

When we came to look into the history of these government business enterprises, we found most of them were created in wars and emergencies for some special needed task. But when the task was completed, each had aboard it an empire-seeking bureaucracy and a large pressure group which benefited from it. With these high inspirations, they developed an extraordinary longevity. One of them lasted thirty-six years and lost money nearly every year. Some of these enterprises are necessary, some are non-competitive.

He debunked the claims that certain of the federal businesses were earning profits. They were exempt from federal taxes, he pointed out, few paid interest or amortization on capital invested by taxpayers, and their accounting in many cases did not include overhead, personnel, pensions, and other obligations shouldered by private competitors. "Our commission," he said, "made the remark that this was a strange proceeding in a government pledged to fair competition. . . . The loss is not wholly the taxpayers' money. It is also a loss by injury to the vitality of the private enterprise system. It is a destruction of freedom."

In the Defense Department alone, the commission proposed the closing out of some one thousand facilities which private industry could provide as well or better. These included meat-cutting plants, bakeries, laundries, clothing manufacture and dry-cleaning plants. Though the commission did not, as some misinterpretations had it, propose the sale of the TVA, it did suggest the transfer of some TVA functions—such as research on chemical fertilizers—to the Department of Agriculture or private industry.

The time had come, Hoover believed, to relinquish or modify sharply some of the banking and credit institutions launched during the depression, among them banks and lending agencies set up during his own Administration. He had not intended them to become permanent fixtures. Government in finance, as he saw it, could be justified only where private services of the same character were not available.

The commission's report on Medical Services drew even more outcries from veterans' organizations than he had expected. The main object of attack was its proposal that free medical aid to veterans for ailments unrelated to their military services—then costing the taxpayers half a billion dollars a year—be stopped.

In one field after another, the Hoover Commission urged that the government retire in favor of private business. It showed that this would produce important savings and, at the same time, fortify the American economic system and yield more taxes. Congress, it even recommended, should study the feasibility of transferring ship construction and repair from the Navy to private shipyards. The Task Force on Business Enterprises had called the existing system "a destructive intrusion into the private shipbuilding industry."

Because the over-all report in effect challenged the trend to Big Government, the howls of pain were loud and prolonged. "Hoover is trying to repeal the New Deal," some Democrats cried. At the Far Left, of course, the commission's candid support of private as against government business revived for a while, at least, the furious anti-Hoover propaganda of the past.

Perhaps 90 percent of the nation's editorial comment, however, was favorable. Impressed by the two commissions, one state after another established its own "Little Hoover Commission." Said the liberal Washington *Post:*

Congress has been handed a hot potato . . . but the non-partisan Hoover Commission has shown no reluctance to tackle politically explosive subjects in the past. It has gained prestige and public respect for that very reason. It would be refreshing if Congress showed comparative objectivity in considering the recommendations of the commission.

The set of proposals that most disturbed Congress and got its priority attention related to the military forces. The commission had recommended that the Defense Department spend more on basic research and development, while saving money by letting private business assume some of its more costly operations. On food and clothing, alone, the commission claimed, $340,000,000 a year could thus be saved.

At least one phase of the commission's efforts won unanimous approval, namely the reduction of red tape—what Hoover called "paper work." Under the prod of his inquiries, some agencies examined their own habitual procedures and acted to simplify them. One agency found that it could reduce the ten reports from those with whom it dealt to three.

Industries affected by government regulation set up committees to analyze the floods of official paper reaching them. Working with the task force and with the agencies involved, these committees helped eliminate paper nuisances costing tens of millions of dollars and consuming enormous time. The job of this particular task force, indeed, was substantially completed through Hooveresque methods of voluntary cooperation before its report was turned in.

In the first week of July 1955 Hoover held a press conference to mark the formal expiration of his commission, now twenty-two months old. The reporters present agreed, sadly, that time and gigantic labors were finally taking their toll of the former President's physique. Overworked veins pulsed plainly in his neck and the hand holding his notes shook noticeably. His hearing, in particular, appeared to have deteriorated considerably.

The Citizens Committee formed after the first commission had remained in existence. It was now reactivated to support the new array of recommendations. Aside from the specific suggestions translated into executive directives and legislative enactments in the next few years, Hoover had given national thinking on many central problems of government

—particularly its invasions of the private business sectors—a new impulse and direction.

In subsequent Washington efforts to economize, the Hoover reports inevitably provided guidance. In a private letter dated July 5, 1962, Secretary of Defense Robert S. McNamara informed the former President that "many of the actions we have taken flow from the recommendations of the Hoover Commission." During a courtesy call on his predecessor at the Waldorf Towers, President Lyndon Johnson told Hoover that he was studying the commission reports in connection with his hopes for trimming the costs of government administration.

Taken together, the two Hoover Commissions represented the most thorough and uninhibited examination of federal machinery and functions in the nation's history. The imprint of the former President's thinking and energy on the government has remained large and deep. A task which many a President and a Congress had dealt with ineffectively for a century had finally been accomplished by an ex-President already in the ninth decade of his many lives.

For the sake of unity and coherence we have dealt with that task, covering eight years, in a single chapter. Now we must backtrack in time to consider other matters.

XXXIII

The Time of Vindication

THE crescendo of Herbert Hoover's restoration to public favor reached a high point on his seventy-fifth birthday, on August 10, 1949. Apparently the magic figure seventy-five offered a welcome occasion for expressing admiration, on the one hand, and on the other for a psychological catharsis: the atonement of an injustice that weighed on the country's conscience.

His birthday in the preceding year, the seventy-fourth, decidedly had not been slighted. He had returned to his native West Branch, Iowa, as guest of the state. Some twenty thousand people crowded into the Quaker village to do him honor. From coast to coast, press and radio fulsomely reported and greeted the event. The subject of Hoover's address was "The Meaning of America," which he had first learned, he said, in his boyhood, then deepened through living in many foreign lands. The core of that meaning was freedom. If preserved, its moral and spiritual essences would assure "centuries of further greatness for America."

But it was the seventy-fifth birthday that somehow crystallized national sentiment and defined the "image" of Hoover which thereafter gained prominence in the public mind. Never before had a living former President been the object of such a vast and sentimental outpouring of eulogy. The dominant emotions, in some cases explicit and everywhere implicit, were regret over past vilification and delight that he was still alive to witness the great change of heart.

Having recalled that "his distinguished career of public service was forgotten in a storm of insult and criticism," *Collier's* editorially declared itself "happy that Mr. Hoover's deserved reward of public esteem has come to him in his lifetime." The Miami *Herald*, to quote one of hundreds of statements in the same vein, wrote:

409

Honesty compels the admission that the American people humiliated their ex-President. Hoover accepted the situation with dignity. He was confident that time would vindicate him. It has. What is particularly gratifying on his seventy-fifth birthday is that he has lived to see the vindication.

A number of Hoover's friends had decided that the three-quarters of a century milestone called for a big birthday party. This thought they relayed to loyal Hoover-men in a number of communities. There was no committee, no chairman, no "program"—just an idea tossed into the air. But it caught on and spread fast. The idea was that the country ought to let its thirty-first President know how it felt about him "while he was still alive to hear it."

The first difficulty was with the Chief himself. It developed that he preferred fishing to parties and had already arranged a fishing expedition for the natal week. Pressures and maneuvering were required before he agreed to speak on August 10 at Stanford University. As the day approached, what was to be a local home-town observance snowballed into a nationwide and even worldwide celebration.

Congress, in a joint resolution extending "its cordial greetings," expressed "admiration and gratitude for his devoted service to his country and to the world," and "hope that he be spared for many years of useful and honorable service." Democrats joined Republicans on the floor of both chambers in presenting oratorical bouquets.

A dozen governors issued eloquent tributes in the name of their citizenry. Literally hundreds of notables from all departments of American life joined the chorus. Some one hundred foreign organizations and governments added their mead of praise.

There were words of homage to Hoover on hundreds of radio programs and birthday editorials in virtually every newspaper in the country. It all amounted to a national reassessment, largely in a spirit of regret and reproof for past abuse, and it reached all but unqualified agreement that Hoover was "a great American" and "a great humanitarian." There was considerably less than unanimity on the conclusion that he was also "a great President." Those who withheld this particular accolade, however, emphasized that he had not been as bad as he was painted, having been falsely and unjustly blamed for sins in the Presidency that he had not committed. The always recurring words in the massive tribute were "integrity" and "selfless service."

David Hinshaw read and analyzed over two thousand of the editorials from all forty-eight states. A year later, in his book, *Herbert Hoover, American Quaker*, he published pagefuls of typical or significant excerpts. Fewer than two dozen, of all, he found, still clung to some of the old anti-Hoover clichés. They were still annoyed with his high collars, which he

410

had long since discarded, and with statements like "prosperity around the corner," which he had never made. A few still resented his handling of the prohibition issue. But 98 percent of the editorial writers played on their typewriters enthusiastic variations on the themes of affection, gratitude, and admiration, with some high notes of reverence.

Running through many of these birthday eulogies, inevitably, was the recognition that Hoover was not a dexterous politician. In this week of celebration, however, that fault rang like a special Hooveresque virtue. "His sin," said one newspaper, "was that he was not also a great politician. Essentially a man of reason and intellect, he was not an emotional leader capable of inflaming the minds of others." Another summed him up as "an honorable gentleman, one perhaps not fitted by nature for the rough-and-tumble hurly-burly of partisan politics, because he would not make tongue-in-cheek promises, because he would not sway with the political winds, because he would not align class against class for political expediency—but nevertheless one of our greatest citizens and one whom history undoubtedly will recognize as one of our greatest Presidents."

2

What follows is an attempt to make what movie people in their own medium call a "montage"—a single eulogy based on dozens cited by Hinshaw, every word drawn from an actual editorial:

There is a man whose name has been vilified but whose countrymen have now come to love and respect him as indisputably our most distinguished private citizen. That man is Herbert Hoover. The sunshine of the nation's gratitude is in his afternoon; full and fair the sunlight falls on Herbert Hoover. The people of the Shadow, his detractors? They have passed "in a desperate disarray over the hills and far away."

The American people acknowledge the high stature of Herbert Hoover, his contributions to the public welfare and his personal virtues of integrity and constancy in the face of unjust and undeserved belittlement and criticism. The American people have slowly become aware of his great worth and the magnitude of the injustice that was done him. He is honored, in truth, not so much as a former President but as a great American.

Not often has there been so widespread and spontaneous a desire to honor such a man in his lifetime. Herbert Hoover is growing in strength among his fellow Americans and to him they turn more often when words of wisdom are needed. He has come to be one of the most respected and admired Americans that ever lived.

People are just beginning to recognize the solid virtue of this man who is so typically American. Herbert Hoover, influenced by the Quaker faith to which he adhered, never developed the capacity to hate those who criticized and reviled him. He hated only those things which he conceived to be wrong, and when he was stirred to anger on this score he was always righteously indignant. Through it all he kept, even as now, his faith in the everlasting righteousness of justice and fair play. He enjoys the admiration and respect now of many people who once hated and abused him. But he has always been what he is today, a fine unselfish public citizen devoted to the welfare of his country and the world.

Like only one or two other statesmen in our history he has been able to go from service to service, making the Presidency only one step in a career which reaches its climax in the total and cumulative record of work done, good causes unselfishly pursued and arduous responsibilities carried through to the end. If ever a man is entitled to feel the deepest kind of satisfaction and content, it is Mr. Hoover at this milestone.

Few men have in their lifetimes undergone such profound fluctuations in public esteem. He has maintained his dignity and composure in victory and defeat. In perspective it can be seen that his public service was all of a piece—patriotic, sincere, humanitarian, and staunchly built on unshakable principle.

The American people are showing a somewhat belated sense of justice in honoring a man who has been viciously and savagely maligned during most of his career. The present high position of Mr. Hoover, along with the great esteem and appreciation in which, regardless of party or class, he is held by the American people generally, is a thrilling demonstration that occasionally the right really does prevail and this appreciation comes before it is too late.

From the peak of achievement he was plunged into a morass of misrepresentation and vilification which would have broken the heart of anyone less valiant. But when abuse was at its highest, Herbert Hoover was at his serenest. And now time is working a revenge for him—the only kind which a man of his Quaker upbringing could accept. Today he enjoys the confidence and esteem of all men of good faith, regardless of creed or party.

It can already be assumed that the name of Herbert Hoover will be recorded with special luster, redeemed from the unjust and undeserved blame that party, parochial politics attached to his courageous, dignified and fundamentally sound efforts to direct the country during his presidential regime. Millions are already sorry for being taken in by the politicians whose tirades made Mr. Hoover the whipping boy of the depression.

Time was when Herbert Hoover was thought cold, but in this also, time has shown us the error. What was so casually and unfairly believed to be chilliness of spirit now is seen to have been something of shyness and something of dignity, alike native to the man's character. Those who flippantly and callously misjudged him were blinded by the disasters of the period. They requited his fidelity by naming him scapegoat. Now they know they were wrong.

Twelve thousand people were gathered on the campus of Stanford University for the birthday party of their most cherished alumnus and neighbor. In his address Hoover said little about himself. Instead, under

the title "Think of the Next Generation," he spoke of trends in government that raise "some grave questions as to our whole future as a nation," and called for a return to certain "principles of government and
morals, if we would preserve the rights and dignity of men to which this
nation is dedicated." He said:

We must wish to maintain a dynamic progressive people. No nation can remain static and survive. But dynamic progress is not made with dynamite. And
that dynamite today is the geometric increase of spending by our governments—
federal, state and local. . . . In the end these solutions of national problems by
spending are always the same—power, more power, more centralization in the
hands of the state.

And in his concluding words, too, there was no allusion to the nationwide tributes of which he was that day the object. He remained on the
plane of impersonal, historic imperatives:

A splendid storehouse of integrity and freedom has been bequeathed to us
by our forefathers. In this day of confusion, of peril to liberty, our high duty
is to see that this storehouse is not robbed of its contents. We dare not see the
birthright of posterity to independence, initiative and freedom of choice bartered
for a mess of a collectivist system.

My word to you, my fellow-citizens on this seventy-fifth birthday is this: The
Founding Fathers dedicated the structure of our government "to secure the
blessings of liberty to our posterity." We of this generation inherited this precious blessing. Yet as spendthrifts we are on our way to rob posterity of its
inheritance.

The American people have solved many great crises in national life. The
qualities of self-restraint, of integrity, of conscience and courage still live in our
people. It is not too late to summon these qualities.

In a number of European cities, also, that birthday was marked by
public meetings. The one in Stuttgart has been described by Lochner in
his book *Herbert Hoover and Germany*. At a gathering for both children
and adults in the ex-President's honor, the principal speaker was Frau
Elly Heuss, wife of the man who subsequently became President of the
Federal Republic of Germany. She addressed herself particularly to the
children:

We want to celebrate a birthday—and our birthday child is already completely grown up: he will be seventy-five years old today! I've been wondering
whether Mr. Hoover this morning thought of the fact that within our area in
Germany many thousands of children even in their vacation camps and hos-
telries are starting out with their little pots and pans in happy anticipation of a
decent, warm Hoover lunch. It must be a beautiful thought for him.

Her audience rose and shouted, "Hoover, *hoch, hoch, hoch!*"

3

Every succeeding birthday, too, was hailed across the nation, as if the accumulation of Hoover's years were a kind of national achievement. Perhaps there are in all of us vestigial traces of ancient patriarchal systems. Or possibly, in Freudian terms, the durable, self-confident Hoover, stern and virtuous, offered a consoling "father image" in times of cold war, nuclear jitters, and other anxieties. However that may be, the habitual sneering at Hoover gave way to no less habitual respect.

Increasingly, with distance and perspective, even the years of the Presidency were reconsidered and found deserving of belated praise. Said a New York editorial on his seventy-eighth birthday: "It is getting dangerous to go on fighting Mr. Hoover. Too many people are coming alive to the fact that he was a great President, just as he is a great man." A popular columnist, Robert Ruark, wrote that same week: "I just wish we could re-run Herbert Hoover for President, because I am certain sure we could win with him and fetch a little sanity back home."

Once, while he was in the Florida Keys for bonefishing, Hoover took ill and was rushed to a hospital. The news was reported in the press, of course. This was the first time in seventy-eight years of life that he remained in a hospital overnight. Clarence Buddington Kelland, the popular novelist, was a guest on the Chief's chartered houseboat. To a fellow Hooverite, Neil MacNeil, he wrote:

Immediately there commenced to arrive a veritable flood of sympathy and good wishes. Telegrams and letters from people of consequence—but the amazing and significant thing was the deluge of printed "get well" cards from all over the nation—cards of the sort one can buy at the corner drug store for a nickel. These from inarticulate people, butchers, bakers, candlestick makers who revered the Chief and knew no other way to express their affection and sympathy. These cards came not by dozens but by thousands, until there were bushel-baskets full of them.

On Hoover's eightieth birthday in 1954, Congress once more attested, in a joint resolution, its affection and gratitude, and the press again confirmed that the Congress was reflecting the sentiments of the citizenry. The ex-President was then in the midst of his second analysis of the Executive branch of the government. The picture of an octogenarian engaged in a great public undertaking—not only the oldest but the hardest-working among the several hundred executives and professional men whom he had mobilized for the job—touched the nation's heart. In the New York *Times Magazine*, R. L. Duffus wrote:

Today Mr. Hoover is not so much an ex-President living on past glory as an active and influential citizen, a sort of one-man "Task Force" working for what he conceives to be the welfare of his country. . . . If he is more widely popular now than he was when he was President, it is not because he has worked at it, but rather because a perception of his character and personality has percolated down to the man in the street.

Collier's featured a birthday editorial that began by identifying Hoover as "one of the most misunderstood and maligned men of our time," and ended on a note of content:

The perspective of years has finally revealed Herbert Hoover to all for what he is—a man to be cherished in a day when "glamor" sometimes serves as a substitute for integrity in public life, a man of wisdom, courage, forebearance and, above all, humaneness and dedication.

The writers of history textbooks have been, as a group, the tardiest in accepting the latterday estimate of Hoover—perhaps, as one of them explained to me, because most new textbooks are rewrites of old ones. It is useful, therefore, to cite one such book which, quite coincidentally, was published in the year of the eightieth birthday. *Recent American History,* by Leland D. Baldwin, said in part:

Hoover has been maligned unjustly as callous, reactionary, inept and even stupid. His policies may or may not have been shortsighted and mistaken, but it is evident that he always kept before him a zeal for promoting human welfare and with this as his guide and principle never flagged or deviated. His shortcomings—if these be such—lay in too great a faith in human reasonableness and in too great a faith that the economic forces which had made us great must continue to operate.

He was an old-fashioned liberal who believed in local responsibility and preferred voluntary association to imposed controls. He believed in democracy and its precious diversities; but he also knew that if two men ride the same horse, one must go on the rump. He was equally opposed to control by special privilege of any economic class and control by Big Government; though he increased the number of service bureaus during his presidency, he actually reduced the total payroll. When he praised rugged individualism he was praising self-reliance, not predatory self-interest.

Since the vocabulary of esteem is limited and repetitive, I resist the temptation of offering more quotations. Suffice that the comment in that year, in editorials and articles and personal messages, was consistent with the "image" established five years before. That image bids fair to blot out and supersede the earlier unpleasant and defamatory stereotype. Future textbooks, it seems a safe guess, will give our school children a more fairminded portrait of Hoover than those still conditioned by the caricatures of the 1930s.

On August 10, 1954, Hoover returned to West Branch, at the invitation of the Iowa state legislature and the governor. Sheaves of congratulatory telegrams and cables from all over the world were awaiting his arrival that morning. Already thousands were beginning to gather in the village. Hoover visited the graves of his parents, then the cottage in which he was born—by now it was a neat, whitewashed shrine maintained by the state of Iowa.

From a platform put up for the great occasion, the governor and other Iowa dignitaries voiced the boundless pride of their state in its native son. Telegrams were read from President Eisenhower and ex-President Truman. The large audience showed almost filial satisfaction that their white-haired guest, at eighty, stood erect and stalwart, clear-eyed, his voice barely touched by the years, his ideas fondly familiar. Said Hoover simply:

I am glad to come to West Branch. My grandparents and my parents came here in a covered wagon. In this community they toiled and worshipped God. They lie buried on your hillside. The most formative years of my boyhood were spent here. My roots are in this soil.

He wanted to discuss, he said—"not in the tones of Jeremiah but in the spirit of Saint Paul"—the forces that make for progress and those "which may corrode away the safeguards of freedom in America." For the corrosions, he said, "the remedies . . . are not revolution" but "mostly jobs of marginal repairs around a sound philosophy and a stout heart," and he warned:

Even if security from the cradle to the grave could eliminate the risks of life, it would be a dead hand on the creative spirit of our people. Also, the judgment of the Lord to Adam about sweat had not been repealed. When we flirt with the Delilah of security for our productive group, we had better watch out, lest in our blindness we pull down the pillars of the temple of free men.

Some years earlier Hoover had published, in the magazine *This Week*, a little essay rejecting "the cult of the Common Man," which has been often quoted and reprinted. He returned to this theme in the West Branch address:

Among the delusions offered us by fuzzy-minded people is that imaginary creature, the Common Man. The whole idea is another cousin of the Soviet proletariat. The *Un*common Man is to be whittled down to size. It is the negation of individual dignity and a slogan of mediocrity and uniformity.

The Common Man dogma may be of use as a vote-getting apparatus. It supposedly proves the humility of the demagogues.

The greatest strides of human progress have come from Uncommon Men and Women. You have perhaps heard of George Washington, Abraham Lincoln, or Thomas Edison. They were humble in origin, but that was not their greatness.

The humor of it is that when we get sick, we want an uncommon doctor. When we go to war, we yearn for an uncommon general or admiral. When we choose the president of a university, we want an uncommon educator.

The imperative need of this nation at all times is the leadership of the Uncommon Men or Women. We need men and women who cannot be intimidated, who are not concerned with applause meters, nor those who sell tomorrow for cheers today.

And in conclusion:

Eighty years is a long time for a man to live. As the shadows lengthen over my years, my confidence, my hopes and dreams for my countrymen are undimmed. This confidence is that with advancing knowledge, toil will grow less exacting; that fear, hatred, pain and tears may subside; that the regenerating sun of creative ability and religious devotion will refresh each morning the strength and progress of my country.

The pattern of nationwide acclaim, its tone becoming ever less political and more affectionate, held true when Hoover reached the age of eighty-five. The *Saturday Evening Post* editorially said:

It is too often forgotten that Herbert Hoover, who celebrated his eighty-fifth birthday August tenth amid glowing tributes from people of all shades of political opinion, was the victim of one of the most vicious, expensive and skillfully engineered smear campaigns in the country's history.

The caption on the editorial read: "Herbert Hoover's Service to the Nation Shames Those Who 'Smeared' Him."

Normally, of course, affection even unto reverence for a former President, rich in years and removed by time from the wars of his prime, would hardly be remarkable. A nation craves heroes, in whom it can see, as in a mirror, reflections of its own most cherished attributes; it is a species of self-flattery. But in Hoover's case there was that long interval of eclipse, contempt, and even persecution. What the American people witnessed and savored, therefore, was a vindication, complete and ungrudging, and suffused by a glow of relief that a wrong had been righted, a blot erased. His life seemed in some measure a comforting morality play, in which Good triumphs over Evil.

Thousands of those who thought they "hated" Hoover were now hard put to remember why. For their "hatred" had been directed against a symbol bearing his name, rather than the flesh-and-blood man. There remained plenty of criticism of his policies, philosophy, and personality, but there was no longer a receptive audience for malice against the thirty-first President.

XXXIV

The "Elder Statesman"

PUBLICATION of the second Hoover Commission report on government operations and functions added substantially to the stature of the ex-President, notwithstanding the opposition it churned up. Even most of those who objected vehemently to some of its specific proposals were impressed by its solidity and coherence, and the boldness of its recommendations.

This was the last significant assignment Herbert Hoover carried out for the government. He was eighty-one. Thereafter he undertook honorific official chores from time to time—like helping entertain visiting royalty or representing the President on state occasions—but it was generally recognized that he was through with official enterprises of large scale.

The idea of retirement, however, never entered his mind. When pressed for his prescription for a long life, his answer was always the same: meaningful work. "I have not retired," he told interviewers repeatedly, "and I don't intend to." Once he explained:

There is no joy to be had from retirement except in some kind of productive work. Otherwise you degenerate into talking to everybody about your pains and pills and the other fellow talks about his. Any oldster who keeps at even part-time work has something worth talking about. He has a zest for the morning paper and his three meals a day. The point is not to retire from work or you will shrivel up into a nuisance to all mankind.

Asked, upon reaching eighty-five, what he was doing with his "spare time," he offered a six-point outline. The first item was: "Watching the dangers which surround our country—hoping to be of occasional service," and the last: "Attending baseball games." In between he listed the writing of four volumes under the title of *An American Epic:* a documented history of American relief and other benevolences since 1914; attending to

418

the affairs of the Boys' Clubs of America and the Hoover Institution on War, Revolution and Peace; serving as chairman, trustee, or in other capacities in about a dozen other institutions.

For completeness, the inventory should have included his continuing indulgence in public oratory, written or personal testimony in response to legislative requests for his opinions, and frequent magazine articles. No, he certainly had not retired. A staff of from six to eight secretaries and researchers could barely keep up with him. Said his longtime secretary, Bernice Miller: "The Chief's idea of a vacation is to work eight hours a day instead of sixteen." Rarely, in fact, did he go on a fishing expedition or to a Bohemian Grove encampment without a backlog of work and a secretary or two to help him.

Between January 1946 and April 1959, a period of a little over twelve years, Hoover made 185 major speeches and a multitude of minor pronouncements. I have no statistics for the subsequent period, except that during his eighty-seventh year (August 1960 to August 1961), despite the encroachments of ill health, he delivered seven full-parade addresses and broadcasts.

Obviously, therefore, he was never silent for long. There were few public issues on which he did not express his always vigorous views. No attempt can be made here to summarize them; nearly all are on record in the eight volumes of his *Addresses upon the American Road:* the last volume embraces his pronouncements from 1955 to 1960 and discloses that domestic and foreign affairs were still under his constant scrutiny.

Though the New Deal slid into the Fair Deal (with unintentional implications that what was "new" had not always been "fair"), and even after the Republicans returned to power in January 1953, the former President continued to protest and warn against the siphoning off of the people's savings by government. Collectivism in any disguise was still his principal target.

While approving both military and economic aid to democratic nations, he was often critical of its proliferation and attendant wastes. Moreover, he demanded that the recipients live up to their ends of the implied bargain.

He had supported Senate ratification of the United Nations Charter as the best that could be obtained under the existing circumstances. But from the start he had many doubts about its efficacy. Among other things he had urged guarantees against American involvement in war without consent of Congress in consequence of UN decisions. But as evidence of Communist misuse of the UN machinery piled up through the years, he became increasingly sharp in his criticism.

Hoover's abhorrence of Communism never faltered. Unlike some other statesmen, he would not permit habit to breed acceptance, nor would he acknowledge the "finality" of Communist rule anywhere. He kept reminding his countrymen that the United States and its democratic allies, having won the war on the battlefields, lost it to Stalin at conferences. That humiliating history, he felt, must not be forgotten or condoned. We could not slough off our share of guilt for the enslavement of millions.

At least two of his foreign policy themes provoked national debates and remained subjects of controversy long after the debates subsided.

The first referred to military strategy. Hoover believed that Western Europe could and should generate its own ground forces, with the United States contributing arms and munitions as long as necessary. Our country should concentrate its industrial and technological resources on air, naval, and nuclear power. If Europe refused to do its full military share, he argued, the chances of its being saved by this country were slight in any case. Our primary duty would then be to make an "impregnable fortress" out of the Western Hemisphere, rather than dissipate our strength on huge armies for overseas warfare. In a broadcast in late 1950 he said:

We are not blind to the need to preserve Western civilization on the continent of Europe. But the prime obligation of defense of Western Continental Europe rests upon the nations of Europe. The test is whether they have the spiritual force, the will, and acceptance of unity among them by their own volition. America cannot create their spiritual forces; we cannot buy them with money.

Even many of those who normally went along with Hoover's views questioned his strategic assumptions. If Europe fell to the Communists, though through its own fault, could an isolated America long survive? Modern weapons, they pointed out, had canceled out the ocean barriers and, indeed, the possibility of an "impregnable fortress" anywhere.

The second set of Hoover proposals that touched off heated debate grew out of his deepening despair over the impotence of the United Nations. The contradictions inherent in an organization built on the premise of "one world," when in fact there were two, were becoming more apparent with every new Soviet veto and every new installment of Communist billingsgate. In an address to the Newspaper Publishers Association in April 1950, Hoover therefore called for what amounted to the expulsion of the Communist bloc:

What the world needs today is a moral mobilization against the hideous ideas of the police state and human slavery. The world needs mobilization against this creeping Red imperialism. The United States needs to know who are with us in the cold war against these practices and whom we can depend on.

I suggest that the United Nations should be reorganized without the communist nations in it. If that is impractical, then a definite New United Front should be organized of those peoples who disavow communism, who stand for morals and religion, and who love freedom.

As was to be expected, the startling suggestion drew instant and violent attacks. Nevertheless, in all the years that followed, Hoover continued to defend the proposal. The United Nations, he complained, has become "a forum for continuous smear on our honor, our ideals and our purposes." It could intimidate the small and the weak but was helpless to restrain the one expanding imperialism on earth.

Hoover did, more and more, retreat from his original concept of a purged United Nations in favor of the alternative—a worldwide organization composed solely of free and unambiguously anti-communist nations. As late as 1962, in his eighty-eighth birthday address at West Branch, he returned to this vision, proposing a Council of Free Nations—more cohesive and stronger than the United Nations. In the meantime, of course, Anthony Eden and others had made equivalent suggestions for a common front for freedom as counterweight to the UN.

Hoover's political and economic views made the headlines and touched off discussion. Yet the main ingredients of his writings and public speaking were "inspirational"—appeals to conscience and patriotism. Whatever else he said, the unvarying theme was America: the traditions that had made the country prosperous and compassionate and therefore a reservoir of strength, material help, and moral guidance to the rest of mankind.

2

When the elder Robert Wagner resigned from the United States Senate in June 1949, the Republican governor of New York, Thomas E. Dewey, offered the seat for the unexpired term to Hoover. The ex-President acknowledged the compliment but declined the interim appointment. The governor's gesture, however, indicated the new status and stature of Hoover within his party. His appearance at every National Republican Convention became almost a ritual of acclaim. Both in 1956 and 1960, the press reported, he drew ovations as enthusiastic as those accorded to President Eisenhower; more so, said some correspondents.

This period, beginning roughly with his seventy-fifth birthday, might be described as Hoover's career as an Elder Statesman. Another of his many lives. At least a little of the flavor of his views and the philosophy from which they stemmed, in these evening years, is provided by his addresses to successive Republican conventions.

Chicago, July 6, 1952: This was the fifth time he had addressed a convention, he said, and "from the inexorable course of nature, this is likely to be the last time." The dominant issue, overshadowing all others, as he saw it, was "the freedom of men," challenged both at home and abroad. He dealt first with the domestic dangers:

The genius of our Founding Fathers which preserved this Republic longer than any Republic in history was the concept of the limitation of powers within our government. One of their strong purposes was to protect free men by restriction of presidential power.

For twenty years we have seen constant attrition of those Constitutional safeguards of free men. I do not need recall to you the "Rubber Stamp Congress"; the packed Supreme Court; war without approval of Congress; and a score of dire secret international commitments without consent of the Senate. And now comes, after one hundred and seventy years, a new discovery in presidential power. That is an "inherent" power to seize anything, any time. All Republican Presidents were densely ignorant of those inherent powers.

Over these twenty years we have seen pressure groups fostered and appeased by Presidents until they intimidate and paralyze the life of the nation. No man has been elected by the people to have such powers. If freedom is to live, we can no more have economic tyranny than we can have political tyranny. Representative government has not been maintained in the mastery of its own house. . . .

The grandeur of a people comes from their moral and spiritual character. Today that grandeur is corroded by this intellectual dishonesty and corruption among public officials. The drip, drip, drip from dishonor in high places plays a part in the increasing crime among the people.

"On this, my last address to you," he wished to speak from his heart on foreign policies, too:

Twelve years ago we were led into a great war crusade on the promise of freedom to men and to nations under the banner of the Four Freedoms and the Atlantic Charter. Then at Teheran, Yalta and Potsdam we sacrificed the freedom of 650 millions of human beings on the altar of appeasement of communism. The souls of one-quarter of mankind have been seared by the violation of that American promise. The ghosts of the Four Freedoms and the Atlantic Charter now wander amid the clanking chains of a thousand slave camps.

Referring to the Declaration of Independence by a convention in 1776, Hoover urged "a new Declaration that will raise the hearts of our people to their spiritual purpose and their eyes into the sunlight of freedom." We must, he said, "revive again hope in a frustrated people" and "recapture the citadels of liberty":

Thus can America be preserved. Thus can it hold the lamp of free men aloft to a confused world. Thus can we wipe out coercion and corruption. Thus can the peace, plenty and security be established and expanded. Thus can the opportunity, and the spiritual future of your children be guaranteed. And thus you will win the gratitude of posterity, and the blessings of Almighty God.

At this 1952 convention, incidentally, Hoover tried hard to maintain an outward neutrality as between Eisenhower and Senator Robert Taft. But his preference was no secret, and at the last moment he issued a statement in Taft's support.

San Francisco, August 21, 1956: Twice before, Hoover told the Republican Centennial Convention, he had indicated that he was making his farewell appearance. That, he said, still did not match the record of the great singer Adelina Patti, who came to America six times for farewell concerts—"But do not get too alarmed over the possibility of three more from me."

His stress was once more on freedom. It was, he said, the most dynamic idea in history and in modern times its true home was in this country. For "ours is a system which holds that human values transcend all others, and that there is a public responsibility to the sick, the veterans, the unemployed, to the aged and to dependent children." The Eisenhower administration, he thought, had made some progress in safeguarding the great heritage, but the battle was as yet far from won.

Instead of the traditional party platform, he suggested, the convention "should make a resounding Declaration of Principles of American Life." The great task of the time, he said, was "to generate a spirit which will rekindle in every American a love not only for his country but a devotion to its true ideals." We must "feed the reviving fires of spiritual fervor which once stirred Americans to live and die for human liberty—Americans who knew no private interest, no personal ambition, no popular acclaim, no advantage of pride or place which overshadows the burning love for freedom of man."

Despite his recitals of many national ills, he attested his undying faith in America:

I have lived a long life. I have witnessed, and even taken part in, many great and threatening crises. With each time they have been surmounted, the American Dream has become more real. . . . If the American people are guided aright, there will be no decline and fall in American civilization.

Chicago, July 25, 1960: Facing the convention, the eighty-six-year-old ex-President was almost apologetic because three times his "affectionate goodbyes did not take," but "unless some miracle come to me from the Good Lord this is finally it." He abstained, on this occasion, from detailed comment on specific events and policies, limiting himself largely to a summons to patriotism:

This nation needs a rebirth of that great spiritual force which has been impaired by cynicism and weakened by foreign infections. Call it nationalism if you will. But there is an American kind of nationalism, which is neither isolationism nor aggression and embedded deep within it is compassion for distress both at home and overseas. It is the kind of nationalism which recognizes changes in the world and requires that we meet them with forward-looking measures. . . .

The spiritual force of which I speak is enshrined in the word *America*. We do not use that word merely as a geographical term. At one time—and even now for millions of Americans—that word summoned to mind the whole background of our nation.

This word *America* recalls that millions of people for over three hundred years have sought our shores as a refuge from oppression. To these millions the word *America* came to mean a civilization unique on earth by the fusion of the attainments of scores of nations. For centuries the word *America* among the great masses of people over the world has been an emblem of hope, of more security in life—and more freedom. . . .

The word *America* means that our wars were not fought for the glory of war but for freedom in the world. It means a country where the doors of opportunity are open to every boy and girl. It means law and order, freedom of choice and callings. It means glorious strides in the advancement of civilization.

The word *America* envisions the rills of freedom springing from our mountains and plains, pouring into a mighty river which refreshes not only our own people but the whole of mankind.

Against this background, Hoover proceeded to castigate those Americans who appeared to be suffering from a sense of guilt over the prosperity and power of their native land: "a multitude of citizens who have sunk to a posture of perpetual apology and seeming shame for ourselves." Despite them he believed that we "can stop this moral retreat" and "lead the attack to recapture the meaning of the word—*America*."

Talking to a reporter on the eve of his eighty-sixth birthday, some days later, he explained: "I made that speech because I hoped to awaken more pride in our country, and an enlightened nationalism as a regenerative force from national apathy and moral slump." That he had touched myriad hearts and minds, he added, was proved by the thousands of approving and thankful letters that had already poured in upon him. They showed, he was sure, "that some force is stirring our people beyond the satisfactions of increasing standards of living and the events of international life."

3

At the World's Fair in Brussels, in 1958, the pavilions of the United States and the Soviet Union stood in close proximity: a symbolic confrontation of the two worlds. High Soviet officials had come to the scene, with their familiar boasts of material achievement; the emphasis of their whole exhibition, indeed, was on material things. The ranking American to visit the Fair, not in title but in prestige, consequently provided a wholesome contrast. For it was Herbert Hoover, who—especially in Belgium—personified friendship and benevolence.

July Fourth was set aside by the Fair authorities to honor American Independence Day. The news that the eighty-four-year-old Hoover was coming over for the occasion as President Eisenhower's personal envoy was hailed throughout Belgium with sincere and unabashedly extravagant jubilation. The country's most famous Honorary Citizen had been a national hero ever since 1914; his reputation was undiminished and untarnished after forty-four years. By common consent the fifth of July was called Hoover Day.

He valued this opportunity, Hoover said in his Independence Day address on the Fair grounds, "to refresh my friendship with the Belgian people, which has now lasted for more than forty-four years." He spoke "On American Ideals" and their importance in a time of totalitarian challenge. The extraordinary success of the American experiment in freedom, he underlined, brought benefits to all mankind: "Our productivity has created great margins which have enabled us to support the freedom of mankind, and to help lift the world's burdens of disaster and poverty." He went on:

In interpreting the ideals of my country, I must include the spirit of compassion towards suffering humanity. It spreads from every American home to all mankind. I need only recall the great famines which have inevitably followed these two score years of world wars. The American people with other nations met these emergencies. But the United States carried the major burdens. By longer hours of labor they stimulated production. They denied themselves food and clothing that more than one billion of peoples all over the world might have the margins on which to live and to hope for a better day.

This spirit of compassion has contributed also to the rehabilitation of many millions of children, diseased and debilitated by famine. Thereby, the world has been saved from the political and moral dangers of millions of distorted bodies and minds. And this compassion has also been extended to Communist Russia.

Even as it has shared its food and goods, Hoover declared, America has shared with the world its scientific discoveries and inventions. He then struck out at the "false legends, misrepresentations and vicious propaganda" being spread about America throughout the free world:

Probably the greatest misrepresentation of our ideals is that we are imperialistically minded and that we daily practice imperialism. It would seem that the world might take account of the Monroe Doctrine, whereby we have aided our Latin American neighbors to secure their freedoms. I could also recall our giving freedom to Cuba and the Philippines and our urging of independence for Puerto Rico.

Moreover, in the last forty years, invariably at the request of nations struggling against oppression or military aggression, our sons have fought and died in three great wars. They died that more freedom would come to mankind and

425

that the world might have a lasting peace. Never after victory did we ask for an acre of territory, except a few military bases to protect the free nations. We have never asked for reparations or economic privileges. On the contrary, we made gigantic gifts and loans to aid nations in war and reconstruction, including Communist Russia. . . . There is no imperialism either in our hearts or in our government.

The following day, Hoover Day, the American guest dominated the news and the hearts of Belgium. He was entertained by the royal family. But the peak point of the celebration was another meeting in the very room where the National Committee for the Relief of Belgium had met regularly during the First World War. It was a re-enactment of the emotional scene, which we have witnessed in an earlier chapter, during Hoover's visit in 1938. Now, however, barely a dozen of the Old Guard were still alive to take part in the proceedings. Hoover spoke with great feeling of those epic days, events, and leaders four decades ago, and his words were carried by radio to a new generation of Belgians.

4

In an age when novelty seems an end in itself, when semantic jugglery often employs the adjective "new" to conceal the real nature of things— the "new" freedom, the "new" liberalism, the "new" morality—it takes both courage and wisdom to adhere to old, tried values. This was Hoover's theme in a broadcast in Des Moines on the occasion of the centennial of his native Iowa. He said in part:

The principal thing we can do if we really want to make the world over again is to try the word "old" for a while. There are some "old" things that made this country.

There is the Old Virtue of religious faith. There are the Old Virtues of integrity and the whole truth. There is the Old Virtue of incorruptible service and honor in public office. There are the Old Virtues of economy in government, of self-reliance, thrift and individual liberty. There are the Old Virtues of patriotism, real love of country and willingness to sacrifice for it.

These "old" ideals are very inexpensive. They even would help win hot and cold wars. I realize such suggestions will raise that cuss word, "reactionary." But some of these things are slipping badly in American life. And if they slip too far, the lights will go out of America, even if we win these cold and hot wars. Think about it. . . .

On Washington's Birthday, 1958, Hoover spoke at Valley Forge as the guest of the Freedoms Foundation and recipient of its highest award for the year. He promised that there would be a "surprise statement at the end of the address"—and I, too, will keep his secret until the reader has absorbed the address. It follows, with only minor deletions—an eloquent summation of Hoover's vision of our America:

We gather here . . . to pay our homage to the 226th anniversary of the birth of George Washington. There is no place which more greatly marks his immortal grandeur than these fields of Valley Forge. This national shrine needs no description; the events enacted here require no recounting to the American people. The very name, Valley Forge, swells within us pride in our Nation.

These peaceful fields hold a glory peculiarly their own. It was not the glory of war for which these fields are remembered. No great battle was fought here. It was not the pomp of victory, for no martial triumph was won here. It was not the scene where peace was signed by which independence of a great nation was won. A thousand other fields mark the tombs of the courage, the glory, the valor, the skill, the martial triumph of our people. Yet the instinct and the judgment of our people after the abrasion of the years has appraised this place as a foremost national shrine.

George Washington and his men at any moment could have surrendered their ideals to the widespread spirit of despair and discouragement. They could have abandoned their claims to freedom. They could have deserted their hopes and forsaken their faith.

Here Washington and his little band of hungry and almost naked patriots kept alive the spark of liberty in the world. They met this, the deepest crisis of the Revolution, with steadfast fortitude; they conserved their strength; they husbanded their resources, they seized the opportunity which, with the turn of the tide, led on to victory. It was a triumph of character and idealism. Here was one of those moral victories that are the glory of the human race. Without such victories the life of man would descend to a sheer materialism for "where there is no vision the people perish." There mankind could claim no distinction, sing no songs, dream no dreams, inspire no hope, and grasp no faith. . . .

An ideal is an unselfish aspiration. It is a thing of the spirit: Our ideals are the cement which binds our society. They provide the mainspring of progress. It is this spirit which has made possible the success of our great democratic experiment. They have tempered our acquisitiveness, have strengthened our sense of civic responsibility, and have made service to our fellow man a part of our national character.

This peculiar significance of Valley Forge should strike with especial force in this particular moment of our national life. To each and every one of us it is an hour of unusual stress and trial. The nation is beset with difficulties and confusions. These temporary reverses in the march of progress have been in part the penalty of the malign inheritances of world forces beyond our control.

Many have doubt and grave concern for the future. But no one who reviews the past and realizes the vast strength of our people can doubt that this, like a score of similar experiences in our history, is a passing trial. From this knowledge must come the courage and wisdom to improve and strengthen us for the future.

Numerous are the temptations under the distress of the day to turn aside from our true national purposes and from wise national policies and fundamental ideals of the men who built our Republic. Never was the lure of the rosy path to every panacea and of easy ways to imagined security more tempting.

For the energies of private initiative, of independence, and a high degree of individual freedom of our American system we are offered alluring substitutes with the specious claim that everybody collectively owes each of us individually a living rather than an opportunity to earn a living—and the equally specious claim that hired representatives of scores of millions of people can do better than the people themselves, in thinking and planning their daily life.

We must not be misled by the claim that the source of all wisdom is in the government. Wisdom is born out of experience, and most of all out of precisely such experience as is brought to us by the darkest moments. It is in meeting such moments that are born new insights, new sympathies, new powers, new skills. Such conflicts as we are in the midst of today cannot be won by any single stroke, by any one strategy sprung from the mind of any single genius. Rather must we pin our faith upon the inventiveness, the resourcefulness, the initiative of every one of us. That cannot fail us if we keep the faith in ourselves and our future, and in the constant growth of our intelligence and ability to cooperate with one another.

The memory of Americans who glory in Valley Forge even as they glory in Yorktown tells us the truth which echoes upward from this soil of blood and tears, that the way to the nation's greatness is the path of self-reliance, independence, and steadfastness in time of trial and stress.

Valley Forge met such a challenge to steadfastness in times and terms of war. Our test is to meet this challenge in time and terms of peace. It is the same challenge. It is the same test of steadfastness of will, of clarity of thought, of resolution of character, of fixity of purpose, of loyalty to ideals and of unshaken conviction that they will prevail.

We, too, are writing a new chapter in American history. If we weaken, as Washington did not, we shall be writing the introduction to the decline of American character and the fall of American institutions. If we are firm and farsighted, as were Washington and his men, we shall progress. If, by the grace of God, we stand steadfast in our great traditions through this time of stress, we shall insure that we and our sons and daughters shall see these fruits increased many fold.

Valley Forge is our American synonym for the trial of human character through privation and suffering, and it is the symbol of the triumph of the American soul. If those few thousand men endured that long winter of privation and suffering, humiliated by the despair of their countrymen, yet held their countrymen to the faith, and by that holding held fast the freedom of America, what right have we to be of little faith? God grant that we may prove worthy of George Washington and his men of Valley Forge.

Then came the "surprise" he had promised. He revealed that this was the identical speech he had delivered at the same place *twenty-seven years earlier*, on Memorial Day 1931.

He was then President of the United States, "the world was in the depths of the greatest economic depression in our history," the American people were confused and discouraged, even as they are at present. Yet

he believed that what he had said in 1931 was equally pertinent in 1958
—and will be twenty-seven years after 1958. The point was not that Hoover clung to his views but that they were basic and timeless. Ours has
been and will be a nation resolutely dedicated to ideals, aware of its
heritage and determined to shield it against the corrosions of doubt and
fear. Though he had been and remained an outspoken critic of his country in the short run, his long-run confidence in its destiny never wavered.

5

On the eve of Hoover's eighty-eighth birthday, a chartered plane flew
him, several members of his staff, and about half a hundred friends from
New York to Cedar Rapids, Iowa, each paying his own fare. On board
were a few of Hoover's colleagues from the Belgian days—their number
by now lamentably small—and others who had worked with him on later
undertakings in relief and government. We were going to the gala birthday party in Hoover's native West Branch, twenty-seven miles southeast
of Cedar Rapids, the following morning.

The men and women in the plane were of diverse backgrounds and
professions, brought together again by their common affection for the
Chief. And they were worried. Hoover was not feeling well, and kept to
himself in the forward compartment. But he summoned his guests, singly
or in twos, for a chat. He was willing to discuss the state of the world and
the nation—anything but the state of his health. When my turn came, our
talk was about the books on which he was then at work.

West Branch (population under a thousand) was gay with red, white,
and blue bunting. A crowd of some forty-five thousand was on hand this
sun-drenched morning of August 10, 1962—more than had ever before
come there to honor the Quaker President. At least half of those shirt-
sleeved men, those women and children, by my own wild estimate, had
not yet been born when Hoover became President. Young and old, they
felt themselves in the presence of a great historical figure.

The formal occasion for the gathering was the dedication of the Hoover
Presidential Library, a beautiful one-story limestone structure built at a
cost of five hundred thousand dollars in private donations to house his
official papers and personal mementos. It was turned over that morning
to the head of the National Archives, to become part of the Presidential
Library System that includes the Eisenhower Library at Abilene, Kansas;
the Truman Library at Independence, Missouri; the Franklin D. Roosevelt Library at Hyde Park, New York; and the proposed Kennedy Library
at Harvard University.

Droves of admirers had traveled to West Branch even from distant
states to attest their admiration for the aged man. Thousands trooped

through the new building. They stood reverently before the cottage in which a President had first seen the light, and before the replica of his father's tiny blacksmith shop across the street. And being normal Americans, they took pride in the fact that so humble a place, eighty-eight years ago, had produced a towering national and international figure.

Dwight Eisenhower was in Europe and expressed genuine regrets that he could not be at the birthday party. But the third of the living ex-Presidents, Harry Truman, Hoover's junior by ten years, had come in from Missouri. Shortly before August 10, the press had reported that a brother-in-law of Truman was seriously ill. Admiral Strauss, who organized the party, thereupon wrote him that, under the circumstances, everyone would understand his absence if he couldn't attend the celebration. To which Truman replied that "the only thing that could keep me from coming would be my own death." At West Branch this day he was jaunty and outgoing, mixed with the crowds and later, from the improvised platform in Hoover Park, spoke of his consistent esteem for his predecessor. In the course of the ceremony a warm message was read from President John F. Kennedy, hailing Hoover's "selfless devotion to public service."

When Hoover was introduced, there were thundering waves of applause. Then the great crowd was quiet, almost subdued. Many of these people had been present eight years before, for his previous visit to West Branch. Now Hoover was a little stooped, visibly feebler, and he half-sat on a high cushioned stool as he delivered his prepared address. His voice was less firm, and every now and then he faltered over a line of type on the teleprompter. His characteristic brand of impromptu humor was still on tap. An Iowa engineering society having awarded him a license entitling him to practice the trade of engineer, he reassured the donors that they had no cause to fear his competition.

A reporter at the scene wrote from West Branch: "Here with the country and the people he loves, Herbert Hoover somehow seems larger than life-sized."

Notwithstanding the strains of the birthday party, Hoover on the return flight that evening seemed in better health and certainly in better spirits. The gathering had been refreshing, for it renewed his strong sense of identity with the American people; for any leader, and especially for a man like Hoover, that is a source of vitality. In the forward compartment, he read the many messages that had come to him and, with a touch of human vanity, he sent out to his friends on the plane some of the more eloquent and some that bore celebrated signatures.

In an editorial the following morning, the New York *Times* spoke for the whole country when it said: "If freedom is today more secure in America than in any other place in the world, Herbert Hoover helped to make it so."

XXXV

The Ninth Decade

HERBERT HOOVER, in his old age, had reason for inner peace and temporal content. The hate-Hoover miasma had been dispersed—the few survivors among those who had whipped up the poisonous fog were themselves ashamed of it. The institutions and organizations especially close to his heart were all doing well. Of course, he was paying the melancholy price of longevity, which is increasing loneliness —the ranks of his first generations of friends were thinning fast. But those who remained were drawn closer around their Chief in a warm community. Though he chose to live alone, Hoover had the love and companionship of a close-knit, devoted family of children, grandchildren, and great-grandchildren; it was, under its Quaker restraints, a family rich in shared affection and admiration.

In the course of an autobiographical article in 1951, the ex-President boasted, in his quiet way, that his sons had already made more money than their father, although they had been able to keep less of it under the new tax conditions. He might have added, and didn't, that they scored so well without financial or other help from himself. Both Herbert and Allan were proud of their father but resolved not to exploit his celebrity.

At the time Herbert, Jr. was designated Under Secretary of State—his only public office—an article about him in *Life* (October 11, 1954) led off with a reference to the famous name he bore. "It has been," the writer, Cameron Hawley, said, "the greatest single influence in his life, both curb and spur, his cross as well as his darkly guiding star." Precisely because of his deep loyalty to his father, Herbert had "a dogged determination to be his own man . . . grimly resolute that no advantage be taken of reflected fame."

This judgment applies equally to the younger son, Allan. An emphatic distaste for the limelight seemed to run in the blood. They both led their

431

own lives, worked hard, prospered immensely, and tried to steer clear of the controversies swirling around their father's head. Increasingly through the years, however, they joined in many of his benevolences, even taking over some organizational chores to lighten his burdens.

His service in the State Department was not of Herbert's seeking. For a long time he had acted as consultant on petroleum problems to many foreign governments, among them Iran. Nationalization of the Anglo-Iranian Oil Company provoked a crisis affecting both the economic and political interests of the United States. By the fall of 1953 the conflict between Britain and Iran was hopelessly snarled. Soviet Russia seemed likely to be the beneficiary of the impasse. At that point John Foster Dulles, Secretary of State, induced Herbert, Jr. to become his adviser on petroleum diplomacy, with the Iranian tangle as his special assignment.

It took nearly a year of intensive negotiations—shuttling between London, Teheran, and Washington—but he succeeded where others had failed. The settlement of the oil dispute brought him a lot of press attention and wide acclaim. He then accepted the appointment as Under Secretary and, because Dulles was out of the country a great deal, frequently served as Acting Secretary. In 1957, though importuned to remain, Herbert chose to return to private life; evidently the experience of his father did not seem to him to recommend a career in government.

This one period in public office was the only time any of President Hoover's offspring "made news" in a big way.

For a year (1928–29) Herbert taught in the Harvard Business School, where he had completed postgraduate courses. He was tempted by the academic discipline but found himself drawn into a variety of exciting and profitable businesses, mostly in electronics as related to radio and aviation. Then, having helped perfect devices for electronic exploration of oil deposits, he specialized more and more in petroleum. The United Geophysical Company, which he founded in 1935, flourished under his direction. He disposed of all his business interests, however, when he became Under Secretary of State.

His brother Allan had majored in economics at Stanford and started his career in a bank. Assigned to manage acreage belonging to the bank, he was soon engaged on his own in large-scale agriculture in California. At the same time he became interested in mining ventures and finally, in the late 1940s, began to devote most of his time to this business.

In October 1955 the New York Board of Trade voted its annual Gold Award for public service to Herbert, Jr. and, because he was then abroad on official business, his father accepted it in his behalf. The elder Hoover, it happened, had received the same award in 1949, so he now said:

There is nothing that makes a father's heart glow warmer than accomplishment of his sons. It took me seventy-five years to achieve such merit as seemed to warrant the Board of Trade to confer this very medal upon me some five years ago. Herbert, Jr. achieved that degree of merit after only fifty-two years. That you recognize that he is better material than his dad was at that age confirms my own view of him.

The light tone veiled real pride. Hoover always took an undemonstrative satisfaction in the achievements of his sons and in the fact that they were involved, with unobtrusive earnestness, in more and more "good works."

In his ninth decade Hoover's life had fallen into a pleasant routine. During the summer he spent a month or two in California, rarely missing the Bohemian Grove encampment in July. Winters came to mean the Key Largo Anglers' Club in Florida, usually with a chartered boat for deep-sea fishing. For the rest, his home was the same commodious apartment at the Waldorf Towers he and Lou Hoover had rented in the mid-thirties, with a set of offices adjoining.

He worked at a small, uncluttered desk in the living room. The walls of the apartment were hung with dozens of framed citations, letters, scrolls, inscribed photographs, and the living room mantlepiece was crowded with a variety of cherished mementos and souvenirs. The late Mrs. Hoover's precious collection of ancient Chinese blue and white porcelains was displayed in corner cabinets.

And always there was vital work in progress—stacks of files and books and printers' proofs overflowing on end tables and sofas. One is impressed with the sheer dimensions of his activities. At a time of life when most men rest on their oars and contemplate the expansive seascape of their past, his mind and spirit remained magnetized by tasks of the present and challenges of the future. Not retreat into leisure but renewed immersion in real problems and adventures—that, in fact, was his recipe for long life.

Politics, except in its broadest sense of national and world trends, seemed steadily to decline in the scale of his interests and preoccupations. Precedence had been regained, in Hoover's evening years, by his humanitarian impulses. His Quaker conscience remained in command of his time and energies. It was an organ so integral to his nature that he was scarcely aware of it, responding to its dictates as automatically as other men respond to the prod of greed or pride or ambition.

But Republicans with a yen for the White House, far from avoiding Hoover as in the past, now made frequent overtures. President Eisenhower's warm feeling for Hoover was genuine and he never missed an opportunity to show it, privately and publicly. In February 1963 the

Jewish Council against Communism, in Los Angeles, was presenting an award to Hoover, *in absentia*. Among the congratulatory messages, one from Eisenhower expressed his "grand admiration and respect" for the older man's "wisdom, sound judgment and dedication to American ideals."

Some days after his election, the late John F. Kennedy met with Vice President Richard Nixon, the defeated candidate, in Florida. The story was front-page news, but the public did not know until weeks later that ex-President Hoover had acted as intermediary, at the request of Joseph P. Kennedy, the winner's father, in arranging the meeting. The elder Kennedy had always counted himself among Hoover's supporters—not quite inside the magic circle of the Hoover cult but conspicuous on its periphery.

Nixon, who is also a Quaker, has told the story in his book, *Six Crises*. He was resting at Key Biscayne after the election. A call came through from Hoover who, in Nixon's words, "never wastes a word in a telephone conversation: no introduction, no amenities, just the substance of whatever is at hand":

I said, "Hello, Chief." He replied: "The Ambassador [Joe Kennedy] has just called me and suggested that it would be a good idea for you and the President-elect to get together for a visit. If you approve of the idea, the President-elect, who is now in Palm Beach, would like to phone you to make the necessary arrangements."

I asked what he thought I should do. He said: "I think we are in enough trouble in the world today; some indications of national unity are not only desirable but essential." I answered that under the circumstances, I would of course be willing . . .

When the Peace Corps was launched, President Kennedy asked Hoover to serve as its Honorary Chairman. Hoover begged off on the ground that he was too busy with urgent writing. On several occasions, while in New York, Kennedy called on Hoover to pay his respects. In the course of his first visit to New York as President, Lyndon Johnson went to the Waldorf apartment for a friendly chat with the ailing ex-President.

Even in periods of illness and convalescence, Hoover kept himself intimately informed of the work of a dozen educational, charitable, and scientific organizations. The Boys' Clubs, Stanford University, the Hoover Institution, the National Fund for Medical Education, the Institute of Nutritional Sciences, the World Rehabilitation Fund, the United Engineering Societies—for these and others he had that sense of personal responsibility most men and women reserve for their private business and family affairs.

Among these organizations, as always, those related to the needs and problems of children and youth had prior call on his services. No doubt his own poverty-ridden childhood, though he made so light of it in his reminiscences, played a role in this lifelong dedication. There was in it also the impulse of an engineering mind to husband the most important resources of humanity—its ever-new generations.

In his eighty-seventh year he was the guest of honor and the principal speaker at the dedication of a handsome new national headquarters of the Boys' Clubs of America in New York, christened the Herbert Hoover Building. He had led the fund drive that made the structure possible and now acknowledged gifts from foundations and the rich. But what he found most touching, he said, "have been the contributions of pennies, nickels and dimes, bricks and handiwork by the boys themselves." His heart went out in understanding to those he called the "pavement boys." On an earlier occasion, in 1956, he had said:

Our civilization has made a difficult environment for these boys by covering their world with bricks and cement. We have equipped it with trucks, cabs, lampposts and policemen. . . . To me, as a boy who grew up ranging the fields, tracking the rabbits and prairie chickens with the help of an unregistered mutt, these places in our cities are especially depressing.

2

In theory Hoover cut down his load of self-imposed labor about the time he reached eighty-four, when he underwent his first serious operation. But in practice he continued to keep a battery of secretaries busy eight or ten hours a day and for himself a ten- or twelve-hour working day and a seven-day work week were more the rule than the exception.

When Hoover was approaching eighty-five, I asked Miss Miller to give me some idea of how the Chief occupied his time. She came through with a memorandum outlining his activities during a recent fortnight. Her boss, it appeared, had returned from Florida and plunged at once into an accumulation of work in New York. In the next two weeks he—

Wrote 371 letters, twenty-eight of them to children seeking help or advice.

Became a member of four public-service committees, after declining invitations to join many others.

Turned down thirty-one invitations to make speeches.

Accepted two awards: an Honorary Membership in the Civil War Commission, and the Hosea Ballou II Silver Medal from Tufts University.

Attended two large public functions: the Stanford Founders' Day Dinner and a Tufts fund-raising luncheon.

Took part, in an advisory capacity, on a Presidential Committee in Washington.

Wrote, in longhand as always, then revised and edited an article for the

Reader's Digest, another for *This Week* magazine, and the Foreword to an *Economic Survey of Mineral Sciences.*

Drafted and revised several times his speeches for the Stanford and Tufts meetings, a broadcast for the Manion Forum, and an address dedicating the Taft Memorial.

Saw thirty-three persons by appointment in connection with public activities and entertained thirty-four guests at luncheons and dinners in his suite.

Worked intensively on histories of global American relief and benevolence since 1914.

Devoted time to fiscal and other problems of several of the organizations with which he is connected.

The memorandum did not specify what he did with his leisure time.

Hoover read and for the most part answered personally between thirty and fifty thousand letters a year. According to those close to him, he actually enjoyed this huge correspondence, most of it with simple people commenting on the state of the world or asking for his advice and opinions. Frequently he would get up in the small hours of the night, take a batch of these letters to his desk, and scribble his brief answers with a lead pencil either on the letter or on a big scratch pad for his secretaries to transcribe in the morning.

"It is the best possible sedative for me," he told Ben Hibbs, who was visiting him in connection with a *Saturday Evening Post* essay on his coming eighty-eighth birthday. "After an hour or so of writing letters, I can usually go back with an easy mind and sleep. I do get my eight hours of rest. I have to."

The Hibbs article, incidentally, reported that the former President during those eighty-eight years had accumulated 468 medals, awards, and other tangible honors, many of them of the very highest distinction. He had accumulated eighty-five honorary academic degrees. Despite his efforts to avoid decorations and tokens, probably no other American received so many, not only domestic but foreign.

In 1930, as President, he had been the first recipient of an award for distinguished scientific services established by several engineering societies, to be known thereafter as the Hoover Medal. Thirty-one years later he made the presentation to the 1961 recipient as part of the dedication ceremonies of a new $12,500,000 United Engineering Center, located at New York's United Nations Plaza. At one point he declared:

We did not deliberately erect this structure in order to keep an eye on the United Nations across the street. But we may hope that the fallout of brevity, unity and constructive action streaming from these rooms might penetrate their assemblies.

Obviously his gentle, whimsical humor had not deserted him in his ninth decade. About three years earlier he was speaking to the New York Chamber of Commerce in a period of business slump. He began by presenting his credentials as an expert in the field:

On the subject of depressions I may mention that once upon a time my political opponents honored me as possessing the fabulous intellectual and economic power by which I created a worldwide depression all by myself. At least I might claim from these tributes that I must know something about depressions.

From his earliest period, in the engineering stage, he had always done some writing. There were various technical articles and, in 1909, his first book, *Principles of Mining*. In his ripest years it became a major avocation. "My purpose," he told a reporter at eighty-seven, "is not like the ancient monks to illuminate the margins of ancient manuscripts. I want to write new ones."

The new one he was writing at the time was tentatively titled *Freedom Betrayed*, a heavily documented history of the American confrontation with Soviet Russia and world Communism since he left the White House. This, in the nature of the subject, included examination of the U.S. entry into World War II and the disposal of the fruits of victory at the key "summit meetings," to use a later term for them, of Allied and Soviet leaders.

By mid-1963 a draft of two volumes was completed, but plans for publication were uncertain. Hoover, indeed, seemed inclined to postpone their release until he had passed from the scene. Meanwhile, at this writing, the whole project remains in abeyance on account of his health.

The shelfful of Hoover books (two of them in collaboration with Hugh Gibson) represent another of his many lives. He was too much of a realist, however, to delude himself that he was a "man of letters" in the creative literary sense. His primary talents in this area were those of lucidity and organization of complex materials. His pages, to do him justice, are studded with felicitous and sometimes even brilliant passages. But he was decidedly not a natural writer and referred to himself, more accurately, as a "historian."

The history with which he dealt is almost entirely that of his own lifetime and from the vantage point of his personal participation in the events. The massive *Memoirs*, published in 1951–52, and the four volumes of *An American Epic*, published between 1959 and 1964, are typical. Basically, that is to say, they are "documentaries," with only enough original narrative and analytical commentary to turn them into cohesive running stories.

The *American Epic* is a detailed account of American relief since 1914.

It carries the record of American benevolence to 1960, a period of forty-four years. The "epic" is largely autobiographical, since in most of the great campaigns against famine and destitution Hoover was the strategist, the commanding general and, in many instances, the prime initiator. Not boastfully but as a matter of plain fact, he could say in an introduction that he was the only one who knew the entire forty-four-year story. In the aggregate, he calculated, the lives of some 1,400,000,000 men, women, and children—equivalent to half the human race—were at stake in these undertakings.

Hoover had constantly emphasized America's instinct for compassion, its readiness to share with the needy the world over. This was one of the key points in his Independence Day address at the Brussels Fair, for instance. These books provide the record in concrete terms. There are few nations which do not owe a debt of gratitude to the United States and therefore to its thirty-first President. Most of them, like Belgium and Germany and Poland, acknowledge the debt. A few, like Soviet Russia and Communist China, have repudiated it as they have repudiated their other debts; but even there, the people's memory is longer than that of their masters.

The Hoover book which drew most attention and readers was *The Ordeal of Woodrow Wilson;* brought out in 1958, it scored high marks by the critics and remained on the national best-seller lists for months. There was an element of drama in the very fact of a book by one President about another, the author a Republican and the subject a Democrat. Hoover, of course, had come to know Wilson well during the crucial war years and their painful aftermath. Though eschewing sentimentality, and again depending largely on documents, he succeeded in conveying both the glory and the pathos of Wilson on the world stage: a Greek tragedy played out with all humankind as its audience.

A large portion of Hoover's voluminous correspondence, the portion in which he took a special delight, has been with children. There was scarcely a mail that did not bring him missives from boys and girls, usually asking for his opinion or advice. In 1962 he decided to put excerpts from the more interesting or significant of these exchanges into a small book, published under the title *On Growing Up.*

The following year, finding himself confined to a sick-bed for many weeks, he passed some of his time of waiting by compiling another small book, this time on his favorite sport. He called it *Fishing for Fun, and to Wash Your Soul.* While it did contain a few new passages, it consisted chiefly of sprightly or philosophic bits on matters piscatory that he had written or said through the years.

Hoover's extraordinary physical vitality was the pride and envy of associates of his own age and even far younger people. It stood extreme and continuing tests of the sort of work, worry, and responsibility that would have shattered the health of other men. But inevitably time began to catch up with him.

He had had gall bladder trouble soon after his seventy-fifth birthday, but seemed to have recovered. Nine years later, in April 1958, the ailment recurred and the gall bladder had to be removed—his first operation. Interviewing him more than two years later, on the eve of his eighty-sixth birthday, a New York *Herald Tribune* reporter described him as "a relaxed, vigorous, almost jaunty Herbert Hoover." In July 1962, with another birthday coming on, Ben Hibbs was able to report in the *Saturday Evening Post* that the Chief's handclasp was still strong, his eyes bright, and that "his omniverous interest in everything under the sun belies his eighty-eight years."

Soon thereafter, however, Hoover developed internal pain, and a malign tumor (polypoid lesion) was removed from the intestines. Ten months after that, on June 4, 1963, he was suddenly seized by massive gastrointestinal bleeding. On both these occasions his life seemed to hang by a thread. The whole country followed the medical bulletins and its alarm was amply justified.

At this writing, early in 1964, as his ninetieth birthday comes closer, Hoover is still convalescing at his Waldorf apartment, under constant nursing care. Though frail and under continuing medication, he appears to be slowly regaining strength. His spirits are good, his mind unclouded. He is not confined to bed, sees his friends, reads a good deal, has two or three guests for dinner most evenings, and keeps up with much of his massive correspondence. Allan Hoover has moved his office to the Waldorf Towers to be near his father.

3

As of the present writing, only one President of the United States lived longer than Hoover—John Adams, who died at ninety-one. Hoover has held the status of ex-President longer than any predecessor. His four years in the White House represent a small fragment of a very long life crammed with important activity both before and after he served as Chief Executive. Yet the question of his qualitative "rating" among Presidents has been raised repeatedly—this kind of historical bookkeeping is a national custom.

On Hoover's eighty-sixth birthday, a number of senators took oratorical note of the occasion on the floor of the Upper Chamber, and the Democratic encomiums were every bit as ardent as those by Republican members. "He is now looked upon as a revered elder statesman," said Mike Mansfield, then Democratic majority whip, and added: "In the light of history, I believe he was a great President; and I think future historians will bear out that statement."

Two years later, in the New York *Times*, Russell Kirk referred to the remarkable reversal of public sentiment on the former President. "Nowadays," he declared, "even Democratic chairmen speak of Mr. Hoover with respect, not to say affection. . . . Though historians of the future will not regard him as the most imaginative of Presidents, they are sure to rate very high indeed his administrative talents and his honesty."

But personally, having studied his many lives with considerable diligence, I lean to the belief that in Hoover's case it will be largely irrelevant how he is ranked in arbitrary assessments of presidential greatness. His life, I am convinced, will be measured less by what he *did*—colossal though it has been—than by what he *was*. Already, in fact, his countrymen instinctively appraise him in moral rather than conventional political terms. They think of him, if at all, not primarily as a President, however rated, but as a great American and a great human being—as a truly *good* man, whose compassion reached out to embrace all humankind.

Hoover, of course, made many mistakes and misjudgments. But none of them can be traced to moral flaws, to appetites for power or glory, to arrogance or to malice. There has been about his actions and reactions, the bad as well as the good, a great sincerity and a great innocence. As with every historical figure, there is room for debate about the wisdom of this or that policy, the validity of this or that conviction. There is no room for argument about Hoover's all-encompassing charity and his high standards of public and private conduct. His probity cannot be rated; it is an incommensurable quality. The mistakes charged against him, when they stand up at all, reflect on his techniques or his views, never on his character.

We have observed that Hoover's brand of liberalism attracted small attention in his earlier years, since most of it was familiar to American ears. Only in the perspective of time did his general philosophy acquire a dimension of the unusual. Why? Because in the intervening years social tendencies in the world, and in America itself, new intellectual fashions, the hardening of totalitarian moods, helped bring into clear and even startling relief the values he defended and, indeed, seemed to incarnate.

Whether these values will survive only the future can tell. As of 1964, they seem again attractive to growing numbers, in Western Europe and in the United States. More and more young people, especially, express renewed concern for the fate of the free economy and a new respect for the moral springheads of American history. The current "conservatism" has about it some of the emotional aura of the radicalism of my own youth. (Hoover after a time adjusted himself to the "conservative" label, but was never quite comfortable with it.)

But there can be no guarantee that the Hoover philosophy will not be submerged in the floodtide of collectivism. Unhappily World War II, in defeating one segment of the encroaching statism, strengthened and inflamed another. It merely switched the primary center of infection from Berlin to Moscow. Perhaps we are irrevocably on what Professor Hayek called "the road to serfdom." Be that as it may, Herbert Hoover seems destined to emerge more sharply and in increasingly heroic stature as champion of the old-style liberalism he called American Individualism.

If the trend to collectivism persists, his primary virtue may then seem to reside in the fact that he represented, in his whole personality, a set of lost values: not quite extinct, but antique and touched by nostalgia. He may well loom in historical perspective as almost a personification of those values, since his life story has been a uniquely American blend of practicality and idealism, of earthly social purposes infused with a spiritual intensity.

"There is no oratory so easy," he wrote in his *American Individualism,* "no writing so trenchant and vivid as the phrase-making of criticism and malice—there is none so difficult as inspiration to construction." One must resist the temptation to see in such discernment the evidence of personal forebodings. At the least, however, he sensed that he was swimming against the tide.

It is altogether likely that in these pages I have been betrayed by ardor into overstatement. Ardor for justice. Yes, justice. A frayed, corny little word, but I offer it without apology to explain any lapse into hyperbole. Reading reams of unconscionable spite aimed at Hoover, matching the man against the ugly myth which prevailed for a long time and still lingers in some places, one is driven to compensatory bias in his favor. Not only justice for a man mocked and maligned but for the things his life connotes: the old-fashioned virtues, decencies, and loyalties.

Hoover has consistently renounced popularity for principle, for duty as he conceived it. As President, and then as ex-President, he never revised or reversed himself under the terror of organized abuse; he never yielded to the temptation of doing the politically profitable thing against his own logic and conscience. At the risk of sounding melodramatic, I dare suggest that his personal experience holds some of the elements of the classic prophet, for it contained a time of crucifixion and a time of resurrection.

There seems little enough danger that this book (and better ones certain to come as Hoover is recorded by abler biographers) will launch a counter-myth of perfection. The man's human failings, especially in the political arena, are too much in evidence for that. He fits into none of the familiar hero patterns. There is nothing flamboyant and melodramatic about his character to win and hold man in the mass. The hallmark of his personality and career is integrity, and that is not exactly a quality to whip up popular adoration.

Not in his feelings but in his manner he remained aloof from the madding crowd, so that for a long time his detractors were able to conceal his physiognomy under masks of their own making. Then, one after another, these masks fell away. Already it is clear that historical revaluation will disclose the real Hoover under the accidental and artificial externals. America has reason to be gratified by this fact—for its own sake, not for Hoover's sake.

What has impressed me profoundly as I studied the data of his life is Hoover's wholeness and genuineness. There is nothing phony, nothing petty, nothing spurious in his story. He has not lived with an eye on opinion polls and philosophical fashions. His view of life and public affairs has not been an improvisation of expediency or a rationalization of self-interest. It is deep-rooted in the American soil. It has evolved naturally, honestly, consistently in the American experience. It is indivisible from our national heritage.

Rarely has such a capacious intelligence as Hoover's been combined with such a great heart and robust spirit. Even more rarely, the democratic process being what it is, has a man so opulently endowed reached the Presidency.

Herbert Hoover is a great monolithic figure. Time has washed off the mud with which he was bespattered—fortunately while he was still alive and active. The granite of integrity underneath became obvious even to the less perceptive of his countrymen.

BIBLIOGRAPHY

Corey, Herbert, *The Truth about Hoover*. Houghton Mifflin, 1932.

Crowther, Samuel, *The Presidency vs. Hoover*. Doubleday, 1928.

DeConde, Alexander, *Herbert Hoover's Latin-American Policy*. Stanford University Press, 1951.

Dexter, Walter Friar, *Herbert Hoover and American Individualism*. Macmillan, 1932.

Emerson, Edwin, *Hoover and His Times*. Garden City Publishing Company, 1932.

Flynn, John T., *The Roosevelt Myth*. Devin-Adair, 1948.

Hard, William, *Who's Hoover?* Dodd, Mead, 1928.

Hinshaw, David, *Herbert Hoover, American Quaker*. Farrar, Straus, 1950.

Hoover, Herbert:

> *Principles of Mining*. McGraw-Hill Book Company, 1909.
>
> *American Individualism*. Doubleday, 1922.
>
> *The New Day: Campaign Speeches of 1928*. Stanford University Press, 1928.
>
> *Campaign Speeches of 1932*. Doubleday, 1933.
>
> *Hoover After Dinner* (compiled by Theodore G. Joslin). Scribner's, 1933.
>
> *The State Papers and Other Public Writings of Herbert Hoover* (collected and edited by William Starr Myers). Doubleday, 1934.
>
> *The Challenge to Liberty*. Scribner's, 1934.
>
> *Addresses upon the American Road:*
>
> > 1933–1938, Scribner's.
> >
> > 1938–1940, Scribner's.
> >
> > 1940–1941, Scribner's.
> >
> > 1941–1945, Van Nostrand.
> >
> > 1945–1948, Van Nostrand.
> >
> > 1948–1950, Stanford University Press.
> >
> > 1950–1955, Stanford University Press.
> >
> > 1955–1960, Caxton Printers.
>
> *America's First Crusade*. Scribner's, 1942.
>
> *Reports on the Commission on Organization of the Executive Branch of the Government*. U. S. Government Printing Office, 1945–47.
>
> *The Memoirs of Herbert Hoover* (3 volumes). Macmillan, 1951–52.
>
> *Reports on the Commission on Organization of the Executive Branch of the Government*. U. S. Government Printing Office, 1953–55.
>
> *The Hoover Commission Report*. McGraw-Hill Book Company, 1949.

The Ordeal of Woodrow Wilson. McGraw-Hill Book Company, 1958.

An American Epic (4 volumes). Regnery, 1959–64.

On Growing Up. William Morrow, 1962.

Fishing for Fun, and to Wash Your Soul. Random House, 1963.

Hoover, Herbert, and Gibson, Hugh:

    The Problems of Lasting Peace. Doubleday, 1942.

    The Basis of Lasting Peace. Van Nostrand, 1945.

Irwin, Will, *Herbert Hoover, a Reminiscent Biography.* Century, 1928.

Joslin, Theodore G., *Hoover Off the Record.* Doubleday, 1934.

Kellogg, Vernon, *Fighting Starvation in Belgium.* Doubleday, 1917.

——, *Herbert Hoover, the Man and His Work.* Appleton, 1920.

Lane, Rose Wilder, *Making of Herbert Hoover.* Century, 1920.

Lyons, Eugene, *Our Unknown Ex-President: A Portrait of Herbert Hoover.* Doubleday, 1948.

MacNeil, Neil, and Metz, Harold W., *The Hoover Report, 1953–1955.* Macmillan, 1956.

McGee, Dorothy Horton, *Herbert Hoover: Engineer, Humanitarian, Statesman.* Dodd, Mead, 1959.

Michelson, Charles, *The Ghost Talks.* Putnam, 1944.

Moley, Raymond, *After Seven Years.* Harper, 1939.

Myers, William Starr, and Newton, Walter H., *The Hoover Administration, a Documented Narrative.* Scribner's, 1936.

Reeves, Earl, *This Man Hoover.* A. L. Burt Company, 1928.

Rothbard, Murray N., *America's Great Depression.* Van Nostrand, 1963.

Spargo, John, *The Legend of Herbert Hoover Who Did Nothing.* 1939.

Strauss, Lewis L., *Men and Decisions.* Doubleday, 1962.

Sullivan, Lawrence, *Prelude to Panic.* Statesman Press, Washington, D.C., 1936.

Train, Arthur, *The Strange Attacks on Herbert Hoover.* John Day, 1932.

Warren, Harris Gaylord, *Herbert Hoover and the Great Depression.* Oxford University Press, 1959.

Wilbur, Ray Lyman, and Hyde, Arthur Mastic, *The Hoover Policies.* Scribner's, 1937.

Wolfe, Harold, *Herbert Hoover: Public Servant and Leader of the Loyal Opposition.* Exposition Press, New York, 1956.

F24